Apprenticeship Companion

Level 5: Operations / Departmental Manager

Tim Webb
PGCE, FBII, FInstLM

THE CHOIR PRESS

Titles in the Apprenticeship Companion series

Level 3: Business Administrator
Level 3: Customer Service Specialist
Level 3: Team Leader/Supervisor
Level 5: Operations / Departmental Manager

Copyright © 2022 Tim Webb

All rights reserved. No part of this publication may be reproduced or transmitted in any form or by any means, electronic or mechanical including photocopying, recording or any information storage or retrieval system, without prior permission in writing from the publishers.

The right of Tim Webb to be identified as the author of this work has been asserted by him in accordance with the Copyright, Designs and Patents Act 1988

First published in the United Kingdom in 2022 by
The Choir Press

ISBN 978-1-78963-289-7

Foreword

Foreword

It would be wrong to suggest that writing this book has been a toil of pleasure. In fact, it has been an enormous challenge, testing the levels of fortitude and stamina to the limits at times. Writing early in the morning and into the darkest hours at night - wearing the letters off the keyboard in the process. However, the time, effort and endeavour will all be worth it, if just one manager of the future finds it a beneficial and effective support resource as they work towards the End Point Assessment of their Management Apprenticeship.

I have taken the materials and resources I have used and developed over the years I have taught management studies, and recompiled it into a format which, I hope, will be of benefit to all who have the stamina to wade through the detail it contains. I have tried to steer clear of the traditional, drab, textbook style and have striven to lighten what can be a very challenging subject.

There is no coincidence it mirrors the structure of the Level 5 Operations Manager Apprenticeship Standard and has been designed to provide the reader with support through each module of the Standard.

Having completed my task, I shall retire to a darkened room and await the feedback of those fearless souls who venture into its depths and upon receiving that feedback, I will decide whether to go and buy a coffee table to display my copy on, or use it to prop open the office door!

Remember – you only get out, what you put in!

Contents

Contents

Foreword 3
Chapter 1: Self-Awareness 7
Self-Reflection 10
Psychometric Tests 12
Management Tools 17
Unconscious Bias 28
Emotional Triggers and Inhibitors 31
Emotional Intelligence 41
Learning Styles 57
Behaviour Styles 69
Reflective Practice 87
Models of Reflective Practice 93
Writing a Reflective Journal 104
Chapter 2: Managing Self 107
Time Management Tools and Techniques 108
Tools and Techniques 111
Time Management Tools 115
Maintaining the Work / Life Balance 128
Time Management Techniques 140
Personal Development Planning (PDP) 153
Setting SMART Objectives 173
Maintaining a Continuing Professional Development log (CPD) 179
Chapter 3: Communication 185
Interpersonal Communication 186
Communication Models 190
Forms of Communication 197
Types of Communication 200
Active Listening 222
Building Rapport 223
Communicating in Challenging Situations 226
Emotional Intelligence 228
Effective Questioning 229
Feedback 237
Feedback Models 238
Escalating Workplace Problems 244
Escalating Customer Complaints 246
Chairing Meetings 249
Key documentation 249
Chapter 4: Building Relationships 261
Stakeholders 262
Stakeholder Management 273
Negotiation Skills 322
Persuasion Skills 328
Influencing Skills 332
Chapter 5: Problem Solving and Decision Making 337
Solving Problems and Making Decisions 338
Scope, Nature and Impact 340
Making Decisions 344

Contents

Data 376
Legislation Affecting Data Management 383
Data Quality 389
Gathering Data 390
Data Collection Methods 391
Benefits of Collecting Data 393
Data Analysis 394
Critical Analysis of Data 397
Ethics and Values 398
Chapter 6: Operational Management 403
Operations Management 404
Mission and Vision Statements 405
Organisational Strategies 408
Key Performance Indicators (KPIs') 414
Business Development tools 419
Operational Business Planning 443
Resource Management 443
Developing Sales and Marketing Plans 445
Management Systems and Processes 450
Contingency Planning and Risk Management 454
Initiate and Manage Change 456
Defining Change Management and Project Management 457
Effective Change Management 462
Open Communication 464
Data Protection 468
Data Security 471
Information Management 473
Data Collection 479
Chapter 7: Leading People 487
Leadership 488
Leadership vs. Management 489
Leadership Styles 494
Leadership Skills 500
Developing Leadership 503
Leadership Theories 510
Summary of Leadership Styles 549
Organisational Culture 553
Leading High-Performing Teams 563
Building a High-Performing Team 564
Adapting a leadership style to different personalities 583
Effective Delegation 586
Communicating with a Team 588
Improving Leadership 590
Supporting the Management of Change within the Organisation 591
Supporting Development through Coaching and Mentoring 592
Coaching and Mentoring Models 597
Barriers to Organisational Learning 614
Assessing Training and Development Needs 617
Training and Development Methods 623
Delivering Training and Development 625

Level 5: Operations / Departmental Manager

Contents

Equality and Diversity 630
Chapter 8: Managing People **631**
Motivating a Team 636
Managing a Large Team 642
Managing Multiple Teams 644
Remote or Multiple Teams 645
Virtual Teams 647
Managing Managers 654
High Performing Teams 658
Communicating and Working with a Team 661
Performance Management 667
Recruitment and Selection 672
Developing People 674
Conducting Appraisals 675
Employee Engagement 676
Dealing with Conflict in Teams 684
Chapter 9: Managing Finance **689**
Business 690
Governance and Compliance 690
Management and Financial Accounting 698
Budgeting and Financial forecasting 709
Planning a Budget 711
Developing the Budget 714
Set and Monitor Budgets 716
Delivering Value for Money 726
Financing Business 731
Glossary of Financial Terminology 733
Chapter 10: Project Management **735**
Projects 736
Project Management 738
Change Management and Project Management 740
Project Management Phases and Processes 743
Project Management Methodologies 744
Delivering the Project 755
Managing Resources 765
Management Tools for Monitoring Progress 768
Managing Project Risks and Issues 770
Reviewing Project Performance 774
Chapter11: Delivering a Project **777**
Project Planning Process 778
Project Plan 780
Project Monitoring 795
Project Control 797
Evaluating a Project 799

Chapter 1: Self-Awareness

Self-Awareness

Introduction

Self-awareness is our ability to recognise our own emotions and their effects on ourselves and others. Without being aware of, and understanding, our own emotions, it will be difficult for us to move into the other emotional competencies like self-management, social awareness, or team leadership.

Self-awareness is being aware of oneself including one's traits, feelings and behaviours.

Self-awareness is the conscious knowledge of ourselves – our character, desires, beliefs, qualities, motives and feelings. Having a good sense of these aspects of ourselves can help us in the workplace, and in our private lives.

We can assess our personal growth and understanding through self-awareness by, for example:

- *being aware of how people and things around us influence us*
- *learning about how we can influence and interact with others*

Developing self-awareness, and understanding our own psychology, is a skill that is part of our personal and professional development. Self-awareness can be applied in our working lives to help us to, for example:

- ***understand emotions more clearly*** – ours and other people's
- ***improve our communication skills*** – and interact with others in the workplace and resolve conflict more effectively
- ***improve leadership skills*** – and our general operational performance
- ***improve job satisfaction*** – by focusing on job roles and tasks that truly motivate us
- ***maximise career development opportunities***

When you look in a mirror – what do you see? Do you see the person you are? The person you want to be or the person you think other people see?

The very first step on the road to deeper self-awareness is to recognise that the image we see is simply a reflection of the packaging we come in! That packaging is about as relevant as the cardboard box your breakfast cereals are delivered in!! – You do not eat the box – it is what is inside the box that matters!!

We seldom look inside the packaging because we are afraid of what we might find, but without absolute honesty, you will never recognise what is really inside.

Level 5: Operations / Departmental Manager

Self-Awareness

We are disinclined to spend time on self-reflection. Even when personal feedback is presented to us, we are not always open to it, because honest feedback is not always flattering.

As we grow up, we base many of our actions, responses and attributes on things that we have learned and been told along the way. For example, we might base our initial education and career choices on what our family members did. However, these choices might not suit our real desires, beliefs or character, and we need to develop our self-awareness to discover more options.

It is quite difficult today to even find time to think about who we are, what our strengths and weaknesses are, our personalities, our habits and values. Consequently, many of us have a low level of self-awareness. Despite this, developing self-awareness is an essential first step toward maximising management skills. It can improve judgment and help identify opportunities for professional development and personal growth.

Self-awareness is also associated with soft skills – There are thought to be five elements to this – Personality, Values, Habits, Needs and Emotions.

These are considered below:

Personality: – *Personalities cannot be changed, but values and needs are based on what we learn about ourselves. Understanding our own personality can help us find in what environment we can be successful. Awareness of our personality helps us analyse such a decision.*

Values: – *It is important that we know and focus on our personal values. When we focus on our values, we are more likely to accomplish what we consider most important.*

Habits: – *Our habits are the behaviours that we repeat daily and often automatically. Although we would like to possess the habits that help us interact effectively with and manage others, we can probably all identify at least one of our habits that decrease our effectiveness.*

Needs: – *Maslow and other scholars have identified a variety of psychological needs that drive our behaviours such as needs for esteem, affection, belonging, achievement, self-actualisation, power and control.*

Emotions: –*Understanding your own feelings, what causes them, and how they impact our thoughts and actions is emotional self-awareness. Persons with high emotional self-awareness understand the internal process associated with emotional experiences and, therefore, has greater control over them.*

The first step on the road to personal development, is to take a long hard look at ourselves and be brutally honest about our true targets and expectations in life.

Self-Awareness

> *If you cannot be totally honest with yourself – you will never be honest with anyone.*

There are many tests and techniques available that help us to identify and understand ourselves in greater depth. They look at our character, qualities, motivation, feelings and so on, so that we can access information about ourselves that is often hidden or undiscovered.

Self-Reflection

Reflecting helps to develop skills and review effectiveness, rather than just carry-on doing things as they have always been done. It is about questioning, in a positive way, what you do and why you do it and then deciding whether there is a better, or more efficient, way of doing it in the future.

In any role, whether at home or at work, reflection is an important part of learning. You would not use a recipe a second time around if the dish did not work the first time. You would either adjust the recipe or find a new and, hopefully, better one. When we do our job, we can become stuck in a routine that may not be working effectively. Thinking about your own skills can help you identify changes you might need to make.

Reflective questions to ask yourself:

> **Strengths** – *What are my strengths? For example, am I well organised? Do I remember things?*
> **Weaknesses** – *What are my weaknesses? For example, am I easily distracted? Do I need more practise with a particular skill?*
> **Skills** – *What skills do I have and what am I good at?*
> **Problems** – *What problems are there at work/home that may affect me? For example, responsibilities or distractions that may impact on study or work.*
> **Achievements** – *What have I achieved?*
> **Happiness** – *Are there things that I am unhappy with or disappointed about? What makes me happy?*
> **Solutions** – *What could I do to improve in these areas?*

Although self-reflection can seem difficult at first, or even selfish or embarrassing, as it does not come naturally, you will find it becomes easier with practise and the end result could be a happier and more efficient you.

Self-Awareness

Self-Reflection Tools

Self-reflection is often used as a management or coaching tool and the process focuses strongly on self-awareness.

Keeping a journal can be a useful tool. Going through the process of writing down our thoughts, experiences and feelings on a regular basis can help us to understand more about ourselves, especially when we review entries at a later date.

Listening to our inner voice can reveal things that we may not have realised previously. Just writing down some of the thoughts as they pass through our mind can be revealing, then reviewing them once a week can add to our self-awareness.

Practising mindfulness helps us to be aware of things going on in our minds, concentrate on the moment and allow unnecessary thoughts to pass through. There are many resources online, some of which are free, that help us to understand and train the mind, to improve concentration and aid stress management.

Strengths and Weaknesses (SWOT test)
Your strengths and weaknesses are the things which you are good at and things you are not so good at or need additional support or training to achieve a higher level of competence.

There are a number of ways in which we can identify our strengths and weaknesses, but the most common is using a SWOT analysis. SWOT stands for Strengths, Weaknesses, Opportunities, and Threats.

These are usually plotted on a chart with four sections.

The strengths and weaknesses are factors which affect you personally. The strengths are the things you are good at, things you can do without support or help. This could include literacy or numeracy, it could include being well organised, etc. Your weaknesses are things you need help or support to achieve. It may be that you can happily read a newspaper, but a textbook may be more challenging. You can perhaps deal with money including making payments and giving change, but more complex calculations you may find difficult and need help. It may also be that you are simply disorganised! These are your strengths and weaknesses!

Opportunities and threats are not about you personally, but about society in general. Opportunities are the things that help you to achieve your targets such as free training courses, help with childcare whilst studying, work experience opportunities, etc. Threats are the things which may prevent you from achieving your targets such as the economic climate, lack of jobs, etc. Both opportunities and threats are matters outside of your control, but you should be aware of these issues.

SWOT Analysis	
Strengths	Weaknesses
Opportunities	Threats

Self-Awareness

Psychometric Tests

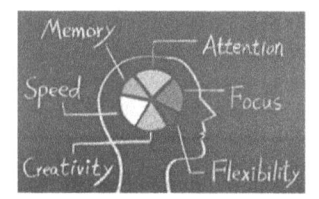

There are many psychometric tests available and it is easy to find them online. They are designed to show someone's personality, mental ability, opinions, strengths, weaknesses and preferences.

They are often used by employers, or prospective employers, to see how an individual's own mix of natural skills and attributes will fit into what the organisation wants.

They can be used as a recruitment selection tool by employers, but they are also useful when developing self-awareness skills. They help to unmask our hidden qualities and habits and focus on our natural abilities and preferences.

Types of Psychometric Testing

There are two main types: personality tests and aptitude tests.

Personality tests explore your interests, values and motivations, analysing how your character fits with the role and organisation. They analyse your emotions, behaviours and relationships in a variety of situations.

Aptitude tests assess your reasoning or cognitive ability, determining whether you have got the right skillset for a role. Usually administered under exam conditions, you will often be given one minute to answer each multiple-choice question. Your intelligence levels are compared to a standard, meaning that you must achieve a certain score to pass.

Myers-Briggs Type Indicator
Have you ever heard someone describe themselves as an INTJ or an ESTP and wondered what those cryptic-sounding letters could mean? What these people are referring to is their personality type based on the Myers-Briggs Type Indicator (MBTI).

The Myers-Briggs Personality Type Indicator is a self-assessment questionnaire designed to identify a personality type, strengths, and preferences. The questionnaire was developed by Isabel Myers and her mother Katherine Briggs based on their work with Carl Jung's theory of personality types. Today, the MBTI inventory is one of the most widely used psychological instruments in the world.

Based on the answers in the questionnaire, people are identified as having one of 16 personality types. The goal of the MBTI is to allow people to further explore and understand their own personalities including their likes, dislikes, strengths, weaknesses, possible career preferences, and compatibility with other people.

When answering the questions, the outcomes are not easy to predict, and we end up with an in-depth and revealing description of our personality.

Self-Awareness

No one personality type is "best" or "better" than another. It is not a tool designed to look for dysfunction or abnormality. Instead, its goal is simply to help you learn more about yourself. The questionnaire itself is made up of four different scales which create the 16 personality types.

Extroversion (E) – Introversion (I)
The extroversion-introversion dichotomy was first explored by Jung in his theory of personality to describe how people respond and interact with the world around them. While these terms are familiar to most people, the way in which they are used in the MBTI differs somewhat from their popular usage.

Extroverts (sometimes spelled extraverts) are "outward-turning" and tend to be action-oriented, enjoy more frequent social interaction, and feel energised after spending time with other people. Introverts are "inward-turning" and tend to be thought-oriented, enjoy deep and meaningful social interactions, and feel recharged after spending time alone.

> *Everyone exhibits extroversion and introversion to some degree, but most tend to have an overall preference for one or the other.*

Sensing (S) – Intuition (N)
This scale involves looking at how people gather information from the world around them. Just like with extroversion and introversion, all people spend some time sensing and intuiting depending on the situation. According to the MBTI, people tend to be dominant in one area or the other.

People who prefer sensing tend to pay a great deal of attention to reality, particularly to what they can learn from their own senses. They tend to focus on facts and details and enjoy getting hands-on experience. Those who prefer intuition pay more attention to things like patterns and impressions. They enjoy thinking about possibilities, imagining the future, and abstract theories.

Thinking (T) – Feeling (F)
This scale focuses on how people make decisions based on the information that they gathered from their sensing or intuition functions. People who prefer thinking place a greater emphasis on facts and objective data.

They tend to be consistent, logical, and impersonal when weighing a decision. Those who prefer feeling are more likely to consider people and emotions when arriving at a conclusion.

Judging (J) – Perceiving (P)
The final scale involves how people tend to deal with the outside world. Those who lean toward judging prefer structure and firm decisions. People who lean toward perceiving are more open, flexible, and adaptable. These two tendencies interact with the other scales. Remember, all people at least spend some time extroverting. The judging-perceiving scale helps describe whether you're extrovert when you are taking in new information (sensing and intuiting) or when you are making decisions (thinking and feeling).

Self-Awareness

The MBTI Types

Depending on where you are on the scale will depend on which letter you are assigned in each category, to create the four-digit code. The resulting personality type can then be checked by the code formed.

Code		Personality Type
ISTJ	=	The Inspector
ISTP	=	The Crafter
ISFJ	=	The Protector
ISFP	=	The Artist
INFJ	=	The Advocate
INFP	=	The Mediator
INTJ	=	The Architect
INTP	=	The Thinker
ESTP	=	The Persuader
ESTJ	=	The Director
ESFP	=	The Performer
ESFJ	=	The Caregiver
ENFP	=	The Champion
ENFJ	=	The Giver
ENTP	=	The Debater
ENTJ	=	The Commander

The characteristics for each personality type are substantial and there is no reason to include them here. The test can be completed online, and the results will be presented after the test for the personality type identified.

How MBTI differs from other personality tests

First, the MBTI is not really a "test." There are no right or wrong answers, and one type is not better than any other type. The purpose of the indicator is not to evaluate mental health or offer any type of diagnosis.

Unlike many other types of psychological evaluation, the results are not compared against any norms. Instead of looking at a score in comparison to the results of other people, the goal of the instrument is to simply offer further information about your own unique personality. While there are many versions of the MBTI available online, it should be noted that any of the informal questionnaires that you may find on the Internet are only approximations of the real thing.

Self-Awareness

The 4 C's of Mental Toughness - Lyons (2015)

Mental Toughness is a personality trait that improves performance and wellbeing meaning that you are more likely to be successful in your personal and professional life.

Mental Toughness is defined as Resilience - the ability to bounce back from setbacks and failures- and Confidence -the ability to spot and seize opportunities. Mentally tough people are more outcome focused and better at making things happen without being distracted by their own or other peoples' emotions.

Mental Toughness can be measured using the MTQ48 psychometric tool, which was constructed by Professor Peter Clough of Manchester Metropolitan University.

It is scientifically valid and reliable and based on a 4C's framework, which measures key components of mental toughness - Control, Commitment, Challenge and Confidence.

Control
Control is your self-esteem - your life's purpose and your sense of control over your life and emotions.

Control is the extent to which you feel you are in control of your life and that you can make a difference and change things.

If you are high on Control, you have a good sense of who you are and what you stand for and are "comfortable in your own skin". You are also better able to control your emotions meaning you can keep your anxieties in check and are less likely to be distracted by the emotions of others or reveal your emotional state to other people.

Alternatively, if you are at the other end of the scale –and low on control –you will feel that events happen to you and are outside your personal control or influence.

Commitment
Commitment is your focus and reliability and being high on commitment means that you can effectively set goals and targets and reliably and consistently achieve them without being distracted. You are strong at establishing routines and habits that enable you to be successful.

Alternatively, if you are at the other end of the scale – and low on commitment – you will sometimes fail or find it difficult to set goals and targets and then prioritise them. You may also find it difficult to focus and be easily distracted by other people and competing priorities. You rarely adopt routines or habits to make you successful.
The Control and Commitment scales together represent the Resilience part of the Mental Toughness definition, namely the ability to bounce back from setbacks and opportunities. This intuitively, as well as scientifically, makes sense because if you face a setback or failure your momentum slows or stops altogether, and you naturally question yourself and revisit your self-identity.

You then need to re-affirm and reassess who you are and then develop some momentum to enable you to bounce back. You can do this by setting and achieving a series of goals

Self-Awareness

and targets, often small and simple at first, to rebuild your confidence and return to your chosen path.

Challenge
Challenge is your drive and adaptability and being high on challenge means that you are driven to be as good as you can be and to achieve your personal best. You see challenges, change, adversity and variety as opportunities rather than threats. You are likely to be adaptable and agile.

Alternatively, if you are at the other end of the scale –and low on challenge –you view change as a threat and so avoid new and challenging situations for fear of failure or wishing not to expend what you perceive will be a wasted effort.

Confidence
Confidence is your self-belief and influence and describes to what extent you believe you can perform productively and proficiently and the ability to influence others.

Being high on confidence means that you have the self-belief to successfully complete on tasks that other individuals with similar ability, but lower confidence would think beyond them. In practice if you are high on Confidence, you will take setbacks, whether internally or externally generated, in your stride. You will keep your head, maintain your routine and often stiffen your resolve.

However, if you are low on confidence, you can easily be unsettled by the setback and feel undermined. Your head could drop. Your internal voice's positive commentary is vital here to counteract this loss of confidence and negativity.

The Challenge and Confidence scales together represent the Confidence part of the Mental Toughness definition, namely your ability to spot and seize an opportunity. This intuitively, as well as scientifically, makes sense because if you are a risk taker you see more situations more clearly as opportunities and are willing to embrace and explore them. If you are confident in your abilities and you easily engage with others, you are also much more likely to convert the potential opportunity of these situations into successful outcomes.

Self-Awareness

Measuring Mental Toughness

The MTQ48 is both popular and versatile used globally across all sectors and in culture, leadership organisational change career transition and stress management situations. It is an ideal measure for those professionals who enjoy and endure high stress public facing roles, comprising uncertainty, pace and rapidly changing priorities. It gives them a profile which they can use as a starting point to reflect and then work on developing their mental toughness using a toolbox of traditional interventions such as visualisation, positive thinking and attentional control and others.

Management Tools

Many of the tools used in management can be useful to use when developing self-awareness. For example, we can learn from:

- *formal feedback from others* – *e.g., formal reviews with a line manager*
- *informal feedback* – *e.g., passing comments from colleagues or customers*
- *360-degree appraisals* – *e.g., a formal review that takes comments from senior managers, customer and colleagues*
- *learning activities* – *e.g., courses on management or career development*
- *development activities* – *e.g., working in a different department or role; taking on voluntary work*
- *attending counselling or mentoring sessions* – *e.g., to focus on personal development*

By finding out about how others view us, in a professional and controlled way, we can learn more about ourselves and the impacts we have on other people.

Feedback Mechanisms

We all need feedback to find out how well we are doing, which is a very important element when developing self-awareness. When feedback is good, it gives us positive reinforcement and gives us the confidence to carry on and develop our strengths further. The negative aspects of feedback are just as useful, if not even more valuable, because they show us where we need to make changes.

When working to improve performance, feedback needs to be collected over time to allow time for objectives to be achieved or to take effect. If the period is too short, there may not be enough data available to be able to measure progress. If too long, energy and motivation to achieve objectives may decrease, and opportunities to improve may be missed.

Self-Awareness

If we do not give and receive feedback, we have no way of knowing how we are doing from an objective point of view. Our efforts need to be measured against outside standards and opinions to reflect a realistic, three-dimensional picture of our performance in the workplace.

Different feedback mechanisms
We all like to feel valued and that our opinions matter. We cannot force people to give us feedback, although we can make sure that we pursue our organisation's policies and procedures for giving and receiving feedback. As managers going through a process of developing self-awareness, we can actively seek out feedback from useful sources that will help us review our progress.

Understanding different feedback mechanisms helps to give insight into:

- *how to maximise the effectiveness of feedback we receive*
- *how to give effective feedback to others – particularly team members*

When giving feedback it is important to consider the person receiving the feedback. If the feedback is positive, it is a good opportunity to give praise and encouragement. This empowers and motivates the team member to continue doing well and not lose focus. They feel valued and respected and will benefit from feeling appreciated and recognised.

When we are asked to give feedback about someone else, it can be a good idea to only say things that we would say to that person's face. This helps us to keep our comment's objective, fair, valid and useful.

> *When delivered tactfully, constructive criticism and genuine praise are both valuable and welcome.*

There are many different mechanisms for giving feedback, including, for example:

Formal Reviews
These provide valuable, organised and focused opportunities for the individual to have detailed conversations with their line manager. Formal reviews usually start with a performance appraisal form that shows objectives, comments and maybe a rating system. The form is then discussed during a meeting when the individual and their line manager can:

- *give and receive feedback*
- *review progress so far*
- *discuss current strengths and issues*
- *set goals and targets for the next stage*

Informal feedback during work activities
Informal feedback can be given at any time – e.g., on completion of a project, at the end of a shift, or when something good or bad happens at work. Opportunities to give informal

Self-Awareness

feedback are usually unplanned and can just be a quick chat, a passing comment, or a spontaneous note or email.

Feedback from peers
Individuals can ask their peers to give them feedback. It can be useful to have feedback from people we work with who can, for example:

- *understand the work environment and requirements*
- *understand how to do the tasks being discussed*
- *give valuable and appropriate information that can be used to make future improvements*

Formal feedback from customers, suppliers or other stakeholders
This can occur when an organisation asks customers, suppliers or other people outside the organisation to give feedback. The information is usually collected on questionnaires, forms or in surveys.

Informal feedback from customers, suppliers or other stakeholders
Customers, suppliers and other people outside the organisation can decide to give spontaneous, informal feedback, verbally or in writing. This could be praise from a customer after a meal, or complaints from a supplier about late payments.

Sandwich technique for delivering negative points
If some of the feedback is negative, this needs to be delivered carefully and objectively. The best way can be to use a sandwich technique, where negative news is put between two bits of positive news, for example:

- *praise the individual for a good aspect of their performance*
- *mention and explain areas that need to be improved, and give guidance and support about how to improve*
- *finish on a high note about positive aspects, plans and hopes for future developments and improvements*

360-degree feedback

360° feedback is a process where feedback is gathered from your peers, your line manager and those who report to you – feedback from all directions. The 180° version omits subordinates. Both types can provide a great insight into the way your behaviour, attitude and approach is perceived by those on whom you have the biggest impact.

Some management roles may be affected - or may impact on - a range of stakeholders both inside and beyond the organisation. If this is the case, then their feedback should be sought too, and their needs considered when creating a Personal Development Plan (PDP).

You will have identified some aspects of your performance, impact and behaviour which have been identified through your self-evaluation which you might wish to gather feedback about. Add a small number of other elements specific to your role and context to ensure the feedback is relevant and sufficiently comprehensive. Then consider your main stakeholders, internally

Self-Awareness

and externally. What 3-5 things about you and your performance have the most critical impact on meeting their needs?

Feedback should be gathered from the right sources. It needs to come from those who have a valid opinion because they know you and are affected by your work and because they are an unbiased source. The feedback will not help if it is vague, distorted or misleading. Compile a list of people who are potential sources of feedback and seek their agreement to participating. Ensure the list of those who agree gives sufficiently comprehensive coverage and is representative of all 360°. If not, find some others.

Analyse the feedback to identify trends, contradictions and clues for your future development. Remember that the perceptions of others are their 'truth'. Whether you agree is irrelevant; this is what they see and how they feel, so take it seriously.

What is the feedback telling you about your behaviour, attitude, approach, impact and performance? What does it say about your style as a leader and manager? To further underpin your analysis of the latter you may wish to research and consider theories on leadership practice e.g., Adair's 'Action Centred Leadership, McGregor's Theory X & Y as well team theories such as Belbin's 'Team Roles'. There are many more...

Gathering feedback from different sources

There are many sources of feedback and it can be collected from, for example:

- **line managers** – e.g., in formal appraisals or informal chats
- **customers** – e.g., in surveys, comments or complaints
- **team members and other colleagues** – e.g., during appraisals or informal discussions
- **training providers** – e.g., in reports and debriefing sessions after completing a unit of a training course or following an observation session
- **coaches and mentors** – e.g., as part of a question-and-answer session after a learning activity or discussion

It is important to look at the feedback in detail and be objective about the comments. Some feedback will be reliable, useful and easily interpreted. For example, structured and informed feedback from a line manager, coach or training provider will be valuable as they have the skills to give useful and constructive criticism.

Self-Awareness

Good Quality Feedback
Good-quality feedback is likely to be based on good knowledge about, for example:

- the individual
- the workplace environment
- observations of the situation and task being reviewed
- the organisation's standards and requirements

This means that the results can be interpreted as being valid and truthful. This gives the individual an honest view of themselves and they can:

- **be positive about the feedback** – *positive feedback is great for confidence and morale, and negative feedback is useful*
- **learn from the issues that need to be improved** – *and appreciate the opportunity to learn something about their performance they might not have seen before*
- **enjoy and accept praise**
- **take confidence from positive comments** – *they are a guide that things are going well and need to continue to the same high standard*

Poor quality feedback
Some feedback is not reliable, however, due to the inexperience of some of those taking part. There may be emotional and over-critical comments from some people due to personal reasons, which may not be honest, valid or useful. For example, customers sometimes leave feedback that is biased, emotional and subjective. When this happens, it is important to interpret the feedback in context, check facts very carefully and look for useful and valid information that can be used as a guide for improving performance.
By gathering feedback from different sources, as happens in the 360-degree appraisal, we can:

- **have access to a three-dimensional picture of ourselves from other people's perspectives**
- **have access to reliable feedback from certain sources** – *so that we can gain useful and valid insight and information*
- **see how some feedback is unreliable** – *and should not be taken too seriously or personally*

Self-Awareness

Coaching Tools

Johari Window

The Johari Window is another tool that can be used to coach the development of self-awareness. It was designed in 1955 by American psychologists, Ingham and Luft.

The idea is that we examine information about ourselves and enter it into the relevant 'pane of the window'. The exercise of entering details can be revealing in itself, but we can work to change the sizes of the windowpanes as a focus for further analysis and personal development planning.

The Johari Window model is a simple and useful tool for illustrating and improving self-awareness. Today the Johari Window model is especially relevant due to modern emphasis on, and the influence of, 'soft' skills, behaviour, empathy, cooperation, inter-group development and interpersonal development. The four Johari Window perspectives are called 'regions' or 'areas' or 'quadrants. Each of these regions contains and represents the information - feelings, motivation, etc - known about the person, in terms of whether the information is known or unknown by the person, and whether the information is known or unknown by others.

A simple version of a Johari Window would be as follows:

1. Open/free area	2. Blind area
Known by the person Known by others Information about the person – e.g., skills, knowledge, experience, behaviour, attitude, feelings	Not known by the person Known by others Things that others know about the person that they do not know or realise themselves – e.g., issues that are deliberately withheld from the person
3. Hidden area	4. Unknown area
Known by the person Not known by others Information that is withheld from others – e.g., feelings, fears, worries, manipulative intentions, secrets	Not known to the person Not known by others Information that has not been recognised or revealed – e.g., a young person's undiscovered talents and attributes that need to be revealed

The idea is to enlarge the open/free area by:

- **reducing the blind area** – *usually achieved through giving and receiving feedback*
- **reducing the hidden area** – *through the process of disclosure*

The four regions, (or areas, quadrants, or perspectives) are as follows:

Self-Awareness

Quadrant 1 - 'Open self/area' or 'free area' or 'public area', or 'arena'
Region 1 is also known as the 'area of free activity'. This is the information about the person - behaviour, attitude, feelings, emotion, knowledge, experience, skills, views, etc - known by the person.

Established employees logically tend to have larger open areas than new employees. New employees start with relatively small open areas because relatively little knowledge about them is shared. The size of the open area can be expanded horizontally into the blind space, by seeking and actively listening to feedback from other employees This process is known as 'feedback solicitation'. Also, other employees can help a new employee expand their open area by offering feedback, sensitively of course.

The size of the open area can also be expanded vertically downwards into the hidden or avoided space by the person's disclosure of information, feelings, etc about him/herself to others. Also, colleagues can help a person expand their open area into the hidden area by asking the person about him/herself.

Managers and team leaders can play an important role in facilitating feedback and disclosure amongst employees, and in directly giving feedback to individuals about their own blind areas. Leaders also have a big responsibility to promote a culture and expectation for open, honest, positive, helpful, constructive, sensitive communications, and the sharing of knowledge throughout their organisation.

Top performing groups, departments, companies and organisations always tend to have a culture of open positive communication, so encouraging the positive development of the 'open area' or 'open self' for everyone is a simple yet fundamental aspect of effective leadership.

Quadrant 2 - 'Blind self' or 'blind area' or 'blind spot'
Region 2 is what is known about a person by others but is unknown by the person him/herself. By seeking or soliciting feedback from others, the aim should be to reduce this area and thereby to increase the open area, i.e., to increase self-awareness. This blind area is not an effective or productive space.

This blind area could also be referred to as ignorance about oneself, or issues in which one is deluded. A blind area could also include issues that others are deliberately withholding from a person. We all know how difficult it is to work well when kept in the dark. No-one works well when subject to 'mushroom management'. People who are 'thick-skinned' tend to have a large 'blind area'.
Colleagues and managers can take some responsibility for helping an individual to reduce their blind area - in turn increasing the open area - by giving sensitive feedback and encouraging disclosure.

Managers should promote a climate of non-judgemental feedback, and colleague response to individual disclosure, which reduces fear and therefore encourages both processes to happen. The extent to which an individual seeks feedback, and the issues on which feedback is sought, must always be at the individual's own discretion.

Self-Awareness

Some people are more resilient than others - care needs to be taken to avoid causing emotional upset. The process of soliciting serious and deep feedback relates to the process of 'self-actualisation' described in Maslow's Hierarchy of Needs development and motivation model.

Quadrant 3 - 'Hidden self' or 'hidden area' or 'avoided self/area' or 'facade'

Region 3 is what is known to oneself but kept hidden from, and therefore unknown, to others. This hidden or avoided self represents information, feelings, etc, anything that a person knows about him/self, but which is not revealed or is kept hidden from others.

The hidden area could also include sensitivities, fears, hidden agendas, manipulative intentions, secrets - anything that a person knows but does not reveal, for whatever reason. It is natural for very personal and private information and feelings to remain hidden, indeed, certain information, feelings and experiences have no bearing on work, and so can and should remain hidden. However, typically, a lot of hidden information is not very personal, it is work- or performance-related, and so is better positioned in the open area.

Relevant hidden information and feelings, etc, should be moved into the open area through the process of 'disclosure'. The aim should be to disclose and expose relevant information and feelings - hence the Johari Window terminology 'self-disclosure' and 'exposure process', thereby increasing the open area. By telling others how we feel and other information about ourselves we reduce the hidden area, and increase the open area, which enables better understanding, cooperation, trust, team-working effectiveness and productivity. Reducing hidden areas also reduces the potential for confusion, misunderstanding, poor communication, etc, which all distract from and undermine team effectiveness.

Organisational culture and working atmosphere have a major influence on group members' preparedness to disclose their hidden selves. Most people fear judgement or vulnerability and therefore hold back hidden information and feelings, which, if moved into the open area, i.e., known by others as well, would enhance mutual understanding, and thereby improve group awareness, enabling better individual performance and group effectiveness.

The extent to which an individual discloses personal feelings and information, and the issues which are disclosed, and to whom, must always be at the individual's own discretion. Some people are more keen and able than others to disclose. People should disclose at a pace and depth that they find personally comfortable. As with feedback, some people are more resilient than others - care needs to be taken to avoid causing emotional upset.

Also, as with soliciting feedback, the process of serious disclosure relates to the process of 'self-actualisation' described in Maslow's Hierarchy of Needs development and motivation model.

Quadrant 4 - 'Unknown self' or 'area of unknown activity' or 'unknown area'

Region 4 contains information, feelings, latent abilities, aptitudes, experiences etc, that are unknown to the person him/herself and unknown to others in the group. These unknown issues take a variety of forms: they can be feelings, behaviours, attitudes, capabilities,

Self-Awareness

aptitudes, which can be quite close to the surface, and which can be positive and useful, or they can be deeper aspects of a person's personality, influencing his/her behaviour to various degrees. Large unknown areas would typically be expected in younger people, and people who lack experience or self-belief.

Examples of unknown factors are as follows, and the first example is particularly relevant and common, especially in typical organisations and teams:

- *an ability that is under-estimated or un-tried through lack of opportunity, encouragement, confidence or training*
- *a natural ability or aptitude that a person does not realise they possess*
- *a fear or aversion that a person does not know they have*
- *an unknown illness*
- *repressed or subconscious feelings*
- *conditioned behaviour or attitudes from childhood*

The processes by which this information and knowledge can be uncovered are various and can be prompted through self-discovery or observation by others, or in certain situations through collective or mutual discovery, of the sort of discovery experienced on outward bound courses or other deep or intensive group work. Counselling can also uncover unknown issues, but this would then be known to the person and by one other, rather than by a group.

Whether unknown 'discovered' knowledge moves into the hidden, blind or open area depends on who discovers it and what they do with the knowledge, notably whether it is then given as feedback, or disclosed. As with the processes of soliciting feedback and disclosure, striving to discover information and feelings in the unknown relates to the process of 'self-actualisation' described in Maslow's Hierarchy of Needs development and motivation model.

Again, as with disclosure and soliciting feedback, the process of self-discovery is a sensitive one. The extent and depth to which an individual can seek out discover their unknown feelings must always be at the individual's own discretion. Some people are more keen and able than others to do this.

Uncovering 'hidden talents' - that is unknown aptitudes and skills, not to be confused with developing the Johari 'hidden area' - is another aspect of developing the unknown area and is not so sensitive as unknown feelings. Providing people with the opportunity to try new things, with no great pressure to succeed, is often a useful way to discover unknown abilities, and thereby reduce the unknown area.

Managers and leaders can help by creating an environment that encourages self-discovery, and to promote the processes of self-discovery, constructive observation and feedback among team members. It is a widely accepted industrial fact that most staff in any organisation are at any time working well within their potential.

Creating a culture, climate and expectation for self-discovery helps people to fulfil more of their potential and thereby to achieve more, and to contribute more to organisational performance.

Self-Awareness

One note of caution about Johari region 4: The unknown area could also include repressed or subconscious feelings rooted in formative events and traumatic past experiences, which can stay unknown for a lifetime. In a work or organisational context, the Johari Window should not be used to address issues of a clinical nature.

The Wheel of Life

The Wheel of Life Exercise is a popular coaching assessment tool because it is a simple yet powerful diagnostic tool.

The Wheel of Life is based on the notion that there are specific categories - or areas of focus - that form the cornerstone of your overall life experience.

The Wheel of Life categories can include:

>**Health:** Your physical health and well-being (can also include your emotional health).
>**Relationships:** Includes your primary intimate relationship, family, and friends.
>**Social:** Includes religious/spiritual communities and other group activities.
>**Financial:** Your ability to manage your money effectively, save, budget, and invest.
>**Professional/Business:** This is your work category, which can break out into a Wheel of Business.
>**Personal Growth:** Although not everyone might have an area of focus for personal development, anyone interested in Self-development does.
>**Spirituality:** This can be its own category or simply the driving force behind all your areas of focus.

These are the basic categories of most people's Wheel of Life.
Additional Wheel of Life categories might include:

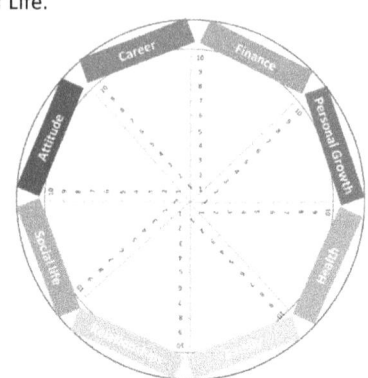

>*Mental State*
>*Attitude*
>*Creativity*
>*Contribution*
>*Lifestyle*
>*Recreation*
>*......... Or anything else that might play a dominant role in your life.*

The entire circle represents your overall life, and each piece represents a different area of focus. It might look something like this:

Self-Awareness

Selecting the Wheel of Life categories
The key is to determine the areas that are most important to *you*.

We all tend to focus on certain areas at the expense of other areas. So, the areas of focus should include both the strengths AND the weaknesses. The reason why all the key areas are important is that many of them hit on basic human needs. Maslow suggests that, when we do not address these basic needs, our lives fall out of balance (that is, we exhibit neurotic behaviour).

Challenge Beliefs
Generally, the reason why we fail to grow in particular areas of our lives is due to subconscious limiting beliefs and a fixed mindset.

Before starting this process, it is important to address your mindset about your intelligence, your skills, your abilities, and your personality. The reason why many people fail to get to grips with these types of coaching exercises is that they start off with lots of preconceived notions.

They answer questions based on what they think they "should" answer as opposed to what is true for them. The key to overcoming this tendency is to clear your mind before you do this exercise.

Assess your current level of fulfilment
After you have identified the major categories for your Wheel of Life, place them into a chart as if they are the pieces of a pie.

We all tend to have certain areas we are more proficient in and we all tend to spend time in these areas, neglecting our areas of weakness.

You may, for example, do an excellent job eating properly, exercising, and staying active (your Health category), but you are terrible at living within your means, paying off your credit cards, saving for the future, and finding more ways to add value (your financial category).

The Wheel of Life exercise brings these discrepancies to your conscious mind.

Self-Awareness

Unconscious Bias

Being aware of the need for inclusivity in the workplace is important, as is an awareness that we need to avoid unconscious bias when making decisions that affect the workforce, customers and other stakeholders. But what do these terms mean?

> *The unintended inclination or prejudice for or against an individual or a group*

Everyone has unconscious bias. It is a natural and unintended influence on how we make decisions, based on unconscious preferences rather than careful, conscious consideration. We naturally favour others who are like us or share the same values – e.g., in looks, attitudes, education, accent, colour, ethnicity, beliefs or work ethic.

Information that influences us can come from many sources – e.g., our own experiences and upbringing; what we read, hear or see around us or in the media; other people we meet; our education and family background; what we have seen and learned in the workplace. Our brains react to information all the time, and they use unconscious shortcuts to speed up decision making processes.

Although unconscious bias can be useful in a dangerous situation, where we must make a split-second decision about survival, it is not a useful attribute when making decisions in the workplace. We need to overcome any instinctive judgements and make conscious, well-rounded and well considered decisions, especially when dealing with colleagues, customers and others.

Unconscious bias can impact on inclusion

When considering our own self-awareness, we need to make sure that our words and actions support inclusivity and make sure that everyone feels valued and included – e.g., minority groups generally; people with disabilities; people from different cultures, ethnic groups or religions; people with unusual skills; people who have a great deal to offer but may not mix easily.

Whilst emotional intelligence can give valuable insight into working relationships, we need to make sure that we do not apply too much of ourselves, and our experiences, when making decisions. This is particularly true when dealing with, for example:

- *recruitment of staff*
- *promotion and career development of team members*
- *evaluating team members and recognising their strengths and weaknesses*

For example, a manager who went to university may favour job candidates who also went to university, even though other candidates are just as suitable for the job. The manager

Self-Awareness

unconsciously remembers how their own university experience shaped and helped them in their career, and they assume that a degree is essential, even if it is not a mandatory requirement in the job description. This is called affinity bias, where the manager feels an affinity with people who have the same life experiences.

In itself, the university experience can be a harmless link that makes for easier communication when getting to know someone. However, if that manager fails to think consciously about all the candidates and just favours the graduates, when there is no operational reason to do so, their action would be discriminatory and potentially liable for legal action. They need to include all suitable candidates in their shortlist, not just the graduates.

Another form of unconscious bias is known as the halo effect, where a positive trait is transferred to someone without any evidence.

For example, a team member who speaks with a 'posh' accent, uses body language very effectively and wears designer clothes may be considered as having better skills, knowledge and experience than they actually have. If selected for an unsuitable role, the manager and organisation could suffer:

- **complaints** – *e.g., from dissatisfied colleagues or customers*
- **increased costs** – *e.g., from additional training or recruitment costs*
- **a bad reputation** – *e.g., from showing poor judgement*

Where unconscious bias is against a protected characteristic under the Equality Act 2010, it can be discriminatory and possibly lead to legal action. The nine protected characteristics are:

- *age*
- *disability or impairment*
- *gender*
- *gender reassignment*
- *marriage or civil partnership*
- *race*
- *religion or beliefs*
- *sexual orientation*
- *pregnancy or maternity*

Discrimination on the basis of these characteristics is illegal, and complaints and legal action could be the serious consequences of forgetting about inclusivity and allowing unconscious bias to affect judgement.

Unconscious thoughts can be based on stereotypes and prejudices, and unconscious bias when selecting people for promotion or recruitment can lead to, for example:

- **discrimination in the workplace** – *e.g., from allowing prejudices to affect judgement when selecting team members for promotion*
- **possible legal action being taken** – *e.g., if a team member is discriminated against on the grounds of a protected characteristic*
- **a less diverse workforce** – *e.g., if people of particular races are overlooked for promotion or recruitment*

Self-Awareness

- **some people's talents being overstated** – e.g., if their image does not reflect the truth about their skills and attributes
- **some people's talents going unrecognised** – e.g., if they are awkward, shy and unable to 'sell' their considerable talents well
- **an inability to adapt to change** – e.g., from holding onto outdated, unhelpful and stereotypical ideas about people and their actions
- **an inability to exploit and develop new markets with diverse customers** – which restricts the chances of stability, success and sustainability for the organisation

Some of these effects apply to the organisation as a whole, but they can all be influenced by unconscious bias on a more personal level. A manager who is unaware of the impact of their own unconscious bias, and how it affects their ability to be inclusive in their outlook, will have an effect on their team members, other teams and the organisation as a whole. Their inability to see how their instinctive prejudices affect people around them can easily lead to resentment, lack of respect and potentially serious consequences for all concerned.

How to avoid unconscious bias

Organisations usually have policies, procedures and training to help their staff treat colleagues, customers and other stakeholders equally and fairly. The main themes are to encourage respect and inclusion, and to make it clear that discrimination will not be tolerated. To support these policies, we can avoid and overcome our own unconscious bias by, for example:

- **being aware that unconscious bias exists**
- **taking our time when making decisions** – to consider issues carefully before making decisions
- **justifying decisions** – with evidence and reasons for making the choices we have
- **following best practice in all aspects of our work**
- **working with a wide range of people** – and getting to know them as individuals
- **being fair and focusing on positive behaviour** – and not making assumptions that might be incorrect
- **challenging negative stereotypes and prejudices** – our own and other people's
- **attending training on diversity, equality and inclusion**

Respect and awareness are the foundations of all good relationships. It is not necessary for people to share beliefs, interests or personal characteristics, they just need to be able to be aware and respect differences without prejudice.

Self-Awareness

Emotional Triggers and Inhibitors

Do you ever react with anger or fear, and say or do things, and then wish you had not? You end up wishing you could take it all back, or rewind it, or get a do-over?

We all have emotional triggers.

An emotional trigger is when someone or something upsets us, and our emotions are triggered. Emotional triggers consist of thoughts, feelings, and events which seem to "trigger" an automatic response from us. The word "trigger" is important because the reaction is deemed to occur automatically. It might seem the emotional reaction is completely involuntary. The truth is that this reaction, like everything else that we do, is a choice. Learning how to identify our personal emotional triggers is the first step to taking control over how we choose to respond.

Have you ever been going through a routine day, only to have something unexpected happen that seems to automatically turn your world upside down? How about driving the car, in a good mood, only to have a sad or sentimental song come on the radio and instantly change your mood? Do you feel the overwhelming urge to do something that you know is not good for you or in line with your most important values when something upsetting happens? These are all examples of being emotionally triggered.

The workplace can be a stressful environment and involve many situations that may trigger strong negative feelings.

It is important for managers not only to be in control of their own feelings, but also help workers de-escalate their emotional situations. This can help maintain workers morale, allow them to perform to their potential, and contribute to a healthy work environment.

For most stressful situations, it is helpful when a manager is able to respond in a calm rational and positive manner. This can help lessen the intensity of workers emotions and encourage them to see the situation more objectively. In contrast, it can be very unhelpful when managers overreact or allow their own emotions into the mix, further fuelling workers emotions.

When managers react in unhelpful ways, it can send a message to workers that the managers are incapable of remaining calm and leading the team through hard times. On the other hand, managers who can help resolve an emotionally charged problem, or demonstrate empathy, can give workers confidence that they are overseen by strong, competent, leaders.

Below are some common situations in which workers may feel scared, angry or sad, as well as examples of unhelpful and helpful ways in which managers can respond.

Self-Awareness

Situations that trigger _fear_ and ways to respond		
Situation	Response is more likely to trigger fear	Responses less likely to trigger fear
A worker makes a costly mistake at work	Blame the worker and question his or her ability to do the job properly	Remind the worker that mistakes happen, help to focus on problem solving
There have been talks about budget cuts and layoffs. Workers are asking you for information.	Thoughtlessly state: I think I have an idea who will be let go but I cannot talk about it	Empathise with their concern. Tell them you will share as much information as you can and keep communication ongoing. If layoffs are inevitable, talk about resources available to those who may need it e.g., Community resources and/or company benefits.
A worker is about to make a presentation but thinks that it will go poorly.	Urge the worker to make a good presentation no matter what, as the whole department depends on it. Reassure the worker that he has prepared well for the presentation, make encouraging comments	I am not concerned at all about your ability to give presentations, I have seen you speaking at meetings and you do a great job
A worker shows up in the manager's office for a performance review. The worker jokes nervously, okay so how bad is it this time?	Ignore the joke and maintain a serious look.	Keep a warm, relaxed expression. Ask if the worker is nervous. Remind them that a review is a positive, growth opportunity
It is a worker's second month on the job, and she seems to have a hard time learning the tasks	Point out that most workers are able to learn the tasks by this time.	Show concern about the worker's progress, but focus on asking what you can provide to help her succeed
Workers on your team are unlikely to meet a looming deadline for an important project	Express your frustration openly to them: my reputation is on the line I will be hacked off if we do not meet the deadline.	Point out the problem in a calm manner, without placing blame on anyone. I accept responsibility as a manager for the delay. Focus on problem solving how can we work together to meet this deadline
A worker reports to you that another worker has been bullying him about his sexuality.	Ask the worker about his sexuality. Do not take his complaint seriously. Express doubt that he is telling the truth	Maintain a calm presence and do not act surprised or shocked. Assume the worker is telling the truth. Express empathy: I am sorry to hear what you are going through Thank the worker for informing. You indicate that you take these complaints seriously and inform the worker of your next steps and actions

Self-Awareness

Situations that trigger _anger_ and ways to respond

Situation	Response is more likely to trigger anger	Responses less likely to trigger anger
You had to choose one worker to promote from several qualified applicants. Today, you announce which worker received the promotion.	Talk about workers in a disrespectful way: I know you have all been drooling over this job. Tell workers that only the successful applicant was qualified, whilst the rest were not good enough	Thank everyone for their interest. Acknowledge the efforts they put into their applications. Acknowledge that it was a tough decision. Remind workers that new opportunities may continue to open up
Your team is delayed in finishing a project because of a worker's negligence	Highlight to the team that it was one of the worker's fault. Show frustration my shaking your head, sighing, and criticising the worker behind his back.	Show team spirit to the workers. De-emphasise the blame from the worker and focus on finishing the project team. Validate feelings of frustration: I can understand that everyone is frustrated they have to work overtime. I really appreciate you for your professionalism and working through this as a team
Your team is expanding and there are not enough offices for everybody.	Allocate new offices to your favourite workers, without consulting the entire group of workers about space allocation.	Make sure the process is transparent as possible. Let workers know the criteria upon which you are basing your choices (possibly workload, seniority or job description). Thank the workers for understanding. Let them know that you are working on providing everyone the space they need.
During a team meeting that you are chairing, two workers engaged in a debate that turns heated.	Joining the argument. Say something disrespectful: okay let us not have a fight over this	Try to de-escalate with words in a calm light-hearted tone: I am glad to see that we all feel strongly about this issue. Retain control over the meeting. Unfortunately, we must move on to other topics. We might need to schedule another meeting just talk about this issue.
A front-desk worker has just been verbally abused by a client and seems upset.	Ask what happened and then walk away, without offering any words of comfort or care	Ask with a caring attitude what happened. Express concern about how the worker was treated. Show empathy to the worker: No one should be treated that way at work. We will need to file an incident report
A worker has just ended a call with a customer and seems very frustrated	Assume that the worker did not handle the call competently: do you need help with handling the phone calls?	Give the worker the benefit of the doubt. Ask what happened. Empathise with the worker. Sometimes it helps the worker, calm down when you paraphrase what they said simply using simpler, calmer words: So, the client got upset and called you stupid because he thought that you had lost his file?
Its late Friday afternoon and you have just given a worker a large and important task which is due for completion by the end of the day.	Tell the worker matter-of-factly about the last-minute task. It is her job, after all.	Recognise that workers need to leave work on time. Acknowledge late notice of the task and thank the worker for understanding. Plan for what is reasonable and feasible to complete.

Self-Awareness

Situations that trigger _sadness (or hurt)_ and ways to respond		
Situation	Responses more likely to trigger sadness or hurt	Responses less likely to trigger sadness or hurt
One of your workers has just been rejected for a grant that he had worked hard to apply for and was hoping to get.	Dwell on the negatives and on the past. Say things that are unproductive: Wow that is too bad. That grant would have helped you a lot. You work so hard for it too. That is two weeks of your life you will never get back.	Empathise with the worker: that is frustrating, because you worked hard to apply for this. Focus on the positives: you did not get the grant, but you put together a good proposal that you can use for future projects.
During a team social event you notice that a worker is trying to mingle with others but is not being accepted	Ignore what you saw and go and mingle with other managers.	Try to make everyone feel included. Make small talk with the worker.
A worker seems ashamed as he is receiving negative feedback from you about his work	ignore what you see, thinking, "that's not my problem". Continue with the negative feedback.	Speak in a respectful, light-hearted tone. Acknowledge what you see. Express empathy with the worker's feelings: it is hard to hear this kind of feedback. But we know that it helps us be better in the long run. How can I help you make improvements?
A well-liked staff member is leaving, and the workers seem sad to see her go	Do not acknowledge her upcoming departure	Acknowledge the situation and the worker's feelings: we are all sad to see her go. Focus on the positives: she is off to a very exciting new job. We will wish her all the best
There has been a massive layoff today in the company and some of the workers although spared, are quiet and sombre.	Focus on the negatives: it is so quiet in here now that some of you are gone. It is going to be a ghost town soon.	Empathise with the worker's feelings. Maintain a neutral attitude. Focus on the positives: the company always tries to find laid off staff other positions within the company.

People tend to be triggered into an anger reaction if they feel:

- Embarrassed
- Humiliated
- Insulted
- Afraid
- Rejected

They can feel this if they feel someone is taking them down, ignoring them or not taking them seriously.

> **Any person who is not treated with respect at all times could react to a trigger you give them.**

Self-Awareness

Consequently, they will regard your actions as being the cause of their reaction, even though they may behave in a manner which is considerably worse than yours. The net result is they will claim you started it!

Inhibitors are things which prevent people from completely losing their temper. Not everyone gets violent when they become angry and this is due to our inhibitions or our inhibitors.

- *self-control*
- *personal values*
- *fear that the other party may fight back*
- *social or legal consequences*
- *experience*
- *training*

Your response such as pointing a finger could be a trigger which leads to an escalation to violence. You must consciously choose to respond to the incident in a way which we de-escalate the situation by thinking about every step you take.

As we become more aware of the triggers in our life which typically lead to an emotional reaction, so we can begin to find ways to manage them. These triggers can come in many forms. It may be our reaction to a mistake made by an employee, or a spill caused by a young child or a reaction to another driver who we consider to have endangered us.

Worse still it could be reaching out to an alcoholic drink or smoking a cigarette, after a trigger, both of which are highly addictive and can have seriously grave repercussions on our health and longevity.

10% of conflict is due to the difference in opinion and 90% is due to the delivery and tone of voice.

It is therefore important that we recognise the triggers, and we manage our emotional response to that trigger. It could be as simple as counting to ten before we react or learning strategies to deal effectively with the problem, so the trigger becomes irrelevant. We know the problems of over-reacting, blowing things out of proportion, or lashing out in anger. But what can we do about it?

Notice When You Get Triggered

If you want to handle your emotional triggers better, you first need to notice when you get triggered. You need to become aware that you have been triggered, and that your emotions are kicking in.

These are some helpful suggestions on things to look out for:

Self-Awareness

Body: *Shallow breathing, rapid heartbeat, and sick to the stomach*
Emotions: *Experiencing a fight-or-flight response, either feeling like a 'rabbit in the headlights' or having an emotional outburst*
Thoughts: *Feeling like a victim, thoughts of blame and judgment, difficulty paying attention*

Triggers almost always have long histories behind them. When we get triggered, it is very often because it brings back something from the past, that *"she's doing that, she's-doing-that-again feeling"*.

Triggers are also very often connected to a perceived inadequacy about ourselves that is a source of pain to us, sort of like a raw nerve. This could be someone simply mentioning one of you identified weaknesses.

When we begin to feel a trigger, you need to manage your emotional triggers and learn to master your emotional responses to negative events.

Impact of behaviour on others
Managers need to always behave professionally and not let personal beliefs or opinions interfere with their judgment and actions. They need to lead by example and be aware of the strengths, weaknesses and needs of people around them.

The way in which you react to a person or situation will directly affect how they react back to you. This is known as stimulus and response.

When we provide a stimulus, it will prompt a response from the person receiving the stimulus – How they respond will directly affect behaviour.

If the response is positive - the situation will de-escalate, whereas, if the response is negative - the situation has the potential to escalate and become more serious.

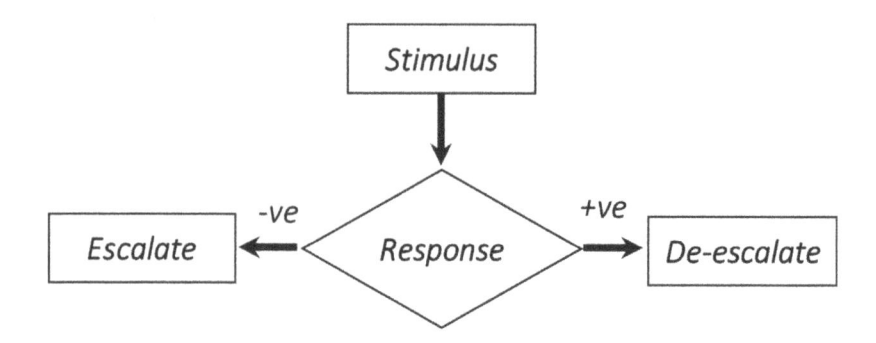

Self-Awareness

The Attitude / Behaviour Cycle

The attitude / behaviour cycle is also known as the Betari Box. It is extremely unlikely that you will have a positive attitude towards everyone you meet. Some people, for any number of reasons, will cause you to have negative feelings towards them. If you have these negative feelings, you will communicate this unconsciously to them and their reaction will be negative.

Once the person has become aware of your negative feeling, they will behave in a negative manner towards you. This will cause your negative feelings to cause you to behave in a negative manner. This will cause them to behave in a negative way which will, in turn, increase your negative feelings and behaviour. And so, the situation continues and deteriorates.
It is very difficult to change your attitude to someone. However, you can easily change your behaviour. You need to learn to behave so your negative feelings do not show, and your behaviour does not reveal and negative traits. This will break the cycle and stop it getting worse.

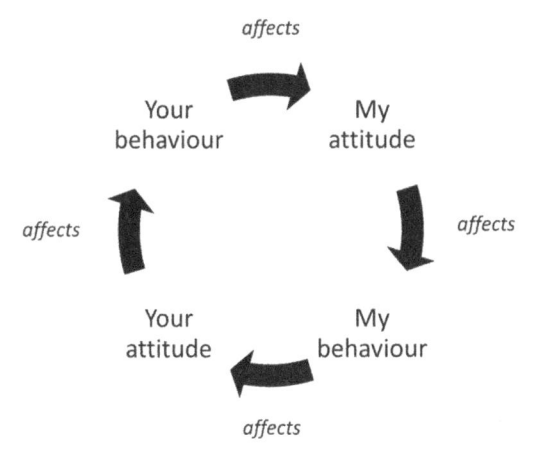

Your behaviour → affects → *My attitude* → affects → *My behaviour* → affects → *Your attitude* → affects → *Your behaviour*

In all activities, managers need to think about how their behaviour:

- *is perceived by others*
- *impacts their own performance*
- *affects working relationships*

Any individual's performance and behaviour can affect other people, but a manager's leadership role puts them in a responsible and influential position. Leaders are nearly always a focus for attention, which makes sense as being visible and vocal are important elements of the role.

However, people can judge leaders harshly, and transfer their loyalty and support elsewhere very quickly. We only have to look at how often sports team managers and coaches are criticised or sacked to know how fragile a leader's position can be.
In the workplace, it is essential to for managers to make sure that their behaviour and leadership skills are of the highest standard so that they can provide effective leadership. As part of the leadership role, managers need to be able to, for example:

Self-Awareness

- *use good communication skills consistently*
- *lead and manage a stable, well-motivated and engaged team*
- *help their teams to meet organisational needs and objectives*
- *offer effective and imaginative solutions to problems*
- *bring energy, enthusiasm and a clear focus*
- *bring a balanced and positive attitude to change*

On a day-to-day level, examples of positive and inspirational leadership behaviour could include:

- **using excellent communication skills** – *able to engage and inspire team members and make them feel valued*
- **being fair and consistent** – *when making decisions or solving problems*
- **good timekeeping and attendance** – *to show commitment to and respect for the team and its objectives*
- **performing at consistently high levels** – *leading the way to achieve deadlines, targets and quality standards*
- **displaying good conduct and behaviour** – *that minimise discomfort, stress, resentment and embarrassment for other team members*
- **following good working practices** – *that avoid unnecessary harm or injury, lost work time or disciplinary procedures*

A manager whose behaviour is positive, inspirational and professional will have the respect of team members, colleagues and other stakeholders. They will be able to deal with plans, strategies, decisions and problems with the positive support of those around them.

On the other hand, a manager whose behaviour is negative for any length of time will soon lose the support of their team and colleagues. They will find it impossible to inspire and lead their team if they do not have their respect and cooperation. For example, a manager who is always late, loses their temper, acts unfairly and inconsistently, will quickly come up against complaints from customers, colleagues and others, and find it very difficult to carry out their operational duties effectively.

From time to time, there will be unexpected circumstances that will adversely affect a good manager's behaviour, such as sudden illness or bereavement. When this happens, because they have a good and loyal working relationship, team members will usually join together to support the manager and help them through the difficult time.

Adapting behaviour to improve the impact on others
Using self-awareness, it is possible to understand the impact of our own behaviour on others and take steps to adapt when necessary. As the psychotherapist Carl Jung said: "There is no cure and no improving of the world that does not begin with the individual himself".

Self-awareness helps us to consciously think about how we influence and interact with others. If things are going well, reflection still helps because it enables us to see what we need to keep

Self-Awareness

doing to maintain good working relationships. If there are problems, however, we need to reflect to see if any of our behaviours are causing issues.

With the help of self-refection, and maybe a discussion with a line manager, we can:

- *identify how our behaviours impact others* – in positive or negative ways
- *consider alternative ways of behaving* – research other ways of behaving
- *try new approaches*
- *collect feedback about effectiveness* – with more reflection or discussion
- *implement further improvements*
- *review regularly*

If team members and colleagues are having problems, the causes may be nothing to do with their manager personally. However, the manager still needs to investigate causes so that they can approach team members in an appropriate manner, to see if they can help or support them with external problems.

Self-Awareness

Reflection

Reflecting helps you to develop your skills and review their effectiveness, rather than just carry-on doing things as you have always done them. It is about questioning, in a positive way, what you do and why you do it and then deciding whether there is a better, or more efficient, way of doing it in the future.

In any role, whether at home or at work, reflection is an important part of learning. You would not use a recipe a second time around if the dish did not work the first time, would you? You would either adjust the recipe or find a new and, hopefully, better one. When we do our job, we can become stuck in a routine that may not be working effectively. Thinking about your own skills can help you identify changes you might need to make.

Reflective questions to ask yourself:

Strengths – *What are my strengths? For example, am I well organised? Do I remember things?*
Weaknesses – *What are my weaknesses? For example, am I easily distracted? Do I need more practise with a particular skill?*
Skills – *What skills do I have and what am I good at?*
Problems – *What problems are there at work/home that may affect me? For example, responsibilities or distractions that may impact on study or work.*
Achievements – *What have I achieved?*
Happiness – *Are there things that I am unhappy with or disappointed about? What makes me happy?*
Solutions – *What could I do to improve in these areas?*

Although self-reflection can seem difficult at first, or even selfish or embarrassing, as it does not come naturally. you will find it becomes easier with practise and the end result could be a happier and more efficient you.

Links between Self-Awareness and Performance

The close link between self-awareness and improved performance is almost irrefutable. Based on the outcomes of your personal research, you will have found a number of instances where your performance falls into a weakness category and clearly needs to be addressed. Furthermore, the impact of your weaknesses will affect not just you and your career, but also the working lives of your team members, other teams, and the wider stakeholders in the organisation and outside it.

Consequently, it is vital that performance is adapted to eliminate the weaknesses identified and immediate steps taken to develop these into strengths. This is best planned and monitored using a personal development plan or PDP.

Self-Awareness

Emotional Intelligence

For decades, researchers have studied the reasons why a high IQ does not necessarily guarantee success in the classroom or the boardroom. By the 1980s, psychologists and biologists, among others, were focusing on the important role other skill sets — needed to process emotional information — played in promoting worldly success, leadership, personal fulfilment and happy relationships.

In 1990, psychologists John Mayer and Peter Salovey theorised that another intelligence underpinned those other skill sets. They coined the term, emotional intelligence, which they broke down into four "branches":

- *Identifying emotions on a non-verbal level*
- *Using emotions to guide cognitive thinking*
- *Understanding the information emotions convey and the actions emotions generate*
- *Regulating one's own emotions, for personal benefit and for the common good*

As a science reporter for the New York Times, Goleman was exposed to Mayer's and Salovey's work and took the concept of emotional intelligence a step further. He argued that existing definitions of intelligence needed to be reworked. IQ was still important, but intellect alone was no guarantee of adeptness in identifying one's own emotions or the emotional expressions of others. It took a special kind of intelligence, Goleman said, to process emotional information and utilise it effectively — whether to facilitate good personal decisions, to resolve conflicts or to motivate oneself and others.

> *Emotional intelligence is the capacity to be aware of, control and express our emotions, and use them effectively in interpersonal relationships. It is the ability to step into someone else's shoes' and see things from their point of view.*

The ability to understand how people feel and react can be extremely useful when managing and leading others, and can be applied on two levels:

- ***personal*** – *understanding our own feelings or reactions*
- ***interpersonal*** – *understanding other people's feelings and reactions*

Emotional intelligence begins with a leader recognising and then managing their own emotions. When a leader can do this, they can begin to improve their own credibility with others. The next step for emotional intelligence is to recognise and manage the emotions of others. Emotional intelligence has the following five dimensions:

Self-Awareness

- **Self-Awareness** - Being aware of your emotions (understanding what you are feeling)
- **Self-Motivation** - Ability to persist in the face of obstacles and setbacks (influencing constructive emotions in yourself)
- **Self-Management** - Ability to effectively manage your emotions and impulses (controlling your destructive emotions)
- **Empathy** - Sensing how others are feeling (understanding what others are feeling)
- **Social Skills** - Ability to effectively handle the emotions of others

Managers and leaders often have to work as a team or develop relationships with colleagues, customers and other stakeholders. A reasonable degree of emotional intelligence can help managers be:

- **empathetic** – e.g., able to put themselves in other people's shoes
- **sensitive to others** – e.g., able to sense and respond to their needs, problems and feelings
- **understanding and sympathetic** – e.g., able to understand the complexities of life and make allowances when things go wrong
- **good at reading other people's emotions correctly** – e.g., able to identify the less obvious causes for emotional outbursts

These skills give leaders a great advantage, especially when they are involved with functions that rely on relationship management. Leaders with good emotional intelligence skills instinctively know how to manipulate situations, inspire and motivate people, and get the best out of them.

Salovey and Mayer's Emotional Intelligence theory

According to their definition, emotional intelligence is the ability to process information about your own emotions and other people's. It is also the ability to use this information to guide your thoughts and behaviour.

Thus, emotionally intelligent people pay attention to, use, understand, and manage their emotions.

According to these two authors, for a person to be categorised as emotionally intelligent, they must have four basic abilities:

- *Ability to perceive and correctly express their emotions and other people's.*
- *Ability to use emotions in a way that facilitates thought.*
- *Ability to understand emotions, emotional language, and emotional signals.*
- *Ability to manage their emotions to achieve goals.*

Self-Awareness

In this particular emotional intelligence theory, each ability has four different stages. However, this process does not necessarily happen spontaneously. On the contrary, it usually requires a conscious effort.

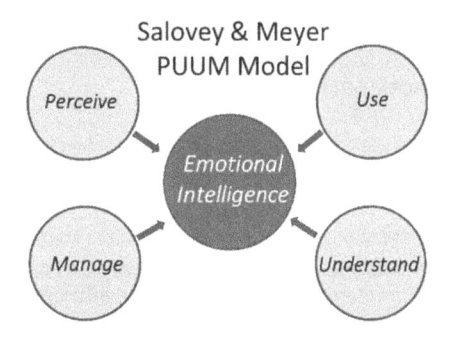

Salovey & Meyer PUUM Model

Perceive — Use — Manage — Understand — Emotional Intelligence

1. Perceiving emotion
Identify deceptive or dishonest emotional expressions.
Discriminate accurate vs. inaccurate emotional expressions.
Understand how emotions are displayed depending on context and culture.
Express emotions accurately when desired.
Perceive emotional content in the environment, visual arts, and music.
Perceive emotions in other people through their vocal cues, facial expression, language, and behaviour.
Identify emotions in one's own physical states, feelings, and thoughts.

2. Facilitating thought using emotion
Select problems based on how one's ongoing emotional state might facilitate cognition.
Leverage mood swings to generate different cognitive perspectives.
Prioritise thinking by directing attention according to present feeling.
Generate emotions as a means to relate to experiences of another person.
Generate emotions as an aid to judgment and memory.

3. Understanding emotions
Recognise cultural differences in the evaluation of emotions.
Understand how a person might feel in the future or under certain conditions (affective forecasting).
Recognise likely transitions among emotions such as from anger to satisfaction.
Understand complex and mixed emotions.
Differentiate between moods and emotions.
Appraise the situations that are likely to elicit emotions.
Determine the antecedents, meanings, and consequences of emotions.
Label emotions and recognise relations among them.

4. Managing emotions
Effectively manage others' emotions to achieve a desired outcome.
Effectively manage one's own emotions to achieve a desired outcome.
Evaluate strategies to maintain, reduce, or intensify an emotional response.
Monitor emotional reactions to determine their reasonableness.

Self-Awareness

Engage with emotions if they are helpful; disengage if not.
Stay open to pleasant and unpleasant feelings, as needed, and to the information they convey.

Goleman's Theory of Emotional Intelligence

One model that explains emotional intelligence was developed by Daniel Goleman, a psychologist and science journalist, following on from Salovey and Mayer's theory.

He contends that Emotional intelligence is twice as important as cognitive intelligence for predicting career success. He suggested high levels of emotional intelligence improve working relationships, help to develop problem solving skills, increase efficiency and effectiveness and catalyse the development of new strategies.

The theory identifies four components:

- **Self-awareness** – *the conscious knowledge of our character, beliefs, emotions, qualities and desires*
- **Self-management and motivation** – *the ability to stay calm under pressure and stay motivated to achieve goals*
- **Social awareness** – *the ability to have empathy and understand other people's emotions and feelings*
- **Relationship skills** – *the ability to influence, negotiate, communicate, build rapport and develop networks*

As the diagram shows, the focus for emotional intelligence is relationship management.

Emotional development can be achieved through, for example:

- *team-building exercises*
- *coaching*
- *training in negotiation and communication skills*

Self-Awareness

In leadership roles, emotional intelligence can provide an extra insight into which approach will be most effective when guiding and inspiring the team to follow. By using emotional intelligence, leaders can:

- *read other people's feelings and reactions more accurately*
- *adapt their approach*
- *employ appropriate skills*

According to Goleman, the higher someone goes in an organisation, the more the emotional skills matter. Senior managers and directors can hire people with the skills and knowledge that the organisation needs, but they need to be very competent in emotional intelligence themselves. Good relationship capabilities become more critical as careers progress.

Petrides and Furnham 2009

"Trait EI" is a new term created by Konstantine Petrides (K.V. Petrides) from the University of London and Adrian Furnham from University College London.

One of the most recent models of EI was published in 2009 by Petrides and colleagues and marks a break from the idea that emotional intelligence is ability-based. Instead, it proposes that people have, as part of their personalities, a number of emotional self-perceptions and emotional traits.

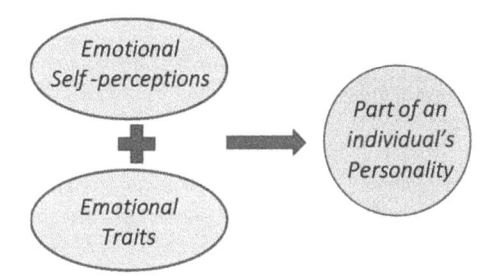

Emotional Self-perceptions + Emotional Traits → Part of an individual's Personality

These traits are not measured in the scientific sense but are instead measured by the respondent's self-report. Of course, this assumes that the respondent can accurately describe his or her own traits.

It is important to note that this model of emotional intelligence can only be viewed in conjunction with a comprehensive exploration of a person's personality. This is distinct from the other models, which posit that EI is a brain-based ability, not an environmental aspect of personality.

Petrides and Furnham identified 15 common components of the different EI models

These are listed below:

Self-Awareness

Component	High scorers perceive themselves as...
Adaptability	flexible and willing to adapt to new conditions
Assertiveness	forthright, frank and willing to stand up for their rights
Emotion expression	capable of communicating their feelings to others
Emotion management (others)	capable of influencing other people's feelings
Emotion perception (self and others)	clear about their own and other people's feelings
Emotion regulation	capable of controlling their emotions
Impulsiveness (low)	reflective and less likely to give in to their urges
Relationship skills	capable of having fulfilling personal relationships
Self-esteem	successful and self-confident
Self-motivation	driven and unlikely to give up in the face of adversity
Social competence	accomplished networkers with excellent social skills
Stress management	capable of withstanding pressure and regulating stress
Trait empathy	capable of taking someone else's perspective
Trait happiness	cheerful and satisfied with their lives
Trait optimism	confident and likely to 'look on the bright side' of life

Travis Bradberry

Travis Bradberry describes EQ as being composed of four core skills, which are often categorised under two umbrellas:

Personal Competence refers to your ability to be aware of and manage your emotions and behaviour. It focuses more on you individually than your interactions with others and is composed of:

Self-awareness – ability to predict, perceive, and be aware of your emotions
Self-management – ability to leverage your self-awareness to positively channel your behaviour

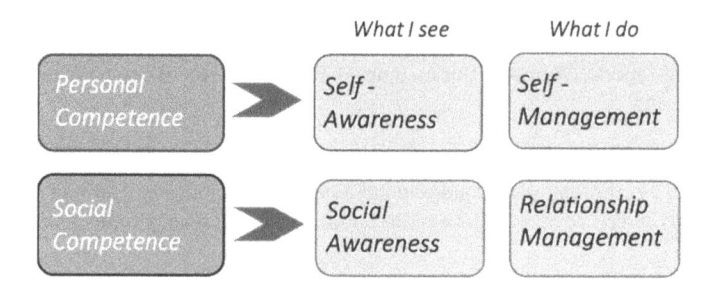

	What I see	What I do
Personal Competence	Self-Awareness	Self-Management
Social Competence	Social Awareness	Relationship Management

Social Competence refers to your ability to understand people's moods, behaviours, and motives to build relationships and effectively interact with others. It is composed of:

Self-Awareness

Social awareness – *ability to pick up on others' emotions and understand what is going on*

Relationship management – *ability to use your social awareness and others' emotions to successfully manage situations*

It stands to reason that you cannot predict emotional intelligence based on how smart someone is. However, it might be tempting to think that because EQ is a flexible set of more qualitative skills, it is directly tied to personality. On the contrary, personality results from hard-wired preferences (e.g., introversion versus extroversion). EQ, on the other hand, can be developed, even if it does not come naturally.

Why is EI important?
Having a heightened degree of emotional intelligence can lead to a range of benefits. On a personal level, increased self-awareness can help you respond to day-to-day situations; self-management skills improve your ability to adapt to change; and heightened levels of social awareness and relationship management can lead to a healthier response from other parties when you are faced with a challenging situation.

High EI also translates to optimal outcomes as a business leader when navigating challenging situations like contract negotiations and terminations, or even in positive cases like company celebrations.

Measuring Emotional Intelligence

1. Are you Self-Aware?
According to Bradberry, being self-aware is your ability to accurately perceive your emotions and stay aware of them as they happen." This self-awareness is important for you to be able to quickly react and adjust in a given situation.

2. Do you have self-control?
Controlling your emotions is key in emotional intelligence. You need to be able to act to act and react based on the situation and not on how you are feeling in that moment. Reacting based on how you feel can come with some not so appealing consequences.

3. Are you empathetic?
Being empathetic takes awareness one step further. Being empathetic is being aware of the emotions of others. You do this by listening carefully and tuning into the non-verbal clues those around you are giving. This gives you the opportunity to build a closer relationship and allows them to related better to you.

4. Do you effectively manage change?
Change is a simple fact of life. How you react to the change is a measure of your EQ and can set you apart from your peers. The one that is able to see the change, adjust to it, help others adjust, and create a positive outcome, will be the one others will look to when future changes occur. If you are a leader or looking to be one, this skill is critical.

Self-Awareness

5. Do you dwell on the past?
If you are stretching yourself reaching for success, you will have some failures. That is part of the price for success. Your emotional intelligence and future success will be measured by how you react to that failure. Do you stay stuck in the label of being a failure or do you rise from the ashes of that failure, a smarter and more confident individual?

6. Do you control your thoughts?
Much research has been done to show that we do indeed talk to ourselves. How we talk to ourselves is a measure of our emotional intelligence. How is your self-talk? Do you berate yourself or put yourself down or do you keep a positive attitude and say the words that will keep you moving forward in a positive direction? Part of your success will come down to the things you say to yourself each day. Take the time to control how you think, and since you will be talking to yourself anyway, why not make the words you speak be inspiring.

7. Do you pay attention?
In 1997, the phrase Weapons of Mass Distraction was coined by the movie comedy with the same name. Today, the weapons of mass distraction come in many forms including texts, emails, and social media. How are you managing these distractions? Are you able to focus for an extended period of time without being tempted to look at your phone or emails? How effective you are at paying attention is a factor that goes into determining your emotional intelligence and the amount you can accomplish throughout each day. Those with a higher EQ accomplish more by not allowing distractions to impair their focus.

Benefits of Emotional Intelligence

It is not the smartest people who are the most successful or the most fulfilled in life. You probably know people who are academically brilliant and yet are socially inept and unsuccessful at work or in their personal relationships.
Intellectual ability or your intelligence quotient (IQ) is not enough on its own to achieve success in life.

Your IQ can help you get into university, but it is your EQ that will help you manage the stress and emotions when facing your final exams. IQ and EQ exist in tandem and are most effective when they build off one another.

Emotional intelligence affects:

Your performance
High emotional intelligence can help you navigate the social complexities of the workplace, lead and motivate others, and excel in your career. In fact, when it comes to gauging important job candidates, many companies now rate emotional intelligence as important as technical ability and employ EQ testing before hiring.

Your physical health.
If you are unable to manage your emotions, you are probably not managing your stress either. This can lead to serious health problems. Uncontrolled stress raises blood pressure, suppresses the immune system, increases the risk of heart attacks and strokes,

Self-Awareness

contributes to infertility, and speeds up the aging process. The first step to improving emotional intelligence is to learn how to manage stress.

Your mental health.
Uncontrolled emotions and stress can also impact your mental health, making you vulnerable to anxiety and depression. If you are unable to understand, get comfortable with, or manage your emotions, you will also struggle to form strong relationships. This in turn can leave you feeling lonely and isolated and further exacerbate any mental health problems.

Your relationships.
By understanding your emotions and how to control them, you are better able to express how you feel and understand how others are feeling. This allows you to communicate more effectively and forge stronger relationships, both at work and in your personal life.

Your social intelligence.
Being in tune with your emotions serves a social purpose, connecting you to other people and the world around you. Social intelligence enables you to recognise friend from foe, measure another person's interest in you, reduce stress, balance your nervous system through social communication, and feel loved and happy.

Developing Emotional Intelligence

1. Self-awareness
If you are self-aware, you always know how you feel, and you know how your emotions and your actions can affect the people around you. Being self-aware when you are in a leadership position also means having a clear picture of your strengths and weaknesses, and it means behaving with humility. To improve your self-awareness:

Keep a journal – *Journals help you improve your self-awareness. If you spend just a few minutes each day writing down your thoughts, this can move you to a higher degree of self-awareness.*

Slow down – *When you experience anger or other strong emotions, slow down to examine why.*

Remember, no matter what the situation, you can always choose how you react to it.

2. Self-regulation
Leaders who regulate themselves effectively rarely verbally attack others, make rushed or emotional decisions, stereotype people, or compromise their values. Self-regulation is all about staying in control.

This element of emotional intelligence, according to Goleman, also covers a leader's flexibility and commitment to personal accountability. Improve your ability to self-regulate by:

Know your values – *Do you have a clear idea of where you absolutely will not compromise? Do you know what values are most important to you? Spend some time examining your "code of ethics." If you know what is most important to you,*

Level 5: Operations / Departmental Manager

Self-Awareness

then you probably will not have to think twice when you face a moral or ethical decision – you will make the right choice.

Hold yourself accountable – If you tend to blame others when something goes wrong, stop. Make a commitment to admit to your mistakes and to face the consequences, whatever they are. You will probably sleep better at night, and you will quickly earn the respect of those around you.

Practice being calm – The next time you are in a challenging situation, be very aware of how you act. Do you relieve your stress by shouting at someone else? Practice deep-breathing exercises to calm yourself. Also, try to write down all of the negative things you want to say, and then rip it up and throw it away. Expressing these emotions on paper (and not showing them to anyone!) is better than speaking them aloud to your team. What is more, this helps you challenge your reactions to ensure that they are fair!

3. Motivation
Self-motivated leaders work consistently toward their goals, and they have extremely high standards for the quality of their work. Improve your motivation by:

- **Re-examine why you are doing your job** – It is easy to forget what you really love about your career. Take some time to remember why you wanted the job. If you are unhappy in your role and you are struggling to remember why you wanted it, try the Five Whys technique to find the root of the problem. Starting at the root often helps you look at your situation in a new way.
- **Make sure that your life and work objectives are fresh and energising.**
- **Know where you stand** – Determine how motivated you are to lead.
- **Be hopeful and find something good** – Motivated leaders are usually optimistic, no matter what problems they face. Adopting this mindset might take practice, but it is well worth the effort.

Every time you face a challenge, or even a failure, try to find at least one good thing about the situation. It might be something small, like a new contact, or something with long-term effects, like an important lesson learned. But there is almost always something positive if you look for it.

4. Empathy
For leaders, having empathy is critical to managing a successful team or organisation. Leaders with empathy have the ability to put themselves in someone else's situation. They help develop the people on their team, challenge others who are acting unfairly, give constructive feedback, and listen to those who need it. If you want to earn the respect and loyalty of your team, then show them you care by being empathic. improve your empathy by:

- **Put yourself in someone else's position** – It is easy to support your own point of view. After all, it is yours! But take the time to look at situations from other people's perspectives.

Self-Awareness

- **Pay attention to body language** – Perhaps when you listen to someone, you cross your arms, move your feet back and forth, or bite your lip. This body language tells others how you really feel about a situation, and the message you are giving is not positive! Learning to read body language can be a real asset in a leadership role, because you will be better able to determine how someone truly feels. This gives you the opportunity to respond appropriately.
- **Respond to feelings** – You ask your assistant to work late – again. Although they agree, you can hear the disappointment in their voice. Respond by addressing their feelings. Tell them you appreciate how willing they are to work extra hours, and that you are just as frustrated about working late. If possible, figure out a way for future late nights to be less of an issue (for example, give them Monday mornings off).

5. Social Skills

Leaders who do well in the social skills element of emotional intelligence are great communicators. They are just as open to hearing bad news as good news, and they are expert at getting their team to support them and be excited about a new mission or project.

Leaders who have good social skills are also good at managing change and resolving conflicts diplomatically. They are rarely satisfied with leaving things as they are, but they do not sit back and make everyone else do the work: they set an example with their own behaviour. Build social skills by:

- **Learn conflict resolution** – Leaders must know how to resolve conflicts between their team members, customers, or vendors. Learning conflict resolution skills is vital if you want to succeed.
- **Improve your communication skills** – How well do you communicate?
- **Learn how to praise others** – As a leader, you can inspire the loyalty of your team simply by giving praise when it is earned. Learning how to praise others is a fine art, but well worth the effort.

To be effective, leaders must have a solid understanding of how their emotions and actions affect the people around them. The better a leader relates to and works with others, the more successful he or she will be.

Take the time to work on self-awareness, self-regulation, motivation, empathy, and social skills. Working on these areas will help you excel in the future!

Self-Awareness

Qualities of people with high EI scores

1. They're not perfectionists.
Being a perfectionist can get in the way of completing tasks and achieving goals since it can lead to having trouble getting started, procrastinating, and looking for the right answer when there is not one. Therefore, people with EI are not perfectionists. They realise that perfection does not exist and push forward. If they make a mistake, they will make adjustments and learn from it.

2. They know how to balance work and play.
Working 24/7 and not taking care of yourself adds unnecessary stress and health problems to your life. Because of this, people with EI know when it is time to work and when to play. For example, if they need to disconnect from the world for a couple of hours, or even an entire weekend, they will because they need the time to unplug to reduce the stress levels.

3. They embrace change.
Instead of dreading change, emotionally intelligent people realise that change is a part of life. Being afraid of change hinders success, so they adapt to the changes around them and always have a plan in place should any sort of change occur.

4. They do not get easily distracted.
People with high EI have the ability to pay attention to the task at hand and are not easily distracted by their surroundings, such as text or random thought.

5. They're empathetic.
Being able to relate to others, show compassion, and take the time to help someone are all crucial components of EI. Additionally, being empathic makes people with EI curious about other people and leads them to ask lots of questions whenever they meet someone new.

6. They know their strengths and weaknesses.
Emotionally intelligent people know what they are good at and what they are not so great at. They have not just accepted their strengths and weaknesses; they also know how to leverage their strengths and weaknesses by working with the right people in the right situation.

7. They're self-motivated.
Were you that ambitious and hard-working kid who was motivated to achieve a goal--and not just because there was a reward at the end? Being a real go-getter, even at a young age, is another quality possessed by people with EI.

8. They do not dwell in the past.
People with high EI do not have the time to dwell in the past because they are too busy contemplating the possibilities that tomorrow will bring. They do not let past mistakes consume them with negativity. They do not hold grudges. Both add stress and prevent us from moving forward.

Self-Awareness

9. They focus on the positive.
Emotionally intelligent people would rather devote their time and energy to solving a problem. Instead of harping on the negative, they look at the positive and what they have control over.

Furthermore, they also spend their time with other positive people and not the people who constantly complain.

10. They set boundaries.
While people with high EI may seem like pushovers because of their politeness and compassion, they have the power to establish boundaries. For example, they know how to say no to others. The reason? It prevents them from getting overwhelmed, burned out, and stressed because they have too many commitments. Instead, they are aware that saying no frees them up from completing previous commitments.

Self-Awareness

EIQ Test

Read the statements below and give yourself a score based on the criteria below. Remember to be as open and honest as possible in order to ensure the most accurate result. When you have completed the assessment, total your scores and check the result in the table below.

Rate yourself on a scale of 1-5 where:

1 = Not true
2 = Generally not true
3 = Generally true

4 = Frequently true
5 = Always true

No.	Statement	Score
1	I find it easy and natural to be aware of my inner feelings, thoughts, and desires	
2	Even when I am very excited about something my passions do not overwhelm my reason.	
3	I experience life through all of my sense and do not filter my experiences through my analytical mind	
4	I experience a healthy degree of motivation, ambition, vitality and zeal in my life.	
5	I welcome opportunities to try to improve my relationships through conversation	
6	People tell me that I am a good communicator	
7	I rarely interrupt people when they are talking to me	
8	I think before I respond even when I am having strong emotions	
9	It is more important to me to hear another's point of view than it is to have them to hear mine	
10	Being right is less important to me than having a sense of connection and understanding	
11	I tend not to hold grudges	
12	I have good conflict management skills	
13	People tell me that I am a good listener	
14	I am willing to be the butt of a joke if it helps someone to trust me	
15	When there is a breakdown in my relationship, I look to what I can do to repair it before I look at how the other person caused it	
16	I can be honest and respectful to people even when I feel angry at them	
17	When it comes to relationships, I DON'T believe that the best defence is a good offense	
18	I do not ever tell people, "You're making a mountain out of a molehill".	

Self-Awareness

No.	Statement	Score
19	I do not tell people that they are too sensitive.	
20	I try very hard to express myself in ways that are respectful to people	
21	I tend to withhold my opinions and advice unless I am sure that they are desired by others.	
22	I tend to NOT dwell on negative thoughts and feelings towards those with whom I am upset or disappointed	
23	When I know that I am wrong I find it easy to apologise	
24	When others admit that they are wrong I am not satisfied until they apologise.	
25	When people do not apologise to me when I think they owe me one, I DON'T insist that they give it.	
26	I do not issue threats and ultimatums to others.	
27	If I catch myself trying to manipulate or coerce someone into giving me my way, I stop doing it and become more honest with what I need or want.	
28	I value openness and am willing to get vulnerable even if my partner is being defensive.	
29	I am quick to forgive and slow to anger.	
30	I can accept and feel comfortable with compliments when I receive them.	
31	I look for learning opportunities in difficult situations	
32	People do not tell me that they think I might have a substance abuse problem	
33	I do not procrastinate	
34	I am basically optimistic by nature	
35	I rarely feel depressed	
36	I am willing to delay gratification until the time is right, even if it is something that I really want.	
37	I live with a strong sense of gratitude.	
38	I am not embarrassed if I cry in front of others.	
39	When things do not go according to plan, I can easily shift gears.	
40	When I am stuck and unable to accomplish something on my own, I am willing to seek out and accept help and assistance	
41	I have enjoyed doing this assessment	
	Total	

Self-Awareness

Total	Level of Emotional Intelligence
190-205	Great job! Keep up the good work!
160-189	Doing well. On the right track!
130-159	Need to focus more on areas that need development or attention
90-129	You have slipped into the danger zone
60-89	Expect relationship breakdowns without significant changes
Under 60	Get to work and probably some help, Now!

Self-Awareness

Learning Styles

As part of our self-awareness, it helps to understand different learning styles. We all have our own preferences, and it is useful to understand which learning styles apply to us so that we can use them during our career development.

During personal and professional development, we frequently check:

- **where we are** – *examining the current role in detail and identifying any skills gaps*
- **where we need to be** – *working out where we need or want to be, deciding and defining ambitions in a clear way*
- **how we plan to get there** – *identifying the learning and development activities and resources that we need to achieve our goals*

Identifying learning styles

Many training providers and organisations have learning style questionnaires to help identify the preferred learning styles of individuals. By analysing the results, they can make sure that the learning materials and activities are compatible with each individual learner's preferences, where possible.

Questionnaires have a range of questions, which can be targeted on the workplace tasks and learning opportunities, or on general activities. For example, when trying a new recipe, tick which way you prefer to learn:

a) *By reading the recipe in a book or online (visual)*
b) *By watching a TV chef make the recipe (visual + auditory)*
c) *By phoning a friend to ask for instructions (auditory)*
d) *By having a go, following my instinct, tasting as I go (kinaesthetic)*

When analysing the results of learning style questionnaires, we will often see that we use a mixture of styles, selected according to the skills and knowledge we need to learn.

When learning about a concept or theory, we may prefer to read about it (visual), look at graphs and graphics (visual), then write our own notes by hand to consolidate our understanding (kinaesthetic).

For a more practical skill, such as learning about how to use a new and complicated photocopier, we may listen to someone else's tips (auditory), watch them use the machine (visual), try it for ourselves (kinaesthetic), and read the instruction manual for more advanced settings (visual).

The Chinese philosopher, Confucius, is thought to have said over two thousand years ago:

Self-Awareness

> *I hear and I forget*
> *I see and I remember*
> *I do and I understand*

For many people, the learning is not successful until they have done the task themselves, which is something we need to consider when choosing development activities.

Types of Learning Styles

We all have our preferred learning styles that we use to develop our skills, experience and knowledge. Some people like to learn by reading about things, others need to see a demonstration to understand something, and others need to try the activity themselves before they remember everything.

We often need repetition before new information can be absorbed and used – e.g., needing several driving lessons before using the car controls become simple to us. Adults usually need more repetition than children, so we should not be embarrassed if we do not understand something straightaway.

There are many theories about learning styles, and here are some brief details about some of the most commonly used theories:

VARK – Visual, Auditory, Reading/writing, Kinaesthetic

People have favourite ways of learning and training needs to be adapted to accommodate these preferences where possible. These four styles are:

- **Visual** – *seeing and watching* – *e.g., seeing pictures of how to make the product, or watching instruction videos*
- **Auditory** – *listening and speaking* – *e.g., being told how to make the product*
- **Reading/writing** – *e.g., reading instructions and writing personal notes*
- **Kinaesthetic** – *touching and doing* – *e.g., touching the components and actually making the product under supervision*

According to this model, people have a dominant or preferred learning style. When training team members, managers need to be prepared to use a combination of all four skills so that everyone's learning style needs can be met.

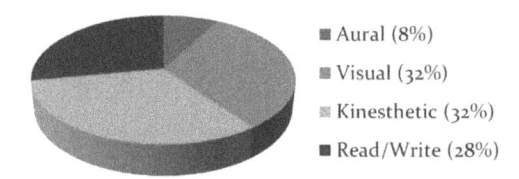

- Aural (8%)
- Visual (32%)
- Kinesthetic (32%)
- Read/Write (28%)

Level 5: Operations / Departmental Manager

Self-Awareness

A visual learner will learn about a subject by looking at graphs, pictures and diagrams, or watching videos or demonstrations. Just being told about what to do will not register. Touching and doing the new activity will help to reinforce the learning at a basic level, but they will need to observe and read up on the details.

A reading/writing learner will learn best from reading instructions, research and information about the subject, and writing notes to help them remember important details.

An auditory learner will absorb the information by listening to their tutor or colleague, asking questions, then listening carefully to the answers.

A kinaesthetic learner needs to touch and do the activity. They may absorb a reasonable amount of information from listening to the tutor or watching a demonstration, but they will not truly understand the subject or activity until they do it for themselves.

VARK	*Very likely to appeal*	*Quite likely to appeal*
Visual – *benefit from seeing materials and watching others*	*Demonstrations* *Shadowing* *Computer-based training* *Internet-based training*	*Delegation* *Role-play* *Classroom-based training courses* *Blended learning* *Distance learning* *Workplace training*
Auditory – *benefit from being able to listen and discuss training*	*Demonstrations* *Shadowing*	*Classroom-based training courses* *Blended learning* *Workplace training*
Reading/writing – *benefit from reading training materials and making notes*	*Training manuals* *Reference books and journals* *Taking notes* *Computer-based training* *Internet-based training*	*Classroom-based training courses* *Blended learning* *Distance learning* *Workplace training*
Kinaesthetic – *benefit from being able to touch and handle items*	*Demonstrations* *Role-play* *Computer-based training* *Internet-based training*	*Job rotation* *Blended learning* *Workplace learning*

Self-Awareness

Gardner's Multiple Intelligences

In 1983, Harvard psychologist, Howard Gardner, developed a theory that stated there are several principles people use to understand and perceive the world.

According to Gardner, intelligence means "the ability to learn, to solve problems". This can be done in multiple ways. Each person has developed other intelligences more strongly, leading to different kinds of cleverness. With his theory of multiple intelligences, Gardner aims to emphasise that teachers must assess their student's learning process in a way that provides a correct overview of their strong and weak suits.

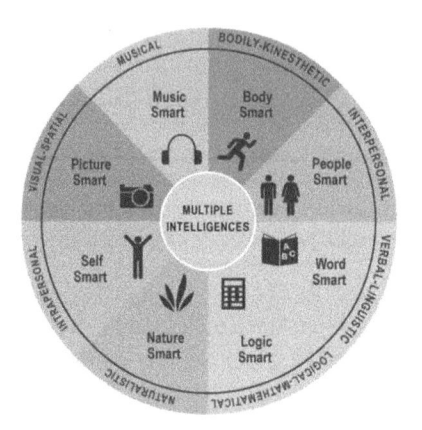

The theory has been refined since, and the main principles are that people use these eight 'intelligences', as can be seen on Gardner's website – www.multipleintelligencesoasis.org:

- **linguistic** – the ability to use spoken or written words, sounds, rhythms or inflections
- **logical-mathematical** – using reasoning and logic as well as numbers and abstract patterns
- **spatial** – spatial awareness and the ability to mentally visualise objects – e.g., as used by an airline pilot or an architect
- **bodily-kinaesthetic** – the ability to use the body control physical movements – e.g., using hands to solve problems
- **musical** – the ability to master beats, tones and rhythms as well as music
- **interpersonal** – the ability to communicate effectively with other people – e.g., to negotiate or develop workplace relationships
- **intrapersonal** – understanding our own emotions, motivation and self-reflection
- **naturalistic** – the ability to make distinctions in the world of nature – e.g., between different types of plants

Self-Awareness

Gardner's Multiple Intelligences	Very likely to appeal	Quite likely to appeal
Linguistic – like to use words, sounds and rhythms	Delegation Demonstrations Role-play Shadowing Coaching and mentoring	Classroom-based training Computer-based training Internet-based training Blended learning Distance learning Workplace training Job rotation Project work
Logical-mathematical – like to use reasoning, numbers and abstract patterns	Training manuals Reference books and journals Taking notes Computer-based training Internet-based training	Classroom-based training courses Blended learning Distance learning Workplace training
Spatial – use spatial awareness and mental visualisation	Role-play Demonstrations Project work Delegation	Classroom-based training Blended learning Workplace training Job rotation
Bodily-Kinaesthetic – benefit from being able to touch and handle items	Delegation Role-play Demonstrations Taking notes	Classroom-based training courses Job rotation Blended learning Workplace learning
Musical – benefit from responding to beats, rhythms, tones and music	Role-play Demonstrations Shadowing	Classroom-based training courses Blended learning Workplace training
Interpersonal – benefit from being able to communicate with other people and develop relationships	Role-play Coaching and mentoring Delegation Job rotation Project work	Demonstrations Shadowing Classroom-based training courses Blended learning
Intrapersonal – benefit from self-reflection and understanding their own emotions	Computer-based training Coaching and mentoring	Internet-based e-training Distance learning
Naturalistic – able to make distinctions in the world of nature	Demonstrations Shadowing Project work	Blended learning Delegation

Self-Awareness

Felder-Silverman Learning Style Model

This model was developed to help engineering students and their tutors, but it can be applied to other industries. The model shows four areas of personality that contribute to learning. A combination of these styles makes up an individual's learning preferences:

- **active or reflective** – how people prefer to process information – e.g., active people like to try things out and work with others in a group; reflective people prefer to think things through and work alone or with a familiar partner
- **visual or verbal** – how people prefer information to be presented – e.g., visual learners prefer videos, pictures and charts; verbal learners prefer written and spoken explanations
- **sensing or intuitive** – how people prefer to perceive or take in information – e.g., sensing learners prefer practical thinking, facts and procedures; intuitive people prefer conceptual thinking, theories and meanings
- **sequential or global** – how people prefer to organise and progress towards understanding – e.g., sequential learners prefer linear thinking and small, incremental steps; global learners prefer holistic thinking, systems and learning in big steps

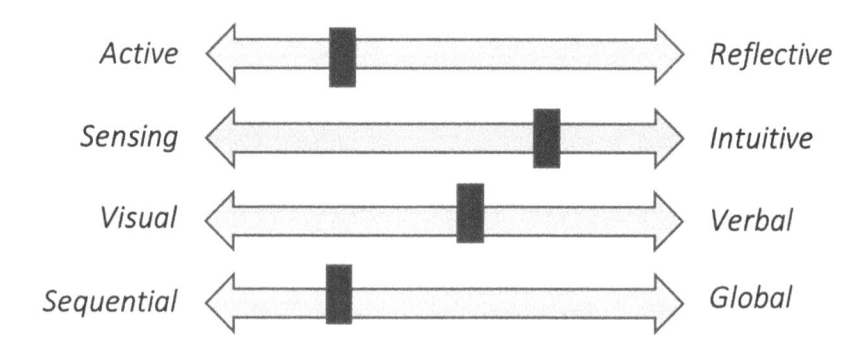

Active	⟵⬛⟶	Reflective
Sensing	⟵⬛⟶	Intuitive
Visual	⟵⬛⟶	Verbal
Sequential	⟵⬛⟶	Global

Self-Awareness

Felder-Silverman	*Very likely to appeal*	*Quite likely to appeal*
Active – like to work things out and work with others in a group	Delegation Demonstrations Role-play Job rotation Project work	Classroom-based training Computer-based training Internet-based training Distance learning Workplace training
Reflective – like to think things through and work alone or with a familiar partner	Computer-based training Coaching and mentoring	Internet-based e-training Distance learning Workplace training
Visual – benefit from seeing materials and watching others	Demonstrations Shadowing Computer-based training Internet-based training	Delegation Role-play Classroom-based training Blended learning Distance learning Workplace training
Verbal – benefit from written and spoken explanations	Delegation Demonstrations Role-play / Shadowing Coaching and mentoring Classroom-based training Workplace training Job rotation Project work	Computer-based training Internet-based training Blended learning Distance learning
Sensing – prefer practical thinking, facts and procedures	Demonstrations Classroom-based training Workplace training Job rotation Project work Delegation	Computer-based training Internet-based training Blended learning Distance learning
Intuitive – prefer conceptual thinking, theories and meanings	Classroom-based training Role-play Computer-based training Internet-based training	Blended learning Workplace learning Distance learning
Sequential – prefer linear thinking and small, incremental steps	Computer-based training Internet-based training Blended learning Distance learning Coaching and mentoring	Workplace training Shadowing Demonstrations
Global – prefer holistic thinking, systems and learning in big steps	Shadowing Demonstrations Workplace training Delegation Role-play	Computer-based training Internet-based training Blended learning Distance learning

Self-Awareness

Kolb's Experiential Learning Cycle

David Kolb developed this theory in 1979. It looks at four points to identify the way people learn:

- **experiencing** – learning and what was felt during the period of learning – e.g., having the first driving lesson and assessing it
- **reflecting** – thinking about how useful the session was – e.g., learned to stop and start safely, learned to change gear smoothly
- **thinking** – looking at ideas and theories that relate to the learning experience – e.g., looking at the functions of the car and the Highway Code
- **acting** – testing the learning – e.g., practising using the gears smoothly when out with an experienced driver

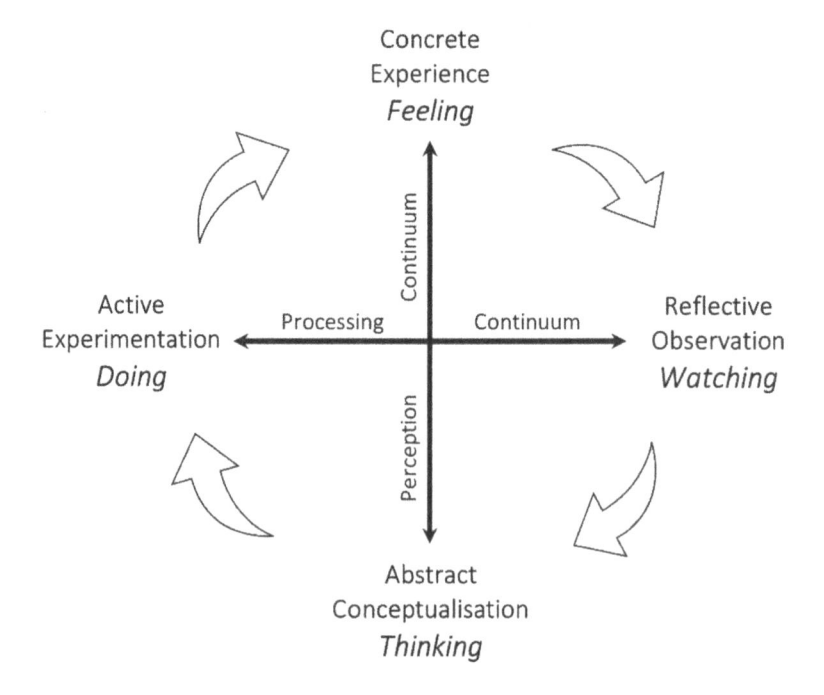

```
                    Concrete
                    Experience
                     Feeling
                        ↑
                        │
                        │ Continuum
                        │
   Active               │              Reflective
Experimentation ←── Processing ── Continuum ──→ Observation
    Doing               │                Watching
                        │
                        │ Perception
                        │
                        ↓
                    Abstract
                 Conceptualisation
                    Thinking
```

Part of Kolb's theory was that this process represents a circle or a spiral where people touch all the bases – i.e., a cycle of experiencing, reflecting, thinking and acting.

Self-Awareness

Kolb's Learning Cycle	Very likely to appeal	Quite likely to appeal
Experiencing – having a go and assessing the experience	Delegation Demonstrations Role-play Job rotation Project work	Shadowing Blended learning Workplace learning
Reflecting – thinking about how useful the new subject or skill will be	Coaching and mentoring	Job rotation Shadowing Project work Classroom-based training Blended learning Distance learning Workplace learning
Thinking – looking for related ideas, theories and different approaches	Job rotation Shadowing Coaching and mentoring Project work	Demonstrations Role-play Classroom-based training Blended learning Distance learning Workplace learning
Acting – testing the learning and practising	Delegation Demonstrations Role-play Job rotation	Project work Classroom-based learning Blended learning Workplace learning

Honey and Mumford's Learning Cycle

Peter Honey and Alan Mumford created a learning cycle as a variation of Kolb's theory in 1986. It is based on four approaches to learning:

- **activists do something** – these people actively enjoy challenges and learning new things
- **reflectors think about it** – these people like to stand back and review learning experiences in a thoughtful manner
- **theorists make sense of it** – these people like to think things through in logical steps
- **pragmatists test it out** – these people like to try new ideas; they enjoy solving problems and making decisions as part of the learning process

These are not seen as fixed personality characteristics. They can be changed at will or through changed circumstances, so each person can go through all four stages:

Self-Awareness

Pragmatist — Planning the next steps
Activist — Having an Experience
Reflector — Reviewing the experience
Theorist — Learning from the experience

Honey and Mumford	Very likely to appeal	Quite likely to appeal
Activists – like to do something	Delegation Demonstrations Role-play Job rotation Project work	Classroom-based training Computer-based training Internet-based training Blended learning Distance learning Workplace training
Reflectors – review progress, analyse and consider options	Delegation Shadowing Coaching and mentoring	Project work Classroom-based training Computer-based training Internet-based training Blended learning Distance learning Workplace training
Theorists – make sense of the options	Shadowing Coaching and monitoring Classroom-based training Blended learning Workplace training	Demonstrations Computer-based training Internet-based training Distance learning
Pragmatists – try out the options, evaluate the experience and progress, then decide how to proceed	Delegation Demonstrations Role-play Job rotation Project work Blended learning	Classroom-based training Workplace training

Self-Awareness

Addressing learning styles in training and development

Our preferred learning styles help us to make the most of the opportunities we have for working towards achieving our goals. We can, for example:

- *get the most out of learning and development activities*
- *enjoy the learning process more*
- *increase the chances of successful completion of training courses and programmes*

To address our learning styles in training and development, we need to:

- *find out about the learning and development activities that are available for our particular learning objectives*
- *select the best ones for our personal requirements*

Learning and Development Activities

There are many learning and development options, based inside or outside the workplace. A combination of activities can be put together to suit the individual's needs, as well as the organisational objectives.

Activities may include, for example:

- **delegation** – *e.g., offering tasks to challenge the individual and give them the opportunity to develop their skills and experience*
- **demonstrations** – *e.g., watching demonstrations about how a new piece of equipment is used, then trying it out*
- **role-play** – *e.g., to practise how to deal with angry customers' complaints*
- **job rotation** – *e.g., training team members on all the tasks performed by the team so that they can develop their skills, keep their interest and motivation levels up, and be able to cover for each other*
- **shadowing** – *e.g., arranging for a trainee to follow an experienced member of staff for a week*
- **coaching and mentoring** – *e.g., giving intensive one-to-one support and guidance; having a senior member of staff as a role model*
- **project work** – *e.g., expanding knowledge and experience by following through all aspects of a project, and not just isolated tasks*
- **classroom-based training courses** – *e.g., a first-aid course at the local college*
- **computer-based training** – *e.g., induction courses to give an overview of the organisation and its policies and procedures*
- **Internet-based e-training** – *e.g., food safety knowledge, followed by an exam at an assessment centre to gain the full certificate*

Self-Awareness

- **blended learning** – *a mixture of different methods – e.g., a computer-based course in Spanish as well as conversation lessons at the local college*
- **distance learning** – *e.g., a course done at work or at home, with the assistance of an assessor or a tutor who may be based miles away*
- **workplace training** – *e.g., internal training sessions on equality and diversity given by colleagues or external trainers*

Analysis of Learning Styles

The most damning criticism, about learning styles comes from researchers in the academic world. Not much comes from those who use learning styles as part of their strategies for learning, training and teaching. It is usually stated in these terms.

> *"There is no evidence that knowledge of one's learning styles is a benefit to learning."*

The absence of evidence is seen as the main issue. But Donald Rumsfeld infamous search for weapons of mass destruction elicited this response.

> *"Absence of evidence is not the same as evidence of absence".*

Using the statement in the heading above this could be rephrased as, "the absence of evidence about the benefits from knowing one's learning style does not mean that benefits don't exist."

There are many aspects of everyday life where there is a lack of evidence. There is not much evidence that the sun will rise tomorrow or that cell phones benefit communication or that there are parallel universes. But lack of evidence means what it says – at this point in time, we do not have any reliable, valid research that would predict that knowing one's learning style is beneficial for learning. That statement does not mean that learning styles are not beneficial and there may be good reasons why that evidence is missing.

Self-Awareness

Behaviour Styles

People have been fascinated with studying behavioural styles for thousands of years. Starting with the early astrologers, theorists have sought to identify these behavioural styles.

In ancient Greece in 400 BC, for example, the physician Hippocrates outlined four temperaments: Sanguine, Phlegmatic, Melancholic, and Choleric.

In 1921, famed psychologist Carl Jung (the first to study personal styles scientifically) labelled people as Intuitors, Thinkers, Feelers, and Sensors.

Since then, psychologists have produced dozens of models of behavioural differences, some with sixteen or more possible behavioural blends.

Companies today are expanding the role of teams in the workplace to empower employees and improve organisational effectiveness. The more we try to work as a team, the more important it becomes to recognise that people exhibit different behavioural styles. The use of the term "behavioural style", is intentional, purposely avoiding the terms "personality" or "attitude", because unless we are psychiatrists or psychologists, we are not qualified to evaluate such things. All that we can see and deal with is a person's behaviour.

There are four major behavioural styles: analytical, amiable, driver and expressive.

Please note these are extreme simplifications of each particular style. It is doubtful that all people of a particular behavioural style exhibit all the characteristics portrayed.

> ***Analytical*** — The analytical style of interaction asserts itself by asking, rather than telling. It is also characterised by a high level of emotional control. It values facts, logic and accuracy, presenting a disciplined and unemotional – some would say cold – face to the world. This manifests in a deep need to be right about things, and therefore a highly deliberative, data-driven approach to decisions. As with all styles, there is a weakness, which is a lack of willingness to state a position until the analytical person is certain of their ground.
>
> This behavioural style is noted for the ability to gather and review data. This style is typical of people in technical positions such as engineering, accounting and information technology. Details and accuracy are important to these people, and they take great pride in providing information that is correct.
>
> > **Skills:** *Analyticals are persistent and do not mind spending extra time to make sure things are right. For the most part, they are orderly and present ideas or solutions in an orderly manner.*
> > **Caution:** *Due to their desire for accuracy and attention to detail, analyticals can come across as indecisive. They can also be critical of solutions that veer from what the "facts" say. They have little use for gut feelings and may go to great lengths to avoid dealing with those who do.*
> > **Favourite word:** *Why?*
> > **Best Performance:** *Allow them sufficient time to gather and interpret information.*

Self-Awareness

Amiable— The amiable style expresses concern for people above all else. Keen to share emotion and not to assert itself over others, building and maintaining relationships dominate behaviour. These concerns manifest a slow, deliberate pace, coming across as sensitive, supportive and dependable. The corollary is a certain nervousness about, and even a resistance to, change. This arises from a deep need for personal security. The weaknesses of this style are the reverse of the strengths of the opposite quadrant: a low willingness to initiate change and act.

Amiables are highly supportive individuals interested in establishing and maintaining relationships in an organisation. This behavioural style is typical of employees in human resources and social or medical services.

> **Skills:** *Amiables are great at achieving consensus within an organisation. They can effectively facilitate groups and bring sides together to develop a win/win solution.*
> **Caution:** *Sometimes an amiable person's desire to reach agreement may cause the person to conform too easily, intent in maintaining relationships rather than reaching the best solution.*
> **Favourite word:** *We.*
> **Best Performance:** *Encourage amiables to initiate and stand behind their ideas. Allow them to maintain relationships in the organisation.*

Driving— The driving style is the typical task-oriented behaviour that prefers to tell rather than ask and shows little concern for feelings. It cares more about results. This is a fast-paced style, keen to make decisions, take power, and exert control. Often uncooperative, this is an efficient, results-driven behaviour, the inevitable compromise of which is to sacrifice personal relationships in the short term and, in extremis, in the long term too. The weakness of this style is evident: a frequent unwillingness to listen and accommodate the needs of others.

Drivers, as the name implies, are often the driving force behind getting things done in an organisation. They are results-oriented individuals who are motivated by goals. Drivers typically gravitate to positions in management and sales.

> **Skills:** *Drivers are effective at time management, seeming to possess an innate ability to devote just the right amount of time and effort to things that need to be done. Drivers rarely struggle with making decisions.*
> **Caution:** *Because they are so driven for success in a timely manner, drivers may neglect the impact that their actions have on others. They may be viewed as willing to do almost anything to get the job done.*
> **Favourite word:** *When?*
> **Best Performance:** *Give them options and probabilities, allowing them to formulate their own decisions whenever possible.*

Expressive— The expressive style is also assertive but uses feelings to achieve its objectives. The behaviour is highly spontaneous and demands recognition and approval, and favours gut instinct in decision-making. At its best, this style comes across as

Self-Awareness

charismatic, enthusiastic and idealistic. At its worst, however, the expressive style can be seen as impulsive, shallow and even manipulative.

Expressives are company visionaries, good at grasping the big picture. Expressives typically gravitate to positions in marketing and strive to get ahead in an organisation. They are truly the "politicians" in an organisation, establishing and using contacts extensively.

>**Skills:** *If you need to develop new concepts, then enlist the help of an expressive. Their ability to size up a situation based on personal experience can assist them in finding creative solutions, perhaps never considered by others.*
>
>**Caution:** *Being so confident of their "gut feelings," they may often ignore or neglect facts that are presented to them. Their lack of attention to detail can be an obstacle.*
>
>**Favourite word:** *I.*
>
>**Best Performance:** *Show interest in their ideas and compliment them, even if you are not sure they are totally deserving of such praise.*

There is no one best behavioural style, and it is not your personal style that is important. What is important is recognising the behavioural style of others so that you can deal with them effectively.

Merrill's People Style Grid

In the early 1960s, two industrial psychologists, David Merrill and Roger Reid wanted to understand whether they could predict managerial, leadership and sales performance. To do this, they explored how people behave in social situations. They chose not to concern themselves with why.

Starting with BF Skinner's ideas of behaviourism and James Taylor's structured list of behavioural descriptions, Merrill and Reid discovered that people's behaviour follows two continua, which they labelled:

Assertiveness
and
Responsiveness.

Assertiveness styles range from 'asking' behaviours to 'telling' behaviours, while our responsiveness varies from 'emoting', or displaying our feelings, to 'controlling' our emotions. From these two dimensions, they defined four behavioural styles that we each display. As with other models, we each have our preferences, but can display all the styles from time to time.

The value of the model lies in using it to assess the people around you and knowing how to get the best from people with each preference.

Self-Awareness

The four quadrants that the two dimensions of assertiveness and responsiveness create, give the four social styles.

- *Analytical*
- *Driving*
- *Expressive*
- *Amiable*

Assessment of Merrill and Reid's Social Styles

Recently, the model has been developed by adding a third, fully integrated dimension: versatility.

This is about how the four styles manifest in the real world, to meet other people's needs. It is closely related to ideas of Emotional Intelligence.

Even as 'just another four-box model', it is a good one. As a result, it has been widely emulated. A similar model uses the styles of Thinker, Director, Socialiser and Relater to replace Merrill and Reid's four social styles, and dimensions of relationship and task orientation, to replace responsiveness and assertiveness.

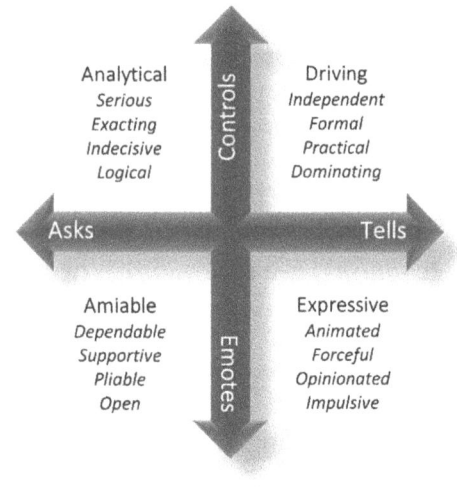

Analytical
Serious
Exacting
Indecisive
Logical

Driving
Independent
Formal
Practical
Dominating

Asks / Tells
Controls / Emotes

Amiable
Dependable
Supportive
Pliable
Open

Expressive
Animated
Forceful
Opinionated
Impulsive

Both models have considerable power in helping managers understand their behaviours and those of other people around them. By adapting their style, the models allow managers to get the best from any social situation. Remembering work is if nothing else… social!

Self-Awareness

DISC Personality Model – William Marston

DISC is a personality model based on the work of psychologist William Marston. Marston found that observable behavioural characteristics can be grouped into four major personality types. Each behavioural type tends to exhibit specific characteristics.

DISC itself is purely an acronym for the four personality types which are:

Dominance – which relates to control, power and assertiveness
Influence – which relates to social situations and communication
Steadiness – which relates to patience, persistence, and thoughtfulness
Compliance – which relates to structure and organisation

Everyone will possess all these personality types, what differs between people is the extent to which they are more or less one type or another.

Essentially a person's 'personality' refers to 'the way they are most often'. Knowing people's DISC helps you to predict how they might respond to information and how they would like to be dealt with by you.

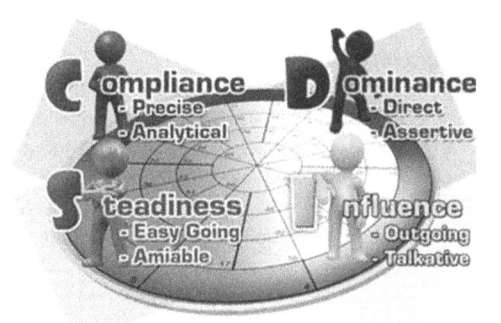

The DISC assessments (worksheets) test a person's preferences using word associations. It would be a good idea to complete the assessments yourself. This will enable you to identify your own DISC type from which you will be able to identify how you may need to adapt your behaviour to suit the individual DISC's of those around you.

Characteristics of the four DISC types

Here is a summary of the four different 'DISC' personality types:

Dominance
Dominance behavioural styles are driven by two governing needs: to control and achieve. Dominance Styles are goal-oriented go-getters who are most comfortable when they oversee people and situations. They want to accomplish many things-now-so they focus on no-nonsense approaches to bottom-line results.

Dominance Styles seek expedience and are not afraid to bend the rules. They figure it is easier to beg forgiveness than to ask permission. Dominance Styles accept challenges, take authority, and plunge headfirst into solving problems. They are fast-paced, task-oriented, and work quickly and impressively by themselves, which means they become annoyed with delays. They are driven and dominating, which can make them stubborn, impatient, and insensitive to others.

Self-Awareness

Dominance Styles are so focused that they forget to take the time to smell the roses.

People who score high on the 'D' type factors enjoy dealing with problems and challenges. These people will often be described as demanding, forceful, egocentric, strong willed, determined, aggressive, ambitious and pioneering.

High 'D' people are often found in leadership positions...this does not mean they are 'good' leaders as their weaknesses often include being poor listeners and being impatient and insensitive to others.
'D' type people are bottom-line people who hate to waste time. They want straight talk and direct answers to their "WHAT" questions

Influence
Influencing behavioural styles are friendly, enthusiastic "party-animals" who like to be where the action is. They thrive on the admiration, acknowledgment, and compliments that come with being in the limelight. Their primary strengths are enthusiasm, charm, persuasiveness, and warmth. They are idea-people and dreamers who excel at getting others excited about their vision. They are eternal optimists with an abundance of charisma. These qualities help them influence people and build alliances to accomplish their goals.

Influencing Styles do have their weaknesses: impatience, an aversion to being alone, and a short attention span.

Interactive Styles are risk-takers who base many of their decisions on intuition, which is not inherently bad. Interactive Styles are not inclined to verify information; they are more likely to assume someone else will do it. People who score high on the 'I' type factors influence others through talking and activity and tend to be emotional. They are commonly described as enthusiastic, magnetic, persuasive, warm, trusting, demonstrative and optimistic.

They like people and thrive in a social scene. It is important that others have a favourable impression of them. Indeed high 'I' people are more interested in people than in accomplishing tasks. Time does tend to get away from them and everything takes a lower priority when they are discussing ideas. They believe everything will be all right and everyone is 'such a nice person'.

They need freedom of expression; they can become easily distracted as they have trouble staying focused. They tend to think in the future. They want answers to their "WHO" questions.

Steadiness
Steadiness behavioural styles are warm and nurturing individuals. They are the most people-oriented of the four styles. Steadiness Styles are excellent listeners, devoted

Self-Awareness

friends, and loyal employees. Their relaxed disposition makes them approachable and warm. They develop strong networks of people who are willing to be mutually supportive and reliable.

Steadiness Styles are excellent team players.

Steadiness Styles are risk averse. In fact, Steadiness Styles may tolerate unpleasant environments rather than risk change. They like the status quo and become distressed when disruptions are severe. When faced with change, they think it through, plan, and accept it into their world. Steadiness Styles-more than the other types-strive to maintain personal composure, stability, and balance. In the office, Steadiness Styles are courteous, friendly, and willing to share responsibilities. They are good planners, persistent workers, and good with follow-through. They go along with others even when they do not agree because they do not want to rock the boat. They are slower decision-makers because of their need for security; their need to avoid risk; and their desire to include others in the decision-making process.

High 'S' people do not like sudden change, they like a steady pace and security. These people are calm, relaxed, patient, predictable, deliberate, stable, consistent and can tend to be unemotional and poker faced.

Steady people get along well with others because they are flexible in their attitude. They may not say anything if they disagree because they like to keep the peace. They like to help others and make good counsellors as they are great listeners.

Steady people like to maintain familiar and predictable patterns. If they receive appreciation, they maintain a high level of performance. They like to feel comfortable with anything new before starting it.

Steady people will want answers to their "HOW" and "WHEN" questions.

Compliance
(This category is also known as 'Cautious' or 'Conscientious') Compliance behavioural styles are analytical, persistent, systematic people who enjoy problem solving. Compliance Styles are detail-oriented, which makes them more concerned with content than style. Compliance Styles are task-oriented people who enjoy perfecting processes and working toward tangible results. They are always in control of their emotions and may become uncomfortable around people who are very outgoing, e.g., Interactive Styles.

Compliance Styles have high expectations of themselves and others, which can make them over-critical.

Their tendency toward perfectionism-taken to an extreme-can cause "paralysis by over-analysis." Compliance Styles are slow and deliberate decision-makers. They do research, make comparisons, determine risks, calculate margins of error, and then act. Compliance

Self-Awareness

Styles become irritated by surprises and glitches, hence their cautious decision-making. Compliance Styles are also sceptical, so they like to see promises in writing.

People who score high on the 'C' type adhere to rules, regulations and structure. They like to do things well and do them well first time. They are slow paced and task oriented.

High 'C' people are commonly described as careful, cautious, neat, systematic, accurate, and diplomatic. Perfection is very important to 'C' people, and they tend to be critical of themselves. They will study privately to learn about a subject before discussing it in public.

People can find it difficult to read high 'C's as they don't show their feelings. They tend to protect their privacy. They make to-do lists. Compliant people want answers to their "WHY" and "HOW" questions.

Identifying other people's DISC personality

If you are just getting to know your staff and clients and have not had time to observe many of their behavioural characteristics, then here are a few tips to help…

D and I people are 'fast' paced; they will speak quickly and fill in any of your personal training forms quickly. S and C people will talk slower and take their time to fill in any forms. C people in particular will be meticulous when filling out any form; they will have very neat handwriting, whereas I people will likely have a big, loopy messy scrawl.

S and I people are people focused and more likely to be chatty. As S type people are team oriented and like to help others, expect them to ask questions about you and talk about and praise others, while the I type person will love to chat about themselves and get the 'goss' on who is doing what, and to whom in the club.

D and C people are task focused, so they will not be too chatty, in fact you may feel like you are pulling your teeth out to get any personal information from them. C people will ask lots of questions about anything relating to their training whereas D people will just want to get on with it. D people will likely be up close and personal and hold direct eye contact with you whereas C people will appear to be less confident or direct with their body language.

Note: DISC is based upon observable behaviours, NOT "personalities" or "temperaments." This distinction is critical because human beings may change their behaviour in the middle of a conversation.

When you learn to adapt to the behaviour that you are witnessing, you will stay in rapport with that person.

People's personalities are deeply ingrained and slow to change, but behaviours can change in the blink of an eye. The way a person is acting at each moment in time will dictate how you should be selling to them.

The table helps to summarise the behavioural characteristics of the different DISC types.

Self-Awareness

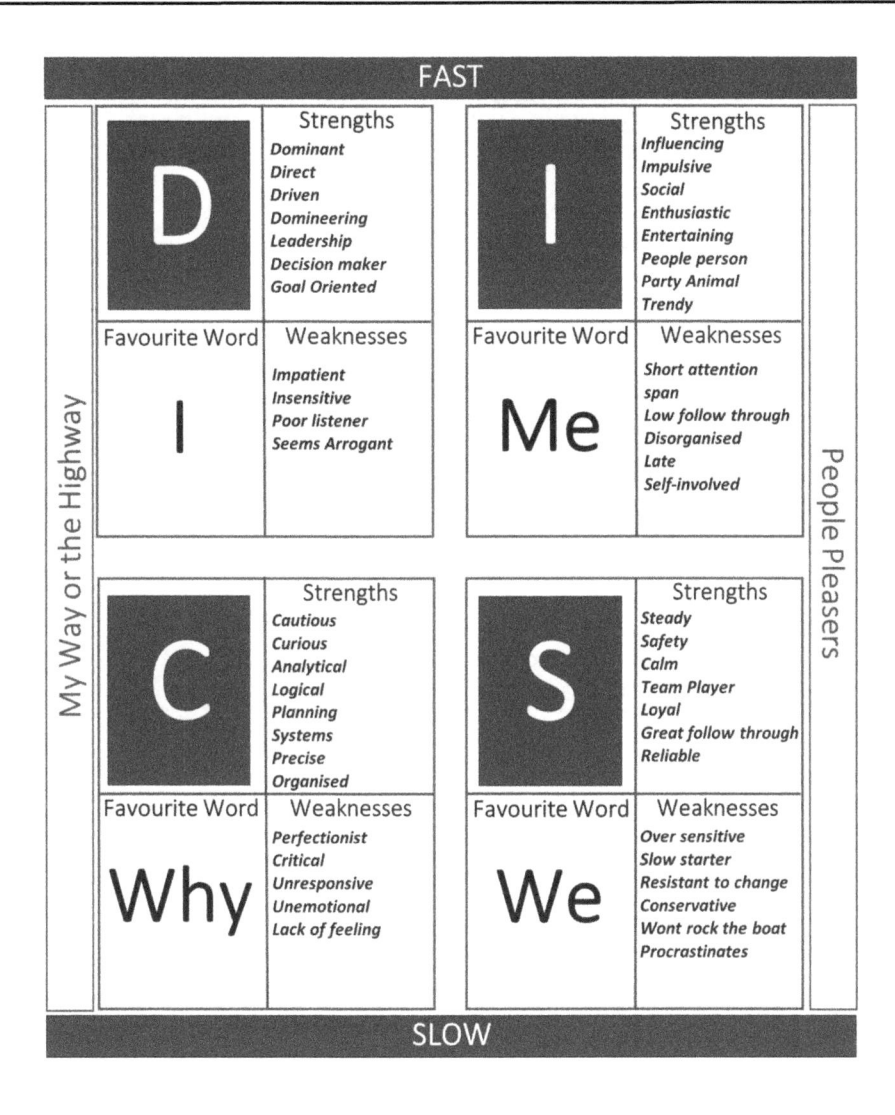

FAST

	D — Favourite Word: **I**	**I** — Favourite Word: **Me**
Strengths	Dominant, Direct, Driven, Domineering, Leadership, Decision maker, Goal Oriented	Influencing, Impulsive, Social, Enthusiastic, Entertaining, People person, Party Animal, Trendy
Weaknesses	Impatient, Insensitive, Poor listener, Seems Arrogant	Short attention span, Low follow through, Disorganised, Late, Self-involved

	C — Favourite Word: **Why**	**S** — Favourite Word: **We**
Strengths	Cautious, Curious, Analytical, Logical, Planning, Systems, Precise, Organised	Steady, Safety, Calm, Team Player, Loyal, Great follow through, Reliable
Weaknesses	Perfectionist, Critical, Unresponsive, Unemotional, Lack of feeling	Over sensitive, Slow starter, Resistant to change, Conservative, Wont rock the boat, Procrastinates

Left axis: **My Way or the Highway**
Right axis: **People Pleasers**

SLOW

Adapting own behaviour to suit employee's DISC

Now in case you have not noticed, different personality styles can clash! A 'D' style person who may appear aggressive and insensitive to others is likely to annoy an 'S' style person who is likely to be very sensitive to the needs of others. A fast talking scatter-brained 'I' type person is likely to annoy a slow thinking 'C' type perfectionist, and vice versa.

Therefore, it is important for you to know and understand your own DISC, so that you do not inadvertently clash with your clients. It also highlights to you where you will need to adapt your typical behaviour to ensure you interact effectively and positively with all your clients, all the time. Here are some guidelines for successful interaction…

Self-Awareness

With Dominant people
Build respect to avoid conflict
Focus on facts and ideas rather than people
Have evidence to support your ideas and advice
Be quick, focused and get to the point
Ask 'what' not 'how'
Talk about how problems will hinder accomplishments
Show them how they can succeed

With Influential people
Be social and friendly with them
Listen to them talk about their ideas
Help them find ways to translate the talk into useful action
Do not spend too much time on the details
Motivate them to follow through to complete tasks
Recognise their accomplishments

With Steady people
Be genuinely interested in them
Create a human working environment for them
Give them time to adjust to change
Clearly define goals for them and provide ongoing support
Recognise and appreciate their achievements
Avoid hurry and pressure
Present new ideas carefully

With Compliant people
Warn them before and generally avoid surprises
Be well prepared. Do not ad-lib with them if you can help it
Be logical, accurate and use clear data
Show how things fit into the bigger picture
Be specific in disagreement and focus on the facts
Be patient, persistent and diplomatic

Self-Awareness

Self-Assessment

Working left to right across the page place a 4 next to the word which most accurately describes you and then a 3, 2 and 1 next to the words that progressively are less accurate at describing you. You must use each number (1-4) once in each row.

How I see myself in an exercise situation (sport or gym) ...

Directing	Influencing	Steady	Cautious
Self-Certain	Optimistic	Deliberate	Restrained
Adventurous	Enthusiastic	Predictable	Logical
Decisive	Open	Patient	Analytical
Daring	Impulsive	Stabilising	Precise
Restless	Emotional	Protective	Sceptical
Competitive	Persuading	Accommodating	Curious
Assertive	Talkative	Modest	Direct
Experimenting	Charming	Loyal	Consistent
Forceful	Sensitive	Sincere	Perfectionist
TOTAL	**TOTAL**	**TOTAL**	**TOTAL**

Self-Awareness

How I see myself at home....

Directing	Influencing	Steady	Cautious
Self-Certain	Optimistic	Deliberate	Restrained
Adventurous	Enthusiastic	Predictable	Logical
Decisive	Open	Patient	Analytical
Daring	Impulsive	Stabilising	Precise
Restless	Emotional	Protective	Sceptical
Competitive	Persuading	Accommodating	Curious
Assertive	Talkative	Modest	Direct
Experimenting	Charming	Loyal	Consistent
Forceful	Sensitive	Sincere	Perfectionist
TOTAL	**TOTAL**	**TOTAL**	**TOTAL**

How my peers see me....

Directing	Influencing	Steady	Cautious
Self-Certain	Optimistic	Deliberate	Restrained
Adventurous	Enthusiastic	Predictable	Logical
Decisive	Open	Patient	Analytical
Daring	Impulsive	Stabilising	Precise
Restless	Emotional	Protective	Sceptical
Competitive	Persuading	Accommodating	Curious
Assertive	Talkative	Modest	Direct
Experimenting	Charming	Loyal	Consistent
Forceful	Sensitive	Sincere	Perfectionist
TOTAL	**TOTAL**	**TOTAL**	**TOTAL**

Level 5: Operations / Departmental Manager

Self-Awareness

Scorecard: Circle the numbers which relate to the totals found in the previous tables.

Exercise Personality				Home Personality				Peers see me			
D	I	S	C	D	I	S	C	D	I	S	C
40	40	40	40	40	40	40	40	40	40	40	40
38	38	38	38	38	38	38	38	38	38	38	38
36	36	36	36	36	36	36	36	36	36	36	36
34	34	34	34	34	34	34	34	34	34	34	34
32	32	32	32	32	32	32	32	32	32	32	32
30	30	30	30	30	30	30	30	30	30	30	30
28	28	28	28	28	28	28	28	28	28	28	28
26	26	26	26	26	26	26	26	26	26	26	26
24	24	24	24	24	24	24	24	24	24	24	24
22	22	22	22	22	22	22	22	22	22	22	22
20	20	20	20	20	20	20	20	20	20	20	20
18	18	18	18	18	18	18	18	18	18	18	18
16	16	16	16	16	16	16	16	16	16	16	16
14	14	14	14	14	14	14	14	14	14	14	14
12	12	12	12	12	12	12	12	12	12	12	12
10	10	10	10	10	10	10	10	10	10	10	10

Reflect on the scores and think how you may need to change your behaviour at home, in the gym and at work. Think about the benefits such a decision may make.

Berne's Transactional Analysis

Before Berne first published his theories on Transactional Analysis, he spent years formulating the framework of this approach. The key to this methodology was a transaction – the fundamental unit of social intercourse. Berne also defined a stroke – the fundamental unit of social action (strokes are discussed in more detail later).

Many of the criticisms of the "science" (or lack thereof) behind psychotherapy was the fact that there was no basic unit for study, measurement, and classification. For example, the study of chemistry was revolutionised with the atomic theory of John Dalton; without the atom as a fundamental unit, the advancement of chemistry as a science would have proceeded slowly or not at all. By identifying and defining a transaction, Berne provided to the psychotherapeutic sciences the "atom" that was needed to allow for rigorous analysis.

Although Berne defined transactions long before he published Games People Play, his description of transactions in Games is the most easily understood:

Self-Awareness

> *"The unit of social intercourse is called a transaction. If two or more people encounter each other... sooner or later one of them will speak or give some other indication of acknowledging the presence of the others. This is called transactional stimulus. Another person will then say or do something which is in some way related to the stimulus, and that is called the transactional response."*

With this definition, Berne defined the basic unit of analysis.

Berne's Three Ego States

In addition to the analysis of the interactions between individuals, Transactional Analysis also involves the identification of the ego states behind each and every transaction. Berne defined an ego state as:

> *"a consistent pattern of feeling and experience directly related to a corresponding consistent pattern of behaviour."*

As a practicing psychiatrist Berne consistently noted that his patients, and indeed all people, could and would change over the course of a conversation. The changes would not necessarily be verbal – the changes could involve facial expressions, body language, body temperature, and many other non-verbal cues.

In one counselling session, Berne treated a 35-year-old lawyer. During the session, the lawyer (a male) said "I'm not really a lawyer; I'm just a little boy." But outside the confines of Dr. Berne's office, this patient was a successful, hard-charging, attorney. Later, in their sessions, the lawyer would frequently ask Dr. Berne if he was talking "to the lawyer or the little boy." Berne was intrigued by this, as he was seeing a single individual display two "states of being." Berne began referring to these two states as "Adult" and "Child." Later, Berne identified a third state, one that seemed to represent what the patient had observed in his parents when he was small. Berne referred to this as "parent." As Berne then turned to his other patients, he began to observe that these three ego states were present in all of them. As Berne gained confidence in this theory, he went on to introduce these in a 1957 paper – one year before he published his seminal paper introducing Transactional Analysis.

Berne ultimately defined the three ego states as: Parent, Adult, and Child. It should be carefully noted that the descriptions of these ego states do NOT necessarily correspond to their common definitions as used the English language.
The following are detailed descriptions of the three ego states:

Parent – The parent represents a massive collection of recordings in the brain of external events experienced or perceived in approximately the first five years of life. Since most of the external events experienced by a child are actions of the parent, the ego state was appropriately called Parent.

Self-Awareness

Examples of recordings in the Parent include:

"Never talk to strangers"
"Always chew with your mouth closed"
"Look both ways before you cross the street"

It is worth noting that, while recording these events, the young child has no way to filter the data; the events are recorded without question and without analysis. One can consider that these events are imposed on the child.

Child – In contrast to the Parent, the Child represents the recordings in the brain of internal events associated with external events the child perceives. Stated another way, stored in the Child are the emotions or feelings which accompanied external events. Like the Parent, recordings in the Child occur from childbirth all the way up to the age of approximately 5 years old.

Examples of recordings in the Child include:

"When I saw the monster's face, I felt really scared"
"The clown at the birthday party was really funny!

Adult – The Adult is the last ego state. Close to one year of age, a child begins to exhibit gross motor activity. The child learns that he or she can control a cup from which to drink, that he or she can grab a toy. In social settings, the child can play peek-a-boo.
This is the beginning of the Adult in the small child. Adult data grows out of the child's ability to see what is different than what he or she observed (Parent) or felt (Child). In other words, the Adult allows the young person to evaluate and validate Child and Parental data. Berne describes the Adult as being "principally concerned with transforming stimuli into pieces of information, and processing and filing that information on the basis of previous experience"

Stated another way, Harris describes the Adult as "a data-processing computer, which grinds out decisions after computing the information from three sources: The Parent, the Child, and the data which the adult has gathered and is gathering"

One of the key functions of the Adult is to validate data in the parent. An example is:

> *"Wow. It really is true that pot handles should always be turned into the stove"* said Jessica as she saw her brother burn himself when he grabbed a pot handle sticking out from the stove.

In this example, Jessica's Adult reached the conclusion that data in her Parent was valid. Her Parent had been taught "always turn pot handles into the stove, otherwise you could get burned." And with her analysis of her brother's experience, her Adult concluded that this was indeed correct. To explain Transactional Analysis to a more mainstream audience, Dr. Thomas

Self-Awareness

Harris developed the following summary. Although this is a very good tool for beginners to learn, keep in mind that this a wildly simplified approach, and can have the effect of "dumbing down" Transactional Analysis.
The summary is as follows:

> Parent – taught concept
> Child – felt concept
> Adult – learned concept

Analysing Transactions

When two people communicate, one person initiates a transaction with the transactional stimulus. The person at whom the stimulus is directed will respond with the transactional response. Simple Transactional Analysis involves identifying which ego state directed the stimulus and which ego state in the other person executed the response.

According to Dr. Berne, the simplest transactions are between Adults ego states. For example, a surgeon will survey the patient, and based upon the data before him/her, his/her Adult decides that the scalpel is the next instrument required. The surgeon's Adult holds out his/her hand, providing the transactional stimulus to the nurse. The nurse's Adult looks at the hand, and based upon previous experiences, concludes that the scalpel is needed. The nurse then places the scalpel in the surgeon's hand.

But not all transactions proceed in this manner. Some transactions involve ego states other than the Adult.

Structural Diagram

Quoting Berne in Games People Play: "The fevered child asks for a glass of water, and the nurturing mother brings it." In this, the Child ego of a small child directs an inquiry to the Parent ego of his/her mother. The Parent ego of the mother acknowledges this stimulus, and then gives the water to the child. In this example, the small child's request is the stimuli, and the parent providing the water is the response. This is nearly as simple as an Adult-Adult transaction.

One of the tools used by a Transactional Analysis practitioner is a structural diagram, as represented on the left. A structural diagram represents the complete personality of any individual. It includes the Parent, Adult, and Child ego states, all separate and distinct from each other. The diagram was developed by Eric Berne before Games People Play when he was developing his theories of Transactional Analysis.

Self-Awareness

Child interacting with a Parent

Transactional Analysts will then construct a diagram showing the ego states involved in a particular transaction. The transaction to the right shows a Parent – Child transaction, with the Child ego state providing the transactional stimulus, and the Adult responding with the transactional response. This transaction matches the Parent – Child example listed above, with the fevered child asking his/her mother for a glass of water.

So far, the two transactions described can be considered complementary transactions. In a complementary transaction, the response must go back from the receiving ego state to the sending ego state. For example, a person may initiate a transaction directed towards one ego state of the respondent.

The respondent's ego state detects the stimuli, and then that particular ego state (meaning the ego state to which the stimuli was directed) produces a response. According to Berne, these transactions are healthy and represent normal human interactions.

Crossed Transaction

However, not all transactions between humans are healthy or normal. In those cases, the transaction is classified as a crossed transaction. In a crossed transaction, an ego state different than the ego state which received the stimuli is the one that responds. The diagram to the right shows a typical crossed transaction. An example is as follows:

> **Agent's Adult:** *"Do you know where my cuff links are?"* (Note that this stimulus is directed at the Respondents Adult).
> **Respondent's Child:** *"You always blame me for everything!"*

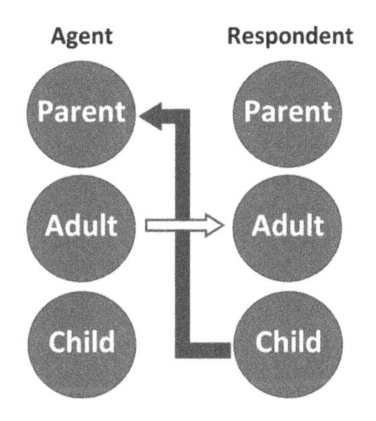

This is one the classic crossed transactions that occurs in marriage. Instead of the Respondent's Adult ego responding with "I think they're on the desk", it is the Respondent's Child ego that responds back.

> *It is important to note that when analysing transactions, one must look beyond what is being said.*

Self-Awareness

According to Berne, one must look at how the words are being delivered (accents on particular words, changes in tone, volume, etc.) as the non-verbal signs accompanying those words (body language, facial expressions, etc.). Transactional Analysts will pay attention to all of these cues when analysing a transaction and identifying which ego states are involved.

The importance of these non-verbal cues can be understood by considering the work of Dr. Albert Mehrabian. Berne passed away in 1970, before Mehrabian's seminal work was published. But Mehrabian's work quantitatively proved the importance of non-verbal cues in communication.

According to Mehrabian, when an individual is speaking, the listener focuses on the following three types of communication:

Actual Words – **7%**
The Way words are delivered – **38%** *(tone, accents on certain words, etc.)*
Facial expressions – **55%**

In the above statistics, the percentage figure indicates the degree of importance the listener places on that type of communication. One can see that facial expressions play a far more important role in communication (and thus, Transactional Analysis) than the actual words exchanged.

Self-Awareness

Reflective Practice

Reflective practice is, in its simplest form, thinking about or reflecting on what you do. It is closely linked to the concept of learning from experience, in that you think about what you did, and what happened, and decide from that what you would do differently next time.

Thinking about what has happened is part of being human. However, the difference between casual 'thinking' and 'reflective practice' is that reflective practice requires a conscious effort to think about events and develop insights into them. Once you get into the habit of using reflective practice, you will probably find it useful both at work and at home.

Reflective Practice is essentially a very old and flexible concept, so it might be called other things. This alternative terminology, which includes some familiar words, can help us to understand and explain its principles and scope.

For example, Reflective Practice might also be called, and is synonymous with:

- *Personal reflection*
- *Self-review*
- *Self-awareness*
- *Self-criticism or self-critique*
- *Self-appraisal*
- *Self-assessment*
- *Intra-personal awareness*
- *Personal cognisance/cognisance*
- *Reflective dialogue*
- *Critical evaluation*
- *Self-analysis of our thoughts, feelings, actions, performance, etc*

Increasingly these principles, terminology, and underpinning theory are defined and conveyed within the term 'Reflective Practice' and its supporting framework of terminology and application.

As such, Reflective Practice is a valuable methodology for using insights and learning from our past to:

- *Assess where we are now*
- *Improve our present and future*

This offers benefits far beyond professional learning and development, for example extending to, and not limited to:

- *Human relationships* - workplace, romance, parenting, etc
- *Rehabilitation*
- *Reconciliation*
- *Mediation*
- *Stress-reduction and management*
- *All sorts of teaching, training, coaching, counselling, etc*

Self-Awareness

- *Parenting*
- *Coping with change and trauma*

We can use Reflective Practice for our own development and/or to help others develop.

Reflective Practice is a very adaptable process. It is a set of ideas that can be used alongside many other concepts for training, learning, personal development, and self-improvement. For example, Reflective Practice is highly relevant and helpful towards Continuous Professional Development (CPD).

History of Reflective Practice

We have already seen that terms such as reflection and critical thinking can mean different things to different people, and this variable characteristic features in the founding ideas of Reflective Practice. This variability is likely to persist.

A major feature in the development of Reflective Practice theory is the evolution of:

- *Simple reflection (contemplation without necessarily having a purpose)*
- *Into critical reflection (contemplation with evaluation)*
- *Into critical thinking or critical reasoning (a balance of reasoning and reflection to assess and develop options and plans)*

Reflection is often thought of as contemplation, rather than critical thinking. Modern dictionary definitions support this. Critical thinking is more often aligned with logical reasoning and enquiry.

Reflective Practice as a Skill

Various academics have touched on reflective practice and experiential learning to a greater or lesser extent over the years. They all seem to agree that reflective practice is a skill which can be learned and honed, which is good news for most of us.

> *Reflective practice is an active, dynamic action-based and ethical set of skills, placed in real time and dealing with real, complex and difficult situations.*
>
> Moon, J. (1999), Reflection in Learning and Professional Development: Theory and Practice, Kogan Page, London.

Academics also tend to agree that reflective practice bridges the gap between the 'high ground' of theory and the 'swampy lowlands' of practice. In other words, it helps us to explore

Self-Awareness

theories and to apply them to our experiences in a more structured way. These can either be formal theories from academic research, or your own personal ideas. It also encourages us to explore our own beliefs and assumptions and to find solutions to problems.

Reflective Learning

Reflective learning is a learned process that requires time and practice. It is an Active process: involving thinking through the issues yourself, asking questions and seeking out relevant information to aid your understanding.

Reflective learning works best when you think about what you are doing before, during and after your learning experience. Reflective learning is therefore not only about recognising your something new, but also about seeing reality in a new way.
Reflection is an important skill to develop and requires you to think about how you are personally relating to what is happening in the workshop or in your work.

The Reflective Learning Process

Identify a situation you encountered in your work or personal life that you believe could have been dealt with more effectively.

Describe the experience

What happened? When and where did the situation occur? Any other thoughts you have about the situation?

Reflection

How did you behave? What thoughts did you have? How did it make you feel? Were there other factors that influenced the situation? What have you learned from the experience?

Theorising

How did the experience match with your preconceived ideas, i.e., was the outcome expected or unexpected? How does it relate to any formal theories that you know? What behaviours do you think might have changed the outcome?

Experimentation

Is there anything you could do or say now to change the outcome? What action(s) can you take to change similar reactions in the future? What behaviours might you try out?

Self-Awareness

Developing and Using Reflective Practice

What can be done to help develop the critical, constructive and creative thinking that is necessary for reflective practice?

It is suggested that there are six steps:

Read - around the topics you are learning about or want to learn about and develop
Ask - others about the way they do things and why
Watch - what is going on around you
Feel - pay attention to your emotions, what prompts them, and how you deal with negative ones
Talk - share your views and experiences with others in your organisation
Think - learn to value time spent thinking about your work

In other words, it is not just the thinking that is important. You also have to develop an understanding of the theory and others' practice too and explore ideas with others.

Reflective practice can be a shared activity: it does not have to be done alone.

Some social psychologists have suggested that learning only occurs when thought is put into language, either written or spoken. This may explain why we are motivated to announce a particular insight out loud, even when by ourselves! However, it also has implications for reflective practice, and means that thoughts not clearly articulated may not endure.

It can be difficult to find opportunities for shared reflective practice in a busy workplace. Of course, there are some obvious ones, such as appraisal interviews, or reviews of events, but they do not happen every day. So, you need to find other ways of putting insights into words.

Although it can feel a bit contrived, it can be helpful, especially at first, to keep a journal of learning experiences. This is not about documenting formal courses, but about taking everyday activities and events, and writing down what happened, then reflecting on them to consider what you have learned from them, and what you could or should have done differently. It is not just about changing: a learning journal and reflective practice can also highlight when you have done something well.

Keeping a Reflective / Learning Journal

learning journal is a collection of notes, observations, thoughts and other relevant materials built-up over a period of time and maybe a result of a period of study, learning and/or working experience. Its purpose is to enhance your learning through the process of writing and thinking about your learning experiences. Your learning journal is personal to you and will reflect your personality, preferences and experiences.

Why use a learning journal?

Self-Awareness

- *To provide a "live" picture of your growing understanding of a subject experience*
- *To demonstrate how your learning is developing*
- *To keep a record of your thoughts and ideas throughout your experiences*
- *To help you identify your strengths, areas for improvement and preferences in learning*

A learning journal helps you to be reflective about your learning, this mean that your journal should not be a purely descriptive account of what you did but an opportunity to communicate your thinking process: how and why you did what You did, and what you know think about what you did.

The Benefits of Reflective Practice

Reflective practice has huge benefits in increasing self-awareness, which is a key component of emotional intelligence, and in developing a better understanding of others. Reflective practice can also help you to develop creative thinking skills and encourages active engagement in work processes.

In work situations, keeping a learning journal, and regularly using reflective practice, will support more meaningful discussions about career development, and your personal development, including at personal appraisal time. It will also help to provide you with examples to use in competency-based interview situations.

Structuring a Learning Journal

Your learning journal may be called several different things: a learning log, a Field work diary or personal development planner. Different subject areas may ask you to focus on different aspects of your experience and may have different formats.

A journal could be a notebook, an electronic document or sometimes recorded verbally on tape. Choose a method that works best for you!

Content of a Learning Journal

A learning journal should focus on your personal responses, reactions and reflections to new ideas or new ways of thinking about a subject that you have been introduced through:

- *Workshops, seminars, training sessions*
- *Research and reading including any visual research including television, film and internet*

Self-Awareness

- Conversations and discussions with other participants, your Manager, Mentor, Coach and other colleagues
- Significant experiences in the workplace

The Process of Reflective Learning

- What do I think about this Issue/topic/ experience?
- Explore my understanding, perceptions and ideas
- Question my assumptions
- Identify anything confusing or difficult to understand
- What more do I need to know to help my understanding?
- Develop and refine my ideas and beliefs
- Identify, locate and interpret relevant Information and resources.
- How can I use this experience to improve my learning, thinking and working?
- e.g., What would I do Differently next time?

What should you write about?
What you think about issues discussed at the learning event?

- Any flashes of inspiration you had
- What you understand so far
- What you find puzzling, difficult or contradictory
- How can you reach a better understanding?
- What do you need to know more about, and how can you go about finding out more?
- What resources have helped you to understand and/or been interesting to use

How do you feel about the way you have approached the subject/topic so far?

What new knowledge, skills or understanding have you gained during the process of writing your journal?

Regarding your long-term development.

- Have you changed your opinions or values during the process/experience?
- How can you improve your learning, thinking and working in the future?

Self-Awareness

Models of Reflective Practice

Part of completing a reflection is an inner sense of discomfort (in fact the first stage of reflection as described by Boyd & Fales 1983) so it is no wonder many people put it off and may even try to get by without it, perhaps carrying out token reflections just to comply with CPD or course requirements.

To begin with, reflecting on your actions is something that requires conscious effort after the event but eventually, according to Johns (2000), it will become an automatic thought process even when you are in the middle of experiencing the event.

When deciding which model to use, it can be helpful to find out what learning style you are according to Honey & Mumford. You can relate these to the knowledge types shown in Carper/Johns' reflective models.

Below is a brief guide to the different models of reflection out there, and which situations they are best geared towards.

Gibbs Reflective Cycle (1988)

Gibbs' Reflective Cycle was developed by Graham Gibbs in 1988 to give structure to learning from experiences. It offers a framework for examining experiences, and given its cyclic nature lends itself particularly well to repeated experiences, allowing you to learn and plan from things that either went well or did not go well. It covers 6 stages:

- *Description of the experience*
- *Feelings and thoughts about the experience*
- *Evaluation of the experience, both good and bad*
- *Analysis to make sense of the situation*
- *Conclusion about what you learned and what you could have done differently*
- *Action plan for how you would deal with similar situations in the future, or general changes you might find appropriate*

Self-Awareness

Advantages: A basic, good starting point, six distinctive stages. Makes you aware of all the stages you go through when experiencing an event.

Disadvantages: superficial reflection- no referral to critical thinking/analysis/assumptions or viewing it from a different perspective (Atkins & Murphy 1993). Does not have the number or depth of probing questions as other models.

Kolb Reflective Cycle (1984)

Kolb's reflective model is referred to as "experiential learning". The basis for this model is our own experience, which is then reviewed, analysed and evaluated systematically in three stages. Once this process has been undergone completely, the new experiences will form the starting point for another cycle.

Concrete experience:
You consciously and physically experience a situation, which makes you realise that you need to reflect systematically in order to learn something new or improve on your existing skill and practice. At this stage you will make a note of the specific situation and just describe what you see, how you feel and what you think.

Reflective observation:
Having written down the description of the experience, it is now time to reflect more deeply on what has happened in that situation. The questions you need to ask yourself are: what worked? what failed? why did the situation arise? why did others and I behave the way we did?

Abstract conceptualisation:
The guiding question for this stage leads on from the questions in the reflective observation stage: what could I have done better or differently? how can I improve? Initially, you try to find different ways for dealing with the situations and think up strategies for when you experience a similar situation again. Also, this is the stage where you should consult colleagues and literature in order to get a better understanding and further ideas.

Active experimentation:
This stage is now practising the newly acquired theoretical knowledge. You take your own reflections and thoughts about improvements as well as the theories back into your practice and try out the new strategies. Some of them will work, others will not, so this is then automatically the basis for the new cycle. As the experiences within the active experimentation stage become the new "concrete experiences".

Advantages: The reflective cycle. Consists of doing, asking how/why, making judgement, testing out.

Disadvantages: Superficial reflection- no referral to critical thinking/analysis/assumptions or viewing it from a different perspective (Atkins &

Self-Awareness

Murphy 1993). Does not have the number or depth of probing questions as other models.

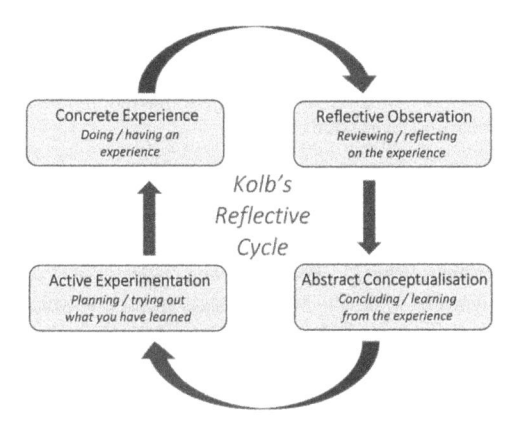

Kolb's Reflective Cycle

- **Concrete Experience** — Doing / having an experience
- **Reflective Observation** — Reviewing / reflecting on the experience
- **Abstract Conceptualisation** — Concluding / learning from the experience
- **Active Experimentation** — Planning / trying out what you have learned

Schön Model (1991)

Schön (1991) distinguishes between reflection-on-action and reflection-in-action in the following way:

Reflection-in-action is concerned with practicing critically. So, a physiotherapy student working with a client on an exercise programme is making decisions about the suitability of particular exercises, which exercise to do next and judging the success of each exercise at the same time as they are conducting the activity.

Reflection-on-action on the other hand, occurs after the activity has taken place when you are thinking about what you (and others) did, judging how successful you were and whether any changes to what you did could have resulted in different outcomes. This is usually the type of reflection which you are asked to write about as part of your studies.

Reflecting on academic or professional practice in this way may make your personal beliefs, expectations and biases more evident to you. This understanding of yourself should help you to carry out your studies more successfully as it makes you aware of the assumptions that you might make automatically or uncritically as a result of your view of the world.

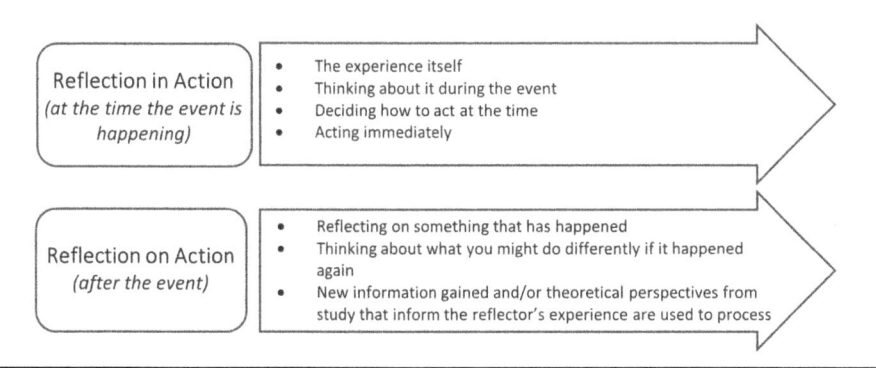

Reflection in Action *(at the time the event is happening)*
- The experience itself
- Thinking about it during the event
- Deciding how to act at the time
- Acting immediately

Reflection on Action *(after the event)*
- Reflecting on something that has happened
- Thinking about what you might do differently if it happened again
- New information gained and/or theoretical perspectives from study that inform the reflector's experience are used to process

Level 5: Operations / Departmental Manager

Self-Awareness

Advantages: Schön described reflection-in-action (in the moment surprise & puzzlement) and reflection-on-action (a cognitive post-mortem after the fact). Professional model: gaining professional artistry and increasing professional confidence.

Disadvantages: highlights the difference between the two types of reflection but does not provide extensive guidance for carrying out either.

Driscoll Model (1994)

This model focuses on 3 stem questions: "What?", "So what?" and "Now what?" Matching these questions to an experiential learning cycle and adding trigger questions which can be used to promote the learning experience and reflect on what was learnt. Below is a list of questions that you may choose to answer in response to the three elements.

What. *(Returning to the event)*

- is the purpose of returning to the event?
- happened?
- did you see? did you do?
- was your reaction?
- did other people do?
- do you see as key aspects of this situation?

So, what. *(Understanding the context)*

- how did you feel at the time?
- how do you feel now? are there any differences? why?
- were the effects of your actions?
- are the positive aspects?
- troubles you? if anything?
- were your experiences in comparison to your colleagues etc.?
- are the main reasons for feeling differently from your colleagues etc.?

Now what. *(Adjusting future outcomes)*

- are the implications for you, your colleagues, customers etc.?
- needs to happen?
- are you going to do about it?
- happens if you decide not to do anything?
- might you do differently if faced with a similar experience?
- information / skills do you need to face a similar experience?
- are your key learning points from this experience and reflection?

Self-Awareness

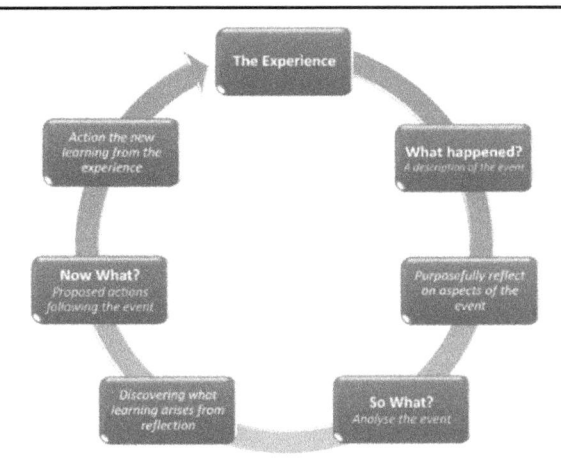

Advantages: Organisational model. Easy to follow cued questions. Easy to remember when you're out and about using the simple "What? So what? Now what?"
Disadvantages: It does not lead to deeper reflection about yourself, only the situation.

Johns' Model for Structured Reflection (2006)

Johns model is based on five cue questions which enable you to break down your experience and reflect on the process and outcomes. John (1995) used seminal work by Carper (1978) as the basis for his model exploring aesthetics, personal knowing, ethics and empirics and then encouraging the reflective practitioner to explore how this has changed and improved their practice.

> **Description of the experience** - *Describe the experience and what were the significant factors?*
> **Reflection** - *What was I trying to achieve and what are the consequences?*
> **Influencing factors** - *What things like internal/external/knowledge affected my decision making?*
> **Could I have dealt with it better?** - *What other choices did I have and what were those consequences?*
> **Learning** - *What will change because of this experience and how did I feel about the experience?*
> **How has this experience changed my ways of knowing?**
> - **Empirics** – *scientific*
> - **Ethics** – *moral knowledge*
> - **Personal** – *self awareness*
> - **Aesthetics** – *the art of what we do, our own experiences*

Self-Awareness

John's Model of Reflection

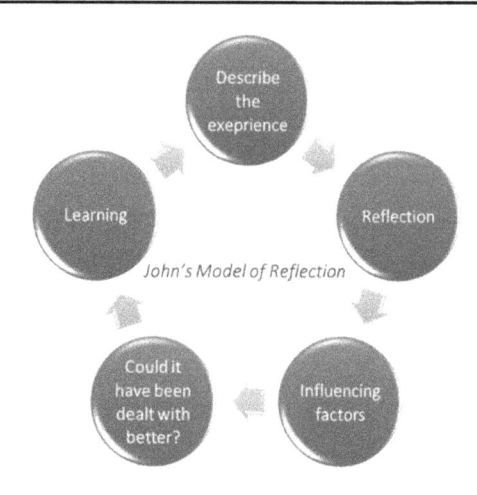

Advantages: Organisational model, examines situations in context of the environment. Provides prompt questions that are easy to follow and can be used in any order (although they follow a natural progression). Can be used by individuals or groups. Based on Carper's (1978) four types of knowing -empirical, personal, ethical and aesthetic- Johns adds a fifth one – reflexivity- to create his model.

Disadvantages: The prompt questions are not rigidly structured which could be confusing for someone inexperienced to know which ones could be omitted and which are salient for their particular reflection. The number of questions means it could be time consuming.

Atkins & Murphy Model [1993]

The Atkins and Murphy model of reflection is, as the name suggests, created by Atkins S. and Murphy K. in 1994. The model was created with the intention to study an individual's experience in order to identify points for improvement, also referred to as reflective practice. It is frequently used by professionals who want to learn continually. It is believed that a proactive attitude towards reflective practice will help improve professional competencies and abilities because it forces people to look at discomforts and next to learn from these experiences.

According to Atkins and Murphy model of reflection, discomforts are essential to make improvements.

However, individuals rather avoid confronting previous behaviours and actions because it is an uncomfortable practice. It requires a proactive attitude to assess things that did not go well, and therefore, reflective practice is preferably avoided. It is however suggested by various researchers who have studied reflective practice models that it will become easier for individuals to perform reflective practice when they continual think about discomforts. The utilisation of this model has shown that by performing reflective practice, a learning effect

Self-Awareness

occurs. This means that it will become easier for reflective practice participants to reflect on past discomforts.

The Atkins and Murphy reflection model identifies the following essential elements for a thorough reflection.
The components are arranged in a circular cycle that goes in a clockwise direction. It starts at awareness and goes to describe, analyse, evaluate, and identify.

Atkins and Murphy model of reflection components

1. Awareness
In the first step of Atkins and Murphy model of reflection it is essential to gain knowledge or awareness about the triggers that have caused discomfort. This step is not yet concerned with the whole situation because this will be described in the following section. Instead, it is now essential to identify one's thoughts and emotions that have resulted from the experience. This means that an individual must be open and express him- or herself vulnerable to identify the discomforts. According to Atkins and Murphy model of reflection, analysing personal feelings and thoughts in this way improves developments. In addition, discomfort can also be a result out of new experiences. This could include a discomfort caused by switching job positions if a new job must be learned.

Key questions to ask in this step could be for example:

- *What happened?*
- *What influenced my emotions?*
- *What were my emotions after the situation occurred?*
- *What was I thinking?*
- *What am now thinking looking back at the situation?*

2. Describe
Now that the personal emotions and thoughts have been analysed, the Atkins and Murphy model of reflection states that it is time to describe the situation. In this step, an individual must analyse the situation and key events that have occurred critically. For example, a particular environmental setting may have caused a trigger for an individual to experience discomfort, but it could be that a different environmental setting has prevented the discomfort from happening. For this reason, it is important to analyse and describe the situation. In this way, a better understanding will be realised why a discomfort occurred, and it will be easier to learn from this discomfort.

The following question could lead as an example to analyse the situation:

- *What was the event?*
- *Where was the event?*
- *When did it happen?*
- *What was my involvement during the event?*
- *What did other people do?*
- *What were the key observations?*

Self-Awareness

3. Analyse
In this step of Atkins and Murphy model of reflection, the individual must now analyse assumptions that he or she made, also referred to as the knowledge of the reflective practice participant. For example, before a situation occurred, the individual might have thoughts about the event. It is in step essential to determine whether the assumptions were correct or false. More importantly, Atkins and Murphy model of reflection states that the participant of reflective practice must additionally explore alternatives. This means that he or she must analyse how the behaviour would have been different in a different setting.

Various questions could be asked to analyse this part of Atkins and Murphy model of reflection such as:

- *What did I already know about the situation?*
- *What were my assumptions about the situation?*
- *How did the reality reflect my assumptions?*
- *What were the differences?*
- *How would I react if something else happened?*
- *In what type of scenarios would the discomfort not occur?*

4. Evaluate
This step of Atkins and Murphy model of reflection may differ from one person to another. It is concerned with personally assessing how the knowledge of the previous step is relevant for improvements. The relevance of knowledge is therefore concerned with identifying if it helps to explain the problem or discomfort. It also deals with assessing how the problem could be solved. For a participant of reflective practice, it can help to analyse different scenarios and potential behaviours, but the positive effects of this way of reflection may differ per individual.

The following could be asked to assess the relevance of knowledge:

- *How does it help to explain the situation?*
- *How does analysing different scenarios influence your thoughts?*
- *How complete was your use of knowledge?*
- *How can your knowledge next time be useful?*

5. Identify
Based on the previously described steps of Atkins and Murphy model of reflection, it is now possible to identify the learnings. By this step, the model has assessed the emotions, situations, assumptions, and knowledge of the reflective practice participant. By integrating all elements, the participant of reflective practice can easily state learnings and make use of these in future situations.

Potential questions to ask in this step:

Self-Awareness

- *What have I learned?*
- *How can my learnings be used in future situations?*
- *How to use Atkins and Murphy model of reflection?*

By using reflective practice theories and models such as the Atkins and Murphy model of reflection, participants of reflective practice create self-awareness and conduct a critical analysis of situations and the related personal emotions and behaviours. However, the Atkins and Murphy model of reflection assumes that development is realised by facing the discomforts. Analysing discomforts can demand some practice because it requires honesty, motivation, and commitment. One must learn to be comfortable with analysing discomforts.

Atkins & Murphy Model

Advantages: Deeper reflections, building on your previous experience. It encourages you to consider assumptions

Disadvantages: It may not be suitable for quick reflections on-the-go or for beginners.

Mezirow Model of Transformative Learning [1981]

Transformative learning theory was developed by Jack Mezirow in the late 1900s. He used this theory to describe how people develop and use critical self-reflecting to consider their beliefs and experiences, and over time, change dysfunctional means of seeing the world. Mezirow was interested in peoples' worldviews and what leads people to change their view of the world.

Mezirow describes transformative learning as "learning that transforms problematic frames of reference to make them more inclusive, discriminating, reflective, open, and emotionally able to change."

The Transformational Learning Theory is described as

Self-Awareness

> *"Constructivist, an orientation which holds that the way learners interpret and reinterpret their sense experience is, central to making meaning and hence learning"* (Mezirow, 1991).

The theory has two basic kinds of learning: instrumental and communicative learning.

- *Instrumental learning focuses on learning through task-oriented problem solving and determination of cause-and-effect relationships.*
- *Communicative learning involves how individuals communicate their feelings, needs and desires*

Meaning structures (perspectives and schemes) are a major component of the theory. Meaning perspectives are defined as:

> *"Broad sets of predispositions resulting from psychocultural assumptions which determine the horizons of our expectations"* (Mezirow, 1991).

They are divided into 3 sets of codes: sociolinguistic codes, psychological codes, and epistemic codes.

A meaning scheme is

> *"The constellation of concept, belief, judgment, and feelings which shapes a particular interpretation"* (Mezirow, 1994, 223).

- meaning structures are understood and developed through reflection.

Mezirow states that "reflection involves a critique of assumptions to determine whether the belief, often acquired through cultural assimilation in childhood, remains functional for us as adults" (Mezirow, 1991).

Reflection is like problem solving and Mezirow talks about how we:

> *"Reflect on the content of the problem, the process of problem-solving, or the premise of the problem"* (Mezirow, 1991).

Through this reflection we can understand ourselves more and then understand our learning better.

Merizow also proposed that there are four ways of learning. They are

Self-Awareness

"By refining or elaborating our meaning schemes, learning new meaning schemes, transforming meaning schemes, and transforming meaning perspectives" (Mezirow, 1991).

Mezirow's original theory has been elaborated upon by others, most notably Cranton (1994;1997) and Boyd (1991). The theory has commonalities with other theories of adult learning such as andragogy (Knowles), experiential learning (Rogers), and Cross.

So, what must happen for a person to change their view of the world? Mezirow believed that this occurs when people face a "disorienting dilemma." Disorienting dilemmas are experiences that do not fit into a person's current beliefs about the world. When faced with a disorienting dilemma, people are forced to reconsider their beliefs in a way that will fit this new experience into the rest of their worldview. This often happens through "critical reflection" in the context of dialogue with other people.

Principles

1. **Adult exhibit two kinds of learning:** *instrumental (e.g., cause/effect) and communicative (e.g., feelings)*
2. **Learning involves change to meaning structures** *(perspectives and schemes).*
3. **Change to meaning structures occurs through reflection about content, process or premises.**
4. **Learning can involve refining/elaborating meaning schemes, learning new schemes, transforming schemes, or transforming perspectives.**

Advantages: First developed in 1981 although has been revised with increasing complexity up until 1997-ish. Personal development model. Involves critically evaluating your assumptions and deep reflection. Frames of reference, from different viewpoints. Reflection on content is shallow but progresses to reflection on process and reflection on premise which leads to deeper reflection, leading to personal development. Suitable when person is motivated for self-directed learning. Mezirow states reflection is only helpful if it leads to a transformation in self or learning from a dilemma.

Disadvantages: This model would only be suitable if someone had the self-motivation and time to integrate the learnings from using this model into their own behaviour and schemas, so is a long-term model in this sense. Focuses heavily on rational and not emotional aspects

Self-Awareness

Writing a Reflective Journal

There is an old saying that "you can't teach an old dog new tricks" and it is certainly true when the "old dog" has a mind which is closed to new learning and experiences. A "old dog" with an open mind will analyse their experiences and use that analysis to influence their reaction and behaviour should the experience occur again.

You will hear the term 'reflective writing' many times as part of your apprenticeship and indeed, it is an integral part of every successful apprenticeship. Without reflecting on something, how will you know whether to do the same thing again or maybe handle a situation differently next time? How will you know when something has gone well, but more importantly, why it went well?

You should update your journal every time you undertake some activity relating to your apprenticeship or PDP. Your reflection may be of a general nature, almost a reflective conversation with yourself or, alternatively, it could be a structured review of your experience over a period of time. Ideally you should follow a structure like the one below.

- *What have you learned or experienced that is new? (Knowledge)*
- *Where did you learn this?*
- *How did you learn it?*
- *How have you, or could you, introduce this into your working life? (Skills)*
- *How might this affect the workplace?*
- *How might this affect you in the longer term?*
- *How might others in the workplace be affected?*
- *How will, or could this affect the way in which you work and how might others be affected by it? (Behaviours)*
- *What have you done differently?*
- *How will others be affected by this change?*
- *Will others benefit from the change?*
- *Will some in the workplace be disadvantaged by the change?*

This is not a definitive list and not everything in the list needs to be addressed every time, but you should feel free to expand and add to this list as you see fit. You should also keep a record of activities which take place around you which are not "normal". You should think about the actions and behaviour of others and reflect on how their activities affected others and the organisation as a whole. Reflect on how it was dealt with and what the outcomes were. Where possible and/or appropriate, ask those who were dealing with the matter why the particular outcome was chosen, what considerations had they made to make the decision – did they reflect on the matter before making the decision?

Be mindful of other workplace issues too. You have a responsibility for staff welfare, safeguarding, PREVENT, Equality and Diversity. Any issue arising under these headings should also be included in your reflective journal whether you were directly affected or involved. What you experience and your views and thoughts upon that experience are likely to affect

Self-Awareness

and influence you in the event it should ever occur, in which case it is important that you have reflected on the experience.

This is not the limit of your learning whilst on an apprenticeship, you will continue to develop your English and Maths skills. Any activity in these areas should also be included and reflected on as this will also form part of your development and progression. If you are asked to interpret data, create spreadsheets, write reports, undertake planning, etc which is an extension of your existing duties, it should be included in your reflective journal.

Warning! Reflective practice is one of the easiest things to drop when the pressure is on, yet it is one of the things that you can least afford to drop, especially under those circumstances. Time spent on reflective practice will ensure that you are focusing on the things that really matter, both to you and to your employer or family.

Chapter 2: Managing Self

Managing Self

Time Management Tools and Techniques

An important skill when developing our careers is time management. It is the process of arranging and controlling how we spend our time, in or out of work.

A study in 2007 covering 2,500 businesses over 4 years in 38 countries identified that wasted time costs UK businesses £80bn per year, which was equivalent to 7% of the gross domestic product (GDP) at the time.

Their findings showed the causes of wasted time were:

- *inadequate workforce supervision – 30%*
- *poor management planning – 30%*
- *poor communication – 18%*
- *IT problems, low morale, and lack or mismatch of skills – 21%*

It is very important to make the workforce as efficient as possible to maximise the organisation's investment in human resources. A 7% increase in productivity and efficiency would be a significant improvement for many organisations.

Effective time management at work can benefit individuals too, and can help workers at all levels to, for example:

- *cut out non-essential activities*
- *be more productive and achieve more within work hours*
- *enhance career development prospects*
- *make tasks more enjoyable and rewarding*
- *meet deadlines more easily*
- *achieve a better work-life balance*

Many managers and team leaders have heavy workloads, considerable responsibility and big demands on their time and expertise. If time is not managed properly, these factors can lead to excessive strain and lack of performance.

On a personal level, effective time management can help managers to, for example:

- *be more organised on a day-to-day basis*
- *be in control of upcoming projects and tasks*
- *have a clearer view of their objectives in the short, medium and long term*
- *maximise efficiency and productivity*
- *enjoy better health as a result of lowering stress and anxiety*

Managing Self

Analysing how time is spent at work

The first step in the process of improving time management is to analyse how we spend our time now. We need to use a planner or diary to note down activities throughout the day so that we can see where the time is being used. At the end of the week, we can take some time to look at the notes and do a thorough review.

We may be unaware of how much time we spend, or waste, on relatively unproductive activities. Our ordinary activities can also waste time if we do not approach them with clarity and focus.

After analysing current activities, we can identify areas of strength, which can be developed further, and areas of weakness that need to be improved. This can be followed by plans about how we can improve our overall productivity, efficiency and well-being.

Areas of our working life to consider can include, for example:

Breaks for coffee, tea etc.
We all need human contact, breaks from work, and time to move around if we spend long periods in one position, often at a desk. However, it is useful to make a note of these short breaks to see their impact over a day or a week.

Meetings and appointments
Meetings can go on for a long time and be an inefficient use of everyone's time. We need to look at the meetings we have attended during the week and maybe ask a few questions:

- *Do we need to meet this often?*
- *Can we cover all of the points in a weekly review rather than having a meeting every day?*
- *Do all of the people need to be there? Colleagues have busy schedules, too. If there are too many attendees, some people may not be heard or have time to speak.*
- *Would a different communication method be more effective, such as email?*
- *Are meetings based on habit rather than need?*
- *Did the meeting run to time?*

Informal meetings or chats with colleagues
Well-meaning colleagues can be a cause of time-wasting, with long chats in the kitchen or the corridor, asking the wrong person for advice and guidance, or being needy and afraid of making decisions on their own.

Workload and task allocation
We can all fall into the trap of spending too much time on tasks that can or should be done by someone else. Some tasks can be delegated – e.g., photocopying, preparing meeting rooms, filing or other administrative routines. The manager may need to dedicate time to

Managing Self

train a new person and monitor and review their work, but the time saved in the long run is worth the investment.

Insufficient preparation and organisation
If we are not properly prepared and organised at work, we can waste a great deal of time looking for things, doing things more than once or missing opportunities altogether. Someone who is disorganised and chaotic can also have a negative impact on colleagues, and they are likely to resent their own time being wasted.

Deadlines
When preparing for deadlines, it is important to organise and plan some projects and tasks in stages. A major project with a long deadline might need a great deal of work, so it is important to achieve smaller deadlines and objectives along the way, so that we are not caught out and forced to work through the night to catch up at the last minute.

Inefficient communication
We need to control our communications and make sure that they are as efficient as possible, as this can save time and aggravation for ourselves and others. Emails in particular are seen as cumbersome and can affect efficiency if they are allowed to dominate work time.

A great deal of time can be wasted if paperwork is disorganised, with time spent moving it around and looking for things. Telephone calls can also be disruptive in some jobs, and they can interrupt the flow of other work and affect achievement levels.

Managing Self

Tools and Techniques

When developing time-management skills, there are several tools and techniques that can help. We have already examined many aspects of time management and how various things and people can waste our time, and here are some examples of recommended time-management techniques:

Set SMART objectives
When addressing issues of time management, one useful technique can be to use SMART objectives. We can set and prioritise these to achieve team goals. By having personal objectives that align with the goals of the team and the organisation, we can work towards a common purpose and increase the chances of the punctual delivery of successful outcomes.

Managers can set their own SMART objectives, integrate these with individual team members' objectives and make sure that all of them work together to achieve the wider goals for the team. Breaking tasks and targets down into small, measurable stages can help each person to focus on the important deadlines and goals that need to be achieved, so that the whole project can move on smoothly. It is like having a three-dimensional view of a team project or objective, with all of the individual goals ending up in the same place.

Write activity logs
It is important to analyse how time is really spent and keeping an activity log can show what we are actually doing each day, as opposed to what we think we are doing with our time. We can note each activity, when it started and finished, and whether we planned to do it at that time, plus some notes if necessary. This sounds like a cumbersome activity, but it is a short-term investment in time to analyse data that can be used to save time and energy in the long term.

For example:

Activity	Start Time	Finish Time	Time Spent	Planned task?	Notes

Assess activities using the Pareto Principle
The Pareto Principle, also known as the 80-20 rule, is a method we can use to assess efforts and activities to see which are the most productive. This can be applied to time management and many other aspects of business – e.g., planning, decision-making, leadership or project management.

General examples of the Pareto Principle include:

Managing Self

80% of output is produced from 20% of input
80% of results come from 20% of effort
80% of profit comes from 20% of the product range

When you review your activity log, you should be able to identify your most productive 20% of effort that produces 80% of your output. By standing back and analysing this, you can plan how to improve our general output and efficiency.

Spend half an hour at the beginning of the day to plan activities
You can use a diary or a planner to schedule when to do things. It is worth setting time aside each morning to do this, so that activities are focused and clear. We need to, for example:

- *go through everything very quickly*
- *make a list of what needs doing and when*
- *avoid handling the piece of paper more than once – e.g., avoid picking up a job, doing a bit, and then putting it back on the pile*
- *avoid starting lots of jobs at the same time – multitasking is usually considered to be inefficient*
- *plan and schedule planning, preparation and creative time for long-term projects – otherwise short-term urgent tasks will always use up all of our time*

Batching similar tasks together can also save time – e.g., setting aside half an hour to make all telephone calls, regardless of their subject.

Accept that emails and telephones do not have to be answered immediately
You need to manage your emails and telephone calls, and not let them manage us. You can have set times for dealing with these, and not let them disturb you when you need to focus and concentrate without interruptions. Even if managers have a customer-facing role, they still need to have time when they are not available, so that they can catch up on other tasks and be proactive about objectives and plans.

You also need to be careful of a growing trend to deal with work emails and other messages during your time off. Many people spend hours each week dealing with emails before or after work. If this is a regular or ongoing occurrence, it is an indication that time management and a workload review are needed.

Factor in some time for interruptions and unplanned activities
By leaving some time available for unplanned activities, important things will not need to be pushed out of the way when something turns up needing attention.

Managing Self

Be prepared to say 'no' sometimes
It is important to examine requests before saying 'yes' to something. You need to find out about what is involved, expectations and deadlines before committing to saying 'yes'. Saying 'yes' does not always work in the long run as the obliging person will often be given too many tasks and not be respected. Someone who says 'no' from time to time, in a firm, fair and objective way, can be taken more seriously, and other people tend to respect their decisions and parameters. If you accept new challenges without question, particularly when you adopt new technology that helps others but not yourself, you open the way for new demands on your time, new interruptions, new tasks and new obligations.

Before each meeting or call, plan exactly what needs to be achieved
This helps to focus your time and effort on what needs to be achieved, and you are less likely to be distracted. Being organised before a call or meeting means that you feel more confident about the objectives, give a more professional impression, and are comfortable about moving things along quickly to achieve your goals.

Delegate effectively
You should delegate appropriate tasks, especially if you have a deputy or assistant within the team. They need to be in a position to take over sometimes, and delegation can help them to learn the tasks and take some of the pressure off you. When official delegation is not appropriate, you can just ask someone nicely if they will help or take over a task for which they are well-suited.

When delegating tasks effectively the manager needs to:

- *identify the work that needs to be delegated*
- *identify the team member's ability to take on the task*
- *identify any skills gaps before they delegate anything*

The manager needs to keep an eye on things to make sure that the delegation has been successful. They need to monitor and review overall progress and discuss feedback with the team member to identify strengths, weaknesses and avoid unnecessary problems. If delegation is not successful, it will not be an effective time-management tool for the manager, so it needs careful planning and monitoring.

Be firm about time spent in meetings
When you take control and explain how you are going to use the meeting and keep it to time, people generally understand and respect you for it. You just need to make it clear at the beginning of the meeting so that people are not offended if you start to bring the conversations and discussions to an end.

Managing Self

Remove distractions when focus is needed

If you can, you need to be able to close the door on people and interruptions when you need to work closely on something and give it your complete focus. You can allocate time when you do not wish to be disturbed, and let your colleagues know so that they can protect and respect your privacy. Just having a rule about a closed door meaning 'I'm busy, please don't come in unless it's urgent' can work if people are told.

If you cannot stop interruptions in your normal workplace, it is worth finding somewhere else to work when you need to be focused. Working in a large, noisy open-plan office, especially if you do not have your own desk, can be a nightmare and an impossible place to work.

Working from home can be an option with some organisations, and you need to discuss your needs and problems with line managers to find a solution when your time is being wasted due to lack of space and privacy.

Managing Self

Time Management Tools

In addition to these techniques, time management tools are also available and one of these is Alan's input processing technique.

This tool consists of a simple flow diagram designed to help you maintain productivity while managing incoming information (inputs).

Alan's Input Processing Technique

It is very easy to be distracted from tasks in the increasingly demanding environment we operate in today. If distraction is an issue for you, Allen's Input Processing Technique may help to improve your productivity.

The model is not complicated, yet it has the potential to help save a significant amount of time every day.

Inputs are the demands which are placed on your time and attention. The way in which these 'inputs' are dealt with will determine how efficiently you utilise your time. Are some inputs allowed to distract you from the task at hand? If they completely ignored, does it mean you are missing out on important information? Whichever you chose you will not be operating at an optimum level.

Using this technique will put a plan in place for how each new input will be processed. Once the plan becomes second nature, there will be no need to waste time analysing every new input – quick decisions will be made allowing you to move on the other matters.

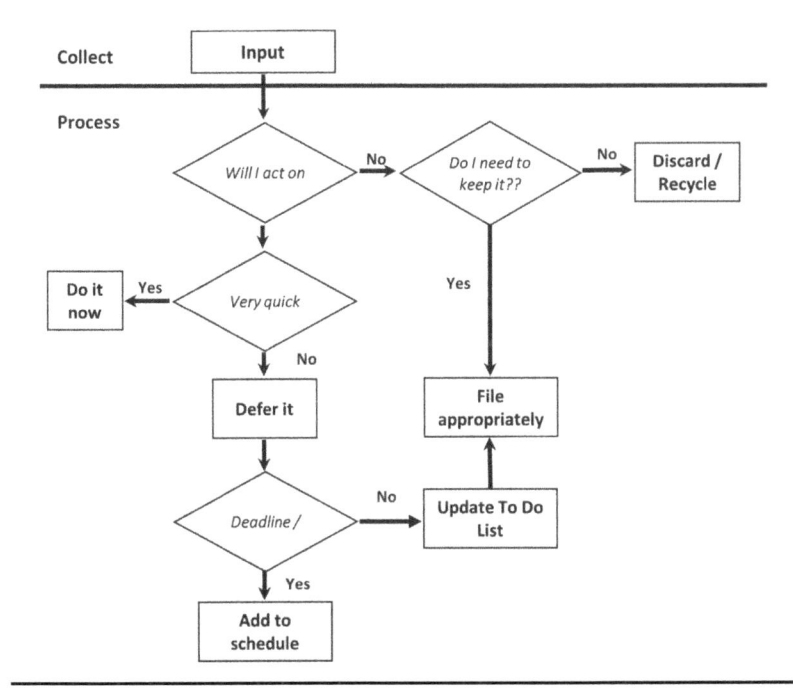

Level 5: Operations / Departmental Manager

Managing Self

Collecting Inputs
The technique starts with collecting the inputs. They will arrive in different forms and through a variety of forms and formats. An email is a clear form of input along with a phone message, a text message, a request for a meeting, a new bill, a customer complaint, etc. It does not matter what form an input is presented –is how you respond that matters

Critical Question
When a new input is received, in whatever form, there is one question which is going to determine how you process it and this is critical. That question is –

Will I act on this?

It is as simple as that. This one question starts the entire process.

If the answer is 'no', then decide whether it is something that needs to be saved for later. If it is to be saved, file it appropriately and move on. If it does not need to be saved – delete it and move on.

Deciding immediately if a new input needs action, avoids having a pile of information which needs wading through at any one time. People fall behind on processing inputs and reach the point where they simply do not have sufficient time to get back on top of it.

Taking Action
If an input needs action, the next question to ask is does it need an immediate response? If the issue is urgent, the decision is simple –complete the task immediately. The urgent inputs are the easiest to deal with as there is no doubt as to when the task should be actioned.

When an input arrives which needs attention, but not immediate attention, it should be deferred to a later time/date. Respond immediately by setting a time and date for the task to be completed. Consider what needs to be done, when it needs to be completed, and how long it will take complete.

When a time and date has been set add it to a calendar or to-do list.

Consistency is Key
Allen's Input Processing Technique helps to deal with inputs in the office, but only if it is consistently applied. It is the kind of tool that must be used every time if it is to save time effectively. Not using it for a day or two will cause a back log and it will be challenging to get back on top once again. Failing to deal with inputs will also result in missing something important – a mistake which could cost money in the long term.

Many people think they are sufficiently organised not to need the benefits of this kind of tool, but rarely is that the case. With an increasing number of inputs using organisational tool is a good choice.

Allen's Input Processing Technique saves time, it can help to reduce stress levels and it can ensure information and assistance needed is received in a timely manner.

Managing Self

Time Management Matrix – Stephen Covey

Another tool you can use is Stephen Covey's time management matrix. The Covey time management matrix can help you to manage your available time more efficiently. The matrix allows you to organise your priorities much better than before.

Covey's system makes use of four different quadrants that allow you to prioritise tasks in relation to their importance and urgency, helping you to decide whether you need to address a task immediately or if you can postpone it. As you can see from the graphic below, the time management matrix is separated into four quadrants that are organised by importance and urgency.

The matrix, also known as Eisenhower's Grid, distinguishes between importance and urgency:

- *Important responsibilities contribute to the achievement of your goals.*
- *Urgent responsibilities require immediate attention.*

These activities are often tightly linked to the accomplishment of someone else's goal. Not dealing with these issues will cause immediate consequences.

	Urgent	Not urgent
Important	Quadrant I DO NOW	Quadrant II PLAN TO DO
Not Important	Quadrant III REJECT AND EXPLAIN	Quadrant IV RESIST AND CEASE

If you apply the matrix to your own professional and private life, you will notice that the majority of your activities can be found within quadrant I and III. Experience shows that quadrant II is neglected by most people, especially in the area of their own personal development.

However, the importance of the second quadrant must not be underestimated. If you notice a big gap in this quadrant, it means that your focus lies too much on the operative aspect, while the strategic perspective is left behind. For this reason, Covey addresses quadrant II as an exceptionally important part of the matrix. Without this quadrant, efficient time management would not be possible, as it requires strategic elements as well.

Managing Self

Quadrants of Covey's Time Management Matrix

The four time-management quadrants

Quadrant 1 – urgent and important
The activities in quadrant 1 can be differentiated into items that could not have been foreseen, and those items that could. The latter can be avoided by developing plans and paying close attention to their execution.

The first quadrant should only contain those activities and responsibilities that require your immediate attention. The space is reserved for emergencies and extremely important deadlines. Should a major crisis arise, you will have to postpone other tasks.

- Crises
- Pressing problems
- Projects that are deadline driven
- Emergencies
- Last-minute preparations

Quadrant 2 – not urgent but important
The items found in quadrant 2 do not have a high urgency but can play an important role in the future. This quadrant is not only reserved for strategic planning, but also to items related to health, education, exercise, and career. Investing time in these areas might not be urgent at the present day, but in the long term, it will be of the greatest importance.

Pay close attention that you have scheduled enough time for quadrant 2 activities, in order to avoid them to become quadrant I items. During so will allow you to increase your capability of finishing your tasks in time

- Planning
- Preparing
- Training
- Exercise, health and recreation

Quadrant 3 – urgent but not important
The third quadrant summarises items that appear to have a high urgency but are not at all important. Some of these activities might be entirely ego-driven, without contributing any value. In fact, these activities are obstacles that stand in-between you and your goals. If possible, try to delegate these items or consider rescheduling them.
If another person is causing you quadrant 3 tasks it could be appropriate to decline their request politely. If this is not an option, try to avoid being constantly interrupted by appointing timeslots to those that often need your help. This way, you can address all their issues at once, without regularly interrupting your concentration.

- Interruptions
- Meetings

Managing Self

Quadrant 4 – not urgent and not important
The fourth and last quadrant contains all those activities that do not contribute any value at all—the obvious time wasters. All the activities contained therein are nothing more than distractions; avoid them as much as you can. You should also try to eliminate all the items in this list, no matter how entertaining.

- Trivia
- Time wasters
- Surfing the Internet without purpose
- Watching TV for hours

Applying the time matrix
When using the Important-Urgent matrix it is recommended to try to maximise the time spent with quadrant II activities. This will allow you (in the long run) to reduce quadrant I activities, as many of them could have been quadrant II activities—if better planning had been implemented.

The objective of using the time management matrix is to question whether a certain activity brings you closer to your goals or not. If this is the case, these responsibilities need to be prioritised over those tasks that might demand your time but do not contribute to your goals. Delay activities that do not contribute any significant output until more important tasks are finished.

Covey's time management grid has many possible applications, two of which will be explained in the following.

Reprioritising your current 'to-do' list
The time matrix can be applied as a tool that allows you to reprioritise the importance and urgency of your current and upcoming tasks. By sorting the tasks and responsibilities into the appropriate grid you will be able to quickly identify activities that need your immediate attention.

One-week assessments
The second approach of using the time management matrix requires a weekly assessment. You will need six blank copies of the matrix, five for each workday and one for your weekly assessment. At the end of each workday, you list all tasks and responsibilities and the amount of time spent. At the end of the week, you summarise the five days of your week in one matrix. Make sure to summarise the amount of time spent on a given task.

After you have summarised the week, you can then evaluate how well the time was spent and whether or not you need to make any adaptations.

Managing Self

Prioritising Work

Individuals, teams and organisations all benefit from people being organised and prioritising work. Benefits include, for example:

- **more efficient use of time** – *e.g., from only touching each file once*
- **improved communication** – *e.g., from everyone knowing and feeling confident about their position and the protocols for communication*
- **improved customer service** – *e.g., from customers knowing that urgent work will be given top priority*
- **fewer complaints** – *e.g., from urgent work being done first*
- **a calmer work environment** – *e.g., from people working more efficiently*
- **respect from colleagues and others** – *e.g., once they accept and understand the rules about interruptions; knowing how and when their issues will be dealt with*
- **better mental and physical health** – *e.g., from not having to 'firefight' all the time*
- **fewer interruptions** – *e.g., as people learn to leave others alone at certain times or if the door is closed*
- **faster meetings** – *e.g., from being more focused and stricter about how the meeting is run*
- **more time to deal with the unexpected** – *e.g., having some flexibility to be able to cope with unplanned tasks and problems*
- **improved promotion prospects** – *e.g., from senior managers being aware of improvements in output or communication skills; from achieving objectives and meeting deadlines with ease*

It is also easier for someone else to take over our work allocation if everything is organised and prioritised, which can be useful for holiday cover, for instance.

In addition to the practical steps, we can take to manage our time more efficiently, we can prioritise our work using one of four methods. This can be a useful exercise that concentrates our attention, for example:

- *at the beginning of each week, day or month*
- *at the beginning of a new project*
- *when deciding how to prioritise objectives*
- *if new tasks suddenly demand attention and need to be fitted in*
- *after an emergency or major interruption* – *to reprioritise work*
- *when events overtake and overcome us* – *to help us refocus and get back on track*

When we have the activity log data, we can analyse how we prioritise activities. This gives us the information we need to be able to stand back, review everything objectively, and then make adjustments to target our efforts and time more effectively.

Managing Self

There are four suggested methods for doing this:

1. Eisenhower / Covey Grid

Enter the findings in the grid to rationalise and prioritise activities.

	Urgent	Not urgent
Important	DO NOW	PLAN TO DO
Not Important	REJECT AND EXPLAIN	RESIST AND CEASE

2. Lakein ABC Priority System

Another theory is the Lakein ABC priority system. Using this system, you need to have brainstorm and write down everything that you need to do – e.g., as a series of spider grams or in lists.

You then allocate each item a value: A (high value), B (medium value) or C (low value). The categories can be broken down further – e.g. A1, A2, B1 and B2. This helps you to remember to:

- *include odd items that we might otherwise forget*
- *focus on the whole workload*
- *prioritise each item so that we can concentrate and not be distracted by less important tasks*

Task	Priority	Allocate
Book dentists	medium value	B1
Pay final reminder gas bill	medium value	B2
Finish report for line manager	high value	A1
Arrange to go to Cinema	low value	C1

Managing Self

3. The 4 D's of Time Management

Simply put, they are:

- *Do*
- *Delete*
- *Defer*
- *Delegate*

Do it.
A simple strategy here is to use the one touch rule. If a task can be completed there and then in a few minutes, then do it. Provided of course it is not a task to delete, delegate or defer. In other words, if it is important for you to do and you have the time to do it, then get it done straight away. Postponing important tasks often leads to procrastination or feelings of anxiety or stress.

You have seen people who paper shuffle. They start with a task and then get side-tracked and start with another, then come back to the first and at the end of the day they were busy, but not productive.

Think about starting your car on a cold morning. You need to let it idle to get warm before you drive it. In the same way each time you pick up or start a task, it takes some time to get into it or get your head around what needs doing. So, if you do not complete the task, then you go through that whole cycle again, each time you pick it up. This wastes time. If it is worth your time, then focus your time and efforts on that one task and get it done and move on.

Delete it.
Check whether the thing requires your attention or is worth your time. If it does not, then simply delete it. An example would be looking at all the email one gets during the day. See which of them are spam or something that you really have no interest in. If you are unsure, then in Outlook as an example, you can have a preview of the emails. Simply bulk delete all the emails that are trash.

If there are some emails that are not important to attend to right now, but you would like to have a look at them later, then you can defer them and move on. Always ask yourself if this particular thing is worth your time. Is it necessary to spend any of your time on it?

Remember the Pareto principle (80/20 rule) and that often people spend 80% of their time on activities that are a waste of time.

Defer it.
There are some tasks that come across your desk that you may just not be able to deal with straight away. It might be an email about booking a family holiday. It is not important during your working day but is important to get done. So, you can defer it and look at the email later in your free time.

Managing Self

Similarly, you might need to meet with a team member to discuss how they can achieve better results in their sales. A very important task, yet it might be able to wait until the sales meeting in a few days. That way you can spend the time until then planning the sales meeting and getting the things done that are more important at that particular point in time.

It might also be that the task is one that cannot be completed quickly and is not of a high priority at that time and as such you can simply defer it. You might even find that some of the tasks that you defer could become obsolete and be deleted.

Delegate it.

Is it important or necessary for you to do the task? Is it your responsibility to do? If the answer is no, then delegate it. You might still be ultimately responsible for the task being done, such as having your accounts done for year end. The buck stops with you! However, it is better to delegate the task of getting the accounts done to the accountant. This is true for many of the everyday tasks that people get involved in. Often people choose to do certain tasks as they are easier or a way of keeping busy and not getting to doing what is really important.

There is a fine line between delegation and abdication. Ensure that there is some measure in place to check that the task has been completed by the person to whom you have delegated. At the same time empower them to do the task and be understanding if the task has not been completed in quite the way you would have done it yourself. Delegating does not just have to be to subordinates. You can delegate across, upwards and to other departments as well. We will look at delegating in more detail in another article.

Implementing the 4 D's of time management

A great way to implement this is to look at your to do list on a daily basis. See which tasks need to be deleted, done, delegated or deferred. Then also do that with each task that comes across your desk during the day.

You may find some tasks stay on your to do list, which you keep on moving on to another day. Ask yourself if that task really is important for you to do. Chances are it may not be.

Thus, by deleting or delegating, you can free yourself from that task that might just have been draining your time. Similarly, it might be a task that you are just procrastinating on. Then ask yourself what it is about the task that keeps you from just doing it.

4. Delegation

There is one final method of managing time and that is to off load all the tasks that could be done by another member of the team. Getting someone else to do the work is a great solution in everyone's book, however, there is the risk it can go horribly wrong leaving you with an even greater problem than when you started, which you will still have to resolve. That is, unless you understand the art of delegation!

Managing Self

The critical steps of successful delegation

1. Define the task
Confirm in your own mind that the task is suitable to be delegated. Does it meet the criteria for delegating?

2. Select the individual or team
What are your reasons for delegating to this person or team? What are they going to get out of it? What are you going to get out of it?

3. Assess ability and training needs
Is the other person or team of people capable of doing the task? Do they understand what needs to be done? If not, you cannot delegate.

4. Explain the reasons
You must explain why the job or responsibility is being delegated. And why to that person or people? What is its importance and relevance? Where does it fit in the overall scheme of things?

5. State required results
What must be achieved? Clarify understanding by getting feedback from the other person. How will the task be measured? Make sure they know how you intend to decide that the job is being successfully done.

6. Consider resources required
Discuss and agree what is required to get the job done. Consider people, location, premises, equipment, money, materials, other related activities and services.

7. Agree deadlines
When must the job be finished? Or if an ongoing duty, when are the review dates? When are the reports due? And if the task is complex and has parts or stages, what are the priorities?

At this point you may need to confirm understanding with the other person of the previous points, getting ideas and interpretation. As well as showing you that the job can be done, this helps to reinforce commitment.

Methods of checking and controlling must be agreed with the other person. Failing to agree this in advance will cause this monitoring to seem like interference or lack of trust.

8. Support and communicate
Think about who else needs to know what is going on and inform them. Involve the other person in considering this so they can see beyond the issue at hand. Do not leave the person to inform your own peers of their new responsibility. Warn the person about any awkward matters of politics or protocol. Inform your own boss if the task is important, and of sufficient profile.

Managing Self

9. Feedback on results
It is essential to let the person know how they are doing, and whether they have achieved their aims. If not, you must review with them why things did not go to plan, and deal with the problems. You must absorb the consequences of failure and pass on the credit for success.

Levels of Delegation

Delegation is not just a matter of telling someone else what to do. There is a wide range of varying freedoms that you can confer on the other person. The more experienced and reliable the other person is, then the more freedom you can give. The more critical the task then the more cautious you need to be about extending a lot of freedom, especially if your job or reputation depends on getting a good result. Take care to choose the most appropriate style for each situation.

It is also important to ask the other person what level of authority they feel comfortable being given. Why guess? When you ask, you can find out for sure and agree this with the other person. Some people are confident, others less so. It is your responsibility to agree with them what level is most appropriate, so that the job is done effectively and with minimal unnecessary involvement from you. Involving the other person in agreeing the level of delegated freedom for any particular responsibility is an essential part of the 'contract' that you make with them.

These levels of delegation are not an exhaustive list. There are many more shades of grey between these black-and-white examples. Take time to discuss and adapt the agreements and 'contracts' that you make with people regarding delegated tasks, responsibility and freedom according to the situation.
Be creative in choosing levels of delegated responsibility, and always check with the other person that they are comfortable with your chosen level. People are generally capable of doing far more than you imagine.

The rate and extent of responsibility and freedom delegated to people is a fundamental driver of organisational growth and effectiveness, the growth and well-being of your people, and of your own development and advancement.

Examples
These examples of different delegation levels progressively offer, encourage and enable more delegated freedom. Level 1 is the lowest level of delegated freedom (basically none). Level 10 is the highest level typically (and rarely) found in organisations.

Level 1. *"Wait to be told." or "Do exactly what I say." or "Follow these instructions precisely."*
This is instruction. There is no delegated freedom at all.

Level 2. *"Look into this and tell me the situation. I'll decide."*
This is asking for investigation and analysis but no recommendation. The person delegating retains responsibility for assessing options prior to making the decision.

Managing Self

Level 3. *"Look into this and tell me the situation. We'll decide together."*
This has a subtle important difference to the above. This level of delegation encourages and enables the analysis and decision to be a shared process, which can be very helpful in coaching and development.

Level 4. *"tell me the situation and what help you need from me in assessing and handling it. Then we'll decide."*
This is opens up the possibility of greater freedom for analysis and decision-making, subject to both people agreeing this is appropriate. Again, this level is helpful in growing and defining coaching and development relationships.

Level 5. *"Give me your analysis of the situation (reasons, options, pros and cons) and recommendation. I'll let you know whether you can go ahead."*
Asks for analysis and recommendation, but you will check the thinking before deciding.

Level 6. *"Decide and let me know your decision and wait for my go-ahead before proceeding."*
The other person is trusted to assess the situation and options and is probably competent enough to decide and implement too, but for reasons of task importance, or competence, or perhaps externally changing factors, the boss prefers to keep control of timing. This level of delegation can be frustrating for people if used too often or for too long, and in any event the reason for keeping people waiting, after they have inevitably invested time and effort, needs to be explained.

Level 7. *"Decide and let me know your decision, then go ahead unless I say not to."*
Now the other person begins to control the action. The subtle increase in responsibility saves time. The default is now positive rather than negative. This is a very liberating change in delegated freedom, and incidentally one that can also be used very effectively when seeking responsibility from above or elsewhere in an organisation, especially one which is strangled by indecision and bureaucracy. For example, "Here is my analysis and recommendation; I will proceed unless you tell me otherwise by (date)."

Level 8. *"Decide and take action - let me know what you did (and what happened)."*
This delegation level, as with each increase up the scale, saves even more time. This level of delegation also enables a degree of follow-up by the manager as to the effectiveness of the delegated responsibility, which is necessary when people are being managed from a greater distance, or more 'hands-off'. The level also allows and invites positive feedback by the manager, which is helpful in coaching and development of course.

Level 9. *"Decide and take action. You need not check back with me."*
The most freedom that you can give to another person when you still need to retain responsibility for the activity. A high level of confidence is necessary, and you would normally assess the quality of the activity after the event according to overall results, potentially weeks or months later. Feedback and review remain helpful and important, although the relationship is more likely one of mentoring, rather than coaching per se.

Managing Self

Level 10. *"Decide where action needs to be taken and manage the situation accordingly. It's your area of responsibility now."*

The most freedom that you can give to the other person, and not generally used without formal change of a person's job role. It is the delegation of a strategic responsibility. This gives the other person responsibility for defining what changes projects, tasks, analysis and decisions are necessary for the management of a particular area of responsibility, as well as the task or project or change itself, and how the initiative or change is to be implemented and measured, etc. This amounts to delegating part of your job - not just a task or project. You would use this utmost level of delegation (for example) when developing a successor, or as part of an intentional and agreed plan to devolve some of your job accountability in a formal sense.

Managing Self

Maintaining the Work / Life Balance

For many people, the traditional picture of a 9 to 5, Monday to Friday job does not exist. Working at home, studying for exams, split shifts, zero-hour contracts, compulsory overtime and reduced hours can make it difficult for us to manage our time. It is more important than ever to take care of ourselves to make sure we have a work-life balance.

Use the Urgent/ Important matrix to help you identify your priorities. You can concentrate on the important tasks and decide whether sometimes tasks are labelled as urgent to make them seem important. The matrix will help you identify those tasks you keep putting off and those that do not really need to be done at all.

Depending on where you put the task, the matrix gives you clarity about how to prioritise and better manage your time.

- *Urgent and Important* – *do now.*
- *Not Urgent but Important* – *plan your time to make sure you are able to complete them.*
- *Urgent but Not Important* – *tasks in this category are often made 'urgent' by someone else, plan ways that you can turn these requests down without upsetting colleagues.*
- *Neither Urgent nor Important* – *stop doing these things, they can be real timewasters and may not need to be done at all.*

The matrix will show if you are achieving the work-life balance you want!

Looking at the causes of wasted time again, you can see ways to help you prioritise work activities and improve your time management. The main word to learn when developing your ability to prioritise is 'No'! This can be surprisingly difficult, but it is worth learning how to say it politely and effectively. It can help you manage interruptions and keep workloads under control.

Breaks for coffee, tea etc.
Just being aware of how long you spend chatting by the kettle can make you realise where you might be losing an hour or two a week. Social interaction and breaks away from the desk or static work area are extremely important, and you should move around at regular intervals. Walking around the office, going to fetch something or popping out for some fresh air are all activities that help maintain good physical and mental health.

However, you might need to change your visits to the kitchen to quieter times when you need to focus and avoid distractions. On other occasions, you can use body language and words to express how busy you are and that you are not stopping to chat today – e.g., avoiding too much eye contact; being polite, friendly and quick; avoiding asking any unnecessary questions. It is a question of balance and being aware of time.

Managing Self

Meetings and appointments
Well-run meetings can be very effective and useful for developing relationships. As the person in charge of the meeting you need to be very clear and assertive about:

- **the objectives of the meeting** – *running to a clear and simple agenda who needs to be there?*
- **the time allocated to the meeting** – *giving a strict timeframe at the beginning of the meeting, and making sure that it winds up on time*
- **keeping the meeting going** – *to make sure that all points are covered and that no one is allowed to 'waffle' too much*
- **how to deal with outstanding points that need action or attention** – *e.g., setting the time for the next meeting, producing and reviewing an action plan*

Informal meetings or chats with colleagues
Being friendly, cooperative and approachable is important, but managers can improve their own time management by, for instance:

- **making sure that people know about other sources of information and advice** – *e.g., encouraging them to look up information themselves*
- **making sure that delegation has been done correctly** – *e.g., if the manager feels 'pestered' by colleagues who are afraid to make a decision*
- **setting some parameters about interruptions** – *e.g., having a policy of closing the door when privacy is needed to deter non-urgent interruptions*
- **setting aside time for the team to discuss their views and queries** – *e.g., just after the team briefing at the beginning of the shift*

It is all about setting reasonable and balanced boundaries so that people can respect the manager's time and space, and not burden them with unnecessary interruptions at inappropriate times.

Workload and task allocation
Some tasks land on your desk at work that are not even part of your job description, action plan or objectives – e.g., being asked to organise an event that would not be part of your normal duties or covering for a colleague who is off work due to long-term sickness.

When this happens, you can usually cope in the short term. However, you need to be proactive and find solutions if the excessive drain on your time, energy and resources continues. Actions could include open discussions with your own line manager about, for example:

- **the current task allocation** – *e.g., discussing how the new tasks impact on other commitments*

Managing Self

- *reviewing and amending action plans, objectives and priorities* – e.g., to agree how long extra work will be needed; to agree changes in work rate or areas of responsibility; to see how to incorporate new tasks into future plans
- *asking for help and support* – e.g., arranging agency cover in the short term; arranging to delegate some tasks to others; agreeing overtime until longer-term solutions can be found; finding other colleagues who can help to share the load

Insufficient preparation and organisation

Preparation is key to getting the most out of a meeting, task or work opportunity. You need to:

- *focus on each meeting, task or project* – so that we know exactly what is expected of us and others
- *do the necessary research in advance* – so that we have all of the facts, figures, ideas and plans ready
- *be well-prepared before we meet and discuss the task with others* – with all of the necessary resources, notes and data ready to use
- *let people know about progress or delays* – it can be better to delay a meeting if something cannot be done in time, rather than waste everyone's time if things are not ready

If you put in the effort to be well-prepared and organised, you can do your job well, be efficient, show your professionalism, inspire trust, make good use of other stakeholders' time, and make a valued contribution to the team and organisation.

Deadlines

When prioritising deadlines, it is important to focus on all deadlines for all tasks and objectives and not just concentrate on the nearest deadline. A Gantt chart can be a useful tool when trying to work out exactly what needs to be done to achieve each deadline.
If a deadline is impossible despite good planning and organisation, it is important to let people know and renegotiate:

- **extensions of the deadlines**
- **the priority of different stages and tasks** – and agree the delivery dates that are achievable
- **extra resources** – maybe more staff, money or physical resources

It is important to reassure other stakeholders that everything possible is being done and that they will be kept informed about progress.

Managing Self

Inefficient communication
To keep emails under control, you can, for example:

- *keep your emails brief and to the point*
- *only send out emails and other messages that need to be sent*
- *only copy messages to people who really need to see them*
- *put a clear description in the subject box to help others to prioritise our emails*
- *discourage others from sending emails that you do not need to see*
- **only open your inbox at set times** – *rather than having it open all of the time, so you are distracted by new messages*
- **have separate folders for emails** – *to prioritise some and keep the rest to be read when time allows*

Paperwork can be prioritised by putting papers in different folders as soon as they arrive. For example, we can have folders marked:

- **urgent** – *deal with today*
- **for action, this week**
- **for information only** – *for things that you need to glance through quickly before filing them away for reference*
- **bills to pay**
- **filing**

Files can also be allocated to specific tasks, projects or subjects – e.g., customer queries, or interviewees for a job.

To prioritise telephone calls, it is better to find a good time to get hold of the person we need rather than wait on hold for a long time. If receiving too many calls, ask the reception staff to take messages at certain times or put the caller through to voicemail. Make sure that reception staff know how to direct calls to the right person.

Managing Self

Workload Management Strategies

At some time or another almost everyone feels as though they have more work than they can cope with. However, not all stress is bad, and it is often cited as a key factor in helping people respond to crises, adapt to change and excel when a peak performance is required, for example, in an interview or presentation. When coping with stress at work, the important thing is not to let your workload grow to the point where you are completely overloaded.

The most common sources of work-related stress include:

1. *Continuous and tight deadlines.*
2. *Dealing with crises on a daily basis.*
3. *An excessive workload.*
4. *Role ambiguity and conflict.*
5. *Constant negative feedback.*
6. *Inadequately trained support staff.*

If you are overloaded, then you need some workload management strategies to remedy the situation.

This will be easier if you have the facts to back up your case and are confident that you are working as effectively as possible by using an appropriate workload management strategy.

The most common sources of work-related stress include continuous and tight deadlines, an excessive workload, role ambiguity and conflict and the need to deal with crises on a daily basis.

If you are overloaded, then you must take steps to remedy the situation. This will be easier if you have the facts to back up your case and are confident that you are working as effectively as possible by using an appropriate time management strategy.

Avoid taking on too much

A significant contributor to workplace stress and overload is the inability to say no, which results in people taking on far more work than they can realistically manage. It is a natural response to want to accommodate requests made by others. You do not want to disappoint them, let them down or give the impression that you cannot be bothered or are too lazy to help.

Sometimes tasks may sound so enticing that you are tempted to take them on and worry about finding the time for them later. This is especially true for work that is some time in the future. However, it is important to think realistically about your workload.

Ask yourself:

Managing Self

> *"are you likely to have any more spare time in the future than you have at the moment?"*

One of the major factors in developing the ability to say no is to realise that if you take on things that you subsequently have not got time to do well, then you will be letting everybody down.

> *A job done badly will reflect poorly on you, your colleague and perhaps the whole organisation.*

It is very easy to agree to take on more responsibility, to be seen as a keen and competent employee. It is much more difficult to admit that overload is a problem and then to take action to remedy the situation. If you feel that you are becoming overloaded, then you may decide to try to negotiate a reduction in your workload.

How to Negotiate your Workload

If you have never questioned the demands of your manager or organisation before, then this may be rather daunting. The most effective tactic may be to restrict your negotiations to a specific task or project that you identify as causing you the worst problem.

Here are some important guidelines to consider when considering workload management strategies:

Specify your objectives precisely
If you felt deluged by low-level customer enquiries, you might suggest: "delegating the handling of first line customer enquiries to the receptionists". This approach provides a framework for the negotiation and prevents the risk of your request being mistaken for a general complaint.

Prepare your evidence
If you can produce a time log detailing the amount of time that a particular task has taken you and can show the associated cost, this will often make for a more convincing case.

Prepare counter arguments to the likely objections
The best way to prepare counter arguments is to look at the situation from your manager's perspective. Seeing things from your manager's viewpoint should help you to devise a solution that they will find acceptable.

Decide in advance what compromise you would accept
If both you and your manager are going to be happy with the outcome over the long-term, then there may need to be some form of compromise. Decide in advance what issues you are likely to need to give ground on.

Managing Self

Become more task-orientated
Some people are primarily task-orientated, whilst others are primarily people-orientated.

Task orientated people often find it easier to say no, as they tend to evaluate requests against task related criteria. They will ask themselves whether or not they are capable of and willing to perform, the requested task. This enables them to make a more objective decision in response to a request.

People-orientated individuals are more likely to ask questions relating to their relationship with other people and their desire not to disappoint them. If you feel that you would like to become more effective at saying no, then try prompting yourself to think more carefully about the task involved each time you are requested to take something on.

Ask yourself questions like:

1. *Can you tackle this task?*
2. *Are you clear about precisely what it entails?*
3. *Have you got the time to take it on?*
4. *Can you do the job well?*
5. *Is there someone else better equipped to do it?*
6. *What happens if you need to disengage from the task due to other commitments?*

If your responses lead you to believe that you would be unwise to take it on, then it is in nobody's interest for you to agree to it. Try to clarify your reasons and explain these in a clear and concise way when declining the request.

Be prepared to say 'no'
In most circumstances you have every right to decline a request. However, if you let yourself worry or dwell on past occasions where you have declined a request, then you are more likely to accept future requests, regardless of their importance.

Consider your response
Try to predict circumstances in which you are likely to be asked to take on extra commitments and prepare some form of response. When requests arrive unexpectedly, ask for time to think about the request before responding.

Do not apologise
Do not fall into the trap of being over-apologetic. Say what you want to say in a clear and concise way but do not sound like you are making excuses. If people get the idea that they can talk you round, then they may persist until they are successful. The other drawback with adopting an apologetic approach is that the requester may feel that your reasons for declining are tenuous and doubt the reasons you have given.

Managing Self

Think ahead
It is a natural assumption that it is easier to book the time of a busy person well in advance, and it is all too easy to accommodate such requests. However, are you likely to be any less busy in 6 months' time than you are in three weeks' time? If your future commitments are uncertain then be very careful about agreeing to things even if they seem to be a long way off.

Saying 'No' to your Boss

There are three common reasons why saying no to your boss is a different proposition to declining requests from colleagues or clients:

> *Firstly, it may appear as though you are refusing to do the normal activities of your job.*
> *Secondly, you may worry about giving the impression of not being as keen as your peers.*
> *Finally, your boss may just overrule your objections and make you do it anyway.*

Generally speaking, there are only two valid reasons for declining work that is passed down.

Firstly, that your existing work will suffer and secondly that the work is beyond your level of competence. This means that any workload management strategies you use must be based on one of these reasons.

It is important to construct a good case to support your argument, you should put your points clearly and concisely and do not come up with too many objections. This invites your boss to use the weakest to undermine your whole case, without giving you the opportunity to counter with your stronger points.

Another useful approach can be to devise a plan for how the task could be tackled, without taking the full responsibility upon yourself. You might even turn a request from your boss into an opportunity to offload some routine work, thereby freeing yourself to address the current request properly. It can assist you greatly to get the boss on-side by sowing the germ of an idea and letting them come up with the plan, before endorsing it as a great way to proceed.

If you feel that you are becoming overloaded, then you may decide to try to negotiate a reduction in your workload. It is helpful to specify your objectives precisely, prepare your evidence and counter arguments and anticipate the need to compromise.
One of the biggest problems many of us face is knowing how to say 'no' to some of the many requests we receive. Task-orientated people tend to make objective, task-related, decisions whereas people-orientated individuals tend to make subjective decisions based on relationships.

Managing Self

The Pomodoro Technique

Getting stuff done is hard, especially if you are self-employed or need to do things for yourself that you usually put off, like paying bills. There always seems to be something else to do: a drawer that could be organised, a phone call to your sister or checking flight prices on a trip you have no intention of taking.

Enter....... the Pomodoro Technique!

This popular time-management method can help you power through distractions, deep-focus and get things done in short bursts, while taking frequent breaks to come up for air and relax. Best of all, it is easy. If you have a busy job where you are expected to produce, it is a great way to get through your tasks. Let us break it down and see how you can apply it to your work.

What is the Pomodoro Technique?

The Pomodoro Technique was invented in the early 1990s by developer, entrepreneur, and author Francesco Cirillo. Cirillo named the system "Pomodoro" after the tomato-shaped timer he used to track his work as a university student.

The methodology is simple: When faced with any large task or series of tasks, break the work down into short, timed intervals (called "Pomodoros") that are spaced out by short breaks. This trains your brain to focus for short periods and helps you stay on top of deadlines or constantly refilling inboxes. With time, it can even help improve your attention span and concentration.

Pomodoro is a cyclical system. You work in short sprints, which makes sure you are consistently productive. You also get to take regular breaks that bolster your motivation and keep you creative.

The Pomodoro Technique is probably one of the simplest productivity methods to implement. All you will need is a timer. Beyond that, there are no special apps, books, or tools required. Cirillo's book, The Pomodoro Technique, is a helpful read, but Cirillo himself does not hide the core of the method behind a purchase. Here is how to get started with Pomodoro, in five steps:

- *Choose a task to be accomplished.*
- *Set the Pomodoro to 25 minutes (the Pomodoro is the timer)*
- *Work on the task until the Pomodoro rings, then put a check on your sheet of paper*
- *Take a short break (5 minutes is OK)*

Managing Self

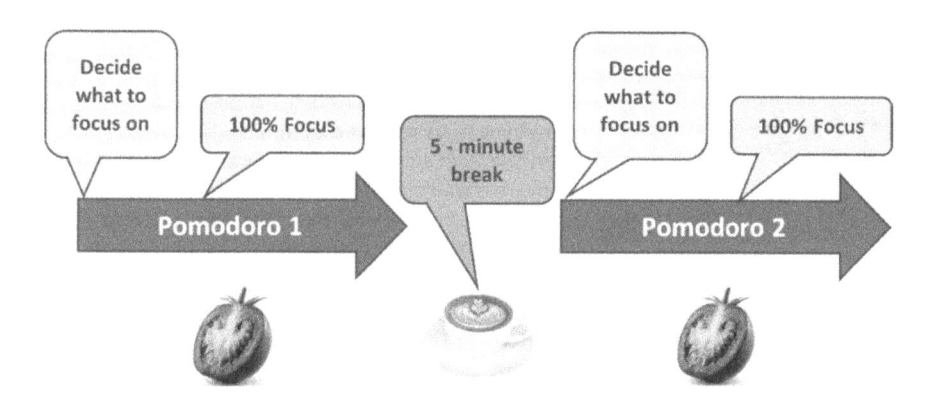

Every 4 Pomodoros take a longer break

That "longer break" is usually on the order of 15-30 minutes, whatever it takes to make you feel recharged and ready to start another 25-minute work session. Repeat that process a few times over the course of a workday, and you actually get a lot accomplished—and took plenty of breaks to grab a cup of coffee or refill your water bottle in the process.

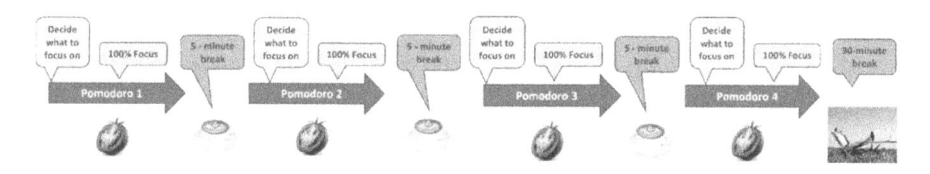

It is important to note that a pomodoro is an indivisible unit of work—that means if you are distracted part-way by a co-worker, meeting, or emergency, you either have to end the pomodoro there (saving your work and starting a new one later), or you have to postpone the distraction until the pomodoro is complete. If you can do the latter, Cirillo suggests the "inform, negotiate and call back" strategy:

- *Inform the other (distracting) party that you are working on something right now.*
- *Negotiate a time when you can get back to them about the distracting issue in a timely manner.*
- *Schedule that follow-up immediately.*
- *Call the other party back when your Pomodoro is complete, and you are ready to tackle their issue.*

Of course, not every distraction is that simple, and some things demand immediate attention—but not every distraction does. Sometimes it is perfectly fine to tell your co-worker "I'm in the middle of something right now, but can I get back to you in....ten minutes?" Doing so does not just keep you in the groove, it also gives you control over your workday.

Managing Self

The Pomodoro Technique is often championed by developers, designers and other people who have to turn out regular packages of creative work. Essentially, people who have to actually produce something to be reviewed by others. That means everyone from authors writing their next book to software engineers working on the next big video game can all benefit from the timed work sessions and breaks that Pomodoro offers.

However, it is also useful for people who do not have such rigid goals or packages of work. Anyone else with an "inbox" or queue they have to work through can benefit as well.

Then it is time for a break, after which you come back and pick up where you left off or start a new batch of tasks. If you build things or work with your hands, the frequent breaks give you the opportunity to step back and review what you are doing, think about your next steps, and make sure you do not get exhausted. The system is remarkably adaptable to different kinds of work.

Finally, it is important to remember that Pomodoro is a productivity system—not a set of shackles. If you are making headway and the timer goes off, it is OK to pause the timer, finish what you are doing and then take a break.

The goal is to help you get into the zone and focus—but it is also to remind you to come up for air.

Regular breaks are important for your productivity. Also, keep in mind that Pomodoro is just one method, and it may or may not work for you. It is flexible, but do not try to shoehorn your work into it if it does not fit. Productivity is not everything —it is a means to an end, and a way to spend less time on what you have to do so you can put time to the things you want to do. If this method helps, go for it. If not, do not force it.

Stress and Workload Management

Everyone has their unique level of over-commitment that leads to stress at work. Knowing when you are approaching this level and taking positive steps to keep control are key to maintaining your performance and productivity. You need to be aware of your stress symptoms.

You may recognise that you become more irritable, indecisive or lack confidence. You could have persistent physical signs, such as, more frequent migraines, indigestion, pains etc.

Your workload negotiations will fall into two main camps, those with your direct boss and those with colleagues. You may employ the same tactics for either group, but you need to be

Managing Self

aware of the higher risks you encounter when negotiating with your manager and be more conscious of the environment your negotiations take place in.

Whoever you are negotiating with you must ensure that you do not feel obliged to accept such tasks or projects unless it brings some benefit to you. The ways to identify and handle such negotiations are described in our free eBook on this topic.

Focus on the benefits to You

When undertaking such negotiations, you must make sure that whatever the outcome you benefit from that decision. It is essential that you approach the underlying reason for such discussions from your own viewpoint. You need to appear sympathetic to request but present your case from a position of strength. This may be returning a past favour, working the request so that there is a mutual benefit to accepting the task or gaining a promise of future help.

You may also choose to accept the task to your workload because it provides a unique opportunity for you to acquire a skill, expand your knowledge base or improve your visibility within the organisation.

If you decide to accept a task part of your decision-making process must assess the impact this additional task will have on your existing deadlines. Finally, clearly define your terms of acceptance and the other person's expectations.

Identify the root cause

You may find that you spend a significant amount of your time in these negotiations. If this is the case, then you must identify their source. The diagram above shows the most common root causes and you will have to take time to assess and prioritise your outstanding tasks and why they remain on your list of things to do.

In each case you will need to ask yourself why these causes keep reappearing and what you can do to eradicate them. If you cannot do this then how you intend to make the cause more manageable.

- *Is someone within the organisation sitting on information causing unnecessary delay?*
- *Is there a problem with the organisation's processes that needs to be fixed?*
- *Why do certain problems keep on reoccurring?*
- *Is there confusion over whose role it is to perform a task?*
- *Are there sufficient resources to perform the task as required?*

By researching such queries, you may find that other people or divisions within the organisation do not realise that they are doing, or not doing something that is having unforeseen consequences elsewhere. Now you have the information you need to prepare your case for not accepting the task.

Managing Self

Time Management Techniques

Time is finite!

We all have the same number of hours each day. You cannot store time, borrow it, or save for later use. You can only decide how to allocate it, spending it on activities of higher rather than low value.

Time management is a game of choices: projects to pursue, tasks to complete, routines to follow.

Adopting good time management techniques in your life is not about squeezing as many tasks as you can into your day. It is about simplifying how you work, getting things done faster, and doing things better. By doing so, you will have more times to play, rest, and doing the things you love. Do not try to work hard, invest in working smarter.

> *"Time management is not a peripheral activity or skill. It is the core skill upon which everything else in life depends."* — Brian Tracy

Below is a list of time management techniques. They are a set of principles, rules, and skills that allow you to put your focus on the things that matter, get more done and help you be more productive.
Use them as a rulebook of your work. You will improve your productivity, accomplish more with less effort, improve your decision-making ability, reduce stress, and ultimately become more successful in your career.

But remember everyone is different. These are the time management techniques that are useful in some people's lives, but you might not agree. Adopt the ones that work for you and always seek to refine your own practices by regularly thinking about how to improve your time management skills.

By writing your own time management rulebook, you will discover that there are really enough hours in a day for everything you would like to do. It just takes a bit of rearranging and re-imagining to find them...

1. Organise work around energy levels
Productivity is directly related to your energy level.

Find your most productive hours — the time of your peak energy — and schedule Deep Work for those periods. Do low-value and low-energy tasks (also known as shallow work), such as responding to emails or unimportant meetings, in between those hours.

For example:

Managing Self

If you are a morning person, do your most critical work when you get in the office. After lunch, your energy might crash a bit, so it is a great time to clean your desk, clean emails or update spreadsheets.
Plan your work around your energy levels, scheduling critical work for peak productivity times.

You should also know your energy levels by day: Tuesday seems to be the most productive day for most people but find your own patterns.

This is how Jeremiah Dillon, head of product marketing for Google Apps for Work, organises his week around his energy levels:

Monday: Energy begins to build after the weekend — *schedule low-demand tasks like setting goals, organising, and planning.*
Tuesday, Wednesday: Peak of energy — *tackle the most difficult problems, write, brainstorm, schedule your Make Time.*
Thursday: Energy begins to ebb — *schedule meetings, especially when consensus is needed.*
Friday: Lowest energy level — *do open-ended work, long-term planning, and relationship building.*

Map your work and energy levels in a spreadsheet for a couple of weeks until you uncover your productivity patterns.

2. Plan your day the night before
Before going to bed, spend 5 minutes writing your to-do list for the next day. These tasks should help you move towards your professional and personal goals.

By planning ahead, the night before, you will be better prepared mentally for the challenges ahead before waking up and there will not be any room for procrastination in the morning. As a result, you will work faster and smoother than ever before. Spend a few minutes each evening before going to bed to write down everything you need to get done tomorrow. Make planning a part of your night-time routine and save yourself time and worries in the morning. Once you wake up, you will be able to just get to work.

3. Start the day with critical work
Mark Twain once said:

> *"If it is your job to eat a frog, it's best to do it first thing in the morning. And, if it is your job to eat two frogs, it's best to eat the biggest one first."*

This is a golden time management technique: Find your most important task for the day and tackle it first. That task should be the one thing that creates the most impact on your

Managing Self

work. Getting it done will give you the momentum and sense of accomplishment early in the day. That is how big life goals are achieved: small continuous efforts, day after day. Each day identify the most crucial tasks to complete and tackle it first. Once you are done, the day has already been a success! How do you find your most important task?
In Elon Musk's words:

> *"Focus on signal over noise. Don't waste time on stuff that doesn't actually make things better."*

Look at your to-do list and decide which tasks help you get close to your goals and make progress in meaningful work. Put these at the top of your list so you can focus on them first. Resist the temptation of tackling the easiest tasks first.

4. Prioritise tasks

Knowing how to prioritise your work is an essential time management technique. Projects, however small or large, need clear priorities. When everything is a priority, nothing is.

You must prioritise your "true tasks" first, the tasks that actually move the needle towards your goals. To help you find them - use the Eisenhower Matrix.

> *Prioritise "true tasks": urgent and important to-dos that have a direct impact on your goals.*

Here is how:

1. Write down all your tasks. Do not worry about the order (for now), just write everything you need to do.
2. Now identify what is urgent and what is important. After each task, mark them with "U" for Urgent and "I" for Important. Tasks can have one, both, or none. If none, you will need to delete them.
3. Now assess value: look at your "I" tasks and identify the high-value drivers of your work. You need to find which tasks have priority over others and how many people are impacted by your work.
4. The next step is to estimate time to complete each task. Order them from most effort to least effort.
5. Finally, insert the tasks into the Eisenhower Matrix. You now have a complete overview of all your work tasks.

5. Delegate or outsource tasks

Using the Eisenhower Matrix, you will find that some tasks are urgent but not important. When that is the case, the best you can do is find someone who can complete these tasks for you. You do not have to do everything yourself. Delegating or outsourcing some tasks can be a great way to multiply your efforts and get more done. Delegate or outsource

Managing Self

urgent but not important tasks to multiply yourself and keep you focused on the most important work. These are the top things you need to know to delegate efficiently:

- *Find to the right person:* whoever you are delegating the tasks to, should have all the necessary skills and is capable of doing the job
- *Provide clear instructions:* write down the tasks in a step-by-step manual be as specific as possible
- *Define success:* be specific about what the expected outcome is and the deadline to have the task completed
- *Clarity:* have the tasks explained back to you and offer clarification when something is unclear, rewriting the specifications if needed

6. Automate repetitive tasks

Technology has finally reached a point where we can automate a lot of our daily operations. By automating a few of your tasks, you save hours per week. You can then use that time for Deep Work or taking breaks. Putting some of your daily tasks on autopilot is key to working smarter. Use technology to automate daily repetitive tasks and use the newfound time to perform Deep Work or rest. Here are a couple of tasks you can automate in under 10 minutes:

- *Create default responses in your email client for emails you keep writing over and over again*
- *Set reminders on your calendar so you never forget anything*
- *Proofread your writing*
- *Use tools to schedule and automate your social media posts in advance*
- *Automatically fill online forms using auto-complete and save all your passwords in one place*
- *Create spreadsheet templates for reports you have to do weekly/monthly*

7. Set time constraints

You become more productive when you allocate a specific amount of time to complete a specific task. That is why we create deadlines.

But Parkinson's law states:

> *"Work expands so as to fill the time available for its completion"*

So, if you reduce the time you have to complete a task, you force your brain to focus and complete it.

Set deadlines even when you do not need to. Scheduling less time to complete tasks and force your brain to focus.

Managing Self

Here is an example:

You have to review and reply to an email, a task that normally takes you around 20 minutes. Reduce the time available to 10 minutes, set a countdown timer and work as hard as you can to beat it.
The timer creates a sense of urgency and pushes you to focus and be more efficient, even if you end up having to go back and add a more time later.

Use deadlines and time limits to your advantage. Even when you do not have a deadline, set one. Your brain will acknowledge it. Knowing you only have one hour to complete a report will ensure you do not waste 20 minutes on Facebook.

8. Eliminate distractions
Distractions hurt your productivity and focus. A study from the University of California Irvine found that it takes an average of 23 minutes and 15 seconds to get back to the task after getting distracted.

Author, Gary Keller, illustrated in "The ONE Thing: The Surprisingly Simple Truth Behind Extraordinary Results" what happens when you get interrupted:

- *When you lose your focus, it can take you twice as long to get back into the groove.*
- *Half an hour completely focused on a task is more productive than 2 hours switching between tasks. Eliminate distractions from your work to avoid task switching costs.*

Here are a few ways to eliminate distractions from your life:

- *Turn off all notifications on your phone, computer, and tablet*
- *Leave your phone in odd places that prevent you from immediately finding it*
- *Work with headphones as people are less likely to approach you with a non-urgent question or gossip if you look plugged in and on-task*
- *If you find interesting articles, save them to Pocket or Instapaper to read later, such as during the commute*
- *The internet is a distracting place. Turn-off your Wi-Fi when your tasks do not require internet connectivity*
- *Do not browse social media at work at all. If you cannot resist, designate "distraction time" and browse it for a couple of minutes. Take out of social media exactly what you want*
- *Use "Do Not Disturb" functions on chat systems, such as Slack, Hangouts, and Messenger*
- *Similarly, use Inbox Pause to stop getting flooded with new emails. Change your inbox to a Gmail to become productive on email*
- *If you have an office, shut the door*

Managing Self

9. Make quick decisions on things that do not matter
We make hundreds of small, medium, and big decisions every day. 90% of the decisions we make do not matter. Success comes from identifying and focusing your energy on the 10%.

Small decisions impact you for a day, such as what to wear or where to eat. Medium impact your life for a year, such as deciding to go back to school or rent a different room. In the long term though, very few decisions matter. Those are the big decisions: they are worthy of serious pondering, discussion, investigation, investment, and decision making.

Invest your focus on big decisions and make quick calls on medium and small decisions.

In "10–10–10: A Life-Transforming Idea", Susy Welch introduces a simple decision-making system. When you have a decision to make, ask yourself the following three questions:

- *How will I feel about this decision 10 minutes from now?*
- *How will I feel about it 10 months from now?*
- *And in 10 years from now?*

Busy people do not spend a lot of time pondering over small and medium decisions. A great time management technique is to train yourself to be quick when making them as well.

10. Track your time
Do you know how much time you spend on each task? Most of us can guess, but our estimates are normally way off. A time-tracking app can help you take out the guesswork and provide real data on your productivity.

RescueTime is a free app that tracks exactly how you spend time on the computer. It is as easy as set it and forget it and you get a report at the end of the week breaking down your productivity. Log in to check other metrics, such as time spent on each task.

Track your time to have real data on your work and uncover insights on how you can improve your productivity.

After a couple of weeks, you will start noticing patterns and knowing where and how your time is leaking. By being aware of how exactly you are using your time, you can devise a plan to attack your leaks and how to get rid of them.

Time tracking is a powerful time management technique that forces you to take a hard look at how your work and how you can optimise it.

11. Beat procrastination with the 2-minute rule
The "2-Minute Rule" is a great way to beat procrastination and get things done. It works for both your professional and personal life.

Managing Self

There are two parts to the "2-Minute Rule":

Part 1: If it can be done in two minutes, just do it. Do not add it to your to-do list, put it aside for later, or delegate to someone else. Just do it.

Here are some examples of tasks you can do in two minutes or less:

- *Answer an email from your boss*
- *Send an update to a colleague*
- *Plan for the day while having your morning coffee*
- *Loading the dishwasher right after the meal*

There are a ton of tiny, seemingly trivial tasks that take less than two minutes, yet you need to do every day.

Part 2: If it takes more than two minutes, start it. Once you start acting on small tasks, you can keep the ball rolling. Simply working on it for two minutes will help you break the first barrier of procrastination.

For example:

- *Write a thousand words every day? Write 50 words in the next two minutes*
- *Meditate for 20 minutes a day? Sit down and meditate for two minutes*
- *Want to exercise for one hour a day? Do jumping jacks for just two minutes*
- *9 out of 10 times I end up working on the task for far longer than 2 minutes (I then continue working using the Pomodoro productivity tool).*
- *Use the 2-Minute rule to beat procrastination: if a task can be done in two minutes, just do it; if it takes more than two minutes, start it.*

12. Say no more often than yes

Most CEOs will tell you that saying "no" is one of the most important time management techniques. Saying "yes" often can be counterproductive, especially when you agree to do things that do not contribute to your work and goals. Your time is a limited resource, and you cannot let people set your agenda in life.

Focus on doing great quality work rather than rushing through it all. Quality wins over quantity every single day.

Warren Buffet said it best:

> *"The difference between successful people and very successful people is that very successful people say no to almost everything."*

Managing Self

But how do you know which things you should say no to? What if you are passing on a life-changing opportunity? Luckily, Buffet has developed a two-step rule to help you set boundaries and become better at decision making:

> Start by writing down your top twenty-five career goals. Once you are done, circle the five most important to you
> The second step is to completely eliminate the other twenty goals. Go ahead and cross them off
> Say "no" by default to anything that does not contribute to your top 5 career goals.

Anything other than the five goals you circled in the first step are distractions getting in the way of reaching what you truly value in life. As such, start saying no to anything that does not contribute to your "true goals".

13. Take advantage of gap time
We have a lot of downtime throughout our days: commuting, lines, waiting rooms, in-between tasks, small breaks in the schedule, etc.

If we add all this time up, we have around 1–3 hours of "gap time" every day. Be as strategic about your breaks as you are about your day in general. While these short periods might not be enough to do Deep Work, we can still work on little things that contribute to your work, development, and growth.

Here are a couple of things you can do to use "gap time" effectively:

- *Learn a new skill, either for your professional or personal life*
- *Read books or articles you saved to Pocket*
- *Organise your computer, folders, calendar or work*
- *Plan your week, tomorrow, or the rest of your day*
- *Listen to a podcast*
- *Learn a language*
- *Take a walk and think and let your mind wander*
- *Take a productive pause to clear your mind.*
- *Use "gap time" effectively to develop new skills, strategic planning, and personal growth.*

By taking advantage of your downtime, you end up getting more done and having more free time for fun after work.

14. 80/20 Your time
The 80 20 rule states that "80% of the output or results will come from 20% of the input or action". In other words, the little things are the ones that account for the majority of the results.

Managing Self

This is one of the best time management techniques you can use to help you regain focus and work on the things that bring the most impact. Do 20% of your tasks bring 80% of the results? Then prioritise your time to work on them.

Use the 80/20 rule in your life and work to prioritise the input that brings the majority of the output.
Here are other questions to ask yourself when using this rule:

- Is 80% of value achieved with the first 20% of effort?
- Are 20% of the emails 80% of the important conversations?
- Do 80% of your distractions come from 20% of sources?
- Do 20% of your tasks give you 80% of the pleasure in your job?
- Is 20% of your team completing 80% of the work?
- Do 80% of problems originate with 20% of projects?
- Are 80% of customers only using 20% of software features?
- Do 20% of customers make 80% of the complaints?

15. Automate decisions
Force your brain to make a lot of decisions and you end up depleting your willpower and suffering from decision fatigue. This hurts your decision-making ability: as the day wears on, you will start making fewer smart decisions. That is why you are more likely to binge-watch Netflix while eating Doritos in the evening.

To avoid mental exhaustion, automate decisions to free yourself from cognitive burden and not rely solely on your self-discipline. Let decisions happen automatically and smart decisions will happen by themselves.

Here are examples of smart decisions you can automate:

- Transfer money to your savings account every time you receive a pay cheque
- Choose all your outfits for the week on Sunday and hang them in order
- Subscribe to a weekly fresh delivery of organic vegetables and fruits to your home
- Standardise the typical daily meals you like the most, saving time in cooking and grocery shopping
- Prepare your sports bag every night and put in your car. If you prefer running the morning, leave your running shoes near the bed
- Automate all electronic gadgets to go into sleep mode at a certain hour

16. Single task
Multitasking is a corporate myth that has evolved over time. The brain is designed to focus on one thing at a time. Switching between tasks can have damaging costs to our work and productivity.

Managing Self

Develop the habit of single tasking by forcing your brain to concentrate on one task and one task only. Put your phone away, close all the browser windows and apps that you do not need. Immerse yourself in this task. Only move to the next one when you are done.

Force your brain to single task in order to do Deep Work and avoid task switching costs.

17. Break down big tasks
From Bird by Bird: Some Instructions on Writing and Life by Anne Lamott:

"Thirty years ago, my older brother, who was ten years old at the time, was trying to get a report on birds written that he'd had three months to write, which was due the next day. We were on holiday and he was at the kitchen table close to tears, surrounded by paper and pencils and unopened books on birds, immobilised by the hugeness of the task ahead. Then my father sat down beside him, put his arm around my brother's shoulder, and said. 'Bird by bird, buddy. Just take it bird by bird.'"

We all have huge tasks that we get tired just thinking about the amount of work needed to complete them. We procrastinate by doing mindless tasks instead of starting them.

To avoid this, break down your larger goals into small manageable tasks with realistically achievable milestones. This will help you map out all the small activities that need to be done and creating a timeline to do them. As a rule of thumb, each small task should take less than one hour to complete.

Break down big tasks into smaller ones to avoid procrastinating and help you stay on track to achieve your final goal. Never put a huge project down as just one to-do on your list. Instead, put bite-sized to-dos that you can do one at a time. Take it "bird by bird".

18. Take fewer (but better) meetings
Meetings are the devil of business. Few people like meetings and most dread them.

The truth is most things do not need a meeting. If the purpose of the meeting is neither to decide or complete an action together, cancel it and communicate by email (e.g., updates on a specific project). As for outside the office meetings, switch to phone calls or video conferences

As for the meeting that you do have to take, make them highly efficient and productive by following these simple rules:

- *Do not schedule more time than needed. Most of the times 20 minutes is the sweet spot*
- *Keep the number of participants small.*
- *Send everyone an agenda and main points the day before*

Managing Self

- Keep conversation on-track by reminding the participants of the topic: "Let's schedule another time to discuss that later if it's helpful since we only have 10 minutes left"
- Group your meetings back-to-back to have a clear start and end point for each one

Only take meetings that have a clear agenda and a decision that needs to be made. To run better meetings, have an end time and keep the number of participants small.

19. Let go of perfectionism
Perfectionism keeps you from being perfect.

It is easy to be caught up in an endless cycle of trying to do everything perfectly. But being a perfectionist can delay your work and make you miss important deadlines. The sooner you realise that delivering high-quality work on time is the most important skill, the faster you will advance on your goals and career.

Perfectionism is actually fear disguised in sheep's clothing, which shows itself as procrastination. Learn to accept that small details do not matter, ship faster, and fix things afterward if needed.

Aiming for perfection is a sure-fire way to delay or never complete a project. Choose to chase "good enough" instead.

In the words of Mark Twain:

> "Continuous improvement is better than delayed perfection."

20. Have a To-Do Not List
In Mathematics, there is a problem-solving technique called inversion. You start with results and work backward to calculate the causes. Inversion is a powerful tool because it forces you to uncover hidden beliefs about the problem you are trying to solve. You need to think how to minimise the negatives instead of maximising the positives.

Let us say you want to improve productivity. Thinking forward, you would list all the things you could do to be more productive. But if you look at the problem by inversion, you would think about all the things you could do that would diminish productivity.

Create your own by writing down all the habits you want to quit and the activities you wish to eliminate from your life. Think about your possible workday — long meetings with people you do not like and boring repetitive tasks — and work from there.

Create a To-Do Not list with all the habits you want to remove from your life. Use it as a guideline of what you do not allow in your life.

Managing Self

- *Do not email first thing in the morning or last thing at night*
- *No morning meetings*
- *Do not say yes unless you are 100% certain you can deliver*
- *Do not drink coffee in the afternoon*
- *Do not agree to meetings or calls with no clear agenda or end time*

The reason why inversion works is simple: what you do not do, determines what you can do.

> *"People think focus means saying yes to the thing you've got to focus on. But that is not what it means at all. It means saying no to the hundred other good ideas that there are. Innovation is saying no to 1,000 things."* — Steve Jobs

21. Batch similar tasks

What does processing all your emails in one sitting and cooking for an entire week on Sunday have in common? They use a productivity trick known as batching.

The main idea behind this time management technique is to collect up a group of similar activities and do them all in one swoop. You can work efficiently on multiple tasks without losing your flow if the activities require similar mindsets. Batching forces your brain to be focused on one type of task at a time.

Batch similar tasks and complete them at one time. Batching reduces the start-up and slow-down time, daily clutter, and improves focus.

To discover which tasks you should stack, start by writing all your activities for the day and week. Now identify the ones that call for similar mindsets and batch them together. Try the batch and rearrange tasks if necessary.

Here are a couple of tasks you should batch together:

- *Outlining all your blog posts for the upcoming week in one sitting*
- *Processing all communications: emails, Slack, and phone calls*
- *Updating several related worksheets at the same time*
- *Completing all your errands — grocery shopping, dry cleaning, post office — at one time*

To process batches faster, work on similar tasks for a set period of time using the Pomodoro Technique.

Managing Self

22. Take time off to recharge

In today's hyper-connected world, it is easy to fall into the trap of being connected 24/7. We feel guilty during the weekend about not working ahead or completing an extra project. All the time

Our body and mind need rest to function properly. Taking time to recharge is crucial to sustaining motivation, passion, and productivity. Quick breaks during a stressful deadline can help you maintain focus, renew creativity, and make you feel more refreshed when you return to your task.

For longer periods of recharging, take regular work vacations of at least a week off throughout the year. Bill Gates, for example, went into seclusion for one week twice a year to focus and plan. Many of Microsoft's innovation ideas came from those "Think Weeks". Schedule breaks throughout your day to help you recharge and take regular vacations throughout the year. Rest is the best medicine for sustainable long-term productivity.

And finally……..

It is so easy to get caught up in our business that we forget to enjoy what we are doing. The ultimate goal of work is enjoyment. You want to spend more time doing things that you enjoy.

Work can and should be fun. It is fun that drives motivation, passion, creativity, and productivity. Dread your job and no time management technique in the world can help you.

Apply these time management techniques as a way to maximise your happiness while at work, not the amount of time you spend working. Use the newfound time in activities you value, such as spending time with your family, working on side-projects, practicing a hobby or developing your skills.

The enjoyment you get from these other activities will in turn fuel your work productivity.

Managing Self

Personal Development Planning (PDP)

At various points in your life, you may be presented with opportunities for personal development: perhaps the chance to work with someone particularly inspiring, or to do something new and unexpected.

But it is also true to say that you make your own luck.

The harder you work, the luckier you get
Attributed to golfer Jerry Barber in 1960

In other words, you have to know what you need to improve to achieve a particular ambition, and then work on it. But if you do so, you will improve. Only by doing so will you have a chance of achieving that ambition.

If you do not know what you need to improve, you cannot work on it.

If you do not plan ahead to develop the skills that you need for your chosen course in life, you will not be able to achieve all that you want.

The reason for planning your personal development is therefore very simple: only you know what you want to achieve, and the key to achieving it is in your hands via the actions you take. Planning what you need to do to achieve your goals is a vital step in the process.

Many people may first come across personal development plans as part of a course of study, or at work. But planning what you need to do to improve or change yourself is not just important in formal situations. It can also help in your personal life too.

Professional growth is all about gaining new skills and experience. That means your development is either related to your current role or the role you want to do next.

Personal development fits alongside professional growth — so if you want to progress in your career, you will need to develop personally first. That is the only way you will be able to handle your fears, take on more responsibility, and succeed with greater challenges.

Professional development is not only about climbing the greasy pole or earning more money. It is also about avoiding stagnation in your career and futureproofing yourself.

When you expand your skills beyond your current role, you are preparing yourself for more and that makes you more valuable to employers. It has never been more important that your personal skill set is developed to meet the demands of today's manager. There is little point in

Managing Self

focussing on developing a team if there is not enough focus on personal development. All leaders and mangers need a broad range of skills in order to led others effectively.

Professional Development can be defined as:

> *"The process of improving and increasing capabilities of staff through access to education and training opportunities in the workplace, through outside organisations, or through watching others perform the job."*

Professional Development is focused on gaining new capabilities and experience and improving the knowledge and skills that improve your potential in your work environment. These are the skills that make you more efficient and effective at your job. It is also suggested that it helps build and maintain the morale of staff members and is thought to attract higher quality staff to an organisation.

> *This means your professional development is either related to your current role or the role you want to do next.*

With changes to our working lives happening every day, be it economic change, amendments in legislation or even the advance of technology, it is important to develop your skillset to remain effective in your career.

Effective professional development involves ensuring your knowledge and understanding of your area of expertise for your career is always at the highest possible level. It is the acquisition of skills and knowledge for career advancement, but it also includes an element of personal development.

Broadly speaking, it may include formal types of vocational education or training that leads to a career related qualification. It can also include informal training and development programmes, which may be delivered on the job in order to develop and enhance skills.

Some examples of professional development are:

- *IT training*
- *Health and Safety*
- *Accountancy or budgeting*
- *Legal knowledge or expertise*
- *Leadership training*
- *Management training*
- *Time management*
- *Handling difficult situations and conflict management*
- *Communication skills*

These could be delivered in many different methods, such as classroom-based learning, eLearning, coaching, consultation, mentoring and more.

Managing Self

Benefits of Personal Development

Personal development is about improving your talents and potential, both in and out of the workplace.
Personal Development can be defined as:

> *"The process of improving oneself through such activities as enhancing employment skills, increasing consciousness and building wealth."*

Personal development sits alongside professional growth — If you want to progress in your career, you will need to develop personally first. That is the only way you will be able to handle your fears, take on more responsibility, and succeed with greater challenges. Personal Development requires us to develop and broaden our knowledge, improve and develop our skills and develop and refine our behaviours to ensure we always perform with the upmost professionalism.

Personal development relates to your life skills. These are what you need in order to achieve your life goals. It focuses on helping you improve your talents, whether they are related to your work or not.

Personal and professional development courses can improve your motivation and help you excel in your domain.
Personal development offers plenty of different benefits. The following are some of the major benefits you can get:

- *Boosting self-awareness*
- *Increasing self-knowledge*
- *Developing your existing skills or learning new ones*
- *Renewing or building your self-esteem or identity*
- *Developing pre-existing talents or strengths*
- *Enhancing your employability*
- *Improve the quality of your life*
- *Positively affecting your social status and wealth*

All these activities can help you make a major difference in your life. Even if you feel helpless, these are skill sets which can help you turn the odds in your favour. By focusing on your personal development, you are able to effectively ensure that you have the right skill sets for you.

Activities suitable for Personal and Professional Development

Managing Self

Personal Development	Professional Development
Emotional Wellbeing	Management Training
Health and fitness	Skill-based training
Communication	Internal Assessment
Motivation	Conflict Resolution
Spirituality	Online Education
Self-belief	Networking
Journaling	Research

Difference between Personal and Professional Development

It is clear from the definition that professional development pertains to enhancing a workforce and/or an individual within a workforce. Often the objectives here are specific to an organisation and its goals at a specific time and the skills that would be required to deliver their products/services.

The second definition indicates that personal development is required where employees, as individuals, seek to update their own knowledge and learn skills that they would like to have.

In the personal context, the activities are more unique to the individual and his/her objectives.

When contrasting personal versus professional development, it is probably easy to see that there is a connection rather than trying to identify differences.

There is a link in that both professional and personal development are similar regarding a drive towards improvement, greater understanding and better effectiveness of individuals' (either an individual or a group).

Additionally, they are alike in that both require effort, time and resources (often money) to get involved in and both regularly reoccur for all individuals and not just professionals.

Whilst personal development might seem separate from your professional life, it could in reality be a great way to achieve your career objectives. It is not just what you learn that could help you thrive at work; by making your commitment to personal development clear to your employer, you will be able to demonstrate dedication and an ability to learn and grow. Whether it is personal development or professional development, you do not need to pick between the two. You should view them in this light:

> *Personal development makes a difference in your life on a daily basis. At almost every stage of your life, you will learn something new which will help you blossom as a person.*

Given this, you do not have to specifically pick one over the other. Your personal development plans might have many aspects of professional development too. Sometimes, the issues can be interlinked as well.

Managing Self

The key to managing your own personal development is knowing your own strengths and areas for improvement. Knowing these can help you to develop your weaknesses and turn them into strengths.

An accurate self-analysis will identify areas for improvement, and it is important to be totally honest with yourself in order to improve on some of your biggest weaknesses.

Personal Development also has a number of business benefits. A study reported that 42% of companies do not believe in using personal development coaches, yet the same study revealed that if these companies had used a coach, they would have increased their income by 46%!

Of those who had received coaching, the survey revealed:

- *62.4% of employees got smarter in goal setting*
- *52.4% of employees became more self-confident*
- *57.1% of employees experienced the lowest levels of stress*
- *25.7% of them left their vices and bad habits behind*
- *33% of employees say they are unlikely to fulfil their career aspirations in their current organisation*

Not only does personal development benefit the business in many ways, but it can also benefit each individual employee in different ways:

Benefits of Development

1. **Mental health/self-esteem** – Personal development not only improves your work life; it also can help you to develop your personal life in a variety of different ways. Keeping track of your positive and negative behaviours can help you to manage them better, preventing negative behaviours and encouraging positives ones. This can help you to become the person you want to be and therefore, improve your self-confidence and performance at work, whilst developing your self-esteem and mental health.

2. **Productivity/motivation** – Personal development can increase your productivity. Becoming aware of your strengths and weaknesses can encourage you to produce higher quality work – seeing improvement in yourself can give you a little confidence boost and motivate you to achieve more!

   Personal development can also guide you to turning your weaknesses into strengths for example, a poor attitude can be turned into a positive one – this can be achieved by recognising the impact and consequences of your attitude and how it can affect others around you. It is certainly not easy but becoming more aware of how others respond to or absorb your mood/behaviour may encourage you to control it – or even turn it into a positive attitude in order to encourage others in the workplace! This should give you the drive that you need to become more productive and work harder to achieve your personal objectives.

Managing Self

3. **Improves Skills** – improving your areas of development will also improve your skills, for example, if you are trying to improve your telephone manner, you can use your personal development tools to keep track of this in order to develop the skill. This could make you a more competent worker and your colleagues may even recognise that you are becoming more dynamic. This could open up opportunities for career growth and promotions. When you are able to identify these needs, you are able to work towards a personal development plan.

Personal development is the foundation for everything that follows. If you focus on developing the core aspects of yourself first, you can actually move forward professionally faster and with greater ease. This is because personal development is where core habits of success are first formed.

Consider this quote by famed author and speaker, Brian Tracy:

> *"Personal development is a major time-saver. The better you become, the less time it takes you to achieve your objectives."*

Remember, you cannot help others until you have helped yourself. If you have ever flown on a plane, you will know that you are meant to put on your own oxygen mask first!

You will soon be able to work on both personal and professional development at the same time and reap new benefits in both. There are no quick fixes, your growth and development is a continuous cycle of reflection and self-improvement. It never ends and that is the whole point.

When you recognise there is always more to learn, you stay grounded, more open to new ideas and better able to manage greater challenges in life.

Finally, neither Personal nor Professional development can be completed satisfactorily without a depth of self-awareness which is far greater than we currently have. By having a thorough understanding of what you need to achieve and how to achieve it, you can develop the necessary skills by way of a solution.

Creating a Personal Development Plan

A PDP is simply a plan, just like any other plan. The only difference is that it relates specifically to you.

When you first start thinking about personal development, it can seem as if you know nothing, and have no skills. You may find this point rather overwhelming! But it is important to bear two things in mind:

Managing Self

- **You do have skills.** You have been learning and developing all your life, and you already have many, many skills.

- **You do not have to improve everything all at once.** In fact, you are much better off not trying to do that.

Focus on just one or two areas at a time, and you will see much larger improvements, and also feel less overwhelmed.

There is a reason why personal development is sometimes called 'lifelong learning': there is no time limit on it!

A good PDP will include:

A clear vision of where you want to be and why

It is really helpful to think about where you want to be and what you want to do. It can be useful to think in terms of different lengths of time: for example, one month, six months, one year, five years.

It is also helpful to make your vision as detailed as possible, across all spheres of life: career, where you want to live, your hobbies and even relationships. The more detail you can include, right down to how you will feel about it, the easier it will be to hold onto your vision when times are hard.

The next step to your personal development plan is to think about what skills you need to develop, and why this is important to achieving your vision.

For example:

- *Do you need certain skills to get a particular job, or to advance in your chosen career?*
- *Are you planning to live abroad, and therefore need to develop your language skills?*
- *Are you struggling to manage a particular situation, and need new skills to help?*
- *Have you been told that you lack particular skills and need to develop them to work effectively with others, or on your own?*

It is important to make sure that the skills you are targeting are clearly linked to a purpose, which is in turn linked to your vision. Without this clarity, your personal development efforts may fail. In particular, you may not concentrate on the right skills, or be fully aware of your timescale.

Development needs can be identified through:

Managing Self

- *analysis of learning styles, and personal and key skills*
- *SWOT analysis*
- *Psychometric tests*
- *Self-assessment*
- *Academic study and research*
- *Workplace goals*
- *Future career, employment/self-employment goals and direction*
- *Personal and social goals*

The difference between where you are now and where you need to be, tells you the magnitude of the task. It also affects how long it will take, and also how much effort you need to put in.

If you are planning to move abroad in a year's time, or go travelling, you may need to develop your language skills. But, if you have already lived in that country for a period and speak the language well, you may not need to do more than keep your language skills up via listening to foreign radio.

If, however, you have never learnt the language, and you are starting from scratch, you may need some intensive language tuition, or even an immersion course, to ensure that your skills develop quickly enough.

You cannot do everything at once.

Instead, you need to prioritise. One very good way to do this is to list all your areas for development, then ask yourself two questions about each one, answering on a scale of one to five:

- *How important is this to me?*
- *How essential is it to develop it now?*

Add together (or multiply) the scores for the two questions for each area, and you will have a much better idea of which areas to focus on first, because they are either more important, or they are more time critical. Leave the other areas for a later date: next year, or even a few years' time.

It sounds obvious, but you need to know how you are going to get from (a) to (b): where you are now, to where you want to be. For example, are you going to enrol on some kind of course? Learn online, go to college or evening class? Just as with your vision, it can be helpful to break this down by time: in a month/six months/a year, what will you have done on the way to your ultimate goals? This makes it easier to check your progress and keep yourself on track.

Creating a Personal Development Plan not only helps you effectively plan for the future and manage your own learning and development, but it can also help give you some direction and move forward in your career.

Managing Self

Planning and delivering your personal development can be thought of as personal strategic thinking and planning – where do you want to be, and how will you get there?

At the heart of the process, there are three questions:

Where am I now?
To answer this question, we need to have a look at our current, personal, situation – e.g., our skills, knowledge and experience; qualifications; job description and tasks; salary package; grade or position at work.

Where do I want or need to be?
Where we would like to be in the future. This can be six months ahead, a year, five years or a period that fits into our future plans. We need to consider our goals, the things we want or need to achieve – *e.g., a higher salary; promotion; increased knowledge and skills in specific areas at work; greater job satisfaction; improved job security; improve employability prospects.*

How will I get there?
The route achieving this is what will be recorded in our Personal Development plan. We need to identify the steps we need to take to begin to work towards our goals. This may include qualifications, a career review, do voluntary work to gain specific experience, ask to broaden experience within current work role, shadow colleagues in order to learn from them, consider the best learning options for you personally.

> **Remember! This is about focussing on your personal goals and set targets that are specific to you and your needs.**

Here are some tips to help you to get started, and then keep going, by focusing on what matters.

1. Why are you trying to develop? - *It is important to understand why you are trying to develop.*
The answers to all the questions about 'what' and 'where' (what should I do? Should I address my weaknesses, or build my strengths? Where should I begin?) all become clearer once you identify why you want to change. It is important to be clear about this purpose, so that you can assess whether your
learning and development activities are moving you closer to your goals. It is also easier to get motivated when you have a clear picture of where you want to be at the end of the process.

2. Planning your development - *Planning your personal development (and documenting your plan) will help to make it more realistic.*
There is something about writing things down that makes the overambitious look ridiculous, and the unrealistic stand out like a sore thumb.

Managing Self

Planning for your personal development, which includes time limits and stages of development, will force you to be realistic about what you can achieve by when.

Of course, writing it down does not bind you irrevocably. Everyone's lives change, and your priorities may well alter after you have developed your plan. A written plan, however, gives you something to look back on and a way of keeping tabs on your goals, even formally altering them if necessary.

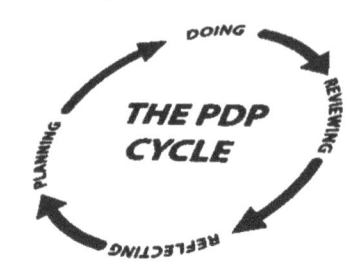

> *I may not have gone where I intended to go, but I think I have ended up where I needed to be.* Douglas Adams

3. Documenting your plans - Writing down your plans and activities enables you to review your progress.

Keeping detailed records may sound like something that you would prefer to avoid. But your personal development plans and activities, if documented carefully, not only enable you to review progress, but also provide a record of your thinking over time.

It is incredibly easy to forget how you felt about things at different stages, and even why you thought a particular goal was important. Carefully documenting your thinking will help to show you what works best, what you have enjoyed and disliked, and quite probably point you towards more suitable activities or areas for development.

4. What works for you? - It is important to find out what personal development methods work best for you.

There are an enormous range of development activities available, from formal training sessions, through online training to experiential learning, reading and discussing ideas with others. As with anything, it is important to find out what works best for you—as in, what you enjoy most and also what helps you to learn and develop quickly and effectively.

5. Focus - What is really important in your personal development?

Personal development is a lifelong process—which is why it is described as 'lifelong learning'. In practice, although it can be hard to remember this, this means you do not have to do everything at once.

Use your vision to identify what really matters now — what you have to do first to achieve your vision — and concentrate on that. Only once you have achieved that, or at least made reasonable progress, should you move on. 'Butterfly-style' personal development, flitting from subject to subject, may keep you interested, but will probably be less satisfying or effective in the longer term.

Managing Self

6. Grasp new opportunities - *Do not be afraid to take opportunities that you had not considered before.*

Not everything in life, or personal development, is predictable. Sometimes you may be offered an amazing opportunity to do something that does not fit with your immediate priorities, but which sounds too good to miss. It is worth considering whether taking this opportunity will slow down your progress towards your ultimate goal and, if so, whether that matters. It is not worth turning something down simply because you have never thought of doing it, and therefore it does not feature in your 'life plans'.

Ultimately, being offered this kind of opportunity probably helps you to define your goals better: if it sounds very exciting and you really want to do it, then do. If it changes your goal and vision, so be it.

> *Our biggest regrets are not for the things we have done but for the things we have not done.* Chad Michael Murray

7. Let personal development evolve - *Your priorities will change — and that is OK*
Few, if any, of us would say that we were exactly the same person at 35 that we were at 15, or even 25. As you grow and change, taking on new responsibilities in work or at home, so your priorities and goals will change. The key is to recognise that this is fine.

What matters is to ensure that your personal development activities continue to take you where you want to go. Regular review and revision of your personal development activities and plans will ensure that they change with your priorities and remain relevant.

There are a number of things that are vital in supporting your personal development, including developing a vision of where you want to be, and planning how you are going to get there.

But alongside these, it is also helpful to take some simple but practical steps to change how you organise your life. These changes will help to give you more time and space to manage your personal development activities. Without that, you may struggle to find the time and energy to improve your skills or study.

Identifying Development Requirements

Skills audits can be used to list the skills that are relevant to a role, then assess ability using a scoring system. The skills tested can be for a current role, to see where improvement is needed, or on a role we want to aim for in the future.

In this example, an experienced fresh produce department manager in a supermarket wants to apply for promotion to deputy store manager. A previous skills audit shows that they perform at a high level in all aspects of their current job, and they want to be considered for promotion. The following skills audit is based on the skills and attributes shown in the organisation's job description for the deputy manager position. This helps them to identify skills gaps that will

Managing Self

need to be addressed if their application for promotion is to be successful. They show their current skills in these areas, with 1 = poor and 5 = excellent.

Skills and attributes	1	2	3	4	5	Action to be taken
Experience of all departments within the store			✓			Need to work in other store areas – see line manager
Evaluating competitors' stores and managing advantage			✓			OK for fresh produce, useful to try other areas competitive
Leadership skills				✓		OK
General staff management skills				✓		OK
Communication skills			✓			Usually very good, but need more at senior management level – ask line manager
Training and coaching skills					✓	One of my strengths
Purchasing and negotiating delivery and discounts	✓					Do not have to do this in current role – ask procurement team if I can shadow them for a day/week?
Ability to promote and generate sales – demonstrations, displays					✓	One of my strengths
Customer service skills					✓	One of my strengths
Budgeting/finance skills		✓				Only have to do a bit – need to shadow someone
Working to the organisation's and industry's standards					✓	OK
Maintaining health and safety in the store-e.g., fire evacuation, first-aid cover, risk awareness, minimising hazards, dealing with dangerous chemicals correctly			✓			OK in my area, do not really need to worry about chemicals here – find out a bit more for rest of store
Quality management – e.g., store cleanliness, customer satisfaction, quality of produce					✓	OK

You can now see the areas that this manager needs to address when preparing to apply for promotion.

Managing Self

The next stage is to prepare a SWOT analysis to identify their development needs in more detail. This shows what they need to do to be able to develop their skills, experience and knowledge to be in a good position to apply for promotion.

The fresh produce department manager could prepare a SWOT analysis along these lines:

Objective: *To be qualified and experienced enough to apply for deputy store manager within 6 months*	
Strengths Worked in trade for 5 years Experienced in fresh produce, frozen food, electrical goods Successfully managed team of 8 staff for 18 months Currently manage budget, staffing, planning, quality control, customer service for fresh produce department Part way through level 3 apprenticeship in leadership and management Good level of general education Ambitious and ready to move forward	**Weaknesses** Have not finished level 3 Little experience of procurement and inventory management Little experience of head office operations beyond normal duties, have gaps in reporting, finance and budgeting skills
Opportunities My line manager (Deputy Manager) has offered to mentor and have access to other operational areas of the store Store manager will let me attend senior store management meetings Study organisation's procurement, finance and budgeting procedures and training materials Do level 4 qualification after finishing level 3 qualification Attend company's Preparing for Senior Management course	**Threats** Might not be enough time to fit in company's course – sit down with diary and line manager to discuss options Colleagues and current team members might be unhappy – explain goals and ask for their help, review as we go to make sure not neglected Level 4 course might be cancelled by college as not enough learners at the moment – discuss options with managers, maybe I can wait until after new job has started

Managing Self

Analyse current skills, knowledge and experience

The normal process for analysing current skills, knowledge and experience is to use a skills audit. This is a simple process which identifies what you are good at what you are not so good at as well as things you may not have done before. The skills audit is a simple process to identify your strengths and weaknesses.

A definitive list is made of the skills that are relevant to the role and it is essential that this list comprehensively covers all the appropriate criteria, otherwise its benefit and effect will be nullified. The existing skill set is then compared to the list and a simple rating system needs to be applied which shows the level of skill for each criterion.

The rating can be from self-evaluation or be done with someone else, such as the line manager.

When deciding which skills to audit, the details can be taken from a variety of sources – e.g., the organisation's own policies, procedures and standards; national occupational standards; essential standards; professional bodies' standards; qualification specifications from awarding bodies. The job description and person specification should go some way to providing some of the elements for this, but the final list should be checked by all parties concerned or involved. Below are two samples of skills audits:

	Personal Audit	1	2	3	4	5
1	Lack confidence in expressing my needs		✓			
2	Manage time effectively			✓		
3	I am competent to lead		✓			
4	I cope with stress well				✓	
5	I do not have the confidence to give presentations			✓		
6	I am patient when teaching and coaching others		✓			
7	I can handle a number of tasks		✓			
8	I do not have the confidence to influence others			✓		
9	I can motivate others			✓		
10	I do not make people do tasks			✓		

Managing Self

Skills required	Current ability (1–5)	Action to be taken
Computing skills	4	Undertake short courses (if possible) to enhance computing skills
Leadership skills	4	Get more involved in communities/societies
Numeracy skills	4	Discuss with lecturers and fellow students on ways to improve
Revision and exam techniques	3	Learn from lecturers and fellow students on techniques to revise and answer exam questions.
Time-management and organisation skills	2	Jot down all activities that need to be done accordingly in a diary
Oral presentation skills	4	Learn to fully utilise and use other presentation aids that are available besides PowerPoint
Critical analysis and logical argument skills	3	Get more involved in group discussions
Selecting and prioritising information when reading	3	Listen to lectures and identify which are the important points
Referencing skills	3	Write more essays and get used to the Harvard referencing style
Summarising skills	4	Need to fully understand the topic
Developing appropriate writing style	3	Read more articles and journals to get used to the writing style so that it can be implemented
Search skills (library and e-resources)	3	Fully utilise the library's 'resources and support' section
Utilising and comprehension	5	Listen more to the way people converse with each other and try and pick up whatever necessary
Proofreading and editing	3	Take another look at the work

Managing Self

Identify development needs and set objectives

The skills audit will help to analyse the current position – where I am I now – and reveal areas that are strong and those that need attention. These can be entered on the PDP, so that we can see our strengths and skills gaps, then start to decide what we need or want to consolidate or improve.

Having analysed where we are now, we can work out where we want to be, then set personal objectives to plan how to improve our performance at work. When setting personal work objectives, it is important to have a realistic number of goals. If overloaded, people feel overwhelmed and are more likely to fail, give up and lose confidence. Honesty about achievements and expectations is important.

It can be useful to support this process with personal reflection and discussions with senior colleagues, maybe during the appraisal process. Once we have established our needs, we can set objectives that support our strengths, address our weaknesses and help us improve our performance.

SWOT Analysis

As well as doing a skills audit and reflecting on our choices, we can also do a **SWOT** analysis to focus our attention on our strengths and weaknesses. These are the things which you are good at and things you are not so good at or need additional support or training to achieve a higher level of competence.

SWOT stands for Strengths, Weaknesses, Opportunities, and Threats.

The strengths and weaknesses are factors which affect you personally. The strengths are the things you are good at, things you can do, without support or help. This could include literacy or numeracy, it could include being well organised, etc. Your weaknesses are things you need help or support to achieve. It may be that you can happily read a newspaper, but a textbook may be more challenging. You can perhaps deal with personal finance including paying bills and managing credit cards, but departmental budgets and cost management you may find difficult and need help with. It may also be that you are simply disorganised! These are your strengths and weaknesses!

Opportunities and threats are not about you personally, but about society in general. Opportunities are the things that help you to achieve your targets such as free training courses, help with childcare whilst studying, work shadowing opportunities, etc. Threats are the things which may prevent you from achieving your targets such as the economic climate, lack of opportunities, etc. Both opportunities and threats are matters outside of your control, but you should be aware of these issues.

Managing Self

SWOT Analysis

Strengths	**Weaknesses**
Opportunities	**Threats**

Managing Self

The Need for Change

When thinking about changes to yourself, or to a team, it can be helpful to use Marshall Goldsmith's 'Wheel of Change'. The need to change can come about from the results that you obtain from a personal or team SWOT, feedback, not hitting KPI's, or as part of your self-reflection processes.

Marshall Goldsmith refers to the wheel of change as:

> *"The variety of options that are presented when wanting to become a better version of ourselves. It illustrates "the interchange of two dimensions we need to sort out before we become the person we want to be: The Positive to Negative axis tracks the elements that either help us or hold us back. The 'Change to Keep' axis tracks the elements that we determine to change or keep in the future. Thus, in pursuing any behavioural change we have four options: change or keep the positive elements, change or keep the negative."*

- **Creating:** This is about all of the positive things that you want to create for yourself (Adding, Inventing) e.g. "I want to go for the promotion in 3-months-time – how do I add to my skills?"
- **Preserving:** These are the elements that we wish to keep in the future (Improving, Maintaining) e.g. "I know that I am good at communicating with key stakeholders – I want to keep improving this"
- **Eliminating:** These are the things that we wish to eliminate in the future (Eradicating, Reducing) e.g., "My time management is not effective because I spend too much time micro-managing my team – I need to let go"
- **Accepting:** The things that we need to accept in the future (Delaying, Making Peace) e.g., "There are certain things that I cannot influence or control – I need to accept this"

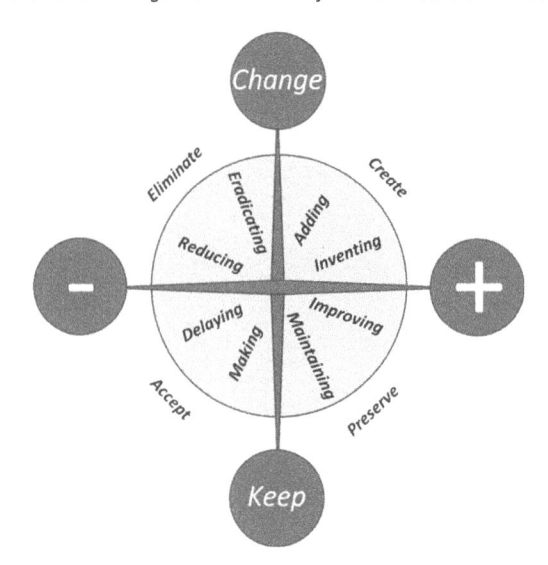

Managing Self

Monitor progress and overcome barriers to learning

SMART objectives help us to monitor progress against the targets mapped out in the PDP. Progress needs to be monitored so that we can, for example:

- ***assess progress against specific targets*** – *to measure development – e.g., looking at dates for handing in assignments and seeing if they are on time*
- ***adjust elements of objectives*** – *to keep them achievable and realistic – e.g., changing timescales following illness*
- ***allocate or seek additional resources*** – *e.g., arranging for one-to-one tuition to learn a language needed for work on time for a newly signed project*
- ***agree further development activities*** – *e.g., work tasks have been done early and there is scope to help out in a different department for a few days*

The PDP needs to be monitored regularly to keep things on track so that problems do not get out of hand. If everything is going well, the positive feedback will be a boost and help to motivate you to carry on. If there are problems, it is vital to catch them early so that they can be dealt with quickly and keep the rest of the PDP intact. Monitoring can be quite informal because it is really keeping an eye on the smaller elements and details of the PDP.

There can be barriers to learning that can stop people engaging in learning and career development activities. We need to identify potential barriers, or threats to progress, and do what we can to mitigate these. There are many things that prevent people from learning new skills, but these barriers may be overcome with some thought. These might include:

Lack of Confidence or Self-Esteem
This is one of the greatest obstacles facing many individuals. However, if this is a problem, ask yourself if there is anyone who would support and help you to take the first steps towards learning a new skill. Often, once the first move is made then the greatest hurdle is overcome. Confidence increases as you develop new skills.

Economic Situation
Your financial situation may seem to be a barrier to developing new skills, but this need not be the case. The internet has lots of free pages and tools and resources that can help you develop specific skills, browse our pages for a comprehensive guide. There may be courses offered in local schools, colleges or universities which are free or offered at a reduced rate for people on a low income. Distance-learning courses allow you to study at home, which can help to reduce the cost of learning. It is even possible to learn a new skill with the aid of books from the local library.

Voluntary work can also provide an excellent opportunity for learning and developing new skills, as can being a member of a local group or society.

Family Commitments
If you have family commitments that prevent you from having the time to learn a new skill, it may be possible for you to enlist the help of a friend or family member

Managing Self

to give you a few free hours each week. Colleges and universities offering vocational training courses may also have free or subsidised crèche places.

Many of these barriers may be more excuses than fundamental blockages. If you are using any of these as reasons for avoiding development, it may be worth looking deeper to see if there are reasons for your thinking, perhaps deeply held values that may be in conflict with personal development.

The first step is often the hardest...

Barriers to personal development are often more in the mind than anywhere else. As you take that first step, remember that the process is described as 'lifelong' for a reason: you are always learning, it is only the level of formality that changes.

Potential barriers to learning:	*Ways to overcome the barrier:*
Lack of time	*Work out exactly how much time will be needed and agree realistic goals* *Discuss doing some study during working hours* *Arrange cover when the individual is in college or doing internal courses* *Create development activities that can be done on the job during normal hours* *Arrange to do part-time courses over a longer period*
Lack of confidence	*Have one-to-one meetings with a mentor or coach (maybe the line manager) to identify the causes of lack of confidence* *Seek positive feedback to reinforce the positive aspects of performance, skills etc.* *Find small learning and development activities to build confidence – e.g., several short courses and seminars rather than a 9-month diploma course*
Fear about standing out from colleagues	*Use positive feedback to reinforce the positive aspects of performance, skills etc.* *Check how well performance measures up against the organisation's standards and expectations* *Encourage team spirit and mutual support between individual team members* *Watch for any bullying or harassment from other team members – act as required*
Worrying about being overworked or overloaded	*Develop time-management skills* *Examine the current and expected workload and check timescales that are realistic* *Make sure that the workload is fair and arrange for extra assistance or cover from others if necessary* *Do not worry if it is necessary to step back and take a break*
Learning styles are incompatible	*Consider changing the development activities – e.g., introduce new activities; appoint different tutors; use different formats to appeal to different learning styles* *Make sure that the content is relevant to the individual and the organisation*
Fear of change – e.g., in technology	*Review the benefits of change, job security, the future of the company etc.* *Find out about all aspects of the plans for change* *Ask to be kept informed, and keep others informed* *Have one-to-one discussions with the mentor/coach/line manager to identify causes of fear and ask for appropriate reassurance and support*

Managing Self

The Cost of Personal and Professional Development

Anything which is beneficial in our lives almost always comes at a cost and that is also true of Development. There can be a personal cost as well as a cost for the organisation. It is, however, true to say that the cost of development is often far outweighed by the benefits it brings.
The costs of development can include any or all of the following:

- *Financial cost of the training*
- *Time spent on training*
- *Expenses involved in attending the training*
- *The cost of providing mentors and coaches*
- *Loss of production whilst training*
- *Cost of replacement staff*

There may also be additional cost with regard to resources. It maybe that new software or machinery needs to be purchased in order to facilitate the development. It may be that structural alterations may be needed to facilitate this or additional resources such as PPE may need to be purchased. It may require that other staff need to be trained first to bring them to a standard whereby they can perform the task being left vacant by another staff member taking up their development.

Setting SMART Objectives

Once areas for personal development have been identified, it is important to set targets. By having our goals and objectives clearly in mind, there is a much greater chance of success. One good way to set goals is to use SMART objectives:

SMART is an acronym that you can use to guide your goal setting.

Its criteria are commonly attributed to Peter Drucker's Management by Objectives concept. The first known use of the term occurs in the November 1981 issue of Management Review by George T. Doran. Since then, Professor Robert S. Rubin (Saint Louis University) wrote about SMART in an article for The Society for Industrial and Organisational Psychology. He stated that SMART has come to mean different things to different people, as shown below.

To make sure your goals are clear and reachable, each one should be:

Specific *(simple, sensible, significant).*
Measurable *(meaningful, motivating).*
Achievable *(agreed, attainable).*
Relevant *(reasonable, realistic and resourced, results-based).*
Time bound *(time-based, time limited, time/cost limited, timely, time-sensitive).*

Managing Self

Some authors have expanded it to include extra focus areas.

SMARTER, for example, includes Evaluated and Reviewed.

How to Use SMART Objectives

1. Specific
Your goal should be clear and specific, otherwise you will not be able to focus your efforts or feel truly motivated to achieve it. When writing your goal, try to answer the five "W" questions:

- What do I want to accomplish?
- Why is this goal important?
- Who is involved?
- Where is it located?
- Which resources or limits are involved?

Example
Imagine that you are currently a marketing executive, and you would like to become head of marketing. A specific goal could be, "I want to gain the skills and experience necessary to become head of marketing within my organisation, so that I can build my career and lead a successful team."

2. Measurable
It is important to have measurable goals, so that you can track your progress and stay motivated. Assessing progress helps you to stay focused, meet your deadlines, and feel the excitement of getting closer to achieving your goal.

- A measurable goal should address questions such as:
- How much?
- How many?
- How will I know when it is accomplished?

Example
You might measure your goal of acquiring the skills to become head of marketing by determining that you will have completed the necessary training courses and gained the relevant experience within five years' time.

3. Achievable
Your goal also needs to be realistic and attainable to be successful. In other words, it should stretch your abilities but still remain possible. When you set an achievable goal, you may be able to identify previously overlooked opportunities or resources that can bring you closer to it. An achievable goal will usually answer questions such as:

Managing Self

- *How can I accomplish this goal?*
- *How realistic is the goal, based on other constraints, such as financial factors?*

Example
You might need to ask yourself whether developing the skills required to become head of marketing is realistic, based on your existing experience and qualifications. For example, do you have the time to complete the required training effectively? Are the necessary resources available to you? Can you afford to do it?

4. Relevant
This step is about ensuring that your goal matters to you, and that it also aligns with other relevant goals. We all need support and assistance in achieving our goals, but it is important to retain control over them. So, make sure that your plans drive everyone forward, but that you are still responsible for achieving your own goal. A relevant goal can answer "yes" to these questions:

- *Does this seem worthwhile?*
- *Is this the right time?*
- *Does this match our other efforts/needs?*
- *Am I the right person to reach this goal?*
- *Is it applicable in the current socio-economic environment?*

Example
You might want to gain the skills to become head of marketing within your organisation, but is it the right time to undertake the required training, or work toward additional qualifications? Are you sure that you are the right person for the head of marketing role? Have you considered your spouse's goals? For example, if you want to start a family, would completing training in your free time make this more difficult?

5. Time Bound
Every goal needs a target date, so that you have a deadline to focus on and something to work toward. This part of the SMART goal criteria helps to prevent everyday tasks from taking priority over your longer-term goals. A time-bound goal will usually answer these questions:

- *When?*
- *What can I do six months from now?*
- *What can I do six weeks from now?*
- *What can I do today?*

Example
Gaining the skills to become head of marketing may require additional training or experience, as we mentioned earlier. How long will it take you to acquire these skills?

Managing Self

Do you need further training, so that you are eligible for certain exams or qualifications? It is important to give yourself a realistic time frame for accomplishing the smaller goals that are necessary to achieving your final objective

Arrange resources and support mechanisms to meet the objectives

Resources and support mechanisms that suit the individual's needs, objectives, circumstances and organisation need to be arranged. These include, for example:

- *development activities*
- *support mechanisms*
- *time and money*

Development Activities

Personal development activities can be based on training or work-based experience. They can also be based on things that are done outside the workplace that develop skills that are used in the workplace.

Generally speaking, development activities can include:

- **completing training courses** – *e.g., in the workplace, via distance learning or from local training providers*
- **working in new areas within the organisation** – *e.g., in different departments or by doing simulation exercises*
- **taking on new challenges and responsibilities at work** – *preferably whilst being supported*
- **attending meetings, seminars, and conferences** *that are not within the normal remit of responsibility*
- **charity work** – *e.g., a finance department manager working in a charity shop to develop customer service skills*
- **working as a volunteer in a different work sector** – *e.g., a catering manager volunteering to work in a hospice to improve communication skills*
- **studying the organisation's policies, procedures, operations and training materials to a deeper level*
- **doing independent research to develop knowledge*

It is worth being imaginative and making good use of the resources and networks of support that are available. Taking part in development activities outside the normal routine of work can be very stimulating, satisfying, rewarding and revealing, taking us into sectors and environments that we would not normally consider. We can be challenged to develop skills that we would not need or use for the current 'day job' that may become useful in the future.

Managing Self

Support Mechanisms

The support mechanisms that people need will vary, but it is important to plan them in advance wherever possible. Support can come from, for example:

- **the line manager** – e.g., to arrange access to new experiences; to give permission for study time in work hours; to act as a mentor or coach
- **the HR and training departments** – e.g., to help with access to courses; to access advice or counselling if there is a problem
- **an outside training provider** – e.g., allocating a course tutor or assessor to guide through a training programme
- **colleagues** – e.g., to help with developmental activities or provide cover during study periods
- **family and friends** – e.g., to give support at home during intense periods of study

It is also important to organise time resources and money before starting on a major programme of career development. Time management is critical, and deadlines need to be managed, so that ordinary activities can continue and still be productive. Finances may also need attention and preparation – e.g., to pay for fees ourselves; to apply for funding via an employer; to arrange for funding via a training provider such as a university or college; to replace income if we have to work part time for a while.

Selecting appropriate Learning and Development activities

We can use a variety of learning and development activities, based inside or outside the workplace, when creating a PDP for ourselves or for our team members. A combination of activities can be put together to suit the individual's needs, goals and areas of weakness.

Activities may include, for example:

- **delegation** – e.g., offering tasks to challenge the individual and give them the opportunity to develop their skills and experience
- **demonstrations** – e.g., watching demonstrations about how a new piece of equipment is used, then trying it out
- **role-play** – e.g., to practise how to deal with angry customers' complaints
- **job rotation** – e.g., training people in a wide variety of tasks to aid flexibility and motivation
- **shadowing** – e.g., arranging for a trainee to follow an experienced member of staff for a week
- **coaching and mentoring** – e.g., giving intensive one-to-one support and guidance; having a senior member of staff as a role model
- **project work** – e.g., expanding knowledge and experience by following through all aspects of a project, and not just isolated tasks

Managing Self

- *classroom-based training courses* – e.g., a first-aid course at the local college
- *computer-based training* – e.g., induction courses to give an overview of the organisation and its policies and procedures
- *Internet-based e-training* – e.g., food safety knowledge, followed by an exam at an assessment centre to gain the full certificate
- *blended learning* – a mixture of different methods – e.g., a computer-based course in Spanish as well as conversation lessons at the local college
- *distance learning* – e.g., a course done at work or at home, with the assistance of an assessor or a tutor who may be based miles away
- *workplace training* – e.g., internal training sessions on equality and diversity given by colleagues or external trainers

Personal Development Plan Content

Your Personal Development Plan should contain the following headings: -

Goal: (What do you want to achieve/change?)	Objectives: (How are you going to do this? SMART)	Resources: (What will you need to do this?)	Performance indicators: (How will you measure the impact?)	Target date: (When will you complete this?)	Review date:

How are you going to achieve each goal? You may have several different actions necessary to achieve one goal.

- *How will you know if you have been successful with each action?*
- *How will you measure success?*
- *When should you have achieved your goal?*
- *Do some goals need to be addressed before others?*

A clear Personal Development Plan is important. Check that your goals are SMART and that your plan is complete. You may find it helpful to discuss your plan with your employer and your tutor.

Please note:
You need to return to your Personal Development Plan on a regular basis to review your progress in completing your goals. If you are able to achieve a goal completely you should give evidence of how you have assessed that it is completed. You may also identify the need for other goals throughout the progression. Any new goals should be added to your development plan. Please also remember that, if a goal needs several actions, each action will need success criteria and a target date.

Managing Self

Maintaining a Continuing Professional Development log (CPD)

It is important to review career development and goals as an ongoing process. This is often referred to as continuing professional development (CPD). CPD links learning directly to working practices. Each time an activity is undertaken that increases skills, knowledge or experience, make a note of it in the CPD log. This helps to show how learning activities work towards achieving the goals we have set out in our overall personal development plan.

A CPD log, will capture useful experiences and assess the practical benefits of what has been learned.

CPD allows us to:

- *review the interrelationship of values* – e.g., ambition, discipline, effectiveness and efficiency
- *review and measure career direction and progress* – e.g., promotion, remuneration, job satisfaction, qualifications and work-life balance
- *measure goals against success*

The CPD Cycle

During the CPD process, we frequently check:

- *where we are* – examining the current role in detail and identifying any skills gaps
- *where we need to be* – working out where we need or want to be, deciding and defining ambitions in a clear way
- *how we plan to get there* – identifying the learning and development activities and resources that we need to achieve our goals

As managers, we need to do this for ourselves and our team members.

The CIPD use a seven-stage CPD cycle to illustrate the process:

Identify – where you have been, where you are now and where you want to be
Plan – how to get these, using clear objectives and monitoring of progress
Act – do the development activities and be open to new experiences
Reflect – routinely reflect upon day-to-day activities
Apply – put theory into practice
Share – share learning experiences and generate insight and support with others
Impact – measure the overall impact of learning on work activities

Managing Self

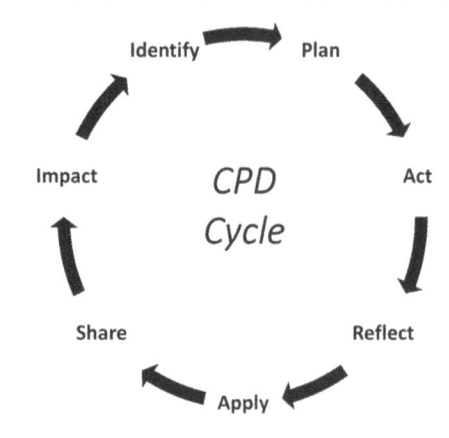

CPD Cycle: Identify → Plan → Act → Reflect → Apply → Share → Impact → (Identify)

Using a CPD log

Keeping a log to track CPD activity is widespread, and many organisations have their own policies and procedures for this. There are many ways of making a CDP log. The main thing to bear in mind is that we may need to show our log to someone else, so it is important to make sure that it is clear and contains sufficient information. It is like a record of evidence that we can use to back up our claims that learning activities have been performed – either in the course of our normal duties or as extra activities.

Some people create their own records, maybe using Word, Excel or Evernote. Some organisations and professional bodies have paper-based or electronic templates or forms for people to use. This is particularly true when there is a legal or contractual requirement for staff or members to maintain evidence about how they keep their skills up to date – e.g., teachers, vets, architects or health professionals. They can be asked at any time to provide their CPD log to prove that their ongoing learning and development are appropriate and up to date. In many cases, it is important to show the number of hours of CPD that have taken place to comply with the organisation's requirements.

Typically, a CPD log needs to show:

- *the person's name*
- *the date of the activity*
- *the type of activity* – e.g., attending a course, reading professional journals or performing a work activity
- *details of the activity* – e.g., the subject covered or task performed
- *how it addresses skills gaps*
- *duration* – e.g., the study hours

Managing Self

Name: Alex Smith				
Date of the activity	Type of learning activity – e.g., course	Details of the activity	Skills gaps addressed	Duration
8 Oct	Evening class – Business English L3 – new course, week 1	Writing informal business emails and reports Grammar & spelling	Email etiquette Using graphs for reports Improved general business writing skills	2.0 hours
11 Oct	Fire drill	Had to clear my section and hand over to fire marshal	Consolidated training from yesterday Understand fire exit routes better	0.5
15 Oct	Bus English L3 week 2	Writing formal business letters and reports Apostrophes and other punctuation	Business report writing General business writing skills	2.0
17 Oct	Reading professional journal	Impact on customers of new consumer laws	Knowledge of legal processes	0.5
19 Oct	Presentation by Sales Director, Q&A	Organisation's approach to changes in consumer laws	Knowledge of legal processes and employer's policies	1.5
			Total	6.5

Managing Self

Evaluating the outcomes of CPD

The Personal Development Plan process needs to be monitored and reviewed to check progress and identify any barriers to learning. The same applies to CPD as well. Whenever we commit time, effort and resources to improvement, we have to make sure that we are achieving something of value.

We need to check:

- **our progress** – *against agreed SMART objectives*
- **our strengths** – *so that we can be confident in our abilities and continue to provide excellent goods and services*
- **areas that need further attention or support** – *so that we can give time, attention and resources to address areas that are weak or unresolved*

In a similar way, organisations also review progress on a wider scale, to make sure that they are getting a return on investment (ROI). Evaluating outcomes and reviewing progress helps individuals and organisations to, for example:

- **measure the additional skills, knowledge and experience gained**
- **identify actual benefits** – *e.g., in terms of output, earnings or increased opportunities*
- **identify potential future benefits** – *e.g., from more courses or putting more people through the same training*
- **identify problem areas as soon as possible** – *e.g., to be able to divert resources and support if required*
- **check that the commitment is still worthwhile and relevant**
- **justify continuing support** – *e.g., in terms of time, money and physical resources*

New skills can be tested in a variety of ways, for example:

- **demonstrating the new skill to an experienced colleague or trainer**
- **measuring feedback** – *e.g., from customers, colleagues or managers*
- **increased output** – *e.g., an increase in sales following training*
- **passing a practical test, exam or appraisal**

New knowledge can be tested with other methods, for example:

- **informal diagnostic tests** – *e.g., quizzes and multiple-choice tests online where the answers are given afterwards*
- **formal multiple-choice exams or tests** – *e.g., under strict exam conditions at work or place of study*
- **assessment by a tutor, assessor or trainer**

Managing Self

- *essays or dissertations*
- *questions in appraisal interviews*

Results cannot always be measured in terms of numbers, quantities or physical evidence. Along the way, managers and their team members may also:

- *define or redefine their limits of authority, now and in the future*
- *improve decision-making processes* – due to the openness developed when discussing and agreeing objectives with others
- *identify areas for improvement for individuals, teams and the organisation that lead to increased productivity and quality*
- *develop better working relationships* – by working together on ways to move forward
- *develop clarity and focus*
- *gain a deeper knowledge of the organisation's operations, policies and procedures*
- *feel engaged in their rules as they focus attention on their goals, and feel motivated to improve and develop*

When evaluating the outcomes of CPD, these need to be considered as well.

Learning activity	Outcome of learning activity	How this was evaluated and/or measured – plus further action if required
L3 Business English course	Passed course Improved, shorter emails to colleagues Improved formal report presentation skills Grammar and spelling still a bit rusty at times	3 exam papers marked externally Positive feedback from line manager and colleagues Feedback and comments at the time and during annual appraisal Keep doing quizzes and online exercises to improve and develop knowledge
Fire drill and H&S ongoing training	Much faster response and more confident in fire evacuation procedures Better knowledge of dangerous chemicals	During drills Knew how to deal with actual dangerous spillage on my shift
Sales legislation training by sales director	Understand consumer rights better Able to deal with complaints more confidently Need to double-check equality and diversity policy at work	Passed online quiz on subject, got 97% Positive feedback from customers when dealing with queries. Line manager pleased with outcome of complaints Check policy against government website on equality and diversity

Managing Self

The main point of CPD is that it becomes a routine task at work, especially if our roles demand that we comply with legal or contractual requirements to log our ongoing learning activities. Many elements of our workplace knowledge and skills need to be kept up to date on a regular basis. CPD, when it is done thoroughly, can provide a useful focus as well as evidence that this is being done.

Chapter 3: Communication

Communication

Communication

Communication is simply the act of transferring information from one place, person or group to another. Every communication involves (at least) one sender, a message and a recipient. This may sound simple, but communication is actually a very complex subject.

Effective communication is about more than just exchanging information. It is about understanding the emotion and intentions behind the information. As well as being able to clearly convey a message, you need to also listen in a way that ensures you gain the full meaning of what is being said and makes the other person feel heard and understood.

Effective communication sounds like it should be instinctive, but all too often, when we try to communicate with others something goes astray. We say one thing, the other person hears something completely different and misunderstandings, frustration, and conflicts ensue (ask your partner or friend!). This can cause problems in your home, school, and work relationships.

For many of, communicating more clearly and effectively requires learning some important skills. Whether you are trying to improve communication with your spouse, kids, boss, or co-workers, learning these skills can deepen your connections to others, build greater trust and respect, and improve teamwork, problem solving, and your overall social and emotional health.

Communication is an essential skill of Leaders and managers

Interpersonal Communication

Interpersonal communication refers to the entire process and practice of exchanging ideas, information, and even emotional experiences that can be shared between people. It is a potent and vital force that is not just all about words. It is an array of cues that come from the voice, body language, facial expressions, and gestures. Effective interpersonal communication is the bedrock upon which relationships in business (and beyond) are built. Good communication is the catalyst for action. When it is done right, it can truly turn ideas into action.

Communication is defined as:

"The meaningful exchange of information between two or more participants"

A meaningful exchange involves 3 stages. The first stage is for the sender to determine

- *What the message will be*
- *who will be the recipient of the message?*
- *and the best channel of communication to use*

Communication

The next stage is for the sender to actually send the message using

- *The appropriate channel of communication*
- *and clear unambiguous language*

The third stage is for the recipient to

- *Receive the message*
- *feedback to the sender*

Though one's own interpersonal communication definition may differ slightly from others, the basic tenets will likely remain the same. Your skills as a communicator will be judged by your mastery of four basic interpersonal communication concepts.

Types of Interpersonal Communication

When it comes to basic elements of interpersonal communication, the various types of possible communication will cluster under four basic categories: verbal, listening, written, and non-verbal communication.

1. Verbal
Whenever you talk or even make an audible sound (like "hmm" of "Ahh!" for example), you are creating verbal communication. Beyond the content of what you are saying and the context in which it is being said, verbal communication also includes additional auditory factors like intonation. This refers to how your voice rises and falls in tone as you speak and can shade how the words are meant to be interpreted.

For example, the phrase "Have a nice day" can take on a number of different meanings when you imagine it said in a friendly way, sarcastically, or even ominously.

2. Listening
Chances are that some point in your life you have been accused of "hearing but not listening" to what someone was saying to you. The distinction between the two concepts might have seemed nuanced at first until the message became clear: hearing is involuntary and effortless whereas listening is focused and intentional.

Hearing is an automatic response that is the result of having working ears. Listening takes more effort. It is purposeful and requires concentration to understand what the speaker is sharing.

3. Written Communication
When you convey a message via written symbols, you are practicing written communication. From emails and text messages to more formal memoranda and reports, written communication is the cornerstone of most information sharing in business.

Communication

When information that is complex or lengthy needs to be shared, it is usually conveyed through written communication. To that end, written communication is often considered more legally valid than spoken words are. That is why it often serves as an "official" mode of communication. Written communication can also include emoji, which can help convey more emotional information and context that can be hard to deduce from the words themselves.

4. Non-Verbal Communication
Getting meaning across without using words either written or spoken is the essence of non-verbal communication. This can be achieved through everything from facial expressions to specific gestures ("jazz hands," anyone?) to body language and certain postures.

To get a sense of how much can be communicated through non-verbal communication, consider that mimes are able to tell entire stories without uttering a word. Moreover, non-verbal communication often complements spoken communication. Gestures like 'air quotes" or shoulder shrugging add additional if not entirely different meanings to what is being said.

How Interpersonal Communication Works

In as much as "it takes two to tango," it takes at least as many (and sometimes many more) for interpersonal communication to occur. In a business setting, interpersonal communication can sometimes quickly devolve into looking like a group attempting to dance the Macarena except everyone is doing the steps in a different order. There are conventions we use to frame our thinking about communication. But it is really far too dynamic a phenomenon to be summed up by a few simple rules.

We often think about communication as having a distinct sender and receiver of a message wherein one person sends a message and the other receives it. The problem with this model is that interpersonal communication seldom occurs so seamlessly — instead, people are more likely to send and receive messages at the same time in a complex, interactive process.

Successful interpersonal communication is achieved through cultivating active feedback. Simply put, feedback consists of the reactions that a receiver conveys to the original sender. Feedback provides the sender the opportunity to adjust their message in order to improve communication.

Feedback occurs not just after someone has made a statement, but often during the communication itself. There are a number of social cues used to indicate that one person is indeed listening to the other — from nodding or expressing affirmative sounds like "mm-hmm" to a variety of interjections and interruptions that shape real-life conversations.

Communication

As messy as this may seem, all of these elements - the spoken words, facial expressions, tone and gestures - are actually part of the overall message. They help shape how it is intended to be interpreted and indicate how it is being interpreted in real-time.

However, there are factors that can distort this process. Communications theorists call this "noise," which is anything that obstructs the meaning of a message. Beyond the literal meaning of noise wherein sounds from the physical world intrude upon the reception of a message (from weak mobile phone connections to the sounds in a crowded cafe), there are other types of noise that can negatively impact communication.

Cultural and language differences can create an added layer of complication that may obscure a communicator's intended message. Similarly, the overuse of jargon or colloquial language can get in the way of the listener understanding what is being communicated.

Much of what influences a message and how it is perceived is the context in which it is shared. The context includes not only the setting of the communication (an office, a restaurant, while walking between locations) but the social factors shared by the communicators. Is one the boss of the other? Are the communicators in question friends or competitors or both?

The relationship and relative social status between two people communicating can affect how a message is received.

Just as important is the way in which a message is transmitted from one person to the other. Is it in-person or over the phone? Text or email? Communication theorists refer to the means of communication as the channel, which can have implications for how the message is meant to be received.

A formal email from a colleague's business email address sets the expectation that the message is an "official" communication. However, a channel like a Facebook message suggests a more social context, which would cue a different, less formal style of interaction. Choosing the appropriate channel for the message can sometimes be as important as the message itself.

Examples of Interpersonal Communication

Humans are a social species — consequently, we are constantly communicating with one another. Research indicates that people speak anywhere from 7,000 to 20,000 words a day to each other. For context, on the higher end of the scale, that is equivalent to chatting out the average novella in the course of a day.

Interpersonal communication is happening all the time and in the business world, it is often one of the most important aspects of your job.

So, if you are wondering to yourself, "What are some examples of interpersonal communication?" Here they are:

1. Phone Calls
In 1876, Alexander Graham Bell, one of the inventors of the telephone uttered the first words ever transmitted over the line. They were to his assistant and are as historic as they

Communication

are mundane: "Mr. Watson, come here, I want to see you." Since then, trillions of words have been spoken into phones daily. How many calls have you made today?

2. Meetings
Whether they are conducted in person, (as in the pre-pandemic days) or on Zoom, meetings have long been a mainstay of the business experience. That said, like the modern saying, "This could have been an email," think twice before requesting someone's time and attention in a group setting.

3. Presentations
The overreliance on "ye olde OHP and slides" may be fading out, but presentations remain a mainstay of the corporate conference room as a well-communicated presentation can be a rallying point for a project and galvanize the team together.

4. Emails and Texting
Some pundits like to bemoan the fact that, as a culture, we spend too much time interacting with screens rather than each other. The fact is, we are using the screens to interact with each other — usually through written communication.

Communication Models

The three most well-known models for communication are Linear, Interactional, and Transactional. As West & Turner (2007) explain, each model sheds light on the development of communication, but emphasises different parts of the communication process.

The models provide pictures, or visual representations, of complex interactions. They are useful because they simplify the basic structure of communication and can help us to understand that structure not just verbal, but also visual. Most importantly, they identify the various elements of communication and serve as a kind of map to show how different parts of the communication process are interrelated.

Linear Models

Linear models explain one directional communication processes.

Originally developed by Shannon & Weaver in 1948, this model describes communication as a linear process. This model describes how a sender, or speaker, transmits a message to a receiver, or listener. More specifically, the sender is the source of the message. A message may consist of the sounds, words, or behaviours in a communication interaction. The message itself is transmitted through a channel, the pathway or route for communication, to a receiver, who is the target or recipient of the message. There may be obstacles in the communication process, or noise.

Communication

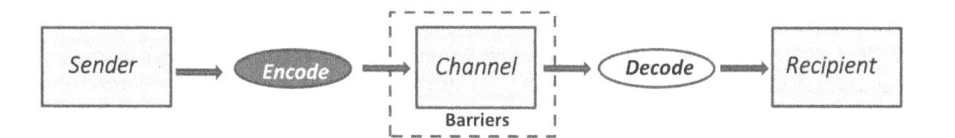

Sender → Encode → Channel → Decode → Recipient
(Barriers)

Noise refers to any interference in the channel or distortion of the message. This is a fairly simple model in which a message is simply passed from sender to receiver.
While the linear model was highly influential during the mid-20th century, this model is perhaps too simple. Its limitations are easy to see if you pause to think about the beliefs about communication, or assumptions, made in this model. First, this model assumes that communication only goes in one direction.

Here, a person can be a sender or receiver, but not both. This is problematic because communication in action is more dynamic than the linear model suggests. In action, communication involves a give and take between senders and receivers in which listeners are not simply passive receptacles for a sender's message. This model is also limited because it provides only one channel for only one message. Finally, it implies that messages themselves are clear-cut with a distinct beginning and a distinct end. However, communication is rarely, if ever, as neat and tidy as a linear model would suggest.

The Shannon Weaver model of communication and involves the following:

- **Sender (information source)** - *is the individual who creates a message and selects the channel and sends the message (the brain)*
- **Channel** - *the medium which is used to send the message (the air)*
- **Receiver (destination)** - *the individual receives the message or the location where the message arrives. The receiver provides feedback depending on the message (the receivers brain)*
- **Noise** - *disturbances from people on the environment that can distract from the message*

The model has been widely used and adapted to different types of communication and is beneficial for identifying the causes of communication breakdowns. For example, messages that are received incomplete due to interference on a telephone line, or the sender and the receiver of an email interpreting its meaning differently.

Aristotle's Model

A framework for thinking about how to improve your communication abilities, by looking at key aspects underpinning a situation.

Aristotle's model of communication is the oldest communication model, dating back to 300 BC. The model was designed to examine how to become a better and more convincing communicator. Aristotle argues we should look at five elements of a communication event to analyse how best to communicate: speaker, speech, occasion, target audience and effect.

Communication

He also identified three elements that will improve communication: ethos (credibility), pathos (ability to connect) and logos (logical argument). Aristotle's model does not pay attention to the role of feedback in communication.

Speaker → Speech → Audience → Effect

Lasswell's Model

Is a basic framework for analysing one-way communication by asking five questions: Who, said what, through which channel, to whom, with what effects?

Lasswell's model of communication tries to understand a communication event by asking five important questions. It looks at who created the message (and what their bias may be), what they said, the channel they said it through (e.g., TV, radio, blog), who they said it to, and what effect it had on the receiver. This model is effective as it provides a very simple and practical way of critiquing a message and exploring five important elements that can help explain the event under analysis in more detail.

Question	Component	How to analyse	Example of component
Who?	Communicator	Control analysis	*Vacuum cleaner salesman*
Says What?	Message	Content analysis	*Promotes his brand of vacuum as the best*
In which Channel?	Medium	Media analysis	*Television*
To whom?	Audience	Audience analysis	*Evening TV viewers*
With what Effects?	Effect	Effects analysis	*Brand awareness, belief that this vacuum is the best, increased sales revenue*

Communication

Berlo's S-M-C-R Model

Berlo's model of communication explains it in four steps: **S**ource, **M**essage, **C**hannel, and **R**eceiver. The unique aspect of Berlo's model is that it gives a detailed account of the key elements in each step that will affect how well the message is communicated:

- **Source:** Elements of the source include communication skills of the sender, their attitude and their culture.
- **Message:** Elements of the message include its content, structure and code.
- **Channel:** Elements of the channel include the senses of hearing, seeing, touching, smelling, etc.
- **Receiver:** Elements of the receiver include their attitude, knowledge and culture.

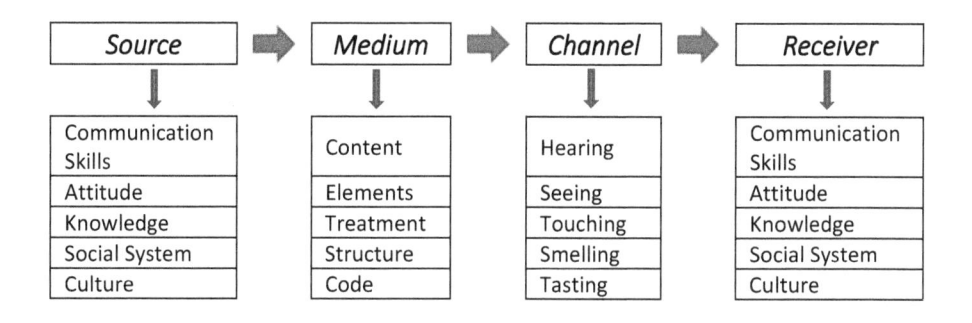

Source	Medium	Channel	Receiver
Communication Skills	Content	Hearing	Communication Skills
Attitude	Elements	Seeing	Attitude
Knowledge	Treatment	Touching	Knowledge
Social System	Structure	Smelling	Social System
Culture	Code	Tasting	Culture

Interactional Models

Interactional (Interactive) models are best for explaining impersonal two-way communication processes.

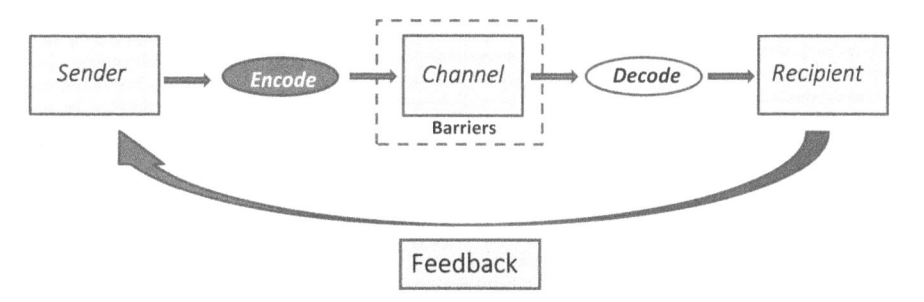

Sender → Encode → Channel (Barriers) → Decode → Recipient → Feedback

In the move to a more dynamic view of communication, interactional models follow two channels in which communication and feedback flow between sender and receiver. Feedback is simply a response that a receiver gives to a sender. Feedback can be verbal (i.e., "yes") or nonverbal (i.e., a nod or smile). Most importantly, feedback indicates comprehension. It can help senders know if their message was received and understood. By focusing on flow and feedback, interactional models view communication as an ongoing process.

Communication

The final feature of this model is the field of experience. The field of experience refers to how environment, experiences, culture, and even heredity can influence how a sender constructs a message. Keep in mind that each person brings a unique field of experience to an interaction. Likewise, each communication interaction is unique.

While the interactional model is more dynamic than the linear model, it still contains some limitations. For instance, this model implies that while people can be both senders and receivers, they cannot do so simultaneously. In real communication, roles are not quite so clear-cut and in fact are much more fluid.

Osgood-Schramm Model

The Osgood-Schramm model explores communication that is equal and reciprocal. It does not differentiate between the sender and receiver but sees each as being in an equal position as message encoders and decoders. This model is best for explaining and examining personal synchronous communication where feedback is immediate (such as face-to-face discussions). As feedback is immediate, noise can be reduced through ongoing clarification of messages during the conversation.

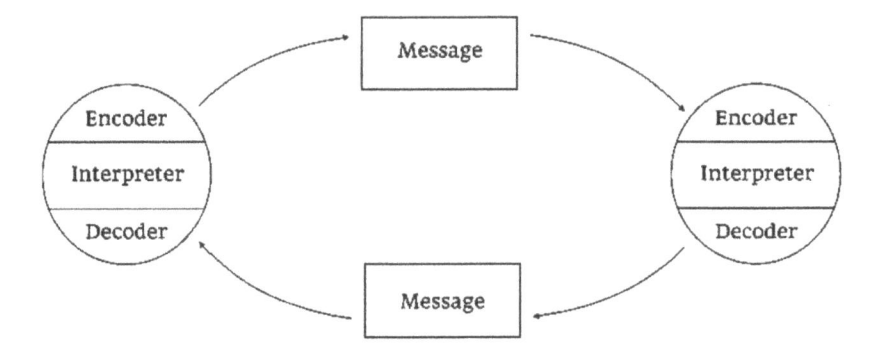

The Westley and Maclean Model

The Westley and Maclean model embraces the importance of feedback in communication. However, it also emphasises the important role of environmental and cultural factors in influencing communication. It shows that the things we say and communicate are influenced by who we are, what our background is, and what perspective we are approaching issues from.

The model considers the *object of orientation* (background, culture and beliefs) of the sender and receiver of messages. It also considers the message to have been received and sent within a broader social context that needs to be considered to know and understand the message.

Communication

X = Environmental Factors
The factors that influence why the message is created in the first place.
A = Sender
The person who sends the message.
B = Receiver
The person who receives the message.
C = Gatekeeper
The editor of the message, such as a newspaper editor. Common in mass communication.
F = Feedback
The return messages sent back to the sender. These can help shape future messages.
X^1 = Sensory Experience
The ways we receive messages, which also shape the content of our future messages.
X^2 = Object of Orientation (Sender)
The beliefs, culture and background of the sender which influence the sender's message
X^3 = Object of Orientation (Receiver)
The beliefs, culture and background of the receiver which influence the receiver's interpretation.

Transactional Models

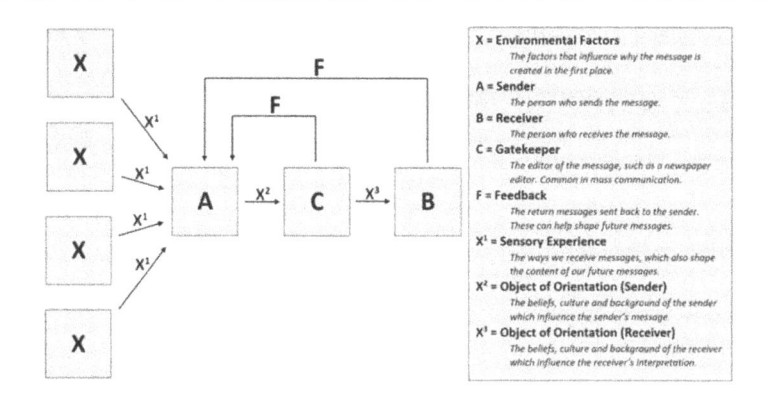

Transactional models explain direct personal communication processes where two-way feedback is immediate.

The transactional is the most dynamic of communication models. One notable feature of this model is the move from referring to people as senders and receivers to referring to people as communicators. This implies that communication is achieved as people both send and receive messages. Fundamentally, this model views communication as a transaction. In other words, communication is a cooperative action in which communicators co-create the process, outcome and effectiveness of the interaction. Unlike the linear model in which meaning is sent from one person to another, also unlike the interactional model in which understanding is achieved through feedback, people create shared meaning in a more dynamic process in the transactional model.

This model also places more emphasis on the field of experience. While each communicator has a unique field of experience, they must also inhabit a shared field of experience. In other words, communicators must share at least some degree of overlap in culture, language, or environment if people are to communicate at all.

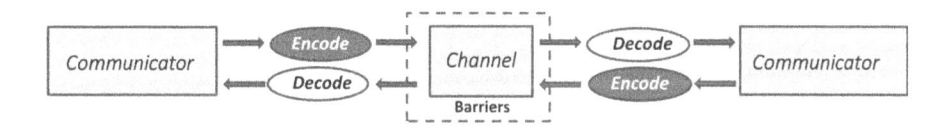

This model also recognises that messages will influence the responses, or subsequent messages, produced in the communication interaction. This means that messages do not stand alone, but instead are interrelated. The principle of interrelation states that messages are connected to and build upon one another. The transactional model forms the basis for much communication theory because:

Communication

1. *People are viewed as dynamic communicators rather than simple senders or receivers*
2. *There must be some overlap in fields of experience in order to build shared meaning*
3. *Messages are interdependent.*

Barnlund's Transactional Model

Barnlund's Transactional Model of Communication highlights the role of private and public cues that impact our messages.

It explores interpersonal, immediate-feedback communication. Central to this approach is the idea that feedback for the sender is the reply for the receiver.

This model also highlights the role of 'cues' in impacting our messages. Barnlund highlights the role of public cues which are environmental cues, and private cues which are a person's personal thoughts and background. With this emphasis on cues, Barnlund's model highlights the factors that influence what we think and say.

Dance's Helical Model

Dance's Helical Model sees communication as a circular process that gets more and more complex as communication occurs, which can be represented by a helical spiral.

The model builds on circular models by explaining how we improve our messages over time by using feedback.

When we communicate with others, their feedback will influence our next statement. We become more knowledgeable with each cycle of communication, enabling up to 'expand our circle', as represented by the increasingly wider and wider circles. The movement up the spiral indicates that each communication practice is new and different from the previous, as communication does not ever perfectly repeat itself.

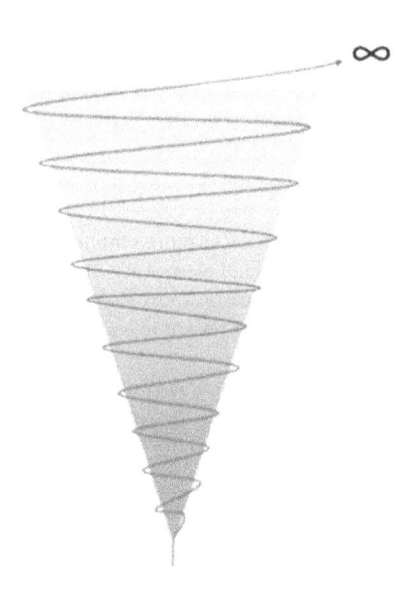

Communication

Forms of Communication

Take a step back and ask yourself:

- *Are you aware that you are communicating every moment? With yourself, with others, with nature?*
- *Are you aware of the various expressions of your communication?*
- *And finally, are you constantly communicating what you want to communicate, in the way you want to do it?*

> *"Communicating every moment? How is that even possible? I don't have my mouth open every minute?"*

We communicate not just verbally, but also non-verbally, and even informally. The entire gamut of the various types of communication channels and expressions we enjoy is outlined in this chart.

As you can see, there are at least 6 distinct types of communication: non-verbal, verbal-oral-face-to-face, verbal-oral-distance, verbal-written, formal and informal types of communication. Add to this the boundless opportunities the internet offers, and you have an almost unlimited range of communication possibilities!

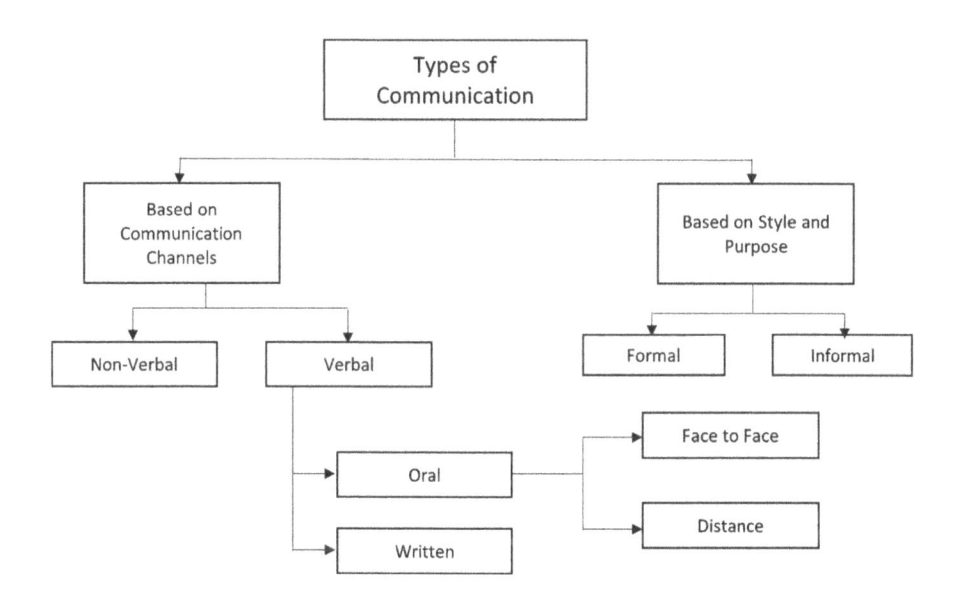

```
                      Types of
                    Communication
                          |
         ┌────────────────┴────────────────┐
    Based on                         Based on Style and
  Communication                          Purpose
    Channels                                |
        |                            ┌──────┴──────┐
   ┌────┴────┐                    Formal        Informal
Non-Verbal  Verbal
              |                         ┌── Face to Face
           ┌──┴──┐
          Oral ──┤
                 │
         Written ┴── Distance
```

Communication

Formal and Informal communication

Some workplace communication requires a formal approach, usually when information is important, sensitive or confidential – e.g., financial reports about the organisation or its customers; staff appraisal interviews; legal letters; formal letters to customers or colleagues; evidence to support a complaint or investigation.

Some workplace communication requires an informal approach, usually when information is not confidential and when it can be shared with people that we know – e.g., a quick question for a colleague or regular customer; sharing information and instructions; during a handover between shifts; announcements that can be made openly; reminders for colleagues or customers.

When choosing the most appropriate form of communication, we need to consider:

- *the type of information being sent*
- *the people who are going to read or hear it*
- *the security and confidentiality of the information*
- *how it will be circulated and shared*

Good communication skills are essential to make sure that:

- *errors and misunderstandings are kept to a minimum*
- *the right level of detail can be provided*
- *the organisation's positive and professional image is maintained*
- *the communication method follows good business practice and is in line with the organisation's policies and procedures*
- *confidentiality is protected, when appropriate*

Formal Communication

This type of communication is also referred to as "official communication" and covers the range of verbal expressions that address a formal need.

This communication is conducted through a pre-determined channel. For instance, a large number of your interactions within your profession, financial communication (from and to your bank, creditors, debtors, etc.) and legal expressions are examples of formal communication. More time-consuming that non-formal communication, as it follows a particular communication protocol.

Even in cases of oral expressions (in meetings, seminars, etc.), it is often backed by written communication that can provide documentation evidence of the oral conversation. (This written communication could be as simple as a minutes-of-meeting, to as complex as a detailed recording.) It is considered a reliable source of information. (So, when you receive a letter from your bank, you had better take notice of it!)

Communication

Formal communication forms the core of our professional lives (though not all professional communication is formal). Hence becoming an expert in this type of communication is central to professional advancement and success.

Below, are simple tips to help you excel in your expression and profession.

- *Begin by clarifying the purpose of your communication.*
- *Whether you use an oral or written expression, always follow a well-defined structure that can be easily understood by your audience.*
- *Keep your tone open, professional and friendly.*
- *End by re-iterating what you expect to cause through this communication: clarification on your stance, answers to questions, a call to action, etc. Also clarify any constraints that apply to this communication (like confidentiality, time-limit for response, etc.)*
- *Finally, thank your audience for their listening. (This works well for written communication too.)*

Informal Communication

Informal communication is surprisingly popular, and often referred to as "the (unofficial) grapevine". This is often by word-of-mouth information. In fact, it is this type of communication that opens you up to unofficial yet provocative information.

- *Informal communication is spontaneous and free flowing, without any formal protocol or structure. Hence this type of information is also less reliable or accurate.*
- *A communication channel that spreads like wildfire, as there are no formal rules to follow.*
- *Mostly oral, with no documentation evidence. Due to this, many undermine the value of informal communication, terming it mere "gossip".*

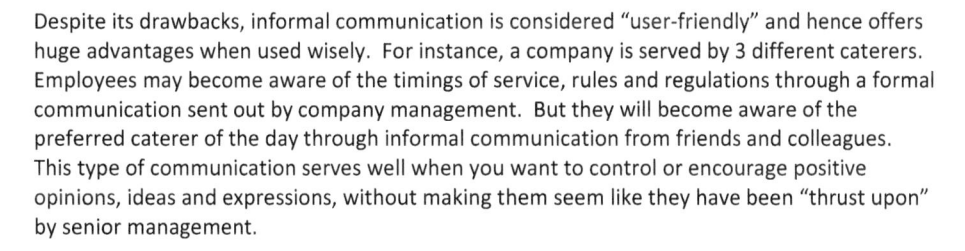

Despite its drawbacks, informal communication is considered "user-friendly" and hence offers huge advantages when used wisely. For instance, a company is served by 3 different caterers. Employees may become aware of the timings of service, rules and regulations through a formal communication sent out by company management. But they will become aware of the preferred caterer of the day through informal communication from friends and colleagues. This type of communication serves well when you want to control or encourage positive opinions, ideas and expressions, without making them seem like they have been "thrust upon" by senior management.

> Note: In modern times, social networks from "unofficial" sources (like your personal Facebook and Twitter feeds, LinkedIn, etc.) are powerful sources of informal communication and are often used to shape public opinion.

Communication

Types of Communication

Oral Communication (Face-to-face)

Face-to-face oral communication is the most recognised type of communication. Here, what you express comes directly from what you say. This can be formal or informal, with your friends and family, in a formal meeting or seminar, at work with your colleagues and boss, within your community, during professional presentations, etc. This type of communication gets better with practice.

- *The more you practice with awareness, the more control you will have on your oral expressions.*
- *Is vibrantly alive! This means that despite all past rehearsals, oral communication offers you a present moment opportunity to tune, revise, revoke and fix what you express. It is the most powerful type of communication and can work for or against you with every expression.*
- *Engages your audience more than other types of communication. The listener (or an audience) often expects to speak back to you with oral communication, enabling two-way communication more than any other channel.*

For better face-to-face communication:

- *Always meet the eyes of your audience with confidence, conviction and openness.*
- *Practice before a mirror to perfect your tone and expressions, so they suit the message you want to convey. These two facets often convey more than your words do.*
- *Practice using role-play. This means that even when you rehearse before a mirror, candidly ask yourself, "Am I ready to receive this message with this tone and expression?" If you are not convinced, your audience will not be either. So, practice again until you get it right.*
- *Consciously engage your audience's participation. This is the strength of this type of communication, so never let your oral expression be a one-way rant to yourself. You can do this by asking questions, getting their opinion and encouraging expression of new ideas.*

Finally, become an active listener. An effective oral communicator not only speaks, but also actively listens to his audience.

Communication

Oral Communication (Distance)

Distance (oral) communication has made the world a smaller and more accessible place. Mobile phones, VOIP, video conferencing, 2-way webinars, etc. are all modern expansions of distance communication, taking its expression to the next subtle level. And in this type of communication, your tone of voice and pace of delivery take priority over other expressions.

For effective oral communication over distance:

- *Give higher priority to your listening. When you fail to listen, you will find that multiple people attempt to speak at the same time, undermining the value of this form of communication.*
- *Speak slightly slower than you would in face-to-face communication. This will make sure that you remain aware of the subtle nuances of your tone, and the receiver has time to grasp what you convey.*
- *Always re-iterate what you understand when you listen. This type of communication misses the non-verbal signals that you would receive in face-to-face communication (that can indicate subtle expressions like anger, friendliness, receptivity, sarcasm, etc.) So, paraphrase what you understand and confirm that this is indeed what the other party also meant to convey.*
- *Where appropriate, wear your friendly face with a smile on your lips and eyes. Feel this friendly face. Your tone will automatically convey your openness and receptivity to the other person. (This may not be appropriate if you expect to convey a warning on the phone, so ensure that your face suits your message.)*

Finally, back this up with written communication where possible. The intention is to confirm the take-away from the communication, so all parties are on the same page. This makes sense even for an informal call with your friend – perhaps you can send a quick text message to re-iterate how pleasurable it was to speak to him, and then confirm the final call-for-action.

Written Communication

A few decades ago, written communication depended on the trusty old postman as we wrote to people who were far away. On occasions, this also included the formal note or legal notice from the bank, landlord, business client, etc. What a surprise then that this type of communication has now taken over every aspect of our world!

Think about it, if you group together the total written communication you engage with in a day – the text messages you send over your mobile, your Facebook and Twitter updates, personal and professional emails, maybe even the blogs you write – it would far surpass any other verbal communication you enjoy.

Communication

It is vital therefore that you are competent in this area and there are 3 rules that can help you get there:

- **Follow a clear structure so your communication is not all over the place.** *This can include a brief introduction, agenda, message body and conclusion. The cleverness and effectiveness of your communication lies in how you are able to capture this structure in your mode of communication (email, text message, quick status update on social media, etc.).*
- **Clarify the context of your communication where possible.** *This might seem like overkill for a harmless text message. But you would be amazed at the amount of seemingly harmless (written) communication that reaches the wrong eyes and ears. Take care to ensure that your context is reasonably clear, no matter who the recipient.*
- **Always err on the side of caution.** *There are very few instances when written communication is purely formal (addressed to professional peers and seniors or third parties), or purely informal (addressed only to your immediate friend/family circle). More often, if falls between these two modes. Hence, play safe by adapting a semi-formal tone, keeping your communication clean (in language and expression) and open (without offending any group). It is far better to have your friends think of you as a "stiff" communicator, rather than have your boss view as an "offensive" communicator!*

Non-verbal Communication

This type of communication is more subtle, yet far more powerful. It includes the entire range of physical postures and gestures, tone and pace of voice, and the attitude with which you communicate.

> *"The most important thing in communication is hearing what isn't said"* Peter Drucker

In the past few decades, body language experts have revealed how the posture you adopt, the hand gestures you endorse, and other facets of your physical personality affect your communication. It is worthwhile to spend a few hours coming up to speed on basic body-language gestures, so you do not inadvertently send mixed messages with your gestures and speech. You can also use this to support your message, making it more impactful.

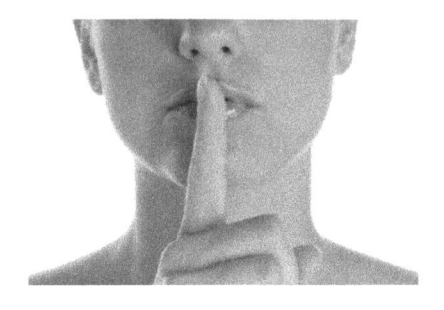

When communicating, always think about:

Communication

- *What you say with your words.*
- *What you share with your postures and gestures.* (However, these can be learnt to express the right message).
- *What you feel inside you, and hence impacts the subtle message you feel compelled to share outside you.*

The first two can be learnt with a little bit of practice. But the third has to be consciously built, so you constantly align yourself to what you want to express.

For instance:

- *When you want your peers to think of you as a friendly person, it is because you genuinely like and care for people.*
- *When you want your team to think of you as a strong leader, it is because you genuinely take responsibility for yourself and the team.*
- *When you want your peers, seniors and others to listen to you, it is because they are convinced that you will genuinely listen to them and factor their thoughts and opinions.*

Communication is a powerful activity that comes to us as naturally as breathing. With a little bit of awareness, our communication can be flawless, so the other person not only receives our message, but is also open to it.

> *"Communication begins with Listening!"*
> Paramahamsa Nithyananda

The next time you find yourself in the middle of a frustrating conversation, focus on your listening. This will help you grasp what your audience wants to hear from you, so you find a way to tailor your communication for your audience to become receptive to it too. When you listen and your audience also listens, you are engaged in the best form of communication!

The influence of non-verbal communication

A huge number of messages are sent non-verbally. These can be transmitted through, for example:

- *posture and body language*
- *gestures and touching*
- *physical appearance*

How people stand, how close they are 'in someone's space', eye contact, fidgeting and hand movements all add to the verbal messages. A person who frowns, looks at the floor and sits

Communication

with their arms folded gives off very negative messages. A person who sits or stands upright, and who smiles and uses good eye contact, is far more approachable and less threatening.

Examples of good and useful body language include:

- **having an open and relaxed posture**
- **facing the person but not standing too close** – about an arm's length away is comfortable for most people
- **smiling when appropriate** – although it is important to be friendly, we need to show that comments are taken seriously
- **using facial expressions to show sympathy or reassurance**
- **using eye contact** – although we need to be aware that some people (and cultures) find too much eye contact inappropriate and threatening
- **being sensitive to the person's own body language**
- **being flexible about our own body language and gestures so that we do not appear threatening or unapproachable**

All gestures and body language support what we are saying and how we are listening. If we say positive things but use negative body language, people will not believe or trust us. They will think that the good things we are saying are untrue. Conversely, if our verbal and non-verbal messages are compatible, our messages are far more convincing and acceptable. Someone who speaks enthusiastically, uses their hands expressively, moves around a stage and stands up straight will be a far more convincing and engaging communicator.

When touching other people, this needs to be appropriate and with the other person's permission if possible. Shaking hands is usually acceptable and encouraged but touching elsewhere needs to be done with caution. If a customer seems to need a helping hand to get up from a seat, for instance, we should offer help and ask if it is all right to hold their arm before we intervene. If our job involves touching people as part of our everyday activities, we will have guidelines about how to ask for permission and deal with difficult situations. If touching is inappropriate or unwanted, it can make communication extremely difficult and ineffective.

Professional behaviour is another important non-verbal influence on communication. We all need to behave in a calm, polite and professional manner at all times in the workplace, however stressed or upset we might feel. This helps to gain respect and cooperation from other people and supports our verbal communication. For example, if staff members are seen running around, screaming and messing about, their words are less likely to be taken seriously. It would be hard to take them seriously if the behaviour is inappropriate and seemingly out of control.

The importance of good personal grooming should not be underestimated. Every member of the organisation needs to make sure that they are:

- **clean and fresh** – body odour and bad breath are off-putting to colleagues, customers and others
- **tidy and presentable** – with clean and tidy hair

Communication

- **correctly dressed** – e.g., in clean uniform or other work clothes
- **wearing the correct footwear** – e.g., safety boots or smart, clean shoes

A smart appearance supports the person delivering verbal messages in the same way that gestures and body language do. We all make conscious and subconscious judgments about each other, especially when we first meet, so it is important to come across as trustworthy, professional and capable in the workplace.

Non-verbal communication can influence verbal communication :

> **in a positive way** – when gestures, appearance, posture and body language are positive and support the verbal messages
>   or
> **in a negative way** – if gestures are negative and undermine the verbal messages

Benefits of effective communication

In a work environment, when communication is effective, it means that we can:

- *send and receive information accurately*
- *share information effectively*
- *give a good impression of ourselves and the organisation*
- *deal with problems effectively*
- *develop useful and productive working relationships with colleagues, customers and others*

Communication is implicit in every function of management and communicating with people is essential in the workplace. These can include:

- **Running meetings and discussions** – e.g., agreeing objectives, discussing the allocation and progress of tasks, dealing with queries.
- **Motivating and leading the team** – e.g., having positive discussions about objectives, listening to feedback from the team and agreeing the way forward, organising team-building activities.
- **Sharing accurate information** – e.g., gathering accurate data from different people and departments, producing accurate leaflets, documents and websites for customers and others.
- **Delegating tasks and implementing plans** – e.g., passing responsibility to team members to move a project forward.
- **Training and coaching the team** – e.g., running training sessions for the whole team, giving one-to-one coaching to an individual to develop their skills.

Communication

- **Creating and delivering reports** – *e.g., progress reviews sent by email to other managers or presenting a report to the team on PowerPoint.*
- **Dealing with customers, visitors and the general public** – *e.g., meeting, greeting and taking care of people visiting the workplace, answering questions and giving out information, dealing with complaints involving the team or its activities.*
- **Giving and receiving feedback** – *e.g., giving praise and support in a staff appraisal interview, receiving and dealing with feedback from customers.*
- **Solving problems** – *e.g., discussing options with the team and the rest of the organisation, monitoring and reviewing progress, negotiating for more time or resources.*
- **Liaising with other managers and directors** – *e.g., discussing administration issues, revising organisational objectives, solving problems and making decisions about changes and progress.*

An organisation is a complex entity, with many stakeholders, each having an interest in how it is run.

Effective communication is vital to make sure that information is shared correctly and that working relationships are positive and well-supported. All stakeholders need to feel that their contributions and opinions matter, and good communication enables information and views to be seen, heard, spoken and shared.

Forms of Written Communication

In written communication, we need to think about reading, writing, pictures, symbols and other visual communication.

There are many instances when we need to use written information in the workplace – e.g., in notes, reports and emails. Written communication can be very important as it is often kept as evidence to show that policies and procedures have been followed. Written communication can also include pictures, symbols and other visual communications – e.g., a scribbled drawing to explain something, or Braille versions of leaflets.

Methods of written communication can include:

Emails
May be formal or informal and are often used in the workplace to:

- **send information to one person** – *e.g., respond to a question*
- **send information to many people** – *e.g., inform all customers on a database about a product*
- **deal with customer's queries, complaints and comments**
- **plan a meeting**
- **report the outcome of a meeting**

Communication

- circulate informal or formal reports
- share information
- make or confirm purchases and orders

When used informally, emails are rather like postcards, memos or short notes. When used formally, emails need to be similar to formal letters. Organisations usually have their own styles, policies and procedures about how to write emails for different situations.

Notes and memos
Notes and memos in the workplace can be very quick and useful. They are generally informal and can be used to, for example:

- **leave notes in the work diary for the next shift** – *e.g., to report problems or make requests for someone to finish a task*
- **share information with colleagues and other stakeholders** – *e.g., to ask a colleague a question*
- **pass on a telephone message** – *e.g., to give a supplier's name, phone number and message to a colleague who was away from their desk*
- **remind people about something** – *e.g., the date, time and location of a meeting or training course*

Notes can be addressed personally or left for everyone to see, depending on who needs to see the contents.

Formal letters
These will be on headed notepaper and will be used in formal situations, especially if a permanent record is needed. They are particularly useful when information is confidential and sensitive and needs to be kept private, for example:

- during disciplinary procedures
- when making a job offer
- when writing to customers, staff or other stakeholders about serious, confidential or sensitive matters

Formal letters reflect the organisation at its most professional and serious, so good grammar, vocabulary and presentation are essential.

Reports
Reports can be formal or informal. An informal report can be, for instance, a completed paper or electronic form that is used for:

- giving daily figures for sales or production
- reporting costs and other measurable statistics
- handover notes

Communication

Formal reports can be printed or sent electronically and will cover subjects such as, for example:

- *annual accounts and accountants' reports*
- *directors' reports for shareholders*
- *research and development* – e.g., test results for new equipment, detailed comparison between two production methods
- *feedback and analysis prepared after an event or project* – e.g., to show achievements, problems and opportunities for improvement
- *staff appraisals*
- *analysis, strategies and plans on how to achieve objectives*

Spreadsheets and Databases

Spreadsheets are used to bring numerical data together – e.g., to analyse expense claims for all employees under different headings, such as travel, subsistence, mileage and hotels.

Databases are used when names, addresses and other personal details and preferences need to be collected and used – e.g., for mailing lists. both systems are flexible and can be amended and updated by people who have authorised access to them.

Drawings, Graphs and Designs

Drawings and designs are used when information needs to be presented in a visual format – e.g., an architect's drawings, a graphic designer's brochure design, a fashion designer's sketches.

Graphs are used when presenting data in a visual and mathematical format – e.g., pie charts to show details of a company's expenditure.

Forms

Most organisations design and use their own forms. The idea is to simplify the process of sharing information so that the person completing the form can do so as easily as possible. The organisation can target the information that they need and want, so that time and resources are not wasted on processing unnecessary answers and data.

Forms can be used for many functions, including, for example:

> *timesheets, mileage and expense claims from staff*
> *requests* – e.g., budgets, maintenance work, for leave and other time off, or new resources
> *surveys and feedback comments from customers*
> *job applications*
> *ideas and suggestions from staff*
> *orders and sales*
> *finance applications* – e.g., when asking for a loan or mortgage

Communication

Information Signs and Notices

Information signs need to be clear and very easy to understand. The language used needs to be straightforward and clearly written to maximise the chances of the message being understood, for example:

- *directions to different departments*
- *instructions about how to operate machinery* – *e.g., how to use the photocopier*
- *instructions about what to wear or how to behave* – *e.g., please be quiet, exam in progress*
- *information for visitors* – *e.g., expected waiting times for their appointments*
- *car park signs*
- *prices and special offers in retail outlets*

Pictures and symbols can be really useful when the information is important, especially if language is an issue. We see them used on information signs all around us at work and in public places, for example:

- *health and safety information in green to imply safety* – *e.g., emergency exit signs and first-aid signs*
- *warning signs in yellow to show danger* – *e.g., yellow trip hazard signs*
- *fire information in red* – *e.g., about fire extinguishers and fire alarms*
- *mandatory (compulsory) information on blue signs* – *e.g., about handwashing or instructions to wear personal protective equipment*

Chemicals will also have symbols on the packaging to back up the information about the product.

Websites

Websites are now common in organisations, and they are a useful way of communicating with an infinite number of people. They use language, pictures, symbols, graphs and other visual elements.

Websites can carry a vast amount of information, including, for example:

- *detailed information about products and services*
- *background information about the organisation and its structure*
- *policies and procedures*
- *photographs and other graphics to give visual examples of the organisation's products and services*
- *legal information*
- *testimonials and other feedback from customers and others*
- *links to related pages, websites or other information connected with the organisation*

Communication

- *availability and booking systems*
- *payment systems*
- *specifications and instruction manuals* – e.g., for staff or customers to use

Websites need to be well-presented and kept up to date. They can reach a wide number of people, so they need to give a good, professional impression of the organisation and its workforce.

Social Media

A great deal of sales and marketing material is now shared using social media. Many organisations now have a team of people whose job is to monitor and manage social media communications so that an instant response can be given if necessary.

Social media can be used to, for example:

- *monitor and react to complaints* – e.g., by train companies if their customers are complaining about a problem
- *let followers and customers know the latest news* – e.g., announcing a new participant at an air show or music festival
- *offer promotions and special offers*
- *encourage followers and customers to engage with the organisation* – e.g., to send their views to a live TV or radio programme, which shows advertisers the level of interest from different people in the audience

Leaflets, Newsletters and Brochures

Leaflets, newsletters and brochures are generally quite formal and need to be factually correct. They can be illustrated and include graphs and technical information and have many uses – e.g., to give instructions and extra information about products and services; promote the organisation's image using glossy pictures, background information, logos and news; keep employees up to date.

Strengths and Weaknesses of Written Forms of Communication

Forms of written communication have different strengths and weaknesses. We need to consider the contents of our message and who is going to read it when we send written communication, including signs and symbols. This helps us to decide which form is most suitable and effective for the situation.

This table has some notes about some of the strengths and weaknesses of written forms of communication:

Communication

Form:	Strengths:	Weaknesses:
Emails	Quick and simple Can be formal or informal Easy to keep a copy and track the messages coming in and going out Provide a clear record of what has been discussed	Cannot always get instant feedback or an answer from the other person – some people do not deal with emails every day, need to check this if the matter is urgent People often get too many emails, so hard to make important ones stand out
Notes in the team diary	Useful central place for handover notes for the next shift Can leave notes for many to see – e.g., manager, team leaders or team members Good way to flag up important dates, times and deadlines Good way to leave reminders – for self or others	Quite public Not suitable for confidential or awkward subjects and details
Spreadsheets and databases	Can be tailor-made for any situation where numerical data or contact details are recorded Can be simple or complicated Access can be open or restricted	Can be tricky to navigate and find if the data and details are not organised logically Some functions are complex and require thorough training and monitoring
Drawings, graphs and designs	Strong visual impact Can explain plans, results and achievements very quickly when data presented correctly Help people to imagine a three-dimensional plan or design	Often time-consuming to prepare Data and parameters can be hard to understand if people are not familiar with the format
Forms	Easy to complete Logical Designed for a specific purpose	Cannot always have room for additional information Questions and boxes might not be entirely suited to the nature of the answers needed
Personal notes	Can give specific information or request Person has a written record	Might be missed if left in wrong place Need to be aware of possible literacy or language issues

Level 5: Operations / Departmental Manager

Communication

Form:	Strengths:	Weaknesses:
Formal letters	Suitable where very personal approach needed – e.g., with a job application Formal permanent record	Usually take longer to prepare, check and send
Information signs and notices	Can pass information to wide range of people – e.g., in the staffroom, customer waiting area, entrance to the building Symbols and colour-coding make them easy to understand Good for general information or announcements	Not suitable for personal or confidential information Some symbols can be harder to understand if they are unfamiliar
Websites	Can be tailor-made for the organisation or department Relatively cheap and easy to use to reach a very wide audience Can hold a vast amount of data, pictures and information Can link to other pages, information and websites	The internal search engine within the website can be inadequate and make it hard to navigate Information can be irrelevant if not kept up to date Website can be hard to find on search engines – e.g., Google
Social media	Quick, easy and inexpensive to operate Can reach extremely large numbers of followers instantly Good for short messages	Needs to be monitored and updated all of the time – especially for customer comments that might need a response Bad news can travel fast – e.g., negative customer feedback or complaints
Leaflets, newsletters and brochures	Can be formal or informal Good for sending information in a permanent form to a large number of people Can be left for people to help themselves – e.g., in a doctor's surgery waiting area	Can go out of date quite quickly Often discarded unread, or hardly read, which is a waste of resources Expensive to produce and store

Communication

Forms of Verbal communication

Forms of verbal communication between individuals and groups can be formal or informal and include:

Face-to-face conversations
Face-to-face conversations can take place in private or in a small group, including, for example:

- *informal and formal meetings to plan and agree objectives*
- *discussions about progress and potential problems*
- *team talks at the beginning of a shift*
- *handovers to other managers*
- *delegating tasks to team members*
- *monitoring and reviewing any workplace activity*
- *conversations with customers* – e.g., about sales or queries
- *conversations with suppliers* – e.g., to discuss problems or plans
- *staff appraisal discussions* – e.g., spontaneous feedback by the team member's workstation, or in a formal interview in the office

Face-to-face communication can be extremely effective, for example: questions can be answered straightaway and in a personal way; people can be reassured and made to feel valued and respected; training sessions can be lively and engaging. It is not always the most time-efficient way of communicating with people, but the personal touch is hard to beat in most workplace situations.

Face-to-face conversations about sensitive, personal or private matters need to be conducted in private to protect dignity and confidentiality.

Telephone conversations
Telephone conversations can cover many of the topics that can be discussed face-to-face. However, in the workplace, telephone conversations can be much quicker and more efficient, especially when staff have additional information instantly available.

Telephone conversations are useful when two-way communication is needed – e.g., to get an answer or instruction from someone.

Typical tasks that can be performed using telephone conversations include, for example:

- *selling products and services* – e.g., cold calls to sell legal or insurance services
- *advising customers about problems* – e.g., bank staff calling about irregular activities on customers' bank accounts
- *dealing with customer complaints and comments*
- *ordering supplies and arranging delivery times*

Communication

- *dealing with supply problems* – e.g., chasing a late delivery
- *sharing information* – e.g., informing colleagues about meetings, changes or updates
- *initial interviews* – e.g., talking to potential job applicants in the early stages of recruitment

Structured formal meetings

Structured formal meetings can be for small or large numbers of people, generally following an established pattern where participants discuss the points listed on an agreed agenda, with someone taking and circulating the minutes (careful notes about the decisions and points made).

Examples of when structured formal meetings are used include, for example:

- *a small annual general meeting (AGM) for a family company with four directors*
- *a large AGM with thousands of shareholders of a public limited company (PLC)*
- *delivering formal reports to key stakeholders* – e.g., giving a quarterly report to trustees of a charity
- *formal disciplinary procedures* – e.g., delivering a final written warning to an employee
- **when accurate records of decisions are needed for legal and compliance reasons** – e.g., if there is a health and safety investigation after an accident, if there is a financial investigation by auditors or a government department
- **when members need to vote on an issue** – e.g., shareholders of a small property company voting to increase funds to cover maintenance of shared areas

Structured meetings show that the organisation is taking matters seriously and treating people and subjects with respect. The notes taken during these meetings can be used to show compliance with rules, regulations and legislation.

Training sessions and lectures

Verbal communication is a key element of training sessions, tutorials, seminars and lectures. The training can be given in person or using electronic devices that use videos of trainers presenting their topic or doing demonstrations. Examples of verbal training sessions include, for example:

- *induction training sessions in a training room at work*
- *'toolbox' talks in the work area* – e.g., briefing sessions on new equipment or procedures

Communication

- *internal training courses* – e.g., refresher training, short and long courses conducted by the organisation
- *external training courses* – e.g., attending colleges or other training providers; working with tutors and assessors when doing distance learning
- *training DVDs, television programmes or online seminars (sometimes called webinars)* – e.g., fire safety procedures; to show staff how to use new equipment; to increase background knowledge
- *one-to-one shadowing or mentoring* – e.g., following and observing an experienced colleague at work
- *demonstrations* – e.g., by the suppliers of new equipment and machinery

Using the Internet
As technology increases its scope and capacity, the Internet is used for verbal communication more and more often. Organisations can use, for example:

- *Skype or other web-based communication systems that use speech – with or without video*
- *videoconferencing systems* – e.g., to have international meetings without delegates needing to travel
- *webinars* – e.g., to learn about new products and services, then discuss them in detail with the supplier's sales team and technical specialists
- *using tablets and other mobile devices for virtual meetings and conversations*

Internet-based communication is very flexible. It can be used in offices or out on the road, for example, with individual staff members having their own mobile devices to stay in touch. Reports can be made away from the office, research can be done, and emails can be sent and received.

Announcements
From time to time, organisations need to make announcements. They are a one-way process to deliver messages, although there might be a questions and answer session straight after the announcement.

Organisations may wish to announce a variety of things, such as:

- *the appointment of key leaders*
- *the launch of new products and services*
- *problems with products that need to be recalled immediately*
- *their apologies and reactions to a disaster* – e.g., following a major accident involving the organisation's customers, employees or products

Announcements can be delivered through:

Communication

- *giving interviews on television or the radio*
- *speaking to print and online journalists* – *e.g., giving interview to the local or national press, or to journalists who publish online articles*
- *at a meeting or conference* – *e.g., announcing changes in directors or objectives*

Presentations

Presentations are also a one-way verbal form of communication, although there is usually the time and opportunity for questions after a presentation. They can be given by one person or by a group of people, depending on the amount of information and the specialist knowledge needed. If the subject will take several hours to present, it can help everyone if there are several presenters – to keep the audience engaged and to give the presenters a break.

Organisations can use presentations for a range of reasons, including:

- *training purposes*
- *to give an update on progress and objectives*
- *to sell products and services*
- *to inform stakeholders about different aspects of the operation*
- *as part of an application for finance* – *e.g., showing banks the current performance and future plans and projections*

Communication

Speaking, Listening and Questioning Skills

To maximise the chances of successful verbal communication, it is important to use effective speaking, listening and questioning skills.

Speaking Skills
The speaker has the responsibility to deliver information and questions in ways that people can understand. If the listener does not fully understand what has been said, they may give inaccurate answers, feel embarrassed and anxious, or pretend that they know what was said. These consequences can affect working relationships, which can be critical when dealing with, for example, colleagues or customers. To aid communication, the speaker needs to:

- **speak clearly and slowly enough for everyone to understand**
- **keep their message simple and straightforward**
- **use language that is appropriate for the listener**
- **consider possible barriers to understanding** – e.g., hearing difficulties or having English as a second language
- **be prepared to repeat or explain if someone does not understand for any reason**
- **be ready to back up speech with hand signals, diagrams and other visual aids**

In addition, the speaker also needs to consider the tone, pitch and volume of their voice, as these will all affect the delivery.

Listening skills
Good listening skills enhance verbal communication and help us to make sure that everyone has understood everything. Active listening skills also help to demonstrate that the other person's views have been heard and are valued.

Active listening skills include:

- *using eye contact*
- *nodding the head in agreement*
- *actively focusing on what is being said*
- *using open body language to show that we are receptive to what is being said*
- *taking notes if the matter is complicated*
- *repeating back key information in a summary of what has been said*

The listener has the responsibility to concentrate and ask questions if they do not understand and use effective, active listening skills.

Communication

Types of question
Questioning focuses the attention on the other person and selecting the right questioning technique for the situation can help us to collect the right information. We can use, for example:

- closed
- open
- probing
- leading
- rhetorical

Question type	Description and examples	Strengths	Weaknesses
Closed	Answered with a 'yes' or 'no' – e.g. Do you work in the customer service department?	Useful when no further detail is required	Answers do not give many clues or depth. The other person is not encouraged to give more detail or express an opinion
Open	They cannot be answered with a 'yes' or 'no' – e.g., Tell me about your recent experience in customer service	Useful when we want the other person to reflect and come up with their own ideas, opinions and suggestions	Answers can be long and may not be focused
Probing	Secondary questions that take the enquiry further – e.g. Following on from that point, can you explain why the customer reacted that way?	Useful to find out more detail and explore in depth. Useful in investigations	Can be intimidating and uncomfortable for the other person, especially if they cannot answer
Leading	A question that prompts and suggests the desired answer – e.g. So, you are saying that you did remember to lock the door when you left? And weren't you going to tell us about next week's meeting?	Useful when we want to guide people to reflect on a particular problem or aspect. Useful when reminding someone else to say something, maybe in a meeting or presentation	The questioner may be reinforcing their own opinion, and may not get an accurate response or agreement
Rhetorical	When no actual answer is needed – e.g. That is better, isn't it?	Useful to help the other person to reflect and maybe commit to a course of action	The other person can feel pressurised

Communication

It is important to use the right type of question for the individual and the situation to be able to obtain useful and relevant information. The following table suggests strengths and weaknesses for these different types of question:

Strengths and weaknesses of verbal communication

As we have seen, different forms of verbal communication have different strengths and weaknesses, and we need to consider the contents of our message and our audience.

Effective verbal communication relies on good speaking skills and good listening skills. The speaker has a responsibility to deliver messages that are clear, straightforward, appropriate and easy to understand.
The listener has the responsibility to concentrate and ask questions if they do not understand.

This table has some notes about some of the strengths and weaknesses of verbal forms of communication:

Form:	Strengths:	Weaknesses:
Face-to-face conversations with colleagues, customers or the public	Instant response Formal or informal Can be confidential if in private Can give good impression of self and organisation Focus on the information tends to be good People feel valued and respected when their views are taken seriously	Not always possible to be in private Timing can be tricky to arrange for formal meetings Can be time-consuming Limit to the number of people who can join in
Telephone communications	Can discuss, make decisions and arrangements in 'real time' People can be accessible – especially using mobiles Texts can be left for someone to read when they are ready – e.g., after a meeting or shift	Not always possible to get through to speak to the person needed Leaving messages is not always effective Texts do not always go through as expected, and might not be read quickly
Structured formal meetings	Predictable structure with agenda and minutes Formal records kept and circulated Useful for legal and compliance reasons	Format can seem quite laboured and 'stuffy', using complicated language and procedures People will not always understand what is happening if the language and format are too difficult

Communication

Form:	Strengths:	Weaknesses:
Training sessions and lectures	Sessions can be lively and engaging for learners and tutors Instant response to queries and feedback Can be adapted to any subject, any learner and any situation Demonstrations help people to learn physical skills Mentoring and shadowing are personal and show current skills	Some people will not understand if the language or delivery are not clear and easy to follow People learn at different paces – some will find sessions too quick, others too slow Limits to the numbers that can be trained in each session Training DVDs and videos can leave learners uninterested and unable to engage
Using the Internet	Relatively inexpensive to run once set up Can have international access Instant, real-time communication Staff can have their own mobile devices – e.g., phones or tablets	Staff can feel as though they are never off duty Some areas around the country do not have good mobile coverage Signals can be disrupted or disconnected at times
Announcements	Good for delivering a clear message Reduced chance of interruptions The speaker usually has control	A one-way process – there usually needs to be an opportunity for people to ask questions or give feedback
Presentations	Can be lively and engaging Formal or informal Can use pictures and other graphics to deliver messages Can be adapted to any topic, audience or situation Can be delivered with or without electronic support	Can be time-consuming to prepare, deliver and attend Not always relevant to people invited to attend Pace and level of information can be hard to judge – flexible approach needed

Barriers to communication

There are many barriers to communication, and these may occur at any stage in the communication process. Barriers may lead to your message becoming distorted and you therefore risk wasting both time and/or money by causing confusion and misunderstanding. Effective communication involves overcoming these barriers in conveying the clear and concise message.

Common barriers to effective communication include:

Communication

- **The use of jargon.** Over complicated, unfamiliar and/or technical terms.
- **Emotional barriers and taboos.** Some people may find it difficult to express their emotions and some topics may be completely off-limits or to boo to below difficult topics may include but are not limited to, politics, religion, disability is (mental and physical), sexuality and sex, racism and any opinion that may be seen as unpopular.
- **Lack of attention, interest, distractions, or irrelevance to the receiver.**
- **Differences in perception and viewpoint.**
- **Physical disability such as hearing problems or speech difficulties.**
- **Physical barriers to non-verbal communication.** Not being able to see the non-verbal cues, gestures, posture and general body language can make communication less effective. Phone calls, text messages and other communication methods that rely on technology are often less effective than face-to-face communication.
- **Language differences and the difficulty in understanding unfamiliar accents.**
- **Expectations and prejudices which may lead to false assumptions or stereotyping.** People often hear what they expect to hear rather than what is actually said and jump to incorrect conclusions.
- **Cultural differences.** The norms of social interaction very greatly different cultures, as do the way in which emotions are expressed. For example, the concept of personal space varies between cultures and between different social settings.

A skilled communicator must be aware of these barriers and try to reduce their impact by continually checking understanding and by offering appropriate feedback

When communicating, think about the following questions:

Why?	What do I want to achieve? What do I want to happen?
What?	What am I going to say or write?
Who?	Who is going to receive the information? Do I need to adapt my communication to make sure that they understand my messages and questions?
When?	When does the communication need to be sent?
Where?	Where am I going to communicate with people? Does it need to be a private place for sharing confidential information?

Communication

Active Listening

Active listening is an integral part of effective communication. You will need to demonstrate active listening with your team members, colleagues, hire managers, customers and stakeholders in the position work for.

Demonstrating active listening involves:

- *giving your full attention to the individual without interrupting them*
- *encouraging them to open up*
- *listening to what they say*
- *paying attention and reacting appropriately to their body language*
- *using your own body language, for example, head nodding, leaning forward and using gestures*
- *understanding their viewpoint and not your interpretation of it*
- *asking questions, if necessary, to gather further information*
- *repeating back phrases to provide confirmation that your listening*
- *summarising what they have told you to check that you fully understood them*
- *giving them the opportunity to let you know if you have not got it quite right*
- *empathising with them*

An effective chairperson needs to:

- *take ownership and not be afraid of chairing the meeting*
- *set high standards*
- *be on time*
- *be courteous*
- *encourage contributions*
- *listen carefully*
- *be fair but firm*
- *be able to work with, lead and manage people, especially during meetings*

When chairing meetings, we need to think about:

- **key documentation** – that supports the participants before, during and after the meeting
- **how to prepare for the meeting** – planning a suitable environment and physical resources, inviting the right people and making sure everyone can prepare effectively
- **following the organisation's procedures** – establishing ground rules for the structure of the meeting
- **making the meeting effective** – keeping it to time and controlling the flow
- **following up after the meeting** – checking that everyone is following up on the decisions and agreed actions

Communication

Building Rapport

It is very important for managers to not only work with others, but also be able to build an effective relationship or rapport with them.   Rapport is a quality that cannot be seen or quantified but its effect can be clearly seen in the strength of the relationship someone has with other people.

Building a rapport with someone involves identifying common ground between two people. This may not be work related, in fact, it is better if it is not just work related. Being able to discuss sport, the environment of fashion helps to build a relationship between two people which transcends the working relationship.

Rapport is an emotional connection or link which is created with other people.

Rapport is defined by the Oxford Dictionary (2018) as:

> *"A close and harmonious relationship in which people or groups understand each other's feelings or ideas and communicate well."*

Rapport is important in both professional and personal relationships.

Employers are more likely to employ somebody with whom they have a good relationship and who they believe will develop a positive relationship with other employees. Relationships are easier to form and develop when there is a deeper connection and understanding between those involved, in other words - there is greater rapport.

When meeting someone for the first time, people engage in small talk before deeper, targeted, conversation takes place. This is the beginning of the rapport building process. This polite conversation strives to find common points of interest between the two as a basis upon which to build a further, stronger, relationship.

> *Building a rapport is easier when there are common interests and there are naturally shared ideas and subjects to talk about.*

After meeting someone for the first few times there may be the feeling that there is no common ground between the two – there is nothing in common. This may mean that working together could be more difficult and communication more awkward because there are no shared frames of reference.

It will require greater effort to build the rapport and develop the relationship, however, it is still possible.

Communication

Getting to know you!
Starting a conversation with a stranger can be a stressful event leaving people lost for words and feeling awkward and self-conscious. This anxiety can be allayed by trying to build a rapport, making the outcome of the meeting more positive. The important thing is to relax and stay calm. By relaxing tension decreases and communication becomes easier.

When meting someone for the first time try to:

- *Choose safe topics to discuss initially such as the weather, road conditions, etc.*
- *Listen carefully to the other persons conversation and try to pick up on things they say which is of personal interest too.*
- ***Try to include a little humour*** – *laughing together about something eases tension quickly, just don't make jokes about other people!*
- ***Be mindful of the body language being displayed and the style of language being used***
- ***Show empathy towards the other person*** – *this reinforces the shared or common ground which exists between the two.*
- ***Make sure the conversation remains light and varied and does not become an interrogation or cross examination.***
- ***The other party will also be seeking to build a rapport*** – *try to meet in the middle.*

Although a great deal of rapport building occurs through conversation some will occur through non-verbal communication too. This non-verbal rapport building is more difficult to manage as it happens without our realising it. There is a tendency to mirror non-verbal signals such as body position, gestures, expressions and the intonation in the voice.

Rapport building is partly an instinctive process and the more comfortable and less threatened the feeling between the two, there more likely there is to be a strong rapport build between them.

Given that this is an instinctive relationship, there is no hiding the situation where rapport does not exist. Both parties will be uncomfortable in each other's company and idle conversation will be very limited and focus will be on the issues to hand.

Active listening is a key tool when establishing a relationship. Listening to what someone says and clarifying understanding where necessary will confirm that the person is being listened to and respond using similar language and terminology which further consolidates the relationship. Lowering the tone of voice and speaking more slowly will also help develop rapport.

Communication

Behaviours which help build rapport

There are certain behaviours that are particularly helpful in building rapport. These include:

- **Lean slightly towards the other.** *Adopt an open body posture with hands and arms relaxed and avoid crossing legs.*
- **Try to make eye contact for around 60% of the conversation** – *don't overdo it or it will become a threatening behaviour.*
- Use active listening
- Smile!
- Use the other person's name a few times to embed it in your mind
- Use an open questioning technique to encourage the other person to speak
- Keep to subjects which are not contentious until the understanding or each other is deeper
- Try to be empathetic
- Use the other persons ideas as a platform to build on
- Avoid stereo typing and don't judge the other person
- **Be honest in all dealings** – *if you are found to have deceived the other person – it will destroy all rapport that existed*
- Try to compliment when appropriate and don't criticise the other person.

Rapport is the basis of all relationships. Being able to build a rapport is therefore a very beneficial skill. Working relationships will be stronger and more effective meaning there is greater tolerance from both parties.

We all know that person who gets on with everyone – they are an expert at building rapport – even though they may not know it!

Communication

Communicating in Challenging Situations

Speaking, listening and questioning skills are essential when managing challenging conversations. As we saw earlier in the workbook, the person leading the meeting needs to, for example:
F
- *speak clearly and slowly enough for everyone to understand*
- *keep their message simple and straightforward*
- *use language that is appropriate for the listener*
- *consider possible barriers to understanding*
- *be prepared to repeat or explain*
- *be ready to back up speech with visual aids*
- *use active listening skills*
- *select appropriate question types* – e.g., open, closed, probing, leading or rhetorical
- *use the appropriate tone, pitch and volume for the situation*
- *support verbal communication with effective body language*

Once the person leading the meeting has planned their approach, they can decide on the speaking, listening, questioning and body language skills that will be most useful for the communication style they want to use.

For example, a manager who is dealing with a complaining customer needs to diffuse the situation, make the conversation less challenging and maximise the chances of a successful outcome. They may concentrate on:

- *having an open and non-confrontational posture*
- *being polite, courteous, patient, apologetic and confident* – to inspire trust
- *listening more than they speak* – using active listening skills
- *using a calm, polite, respectful but confident tone of voice*
- *using open, closed and rhetorical questions* – maybe with probing questions if more detail is required

On the other hand, a manager who is giving a second verbal warning to a team member may choose to use a more assertive approach. They still need to be polite, but they may also concentrate on:

Communication

- *using dominant body language* – such as strong eye contact
- *good speaking skills with a strong tone of voice*
- *being firm and assertive*
- *expressing their disappointment* – that the first verbal warning did not seem to work
- *a range of question types* – including leading and probing questions

Communication methods and styles need to be calm, fair and professional so that, for example:

- *everyone concerned can work together afterwards*
- *the challenging conversation is less likely to lead on to further complaints or accusations of harassment and bullying*
- *the good reputation of the individuals and the organisation are maintained*

Communication

Emotional Intelligence

Emotional intelligence is the ability to understand the way people feel and react, then use the skill to make good judgements, avoid issues or solve problems. This ability can be extremely useful when managing and communicating with others, and can be applied on two levels:

- *personal* – *understanding our own feelings or reactions*
- *interpersonal* – *understanding other people's feelings and reactions*

People with a reasonable degree of emotional intelligence can be, for example:

- *empathetic* – *able to put themselves in other people's shoes*
- **sensitive to others**
- **understanding and sympathetic**
- *good at reading other people's emotions correctly*

In the workplace, we often have to work as a team or develop relationships with colleagues, customers and other stakeholders. Being aware of how people think and react can be essential. When looking at different forms of communication and how they are used, emotional intelligence can provide an extra insight into which form, and approach will be most effective.

Using Emotional Intelligence

Whatever our approach, we need make allowances for the other person's feelings when managing challenging conversations. The chances are that they will be nervous, afraid, uncomfortable, aggressive or defensive. By using our emotional intelligence, we can read their feelings and reactions more accurately and adapt our approach and employ appropriate skills.

People can be challenging to deal with for many reasons. They may have, for example:

- **additional needs or requirements** – *e.g., impaired vision, hearing or mobility issues*
- **poor communication skills** – *e.g., learning difficulties that make communication difficult*
- **language or cultural barriers** – *e.g., making them upset because they find it hard to express themselves in English*
- **personal problems** – *e.g., issues with alcohol, drugs or a medical condition; childcare or family problems; difficult living conditions*
- **they may have an incident, emergency or trauma** – *e.g., reacting badly if they (or a person close to them) have been involved in an accident, injury or serious illness*
- **dissatisfaction and disappointment** – *e.g., reacting emotionally when there is a problem with the product or service*
- **impatience** – *e.g., being short-tempered if they are not dealt with straightaway*
- **indecision** – *e.g., uncertainty about how to proceed, what they want or how to solve problems*

Communication

- ***being overly assertive, confident or intimidating*** – e.g., coming across as a bully when talking
- ***being too talkative*** – e.g., making problems unnecessarily complicated, hard to identify and deal with

By being aware of background information, it is possible to use our emotional intelligence to 'step into their shoes', understand their viewpoint and take appropriate measures to achieve the objectives of the conversation. This skill of using empathy and understanding can be extremely useful. It helps us to amend our approach, diffuse problems and use the listening, speaking and questioning techniques that will be most effective.

We also need to be aware that some people find it extremely hard to use and understand emotional intelligence, and we cannot assume that we all have the same ability to 'put ourselves in someone else's shoes' when we are involved with challenging conversations.

Effective Questioning

Asking good questions is productive, positive, creative, and can get us what we want!

Most people believe this to be true and yet people do not ask enough good questions. Perhaps one of the reasons for this is that effective questioning requires it be combined with effective listening.

Effective Questions

Effective questions are questions that are powerful and thought provoking. Effective questions are open-ended and not leading questions. They are not "why" questions, but rather "what" or "how" questions. "Why" questions are good for soliciting information but can make people defensive so be thoughtful in your use of them. When asking effective questions, it is important to wait for the answer and not provide the answer.

When working with people to solve a problem, it is not enough to tell them what the problem is. They need to find out or understand it for themselves. You help them do this by asking them thought provoking questions. Rather than make assumptions find out what the person you are talking to knows about the problem.

For example:

> *"What do you think the problem is?"*

Behind effective questioning is also the ability to listen to the answer and suspend judgment. This means being intent on understanding what the person who is talking is really saying. What is behind their words? Let go of your opinions so that they do not block you from learning more information. Pay attention to your gut for additional information.

Communication

Powerful Questions
The following are examples of typical questions. These questions can help you improve your communication and understanding of the client or staff member.

Identification of issue:
These questions can be used in staff interviews and meetings, settlement negotiations and to work with others in solving problems.

> What seems to be the trouble?
> What do you make of _____?
> How do you feel about _____?
> What concerns you the most about _____?
> What seems to be the problem?
> What seems to be your main obstacle?
> What is holding you back from _____?
> What do you think about doing X this way?

Obtaining further information:
These questions can be used to find out what someone has already done to resolve a work problem.

> What do you mean by _____?
> Tell me more about _____
> What else?
> What other ways did you try so far?
> What will you have to do to get the job done?

Outcomes:
These questions can be used in settlement negotiations or while working with staff to plan how to do something.

> How do you want _____ to turn out?
> What do you want?
> What is your desired outcome?
> What benefits would you like to get out of X?
> What do you propose?
> What is your plan?
> If you do this, how will it affect _____?
> What else do you need to consider?

Taking Action:
These questions can be used in working with staff.

> What will you do? When will you do it?
> How will I know you did it?
> What are your next steps?

Communication

Listening as Part of Effective Questioning

When staff are listened to, they feel understood and are more trusting of you. Effective listening is a skill that requires nurturing and needs development. Since managers are "smart", the temptation is to get by with listening at a minimal level. To connect with your staff and have them experience you as an effective manager requires you to maintain superior listening skills along with asking effective questions.

Consider the following different levels of listening:

Level 1 Listening:
When we are listening at level 1 our focus or attention is on how the words the other person is saying affect ourselves with minimal concern for the person talking. We listen for the words of the other person to see how they affect us. The attention is on me - what are my thoughts, judgments, issues, conclusions and feelings. There is no room to let in the feelings of the person being "listened" to. When listening at level 1 our opinions and judgments arise. Level 1 listening is appropriate when you are gathering information for yourself like getting directions or ordering in a restaurant or a store.

Level 2 Listening:
When we listen at level 2, there is a deeper focus on the person being listened to. This often means not even being aware of the context. Our awareness is totally on the other person. We notice what they say as well as how they say it and what they do not say. We listen for what they value and what is important to them. We listen for what gives them energy or sadness or resignation. We let go of judgment. We are no longer planning what we are going to say next. We respond to what we actually hear.

Level 3 Listening:
When we listen more deeply than the two levels described above, in addition to the conversation we take in all information that surrounds the conversation. We are aware of the context and the impact of the context on all parties. We include all our senses, in particular our intuition. We consider what is not being said and we notice the energy in the room and in the person we are listening to. We use that information to ask more effective questions.

Communication

Listening skills as part of effective questioning

Articulating
Attention and awareness result in articulation and succinctly describing what we have learned from the employee. Sharing our observation clearly but without judgment does this. We can repeat back to our employee just what they said. We can expand on this by articulating back to them what we believe they mean. This helps a person feel heard. For example: "What I hear you saying is . . ."

Clarifying
Clarifying is a combination of asking and clearly articulating what we have heard. By asking questions the employee knows we are listening and filling in the gaps. When the employee is being vague, it is important for us to clarify the circumstances. We can assist them to see what they cannot see themselves by making a suggestion. For example: "Here's what I hear you saying. Is that right? "

Being Curious
Do not assume you know the answer or what the employee is going to tell you. Wait and be curious about what brings them to see you. What motivates them? What is really behind the meeting? Use your curiosity so that your next question can go deeper.

Silence
Giving the person we are listening to time to answer questions is an important aspect of listening. Waiting for the employee to talk rather than talking for them is imperative for an effective listener.

Types of Question

Although there are numerous reasons for asking questions, the information we receive back (the answer) will depend very much on the type of question we ask.

Questions, in their simplest form, can either be open or closed - this section covers both types but also details many other question types and when it may be appropriate to use them, in order to improve understanding.

Closed Questions
Closed questions invite a short, focused, answer- answers to closed questions can often (but not always) be either right or wrong. Closed questions are usually easy to answer - as the choice of answer is limited - they can be effectively used early in conversations to encourage participation and can be very useful in fact-finding scenarios such as research.

Closed questions are used to force a brief, often one-word answer.

- *Closed questions can simply require a 'Yes' or 'No' answer, for example: 'Do you smoke?', 'Did you feed the cat?', 'Would you like a cup of tea?'*

Communication

- *Closed questions can require that a choice be made from a list of possible options, for example: 'Would you like beef, chicken or the vegetarian option?', 'Did you travel by train or car today?'*
- *Closed questions can be asked to identify a certain piece of information, again with a limited set of answers, for example: 'What is your name?', 'What time does the supermarket open?', 'Where did you go to University?'*

Open Questions
By contrast, to closed questions, open questions allow for much longer responses and therefore potentially more creativity and information. There are lots of different types of open question; some are more closed than others!

Open-ended questions prompt a conversation because they cannot be answered with one-word answers. An example of an open-ended question would be "Where do you want to be in five years?" The answer to this question varies from person to person and can only be answered with a unique perspective that usually prompts a longer conversation.

You might be familiar with open-ended questions, but maybe not closed-ended questions, which you usually want to avoid.

Open-ended questions prompt the beginning of a longer conversation by asking questions starting with "why," "how," and "what if?" Closed-ended questions can be answered with single-word answers, such as "yes" or "no."

How to ask Open Questions
If at the end of the meeting, you ask a team member, "Did you find this meeting helpful?" that's a closed question since they can only answer "yes" or "no." While it is good to know that they found the meeting helpful, unless they volunteer some elaboration to their answer, you do not know in what ways they experienced value. Maybe they are just being polite.

On the other hand, you could ask, "We've been through a bit of a process to get to this point, can you tell me the value you feel you've received by going through this entire process?"

The team member will now clearly articulate their perception of the process, which helps you to get an even clearer picture on the outcome. In addition, asking your team member about value actually helps them reinforce it in their own minds. The net result is you become more preferable to them and reinforce your position in their mind.

Tell, Explain and Describe (TED) Questions
When using probing questions, TED can become your best friend. TED stands for three simple words that will help you get the answers you are looking for: Tell, Explain and Describe.

Some examples could include:

Communication

- *Tell me, how will that affect you?*
- *Tell me, has this happened before?*
- *Tell me, what was your main motivation for calling?*
- *Explain to me, what impact has this had on your…?*
- *Explain to me, how did this situation begin?*
- *Explain to me, what difficulties did you face when you tried to…?*
- *Describe how you felt about that*
- *Describe how it looks*
- *Describe your ideal outcome*

TED questions should be used at any moment when you feel as though you have heard something that they would like some more information on. They are used best interjected between open and closed questions." These probing TED questions help to pinpoint the relevant insight from an employee's open response. The style of wording helps to prompt the employee into giving you all the relevant information in regard to your query.

By starting a question with one of these words, you are essentially demanding an answer from the customer without letting them know that you are. However, the key point Is listening - There is absolutely no point asking questions if we are not prepared to listen.

Leading or 'Loaded' Questions
A leading question, usually subtly, points the respondent's answer in a certain direction.

Asking an employee, 'How are you getting on with the new finance system?' This question prompts the person to question how they are managing with a new system at work. In a very subtle way, it raises the prospect that maybe they are not finding the new system so good.

'Tell me how you're getting on with the new finance system' is a less leading question – the question does not require any judgement to be made and therefore does not imply that there may be something wrong with the new system.

Children are particularly susceptible to leading questions and are more likely to take the lead for an answer from an adult. Something simple like, 'Did you have a good day at school?' points the child towards thinking about good things that happened at school. By asking, 'How was school today?' you are not asking for any judgement about how good or bad the day has been, and you are more likely to get a more balanced, accurate answer.

This can shape the rest of the conversation, the next question may be, 'What did you do at school?' - the answer to this may vary based on the first question you asked – good things or just things.

Communication

Recall and Process Questions

Questions can also be categorised by whether they are 'recall' – requiring something to be remembered or recalled, or 'process' – requiring some deeper thought and/or analysis. A simple recall question could be, 'What is your mother's maiden name?'. This requires the respondent to recall some information from memory, a fact. A schoolteacher may ask recall questions of their pupils, 'What is the highest mountain?' Process questions require more thought and analysis and/or a sharing of opinion. Examples include, 'What skills can you bring to this organisation that the other applicants cannot?' or 'What are the advantages and disadvantages of asking leading questions to children?'

Rhetorical Questions

Rhetorical questions are often humorous and do not require an answer.

> *'If you set out to fail and then succeed have you failed or succeeded?'*

Rhetorical questions are often used by speakers in presentations to get the audience to think – rhetorical questions are, by design, used to promote thought.

Politicians, lecturers, priests and others may use rhetorical questions when addressing large audiences to help keep attention. 'Who would not hope to stay healthy into old age?', is not a question that requires an answer, but our brains are programmed to think about it thus keeping us more engaged with the speaker.

Funnelling

We can use clever questioning to essentially funnel the respondent's answers – that is ask a series of questions that become more (or less) restrictive at each step, starting with open questions and ending with closed questions or vice-versa.

- "Tell me about your most recent holiday."
- "What did you see while you were there?"
- "Were there any good restaurants?"
- "Did you try some local delicacies?"
- "Did you try the Clam Chowder?"

The questions in this example become more restrictive, starting with open questions which allow for very broad answers, at each step the questions become more focused and the answers become more restrictive.

Funnelling can work the other way around, starting with closed questions and working up to more open questions. For a counsellor or interrogator these funnelling techniques can be a very useful tactic to find out the maximum amount of information, by beginning with open questions and then working towards more closed questions. In contrast, when meeting somebody new it is common to start by asking more closed questions and progressing to open questions as both parties relax.

Communication

Responses to questions
As there are a myriad of questions and question types so there must also be a myriad of possible responses. Theorists have tried to define the types of responses that people may have to questions, the main and most important ones are:

A direct and honest response – this is what the questioner would usually want to achieve from asking their question.

A lie – the respondent may lie in response to a question. The questioner may be able to pick up on a lie based on plausibility of the answer but also on the non-verbal communication that was used immediately before, during and after the answer is given.

Out of context – The respondent may say something that is totally unconnected or irrelevant to the question or attempt to change the topic. It may be appropriate to reword a question in these cases.

Partially Answering – People can often be selective about which questions or parts of questions they wish to answer.

Avoiding the answer – Politicians are especially well known for this trait. When asked a 'difficult question' which probably has an answer that would be negative to the politician or their political party, avoidance can be a useful tact. Answering a question with a question or trying to draw attention to some positive aspect of the topic are methods of avoidance.

Stalling – Although similar to avoiding answering a question, stalling can be used when more time is needed to formulate an acceptable answer. One way to do this is to answer the question with another question.

Distortion – People can give distorted answers to questions based on their perceptions of social norms, stereotypes and other forms of bias. Different from lying, respondents may not realise their answers are influenced by bias or they exaggerate in some way to come across as more 'normal' or successful. People often exaggerate about their salaries.

Refusal – The respondent may simply refuse to answer, either by remaining silent or by saying, 'I am not answering'.

Communication

Feedback

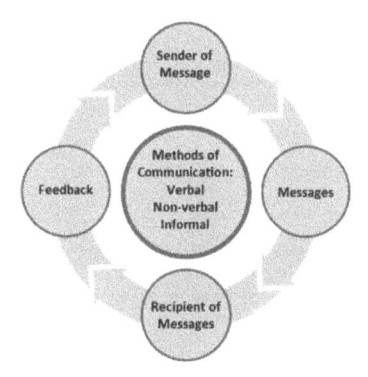

If you have been telling people the same things over and over again, it is possible you have not been telling them the right things.

It is vital when giving feedback to employees to make it so that it is useful to them. It is even more vital when this feedback goes to team members working on a project. Because successful project management requires good communication – both with stakeholders and with members of the team, then it is important to be able to give feedback to those individuals that reinforces the behaviour you would like to see them exhibit.

Delivering constructive feedback is an important element of effective communication, especially when managing challenging conversations.

There are many theories and versions of communication cycles that show how sharing information is a continuous process, but the principles are broadly the same:

There will be many types of feedback in the workplace – e.g., complaints and praise from customers, comments in staff appraisal interviews, or discussions in a progress review.

Feedback helps us to:

- *find out what went well – so that we know we are going in the right direction and can build on our strengths*
- *find out things that need to be improved*

Points to consider when giving feedback include, for example:

- *the value of constructive feedback*
- *following a feedback model*
- *how to give negative feedback*
- *environment and communication techniques*

Environment and Communication techniques

As we have seen already, environment and communication techniques are important when managing challenging conversations, and these apply when giving feedback too. For the feedback to be useful and well-received, discussions need to take place in private, where noise and distractions are kept to a minimum. The choice of speaking skills, active listening skills and questioning techniques need to be focused on the individual and a positive outcome.

Communication

Feedback Models

Feedback models help new managers and team leaders to develop their feedback skills. There are several different frameworks which can help guide managers and leaders.

STAR feedback model

One type of effective model for such feedback is known as the STAR model. The purpose of this model is to help you to visualise a pattern of giving good positive feedback and encouraging individuals to take initiative and complete their tasks efficiently.

If you visualise a star, much like the one in the image to the right, you can divide that star into three sections. the top point of the star, the left two-star points, and the right two-star points. The top point represents the situation or task at hand. the left two points refer to the action that was taken, and the right two points stand for the result of that action.

ST – The Situation or Task
The first part of being able to interpret and use feedback given is to understand the situation or task. What happened that alerted you to the necessity of taking care of this situation? In order to be able to determine the sort of feedback that is appropriate, you will need to take a minute to define what happened and what that meant in terms of the project. By defining the situation or task that occurred, you can pinpoint exactly what it is you need to address when it comes to the individual to whom you are providing feedback. For example, a situation might involve an employee who has arrived late to work every day for a week.

A – The Action
What action was taken? Was that action good or bad? What action should have been taken? It is important to identify the action involved with the situation. When the action you are reviewing was positive, note that it was positive. When the action was negative, explain first what should have happened. In keeping with the current example, you would tell the tardy employee that he or she should have arrived on time. If it is a case of an employee who had provided outstanding ideas in a meeting, then point out the exact action that employee took that was worthy of praise.

R – The Results
Next, you need to look at the results that action lead to. What happened as a result of that action? For example, if the employee provided many good ideas during the brainstorming session that impressed stakeholders, tell them! By acknowledging the situation, action, and results that turned out well, you will increase their motivation and commitment to the task.

When you are providing an employee with positive feedback using the STAR model, you will put everything together and deliver the feedback. For example, the following might be said when giving feedback using this model:

Communication

The other day, when things went wrong in the factory, you did not panic. Instead, you kept a calm head and patiently determined what the cause of the problem was. This resulted in keeping other employees calm and helped us to solve the problem much faster.

You can see in this example that by acknowledging the situation, identifying the action, and praising the results, that you will be better able to encourage similar action in the future from employees.

When it comes to providing negative feedback, make sure you identify both the actual action and result and the desired action and result. For example:

When I sent this proposal back to you for adjustments and with questions, you did not correct the problems or respond to the questions, and therefore I cannot accept the proposal. If you had made the needed adjustments and responded to the questions effectively, then I would have been able to approve the project proposal.

In this example, both the undesired and desired actions and results are identified. By doing this, it makes it much easier for employees, stakeholders, and project team members to understand what needs to be done and why it needs to be done.

By providing effective feedback on a regular basis, you can improve the productivity and effectiveness of your team.

CORBS Feedback Model

The principles of CORBS feedback model are as follows:

- ***Clear statement*** – *give clear and concise information.*
- ***Owned by the person speaking*** – *your own perception, not the ultimate truth. How it made you feel. Use terms such as "I find" or "I felt" and not "You are".*
- ***Regular*** – *give immediately or as close to the event as possible. NEVER delay*
- ***Balanced*** – *balance negative and positive feedback. DO NOT overload with negative feedback.*
- ***Specific*** – *base your feedback on observable behaviour. Behaviours that the recipient can change.*

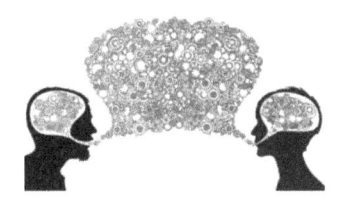

Communication

Situation, Behaviour, Impact Model

Imagine that you recently gave some feedback to a member of your team. You told him that his KPI's are great, but he needed to improve his people skills.

You follow up a few weeks later to find out why he has not made any changes. You discover that he did not understand what he could do to improve – your feedback simply prompted more questions. He was left thinking "What's good about achieving the KPI's and how can I do more?" and "What's wrong with my people skills?"

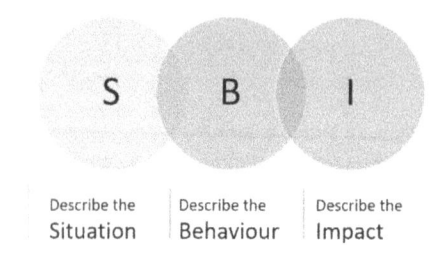

The Situation – Behaviour – Impact (SBI) Feedback tool helps people deliver more effective feedback. It focuses your comments on specific situations and behaviours, and then outlines the impact that these behaviours have on others.

The SBI Feedback Tool outlines a simple structure that you can use to give feedback:

1. *Situation.*
2. *Behaviour.*
3. *Impact.*

When you structure feedback in this way, people will understand precisely what you are commenting on, and why. When you outline the impact of their behaviour on others, you are giving them the chance to reflect on their actions and think about what they need to change. The tool also helps you avoid making assumptions that could upset the other person and damage your relationship with them.

Applying the Tool

1. Situation
When you are giving feedback, first define the where and when of the situation you are referring to. This puts
the feedback into context and gives the other person a specific setting as a reference.

2. Behaviour
Your next step is to describe the specific behaviours that you want to deal with. This is the most challenging part of the process because you must communicate only the behaviours that you observed directly.

You must not make assumptions or judgments about those behaviours. These could be wrong, and this will undermine your feedback. For example, if you observed that a colleague made a mistake, you should not assume that they had not prepared thoroughly. You should simply comment that your colleague made mistakes – and, ideally, you should note what the mistakes were. Do not rely on hearsay or gossip, as this may contain other

Communication

people's judgments. Again, this could undermine your feedback and jeopardise your relationship.

The examples below include a description of behaviour:

- *"During yesterday morning's Daily Review Meeting, when you talked about the night shift KPI's, you were uncertain about why a line had a negative score, and your calculations were incorrect."*
- *"At the team meeting on Friday afternoon, you ensured that the meeting started on time and all your research was correct, and each of the managers' questions were answered."*

Aim to use measurable information in your description of the behaviour. This helps to ensure that your comments are unbiassed.

3. Impact
The last step is to use "I" statements to describe how the other person's action has affected you or others.

For example:

- *"During yesterday morning's Daily Review Meeting, when you talked about the night shift KPI's, you were uncertain about why a line had a negative score, and your calculations were incorrect. I felt a bit embarrassed because my manager was there. I'm worried that this has affected the reputation of our team."*
- *"At the team meeting on Friday afternoon, you ensured that the meeting started on time and all your research was correct, and each of the managers' questions were answered. I am proud that you did such an excellent job and put us in a good light. Keep up the great work!"*

Next Steps

Once you have delivered your feedback, encourage the other person to think about the situation and to understand the impact of their behaviour. Allow the other person time to absorb what you have said, and then go over specific actions that will help him or her to improve.

Communication

Pendleton's Model of feedback

Pendleton's Rules are structured in such a way that the positives are highlighted first, in order to create a safe environment. Therefore, the recipient identifies the positives first.

This is followed by the leader reinforcing these positives and discussing skills to achieve them.

"What could be done differently?" is then suggested, first by the recipient and then by the leader giving feedback.

The advantage of this method is that the recipient's strengths are discussed first. Avoiding a discussion of weaknesses right at the beginning prevents defensiveness and allows reflective behaviour in the recipient. There are some deficiencies in the rules. They create artificiality and rigidity by forcing a discussion of the recipient's strengths first. Therefore, an opportunity for an interactive discussion of topics that might be relevant to the recipient is lost.

There is also inefficient use of time because the same topic is discussed twice in its entirety: first to discuss the strengths and then the weaknesses.

Phase	Supervisor	Recipient
Positive Aspects		Tells what went well
	Complements on what went well	
Areas for Improvement		Tells what went wrong and what could be done better
	Complements on what could be done better	
Action Plan for Improvement		Tells action plan
	Approves action plan with modifications	
Summary		Summarises the key points
	Complements if necessary	

To someone expecting primarily negative feedback, the discussion of strengths may appear patronising, which makes the feedback more stressful and, perversely, a disproportionate amount of time may be spent discussing strengths to soften the impact of the negatives.

A judgemental tone may also creep into the feedback when "What was done correctly and what was incorrect?" is discussed, which goes against the non-evaluative and formative nature of feedback.

Communication

The value of constructive feedback

For feedback to be useful, it needs to be constructive, not destructive. If there are problems and weaknesses that need to be addressed, people need to be advised of these tactfully and shown how to improve.

People can see feedback as criticism and may react negatively. They can become defensive, make excuses, choose not to hear or take the feedback seriously. Destructive or negative feedback that is handled poorly can leave people feeling bad, hopeless and worthless. They can feel they are left without any useful information or ideas on which they can build. However, people often respond positively to constructive feedback because it concentrates on, for example:

- **the individual's needs and abilities** – *increasing self-awareness and offering them what they need to develop in the workplace*
- **positive messages** – *providing useful information about performance and how to develop*
- **being supportive** – *offering encouragement and developing working relationships and trust*
- **behaviours and actions rather than the person** – *making the issues less personal*
- **helping people to feel valued, respected and engaged in the workplace processes** – *to aid team building and motivation*

Delivering negative feedback

Negative feedback does not need to be avoided; it just needs to be handled well. If a manager only gives positive feedback, people will distrust their judgement after a while, as nobody is perfect and there must be some things that need correction and development. When giving negative feedback, it is useful to use a sandwich technique. For example:

- *give some positive comments about something that has gone well*
- *deliver the negative feedback tactfully, maybe following the CORBS model*
- *finish with some positive feedback and comments, maybe about the future*

This enables the recipient to be given the negative comments and end the conversation with an uplifting, positive comment that makes them feel valued and committed to the team.

Communication

Escalating Workplace Problems

Working within the limits of authority is important, and this applies to managing challenging conversations as well. We all need to know when to escalate a problem to someone else. The limits of authority, and how to escalate a problem that is outside those limits, will be set out in, for example:

- *the employment contract*
- *the job description*
- *organisational policies, procedures or standards*
- *training materials*

The organisation's procedures will show when staff need to escalate a problem. For example:

- *when a decision is needed that is outside their limits of authority*
- *when a customer or another stakeholder requests something that is outside the limits of their responsibility*
- *when dealing with complaints or problems that are outside the limits of authority*
- *when they do not have enough knowledge, experience or skill to be able to deal with something on their own*
- *when there is not enough time to deal with something properly*
- **when there is a threat to health and safety** – *e.g., if someone becomes aggressive, very upset or unwell during a challenging conversation*

The job titles can vary, but employment contracts, job descriptions and training materials should show the chain of command, or management structure, of the organisation. For example:

- **team members will usually escalate problems to their team leader, or supervisor**
- **team leaders and supervisors might refer a problem to their shift manager or a specialist from another department** – *e.g., a quality control team leader for help with product testing*
- **managers will escalate to more senior managers or subject specialists**

Working within the limits of authority and escalating problems when appropriate protects:

- **the people involved with the conversation** – *by making sure that they act legally and are fully supported in their decisions and promises if they have worked in line with the organisational procedures; by making sure that their legal rights have been observed and respected*
- **the organisation** – *helping it to maintain a good reputation for being fair and consistent*

Communication

Employers value employees who can operate independently and do not need to be micromanaged.

Similarly, particularly among employees with some level of management responsibility or who aspire to such responsibility, there is often a desire to handle things on their own without asking supervisors for help. At the same time, managers are there for a reason, and it is important for employees to know when they can and should escalate issues up the chain of command.

The employee has reached their level of authority

This is perhaps the most common situation when escalation is appropriate or necessary. Employees should not be expected to make decisions that are above their pay grade. Instead, they should bring these issues to their managers, who can make the call or escalate further as needed.

How do employees know when they are bumping up against their level of authority?

Their job descriptions should convey some indication. In addition, though, direct supervisors and managers need to help employees understand where their decision-making authority may end and when they need to turn to their managers for support. Citing specific examples and providing real-time feedback are both good ways of coaching employees.

Cross-department support is needed

Sometimes, the solution to a problem requires input across departments or business units, and an employee may need to engage his leadership team to engage the appropriate resources.

Maintaining Relationships

It can be awkward for employees to be the ones to say "no" to an important customer. This is particularly true when employee-customer contact is frequent and long term. In these situations, it can help maintain that close relationship if the employee can take an issue to his manager and let the manager deliver the bad news—obviously with the appropriate explanation.

This lets the employee demonstrate that he advocated for the customer while insulating that employee from the unwelcome decision.

Again, supervisors and managers can help employees understand when this handoff is indicated by conveying clear expectations and providing feedback.

Independence is important for employees and employers alike, but there are always going to be situations when employees need to escalate issues to their boss, their bosses, etc. This is true at any level of the organisation.

Communication

Escalating Customer Complaints

Causes of Customer Escalation
A survey revealed that the top seven reasons customers escalate complaints are staff lack of knowledge, being told no without any apparent reason or explanation, the employee lacking confidence, the staff member having a negative or disagreeable attitude, not receiving an apology, the employee not communicating clearly and not adapting to the pace of the customer.

Handling Cases
Have a clear strategy in place for when complaints should be escalated. The more you empower an employee to resolve an issue on his own, the less you will have to deal with escalated complaints. Encourage staff to listen more closely to customer concerns so they can effectively handle objections and satisfy the customers' needs. Staff should never take things personally. A customer may be having a bad day or just be a grouch. Advise Staff to adopt a helpful mentality and treat every customer with respect. This should disarm customers who may not be in a good mood.

Dispute Resolution
The best resolutions to escalations are those where both you and the customer come to a consensus on what needs to be done to make the issue right. Once you have verified with the customer that this will resolve the issue for her, take the necessary steps to fix the matter.

This is your time to go above and beyond to impress the customer. You already know her experience has been less than ideal. Once you have done what is necessary to resolve the matter, verify once more that the customer is now satisfied. You should also confirm if the customer will continue patronising your business.

Other Considerations
Closely monitor escalations within the business. These types of scenarios should be the exception not the rule. If you are receiving multiple escalations, you must get to the root cause of these. Understand if there is a particular employee where most of these are coming from or if the problem is more widespread. Address the issues with the appropriate training, coaching and feedback. A decrease in escalations means your staff are becoming better at satisfying your customer's needs.

Reasons why escalation does not take place

No one likes escalating problems to their boss. It is kind of smacks of 'I can't deal with this myself and need help' and most of the managers I know would rather struggle on than ask for help in most situations. When they do ask, you know it is a huge deal and definitely worthy of their senior manager getting involved.

So, what kind of situations is escalation appropriate for?

Here are 5 scenarios where it pays to escalate.

Communication

1. When you do not know who will make the decision
You have done all you can to resolve the matter but when money needs to be spent that could be outside your remit. Someone else has that authority and you need to know who they are. If no one around you can give you a straight answer about who has the final say on design, sign off, functionality, branding and so on, then that is a red flag for an escalation.

When you escalate this to your boss, be conscious of the fact that it might be them who is the right person to make the decision and approach the conversation carefully!

2. When you cannot break down the groups
Teams that work in groups are difficult. If you have done everything in your power to get them to work together: regular team meetings, cross-functional workshops, bringing people together in person and virtually – and nothing is working, then escalation might be the answer.

You do not want this to come across to your boss as 'I can't make my team play nicely together' so be sure you have a real problem before you take up your sponsor's time with it. Equally, it helps if you go to them with a solution in mind, and a list of the things you have tried that have not made a difference.

3. When you cannot control the changes
As a manager you have a strong change control process, and you are great at communication upwards and ensuring the team do not engage with tweaks and changes. But sometimes you get a stakeholder (or even the boss themselves) who says: "I don't care, just do it." Be honest, you have probably met someone in your career who has this attitude. They can pull rank and get new stuff included in the scope of their project because they are who they are, and no one says no to them. Or because the client they work with is the most important client for the business.

Changes are fine, as long as they are managed in a reasonable and controlled way. It is the changes that come from people with greater authority and influence than you, who do not seem to get that you cannot use nine women to deliver a baby in a month. When you cannot 'just do it' within your existing scope, time, budget and quality targets then you need help to resolve that. Hopefully, your manager or someone senior will be able to get through to your stakeholder that it is not possible and that the options are... whatever the options are.

4. When you cannot meet unrealistic expectations
A bit like the previous point above: you will sometimes come across stakeholders who want too much for what they are prepared to offer in return. It will either be a tiny budget or a tiny timescale. Everyone wants their project faster and cheaper and, in many respects, it is your responsibility to ensure that you can schedule work appropriately and to use your budget management skills to deliver that. But when you have exhausted schedule compression, crashing, paying overtime and adding extra people to the team, there comes a point where you just cannot get any faster. If your stakeholders are still demanding that you shave days off the delivery milestone, it is time to escalate.

Communication

Before you do so, make sure you have sat with them to explain why you cannot do things faster and what you have done to ensure the work takes as little time as possible. Or costs as little as possible if the challenge is on the budget. It may just be an issue of education. Not everyone knows how projects are put together and what goes into getting the work delivered on time.

5. When you cannot manage the politics

All workplaces have politics – it is simply the nature of the organisation. If you are lucky, you will not notice them because they are positive and the relationships at play work in favour of your department. If you are not so lucky the gossip, power plays and in-fighting will bring your work to a halt.

Sometimes you can handle conflict (because that is what it is) yourself. It depends on the severity of the situation and the people involved. It might just take a conversation with the line managers involved, focusing on the overall business benefits and highlighting what their teams will get out of the project. But when you cannot handle the discussions yourself, or the people involved are way above your pay grade, then that is the time to escalate. Issues on work tasks are normal: you are going to hit some problems that you cannot deal with alone. Once you have exhausted the channels that are open to you, it is time to consider your next options. You could struggle on in a difficult situation, putting more pressure on the team and delivering less and less. Or you could ask for help – which is effectively what an escalation is.

A good manager will never mind that you have asked for their advice and intervention. If you know what you need them to do, ask them to do it. If you do not, tell them what you have tried and what you think might be the next steps, and ask for their help in working out whether that is the right path.

Escalations can be awkward conversations as you do not want them to come across as if you are not in control or you are blaming someone else for issues outside your responsibility. Stay factual, talk about the implications for the project in terms of impact on key success criteria and take the emotions out of the conversation. Get over the awkwardness and you could find that your problems disappear quickly once your sponsor has resolved the issue on behalf of the team.

Communication

Chairing Meetings

Meetings offer the opportunity for employees to get together to share business information, generate ideas, plan future events and celebrate success. Whether meetings are face-to-face, by videoconference or webinars, employees have the chance to exchange information. You should make sure you are fully prepared for the meeting, carrying out any research in advance and making sure you have all the information that you need for each agenda item.

You need to create and communicate the agenda to all participants in good time, which enables them to plan their contribution, if required, and add agenda items if they wish. Depending on the method you use for the meeting, you may need to check the availability of the meeting room and of any equipment you wish to use to enhance your communication and ensure that it set up and working correctly beforehand.

When chairing the meeting you should communicate clearly using the appropriate aspects of verbal and non-verbal communication. You will also need to actively listen to what is being said by members of the team and, if you are unsure of any points, ask questions to clarify your understanding.

Showing respect for other people's ideas and opinions is important, it is also important that you make sure you pass on your information in a clear and professional manner, using your own knowledge and experience.

As the chair of the meeting, you will be responsible for ensuring that it stays on track and does not stray too far from the agenda. Additional time should have been allowed at the end for any other business to be discussed, therefore some items can be added, and anything nonurgent may be deferred to the next meeting or allocated to member of the team as an action.

You will need to agree for a participant of the meeting to take the minutes, recording the key items and actions to be taken, will be responsible for them and when they are to be completed by. The person produces the minutes will need to be able to use effective written communication and you may need to support them with this. You should clarify key points after each agenda item and check that all participants understand their roles. Meeting minutes should be checked for accuracy, and then agreed or amended accordingly

Key documentation

When organising a meeting, the person leading it will often generate and circulate an agenda in advance. This is a list of points that they are expecting to cover, in order, within the time allocated to the meeting.

The agenda is based on the organisational objectives that the people attending need to discuss. For example, a quarterly meeting between department managers and team leaders to review activities could result in these items being on the agenda:

Communication

1. ***Welcome and introduction*** – *from the senior manager holding the meeting*
2. ***Minutes from the last meeting*** – *to be agreed and signed off as being accurate*
3. ***Apologies*** – *from people who cannot attend the meeting*
4. ***Production output for the last two quarters*** – *to compare and analyse*
5. ***Problems arising*** – *e.g., delays, staffing issues or problems with suppliers*
6. ***Forecasts and targets for the next quarter***
7. ***Anticipated resources needed and potential problems***
8. ***Review draft targets for the following year***
9. ***Recruitment plans for the following year***
10. ***Training courses planned for the following year***
11. ***Any other business (AOB)*** – *for people to add things that need to be discussed*

It can be useful to put the expected time next to each item, so that people can see how long has been allocated. Also, it is helpful to show who will be leading each item. This helps to focus attention and identify speakers that may not be known to all of the attendees. For example, items 1, 2, 3 and 11 would be led by the chairperson, but items 7 and 8 about forecasts and targets would be led by the sales director.

It is important to have a meeting agenda that addresses the objectives of the organisation so that, for example:

- **the meeting is focused, structured and has direction** – *to keep things moving as people can see how much business needs to be covered, and in what order; to avoid people spending valuable time talking about issues that are nothing to do with the objectives; to keep the meeting on time*
- **people can see what needs to be prepared before the meeting** – *e.g., reports and figures that are going to be discussed*
- **participants can anticipate questions they may want to ask** – *e.g., by having advance warning that they will discuss specific problems with other managers*

Having an agenda shows that the meeting is serious and will be run well. Everyone's time is precious, and it is important to use the time wisely and efficiently, making the most of the opportunity to share information, review objectives and agree the ways forward.

During formal meetings, someone will usually take the minutes. These are brief or detailed notes that are written up after the meeting as a true representation of what was discussed and agreed. They are often sent out soon after the meeting, so that everyone can see the points that have been agreed. The minutes are checked and agreed at the next meeting to make sure that they are accurate. They can also be used when writing the agenda for the next meeting, to check that actions have been completed, and to show which subjects and objectives need to be reviewed again.

The evidence recorded in minutes can be used for serious purposes. For example, they may be used during legal action, such as a disciplinary process, and need to be truthful and accurate. Minutes can also help when managing projects and tasks, to provide evidence of decisions and agreed actions.

Communication

Other key documentation needed will depend on the purpose of the meeting, who is attending and the format that is most suitable for sharing information.

The following table shows examples of documents, type of meeting where they might be used and when they might be circulated:

Documents:	Examples of their purpose:	Type of meeting where they might be useful:
Agenda	To list the points to be covered during the meeting	Any meeting, especially formal meetings or if several people are expected to attend
Minutes	Detailed notes that need to be agreed at formal meetings	Meetings between directors, trustees or shareholders, or when there is a statutory or regulatory requirement to log and approve the minutes
Briefing notes or handouts	Detailed information that people need to read before or after the meeting – e.g., about new products and services	Any meeting, especially management, sales or training meetings
Reports – including graphics, pictures, graphs and tables	Formal or informal reports about any business function – e.g., sales figures, production data sheets, organisational operations, market research analysis, feedback questionnaires and data	Any meeting, especially management, videoconferences, sales, team and directors' meetings
Workbooks	Training materials – e.g., to give to learners to use during training meetings as samples to discuss when planning and organising training with other team leaders or managers	Team, training and management meetings
Forms	To collect information in a structured manner – e.g., order forms or application forms	Meetings with customers or suppliers; team meetings for HR or training purposes
Contracts or agreements	Legally binding documents between parties	Meetings with customers, suppliers or members of staff
Instructions	To include within operational procedures and training manuals	Team or training meetings
Brochures and other marketing materials	To provide detailed information about the organisation's products and services	Meetings with customers or suppliers

Some key documents need to be made available before the meeting so that people can be fully prepared, for example:

Communication

- *the agenda*
- *briefing notes*
- *reports and materials for people who have been involved with their preparation* – *e.g., so that they can get to know their material before they present their part of the report during the meeting*

Many key documents only need to be made available during the meeting to support the information being discussed. These could include, for example:

- *copies of the agenda for people who have not seen it*
- *reports*
- *handouts, workbooks and other training materials*
- *contracts*
- *samples of marketing materials*

All of the key documents can also be circulated to appropriate people after the meeting. If people have not attended the meeting, they may need to be informed about all of the points, decisions and information that were discussed so that they can comment and stay up to date. If people did attend the meeting, they may need additional documents after the meeting that confirm what was agreed and what follow-up actions are needed. These could include, for example:

- **minutes** – *draft or agreed*
- **forms** – *that need to be completed*
- **further reports** – *to show progress and update follow-up actions*

When circulating key documentation, it is important to make sure that it is appropriate to share it. For example, care needs to be taken to make sure that:

- *the recipient is authorised to receive it*
- *the information is relevant to them*
- *confidentiality is not breached*
- *the information is current and correct*
- *the documents are sent out at the right time*
- *the information is sent in a suitable format* – *e.g., secure email or by post*

Preparing for a meeting

There are several things that need attention when preparing for a meeting, and these should be set out in the organisation's procedures. When arranging a meeting, we need to know the answers to the following questions:

Communication

When will the meeting take place?
The date, time and duration of the meeting are important so that:

- people can be invited to the meeting
- the room can be booked or reserved
- resources can be arranged
- people know how long the meeting is expected to run
- time zones can be checked for international video conferences

Why is the meeting happening?
It helps to know why the meeting is taking place as it enables us to:

- make sure that standard procedures are being followed
- plan to deal with typical problems and issues
- **answer questions about the purpose of the meeting** – e.g., if people call for details or to check if they should come

The meeting could be, for example:

- **an information meeting** – e.g., to cascade information down to the attendees whose primary involvement is to take notes, and maybe ask relevant questions
- **a decision-making meeting** – e.g., where people need to prepare their reports, data and arguments to make their contribution to the group
- **a combination** – e.g., team or divisional meetings that involve sharing information, drawing conclusions and making decisions

Who is coming to the meeting?
We need to know who is supposed to attend the meeting so that:

- **the right people can be invited** – e.g., with written invitations, by email, using a list on the wall in the staff room or electronic meeting planners
- **resources can be planned** – e.g., the right size of meeting room, car parking capacity, or the right number of coffee cups
- an attendance list can be prepared
- name badges can be prepared if needed
- **special requirements can be accommodated** – e.g., wheelchair access, hearing loops for those with impaired hearing, or translation services
- someone can be tasked to take notes for the minutes

Where will the meeting happen?
Details of the location of the meeting need to be considered so that:

- people can be told where the meeting will be
- maps and directions can be sent out if necessary

Level 5: Operations / Departmental Manager

Communication

- *planners can make sure that the location is big enough and has all the necessary equipment*
- *parking and transport can be arranged if needed*
- *any security and access issues can be dealt with in advance* – e.g., getting security passes for people who do not normally have access to the location
- *people with access problems can be informed and assisted as required*

Which resources and facilities are needed?

As we find out more about the 'when, why, who and where' of the meeting, the resources and facilities that are needed start to become clear. Once the venue has been established, planners who organise the meeting might need to consider the following:

- **invitations** – asking the person to accept and state any special access or dietary requirements
- **furniture** – e.g., the number and placement of chairs and tables
- **technical equipment** – e.g., PowerPoint, screens, microphones, sound system, videoconferencing system, other audio-visual aids (known as AV)
- **special access requirements** – e.g., ramps and space for wheelchairs
- **catering** – e.g., tea, coffee, water, snacks or meals
- **security and car pass** – e.g., to gain access to a secure site such as a military base
- **name badges and attendance lists** – e.g., a list of names and contact details so that colleagues can see who attended and follow them up
- **agenda** – a list of points to be covered, usually produced by the person holding the meeting
- **copies of the minutes of the last meeting** – e.g., to hand around in a formal meeting to be agreed and signed; for people to check that previously agreed points have been actioned
- **briefing notes** – e.g., detailed information that people need to read before or after the meeting
- **stationery** – e.g., pads and pens
- **literature** – e.g., notes, reports, workbooks, forms or brochures
- **the budget for resources** – e.g., the food budget per head

Some of these things need to be organised and planned well in advance of the meeting, and the chairperson, or chair, needs to be aware of the whole process. They need to be confident that all points are being covered. By preparing thoroughly, we can make sure that:

- *there is a suitable environment*
- *the right people are invited*
- *people can prepare themselves and contribute effectively*

Communication

Facilitating a meeting

Having taken care of the practicalities of preparing for and arranging a meeting, the chairperson needs to use their skills to make sure that the meeting is effective. The need to, for example:

- *use leadership skills*
- *use effective communication skills*
- *follow the organisation's procedures*
- *guide the meeting*
- *manage time*
- *control speakers when necessary*
- *make sure that information has been recorded*

Leadership skills

Leaders inspire and motivate people – they focus on people and set new directions for a group to follow. When chairing a meeting, the leadership skills used can include, for example:

- *personal and interpersonal skills to get the most out of the people at the meeting*
- *analysing results and trends, forecasting, innovating and giving direction for change*
- *communicating visions and plans*
- *encouraging, praising, developing and inspiring team members*

The chairperson's leadership style can be important. For example, using Kurt Lewin's theory of leadership styles, the chairperson may employ one or all of the following styles:

- **autocratic** – *expecting others to do things in their way*
- **democratic** – *allowing other people to be involved in the decision-making process*
- **laissez-faire** – *trusting their team's capabilities, willing to stand back and let the team get on with the tasks*

A mixture of all three styles will often be needed when chairing a meeting. Strong, autocratic leadership can be used to keep things on time and to make sure that the points on the agenda are covered. The democratic style can help to involve and engage other people, gaining their trust and commitment and making the most of what they have to offer. The laissez-faire style is important when delegating tasks and can be used when the chairperson knows that they can trust people to take ownership of tasks and follow-up actions.

Communication

Using effective communication skills

Communication skills are covered in detail in another workbook, but the skills that are useful when chairing a meeting can include, for example:

- **questioning techniques** – *e.g., using a mixture of open, closed, probing, leading and rhetorical questions*
- **listening skills** – *e.g., using active listening techniques*
- **building rapport** – *e.g., developing working relationships and gaining the confidence of others*
- **emotional intelligence** – *e.g., recognising, understanding, managing and influencing emotions*

Good communication skills help to ensure that all participants take an active role in the meeting and contribute effectively.

Following the organisation's procedures

Organisations often have procedures about how meeting should be run. These are the ground rules that everyone needs to accept and follow to make the meeting productive and effective. For example, procedures could ask people to:

- *switch off mobile phones*
- *introduce themselves*
- *avoid interrupting other people*
- *stick to the agenda*
- *not talk amongst themselves*
- *start on time and stay until the end*

Some meetings are run on a formal basis where all questions go 'through the chair'. This means that all participants have to address their questions and comments to the chairperson, then wait for the chair to give them their turn.

Guiding meetings and managing time

The most important tasks for the chairperson are to guide meetings and keep them running to time. People attending meetings become irritated, uncomfortable and resentful if meetings are not run well. For example, nobody appreciates spending their time in a meeting that:

- *goes on too long*
- *does not have clear objectives*
- *does not cover all of the items on the agenda*
- *does not stick to the agenda – except for time allocated to 'any other business'*
- *does not allow people to speak and get important points across*
- *feels boring and irrelevant*

Communication

- *wastes time by letting some people speak for too long, or in too much detail*
- *gets out of hand with too many interruptions, inappropriate language or emotional outbursts*
- *does not have clear outcomes about decisions, changes, future actions or new responsibilities*

The chairperson needs to plan well, be focused on the objectives and be aware of people's expectations. They need to take command every so often to keep the meeting on track and make sure that time is spent effectively. For example, the chairperson needs to:

- **make sure that the right people are invited to attend** – e.g., to present and share information and take part in making decisions
- **make sure that everyone has access to the information they need** – e.g., to be able to prepare, share information and take away material that needs to be studied later
- **make sure that everyone is clear about the objectives of the meeting** – e.g., to keep everyone focused and engaged; to manage expectations
- **follow the agenda and cover all of the points listed** – e.g., make sure people do not get side-tracked too much by irrelevant topics and details
- **use good listening and questioning techniques** – e.g., to encourage people to contribute effectively and share information fully
- **guide the speakers** – e.g., to introduce themselves, make their points and stick to the agenda
- **summarise decisions and future actions** – e.g., to set the date and objectives of the next meeting; to clarify what has been agreed and what follow-up actions are required

Controlling the meeting can be quite difficult as there needs to be a balance between getting enough information from people without getting too much. The amount of time given to each item on the agenda will depend on its complexity and the information that people need to discuss. If an item is taking too long, for example, the chairperson can announce that they will allow five more minutes of discussion, bring the matter to a close, move on to the next item and arrange for the matter to be discussed again in another meeting, if necessary.

Controlling speakers when necessary
This can be the hardest task for the chairperson, and they need to make sure that the meeting is balanced and that everyone gets a chance to contribute.

To keep the meeting in balance, the chairperson needs to be ready to take command and not be afraid to chair the meeting. The following table gives some examples of problems that may occur, along with some suggested solutions:

Communication

Problem:	Suggested solutions:
New or shy people do not contribute to the meeting	Invite new people to introduce themselves Ask questions – their silence may not mean that they agree with what others are saying
People from minority groups or who have unpopular views are not heard	Make sure that they are invited to air their views Insist that others give them time to speak, even if they disagree Ask if anyone who has not spoken yet wishes to comment
People interrupt each other	Be firm and consistent Acknowledge the interruption but avoid being drawn in Ask the person who is interrupting to wait until the first person has finished, then go back to them to air their points of view
People talk amongst themselves	Stop the chatter politely at first, then firmly – it is distracting and discourteous Be firm about them waiting for their turn to speak Emphasise the importance of listening to what the speaker has to say
Speakers talk for too long or get side-tracked away from the topic	Again, be firm and consistent Thank them for their contributions and for raising interesting points, then explain you want to ask others to comment
People criticise decisions or each other in a negative way	Be firm about looking for solutions not problems Ask for suggestions about how things could be improved Ask the critic what they would do to resolve the issue
People argue or make emotional outbursts	Stop the discussion Identify areas where there is agreement Summarise the issues and suggest ways forward Take the focus away from individuals and concentrate on the broader issues

Communication

Recording information

The chairperson needs to work with the person taking the minutes to make sure that an accurate record is kept. Minutes need to be written up in line with the organisation's procedures, especially if there is a legal requirement to have a true representation of the points covered and agreed in the meeting.

The chairperson needs to make sure that a suitable minute-taker:

- *attends the meeting*
- *is fully briefed and able to handle the information*
- *keeps up with all of the points made and agreed*
- *writes up their notes as soon as possible after the meeting*

The chairperson and other participants can openly ask for certain, important points to be noted in the minutes during the meeting – e.g., to record a disagreement with a decision or to highlight points that affect people who could not attend the meeting.

Follow-up actions

After meetings, the chairperson's managerial input continues. They need to:

- *communicate recorded actions*
- *take follow-up action, when required*
- *make sure other people complete follow-up actions*

Communicating recorded actions

The chairperson needs to make sure that information has been circulated after meetings. This is important for:

- **people who attended the meeting** – *e.g., so that they can go ahead and action the points that are their responsibility, as shown in the minutes*
- **people who did not attend the meeting** – *e.g., so that they can see what was agreed and what they have to follow up*
- **compliance** – *e.g., as part of a legal process where people need to be informed of decisions and agreed actions*

Documents could include minutes and any other relevant key documents and can be sent in the paper-based or electronic format set out in the organisation's procedures. If it is critical to know that people have received minutes and documents, there may be procedures where the recipient needs to acknowledge receipt.

Communication

Taking follow-up action
As a leader, the chairperson needs to make sure that they follow up decisions and actions that affect them. For example, if the chairperson has agreed to research something and report their findings within a week of the meeting, they need to make sure that they do this on time or report why they are late if there is a problem. They need to lead by example to maintain credibility and other people's trust and confidence.

Making sure other people take follow-up action
The chairperson needs manage other people to make sure that they follow up decisions and agreed actions. If they have delegated responsibility for follow-up actions, the chairperson needs to keep an eye on progress, and help to provide support and resources if there are problems.
The minutes are a useful guide as to who needs to take action, the details of what they should do and the timescale they need to follow. The chairperson, other managers, leaders or decisionmakers can use them as a tool when planning and monitoring progress.
The agenda of the next meeting is another useful tool to encourage people to complete agreed actions. It usually includes a reference to the actions agreed in the previous meeting, and this provides a focus to make sure that follow-up actions are not overlooked.

Chapter 4: Building Relationships

Building Relationships

Stakeholders

A stakeholder is an individual, a group of people, or an organisation who can affect or be affected positively or negatively by your business.

Before you can engage stakeholders, you first need to identify them. Then analyse them to place them into appropriate groups. This will then help develop the right plan for communicating with the groups.

The benefits of identifying the right stakeholders and properly analysing them is that:

- *You will improve the quality of the business, as stakeholders can give you vital information and make sure you do not miss anything important*
- *You can avoid delays by making stakeholders supporters rather than obstacles to getting approval*
- *Supporters could provide you extra resources for the business.*

Failing to identify and engage the right stakeholders could potentially result in your business going over budget, missing important deadlines, wasting the time and energy of the people delivering the production and ultimately, the business being labelled a failure and shelved.

In business, a stakeholder is any individual, group, or party that has an interest in an organisation and the outcomes of its actions. Stakeholders are individuals, groups and entities affected by the operation of your business.

Strong relationships with core stakeholders are key to long-term profit and business success.

The term "stakeholder" has been coined because of the fact that the people who fall into this category have some interest of stake in the business.

Understanding Stakeholders

Stakeholders can be internal or external. Internal stakeholders are people whose interest in a company comes through a direct relationship, such as employment, ownership, or investment. External stakeholders are those people who do not directly work with a company but are affected in some way by the actions and outcomes of said business. Suppliers, creditors, and public groups are all considered external stakeholders.

Building Relationships

Internal Stakeholders

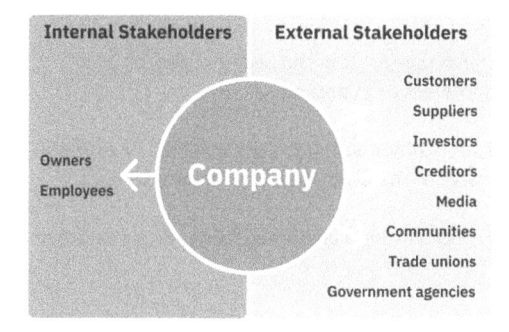

Investors are a common type of internal stakeholder and are greatly impacted by the outcome of a business. If, for example, a venture capital firm decides to invest £5 million into a technology start-up in return for 10% equity and significant influence, the venture capital firm becomes an internal stakeholder of the start-up. The return of the company's investment hinges on the success, or failure, of the start-up, meaning it has a vested interest.

External Stakeholders
External stakeholders are a little harder to identify, seeing as they do not have a direct relationship with the organisation. Instead, an external stakeholder is normally a person or business affected by the operations of the organisation. When an organisation goes over the allowable limit of carbon emissions, for example, the town in which the company is located is considered an external stakeholder because it is affected by the increased pollution.

Conversely, external stakeholders may also sometimes have a direct effect on a business but are not directly tied to it. The government, for example, is an external stakeholder. When it makes policy changes on carbon emissions, continuing from above, the decision affects the operations of any organisation with increased levels of carbon.

Issues with Stakeholders
A common problem that arises with having numerous stakeholders in an enterprise is their various self-interests may not all be aligned. In fact, they may be in direct conflict. The primary goal of an organisation, for example, from the viewpoint of its shareholders, is to maximise profits and enhance shareholder value. Since labour costs are a critical input cost for most organisations, it may seek to keep these costs under tight control. This might have the effect of making another important group of stakeholders, its employees, unhappy. The most efficient organisations successfully manage the self-interests and expectations of their stakeholders.

Stakeholders vs. Shareholders
Stakeholders are bound to an organisation with some type of vested interest, usually for a longer term and for reasons of greater need. A shareholder, meanwhile, has a financial interest, but a shareholder can sell their shares and buy different shares or keep the proceeds in cash; they do not have a long-term need for the organisation and can get out at any time.

For example, if an organisation is performing poorly financially, the vendors in that organisation's supply chain might suffer if the organisation no longer uses their services. Similarly, employees of the organisation, who are stakeholders and rely on it for income, might lose their jobs. However, shareholders of the organisation can sell their shares and limit their losses.

Building Relationships

The term stakeholders should not be confused with the term customer. It may be useful to recognise a subtle difference between them

A stakeholder is identified as anyone who has a vested interest in the business and/or is impacted by the business and benefits from this interest or in packed

A customer on the other hand is identified as anyone either within the organisation or external to the organisation who purchases or is the end user of the product or service provided.

It stands to reason therefore that a stakeholder is not always a customer; however, a customer will always be considered a stakeholder.

Stakeholders could be:

- Customers
- Owners of the Business
- Wholesalers
- Employees
- Management Teams
- Suppliers
- Shareholders
- Business Partners
- Regulating Bodies
- Competitors
- The Media

To take the classification of a stakeholder one step further, consideration can be given to identifying them as either primary, secondary, or tertiary.

Primary stakeholders are those who influence the actual root of the business, including business managers, external regulatory bodies, and employees.

Secondary stakeholders would be those who receive the benefits less directly and would include delegates attending one of the training programs provided by the business.

Tertiary stakeholders include corporate clients as they are affected more indirectly than those within the primary and secondary groups.

Primary Stakeholders

Primary stakeholders are usually stakeholders within the organisation. They are also referred to as internal stakeholders. These stakeholders are involved in economic transactions of the organisation.

Examples include:

- Customers
- Shareholders
- Suppliers
- Creditors
- Investors
- Employees

Building Relationships

The interests for primary stakeholders are significant, particularly when it comes to investors and creditors. The article on financial accounting shows that these two stakeholders are primary users of financial pieces of the organisation. Shareholders own the organisation, and their interests carry much weight. Together, they decide what the course of the organisation looks like.

Secondary Stakeholders

Secondary stakeholders are generally external interested parties, people outside the organisation. Although these stakeholders do not directly participate in economic activities with the organisation, they are affected by its business activities, and thus crucial to take into consideration while performing the stakeholder analysis. Because the impact of those activities can be significant, these stakeholders also receive a lot of attention.

Examples of secondary stakeholders include:

- Communities
- Activists
- The public
- Media
- Trade unions
- Governments
- Competitors

Stakeholders in other Business Situations

It is important to understand that there are different stakeholders in different contexts and situations. On a corporate level, an organisation-wide level, the stakeholders are other people than in the smaller departments of an organisation.

Financial Accounting

Information gained through financial accounting is shared with external users. These stakeholders mainly include investors and creditors.

Project Management

Stakeholders play an important role in project management as many people generally have an interest in a project. Primary stakeholders are people who have an immediate effect on the success and failure of a project, such as the project members or sponsors. Typical stakeholders in project management are:

- Customers
- Project manager
- Project team
- Sponsor

Building Relationships

Identifying Stakeholders

It is essential to map the various stakeholders because they might have a significant impact on the success of an organisation, project, or other process. Conducting a stakeholder analysis is a fixed part of effective stakeholder management. There are three steps that must be followed in the stakeholder analysis.

Step 1: Identify all stakeholders

To be able to communicate with the stakeholders, they must first be identified. Therefore, it is important to make sure that both the primary and secondary stakeholders have been identified. When making a list, think of everyone who might have influence on or might be influenced by the project. People who benefit from the success or failure of a project or organisation are also important.

- *Who might have a negative impact on the success of the project or organisation?*
- *Have both the supporters and opponents been identified?*
- *What is the relationship between these stakeholders?*

Step 2: Assess the stakeholders and sort them by influence

When the stakeholders have been identified, it is important to sort them based on their impact and power. The groups of stakeholders can subsequently be divided across the stakeholder matrix. This will be explained in the next section.

Step 3: Understand the stakeholders

It is important for the project manager or business manager to know what the stakeholders think of a project, and what they like or dislike about it. This enables the manager to develop a perspective on what the stakeholders expect to gain from the project. Ask yourself the following questions:

- *Do stakeholders have a financial or other interest?*
- *Which information is valuable to them and how can this best be communicated to them?*
- *What is their opinion?*
- *Who or what influences their opinion?*
- *Are there mutual relationships between stakeholders that might change this opinion?*
- *How could possible hostile actions be avoided?*

The information that is gained here is used to get an idea of exactly which stakeholders exert how much influence, and how these stakeholders can best be handled. After all stakeholders and their interests and influence have been established, these can be included in the stakeholder matrix.

As a first step, you can kick start stakeholder identification by asking the following questions in a brainstorming session:

Building Relationships

- Who is affected positively and negatively by the organisation?
- Who has the power to make it succeed (or fail)?
- Who makes the decisions about money?
- Who are the suppliers?
- Who are the end users?
- Who has influence over other stakeholders?
- Who could solve potential problems with the organisation?
- Who is in charge of assigning or procuring resources or facilities?
- Who has specialist skills which are crucial to the organisation?

It is surprisingly easy to forget about a minor stakeholder who then exercises a disproportionately large influence on success after they feel like they have not been adequately consulted. It happens in countless businesses every day. For this reason, stakeholder management is used to obtain, or maintain, stakeholder support for the business.

Stakeholder Register

The first step in managing a relationship with stakeholders is the creation of a Stakeholder Register. This is a listing of the stakeholders identified as a result of the Stakeholder Identification process.

Stakeholders can be subdivided into four categories according to their general needs:

1. *Upwards* – Executives, project sponsor, and investors
2. *Sideways* – External stakeholders who have an interest in the project
3. *Outwards* – Other managers and activities which compete for limited project resources
4. *Downwards* – The team itself, subcontractors, and suppliers

Upwards

The upwards category is involved in the initiating and funding of the business, and they have a business interest in its success.

It contains 5 groups of stakeholders:

1. **Executives**
   Management of the parent organisation has a desire to see the business succeed within budget and schedule. They probably formed the business and funded it. Generally speaking, they do not like forming new businesses or changing existing ones, with some exceptions, like when it has identified new market opportunities that could be exploited for an additional cost.

2. **Business Sponsor**
   The business sponsor is the organisational contact for the parent organisation. They are the first point of contact outside the main business. They wish the see the business

Building Relationships

to succeed, in fact, they were often the person who championed its formation and drummed up support for its initiation and funding. The sponsor's needs are similar to the executive's; however, they have additional communication requirements. They need to be aware of the development status so that they can decide what, if any, issues need to be escalated to the next executive level.

3. *Lenders*
   Many businesses obtain loans to fund their operations. The lender's primary need is to see their money returned with interest. Beyond that, they wish to be communicated with regularly so as to satisfy themselves that the business is able to pay the loan back. With the exception of certain high-risk lenders, banks do not wish to assume the business risks.

4. *Creditors*
   Some businesses have been funded using bonds, or similar types of debt. Investors in these instruments, like lenders, also do not wish to assume the businesses market or other risks. However, they wish to see a fixed income throughout the term of their investment, and they wish to see the value of the bond grow as the business succeeds. Thus, they are somewhat invested in business success.

5. *Shareholders*
   Shareholders who own stock in the business or the organisation that initiated it have fully exposed themselves to the risks of business failure. Although sometimes they receive small pay-outs in the form of dividends, these are minor and do not represent a significant portion of their motivation for making the investment. Rather, they wish to see the businesses products or services succeed in the marketplace, which will result in large returns on their investment. Likewise, if the project fails there is a large negative return.

Outwards

This category contains traditional business stakeholders who have a stake in the organisation. Their needs vary according to how the project affects them.

1. *Customers*
   The most important stakeholder is the customer. They must purchase the product or service that the business creates, or it will be a failure. For many businesses, the sponsor is the customer who pays for the business's products. For example, for a road construction project the government agency who is building the road is the customer who takes delivery from the contractor who built it. Enough market research should have been completed prior to starting the business in order to make the decision to proceed with the it but the business itself may require information flow back to the parent organisation to refine that market research with new information. Also, market research may be appropriate within the business itself if the budget exists for it.

2. *End Users*
   Often the end users of the businesses products and services are the same as the customers, but sometimes they are not. For example, software development

Building Relationships

companies often have as a customer the owner who pays for the development of the product, who is different than the end user who uses the software product.

End users require their lives to be enhanced in a meaningful way. They wish to improve an area of their life with the minimal amount of inconvenience and cost. The business must consider the ways in which the end user's lives change because of the business and what features and innovations could add benefit for them at an acceptable cost.

3. *Government Agencies*
It is rare these days that a business can be started that does not require some form of government permits and approvals. Large infrastructure, mining, and oil projects require years of consultations from many different agencies culminating in many different permits, before they can break ground. These regulatory agencies do not wish to stop businesses. Rather, they seek to find acceptable middle ground between the proponent business and a group of specific stakeholders that might be opposed to the project.

Usually, they take the businesses design information and advertise it to the stakeholder group. They then hold consultation sessions and bring requests for changes back to the proponent. If the opposition is extremely fierce, they could withhold permits, however this rarely happens. When the stakeholder group is satisfied, or at least sufficiently satisfied to the regulatory agency, the permits are granted.

4. *The General Public*
The general public is not usually a stakeholder in most business, with a few exceptions like road construction projects where the public is inconvenienced. But most business have some form of interface with the general public something could go wrong that would affect the public, and this possibility usually represents a significant expense. The possibility of it happening might be small, but the consequences are very high, hence it might be worth giving some passing thought or performing a risk analysis on it.

Sideways

This group contains stakeholders that are in competition with the business's resources.

1. *Other managers*
Many organisations have other businesses that compete for limited resources to perform their functions. These businesses become stakeholders that need to be monitored and controlled during business operations to ensure that the business has the resources it needs, when it needs them. The other managers wish to run their businesses and must be consulted regularly. In a perfect world, all the resources would be available right when we need them, but unfortunately, it is not a perfect world.

2. *Technical / Department managers*
Department managers often provide the resources used by a business. They are the owners of the resources, and they usually have some form of operations / maintenance role in which they use the resources. They want their normal activities to continue

Building Relationships

without impact (or with minimal impact) and their resources returned in the condition in which they delivered them to the business

3. *Local committees and boards*
   Many businesses have committees and boards that impact their activities. For example, development review boards for new housing projects, technical committees for a review of building codes, or an environmental review board for an industrial development. These boards have a desire to maintain the standards in a certain area. The business must appease their desires, but their power to stop the business can range from nil to full.

4. *Unions and Trade organisations*
   Unions wish to improve workers' pay and satisfaction levels. Some businesses in unionised organisations must be familiar with and abide by union legislation. Trade organisations wish to provide employment for their members.

Downwards

The downwards category contains those stakeholders that produce the business products and services. They wish to be fairly treated and compensated and operate the business with a slightly better chance at being part of the next one.

1. *The Production Team*
   The production team puts in the work that produces the products or services for the customer. They are one of the most important pieces of the puzzle who require the most day-to-day management time of the management. Often each member of the Production Team has different needs, but they all want two main things:

   - *To feel that they are making an important contribution.*
   - *To operate the business with slightly better prospects of being chosen for the next one* (or a better job). This means that they must be developed in the form of training. New knowledge, skills, and additions to a portfolio are not a nice-to-have bonus, rather they are a necessity that is integral to business success.

2. *Suppliers*
   Most businesses have suppliers who provide resources in the form of equipment, materials, or tools to allow it to achieve its goals. These suppliers have two main desires:

   - *To be paid fairly for their products and services*
   - *To serve the business with a slightly better chance at receiving work in future projects (i.e., a good reference)*

3. *Contractors*
   Contractors are similar to suppliers, but they involve a manpower component. For that reason, contractors have the same needs as suppliers with the exception of one additional one. Their needs are:

Building Relationships

- *To be paid fairly for their products and services*
- *To be treated fairly and with respect*
- *To serve the business so as to have a slightly better chance at receiving work on future projects (i.e., a good reference)*

Stakeholder Analysis

Before a business can consider the needs and expectations of its stakeholders in the course of its planning, it must identify those stakeholders and sort them in their order of importance to the business.

One method to accomplish this is to list the stakeholders and then determine the degree of their interest and influence in the business. If stakeholders have a high degree of interest, the business needs to communicate with them on a regular basis and keep them informed about its activities. The business also needs to keep them placated.

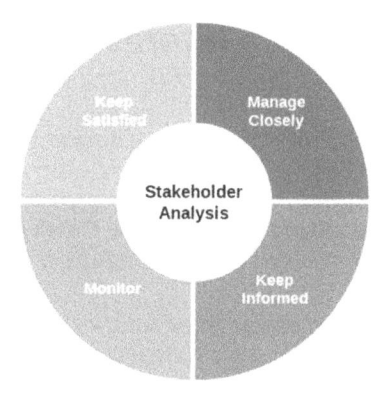

Prioritising Stakeholders

Having produced a list of people and organisations that are affected by your work. Some of these may have the power either to block that work or to advance it. Some may be interested in what you are doing, while others may not care, so you need to work out who you need to prioritise.

You can map out your stakeholders, and classify them according to their power over your work and their interest in it, on a Power/Interest Grid

Building Relationships

```
High ↑
        |
  Power |   Keep Satisfied    |    Manage Closely
        |---------------------|---------------------
        |       Monitor       |    Keep Informed
        |   (Minimum Effort)  |
  Low   |_____|_____→
        Low        Interest              High
```

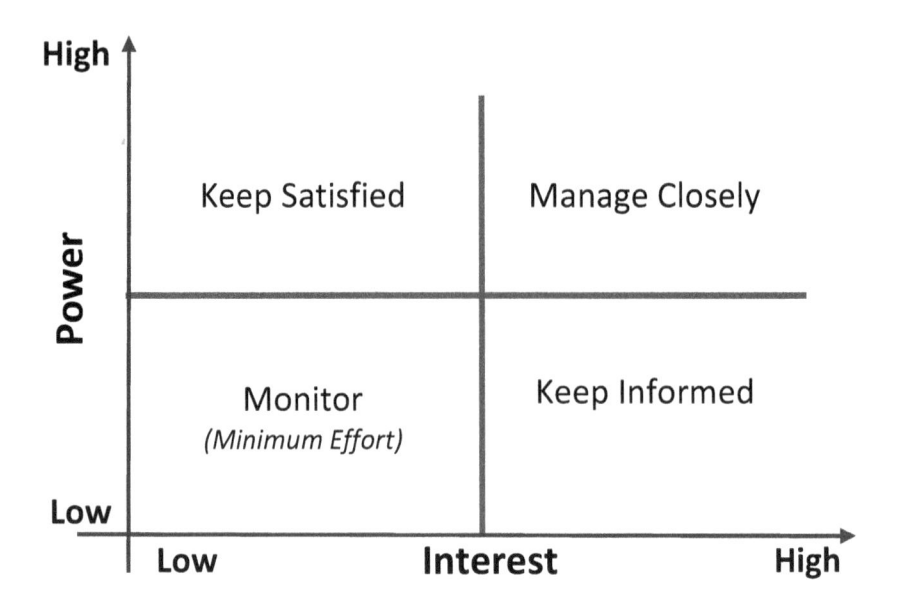

The position that you allocate to a stakeholder on the grid shows you the actions you need to take with them:

- **High power, highly interested people (Manage Closely):** *you must fully engage these people and make the greatest efforts to satisfy them.*

- **High power, less interested people (Keep Satisfied):** *put enough work in with these people to keep them satisfied, but not so much that they become bored with your message.*

- **Low power, highly interested people (Keep Informed):** *adequately inform these people and talk to them to ensure that no major issues are arising. People in this category can often be very helpful with the detail of your project.*

- **Low power, less interested people (Monitor):** *again, monitor these people, but do not bore them with excessive communication.*

Building Relationships

Stakeholder Management

Managing stakeholder relationships is paramount to success. To ensure an effective relationship can be established and developed, understand the emotions of stakeholders and what is important to them is key. As emotions run behaviours, it is necessary to understand the drivers of any stakeholder. To this end you must accept that the emotions of stakeholders are important. It should be understood that facts and figures alone will not determine the outcome of a discussion or a decision. Feelings are just as important in many decisions will be made based on how stakeholder feels about the facts, the project and the people involved.

Key elements of stakeholder management

There are several actions that you can take to manage stakeholder relationships effectively:

- *communicate*
- *plan*
- *consult*
- *show empathy*
- *mitigate risks*
- *negotiating compromise*
- *recognise successes*
- *take ownership*

Businesses will enter into a contract to supply their stakeholders with the service or product, whether that contract is verbal, or implied as in identified in the sale of goods act or written and qualified in a service level agreement (SLA). It will include:

- *the quality of the service or product*
- *a reasonable cost of the service or products be provided*
- *a reasonable timescale for the provision of the service or product*

The agreement, or offer, is understood, agreed, and expected by the provider and the customer. Thus, most methods of meeting the stakeholder's expectations of qualified, understood and agreed upon prior to the exchange of payment for goods or services.

With any stakeholder, the offer must be constantly reviewed in terms of meeting the stakeholder's requirements by,

- *measured in monitoring the offer*
- *predicting potential changes (required by the stakeholder)*
- *seeking to continually improve the offer*

The next logical step would be to identify how the business and its function impact on the various stakeholders and from this it would be possible to determine the priority allocated to

Building Relationships

each stakeholder, recognising of course that depending on the circumstances, those priorities are likely to alter (be dynamic).

There will be occasions when one stakeholder will assume priority over another, and the situation may well reverse later. It is all too easy to prioritise the stakeholder who complains the loudest and most often when the product or service is not within their expectations, or the one who you feel will benefit you or the business the most. However, it is important to acknowledge the views of all stakeholders and manage their needs, expectations, and views appropriately.

Everyone, even businesses, can become complacent, and believe that what they are doing now is sufficient and as the stakeholder is not making a fuss than they must be supplying a more than satisfactory product or service. The competent operation/departmental manager and business would be well advised to prudent periodically check the offer to the stakeholders to ensure their satisfaction. Perhaps the first the business will know of the stakeholder's dissatisfaction is when they cease to be a stakeholder. How often have you complained, or more likely, just walked away and sourced a different product or service provider?

Benefits and Challenges of Stakeholder Management

The benefits of working with stakeholders are many, however, they do need to be closely managed to ensure that everyone is pulling in the same direction. Disagreements and disparity between stakeholders will lead to conflict which could have a severely detrimental effect on the business.

Benefit: Business Experience

Internal stakeholders with a large, vested interest in a business often sit on the board of directors. This stakeholder's value is partially his business experience and partially his book of business relationships. The business acumen an experienced business leader has is highly beneficial for a business owner. Not only can the stakeholder offer mentoring advice, but the stakeholder can also help guide the company to grow properly and not make costly mistakes along the way.

Challenge: Representing own Interests

There are times when stakeholders are focused on their own interests. This is common but not exclusive to external stakeholders. Often, external stakeholders are community groups or political appointees who might not act in a company's best interest if the company is not offering anything that helps the stakeholder with his constituents. Even an internal stakeholder, such as an inexperienced investor, might vote against a proposal for growth in fear of losing money. He is focused on his own financial needs and not on the needs of the business.

Building Relationships

Benefit: Anticipate Potential Problems
Stakeholders help a business owner anticipate things that might go wrong. Stakeholders often come from a variety of backgrounds and levels of experience, which help them see a bigger picture that a business owner might not see. This is one reason that some small businesses owners bring an accountant or a lawyer onto the board of directors so they might be able to foresee potential legal or financial issues. It is also possible that a stakeholder has experience with a potential vendor the company needs and can provide valuable first-hand testimony to working with the vendor.

Challenge: Block Progress
Blocking progress is also frequently found when external stakeholders fear that a business' actions will harm their interests. A university might not want a medical marijuana centre within a specific proximity to the campus. The university is the external stakeholder and might be able to petition to block business permits for the business.

Business owners should anticipate problems like this and have a plan to appease external stakeholders that have concerns about the business. Smart business owners approach potentially antagonistic stakeholders before a problem starts, and then they build a relationship to take a disadvantage and make it an advantage.

By having a good working relationship with Stakeholders, you might expect the following benefits:

- **Fewer surprises.** How many times have you been caught off guard by a stakeholder? A powerful individual, out of the blue, entered your project world and exerted his or her influence in ways that caused rework and additional cost, resulting in team morale issues.
- **Better understanding of needs.** Businesses are unique endeavours resulting in a unique product, service, or result. Unique means we are creating something new or modifying existing products and services. Certain individuals, teams, and organisations will be impacted. Each of these stakeholders has needs. The best managers identify and seek to understand those needs early in the process.
- **Better understanding of concerns**. Stakeholders also have concerns. Ask them and they will tell you about potential events or conditions that may hinder your progress. Other stakeholders can explain how the project may impact their roles and responsibilities.
- **Time invested in the right places.** You may be a hard-working manager, working late evenings and weekends. The question is: Are you working on the right things? With the stakeholder's input and regular feedback, you can ensure that you are working on things that have the greatest value to the business
- **Happier stakeholders.** Any chance that you will make all the stakeholders happy? Probably not. However, you will have a much better chance of keeping stakeholders happy and satisfied if they are properly involved in your business. Less stress for your stakeholders translates into less stress for you as the manager.
- **Improved communication**. Stakeholder management includes the identification of your stakeholders and seeking to understand their preferences. Armed with this stakeholder information, project managers can develop a better communications plan.

Building Relationships

- *Better management of expectations.* Individuals, groups, or organisations believe that certain things are going to happen in the future, based on gossip, hearsay, and a few facts. Competent managers seek to understand and to shape the stakeholder's expectations, guarding against costly false expectations.

As important as stakeholders can be to the success of a business, they can often impact operations for a variety of reasons:

- *Looking out for number one.* Perhaps it is only human nature for people to often place their own interests above those of the business they claim to support. Whenever the issues of money and power intersect, even the best-intentioned individuals can make or force decisions that protect their own pocketbooks or their standing with their own constituents.
- *Standing in the way of progress.* People are often wary of change, and in today's business climate, change is happening at a breath-taking pace. Communication and technological advances are radically affecting relationships between individuals, companies and even countries. For instance, labour and management are often at conflict on key issues, from the impact of globalisation on workers' rights to the effect of automation on jobs traditionally performed by human workers.
- *Fearing Failure.* Factors that can contribute to a party interfering with a business' operation out of a fear that things will not work out is an issue. This is caused by a lack of effective communication in which parties are not kept abreast of developments, creating a lack of control over key decisions, or limiting the responsibilities and power of interests used in exerting a large amount of influence.

As a consequence, it is clear there are merits and demerits in the association, although there is an inevitability about is as there would be no business without stakeholders!

The solution is to produce a Stakeholder Engagement policy and stick to it.

Social responsibility
Identifying and engaging with stakeholders is key for socially responsible investors and result in improved relationships. With social responsibility at the core of their values, it is vital that you keep this in mind and engage accordingly.

Risk management
An active relationship with stakeholders that involves ongoing dialogue allows companies to anticipate any potential problems or issues. If an issue can be detected early, it can be mitigated perhaps before it even becomes a problem.

Solution orientation
Dialogue also allows companies to be part of the solution in terms of any issues that may arise and reduces the risk of negative exposure.

Innovation
Sustainable business practices are increasingly in demand by consumers—being ahead of this trend is beneficial to public image and could potentially open new markets. By being

Building Relationships

ahead of the curve and generating a solid stakeholder engagement policy, your company will position itself as a thought leader and will have influence in your industry.

Proven results
Measurable results and testimonials can not only lead to good exposure for your company, but you will also be able to present to your stakeholders how you have engaged with them and the good that has come out of it.

Positive exposure
Practicing sustainable business often leads to praise from stakeholders (who have often changed their perspective on the proponent of a project and the company), which can lead to enhanced employee morale.

Limiting Stakeholder Conflict

The following are suggestions of steps to take to limit conflict and promote harmony between stakeholders and the business

- *Provide all stakeholders with full opportunities to share their views, needs and knowledge on business*
- *Build consensus through bringing together a diverse range of stakeholders to share needs, information, ideas, and knowledge and harmonise the objectives of individual groups to reach common societal goals*
- *Provide all stakeholders and the public with appropriate information so that they can understand the process, the issues, and values*
- *Enable participants to influence the outcome by including them in the process of risk assessment as well as in the processes of shaping, developing, identifying, and implementing business strategies*
- *Enhance understanding between stakeholder groups, thus reducing potential conflicts and promoting effective cooperation*
- *Build stakeholders commitment and a feeling of ownership to enhance the effectiveness of flood management strategies and individual flood management measures*
- *Ensure implementation of business management plans with full public support*
- *Increase sustainability of plans and associated decisions*
- *Build resilience in local communities*
- *Bring autonomy and flexibility in decision-making and implementation*

Building Relationships

Working with Stakeholders

Working with stakeholders can be an important factor guaranteeing the success of your organisation.

You should, however, think carefully about how you involve stakeholders in the running of the organisation, ensuring that individuals who have responsibility for the organisation have the appropriate freedom to make decisions while allowing stakeholders the opportunity to contribute.

In legal terms, stakeholders can be thought of in three categories: constitutional stakeholders, contractual stakeholder, and third-party stakeholders.

Constitutional stakeholders
In most organisations there are two main constitutional stakeholders; the shareholders and the individuals who sit on the board of the organisation.

In law, shareholders generally have the powers to amend its constitution, to change its name, to wind it up and to appoint and remove individuals to the board of the organisation. In most organisations shareholders also have the right to receive a return from the organisation. Others, particularly charities, are generally prevented from paying any benefits to members.

Sometimes the word "members" is used for individuals who do not have any constitutional rights but simply have a contractual right to receive certain benefits from an organisation. These benefits might include access to a stately home or a newsletter. It is important that organisations maintain a clear understanding of the different types of membership.

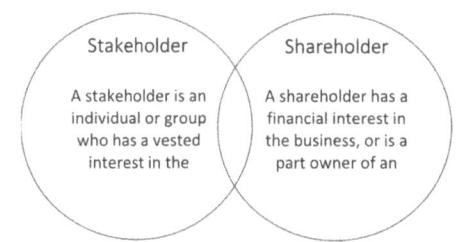

Stakeholder: A stakeholder is an individual or group who has a vested interest in the

Shareholder: A shareholder has a financial interest in the business, or is a part owner of an

Contractual stakeholders
This category includes staff, funders, and customers. These are all individuals and organisations that have a formal relationship with the organisation. Sometimes it may be appropriate to add to it, for example, some organisations are staff co-operatives (Co-operatives UK refer to this as 'worker co-operatives') so that all staff are also members.

Third party stakeholders
This category can include everyone else affected by your organisation. This might include neighbouring businesses, the local authority or people who live locally.

Building Relationships

Pros and Cons of stakeholder involvement

PROS
- Giving stakeholders a sense of ownership can encourage them to support the enterprise.
- Involving employees can be good for staff morale and reduce staff turnover.
- Closer engagement can help with raising finance from stakeholders.
- Services can be better tailored to user/customer needs when there is a greater opportunity for direct input and/or feedback.

CONS
- Decision-making can be slower because a wider group of people need to be consulted.
- Stakeholder representatives may find it difficult to reconcile the interests of their stakeholder group with those of the organisation.
- Close involvement with the day-to-day running of the organisation can be a burden for stakeholders.
- Stakeholders may not want to be involved - stakeholder apathy.

Charities, co-operatives, and social enterprises often involve their stakeholders to a greater extent than many private businesses. This can often be a great source of strength to the organisation. However, it is worth giving careful thought to exactly how people can become involved, to ensure the organisation can be run effectively. Stakeholder involvement is not an 'all or nothing' process, and there are several ways in which people can be involved, from being consulted to taking full control of the business. No method is necessarily 'better' or 'worse' than any other, and different levels of involvement will be appropriate for different groups or situations. You can include a wide variety of different methods of involvement in your organisational structure.

Stakeholders and conflicts of interest

Many charities, social enterprise and co-operatives have stakeholders on their boards. Indeed, the Charity Commission encourages this because of the benefits they can bring. However, the charity board members are under a legal duty to act only in the interests of the charity. They cannot make their decisions based on:

their own personal interest
or
their relations with, or loyalty to, another person or organisation.

Building Relationships

From time-to-time board members may find themselves in a situation where the interests of their organisation conflicts with their own personal interest, or the interests of another person or organisation with which they have links. This situation is called a conflict of interest. A conflict of interest automatically exists in the case of most stakeholders who are board members. For example, a board member who is a service user of the charity has a personal interest in the activities of the charity.

Conflicts of interest can also arise with board members appointed by a local Council with financial or other links with the charity, social enterprise or co-operative.

Examples of ways to manage conflicts of interest include:

- *keeping a register of board members' interests*
- *having board members declare any conflict of interest that may arise*
- *having those board members with a conflict of interest leave the board meeting at which the matter is discussed and not taking part in the vote*
- *having only a minority of board members who are also service users/beneficiaries*

It is very important to manage conflicts of interest and comply with your constitution. If conflicts of interest are not properly managed, the decisions of the board may be invalid. If the organisation is a charity, the Charity Commission may also argue that the failure to properly manage conflicts of interest means that the organisation is not demonstrating sufficiently clearly that it is run for public rather than private benefit.

Conflict

MANAGER Wants to raise selling prices to maximise profits	CUSTOMER Will not want to pay more for their goods
OWNER Wants to re-invest profits into the business	SHAREHOLDER Will want the profits shared out to them
OWNER Wants to pay lower wages to their employees to maximise profits	TRADE UNION Trade unions who represent the employees will not be happy with this
OWNER Wants to buy stock from suppliers at minimum prices	SUPPLIER Will want to make maximum profits.

Building Relationships

Stakeholder Engagement

Stakeholder engagement and stakeholder management are arguably the most important ingredients for successful relationship, and yet are often regarded as a fringe activity or one that can be outsourced to business-as-usual functions. Managers depend on people to respond to the outputs and benefits that they deliver.

People will only respond if they are engaged.

The phrase "stakeholder management" implies that these people can be made to respond positively to an organisation, but the truth is that a manager frequently has no formal power of authority and therefore has to rely on engagement to achieve his/her objectives.

Communicate
Before aiming to engage and influence stakeholders, it is crucial to seek to understand the people you will be working with and relying on throughout the phases of the relationship. Sharing information with stakeholders is important, but it is equally important to first gather information about your stakeholders.

Consult, early and often
A relationship, particularly in the early stages, may be unclear to its stakeholders for example, in terms of purpose, scope, risks and approach. Early, then regular consultation is essential to ensure that requirements are agreed and a delivery solution is negotiated that is acceptable to the majority of stakeholders.

Remember, they are only human
Humans do not always behave in a rational, reasonable, consistent, or predictable way and operate with an awareness of human feelings and potential personal agendas. By understanding the root cause of stakeholder behaviour, you can assess if there is a better way to work together to maintain a productive relationship

Plan it!
A more conscientious and measured approach to stakeholder engagement is essential and therefore encouraged. Investment in careful planning before engaging stakeholders can bring significant benefits.

Relationships are key
Developing relationships results in increased trust. And where there is trust, people work together more easily and effectively. Investing effort in identifying and building stakeholder relationships can increase confidence across the project environment, minimise uncertainty, and speed problem solving and decision-making.

Simple, but not easy
Over and above conventional planning, using foresight to anticipate hazards, and taking simple and timely actions with stakeholders can significantly improve project delivery. Although this principle is self-evident, in practice is still only rarely done very well.

Building Relationships

Just part of managing risk
Stakeholders are important influential resources and should be treated as potential *sources* of risk and opportunity within the project.

Compromise
The initial step is to establish the most acceptable baseline across a set of stakeholders' diverging expectations and priorities. Assess the relative importance of all stakeholders to establish a weighted hierarchy against the business requirements and agreed by the management.

Understand what success is
Success means different things to different people and you need to establish what your stakeholder community perceives success to be for them in the context of delivery.

Take responsibility
Stakeholder engagement is not the job of one member of the team. It is the responsibility of everyone to understand their role and to follow the right approach to communication and engagement. Good governance requires providing clarity about stakeholder engagement roles and responsibilities and what is expected of people involved in the project.

Planning for stakeholder engagement

A good stakeholder engagement plan contains the following parts:

Stakeholder list / Register
The first step in any stakeholder engagement plan is to list the stakeholders. But it is important to be thorough because it is easy to underestimate the ability of a minor stakeholder to trip up the organisation when they are not being communicated with adequately. The Stakeholder Register fits in here and it is created as part of the Identify Stakeholders process.

Aspects
Many stakeholders will be involved in only certain aspects of the organisation.

Contact name(s)
It is important to be in contact with the correct people. Large organisations or government (regulatory) stakeholders have many layers of bureaucracy which can result in delays when the primary decision maker is not being communicated with directly.

Areas of Influence
This is where the stakeholder's "stake" is defined. How do their interests overlap with the project? What are their business goals and how does your project interfere with them? Why is this stakeholder interested in your business? There can be no meaningful stakeholder engagement without understanding each other's viewpoints.

Building Relationships

Power
Each stakeholder has a unique ability to stop and/or change the organisation. What is that ability? Where does it derive from, and how can it be controlled? Sometimes the stakeholder's power over the organisation can be removed, but this comes at a cost, both monetary and in stakeholder satisfaction (they could become very unhappy and influence other stakeholders).

Engagement approach
The strategy for engaging the stakeholder must be outlined in detail. The types and frequency of communication, for example weekly emails, monthly phone calls, or weekly face to face meetings. The content of those communications, for example a weekly update that contains project progress, design information, and open house plans.

Developing a Stakeholder Engagement Plan

There are five steps to developing a stakeholder engagement plan:

Classify Stakeholders
As an initial step in stakeholder analysis, classifying the stakeholders into defined groups can assist in the next, more detailed steps. Stakeholders can be classified into supporting or opposed, for example, a business investor is a supporter and an environmental action group is opposed. They can be divided into Upwards/Sideways/Outwards/Downwards, for example, upwards are executives from the parent organisation, sideways are suppliers and contractors, outwards are other businesses competing for limited resources and downwards are the delivery team, suppliers, and contractors.

Develop Power/Interest Grid
This is the primary stakeholder analysis tool. It contains the power of the stakeholder on the y-axis, which is the ability of the stakeholder to stop and/or change the project, and the interest level of the stakeholder on the x-axis, which is the amount of overlap the stakeholder's interests have with the project. This defines the stakeholder's "stake" in the project.

Define Power
Although the stakeholder's location on the chart is important, a verbal analysis of the power of the stakeholder is imperative to get a sense of how much influence the stakeholder has. For example, a government regulatory agency usually has extremely high power to stop the business – they can withhold their approval and stop the project immediately. The success of the business is heavily dependent on keeping them informed on an ongoing basis.

Define Interest
Once again, the location of the stakeholder on the chart is expanded and analysed to determine what their interest in the business really is. The stakeholder's business interests are analysed and prioritised. Their needs and wants are described to a point where the stakeholder is well understood by the management team.

Building Relationships

Develop the Stakeholder Communication Plan
The stakeholder communication needs are itemised based on the power and influence analysis. The type of communication and its frequency is specified. The other parts of the stakeholder engagement plan are more administrative in nature.

Developing a strategy for Stakeholders

Certain decisions made by organisations will affect and be of interest to many different stakeholder groups. For example, if a council wanted to build a memorial to honour local war veterans, they may consult relatives about the project, collaborate with a local sculptor on the design and inform the media to help promote its launch.

But not all stakeholder groups are created equal. Some may need to be kept updated daily on developments, while others only require occasional contact.

A stakeholder engagement strategy will help you plan how often you need to communicate with the different groups and decide which tools to use for each one.

Importance of Stakeholder Engagement

The stakeholder engagement plan is the foundation for achieving stakeholder buy-in for the project.

Of course, the plan must be tailored to the size of the business, as with all parts of the Business management plan. For the smallest possible business, where one person writes a report for one sponsor, a written stakeholder engagement plan is probably not necessary. But the concept is still present – the single stakeholder must be managed in order to achieve their buy-in.

For large businesses, such as infrastructure projects, stakeholder engagement is a major undertaking. The many stakeholders all have different needs and wants, and their power and interest in the project are all unique, requiring specialised consultation requirements. The stakeholder engagement plans are given to the management team, and potentially the parent

Building Relationships

organisation for approval prior to implementation. The plans are then put into action and the project management team are continuously updated regarding the status of each stakeholder.

Improving Stakeholder Engagement

For businesses that need it, detailed stakeholder engagement plans are indispensable. But often the secret to success is in the continuous improvement of the stakeholder consultation process rather than in rigid adherence to a plan. That is, there is a creative component rather than a purely analytical one.

In that spirit, the following three steps to improve stakeholder engagement for all projects:

Show the stakeholder you care
Stakeholders understand that someone wants to win them over, and that the organisation probably has a plan to do just that. Believe me, there are many, many projects out there where organisations have engaged stakeholders with an aggressive, empathy-free attitude attempting to strong arm the stakeholder into project approval. This tends to drive stakeholders further into their trenches and develop their opposition. Even if you have the power to stop their concerns, they often exercise their right to spread bad word of mouth, which takes enormous amounts of time and money to neutralise. A little bit of empathy costs nothing but accomplishes great strides in addressing project opposition.

Emphasise the human aspect
Private sector projects are undertaken by organisations that hope to enhance their bottom line, to increase their profits. Government and public organisations also have goals that sometimes overlap with stakeholders with conflicting interests. But it is not only about the money. Even private sector projects have a societal benefit – the employment of the staff, that is, the business is a crucial piece in the generation of prosperity to society. In other words, there are people on both sides. Stakeholders should be consulted in a way that communicates the benefits to society rather than purely increasing investor profits. Of course, some businesses might be structured so as to be excessively profit driven at someone else's expense, in which case the management team needs to ask themselves if they need to change their plan.

Give stakeholders a voice
More than anything else, people want to be heard. It is amazing what type of transformation takes place when a stakeholder is allowed to voice their concerns and realises that it is being heard. But therein lies the rub. Most stakeholders are well attuned to the possibility that they will be listened to and ignored.

The transformation occurs when they truly believe that the management team has considered their concerns and tried very hard to implement them. And this belief is not accomplished by the development and rigid implementation of a plan.

Building Relationships

Role of the manager in managing stakeholder relationships

The role of the manager is paramount to the success of the relationship with the shareholder. The following list defines the key areas to which all managers should be attuned

Clearly communicate the scope of the business
Tell stakeholders the process you will use to communicate information to them right from the start. Also, clearly explain how you will engage with them in decisions. People are more willing to listen when you tell them their influence over the final outcome, the decision-making process, what is negotiable and what is not.

Gain the trust of stakeholders right from the start
Stakeholder relationship management includes communicating with people early and often, so they fully understand the benefits of your project. Understanding a situation means people are more likely to support you when necessary. It also means even if stakeholders do not agree with the final decision, they have the benefit of understanding the process, history and the trade-offs made. Therefore, they will be less likely to aggressively object at the final stage.

Stay consistent with your messaging
Confusing stakeholders is incredibly dangerous. Inconsistent messaging can lead to public outrage, loss in trust, and a negative reputation. Stakeholders value consistent messaging and want to know they can rely on you for the most current and up-to-date information. If there is a hurdle to overcome, your stakeholder will be more willing to help overcome the problem rather than blame the issue for coming up.

Meet stakeholders who are resistant to change
All projects will include people who love, hate, or want to shape or want to mould the project idea. It is our job to find a way to balance these differing views. One of the worst things that can happen is you have gone through your engagement process, made a final decision and then you receive angry phone calls and emails about the project outcomes. To prevent this from happening, it is important to regularly meet with key stakeholders who are resistant to change. The meeting could be in person, by email or through a phone-call. Involving stakeholders in decisions and listening to concerns re-emphasises the benefits of the potential change.

In the instance where stakeholders are resistant to change, it is important to discuss the project scope. Some things are not negotiable and it is important to show stakeholders what influence they do have to shape the project.

Use data management systems to summarise key information
It all comes down to the power of reflection. If you have a meeting with a stakeholder then write a summary of the event. What was the meeting about? What were the key findings? Are there any actions? When is the next meeting? Use your data management system to its full potential.

Keep surprises to a minimum
Some of us love surprises but placing your stakeholders off-guard can result in a huge mistake and can cost you from building positive stakeholder relationships. Most

Building Relationships

stakeholders like to be given an early view of risks and issues. However, this does not mean you need to present every issue as it occurs. Go into the meeting solutions-based rather than problem-focused. Create various options to resolve the issue and then ask stakeholders to add their input to create an informed decision about the next step.

Collaborating with Stakeholders

A collaborative team is a slightly different version of a traditional team because its members have differing skill sets. Although the members have varying areas of expertise, they still share similar goals, resources, and leadership. With their diverse set of specialised skills, they should be able to problem-solve as a group.

Collaborative leaders can span the scope of your business by engaging stakeholders outside of their direct control and getting them to work as a team with a common goal. When businesses talk about collaboration, they mean stakeholders at all levels all of whom have a stake in the outcome.

This strategy is more about facilitating the group effort than about making decisions for the group. In other words, a collaborative leader leads the group's process, not the group itself.

Therefore, when we talk about collaboration itself, we are talking about problem-solving with a group of people with different skillsets. However, what makes this type of group work compelling and successful can also make it fail. Different skill sets often come attached to people who think differently from each other, which can make communication among them difficult. Moreover, they frequently possess different priorities, which can cause surges of disagreement.

A big part of collaboration is coordination. Coordination is about achieving efficiency and about telling participants how and when they must act. This concept is similar to collaboration and teamwork because its goals are the same. Of course, cooperation is an integral element of teamwork, collaboration, and coordination. Cooperation usually consists of two or more people sharing ideas or activities. You often share the information you generate from cooperation - while it is sometimes required, it is an informal process. Compared with teamwork, collaboration, and coordination, cooperation is the activity that requires the least amount of shared purpose and dependence on team members.

Communication is another key element of working together. It is the well-mannered approach to the workplace, requiring all members to talk to each other. It involves interacting in whatever way works best for you and your team personality and relationship-wise.

Stakeholder collaboration means working together with stakeholders from across the business to achieve a shared goal. Although similar to teamwork, a collaborative partnership is not hierarchical – everyone has equal status, no matter their seniority (though you may elect one person to organise the collaborative project)

Level 5: Operations / Departmental Manager

Building Relationships

Collaboration a great way to encourage stakeholders to share knowledge and resources. You can use it to pool your negotiating power, to coordinate strategies, or to create new products, for instance.
Second, it can provide great opportunities for cross-skilling and networking and can even improve engagement levels. One study shows that people who work collaboratively stick to their tasks 64 percent longer than those who work alone.

There are a two main types of collaboration, depending on what you hope to achieve. These are:

Open collaboration.
You invite people from inside or outside the business to generate ideas or to solve a problem. Open collaborations work best for big, wide-ranging challenges as they allow anyone to respond. This enables you to access a diverse spectrum of opinion and expertise.

Closed collaboration.
Closed modes work best when you have a specific problem to solve which requires specialist skills or knowledge. As a result, closed collaborative groups tend to be much smaller than open ones.

Both of these types of collaboration are suitable for use with stakeholders allowing access to their skills, knowledge, and network, to resolve issues within the organisation.

Other types of collaboration include:

Cross-functional collaboration. *This involves working with people who have different job functions (marketing, technology, or customer service, for instance) to achieve a common goal.*

Cross-cultural collaboration. *Here, you work with people from other countries or cultures to learn more about different markets and encourage innovation.*

Virtual collaboration. *Apps like Skype™, Slack™, Asana™ and Google Docs™ have made it easier than ever for people to come together and collaborate, even if they work in different offices or countries.*

Once again, all of these can be used to foster stakeholder collaboration and reap the benefits and rewards of the combined knowledge, expertise, and experience which the collectively hold.
Stakeholder collaboration can bring huge benefits to any organisation if it is managed correctly. While good collaboration can result in new and creative ideas and discoveries, poor collaboration can be more damaging than no collaboration at all – it can waste time, energy, money, and resources. It is therefore vital that stakeholder collaboration is carefully managed and controlled to avoid it becoming toxic to the organisation.

When planning collaborative working with stakeholders, consider the following:

Building Relationships

Define the Purpose
First and foremost, you need to have a strong shared purpose. Only when you know what you are working toward can productive collaboration begin.

So, before you set up a collaborative working, take some time to identify and clarify what you want the group to achieve. This will give people focus and direction.

Choose Open or Closed Collaboration
Your choice will depend on the problem that you need to solve. If you want to get ideas for a new product, for instance, you might want to invite responses from stakeholders across the business, as well as your customers. If this is the case, open collaboration will likely be the most suitable.

A great example of successful open collaboration is Lego's Create and Share website. It allows Lego community members to share their designs with each other and the company. When support for an idea reaches 10,000, the company then evaluates it and produces it under its Lego Ideas label.

In contrast, if your purpose is to perfect a product or process that requires specialist knowledge, closed collaboration will likely work best. This is because you will need to limit the number of collaborators to only those who have specialist knowledge of the topic.

For instance, if you wanted to improve the efficiency of your production line, you might choose to collaborate with those stakeholders who have production experience as well as an external machinery designer. This will ensure that you get exactly what you want and may even result in a new innovation that gives you an edge on your competition.

Involve the Right People

Once you have set your goals, you need to identify the people who are best placed to achieve them. This is particularly important when you use closed collaboration.

Think about stakeholders who have relevant expertise, experience, and skills, or who are good at challenging assumptions and can contribute different perspectives.

Although collaboration is about equal participation, it can be useful to appoint someone to organise and lead the project so that it stays on track. Assign roles within the group of stakeholders too. Research has shown that this encourages stakeholders to take responsibility, and avoids time being wasted on negotiating responsibilities or "protecting turf."

Achieve "Buy-In"
While some stakeholders will jump at the chance to collaborate, others may not be so keen. They might see it as an imposition on their time and be worried about the extra work or stress that it could bring.

Building Relationships

Before asking someone to collaborate, think about how it can benefit him or her as well as the organisation. Identifying the wider strategic goal, like fine-tuning a process to increase income, can be persuasive, but so can outlining the personal benefits to individual collaborators, such as recognition, the opportunity to learn new skills and improving career progression.

Encourage Collaborative Behaviour
Collaboration can demand a lot from people. It means being open-minded, listening to other people's opinions and putting personal agendas to one side. So, it is essential that you try to encourage collaboration across your stakeholders and the organisation. This can be achieved by:

Leading by example. People watch how you act. If you are not afraid to listen to new ideas and offer solutions – even when it makes you vulnerable – you will encourage others to do the same.

Building trust. Collaboration can stall when people do not feel able to open up. Combat this by setting up team building activities and encouraging stakeholders to give honest and constructive feedback. This will help to strengthen stakeholder team bonds, to create a sense of shared responsibility and to give people the confidence to speak up.

Fostering a creative culture. Creative thinking underpins good collaboration. It can help to drive innovation and allows you to avoid groupthink. Encourage this behaviour by making use of creativity tools and processes.

The Pitfalls of Poor Collaboration

You might find that collaborative efforts come from the same stakeholders, time, and time again. In fact, research suggests that 20 percent to 35 percent of value-added collaborations come from only 3 percent to 5 percent of stakeholders.

Be careful not to rely too heavily on these "extra milers " – stakeholders who go that "extra mile" to help out and consistently work to make improvements. If you do this, it can lead to stakeholders taking on too much and becoming overwhelmed. This is known "collaborative overload" or "generosity burnout."

To avoid this, break down barriers that prevent more people from collaborating – silos, for example, or "that's-not-how-we-do-it-here " attitudes. Also, allow and expect stakeholders to say "no" to your collaboration requests, and recognise and reward people when they make positive contributions.

Collaboration is a key factor in building relationships with stakeholders because it works. People thrive in environments which free them to communicate and work together. When the company environment is focused on collaboration, all stakeholders naturally feel a part of something bigger than themselves. The best way to transition from an individual to a collaborative mindset is to afford each stakeholder the opportunity for active participation in the organisation dynamic.

Building Relationships

Building Collaborative Working with Stakeholders

The following are constructive ways to engender collaborative working across stakeholders and the organisation

Create a clear and compelling cause.
To create cohesion, stakeholders must be provided with a convincing reason to be a part of the company mission. The more compelling and exciting the mission, the easier it is to inspire stakeholders to want to be a part of what the company aspires to accomplish. When they are given a clear and gripping cause to be involved with, stakeholders naturally become as passionate about the goals and objectives as the leaders. If stakeholders do not care or are unclear about the goals and objectives presented to them, they will find all kinds of reasons not to work together. For collaboration to work, the vision and purpose must be clear.

Communicate expectations.
Collaboration must be communicated to Stakeholders as the minimum standard. To foster this, stakeholders must be provided with defined individual and collective roles and responsibilities they will hold within the team. When they have a clear understanding of their position, each stakeholder will work more effectively and without accidentally stepping on another person's toes creating unforeseen conflicts. In a collaborative environment, each stakeholder experiences what it means to take part in the shared responsibility of results. With this type of focus, what starts out as a goal becomes a crusade with the experience of success changing from an individual achievement into a bonded group experience building camaraderie and morale.

Establish goals.
To drive success in stakeholders it is important to set measurable goals for each on a quarterly basis. The purpose of these goals is to provide stakeholders with achievable wins. These wins have a magical way of breaking down barriers and creating positive momentum individually and collectively. Furthermore, it is imperative to re-evaluate goals and redirect whenever necessary. At each quarter's end, the outcomes of quarterly goals must be made available as a way to measure and celebrate progress, and to determine where improvements need to be made. Working with this type of transparency decreases confusion, finger-pointing, and the disintegration of stakeholder cohesion.

Leverage stakeholder strengths.
To empower each stakeholder, it is a great strategy to work with their strengths rather than working around their weaknesses. It is a good idea to have each member take a personality test such as the Myers-Briggs and hold a team roundtable to share results. This is a great bonding exercise because the results allow each person to get to know themselves and their fellow stakeholders in a much deeper way. It also gives stakeholders information about who to go to and for what, based upon each person's individual strengths. When stakeholders are connected in this way, each member is set up for success because they are each assigned tasks that play to their respective strengths.

Foster cohesion.
Cohesive teams are more successful. They are successful because each person on the team is included in as many large decisions as possible. When stakeholders feel this type of

Building Relationships

inclusion, they feel the perceived significance of their role, causing them to naturally perform better. To be the most effective, stakeholders should participate in regular "huddles" where each member discusses their goals and objectives for period. This helps to avoid duplication of effort and competition between stakeholders. These huddles keep everyone on the same page and enables stakeholders to re-direct their efforts as needed.

Encourage innovation.
For stakeholder teams to grow, they must be encouraged to brainstorm and question the status quo in an open and non-judgmental environment. Stakeholders must be coached and led to believe the challenges and obstacles they face can and will be overcome. When a "can-do" attitude is instilled, it motivates stakeholders to live up to those "can-do" expectations. It is also important to ask stakeholders for their thoughts, their reasoning, and ideas on a regular basis. The more connected and understood they feel to the organisation, the more motivated they will be to perform, impress, be creative and to exceed expectations.

Keep promises and honour requests.
Most requests and promises are held sacred within a team, but often considered optional between the organisation and its stakeholders. Taking a request from a stakeholder seriously and demonstrating that the organisation is working to do what they say they are going to do, goes a long way towards building trust and blurring boundaries. The question every stakeholder asks of another is, can I count on you? Will you be there when I need you? Do you care about this as much as I do? When the organisation and its stakeholders feel they can depend upon each other, business grows, relationships grow as does revenue.

Encourage stakeholders to socialise outside of work.
We all lead busy personal lives and the thought of having one more corporate event we are obligated to attend can add stress. However, socialising with stakeholders outside the office is an effective way to open channels of communication, to create a better understanding and break down any walls of pre-judgemental or mistrust between stakeholders.

When stakeholders learn they share common interests or wrestle with some of the same challenges outside of work as others, they experience their stakeholders as more real, which helps to decrease individual bias, stereotyping and false objectifying. When we see our stakeholders as human, it makes it more difficult to point the finger at them.

Recognise, reward, and celebrate collaborative behaviour.
The legends of athletic dynasties or standout corporate successes consist of incredible collaborative efforts. Stakeholders often sit in conversation reminiscing over how it all came together. Whether shared through video, newsletter, podcast, annual report or seminar, stories of great collaboration break down the walls of individualism and honour the collective accomplishment. Attaching performance rewards and bonuses to

Building Relationships

collaborative efforts sends the right message to stakeholders about the values that are driving the business.

Establishing a collaborative environment is just the beginning of a more successful venture. For collaboration to work it must be consistent and purposeful, with resources and rewards dedicated to its success. You may have many standout successes in your company already; but you can increase your productivity exponentially by getting stakeholders to work as a collaborative team. When stakeholders feel they are a part of something exceptional they are more than willing to work together to get the ball across the goal line. Collaboration works because there is nothing more meaningful, bonding or growth promoting than a shared win.

Building Relationships

Managing Stakeholder Conflict

There is a conflict between stakeholders raging. Emails are flying and tempers are fraying. Maybe they cannot agree on what requirements should say, or on what solution to implement, or on the project schedule.

Whatever the problem is, you have a big mess on your hands. What do you do?

Types of Conflict

The first step after identifying that a conflict in the requirements has arisen is to determine what is the nature of the conflict. There are a few common types of conflicts that occur which are closely related to the reasons they occur.

The first type of conflict is a "data conflict". This is typically where all stakeholders are not agreeing to a requirement that is specified in a certain way. For example, the business stakeholder might want to retrieve 1000 records at a time in real-time whereas the technology stakeholder knows this is practically impossible and not feasible.

The second type of conflict is a conflict of interest. This type of conflict arises when two or more stakeholders have different priorities or goals within their own business area, which is determining the requirements they are asking for. An example of this could be that the customer services stakeholder is asking to be able to see all personal customer data when supporting a customer on the phone where the company's Data Privacy stakeholder is saying that the personal information of their customers is sensitive and should not be available in its entirety to the customer services representatives.

The third type of conflict is referred to as a "conflict of value". This type of conflict arises when the stakeholders have different values or beliefs about what is acceptable or not acceptable. For example, one stakeholder might believe it is acceptable to ask a customer to enter their cultural heritage, as a mandatory field on the screen during an online application for life insurance whereas the other stakeholder might believe this is an unacceptable request and should only be an optional field for the customer to provide if they choose to.

The fourth type of conflict is referred to as relationship conflict. This is the type of personal relationship conflict where two stakeholders do not get along. This causes some emotional anxiety during requirements meetings and often these types of stakeholders will try and force requirements on to the project purely based on "winning" the conflict with another stakeholder.

The fifth type of conflict is a "structural conflict" which is when a more senior team member or stakeholder continuously rejects the requirements contributions made by their less senior colleagues.

Building Relationships

In most cases the conflicts that arise within the context of requirements management are a combination of these different types of conflicts. It is however important to understand the different types of conflicts to be able to effectively resolve the conflicts.

Sources of Conflict

Before we can resolve conflicts in business, we need to know the reason for the conflict. Research on conflict started in the 1970s and has shown an evolution over the past 30 years that matches the maturing state of management. In 1975, Thamhain and Wilemon identified the following seven potential sources of conflicts in projects (Brown, 2009):

- *Schedule conflict,*
- *Conflict of priorities,*
- *Resource conflict,*
- *Technical conflict,*
- *Conflict over administration,*
- *Personality conflict, and*
- *Cost conflict.*

Harrison and Lock grouped the factors that cause conflicts into the following three classifications (Harrison & Lock, 2004):

- *Structure of the organisation*
- *People's self-interests*
- *Individuals.*

We could then surmise that the source of conflicts may not be as easily determined as we might have once thought. It would appear that, while schedule and costs may always be with us as constraints in business, conflict is centred on the underlying perspectives of the people involved and how they interact. Thus, the motivations of the relevant stakeholders will play a large part in establishing their expectations and will be key to a project manager's strategy in managing any conflicts between those expectations.

> *There are two aspects of motivation for human behaviour: resistance to change, and trust.*

Resistance to Change

Change is at the heart of all business projects. After all, the very nature of projects suggests that something is different at the end from the beginning. If we are producing a tangible product, we assume that someone will then use it. If the project delivers an evaluation of business processes, the expectation is that any recommendations for improvement will be implemented. Stakeholders will react differently to these changes, depending upon how the change affects them.

Building Relationships

Before asking anyone to accept change, we need to understand how they came to be in their current position. From an organisational perspective, knowing why the current culture exists is a prerequisite for determining the potential direction for its evolution. Similarly, if we understand why a person holds a certain view, we can develop insight into how that view could change.

Not everyone will be readily convinced that the resulting changes will benefit them. They may feel emotionally tied to the current state and hesitate from leaping into the new one.

Schuler lists the following ten reasons why people resist change (Schuler, 2003):

1. *The risk of change is seen as greater than the risk of standing still.*
2. *People feel connected to other people who are identified with the old way.*
3. *People have no role models for the new activity.*
4. *People fear they lack the competence to change.*
5. *People feel overloaded and overwhelmed.*
6. *People have a healthy scepticism and want to be sure that new ideas are sound.*
7. *People fear hidden agendas among would-be reformers.*
8. *People feel that the proposed change threatens their notions of themselves.*
9. *People anticipate a loss of status or quality of life.*
10. *People genuinely believe that the proposed change is a bad idea.*

In addition to Schuler's list, resistance can also be due to rational or behavioural reasons.

Regardless of the reasons for any resistance to change, one of the most important means of overcoming the resistance is to listen to the concerns of the relevant stakeholders. These concerns may lend themselves to improvements in project planning, such as risk mitigation. In addition, the management team, in conjunction with the leaders of the organisation, need to clearly explain both the reasons and the urgency for the change, as well as the impact if the change is not accepted. This would be in line with the general role of top management, which is not only to establish goals, both for the organisation and the managers, but to provide guidance and support in meeting the business objectives.

When we communicate effectively with stakeholders, we lay a foundation for trust, which can assist in both preventing and resolving conflicts.

Trust

To satisfy stakeholder expectations, we must first understand what those expectations are. Discovery of both the initial expectations, and any changes in those expectations, often relies upon the existence of a good relationship between the stakeholders, the project manager and/or project team.

Lewis Ireland's first principle for good customer relationships is to develop a sense of trust. If we expand his definition of customers to include all stakeholders, then trust becomes imperative for revealing and managing expectations.

Building Relationships

How do we build trust? Burtonshaw-Gunn, (2008) offers these suggestions:

- *Go first: lead the relationship by example.*
- *Illustrate the topic by drawing on relevant examples.*
- *Listen for what is different, not for what is familiar.*
- *Be sure your advice is being sought.*
- *Say what you mean.*
- *When you need help, ask for it.*
- *Show an interest in the person and what is important to them.*
- *Respect other cultures if different to your own.*
- *Use compliments, not flattery.*
- *Show appreciation.*

Once we have a trusting relationship with stakeholders, we are in a good position to discuss their expectations and to work with them to resolve conflicts regarding these expectations.

One of the key elements in building trust is effective communication. This may be described as "negotiating and influencing (stakeholders') desires to achieve and maintain the goals".

The means of conducting this communication can be achieved through various dimensions, listed as follows

- *Internal and external,*
- *Formal and informal,*
- *Vertical and horizontal,*
- *Official and unofficial,*
- *Written and oral, and*
- *Verbal and nonverbal.*

Consequently, managers can choose from an array of communication methods to convey messages, elicit feedback, and work to resolve differences, directly or indirectly (such as through project team members or other stakeholders).

This kind of situation shows why "soft skills" like negotiation and diplomacy are so important for a manager. You will often encounter situations where you are expected to broker a solution between warring parties.

Listen, do not speak.

Sometimes it is best to *just be quiet*. One of the things most likely to escalate a conflict is having a stakeholder feel like nobody is listening. When a stakeholder is talking with you as

Building Relationships

the manager, they may feel like trying to convince you that they are right. Just listen to what they have to say.

Then show them you understand and have heard them loud and clear. A helpful tactic is to "reflect" the content of what they said back to them, which shows them that you "get it." You could say: *"Let me make sure I understand what you're saying. You said [insert what they said, in your own words.]."* This is also known as active listening.

You will often get a calmer stakeholder because you have communicated that you understand 100% of the point they are trying to make. Sometimes that is enough to start a dialogue about resolving the conflict.

Provide a forum for resolution of the conflict.
Sometimes the way to manage conflicts between stakeholders is to let them "duke it out" (respectfully, of course.) You can call a meeting of stakeholders together to allow everyone an opportunity to air their views.

During such a meeting you will play the role of facilitator, and perhaps help smooth ruffled feathers. Keeping the discussion civil is key. Again, make sure everyone has an opportunity to feel heard.

You should also make sure the meeting continues being productive and driving towards a resolution. If people seem stuck, you can employ one of the other strategies listed here to see if you can get to the solution. Otherwise, people may need to separate for a while and think about the issues before getting back together to resolve the problem.

Look for the win-win.
When things seem stuck at an impasse, it is time to put your knowledge of the business domain to work. Try to find a way out of the conflict that provides each of the stakeholders at least some of what they are looking for. The more the better.

Get each of the stakeholders to prioritise the most important things they want to get out of a resolution to the conflict. Find the areas of agreement and see if you can cobble together a compromise.

A win-win situation is likely to have some "loss-loss" for the arguing stakeholders too. Neither party is going to get everything they wanted. Where possible, explain how the upsides of a win-win approach beat the downsides, or how the downsides can be managed or mitigated.

Bend the laws of reality.
Sometimes, what is needed is to change one of the "laws of reality." (Hey, we already knew that managers are superheroes, right?)

Every organisation has a series of "laws" that govern how it does business. They generally revolve around time and schedule, money, and availability of staff. Conflicts between stakeholders can arise when you are unable to meet conflicting needs while still following these "laws" of the organisation.

Building Relationships

If you can, look for ways to change these "laws of reality" in some way to help resolve the problem. If the conflict is over which resource to pay for when the business can only pay for one, is it possible to get the money to pay for both?

These "laws" will NOT be easy to change if it is possible at all. Either you or the affected stakeholders may need to appeal to upper management to approve the proposed change. But it may be worth a shot, depending on your organisation.

Advocate but do not choose sides.
Whatever you do, do not choose sides, or appear to do so. Doing so will cause one of your stakeholders to feel betrayed, and you definitely do not want that. It could permanently affect your relationship with the individual.

If you have a point of view or a proposed way forward, by all means feel free to advocate for that view. But you should always make clear that the final decision is for the stakeholders to make, and your job is to help bring things to closure.

Get help.
If all else fails and people are still yelling at each other, it is time to escalate. Eventually this becomes a job for someone who has the power to compel a decision one way or the other.

You should only do this as a last resort. Consider conflicts between stakeholders as a way of honing your negotiating skills and becoming a master of conflict resolution. But no matter how experienced you are, sometimes you just need intervention to break the logjam.

When that happens, try to keep the escalation as quick and painless as possible. When senior management gets brought in to resolve conflicts between stakeholders, they may ask you to explain what is going on. Staying as neutral as possible makes it likelier to keep stakeholders friendly to you. When the ruling comes down from above, close the subject and move on.

Building Relationships

Conflict Resolution Techniques

Agreement
Agreement is when the stakeholders work together to negotiate a solution to the conflict. This involves discussion of each other's views in order to try to persuade people experiencing the conflict to agree a workable solution.

Compromise
This technique is about using alternative parts of various solutions to try and come up with a solution that could be a compromise for all stakeholders but an acceptable solution to go forward with.

Voting
This technique is simply to ask all stakeholders involved with the requirements and/or the conflict itself to vote on a set of alternative options for a solution. The solution with the most votes is accepted as the resolution for the conflict.

Definition of Variants
This technique is a way that is selected to develop the solution where the different stakeholders can apply their own variants to the solution as parameters. This way the different stakeholders get their preferred solution implemented.

Overruling
This technique is aligned with the organisational hierarchy. The more senior stakeholder's requirements or proposed solution is the one that will be taken forward as the resolution.

Consider all facts (CAF)
This technique is about collecting all facts and influencing factors relating to the requirements that are in conflict. These facts and factors are then prioritised in readiness to be used as an input into the "Plus-Minus-Interesting" or PMI technique.

Plus-Minus-Interesting or PMI
With this technique all the positive and negative repercussions of a solution alternative is being analysed. Two categories, one for Plus and one for Minus are developed in order to list the Positives and Negatives. When a fact or factor is neither a positive nor a negative item, it is placed in the interesting column.

Decision Matrix
This technique to resolve a requirements conflict comprises of a comparison matrix of all key criteria that needs to be considered against each solution alternative. By compiling this comparison information in a matrix format, it often highlights which is the best solution to choose. This therefore resolves any conflicts with the collated information provided.

Building Relationships

Thomas-Kilmann Conflict Mode Instrument

The Thomas-Kilmann Conflict Mode Instrument assesses an individual's behaviour in conflict situations—that is, situations in which, two people's interests appear to be incompatible.

In conflict situations, we can describe a person's behaviour along two basic dimensions:

(1) assertiveness, the extent to which the individual attempts to satisfy his or her own concerns, and
(2) cooperativeness, the extent to which the individual attempts to satisfy the other person's concerns.

These two dimensions of behaviour can be used to define five modes of dealing with conflict. They also provide detailed information on how to use these different conflict-handling styles effectively.

These five conflict-handling modes are shown below:

Dealing With Conflict

```
Assertiveness ↑
              |   Competing              Collaborating
              |
              |           Compromising
              |
              |   Avoiding              Accommodating
              |_____→
                          Cooperativeness
```

The Interest-Based Relational Approach

When conflict arises, it is easy for people to get entrenched in their positions and for tempers to flare, voices to rise, and body language to become defensive or aggressive. You can avoid all of this by using the Interest-Based Relational (IBR) approach.

Roger Fisher and William Ury developed the IBR approach and published it in their 1981 book, "Getting to Yes." They argue that you should resolve conflicts by separating people and their emotions from the problem. Their approach also focuses on building mutual respect and understanding, and it encourages you to resolve conflict in a united, cooperative way.

Building Relationships

- First priority is to protect the relationship
- The other person is not necessarily the problem
- Listen more than talk
- Show empathy
- Work with facts not

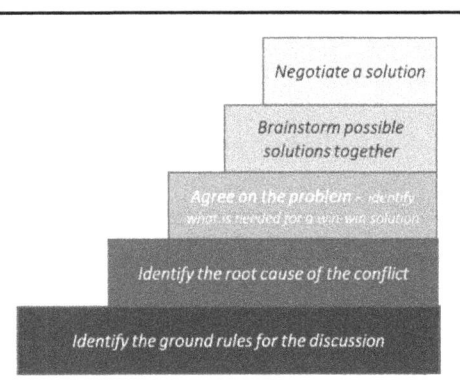

Pyramid (bottom to top):
- Identify the ground rules for the discussion
- Identify the root cause of the conflict
- Agree on the problem – identify what is needed for a win-win solution
- Brainstorm possible solutions together
- Negotiate a solution

The approach is based on the idea that your role as a manager is not simply to resolve conflict but to ensure that team members feel respected and understood, and that you appreciate their differences. In essence, it helps you to manage conflict in a civil and "grown up" way.

During the process, your focus should be on behaving courteously and consensually, and on insisting that others do the same. Your priority is to help each side develop an understanding of the other's position, and to encourage both to reach a consensus – even if that means agreeing to disagree.

To use the IBR approach effectively, everyone involved should listen actively and empathetically, have a good understanding of body language, be emotionally intelligent, and understand how to employ different anger management techniques. In particular, you and the conflicting parties need to follow these six steps:

1. **Make sure that good relationships are a priority.** Treat the other person with respect. Do your best to be courteous, and to discuss matters constructively.
2. **Separate people from problems.** Recognise that, in many cases, the other person is not "being difficult" – real and valid differences can lie behind conflicting positions. By separating the problem from the person, you can discuss issues without damaging relationships.
3. **Listen carefully to different interests.** You will get a better grasp of why people have adopted their position if you try to understand their point of view.
4. **Listen first, talk second.** You should listen to what the other person is saying before defending your own position. They might say something that changes your mind.
5. **Set out the "facts."** Decide on the observable facts that might impact your decision, together.
6. **Explore options together.** Be open to the idea that a third position may exist, and that you might reach it jointly.

You can often prevent contentious discussions from turning bad by following these guidelines, and they can help you avoid the antagonism and dislike that can cause conflict to spiral out of control.

However, bear in mind that the IBR approach may not be appropriate for all situations. For example, you may not be able to resolve differences in such a consensual, collaborative way if

Building Relationships

your organisation is in a crisis. On these occasions, you may have to "pull rank" as a leader and make quick decisions about disputes and conflicts.

Putting the IBR Approach into Practice

Follow each of the six steps of the IBR approach by applying them to a conflict resolution scenario.

Imagine that you run a paper product manufacturing company and you work closely with two managers, Roger, and Juanita. Roger heads up production and is eager to buy a new machine that will increase his department's output. Juanita works in purchasing and is keen to reduce costs. She understands Roger's motivation but informs him that the organisation will not be making any new purchases. This has created conflict and tension that is spreading throughout the workplace.

Step 1: Make Sure Good Relationships Are a Priority

As a manager, your priority in any conflict situation is to take control early and maintain good relationships within your team. Make sure that everyone understands how the conflict could be a mutual problem, and that it is important to resolve it through respectful discussion and negotiation, rather than aggression. Make it clear that it is essential for people to be able to work together happily, effectively and without resentment, so that the team and organisation can function effectively.

So, in our example situation with Roger and Juanita, you might facilitate a face-to-face meeting with them to clarify the importance of good relationships and to identify the main problems. Tell them that you respect their points of view, and that you appreciate their cooperation and desire to resolve the situation. You should also make it clear that everyone needs to work together to build and preserve relationships that allow the organisation to achieve its goals.

Step 2: Separate People from Problems

At this point, it is important to let team members know that conflict is rarely one-sided, and that it is best to resolve it collaboratively, by addressing the problem rather than the personalities involved. The problem is caused by neither person, but they do need to work together to resolve it.

So, in our example, Juanita may initially think that Roger is the problem. She believes that he is being defensive and demanding, but you should point out that she is focusing on the person instead of the problem. The problem is whether the organisation can afford the new equipment.

Step 3: Listen Carefully to Different Interests

It is important that everyone understands each party's underlying interests, needs and concerns. So, take a positive stance, keep the conversation courteous, and avoid blaming anyone.

Building Relationships

Ask for each person's viewpoint and confirm that you need his or her cooperation to solve the problem. Ask your team members to try to understand one another's motivations and goals, and to think about how those may affect their actions.

Encourage everyone to use active listening skills, such as looking directly at the speaker, listening carefully, nodding, and allowing each person to finish before talking. By following these guidelines, everyone will be able to hear and understand one another's positions and perceptions. Focusing on listening will also help to prevent the conversation from becoming heated and getting out of hand.

Once everyone knows that their views have been heard, they are more likely to be receptive to different perspectives. In our example, perhaps Juanita did not realise the amount of pressure that Roger was under to meet his production targets. Similarly, Roger may have assumed that Juanita was being unfair when she actually had a mandate to cut costs.

Step 4: Listen First, Talk Second
Encourage each team member to listen to other people's points of view, without defending their own position. Make sure that each person has finished talking before someone else speaks, emphasise that you want to resolve the situation through discussion and negotiation, and ensure that listeners understand the problem fully by asking questions for further clarification.

Be sure to focus on work issues and leave personalities out of the discussion. You should also encourage everyone to:

- *Listen with empathy, and to see the conflict from each participant's point of view.*
- *Explain issues clearly and concisely.*
- *Encourage people to use "I" rather than "you" statements, so that no one feels attacked.*
- *Be clear about their feelings.*
- *Remain flexible and adaptable.*

Once you have listened to everyone is needs and concerns, outline the behaviours and actions that you will or will not tolerate, and gain the opposing parties' agreement to change.

In the example, Juanita and Roger were both keen to get their opinions across, so they did not listen to what the other had to say. Once they did listen, they began to understand the situation more clearly.

Step 5: Set out the "Facts"
This sounds like an obvious step, but different underlying needs, interests and goals can often cause people to perceive problems differently. You will need to agree the problem that you are trying to solve before you can find a mutually acceptable solution, and you should agree the facts that are relevant to the situation.

Building Relationships

Sometimes, people will see different but interlocking problems. So, if you cannot reach an agreement, you should aim to understand the other person's perception of the problem.

Step 6: Explore Options Together
By this stage, you may have resolved the conflict. Each side will likely understand the other's position better, and the most appropriate solution might be obvious.

However, you may also have uncovered some serious differences. This is where a technique like win-win negotiation can be useful, so that you can find a solution that satisfies everyone. Or you might need to take action to change the fundamental circumstances that have caused the conflict.

By asking each team member to help generate solutions, you ensure that everyone feels included and that they are more likely to be satisfied with the outcome. Brainstorm ideas and be open to all suggestions, including ones you might not have considered before.

Conflict in the workplace can destroy good teamwork. When you do not manage it effectively, real, and legitimate differences between people can quickly get out of control, which can result in an irretrievable breakdown in communication.

The Conflict Layer Model

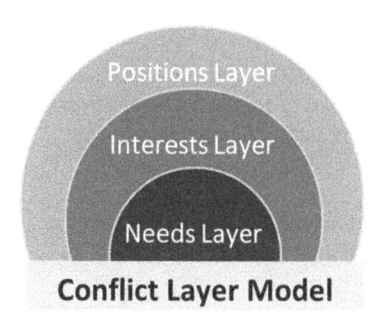

Conflict Layer Model (Positions Layer, Interests Layer, Needs Layer)

Negotiations are at the heart of many businesses. If you are working in the role of a business manager, it is likely you need to negotiate deals on a regular basis. Whether you are negotiating compensation packages with employees, or you are working on a purchase agreement with a supplier, successful negotiation can lead to a positive outcome for all involved. Despite what many believe to be true, negotiation does not have to come down to a winner and a loser – both sides can get what they need out of the deal when communication is emphasised.

The Conflict Layer Model is a helpful way to look at any negotiation process. One of the problems commonly found in negotiation is the fact that one or both sides may not be willing to say what they are really looking for in the deal.

Salary negotiations are a great example of this problem. An employee may be too nervous to openly state the pay rate they desire, as they do not want to appear greedy or unrealistic. As a result, the negotiations could go back and forth without ever really getting to the point. In the end, the employee will probably not get their desired salary, and they may quickly start looking for new employment.

Building Relationships

A better option would be to have the needs of all involved laid bare on the table. When everyone involved in the negotiation knows what the other side is looking for, serious negotiation can begin.

While it is usually impossible for everyone to get exactly what they want, reasonable compromises may be attainable with the lines of communication open. By using the Conflict Layer Model, you may be able to get down to serious negotiations sooner rather than later. As you might imagine from the name of this model, there are layers which make up the construction of this negotiation tool. Specifically, there are three layers which need to be understood before you can apply the model successfully. Those three layers are listed below.

Positions
The outer layer of the Conflict Layer Model is known as the positions. When negotiations begin, each side in the room will take up a position. While that might seem like a positive step, the problem lies in the fact that these positions are often not exactly what each side really wants out of the deal. Rather than stating openly what you are looking for, you may decide to represent a specific position based on how you want to appear.

Going back to our example of salary negotiations, an employee may state that they are looking for a wage which is 10% – 20% lower than what they actually desire. This employee may simply be embarrassed to ask for the kind of money they feel they deserve, so they will start out with this lower demand. Choosing a hard line, the company representation might offer numbers even lower than this initial request. At this point, each side will be standing behind a position which does not necessarily represent their true feelings or desires on the matter.

Interests
Moving to the middle layer of the model, the interests of each side are the reasons they use to back up their chosen positions. An employee may point to certain accomplishments in order to justify a salary increase, or they may point to the salary of an employee with similar responsibilities.

Whilst these interests will be based in fact, they might not actually be the truth in terms of what each party desires. While negotiations remain in this middle layer, they will still be stuck and unlikely to lead to a meaningful resolution.

Needs
Finally, we get to the core of the negotiation. At the needs layer we will find exactly what both sides are truly looking for in the process. This is where the employee is completely honest about the compensation that he or she desires, and it is also where the company is open about the kinds of offers it can make. As you might expect, this is where deals can begin to take shape. Without working all the way to the needs level, it will be difficult to successfully strike an accord that makes everyone happy at the end of the day.

It should be clearly stated that the Conflict Layer Model is not always going to be the best way to approach a negotiation. When the two parties involved in a negotiation are not working toward the same goal, it may be necessary to be more guarded than this model would provide. For instance, if a company goes into negotiations with another business by stating openly how

Building Relationships

much they are willing to pay for a particular good or service. That company is giving away all of their bargaining power. There is a certain strategy that should be employed in specific negotiations which would run counter to the way talks can work in the Conflict Layer Model.

The example of an employee and employer used above illustrates a time when both sides can benefit from being honest. While the employee wants as much money as possible and the employer wants to save money, these two parties are still working toward the same end. If the company is successful, everyone at the bargaining table is going to succeed. The employee wants to maximise his or her earnings, and the business wants to retain a valued, talented individual. If these two parties can be honest with one another in order to find common ground, it should benefit the organisation as a whole.

The Conflict Layer Model is not going to be the right way to approach every negotiation. It will, however, be the suitable method for a number of situations in which hard-line negotiating is not necessary. Think about the stakes and the parties involved in each negotiation you enter and use this method when you deem it is appropriate.

Bell and Hart's Eight Causes of Conflict

Workplace conflicts are a common problem in many workplaces. Unfortunately, workplace conflicts can lead to a number of negative influences not only on individual employees, but the business itself. Conflict in the workplace can lead to negative behaviours, such as physical or verbal fighting, in addition to lower workplace productivity due to job-related stress and dissatisfaction.

Causes of Workplace conflicts, or workplace tension, can be caused by a number of different factors. These factors may be minor, such as an employee who has a consistently cluttered work desk, to major, such as employee who is undermining their co-worker's ability to work.

Conflicting Resources → Conflicting Types → Conflicting Perceptions → Conflicting Goals → Conflicting Pressures → Conflicting Roles → Different Personal values → Unpredictable Policies

In 2000-2002, psychologists Art Bell and Brett Hart conducted a study on workplace conflicts and workplace tension. Their study was intended to root out the most common causes of workplace tension, which would allow employers--and employees--better understand, and hopefully create a successful conflict resolution for, what is causing tension in the workplace. Hart and Bell narrowed down the causes of conflict to eight different factors:

- *conflicting resources*
- *conflicting styles*
- *conflicting perceptions*
- *conflicting goals*
- *conflicting pressures*
- *conflicting roles*
- *different personal values*
- *unpredictable policies*

Building Relationships

These eight classifications can be used by employees or employers to help better understand what may be causing conflict in the workplace by looking at the root of the problem rather than what may be happening on the external surface of the issue.

Consider the first three of these eight conflict classifications.

Conflicting resources
Resources in the workplace include physical resources--such as office supplies or space for meeting rooms--in addition to mental resources, such as assistance from co-workers or a workplace assistant. Employees need access to certain types of resources in order to perform their jobs well.

When more than one person needs access to the same particular resource, this can cause a conflict. For example: An employee is using the only work fax machine to fax ten different important letters from her department to a client. Another employee rushes into the same area and needs to use the fax machine to fax an important document which is due within minutes. Both of these employees require the use of the fax machine, but because one employee is already using the machine and the second employee feels that they "deserve" to use it, due to a time crunch, this can cause a conflict between the two employees.

Employers can help resolve conflicts which are caused by conflicting resources by creating consistent, fair policies regarding the use of physical resources, such as fax machines or office spaces, in addition to providing enough mental resources to support all employees fairly. For example: An employer who sees that employees frequently have conflicts over the use of a fax machine might decide to purchase several more machines for the office, or if that is not an option, create a clear-cut policy towards using the machine, such as "one document per employee at one time," to allow a faster rotation.

Conflicting Styles
"Styles," in the workplace context, refers to how people work according to their own individual personality and needs. Some people, for example, might create strict schedules and deadlines for themselves in order to get everything done promptly; other people might consistently avoid creating schedules and leave their work to be done at the last minute. Some people might enjoy having strict, structured work times, while others may get work done at their own pace and on their own time.

In the workplace, a conflict of styles may occur when people are working together on a work-related project or assignment, or work within the same department. For example: A marketing department at an office firm is given an assignment which requires employees to pair-up and create at least one different advertising campaign per pair. One person in the pair may want to create a schedule and work consistently to ensure that the project is completed well before the deadline, while the other person in the pair is more laid-back and wants to work on the project "whenever," aiming to get it done just before it is due to be proposed. This can create a conflict caused by the conflicting styles of the employees, who would each get frustrated by the other employee's desire to work in a different way. Employers can help reduce or prevent conflicts caused by conflicting work styles by taking individual employee's styles into consideration when creating groups or pairs. Instead of

Building Relationships

pairing two employees with conflicting styles, for example, the employers could deliberately pair two employees who both share a strict schedule style of working.

Conflicting Perceptions

The way people see the world--people, events, and experiences--is called their perception. In the workplace, conflicts of perception may occur for a number of reasons. One common example occurs when an employer gives a certain employee an assignment that would normally be given to another employee.

From the employer's perception, they gave the specific employee the assignment because they felt the first employee would be overloaded due to their current work projects. However, the perspective of the person who would have ordinarily been given the assignment may see things differently: they may feel as if they are being slighted, ignored, or even punished for some sort of minor infraction because they were not given the assignment. This may then in turn cause a conflict between the employee who would normally have been given the assignment and the employee who was given the assignment, due to the perceived slight on part of the employer.

Conflicts in perception may be resolved by employers and employees encouraging open, clear lines of communication. In the previous example, the employer could have talked to the first employee about why the decision was being made to give their normal assignment to another person—this would have changed the perception of the employee, preventing a conflict between the employee and their employer, as well as between the employee and the second employee.

Conflicts in the workplace are a common problem experienced by many employers and employees. Workplace conflicts can negatively influence the workplace in many different ways. They can lead to fighting, such as verbal gossip or even physical altercations in more extreme circumstances; workplace conflicts can also cause a lowered job satisfaction and lower productivity.

Conflicting Goals

Goals in the workplace are usually related to deadlines, quotas, and overall goals which employees are expected to meet. Goals may be set in place by company heads, managers, supervisors, team members, or anyone given the authority to set a goal for another employee or a group of employees. Conflicting goals generally occur when an individual or group is given a goal by one person—such as a manager—that conflicts with the goal given by another person, such as a team leader or even another manager.

For example: *One manager might tell an employee that their goal is to get their work done as fast as possible, while another manager might tell that same employee that their goal is to do the work to the utmost of their ability, regardless of speed. These two conflicting goals can create tension between the employee and their managers, as well as tension between the two managers in the example.*

Employers can help prevent or resolve these conflicting goals by making sure that anyone with the authority to set a goal knows that it may not conflict with other goals. They can also encourage open liens of communication between employees and their superiors, in

Building Relationships

order to ensure that an employee will feel that it is acceptable to let someone—such as a manager—know when a goal is conflicting.

Conflicting Pressures

In the workplace, pressures are created by something that needs to be done—usually within a certain timeframe. For example, an employee may need to finish a report by a certain time or complete a certain amount of work before a certain time. When one employee's pressures conflict with another employee's pressures, this creates a conflict. For example: One employee may need a report from their co-worker by noon in order to relieve their own deadline pressure—but that second co-worker is already working on a different report that they need to give to someone else by noon. Conflicting pressures are similar to conflicting goals, except that pressures occur within specific deadlines or timeframes.

Employers can help prevent conflicting pressures by encouraging open communication and being willing to reschedule or move deadlines around to ensure that their employees are not experiencing conflicting pressures.

Conflicting Roles

In the context of the workplace, a "role" is a combination of the normal responsibilities and duties of an employee. For example, an employee in the advertising department will have a role related to assignments and work related to advertising; while an employee in the sales department will have a role related to increasing and understanding a business's sales. Sometimes, however, employees are given tasks or assignments which are outside the realm of their normal role but within the realm of someone else's role. When this occurs, it is often perceived as "invading territory," which can cause a power struggle and conflict between the individuals involved.

> Example:
> An employer decides to give an assignment related to creating a commercial slogan to someone in the sales department, instead of someone in the marketing department who is ordinarily given this task. The person in the marketing department may feel that the person in the sales department has invaded their territory, or their role, creating a conflict because they may feel as if their position is being threatened.

Employers can help prevent conflicts caused by conflicting roles by ensuring that they clearly explain the reasoning behind any decisions which may be perceived as changing employee's ordinary roles.

Different Personal Values

Personal values are a combination of an individual's personal morality, ethics, and values. Conflicts related to personal values in the workplace are usually caused by employees being asked to do something which conflicts with their own personal values. For example, an employer might ask an employee to create an ad-campaign which conflicts with their own sense of morality. This can cause conflict because an employee may be pressured to

Building Relationships

accept the assignment because they worry, they might be reprimanded or even fired from their position if they say no.

Employers can help prevent conflicts related to different personal values by prating ethical leadership—or by avoiding asking employees to perform actions which go against their personal values whenever possible.

Unpredictable Policies

Consistent workplace policies create a sense of consistently and fairness among employees. For example, if every employee is held up to the same standards created by workplace policies, they will know that their workplace if fair. However, if policies are not enforced consistently in the workplace—for example, if one employee is not reprimanded for doing the same thing that another employee was reprimanded for—this can cause conflicts due to the perception of unfairness and unpredictability.

Employers can prevent conflicts caused by unpredictable policies by ensuring that they are fair and consistent with all of their rules, regulations, and policies in the workplace.

Guidelines to reduce conflict with team members regarding performance

- *Set up a meeting between the conflicting parties to discuss the issue.*
- *Let them know that you are there to work together to find a solution, and that they need to focus on the problem, not the person.*
- *Ask them to listen carefully to one another's point of view, and to use active listening skills, so that everyone feels heard.*
- *Be clear about the facts and then work together to agree on a resolution.*
- *Get practice by focusing on a relatively mild conflict first, and then try it on a more significant one.*

It is wise to remember that when arranging to meet with an individual to discuss issues of conflict, they may be apprehensive and therefore talking to them informally before meeting, encouraging them to prepare their thoughts and notes, may contribute to a smooth meeting with a swift resolution. This is particular so with members of your team. The following processes will allow to successful mediation.

1. **Prepare to resolve the conflict** - *do not ignore it, discuss it and act on it. Agree a process for communication and resolution*
2. **Understand the conflict** - *establish opinions, establish the facts, and meet with individuals/groups to establish their views and beliefs. Remain neutral, do not judge opinions, listen, and understand. Bring the individuals/groups back together to discuss the solutions.*
3. **Reaching agreed action** - *bringing all of the facts together and discussing assumptions will enable the team to reach a decision. Remember to celebrate successful outcomes.*

Steps 2 and 3 may be repeated, if necessary, to gain further information for a resolution to be reached

Building Relationships

If a resolution is not possible you may want to look at negotiating a win-win situation, this means identifying goals, trading assets, looking at alternative opportunities and considering other consequences. In this case, both parties should benefit from the agreed action and be happy with the results.

As an operations/departmental manager, on occasions you will need to manage issues around that practice or the non-achievement of business or personal development goals. In the circumstances, it is important to reduce the risk of conflict between you and the team member. The following table shows a process for reducing conflict during formal meetings.

Preparation	Refer to a list of previously agreed objectives and any notes on performance against these during the period. Form views about the reasons for success or failure. Decide where to give praise. Identify any areas for improvement in any thoughts on steps to improve. Consider any changes that may have taken place within the individuals working environment. • Ask individuals to prepare to identify achievements and problems. • Ask individuals to be ready to assess their own performance at the meeting. • Ask individuals to prepare notes on any points they wish to raise. Remember to keep notes of items discussed and agreed for the final phase.
Creating the atmosphere	Choose a location with care. Choose a time with care. Consider the most appropriate table/chair layout. Start with a friendly general discussion to relax the individual.
Working to a structure	Plan a meeting to cover all the points identified during the preparation phase. Allow time for the individual to express themselves fully.
Using positive feedback	Motivate them by recognising their achievements. Begin with praise for a specific achievement, but it must be sincere and deserve. Praise will relax the individual.
Letting them talk	It enables to get things off their chest. Allows and to feel that they are getting a fair hearing. Use open-ended questions. Encourage them to be expansive.
Encourage self-appraisal	This allows you to see things from their point of view on will provide the basis for discussion. Ask questions such as: • How well do you feel you have done? • What do you feel are your strengths? • What do you like the most/least about your job? • Why do you think that went well? • Why do you think that did not go well?

Building Relationships

Performance not personality	Based discussions on performance on hard evidence. Do not base discussions on opinion. Refer to actual results or behaviour and compare it with expected results or behaviour. Ensure individuals are given time to explain why something did or did not happen.
Encourage analysis of performance	Do not hand out praise or blame. Jointly analyse reasons success or lack of success. Agree what could be done in the future to repeat success or prevent lack of success. Agree what can be done in the future to achieve expected performance.
No unexpected criticisms	There should be no surprises. Discussion should only be with events or behaviours noted at the time they occurred. Fish feedback should be immediate-do not wait until the review! The purpose of the review is to review the performance period and look forward.
Agree objectives and action plan	If the above are followed, the action plan in its agreement will have been taking place throughout the review and it now needs to be agreed. End the meeting on a positive note.

Building Relationships

Measuring Stakeholder Satisfaction

The first clue to understanding the importance of stakeholder management is in the term itself. There can be a small amount of people carrying out the daily legwork in your organisation, but a large amount of people with stakes in its success. For some, these stakes can be very high.

> *Stakeholders determine whether your organisation is successful, and each one has their own definition.*

Collaboration managers use a variety of methods to measure stakeholder satisfaction. Each method allows the manager to gather stakeholder input that ensures the business stays on track throughout each of its different phases. Conducting surveys, meetings, and interviews with stakeholders on a regular basis helps increase the likelihood of success.

The only way we can know what our stakeholders feel about the organisation is to ask them. This can be done in a number of ways

The Importance of Feedback

Getting different perspectives on our behaviour and performance can be a powerful method for self-reflection. It can be a driving force behind understanding ourselves, increasing our choices and making decisions about any changes we may wish to make. Stakeholder feedback differs slightly from 360-degree Feedback due to the audience being targeted. Unless designed as such, stakeholder feedback does not need to seek views from people you interact with at different hierarchical levels. Instead, questions are asked which normally relate to a specific role or service provided and/or behavioural and attitude factors. You would then identify stakeholders who would be best placed to respond to that question, regardless of their level.

Responses are normally analysed using a scoring or value judgement system. This allows you to gain a set of standardised results, which you can then analyse to help you reflect upon your performance. You should also assess yourself using the same feedback method.

Some areas for consideration when undertaking stakeholder feedback:

- *Open, honest feedback can sometimes be hard to hear. It is important to identify and agree the criteria you will use, your respondents and how the process will work.*
- *Consider the tool you are going to use to best analyse your results. For example, if you are using a numerical scoring system for responses (such as 1 – do not agree, to 6 – Agree totally) it may be a spreadsheet is the best way of recording the information to analyse. You may find numerical feedback more appropriate than descriptive feedback in most instances.*
- *You should ensure your respondents are aware of any confidentiality, equality and discrimination issues when making their responses.*

Building Relationships

- *Once you have received your feedback, it is important you analyse this so you can look for positive feedback and possible future developmental areas where the feedback may not be so positive.*

Giving good, constructive feedback is probably one of the most important things a leader can do for their team. Whether providing feedback to encourage improvements or simply praising a job well done, feedback is an underrated, underutilised management tool that can make a world of difference to staff and business performance.

Feedback Defined

The term 'feedback' is used to describe the helpful information or criticism about prior action or behaviour from an individual, communicated to another individual (or a group) who can use that information to adjust and improve current and future actions and behaviours.

Feedback occurs when an environment reacts to an action or behaviour. For example, 'customer feedback' is the buyers' reaction to a company's products, services, or policies; and 'employee performance feedback' is the employees' reaction to feedback from their manager – the exchange of information involves both performance expected, and performance exhibited.

Who would dispute the idea that feedback is a good thing? All can benefit from feedback. Both common sense and research make it clear – feedback and opportunities to use that feedback helps to improve and enhance, whether an individual, group, business, business unit, company, or organisation – and that information can be used to make better informed decisions. It also allows us to build and maintain communication with others.

> *Effective feedback, both positive and negative, is very helpful.*

Feedback is valuable information that will be used to make important decisions. Top performing companies are top performing companies because they consistently search for ways to make their best even better. For top performing companies 'continuous improvement' is not just a showy catchphrase. It is a true focus based on feedback from across the entire organisation – customers, clients, employees, suppliers, vendors, and stakeholders. Top performing companies are not only good at accepting feedback, but they also deliberately ask for feedback. And they know that feedback is helpful only when it highlights weaknesses as well as strengths.

Effective feedback has benefits for the giver, the receiver, and the wider organisation. Here are five reasons why feedback is so important.

Building Relationships

1. Feedback is always there
If you ask someone in your organisation when feedback occurs, they will typically mention an employee survey, performance appraisal, or training evaluation. In actuality, feedback is around us all the time. Every time we speak to a person, employee, customer, vendor, etc., we communicate feedback. In actuality, it is impossible not to give feedback.

Businesses do not need to go through a lot of hassle in order to gather feedback. It is always available for them and they just need to look for a way in order to gather and manage feedback in an appropriate manner. Businesses can also gather feedback in many different ways. It is up to the business owners to think about the most convenient method that needs to be followed in order to gather feedback.

2. Feedback is effective listening
Feedback is similar to effective listening

> *"Employees don't leave bad companies; they leave bad managers."* Marcus Buckingham

A recent survey uncovered the top ten reasons why people quit their jobs.

The top three included feeling undervalued, having a bad manager and poor communication. All of which can be fixed with a strong internal feedback system.

It does not matter how well your employees are performing, how well they are liked, or how great they treat your customers. If your business does not meet the feedback expectations of your employees, you could be putting the entire future of your business at stake.

Feedback can be gathered in different ways. Collecting verbal feedback via a survey is one of the most popular techniques out of them. In fact, collecting verbal feedback is almost similar to effective listening. The business owners can gather a lot of information from feedback, which can help them to focus on future development.

Whether the feedback is done verbally or via a feedback survey, the person providing the feedback needs to know they have been understood (or received) and they need to know that their feedback provides some value. When conducting a survey, always explain why respondents' feedback is important and how their feedback will be used.

3. Feedback can motivate
Feedback has the potential to motivate business owners as well. Through feedback, the business owners will be able to get to know where they are not doing well. It is possible for the business owners to trust feedback that they get from the customers as well. Then they can think of making required changes in the business in order to adapt accordingly and provide more value to the customers. This is one of the most convenient methods available for the businesses to increase the potential customer base as well. That is because it can help the businesses to cater the specific needs and requirements of the customers.

Building Relationships

By asking for feedback, it can actually motivate employees to perform better. Employees like to feel valued and appreciate being asked to provide feedback that can help formulate business decisions. And feedback from client, suppliers, vendors, and stakeholders can be used to motivate to build better working relations

4. Feedback can improve performance
Most of the businesses do not have a clear understanding whether they are performing in an effective manner or not. Feedback can assist them to get to know about it. However, the business owners need to be careful not to ignore feedback as criticism. What is viewed as negative criticism is actually constructive criticism and is the best kind of feedback that can help to formulate better decisions to improve and increase performance.

5. Feedback is a tool for continued learning
For an employer/employee relationship to work well, both parties need to be willing to learn from each other. Seizing learning opportunities can provide an exceptional springboard for business and personal growth. It is possible to get feedback from customers on a regular basis. Therefore, it can be considered as an excellent tool available for the businesses to engage with continuous learning. In other words, businesses can develop new products or services or rebrand the existing products based on feedback.

Regular feedback sessions, both scheduled and impromptu, allows us to reflect on our behaviours, and, if appropriate, upgrade or change the way we do things. Seeing ourselves from someone else's point of view can be a truly enlightening experience.

Negative feedback, however, can have the opposite effect. Using feedback as a tool to berate a colleague or staff member, should never be employed as a leadership tactic. If someone is awful at their job, making them feel horrible about themselves will only serve to make things worse. In cases of poor performance, a more formal feedback stance or training route should be considered.

Feedback Fuels Change

Business processes need to change for many reasons; to make cost savings, to create efficiencies, to provide better service to clients... the reasons for change are endless.

When a business is experiencing a period of change, feedback is a crucial element of the change process. If change is not the direct result of external feedback, then it is important to source opinions from those who matter to your business: employees, customers, and stakeholders.

Invest time in asking and learning about how others experience working with your organisation.

Continued feedback is important across the entire organisation in order to remain aligned to goals, create strategies, develop products and services improvements, improve relationships, and much more.

Building Relationships

Continued learning is the key to improving

Most of the world's most prominent organisations use customer and stakeholder feedback to make improvements to their products and services. No matter what the size of your business, do not lose sight of the opinion of those that spend their time, money, and resources with you.

Value of Stakeholder Feedback

Understanding your stakeholders is vital in modern-day business. This includes listening to the views and beliefs of stakeholders as well as seeking their feedback. After all, these are the people who will shape and influence future successes (or failures). Keeping every stakeholder on-side can be difficult but can be hugely beneficial.

What is it?
The key to keeping stakeholders on-side is consultation. This involves the development of constructive and productive long-term relationships. Stakeholder consultation aims to build relationships based on mutual trust and benefits. Listening to and understanding the views and feedback from stakeholders can help shape and improve the overall operations of a business.

Stakeholder consultation can be project-based or on-going. Specific project-based consultation is generally used for the development of new products and services. For example, a company may consult with customers to establish specific needs of the target market. On-going consultation, however, is generally used to track the progress of a company in regard to stakeholder expectations and to maximise buy-in. For example, a company may consult with stakeholders regarding changes to the company's direction or its branding.

What are the benefits?
The benefits of stakeholder consultation are clear, with some of the most significant reasons listed below:

- *Enable more informed decision making*
- *Lead to greater stakeholder satisfaction*
- *Improves chances of project/initiative success*
- *Promote open, two-way communication*

The 4-Step Process

The stakeholder consultation process is an opportunity for key groups to be kept informed, and for their views and feedback to be heard. It is important that any consultation is thoroughly planned with clear objectives set at the beginning.

Regardless of the aims and objectives of the stakeholder consultation, the process typically consists of four steps: Planning, Process, Presentation and Promise (the 4Ps).

Building Relationships

Planning
The "planning" stage is where the aims and objectives of the stakeholder consultation are discussed and agreed upon. After the aims and objectives have been determined, the "planning" stage is used to discuss how the process will be carried out. Process owners allocate resources and select an appropriate consultation method. Several questions need to be asked at this stage to ensure every facet of the process is considered.

> *Why do we need to consult?*
> *Who are we consulting?*
> *What resources do we have?*
> *How are we going to do it?*
> *What materials will be needed?*

Process
The "process" stage is where the stakeholder consultation is actually carried out. It is important at this stage to develop effective two-way communication with the stakeholders in order to promote open and honest sharing of views and beliefs. The process and data will then need to be accurately recorded for the final stages.

Presentation
The "presentation" stage is where the data gathered is analysed and reported on. The aims of this stage are to ensure the data is an accurate representation of the stakeholder views, and to prepare the report ready for presentation. The report is typically presented to the process owners, such as the company itself or policy makers. However, feedback will also be provided to those who took part in the process.

Promise
Lastly, the "promise" stage is where actions are put in place in response to the information gathered. The 'promise' of action on the back of the stakeholder consultation process helps drive the development of a long-term relationship based on transparency and collaboration.

Methods of stakeholder consultation are largely the same as those used for market research. The key question is whether the consultation requires depth of knowledge or breadth of knowledge. The answer generally determines which method will be chosen. If depth of knowledge is required, a qualitative study is usually appropriate. These are studies which encourage open styles of discussion and debate. The most common methods used to gather depth of information are focus groups, individual depth interviews and observation (or ethnography). If breadth of knowledge is required, a more quantitative study is usually appropriate.

These are studies which encompass large number of respondents but are restricted to closed style questions, aimed at providing generalist viewpoints. The most common methods used to gather breadth of information are online surveys, telephone surveys, and short street interviews.

As understanding stakeholders becomes more and more important for businesses, stakeholder consultation will become a vital process to maximise success. Stakeholder consultation can be

Building Relationships

used to evaluate reactions and to track the perceptions of a company's activities and ensure collaboration and partnership with all stakeholders. The long-term effectiveness of an organisation can depend on its relationships with stakeholders, ensuring commitment and buy-in to any future strategies and challenges. This makes for a more informed organisation that is responsive to the needs of all its users and stakeholders.

Gathering Stakeholder Feedback

Gathering feedback from internal stakeholders in your organisation is fundamental to developing a successful product. Remember that team members are also internal customers, and will likely be as or more vocal than your external customers about your product — they have a lot to say, but where and how should they say it? Let us look at some ways to gather feedback from stakeholders.

While product teams rely on a combination of several communication channels to share feedback with colleagues, others find it better to pick one and stick with it. Here are a few common feedback communication channels and a brief look at the pros and cons of each so you can make a considered choice about what works best for you:

1. Interviewing Stakeholders
Interviewing stakeholders individually allows managers to gather feedback privately from people who have the ability to impact the organisation. Managers should use this opportunity to handle both negative and positive input in a more controlled environment. Taking the time to interview stakeholders or sponsors makes sense when a stakeholder cannot attend a group meeting due to time constraints or other scheduling conflicts. This method of grading stakeholder satisfaction with progress allows managers to receive potentially sensitive information out of public view, such as a recommendation that resources be terminated, or the organisation's scope be significantly altered.

Pros:	Cons:
Convenient for stakeholders to use. Feedback can be shared virtually anytime. You can search feedback later.	Does not aggregate data or provides analytics. Requires extra manual work to extract the feedback.

2. Focus Groups
Running brainstorming sessions to get input from stakeholders involves scheduling meetings and facilitating discussions about the team's progress toward achieving the organisation's goals. Topics typically include the presentation of status reports, quality data and project outcomes, such as prototype products.

Conducting an effective focus group usually involves comprehensive planning including setting an agenda, preparing specific questions to ask stakeholders, encouraging collaboration, and calling for action from participants. Project managers should encourage all participants to provide candid input reflecting their perspective. This method of measuring stakeholder satisfaction with progress allows project managers to get timely

Building Relationships

input for all stakeholders at once, enabling the project team to avoid costly mistakes or rework later.

Pros:	Cons:
Opportunity to provide product updates/share what is next on your roadmap.	Getting everyone in the room at the same time can be hard and inconvenient.
Allows you to ask follow-up questions. You can clarify feedback with those who have shared it	Can lead to confusion if stakeholders have to hold onto feedback for a month before relaying it..

3. Feedback Reports

In lieu of (or in addition to) facilitating a feedback meeting, have every team generate a customer feedback report every two weeks or so and share it with your team.

Pros:	Cons:
Contains both qualitative and quantitative data.	Time-consuming and possibly inconvenient for customer teams to produce.
It is a resource you can return to for information when you need it.	Does not look at long-term feedback trends.

4. Collaborative Spreadsheets

You can ask customer-facing teams to enter feedback directly into a spreadsheet within Google Sheets or a similar tool.

Pros:	Cons:
Customer teams can share feedback at any time.	May be inconvenient for customer teams to use, which could result in them sharing less feedback.
Good for gathering and both qualitative and quantitative feedback.	Hard for customer teams to know whether the product team is reading their feedback

5. Feedback Collection Platforms

Using surveys to gather and measure stakeholder satisfaction with project progress involves selecting a tool, such as Zoomerang, SurveyMonkey or Qualtrics, to create and deploy an online survey. To design an effective survey, the manager should generate a short list of questions to gather input. The manager should provide a menu of choices, such as a satisfaction rating scale including the options "Completely Satisfied," "Satisfied," "No Opinion," Dissatisfied," and "Completely Dissatisfied." Then, the manager must provide clear instructions on how to complete the survey, when feedback is requested and how the feedback will be used. This method of measuring stakeholder satisfaction allows project managers to create sophisticated charts of responses and analyse input to take decisive action.

Building Relationships

Pros:	Cons:
Highly scalable. Can aggregate qualitative and quantitative data from every feedback source in one place, making it easy to access and use to make decisions.	Cost may be a concern if your budget is tight. Customer teams may require a bit of training to help them understand how the system works.

All of these communication channels come with their benefits and disadvantages, and the right approach is probably some combination of several. It is up to you and your team to decide which recipe of channels works best for you.

Negotiation Skills

Implicit in all conflict resolution are specific interpersonal skills, one of which is Negotiation Skills.

Negotiation is a method by which people settle differences. It is a process by which compromise, or agreement is reached while avoiding argument and dispute.

In any disagreement, individuals understandably aim to achieve the best possible outcome for their position (or perhaps an organisation they represent). However, the principles of fairness, seeking mutual benefit and maintaining a relationship are the keys to a successful outcome.

Specific forms of negotiation are used in many situations: international affairs, the legal system, government, industrial disputes, or domestic relationships as examples. However, general negotiation skills can be learned and applied in a wide range of activities. Negotiation skills can be of great benefit in resolving any differences that arise between you and others.

Stages of Negotiation

In order to achieve a desirable outcome, it may be useful to follow a structured approach to negotiation. For example, in a work situation a meeting may need to be arranged in which all parties involved can come together.

The process of negotiation includes the following stages:

- *Preparation*
- *Discussion*
- *Clarification of goals*
- *Negotiate towards a Win-Win outcome*
- *Agreement*
- *Implementation of a course of action*

Building Relationships

1. Preparation
Before any negotiation takes place, a decision needs to be taken as to when and where a meeting will take place to discuss the problem and who will attend. Setting a limited timescale can also be helpful to prevent the disagreement continuing.

This stage involves ensuring all the pertinent facts of the situation are known in order to clarify your own position. In the work example above, this would include knowing the 'rules' of your organisation, to whom help is given, when help is not felt appropriate and the grounds for such refusals. Your organisation may well have policies to which you can refer in preparation for the negotiation.

Undertaking preparation before discussing the disagreement will help to avoid further conflict and unnecessarily wasting time during the meeting.

2. Discussion
During this stage, individuals or members of each side put forward the case as they see it, i.e., their understanding of the situation.

Key skills during this stage include questioning, listening, and clarifying.

Sometimes it is helpful to take notes during the discussion stage to record all points put forward in case there is need for further clarification. It is extremely important to listen, as when disagreement takes place it is easy to make the mistake of saying too much and listening too little. Each side should have an equal opportunity to present their case.

3. Clarifying Goals
From the discussion, the goals, interests, and viewpoints of both sides of the disagreement need to be clarified.

It is helpful to list these factors in order of priority. Through this clarification it is often possible to identify or establish some common ground. Clarification is an essential part of the negotiation process, without it, misunderstandings are likely to occur which may cause problems and barriers to reaching a beneficial outcome.

4. Negotiate Towards a Win-Win Outcome
This stage focuses on what is termed a 'win-win' outcome where both sides feel they have gained something positive through the process of negotiation and both sides feel their point of view has been taken into consideration. A win-win outcome is usually the best result. Although this may not always be possible, through negotiation, it should be the ultimate goal.

Suggestions of alternative strategies and compromises need to be considered at this point. Compromises are often positive alternatives which can often achieve greater benefit for all concerned compared to holding to the original positions.

Building Relationships

5. Agreement
Agreement can be achieved once understanding of both sides' viewpoints and interests have been considered.

It is essential to for everybody involved to keep an open mind in order to achieve an acceptable solution. Any agreement needs to be made perfectly clear so that both sides know what has been decided.

6. Implementing a Course of Action
From the agreement, a course of action has to be implemented to carry through the decision.

Failure to Agree

If the process of negotiation breaks down and agreement cannot be reached, then re-scheduling a further meeting is called for. This avoids all parties becoming embroiled in heated discussion or argument, which not only wastes time but can also damage future relationships. At the subsequent meeting, the stages of negotiation should be repeated. Any new ideas or interests should be considered and the situation looked at afresh. At this stage it may also be helpful to look at other alternative solutions and/or bring in another person to mediate.

Win-Win Negotiation

Do you dread entering a negotiation? Do you worry that what you want will not match what the other person wants to give? Do you worry about having to "play hardball" and souring a good working relationship? After all, for someone to win, someone else has to lose, right? Well, not necessarily.

Chances are, you can find a solution that leaves all parties feeling like winners by adopting the aptly named "win-win" approach to negotiation.

What Is Win-Win Negotiation?
A win-win negotiation is a careful exploration of both your own position, and that of your opposite number, in order to find a mutually acceptable outcome that gives you both as much of what you want as possible. If you both walk away happy with what you have gained from the deal, then that is a win-win!

Building Relationships

In an ideal win-win situation, you will find that the other person wants what you are prepared to trade, and that you are prepared to give what he or she wants. If this is not the case, and one of you must give way, then it is fair to negotiate some form of compensation for doing so. But both sides should still feel comfortable with the outcome. People's positions are rarely as opposed as they may initially appear, and the other person may have very different goals from the ones you expect! So, try to keep an open mind and be flexible in your thinking.

Principled Negotiation Within the Win-Win Scenario

Establishing a strong position is a good starting point for a negotiation. But if you become too entrenched, conflict can quickly arise and the discussion may break down.

You can avoid this by using a form of win-win negotiation called "principled negotiation."

Roger Fisher and William Ury developed this approach in their 1981 book, "Getting to Yes." They identified five steps of principled negotiations and argued that negotiations are successful when they encourage cooperation toward a common goal.

Consider the five stages of principled negotiation:

1. Separate People from the Problem

First, avoid identifying your opposite number as your "opponent." Be sure to focus on the issue at hand and try to ignore personality differences. To do this, be aware of three factors: perception, emotion, and communication.

According to Fisher and Ury, perception means "putting yourself in their shoes," so you are better placed to see common ground or a compromise solution. You may be convinced that your position is fair, reasonable and "right," but it is likely so will the other person.

Examine and acknowledge your emotions, and to ask yourself why you feel the way you do. For example, could a previous bad experience in a negotiation be affecting your behaviour in this one? Remain calm during the negotiations, as this will aid your decision-making processes. Observe the emotions of the other party and try not to respond in kind if the discussion becomes "heated."

Instead, use your emotional intelligence skills to understand why the debate has taken this turn, and try to understand each party's underlying interests, needs and concerns.

Finally, make sure that your communication is clear and precise, to avoid misunderstandings. Use active listening techniques, such as looking directly at the speaker, listening carefully, and allowing each person to finish before you respond.

2. Focus on Interests, not positions

People are seldom "difficult" just for the sake of it, and almost always there are real and valid differences sitting behind conflicting positions. The way that each person sees the issue may be influenced by many factors, such as their values, beliefs, status, responsibilities, and cultural background.

Building Relationships

Try to keep the conversation courteous and avoid attributing blame. Once everyone knows that their interests have been considered, they are more likely to be receptive to different points of view.

For example, if you are negotiating with your boss to get more resources for your team, consider that he may be under pressure to reduce costs. If you look beyond your two positions, you may find that you have a common interest, such as increasing your team's productivity.

3. Invent options for mutual gain
By now, each side will likely have a better understanding of the other's interests, and a solution might be obvious. You may even be on the verge of agreement. If not, stay open to the idea that a completely new position may exist and use the negotiation process to explore your options.

To return to our example, let us say that you have identified increased productivity as a mutual interest, but your company cannot afford new staff or equipment. You could see this as an opportunity to assess working practices, training opportunities, and inexpensive ways to increase efficiency. Brainstorm as many ideas as you can to find a solution to the problem. Be receptive to all suggestions, then develop the most promising ones into new proposals that you can bring to the negotiating table.

4. Use objective criteria
This is not just "setting out the facts," as different underlying needs, interests, opinions, and goals can cause people to interpret facts differently, or cause you to select only those facts that support your position.

For example, during an interdepartmental negotiation in your company about the launch date of a new product, you become convinced that rushing it to market as early as possible is the best option. There is a danger your position could become entrenched, and your willingness to listen lessened.

Yes, there is some evidence to support this view within the marketing data, but also indications that delaying the launch until later in the year, to coincide with a national holiday, would also be good for sales in the longer term. It would also give your marketing team more time to prepare a campaign.

Try to agree on a set of objective criteria that provide a framework for your discussion. These could include measurements such as legal standards, market value, a mission statement, or contractual terms. Agreeing on standards demonstrates shared values, and a commitment to reaching an agreement.
Returning to our first example, both you and your boss could agree on a budget as a basis for discussion regarding more resources for your team and proceed on the basis that any changes must be made within these financial limitations.

Building Relationships

5. Know your BATNA (Best Alternative to a Negotiated Agreement)
Your BATNA is your favoured fallback option if you cannot get everything that you want. This is not the same as a "bottom line," which is a fixed position that can limit your options and may prevent you from discovering a new course of action.

Instead, think through what might happen if the negotiation does not achieve your desired result, and select the most attractive alternatives. Evaluate these alternatives and at the end of that process, the most promising alternative solution is your BATNA.

If you start the negotiation with a "bottom line" demand for two extra departmental staff members, and your company refuses, the negotiation falls at the first hurdle. However, if you started with this request, but your BATNA was to achieve a commitment to training and updated software, you would be in a better position to get a good result.

Win-Win Versus Win-Lose Negotiation

In a negotiation where you do not expect to deal with the person concerned again, and you do not need their continued goodwill, it may be appropriate to seek a "bigger piece of the pie" for yourself. This "win-lose" approach, often called "distributive bargaining," is usually used for negotiating the price of goods or services (for example, a house or a car).

Similarly, when the stakes are high, it may be appropriate to use legitimate "gamesmanship" (pushing the rules to their limits) to gain advantage, but without crossing the line into brinkmanship. But, when you want to have an ongoing, productive relationship with the person you are negotiating with, these techniques can have serious drawbacks:

One person "playing hardball" puts the other person at a disadvantage. This may lead to reprisals later.
If the losing party needs to fulfil some part of a deal, they may decide to become uncooperative and awkward.

Using tricks and manipulation during a negotiation can undermine trust and damage teamwork.

Win-win negotiation can enable both parties in a discussion to feel that they have made a satisfactory deal, and that neither is the "loser."

It is particularly useful when you have an ongoing relationship with the other party, and you wish to remain on good terms.

> WIN WITH HUMILITY
> AND LOSE WITH GRACE

Building Relationships

Persuasion Skills

How often have you needed to persuade others to do something?

It is a situation that arises almost every day, whether it is getting your teenager to tidy their room, or your toddler to get dressed, or a colleague to attend a meeting on your behalf. Some people seem to be able to do it effortlessly, and almost without anyone noticing, whereas others fall back on the power of their position to enforce what they want.

Persuasion skills can be learnt just like any others, and they are a key part of being able to influence others to achieve your goals and objectives.

Ways to Influence and Persuade

Nagging
We all know people who aim to persuade by talking constantly. They seem to think they can grind others into submission, by simply reiterating their point of view constantly. This, basically, is nagging. And it does sometimes work, of course, because their colleagues or family give in solely to get some peace. But as a general rule, others persuaded in this way probably have not bought into the idea and are not committed to it.

This means that when the going gets tough, the idea could easily just wither and die.

Coercion
Others fall back on the power of their position, and order others to do what they want. This, in its most unpleasant sense, is coercion. Again, their family or colleagues will not necessarily like what they are doing. If it is hard, they may well give up. More orders will be issued, to rescue the idea, but again, may be unsuccessful, because those involved are doing it because they have to, not because they want to.

A Better Way
The 'Holy Grail' of persuasion, then, is to get others to buy into the idea, and want to do it your way. And the best way of doing that is in a way that others do not notice. But how?

The fable of the sun and the wind is a good example:

> *The wind and the sun decided to have a competition to decide once and for all who was stronger. They agreed that the winner would be the one who could persuade a man to take off his coat. The wind blew and blew, but the man only held on more tightly to his coat. Then the sun shone gently down, and within minutes, the man took off his coat.*

The moral here is that you cannot force someone to do what they do not want to do; instead, the art of persuasion is to get them to want what you want.

Building Relationships

Persuasion Unseen
Consider this example of a group of students choosing a leader for a group task.

> *The group had agreed on the ideal type of person, and there were two obvious candidates within the group, Sue, and Steven.*
>
> *Sue suggested that Steven should take on the task, and he accepted happily. Decision made. Everyone smiled, except for one member of the group, John.*
>
> *John, who had until that moment been silent, said: "Steven, don't forget to let us know what you want us to do to help. With your new job, you are going to have a lot on, and you'll need to make sure you get us organised or we won't get it all done."*
>
> *Steven looked thoughtful, and then said, "You know, on reflection, I'm not sure I've got time to do this as well as starting my new job. I have got a lot on, as you say. Maybe it would be better if Sue did it."*
>
> *Everyone looked at Sue, who said that she would take it on if the group wanted. They all agreed that would be best.*
>
> *Sue later asked John privately why he had intervened when the group had already decided on a leader. He said that he thought she would do it better than Steven and get a better result for the group.*

In this example, John had used his persuasion skills very subtly to get what he wanted and created a win-win situation from a potentially unpleasant conversation.

Steven was happy that the group had acknowledged his skills, and equally happy that he was not leading the task.

In fact, at the end, he wanted Sue to lead it, without John ever having to risk upsetting him by saying that he thought Sue would be better.

Successful Persuasion

Research shows that there are a number of things that people like about successful persuaders.

Kurt Mortensen's research suggests that these elements are largely emotional. They include keeping promises, being reliable and taking responsibility, being sincere, genuine, and honest, knowing their subject, and believing in it, building rapport, and being entertaining, as well as not arguing and providing solutions that work.

The key skills for successful persuasion, then, are pretty wide. First of all, successful persuaders tend to have high self-esteem and good Emotional Intelligence more generally. They really believe that they will succeed.

Building Relationships

You also need to remain motivated and believe in yourself and your ideas. See our pages on Self-motivation for more. Additionally, you need to understand how your audience thinks.

Key skills here include Empathy, and good Listening Skills, including Active Listening.

> *If you listen, your audience will usually tell you what and how they are thinking.*

It also helps to be able to build rapport; people like those who take time to become a friend, as well as an influencer. It follows, really: if we are honest, we would all much rather do what a friend suggests than someone we dislike, however sensible the idea. Building rapport also helps to build trust.

Good persuaders or influencers also have very good Communication Skills.

It is essential that you can get your point across succinctly and effectively, otherwise you are never going to persuade anyone of the merits of your position.

The final skill of good persuaders is being organised. They do their homework; they know their audience and they know their subject. They have taken time to organise themselves and think about what they want to achieve.

It takes time, but develop these skills, and you will start to develop 'authentic power', which means that you have power because people believe in what you are saying. Once you have that, you are likely to be much more successful in persuading and influencing others, whether at home or at work.

Building Relationships

Barriers to Successful Persuasion

One way to think about what works in persuading others is to think about what does not work first.

In his book Persuasion IQ, Kurt Mortensen lists ten obstacles to successful persuasion:

1. Thinking that you are better at persuasion than you are, and therefore failing to hone your skills. Instead, take a long, hard look at yourself, and see where your skills need to be improved.
2. Trying too hard to persuade. Seeming too keen probably puts people off faster than anything else.
3. Failing to put in the effort required to get what you want. Nothing, or at least not much, is free in this world.
4. Talking too much. Stop, and just listen to the people you need to persuade.
5. Providing too much information, which just confuses people, and makes them think you are trying to blind them with science. What, they ask, are you not telling them
6. Getting desperate. Like insincerity, people can spot fear at a distance, and do not like it.
7. Being afraid of rejection. This can even stop people from trying to persuade in extreme cases.
8. Not being prepared. You cannot 'wing it' every time. Your audience will see through you and will think that you value your time more highly than theirs.
9. Making assumptions about your audience, and then not being prepared to reassess when new evidence emerges.
10. Forgetting that the whole conversation is important. You need to engage in order to persuade, right from the beginning.

Building Relationships

Influencing Skills

As organisational hierarchies and layers diminish, developing personal effectiveness and influencing skills is essential in today's workplace. Success and outcomes can only be achieved through, with and from others. Being able to influence without formal authority is an essential skill, and we cannot do this without confidence, clarity of purpose and the communication skills to fully express ourselves. And as leaders our roles require that we draw on who we are, as well as what we do to inspire and engage our people.

But influencing skills is not just about getting others always to agree to our point of view – we may be able to influence them to cooperate with us AND they may not always agree with us. It is not about winning at all costs and having to get our own way all of the time. It is not about forcing or getting others to change – we cannot change others.

Influencing skills IS about behaving in ways that offers others the invitation to change (their behaviour, attitudes, thoughts, and ways) and/or accommodate your own wishes whilst accepting that they may be unable to or unwilling to or are unprepared to meet our request to be influenced.

Definitions of influencing skills

> *"It is not the ability to get someone to do what you want them to do, it's the ability to get yourself to do what you want to do"*

Whether we like it or not, the fact is we are using influencing skills all the time and not just by our actions. Our very presence at a meeting may influence people positively or negatively. The style or nature of our presence, what we say or how we say it and the attitude we (unconsciously or otherwise) project speaks volumes.

> *"It is everything we say or don't say, do or don't do, are or are not, that modifies, affects, or changes someone else's behaviour, thoughts, or actions, consciously or unconsciously, for good or for ill"*

The smarter we can get at knowing what we do, or what it is about us, that impacts on others, the more personally effective and powerful we can become.

Ten key influencing skills

> **Observation** – *paying attention to non-verbal behaviour – what is not said, how a person may be feeling, paying attention to your own thoughts, feelings, hunches, and intuitions*

Building Relationships

Interpretation – *to understand and respond to non-verbal behaviour – what do particular body signs, changes in skin colour, breathing, demeanour, etc.*

Active Listening – *to hear what is said and to hear what is implied or not said as well as being able to communicate in your own words what the other person has said and reflect their feelings as well as summarising checks for clarity and agreement.*

Feedback – *offer feedback to the other person about what you see, interpret, hear as well as what you feel and intuit. Elicit feedback from others to develop your own self-knowledge and your impact on others.*

Awareness – *be aware of yourself, moment by moment, particularly of behaviour patterns which are counter-productive, your limiting thoughts, beliefs, and reactions.*

Choices – *recognise at any moment that, if how you are behaving is unproductive, you can change your own thoughts, feelings, and behaviours.*

Self-confidence – *to feel confident about yourself in the face of resistance or conflict. This confidence should be based on acceptance of self and not on felt superiority to the other person.*

Timing – *be able to get the timing right such as when to give feedback and when not to, when to use choice 'A' or 'B', when to retreat or be persistent and when to let go completely.*

Intuition – *trust your own feelings or hunches about the likely patterns of the other person's behaviour, to listen to your positive, inner voice.*

Other's Viewpoint – *to look at your objectives (what you want) from the other person's point of view. You cannot control or order them to agree so decide what is in it for them, sell them the benefits, consider their feelings, and be prepared to alter your position.*

Today's working environment depends very much on relationships and influencing skills – both working with and through other people. It is rare that you can be personally effective and influence others positively without the reciprocal giving to and taking from others that creates opportunities for your growth and your effectiveness – and you can only achieve this if you have the support and challenge that only other people can give you.

How to develop influencing skills

We often have to persuade and influence those over whom we have no real authority. The question is how to do this in an effective and subtle way? A subtle, empathetic approach is recommended rather than a more direct or forceful style

Influencing requires empathy

Building Relationships

Give the other party the impression that you have met them halfway or further. A subtle, empathetic approach is recommended rather than a more direct or forceful style.

If you can give the other party the impression that you have met them halfway or further, that they have bought into or even come up with the idea themselves you will get real support and longer lasting results.

Successful influencing is about making a connection and appealing to the heart as well as the head. It is about identifying personal triggers and adapting your style to others to get the best results from the people you are trying to influence.

Seven tips to develop your influencing skills

A combination of communication and interpersonal skills will help you to get the results you need. Below are some practical hints to help develop your powers of influencing whether you need a decision from your boss, an "awkward" peer to help you or a client to accept your new prices.

1. **Create Rapport**
   Create rapport with the person you are trying to influence – it may sound like common sense but if they like and trust you there is a greater possibility that you will be able to persuade them

2. **Listen**
   Listen and show you are listening. If someone feels valued, they are more likely to be persuaded to your point of view

3. **Ask the right questions**
   Use questioning techniques to lead people towards the answers you want. The art of influencing does not come naturally

4. **Be aware of body language**
   Mirror the other person's body language to create better rapport

5. **Sell the benefits**
   Sell the benefits of your argument to the other person and try to see your position from their perspective

6. **Be relaxed**
   A relaxed and natural demeanour is more likely to achieve a successful outcome rather than an emotional or demanding approach. Demonstrating a natural confidence will help to persuade others that your ideas are good

7. **Invest your time**
   Influencing is not a quick fix. It can take time to develop empathy and awareness, but you are more likely to get what you want if you play a long game

Building Relationships

The art of influencing does not come naturally to everyone. There are many sources of help for you to develop your influencing skills. Check out some great online resources and videos, LinkedIn groups and, of course, training is always an option to help you hone and develop your influencing skills.

Chapter 5: Problem Solving and Decision Making

Problem Solving and Decision Making

Solving Problems and Making Decisions

Every day the average manager will make hundreds of decisions. Very often, these will be minor inconsequential matters which had the questioner thought, they could have solved the problem for themselves. Sometimes however, the decisions are more important. The consequences and implications of a wrong decision could have serious repercussions on the organisation. In the case of a doctor, a fireman or a pilot, the consequences could be so grave as to be life threatening.

Problem solving skills include:

- *Thinking logically/mathematically*
- *Reasoning*
- *Using what you know to work out something you don't know*
- *Working systematically*
- *Using visual clues, such as worked examples and videos*
- *Making choices*
- *Making modifications*

In business the decisions are less likely to be life threatening but can still have serious implications for the organisation, the employees and the stakeholders. As a consequence, it is important that problems are resolved and important decisions are made only after careful consideration and thoughtful reflection.

The difference between problem-solving and decision-making

There is a difference between problem-solving and decision-making. They are closely linked skills that are very important in leadership and management roles, but they are not the same.

The Dictionary, definitions are:

> *Problem-solving – the process of finding solutions to difficult or complex issues*
> *Decision-making – the action or process of making decisions, especially important ones*

> *Decisions need to be made about how problems are going to be solved.*

When a problem needs solving, a series of decisions must be made along the way.

For instance, if the problem needing a solution is how to pay for a new sofa ordered for delivery in six months' time, decisions need to be made about how the money will be accrued to pay for it.

Level 5: Operations / Departmental Manager

Problem Solving and Decision Making

Problem-solving skills are needed to find possible solutions to the problem:

- *using savings that are set aside for something else* – e.g., a new car
- *reducing current essential costs* – e.g., money spent on bills or travel expenses
- *reducing the money spent on non-essential items* – e.g., take-aways and socialising
- *increasing income* – e.g., from overtime or a second job
- *borrowing money* – e.g., taking out a loan

There are many methods that could be used to solve the problem, and we can quantify the different options to show much each one could add to our sofa fund. To fully solve the problem, we need act, not just write down the options.

Before taking action to resolve the problem decision-making skills are needed to make the most suitable choices.

This is a process and needs to be considered in more detail. Each proposed action must be considered in detail before a decision can be made as to which is the best one to take.

For example, if increasing earnings is under consideration questions that need to be answered could include:

- Does the employer have any extra work? Is overtime available?
- How much extra would be generated after tax and national insurance?
- How many hours would be needed to generate the money needed?
- How much would be spent on travel, parking costs and additional expenses for the extra shifts?
- How might doing so much overtime affect other aspects of life– e.g., health, relationships or social commitments?
- Is there scope to take on a second job for a while to pay for the sofa?
- How would such a job be found and what would it pay?

Problem Solving and Decision Making

Scope, Nature and Impact

There are three elements to all problems, which must be understood before any remedial action can be taken. These are the Scope of the problem, the Nature of the problem and the Impact the problem could have.

Understanding the nature, scope and impact of a problem

Having a 360° view of a problem is critical when managers solve problems and make decisions. The more information and data they have at their disposal, the more informed they will be, making them more likely to make appropriate decisions.

When assessing a problem, a manager needs to go through a series of processes that are not dissimilar to those made by a doctor when making a diagnosis.

When diagnosing the patient, a doctor needs to:

- *examine the patient*
- *question them*
- *check mobility*
- *check temperature*
- *assess the scope and impact of the problem*
- *perform or request further tests* – e.g., blood tests or scans
- *research extra information if they cannot make an instant diagnosis*
- *consult with colleagues*
- *ask specialists for advice and guidance*

Very often, the diagnosis can be made and a treatment plan can be put in place. However, sometimes the diagnosis is not straightforward, and the doctor will have to try different options before the best form of treatment can be found.

The same sort of processes apply in management.

Managers need to investigate and assess problems thoroughly before they can make decisions about the possible solutions.

Problem Solving and Decision Making

Typical problems might include:

- **Equipment failure** – e.g., production machinery, lifts, ITC equipment or vehicles
- **Accidents involving equipment** – e.g., using equipment incorrectly and damaging it
- **Accidents involving people** – e.g., staff or customers having slips, trips and falls in the workplace; injuries after lifting incorrectly; ladders and steps slipping
- **Problems with physical resources** – e.g., insufficient resources; delays in the supply chain; damaged goods; poor-quality supplies; late or missing deliveries
- **Problems with human resources** – e.g., insufficient skills, knowledge or experience to be able to deal with tasks; staff absences causing delays and cancellations
- **Missed deadlines** – e.g., failing to deliver tasks, products, services or reports on time due to poor time management, bad weather or staff problems
- **Customer complaints** – e.g., faulty goods; late deliveries of products; receiving rude service; not having their telephone calls answered quickly; letters and emails not being answered
- **Difficulties with working relationships between colleagues** – e.g., arguments or disharmony within a team; harassment, bullying or discrimination; communication problems

The Nature of the problem

When analysing problems, the first thing a manager needs to know is the nature of the problem

A manager needs to know what the problem is. They need to ask questions, such as:

- Is the problem a life-threatening emergency?
- Has anyone been hurt or affected by the problem?
- Is the problem urgent?
- Have emergency procedures been put into action?
- What is the background to the problem?
- When, where and how did things go wrong?
- Has the problem happened before – if so, how was it handled before?

For example, if there is a fire in one of the offices, the manager initially needs to know what is happening, who is involved, if everyone is safe and if emergency services have been called.

Soon after the initial actions, managers need to look at how, when and why things went wrong.

Problems can be put into three broad categories:

- **Critical problems** – where immediate action and decisions are required
- **Non-critical problems** – not urgent and often routine, these still need early attention to stop them becoming crises

Problem Solving and Decision Making

- **Opportunity problems** – *where there is an element of choice that is driven by opportunity to improve rather than by routine or crisis*

The Scope of the problem

Having full details about the nature of the problem enables managers to assess the scope of the problem.

When considering the scope of a problem, managers look at the potential size of the problem:

- **exactly what is affected?** – *e.g., a small work area or the whole building; the stock on a shelf or a full warehouse that contains six months' supply of materials; the budget and deadlines*
- **exactly who is affected?** – *e.g., one person, a small team, a large department or the whole organisation; suppliers or customers; two people or 20,000 people*
- **who might be able to solve the problem?** – *e.g., are solutions within the scope of the manager's limits of authority, or will senior managers and external specialists be required?*

In this process, managers will look at how big the problem is, or how big it could be. They will look at how far the problem could affect:

- the team and others in the organisation
- customers and suppliers
- production and delivery of goods and services
- the building, infrastructure, machinery and equipment
- objectives, deadlines and budgets

INVESTIGATE THE SCOPE OF THE PROBLEM.

Using the same example, if there is a fire in an office, there is scope for the fire to spread throughout the rest of the building, threaten the health and safety of anyone in the area, destroy equipment, machinery and supplies and destroy jobs, customer relations and the business.

Problem Solving and Decision Making

The Impact of the problem

The impact of the problem is the knock-on effect of the problem. Managers need to be able to step back and analyse everything objectively and consider the wider impact of the problem and the possible solutions. This helps them to work out plans and strategies about how to overcome the problem.

The impact of problems can vary and it might not be possible to predict every outcome. The best that managers can do if they cannot assess the full impact of a problem is:

- **work on the basis of the impact being minimal** – *and plan actions and solutions for the best outcome*
- **be ready for maximum impact** – *and have outline plans in case they have to deal with the worst outcome*
- *Some problems only have a short-term impact.*
- *If temporary solutions can be found, or if the problem is routine and can be fixed quickly, the short-term impact might be minimal.*
- *Some problems have a long-term impact.*
- *The problems might be very difficult and expensive to solve and there could be a long-term impact and far-reaching consequences on finances, jobs, customer relations, the local area and so on.*

Following the office fire example, if the fire is put out quickly with no injuries or major damage, the impact effects could include:

- *Disruption to that day's activities only*
- *Inspections by fire officers and health and safety experts before being allowed to use the office again*
- *Time spent cleaning up and redecorating if necessary*
- *Some lost materials* – *e.g., paperwork*
- *Staff being upset but unhurt and unaffected by smoke due to a swift exit or extinguishing of the fire*
- *Replacing fire-fighting equipment immediately*
- *Operational changes following analysis of the causes of the fire*

If the fire cannot be put out quickly and safely and spreads to the entire factory that employs 100 people, the impact effects could also include:

- *Short-term emergency medical care for a large number of people*
- *Long-term health issues for some people* – *e.g., lung damage after smoke inhalation*
- *Destruction of the whole building and its contents*
- *Long and detailed investigations by police, fire officers, insurance assessors, health and safety specialists, legal representatives and others*

Problem Solving and Decision Making

- *Serious financial and legal consequences for the organisation, directors, managers and others*
- *Loss of jobs for all employees if the business cannot recover*

This example is extreme, but it does show how far-reaching the scope and impact of a problem can be.

Making Decisions

Some decisions will be so routine they are made without giving them much thought. But difficult or challenging decisions demand more consideration. These are the sort of decisions that involve:

- **Uncertainty** – Many of the facts may be unknown.
- **Complexity** – There can be many, interrelated factors to consider.
- **High-risk consequences** – The impact of the decision may be significant.
- **Alternatives** – There may be various alternatives, each with its own set of uncertainties and consequences.
- **Interpersonal issues** – You need to predict how different people will react.

When making a decision that involves complex issues like these, problem-solving will be needed, as well as decision-making skills. It pays to use an effective, robust process in these circumstances, to improve the quality of your decisions and to achieve consistently good results.

Problem-solving and decision-making techniques

Problem-solving and decision-making can be quite complicated processes – especially if the nature, scope and impact of the problem are considerable. When making the right decisions about which solutions to try, it can help to use a particular technique to evaluate the options.

Model	Key Features	Best Used
Algorithm model	Analytical in nature Clear Yes or No Answers	More effective in fault finding areas as fact-based results are produced
Plus, Minus, Implications Model	Based on judgements rather than facts Involves qualitative data	More effective when a rapid response or quick decision is needed
Six thinking hats	Group decision making sessions Key roles are identified for team members and may include members who are not involved	More effective when diverse input is needed as in larger organisation

Problem Solving and Decision Making

It is recognised that there are four basic rules that exist when considering potential outcomes and the impacts of decisions, and that one of these rules will always apply:

1. **Pessimistic rule** - choose the option that results in the highest possible outcome for the least likely option (worst case scenario)
2. **Optimistic rule** - choose the option that results in the best possible outcome (best case scenario)
3. **Expected value rule** - choose an option based on an estimate of the likelihood of a situation occurring (what if scenario)
4. **Opportunity rule** - consider the likely or potential opportunities that can be lost by applying any of the other rules (lost opportunities scenario)

There may be occasions when more than one rule will be integral to the process for making a decision, none more so than when using the six thinking hats model.

Algorithm Method

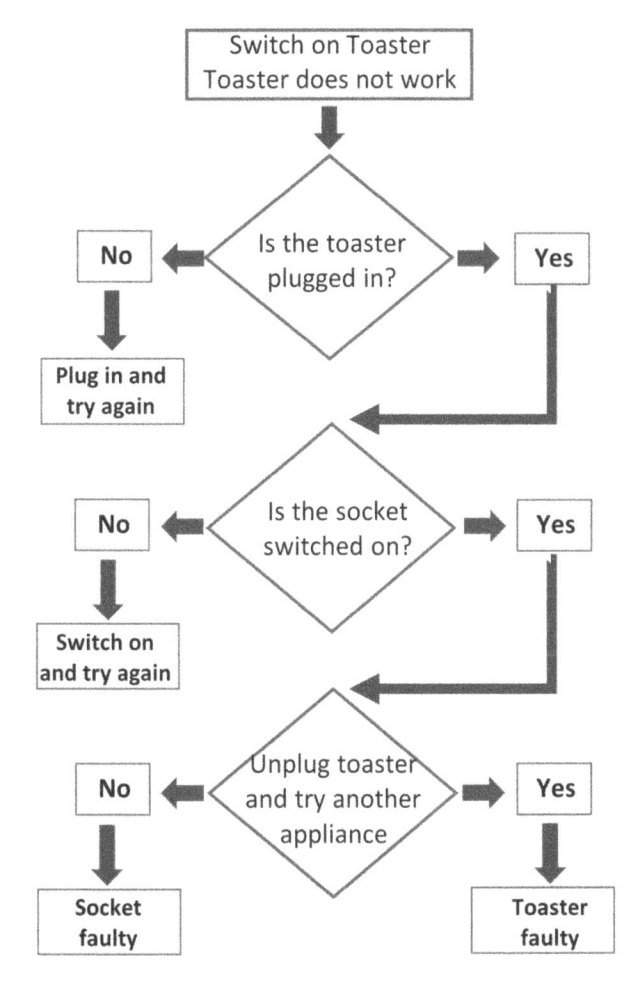

```
          Switch on Toaster
          Toaster does not work
                   │
                   ▼
    ┌──── Is the toaster ────┐
    No     plugged in?     Yes
    │                        │
    ▼                        │
Plug in and                  │
try again                    │
                             ▼
    ┌──── Is the socket ─────┐
    No    switched on?     Yes
    │                        │
    ▼                        │
Switch on                    │
and try again                │
                             ▼
    ┌──── Unplug toaster ────┐
    No   and try another   Yes
    │      appliance         │
    ▼                        ▼
  Socket                  Toaster
  faulty                   faulty
```

Problem Solving and Decision Making

PMI - Plus, Minus, Interesting

PMI (plus, minus, interesting) is a brainstorming, decision making and critical thinking tool. It is used to encourage the examination of ideas, concepts and experiences from more than one perspective. PMI was developed by Dr. Edward de Bono, a proponent of lateral and critical thinking.

Determining the Pros and Cons

A PMI strategy can help you to:

- *to brainstorm ideas*
- *make decisions quickly by analysing and weighing the pros and cons*
- *reflect upon or evaluate a product or processes after the fact*
- *identify strengths and weaknesses for future improvement*

To complete, make a chart of three columns - "Plus", "Minus" and "Interesting."

Plus	Minus	Interesting

Step 1. Consider the Plus Points
Simply enumerate all of the positive things. Do not critique along the way, simply spill out all conceivable positive points.

Step 2. Consider the Minus Points
Enumerate all of the negative things. Again, do not critique. Simply spill out all the negative points.

Step 3. Consider the Interesting Points of the Situation.
List all the interesting points. Rather than positive or negative, they are simply points of interest that attention should be directed towards.

Step 4. Make the conclusion
Make the judgement based on the three important aspects: the positives, the negatives, and the interesting which have been identified and organised.

Problem Solving and Decision Making

It is a great tool for critical thinking, focussing your attention, evaluating and analysing. After you have used this technique, you should be in a better position to make your decision.

Edward de Bono's - Six thinking hats

If a manager is naturally optimistic, then chances are they will not always consider potential downsides. Similarly, if they are very cautious or have a risk-averse outlook, they might not focus on opportunities that could open up.

Often, the best decisions come from changing the way that people think about problems and examining them from different viewpoints.

Edward de Bono's - Six thinking Hats

Facts	Emotion	Benefit	Ideas	Planning	Judgement
neutral	emotional view	logical positive	creativity	process control	logical negative
neutral and objective, concerned with data, facts, figures, and information	the intuitive view, hunches, "gut" feeling	optimistic, sunny, and positive covers hope	associated with energy, fertility, growth, new ideas. Switches around the normal superiority of the Black Hat	the organising hat (start and finish) controls the use of the other hats	careful and cautious, the "judgement" hat

"Six Thinking Hats" can help look at problems from different perspectives, but one at a time, to avoid confusion from too many angles crowding thinking.

> *Decision makers often wear many hats in order to devise a well-rounded solution.*

It is also a powerful decision-checking technique in group situations, as everyone explores the situation from each perspective at the same time. It forces thinking outside habitual styles, and to look at things from a number of different perspectives and gain a more rounded view of the situation.

Successful solutions or outcomes can often be achieved from a rational, positive viewpoint, but it can also pay to consider a problem from other angles. For example, looking at it from an emotional, intuitive, creative or risk management viewpoint. Not considering these

Problem Solving and Decision Making

perspectives could lead to underestimating people's resistance to the plans, fail to make creative leaps, or ignore the need for essential contingency plans.

Using the six thinking hats model

Six Thinking Hats can be used in meetings or alone. In meetings, it has the benefit of preventing any confrontation that may happen when people with different thinking styles discuss a problem, because every perspective is valid.

Each "Thinking Hat" is a different style of thinking.

- **White Hat:** with this thinking hat, the focus is on the available data. Look at the information to hand, analyse past trends, and see what can be learnt from it. Look for gaps in knowledge and try to either fill them or take account of them.

- **Red Hat:** The Red Hat looks at problems using intuition, gut reaction, and emotion. Also, think how others could react emotionally. Try to understand the responses of people who do not fully know the reasoning.

- **Black Hat:** Black Hat thinking, looks at a decision's potentially negative outcomes. Look at it cautiously and defensively. Try to see why it might not work. This is important because it highlights the weak points in a plan. It allows them to be eliminated, alter them, or prepare contingency plans to counter them. Black Hat thinking helps to make the plans "tougher" and more resilient. It can also help spot fatal flaws and risks before embarking on a course of action. It is one of the real benefits of this model, as many successful people get so used to thinking positively that they often cannot see problems in advance. This leaves them under-prepared for difficulties.

- **Yellow Hat:** this hat helps positive thinking. It is the optimistic viewpoint that helps see all the benefits of the decision and the value in it. Yellow Hat thinking helps to keep going when everything looks gloomy and difficult.

- **Green Hat:** The Green Hat represents creativity. This is where creative solutions to a problem are developed. It is a freewheeling way of thinking, in which there is little criticism of ideas.

- **Blue Hat:** this hat represents process control. It is the hat worn by people chairing meetings, for example. When facing difficulties because ideas are running dry, they may direct activity into Green Hat thinking. When contingency plans are needed, they will ask for Black Hat thinking.

A variant of this technique is to look at problems from the point of view of different professionals (for example, doctors, architects or sales directors) or different customers.

Problem Solving and Decision Making

An example of Six Hat thinking

The directors of a property company are considering whether they should build a new office block. The economy is doing well, and the vacant office spaces in their city are being snapped up. As part of their decision-making process, they adopt the Six Thinking Hats technique.

Wearing the White Hat, they analyse the data that they have. They can see that the amount of available office space in their city is dwindling, and they calculate that, by the time a new office block would be completed, existing space will be in extremely short supply. They also note that the economic outlook is good, and steady growth is predicted to continue.

Thinking with a Red Hat, some of the directors say that the proposed building looks ugly and gloomy. They worry that people would find it an oppressive or uninspiring place to work.

When they think with the Black Hat, they wonder whether the economic forecast could be wrong. The economy may be about to experience a downturn, in which case the building could sit empty or only partially occupied for a long time. If the building is unattractive, then companies will choose to work in other, more attractive premises.

Wearing the positive Yellow Hat, however, the directors know that, if the economy holds up and their projections are correct, the company stands to make a healthy profit. If they are lucky, maybe they could sell the building before the next downturn or rent to tenants on long-term leases that will last through any recession.

With Green Hat thinking, they consider whether they should redesign the building to make it more appealing. Perhaps they could build prestige offices that people would want to rent in any economic climate. Alternatively, maybe they should invest the money in the short term, then buy up property at a lower cost when the next downturn happens.

The chairman of the meeting wears the Blue Hat to keep the discussion moving and ideas flowing, encouraging the other directors to switch their thinking between the different perspectives.

Having examined their options from numerous viewpoints, the directors have a much more detailed picture of possible outcomes and can make their decision accordingly.

A 5-Step Approach

Some problems are small and can be resolved quickly. Other problems are large and may require significant time and effort to solve. These larger problems are often tackled by turning them into formal projects.

> *"A project is a problem scheduled for solution."*
> - Joseph M. Juran

Whether the problem you are focusing on is small or large, using a systematic approach for solving it will help you be a more effective manager.

Problem Solving and Decision Making

This approach defines five problem solving steps you can use for most problems...

- *Define the Problem*
- *Determine the Causes*
- *Generate Ideas*
- *Select the Best Solution*
- *Take Action*

Define the Problem
The most important of the problem-solving steps is to define the problem correctly. The way the problem is defined will determine how attempts are made to solve it. For example, a complaint is made about a team member from a client, the solutions identified will be different based on the way the problem is defined.

If you define the problem as poor performance by the team member you will develop different solutions than if you define the problem as poor expectation setting with the client.

Determine the Causes
Once the problem is defined, dig deeper and start to determine what is causing it. Use a fishbone diagram to help perform a cause-and-effect analysis.

If the problem is considered as a gap between where the business is now and where it wants to be, the causes of the problem are the obstacles that are preventing closure of that gap immediately.

This level of analysis is important to make sure solutions address the actual causes of the problem instead of the symptoms of the problem.

> *If the solution fixes a symptom instead of the actual cause, the problem is likely to reoccur since it was never truly solved.*

Generate Ideas
Once the hard work of defining the problem and determining its causes has been completed, it is time to get creative and develop possible solutions to the problem. Two great problem-solving methods to envisage solutions are brainstorming and mind mapping.

Select the Best Solution
Once several ideas have been identified that can solve the problem, one problem solving the best way to identify the most appropriate solution to the problem is a simple trade-off analysis.

To perform the trade-off analysis, define the critical criteria for the problem that can be used to evaluate how each solution compares to each other. The evaluation can be done using a simple matrix. The highest-ranking solution will be the best solution for this problem.

Problem Solving and Decision Making

Take Action
Once the solution for implementation has been identified, it is time to act. If the solution involves several actions or requires action from others, it is a good idea to create an action plan and treat it as a mini project.

Using this simple five-step approach can increase the effectiveness of your problem-solving skills.

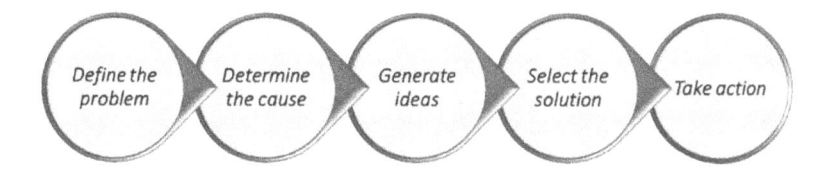

Define the problem → Determine the cause → Generate ideas → Select the solution → Take action

Kepner Tregoe Method

When problems occur in an organisation there are many pressures to solve the problem as quickly as possible. Decisions can be made spontaneously in the hope the problem may be fixed without first fully considering the issue which caused the problem in the first place. The KT-method allows the problem to be fully analysed making the decision relate to the solution.

When dealing with a problem there are four key questions to be asked:

1. What happened?
2. Why did it happen?
3. What is the response?
4. What will be the outcome?

Kepner and Tregoe devised four rational processes as a means of answering the questions:

Situation analysis - answers the question: **What is going on?**
The process includes identifying concerns, breaking down the issues into workable units, setting priorities, planning the next steps, and selecting the right people to resolve the problem. Situation analysis prioritises concerns and focusses on the true issue.

Problem analysis - answers the question: **What went wrong?**
Problem analysis is a way of finding the root cause of a problem by using both logic and data. It helps focus on the right data and avoids the temptation to identify the wrong cause before all the relevant facts have been reviewed. It requires that the problem be described, identifies and assess possible causes and analyses them to identify the root cause of the problem before remediation starts.

Decision analysis - answers the question: **What are the alternatives?**
Decision analysis is a defined process to systematically consider the best, balanced decision when the merits of alternatives is unclear. It clarifies purpose, evaluates

Problem Solving and Decision Making

alternatives, assesses the risks and benefits, and identifies the optimum choice. The use of Decision analysis clarifies the decision-making roles and responsibilities, identifies the appropriate performance objectives for each decision and provides clarity for making recommendations.

Potential Problem / Opportunity analysis - answers the question: **What might go wrong?**
Potential Problem Analysis anticipates issues and therefore change and improve the future, rather than walking into problems along the way. It identifies potential problems and the possible causes allowing mitigation and contingencies to be prepared.

Kepner Tregoe assert that, different tasks involve different problems, which therefore need different approaches to resolve them. A situation analysis clarifies the differences in all these processes and enable the search for suitable solutions. This situation analysis also illustrates the need, importance and urgency of the various tasks. When the tasks which are to be prioritised are identified preparations can be made for potential problems. Using problem analysis early, allows a process to be created which prevents the risk of future problems or in emergencies and limits the damage.

The KT-Method not only identifies the cause of problems, it also identifies the things which cannot be the cause. As a result it significantly increase clarity in the identification of causes.

The KT-Method is still used today to identify problems and the potential causes. As a result, it helps explain problems and improve the understanding of those problems across the organisation which in turn, improves communication with stakeholders, quality of production, customer service and problems related to routine maintenance.

Other Techniques Available

There are many techniques that we can use to help us find suitable solutions and make effective decisions. Such as:

- *SWOT analysis*
- *PESTLE analysis*
- *Root cause analysis*
- *The Simplex Process*
- *Paired comparison analysis*
- *Weighted grid analysis*
- *Gantt charts*
- *PDCA cycle*

Problem Solving and Decision Making

SWOT Analysis

One technique is to perform a SWOT analysis. Managers can produce these in a simple way to help to clarify their thinking and focus their attention on all aspects of the problem. A SWOT analysis is particularly useful for gathering, interpreting and analysing information. For each realistic possible solution, managers can analyse the following:

- S – Strengths
- W – Weaknesses
- O – Opportunities
- T – Threats to success

If a car has been breaking down and causing problems, a SWOT analysis could show, for example:

	Option A – have it fixed every time to keep it going for as long as possible – maybe another year	Option B – replace the car with a brand-new, up-to-date version that should last ten years	Option C – replace it with a second hand, model that should last five years
Strengths	Not too expensive to run The problems are well-known and familiar	Good reliability Up-to-date technology Good warranty support	Reasonable cost Its service history should indicate reliability Know how to operate it
Weaknesses	Cost of repairs Frequent disruption of your life that cannot be planned Drop in your efficiency and performance	Very expensive May have to make sacrifices Will be difficult to look after properly	Does not benefit from the most up-to-date technology and design Only a short warranty Could develop problems at any time
Opportunities	Easy to arrange with garage for repairs	Three possible suppliers Available in about two months	Plenty available if researched online Could be bought quickly as changes to storage arrangements not needed
Threats to success	Garage staff may refuse to repair it when it breaks again Repair costs are high Wages could be lost due to delays	Cost and budget constraints Might be outdated after a few years Personal benefits may not justify the cost	Cost might not be justifiable if planning to keep it for less than five years

Problem Solving and Decision Making

Although a SWOT analysis does not give a magic answer to the problem, it does help managers to identify the pros and cons of each option. Once they knew their budget constraints and the long-term organisational targets that could be affected by the vehicle in the example, managers would be able to make the best decision to solve the problem.

PESTLE Analysis

Another system that could be used when making well-informed decisions is a PESTLE analysis. This can be particularly useful when there are areas of concern outside of the control of the organisation, and for gathering, interpreting and analysing information.

For example, if the problem is that the company has outgrown its present site, it will have to consider many things that are outside its control. When doing a PESTLE analysis, managers would look at these areas:

P   Political – e.g., government funding for expanding in the same area or setting up in a different location

E   Economic – e.g., the overall economic climate and whether stakeholders would support investment and expansion if the economy is slow or in recession

S   Social – e.g., the effect on the local population if the company moves away/stays put and expands

T   Technological – e.g., the scope for using new technology as part of the expansion plans

L   Legal – e.g., legal requirements about redundancies or relocation of staff

E   Environmental – e.g., the regulations on emissions and waste management in the current area and the potential new area

Paired Comparison Analysis

This type of analysis is useful when managers need to work out relevant factors when choices are quite different from each other – rather like the classic case of comparing apples and oranges.

An example could be someone having to choose which type of charity to support – an animal charity, a bequest for university, a children's charity or disaster relief.

There are six stages:

Problem Solving and Decision Making

Stage 1 – make a list of things that need to be compared, assign each option a letter – e.g. A for Animals, B for Bequest, C for Children and D for Disaster.
Stage 2 – put the letters in a grid and block out squares where data would be duplicated.

Stage 3 – within each cell, compare the options and decided which is most important – e.g. A is more important than B in the above grid.

Stage 4 – give the letter a rating to show how important the choice is – e.g., from 0 for no importance to 3 for extremely important – A has been given rating 1 in the above grid.

Stage 5 – consolidate results by adding up the values for each of the options – maybe converting them to percentage values. In the example:

A = 1 (10%)	C = 5 (50%)
B = 0	D = 4 (40%)

Stage 6 – use common sense and manually adjust, as necessary. In the example:
After comparing the results, the person decides to make their main donation to the children's charity, with some going to disaster relief.

	A – Animal charity	B – Bequest for university	C – Children's charity	D – Disaster relief
A – Animal charity	XXXXXXXXXX	A1	C2	D2
B – Bequest for university	XXXXXXXXXX	XXXXXXXXXX	C2	D2
C – Children's charity	XXXXXXXXXX	XXXXXXXXXX	XXXXXXXXXX	C1
D – Disaster relief	XXXXXXXXXX	XXXXXXXXXX	XXXXXXXXXX	XXXXXXXXXX

Weighted Grid Analysis

A grid analysis is a useful technique to use when deciding, especially when there are numerous factors and alternatives to consider. There are several steps:

Step 1 – list the options as row labels and the factors as column labels
Step 2 – work out the relative importance of the factors in the decision and show them as numbers to give each factor a weight – e.g., from 1 (not important) to 5 (extremely important)
Step 3 – work through and score each option for each of the important factors – score from 0 (poor) to 3 (very good)
Step 4 – multiply each of the scores to reveal the relative importance
Step 5 – add up the weighted scores – the highest score 'wins'

Problem Solving and Decision Making

For example: a manager is deciding where to purchase a new computer to run the production line that is in operation 24 hours a day, 7 days a week. As it is a long-term investment, the quality of the machine and the back-up service from the supplier are extremely important.

	Factor 1 – Cost	Factor 2 – Availability	Factor 3 – Delivery time	Factor 4 – Quality	Factor 5 – 24/7 Support	Total
Weighting:	4	3	3	5	5	
Suppliers						
IBN	2	3	1	2	1	
Dill	3	2	2	2	3	
EP	2	3	2	3	0	
Toshiva	1	3	2	2	2	
Suny	2	2	3	2	2	

Then multiply the figures by the weights….

	Factor 1 – Cost	Factor 2 – Availability	Factor 3 – Delivery time	Factor 4 – Quality	Factor 5 – 24/7 Support	Total
Weighting:	4	3	3	5	5	
Suppliers						
IBN	2 x 4 = 8	3 x 3 = 9	1 x 3 = 3	2 x 5 = 10	1 x 5 = 5	35
Dill	3 x 4 = 12	2 x 3 = 6	2 x 3 = 6	2 x 5 = 10	3 x 5 = 15	49
EP	2 x 4 8	3 x 3 = 9	2 x 3 = 6	3 x 5 = 15	0 x 5 = 0	38
Toshiva	1 x 4 = 4	3 x 3 = 9	2 x 3 = 6	2 x 5 = 10	2 x 5 = 10	39
Suny	2 x 4 8	2 x 3 6	3 x 3 9	2 x 5 10	2 x 5 10	43

In this example, Dill come out as the favoured supplier.

Problem Solving and Decision Making

Gantt Charts

Gantt charts are often used in project management to show activities against time. They are extremely useful when the problems are complex and interconnected, with various deadlines and targets that have an effect on each other and are frequently used as planning tools.

Managers need to start by breaking down the overall problem into smaller tasks or activities. Each activity is represented by a bar, and its position and length illustrate the start and end dates. Gantt charts enable managers and others to see:

- *what the activities are*
- *when activities and whole projects begin and end*
- *how long each activity is scheduled to last*
- *where they overlap, and by how much*

Task	Sept 19	Oct 19	Nov 19	Dec 19	Jan 20	Feb 20	Mar 20	Apr 20
Planning		xxxx	xxxx					
Research			xxxx	xx				
Design				xxxx				
Implementation					xxxx	xxxx		
Review							x	xx

Gantt charts can become exceptionally large in size as well as content and depending on the problem, can become hugely complex. If this is the case, try using additional colours symbols etc to better identify the areas involved.

When making decisions, they are a flexible tool that can be used to show all of the variables and how they need to work together. In the example above, for instance, the manager can see how the design process has to be finished by the end of December, so that it does not delay the implementation start date at the beginning of January.

Root Cause Analysis (RCA)

This is a method of finding possible solutions by identifying the root causes of faults or problems. It is also referred to as cause-and-effect analysis and makes use of fishbone diagrams, herringbone diagrams and Ishikawa diagrams, named after Professor Kaoru Ishikawa, a pioneer of quality management in the 1960s.

The technique can be used to:

- *discover the root cause of problems, especially for complicated problems*
- *reveal 'bottlenecks' in a process that are causing delays*
- *identify where and why a process does not work*
- *improve quality control*

Problem Solving and Decision Making

Step 1 – identify the problem – e.g., what the problem is, who is involved, where and when it occurs.

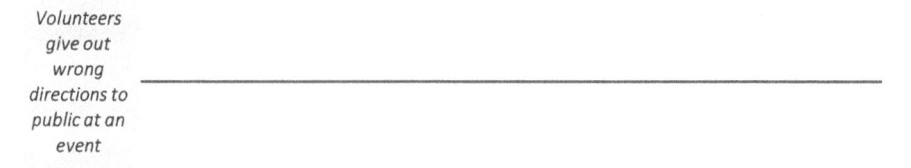

Volunteers give out wrong directions to public at an event
_____

Step 2 – work out the major factors involved – e.g., systems, equipment, materials or external forces.

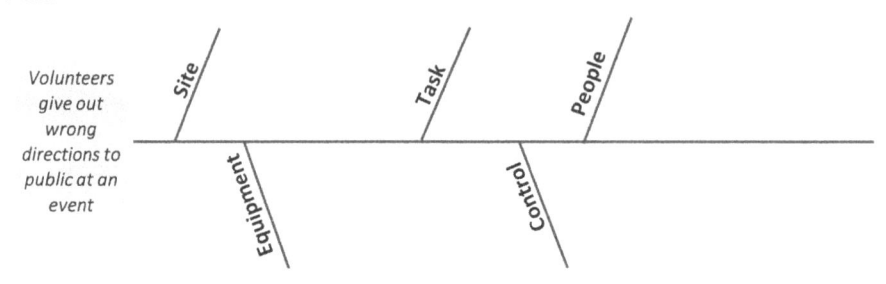

Volunteers give out wrong directions to public at an event

Branches: Site, Task, People, Equipment, Control

Step 3 – identify possible causes – e.g., brainstorm the different problems in Step 2 and add them to the diagram.

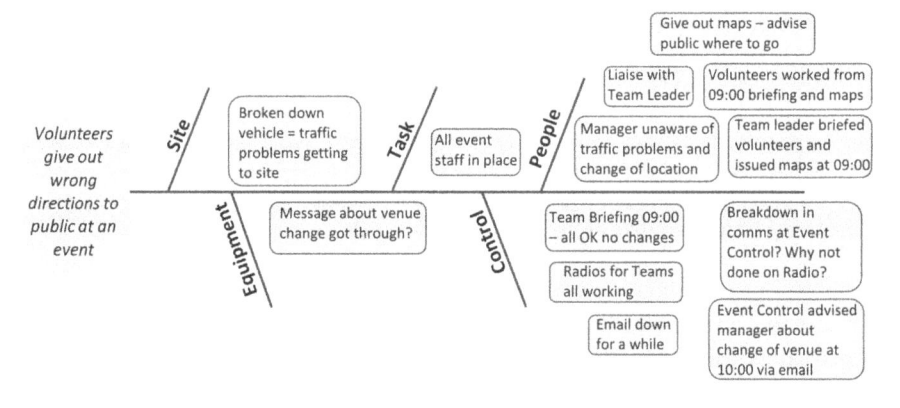

Volunteers give out wrong directions to public at an event

- **Site**: Broken down vehicle = traffic problems getting to site
- **Task**: All event staff in place
- **People**:
  - Give out maps – advise public where to go
  - Liaise with Team Leader
  - Volunteers worked from 09:00 briefing and maps
  - Manager unaware of traffic problems and change of location
  - Team leader briefed volunteers and issued maps at 09:00
- **Equipment**: Message about venue change got through?
- **Control**:
  - Team Briefing 09:00 – all OK no changes
  - Radios for Teams all working
  - Email down for a while
  - Breakdown in comms at Event Control? Why not done on Radio?
  - Event Control advised manager about change of venue at 10:00 via email

Step 4 – analyse the diagram – e.g., look at all of the possible causes and look out for problem areas that have a knock-on effect on other issues.

In this example, we can see that:

- *traffic problems caused delays*
- *volunteers worked from notes and maps given out at their 09:00 briefing*
- *the manager was informed about the change of venue at 10:00 via email*
- *email was down for a while and the message was not received or actioned*

Level 5: Operations / Departmental Manager

Problem Solving and Decision Making

The manager would need to make further investigations to see why the communication failed from event control and why there was no backup plan to let people know about the changes.

The Problem-Solving Cycle (PDCA)

The problem-solving cycle is a frame of reference for using various problem-solving methods. In this model there are six phases in problem solving:

- Naming the problem
- Analysing
- Goal setting
- Searching for solutions
- Planning
- Evaluation

What Is PDCA?

PDCA, sometimes called PDSA, the "Deming Wheel," or "Deming Cycle," was developed by renowned management consultant Dr William Edwards Deming in the 1950s. Deming himself called it the "Shewhart Cycle," as his model was based on an idea from his mentor, Walter Shewhart.

Deming wanted to create a way of identifying what caused products to fail to meet customers' expectations. His solution helps businesses to develop hypotheses about what needs to change, and then test these in a continuous feedback loop.

The four phases are:

Plan: *identify and analyse the problem or opportunity, develop hypotheses about what the issues may be, and decide which one to test.*
Do: *test the potential solution, ideally on a small scale, and measure the results.*
Check/Study: *study the result, measure effectiveness, and decide whether the hypothesis is supported or not.*
Act: *if the solution was successful, implement it.*

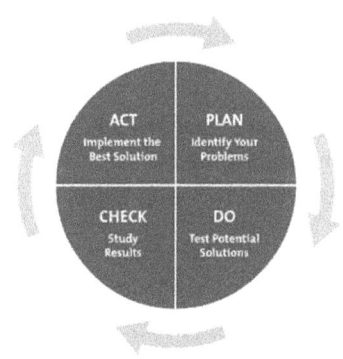

Problem Solving and Decision Making

The PDCA cycle helps solve problems and implement solutions in a rigorous, methodical way. Follow these four steps to ensure the highest quality results.

1. Plan
First, identify and understand the problem, or the opportunity to be taken advantage of. Using the first six steps of The Simplex Process can help to achieve this, by guiding through a process of exploring information, defining the problem, generating and screening ideas, and developing an implementation plan.

At the final part of this stage, state quantitatively what the expectations are if the idea is successful and the problem is resolved. The process returns to this point after the Check stage.

2. Do
Once a potential solution is identified, test it with a small-scale pilot project. This will allow the opportunity to assess whether the proposed changes achieve the desired outcome, with minimal disruption to the rest of the operation if they do not. For example, organise a trial within a department, in a limited geographical area, or with a particular demographic.

3. Check
At this stage, analyse the pilot project's results against the expectations that were defined in Step 1 to assess whether the idea has worked or not. If it has not worked, return to Step 1. If it has worked, move on to Step 4.

Try out more changes and repeat the Do and Check phases – do not settle for a less-than-satisfactory solution.

Move on to the final phase (Act) only when genuinely happy with the trial's outcome.

4. Act
This is where the solution is implemented. But remember that PDCA / PDSA is a loop, not a process with a beginning and an end. This means that the improved process or product becomes the new baseline, and the search continues to find ways to make it even better for the organisation or customers.

When to use PDCA
The PDCA framework can improve any process or product by breaking it into smaller steps. It is particularly effective for:

- *Helping to improve processes.*
- *Exploring a range of solutions to problems and piloting them in a controlled way before selecting one for implementation.*
- *Avoiding wastage of resources by rolling out an ineffective solution on a wide scale.*

The model can be used in all sorts of business environments, from new product development, project and change management, to product lifecycle and supply chain management.

Problem Solving and Decision Making

Pros and Cons of PDCA
The model is a simple, yet powerful way to resolve new and recurring issues in any industry, department or process. Its iterative approach allows solutions to be tested and results assessed in a waste-reducing cycle.

It instils a commitment to continuous improvement, however small, and can improve efficiency and productivity in a controlled way, without the risks of making large scale, untested changes to processes.
However, going through the PDCA cycle can be much slower than a straightforward, "gung-ho" implementation. So, it might not be the appropriate approach for dealing with an urgent problem or emergency.

It also requires significant "buy-in" from team members, and offers fewer opportunities for radical innovation, if that is what the organisation needs.

8D Report

What is an 8D Report?
The 8D Report is a problem-solving approach for product and process improvement. Furthermore, 8D Methodology is used to implement structural long-term solutions to prevent recurring problems. The 8D Report was first used in the automotive industry.

Eight Disciplines
The 8D Methodology mainly focuses on solving problems and comprises 8 steps or disciplines. It helps quality control staff find the root cause of problems within a production process in a structured manner so that they can resolve the problem(s).

In addition, it helps implement product or process improvements, which can prevent problems.

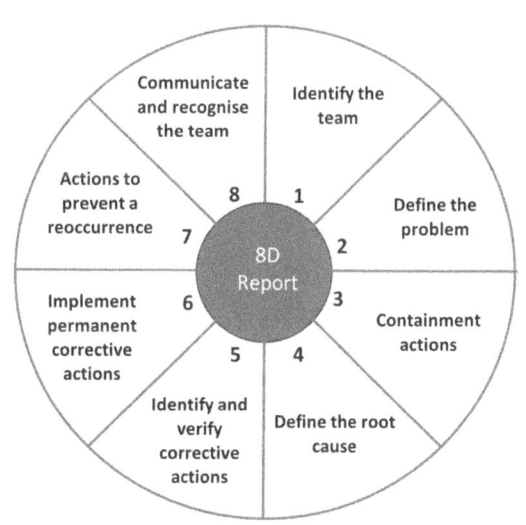

Problem Solving and Decision Making

D1 – Create a team
Mobilising a good team is essential. The team must preferably be multidisciplinary. Due to a varied combination of knowledge, skills and experience, one can look at a problem from different perspectives.

Besides having an effective team leader, it is also advisable to record team structure, goals, different team roles, procedures and rules in advance so that the team can begin taking action quickly and effectively, and there is no room for misunderstandings.

D2 – Describe the problem
Define the problem as objectively as possible. The 5W2H analysis (who, what, when, where, why, how, how much) is a welcome addition to the problem analysis and can help to arrive at a clear description of the problem.

D3 – Interim containment action
It may be necessary to implement temporary fixes. For example, to help or meet a customer quickly or when a deadline has to be met. It is about preventing a problem from getting worse until a permanent solution is implemented.

D4 – Identify the root cause
Before a permanent solution is found, it is important to identify all possible root causes that could explain why the problem occurred. Various methods can be used for this purpose, such as the fishbone diagram (Ishikawa) which considers factors such as people, equipment, machines and methods or the 5 whys method. All causes must be checked and/ or proven and it is good to check why the problem was not noticed at the time it occurred.

D5 – Developing permanent corrective actions
As soon as the root cause of the problem has been identified, it is possible to search for the best possible solution. Again, various problem-solving methods can be used such as value analysis and creative problem solving. From here, permanent corrective actions can be selected and it must be confirmed that the selected corrective actions will not cause undesirable side effects. It is therefore advisable to define contingency actions that will be useful in unforeseen circumstances.

D6 – Implementing permanent corrective actions
As soon as the permanent corrective actions are identified, they can be implemented. By planning ongoing controls, possible underlying root causes are detected far in advance. The long-term effects should be monitored and unforeseen circumstances should be taken into account.

D7 – Preventive measures
Prevention is the best cure. This is why additional measures need to be taken to prevent similar problems. Preventative measures ensure that the possibility of recurrence is minimised. It is advisable to review management systems, operating systems and procedures, so that they can be improved procedures if necessary.

D8 – Congratulate the team

Problem Solving and Decision Making

By congratulating the team on the results realised, all members are rewarded for their joint efforts. This is the most important step within the 8D method; without the team the root cause of the problem would not have been found and fixed.

By putting the team on a pedestal and sharing the knowledge throughout the organisation, team motivation will be high to solve a problem the next time it presents itself.

A strength of the 8D Report is its focus on teamwork. The team as a whole is believed to be better and smarter than the sum of the qualities of the individuals. Not every problem justifies or requires the 8D Report. Furthermore, the 8D Report is a fact-based problem-solving process, which requires a number of specialised skills, as well as a culture of continuous improvement. It could be that training of the team members is required before 8D can work effectively within an organisation. The team must recognise the importance of cooperation in order to arrive at the best possible solution for implementation

Facts, Optimism, Creativity, Understanding, Solve (FOCUS)

The FOCUS model is valuable in problem solving because it uses a team-based approach to resolving issues which works well for solving cross-departmental issues. The approach also encourages people to rely on objective data rather than on personal opinions which increases the quality of the outcome.

The FOCUS model has five steps:

Find the problem.
Organise a team to deal with the problem.
Clarify the problem.
Understand the problem.
Select a solution.

Facts/Problem Definition
The objective is to clearly state the problem and break it into manageable parts. Present facts in unambiguous, concrete terms, separate from assumptions, and differentiate relevant from irrelevant information. Seek all available facts to answer who, what, when, where, why, and how of the situation.

- *Differentiate fact from opinion*
- *Specify underlying causes*
- *Consult each faction involved for information*
- *State the problem specifically*
- *Identify what standard or expectation is violated*
- *Determine in which process the problem lies*
- *Avoid trying to solve the problem without data*

Problem Solving and Decision Making

Optimism/Problem Orientation
The objective is to develop a sense of optimism regarding problem-solving ability. This includes instilling a belief that one is sufficiently skilled to solve problems, as well as instilling a sense of motivation to engage in problem-solving process while simultaneously regulating emotional experiences to maintain a sense of confidence.

Creativity/Generation of Alternative Solutions
The objective is to actively brainstorm multiple solutions to the problem of highest priority.

- Postpone evaluating alternatives initially
- Include all involved individuals in the generating of alternatives
- Specify alternatives consistent with organisational goals
- Specify short- and long-term alternatives
- Brainstorm on others' ideas
- Seek alternatives that may solve the problem

Understanding/Decision-making
The objective is to outline the process needed to make an informed, wise, and appropriate choice that maximises the probability of a positive outcome. Deciding about the "best" strategy to try and solve the problem requires a thoughtful consideration of gains and benefits of the best available strategies.

Solve/Implementation & Verification
The objective is solving the problem and then systematically reviewing the outcome to determine how the solution worked and the degree to which the actual outcome approximates the expected one. This self-monitoring is crucial for learning what made a solution effective or ineffective and how to implement a similar solution or use a different solution in the future.

Problem Definition Process

Problem Definition Process is a tool that can be used to compare different problems, for example, within an organisation or in a project, and can highlight general problems that were previously unclear.

What initially appears to be the whole problem is often only a part or a symptom of a larger, deeper, and more complex issue. The problem definition process helps to visualise the problem, by presenting it from different angles and to help define the broader context and associated problems.

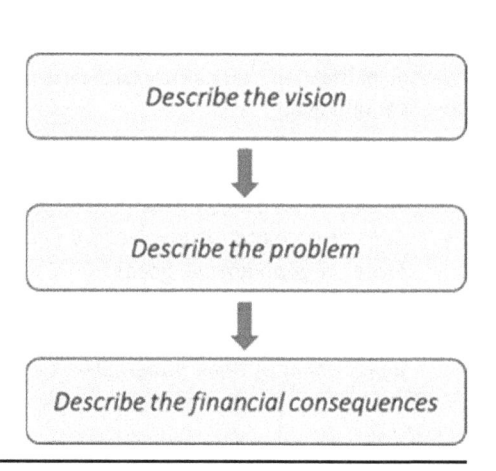

Describe the vision
↓
Describe the problem
↓
Describe the financial consequences

Problem Solving and Decision Making

Implementing the Problem Definition Process is especially effective when all stakeholders are involved. In this way, one can develop valuable insights about the size of the problem and its possible consequences. In addition, one can develop ideas about creative solutions, even if the solutions are not part of the problem definition process. However, defining the problem is essential before switching to, for example, a Root Cause Analysis, making an Ishikawa diagram or performing a cause-and-effect analysis.

Approaching the problem with sufficient background information is advantageous, in that one can spot previously unforeseen issues.

Steps in the Problem Definition Process

1. Describe the vision
Start by describing how things should work in the most ideal situation. Before the problem is described or treated, a few sentences should be used to explain what the situation would be if the problem did not exist.

Take, for example, the check-in protocol of a small airline. If every passenger has to check in at the airport, long queues develop as a result and this takes up a lot of time. An inefficient check-in protocol is time consuming and entails extra costs. This is a problem. After all, the aircraft has to depart as soon as possible. The check-in protocol must therefore be optimised, while making the situation understandable for all passengers.

2. Describe the problem
Accurately describing the problem is often half the work. Summarise the problem briefly and position the key information at the beginning of the single-phrase problem definition. In the case of the airline company, this could be that: The company's current check-in protocol is inefficient in use. By wasting man-hours, the current protocol makes the company less competitive and a slower check-in process creates an unfavourable brand image.

3. Describe the financial consequences of the problem
Once the problem is defined, it must be explained why it is a problem. After all, nobody has the means to solve every small problem. For example, if the airline transports 50 passengers per day, and if the current check-in protocol wastes about 6 minutes per passenger, this results in a loss of about 5 hours per day, which amounts to £100 per day, or £36,500 per year. A cost-benefit analysis, for example, can show whether the investment into an online check-in portal can be recouped.

Using Lean's "5 times why" method (who, what, where, when and why) when defining the problem definition, all five W's should be fully answered.

Problem Solving and Decision Making

- Who causes or can influence the problem?
- What would the situation be if the problem did not exist, and what is the situation in the future if the problem persists?
- Where does the problem take place?
- When does the problem have to be solved?
- Why is it important to solve the problem?
- What are some questions that can be asked here?
- Is the problem temporary or permanent?
- How many people are affected by the problem?
- Does this analysis of the problem possibly affect existing knowledge, practices or protocols?
- Polish the problem definition

Some tips for improving the problem definition are:

Be concise
One thing to keep in mind when writing the problem definition is to keep it as short and clear as possible. The problem definition must not be longer than necessary and must be understood by everyone who reads it. Use clear, direct language and do not get stuck in small details. Only the essence of the problem should be dealt with.

Write for others
Since it is likeliest that different parties will be dealing with the problem, it is important that everyone interprets the problem in the same way. Therefore, adjust the tone, style and diction accordingly. Ask yourself: for whom am I writing this? Do these people know the same terms and concepts as I do? Do these people share the same attitude as I do?

Avoid using jargon
As mentioned above, the problem definition must be written in such a way that everyone interprets it correctly. This means that, unless it can be assumed that the reader does have the right knowledge, technical terminology should be avoided, or these terms should be explained.

To summarise
Problems do not often solve themselves, which is why it is crucial to address problems without wasting time or inciting other inefficiencies. Since more than one party is usually working on a solution to the problem, the problem definition is the most important part of the solution because different interpretations of the problem cause a lot of uncertainty.

Use the Problem Definition Process to define the problem definition. By describing the ideal situation, explaining the problem and determining the consequences using the "five times why" method, one will be able to think 'outside the box' and ensure that the solution is a best fit for the problem.

Problem Solving and Decision Making

A Systematic Approach for Making Decisions

In live business situations, decisions can often fail because the best alternatives are not clear at the outset, or key factors are not considered as part of the process. To stop this happening, problem-solving and decision-making strategies must be brought together to clarify understanding.

A logical and ordered process can help do this by making sure all of the critical elements needed for a successful outcome are addressed.

Working through this process systematically will reduce the likelihood of overlooking important factors.

A seven-step approach takes this into account:

- *Create a constructive environment.*
- *Investigate the situation in detail.*
- *Generate good alternatives.*
- *Explore the options.*
- *Select the best solution.*
- *Evaluate the plan.*
- *Communicate the decision and take action.*

This process will ensure a good decision in a complex situation but may be unnecessarily involved for small or simple decisions. In these cases, focus on the tools in Step 5.

Step 1: Create a Constructive Environment
Decisions can become complex when they involve or affect other people, so it helps to create a constructive environment in which to explore the situation and weigh up your options.

Often, when responsible for deciding, there is reliance on others to implement it, so it pays to gain their support. If it is most appropriate to make the decision within a group, conduct a Stakeholder Analysis to identify who to include in the process.

To build commitment from others, make sure that these stakeholders are well represented within the decision-making group (which will ideally comprise five to seven people).

If there is uncertainty about how much say other people should have in the final decision, use the Vroom-Yetton-Jago Decision Model to decide whether to consult them or to give them a vote.

Encourage people to contribute to the discussions, debates and analysis without any fear of the other participants rejecting their ideas. Make sure everyone recognises that the objective is to make the best decision possible in the circumstances – this is not the time for people to promote their own preferred alternative.

Problem Solving and Decision Making

The Charette Procedure is a systematic process for gathering and developing ideas from many stakeholders. Alternatively, consider using the Stepladder Technique to introduce more and more people to the discussion gradually, while ensuring that everyone gets heard.

Step 2: Investigate the Situation in Detail

Before beginning to decide, make sure that the situation is fully understood. It may be that the objective can be approached in isolation, but it is more likely that there are a number of interrelated factors to consider. Changes made in one department, for example, could have knock-on effects elsewhere, making the change counterproductive.

Start by considering the decision in the context of the problem it is intended to address. Use the 5 Whys technique to determine whether the stated problem is the real issue, or just a symptom of something deeper. Root Cause Analysis can be used to trace a problem to its origins.

Once the root cause is identified, define the problem to extract the greatest amount of information from what is known, and use Inductive Reasoning to draw sound conclusions from the facts. The Problem-Definition Process can be used to gain a better understanding of what is going on.
As well as this, consider using CATWOE to explore the problem from multiple perspectives, and to make sure no important information is being missed.

Step 3: Generate Good Alternatives

The wider the options are explored, the better the final decision is likely to be. Generating a number of different options may seem to make the decision more complicated at first, but the act of coming up with alternatives forces a deeper dig and looking at the problem from different angles.

This is when it can be helpful to employ a variety of creative thinking techniques. These can help step outside the normal patterns of thinking and come up with some truly innovative solutions.

Brainstorming is probably the most popular method of generating ideas, while Reverse Brainstorming works in a similar way, but starts by asking how you can achieve the opposite outcome from the desired one and then turning the solution on its head.
Other useful methods for getting a group of people producing ideas include the Crawford Slip Writing Technique and Round-Robin Brainstorming. Both are effective ways of ensuring that everyone's ideas are heard and given equal weight, regardless of their position or power within the team.

Do not forget to consider how people outside the group might influence, or be affected by, the decision. Tools like the Reframing Matrix, which uses 4Ps (Product, Planning, Potential, and People) can be used as a way to gather different perspectives.

Problem Solving and Decision Making

Ask outsiders to join the discussion or use the Perceptual Positions technique to encourage existing participants to adopt different functional perspectives (for example, having a marketing person speak from the viewpoint of a financial manager).

If there are very few or unsatisfactory options, try using Concept Fans, to take a step back from the problem and approach it from a wider perspective, or Appreciative Inquiry, to look at the problem based on what's "going right" rather than what's "going wrong." This can help when the people involved in the decision are too close to the problem.

When ideas start to emerge, use Affinity Diagrams to organise them into common themes and groups.

Step 4: Explore the options
When there is a good selection of realistic alternatives, it is time to evaluate the feasibility, risks and implications of each one.

Almost every decision involves some degree of risk. Use Risk Analysis to consider this objectively by adopting a structured approach to assessing threats and evaluating the probability of adverse events occurring – and what they might cost to manage.

Then, prioritise the risks with a Risk Impact/Probability Chart, this will direct focus to the ones that are most likely to occur.

Another way to evaluate the options is to consider the potential consequences of each one. The ORAPAPA tool helps evaluate a decision's consequences by looking at the alternatives from seven different perspectives. Alternatively, conduct an Impact Analysis or use a Futures Wheel to brainstorm "unexpected" consequences that could arise from the decision.

Other considerations are whether the resources are adequate, the solution matches the objectives, and the decision is likely to work in the long term. Use Star bursting to think about the questions to evaluate each alternative, and assess their pros and cons using Force Field Analysis or the Quantitative Pros and Cons approach.

Weigh up a decision's financial feasibility using Cost-Benefit Analysis.

Step 5: Select the Best Solution
Having evaluated the alternatives, the next step is to make the decision. If one particular alternative is clearly better than the rest, the choice will be obvious. However, if there are still several competing options, there are plenty of tools that will help decide between them.

Use Decision Matrix Analysis to compare them reliably and rigorously. Or, to determine their relative importance, conduct a Paired Comparison Analysis to decide which ones should carry the most weight in the decision.

Problem Solving and Decision Making

Decision Trees are also useful when choosing between different financial options. These help lay options out clearly and bring the likelihood of the project succeeding or failing into the decision-making process.

If the decision criteria are subjective, and it is critical that consensus is reached, Multi-Voting and the Modified Borda Count can help the team reach an agreement.

When anonymity is important, decision-makers dislike one another, or there is a tendency for certain individuals to dominate the process, use the Delphi Technique to reach a fair and impartial decision. This uses cycles of anonymous, written discussion and argument, managed by a facilitator. Participants do not meet, and sometimes they do not even know who else is involved.

If it is an established team, use Hartnett's Consensus-Oriented Decision-Making Model to encourage everyone to participate in making the decision. Or, if working with several different teams, or a particularly large group, assign responsibility for each stage of the decision-making process with Bain's RAPID Framework, so that everyone understands their responsibilities and any potential in-fighting can be avoided.

Step 6: Evaluate Your Plan

With all the effort and hard work already invested in evaluating and selecting alternatives, it can be tempting to forge ahead at this stage. But now, more than ever, is the time to "sense check" the decision. After all, hindsight is great for identifying why things have gone wrong, but it is far better to prevent mistakes from happening in the first place!

Before starting to implement the decision, take a long, dispassionate look at it to be sure that the process has been thorough, and that common errors have not crept into the process.

The final decision is only as good as the facts and research used to make it. Make sure that the information is trustworthy, and that data has not been "cherry picked". This will help avoid confirmation bias, a common psychological bias in decision making.

Discuss the preliminary conclusions with important stakeholders to enable them to spot flaws, make recommendations, and support the conclusions. Listen to intuition, too, and quietly and methodically test assumptions and decisions against experience. If there are doubts, examine them thoroughly to work out what is causing the doubt.

Use Blindspot Analysis to review whether common decision-making problems like over-confidence, escalating commitment, or groupthink may have undermined the process. Consider checking the logical structure of the process with the Ladder of Inference, to make sure that a well-founded and consistent decision emerges at the end.

Step 7: Communicate the Decision, and take Action

Once the decision is made, communicate it to everyone affected by it in an engaging and inspiring way.

Problem Solving and Decision Making

Get them involved in implementing the solution by discussing how and why the decision has been arrived at. The more information provided about risks and projected benefits; the more likely people will be to support the decision.

If people point out a flaw in the process as a result, have the humility to welcome their input and review the plans appropriately – it is much better to do this now, at minimal cost, than having to do it expensively (and embarrassingly) if plans have failed.

> *Although problem solving and decision making are different processes, it is often necessary to combine them when making a complex decision.*

The Simplex Process

The Simplex process is not dissimilar to the Systematic Approach for making decisions detailed above.

When solving business problems, it is easy to skip over important steps in the problem-solving process, meaning good solutions can be missed, or, worse still, fail to identify the problem correctly in the first place.

One way to prevent this happening is by using the Simplex Process. This powerful step-by-step tool which helps identify and solve problems creatively and effectively. It guides users through each stage of the problem-solving process, from identifying the problem to implementing a solution.

> *This helps ensure solutions are creative, robust and well considered.*

The Simplex Process was created by Min Basadur, and was popularised in his book, "The Power of Innovation." Rather than seeing problem-solving as a single straight-line process, Simplex is represented as a continuous cycle. This means that problem-solving should not stop once a solution has been implemented. Rather, completion and implementation of one cycle of improvement should lead straight into the next.

It is suitable for problems and projects of any scale. It uses the eight stages shown below:

Problem Solving and Decision Making

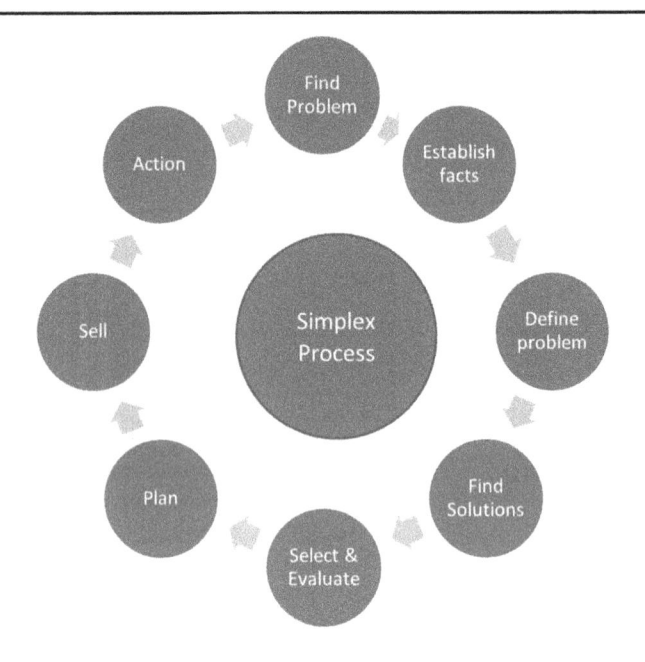

Simplex Process diagram with the following stages around a central "Simplex Process": Find Problem → Establish facts → Define problem → Find Solutions → Select & Evaluate → Plan → Sell → Action

1. Problem Identification
Finding the right problem to solve is sometimes the most difficult part of the resolution process. Problems provide the opportunities for change and improvement, making problem finding a valuable skill. Problems may be obvious. If they are not, they can often be identified using trigger questions like the ones below:

- *What would customers want us to improve?*
- *What are they complaining about?*
- *What could they be doing better if we could help them?*
- *Who else could we help by using our core competences?*
- *What small problems do we have which could grow into bigger ones?*
- *Where could failures arise in our business process?*
- *What slows our work or makes it more difficult?*
- *What do we often fail to achieve?*
- *Where do we have bottlenecks?*
- *How can we improve quality?*
- *What are our competitors doing that we could do?*
- *What is frustrating and irritating to our team?*

These questions deal with problems that exist now. It is also useful to try to look into the future. Think about how markets and customers might change over the next few years and the problems the organisation may experience as it expands; and social, political and legal changes that may affect it. (Tools such as PESTLE or PEST Analysis will help to do this.)

Problem Solving and Decision Making

It is also worth exploring possible problems from the perspective of the different "actors" in the situation – this is where techniques such as CATWOE can be useful.

At this stage there may not be enough information to define the problem precisely. This should not be an issue until you reach step 3!

2. Fact-Finding
The next stage is to research the problem as fully as possible. This is where you:

- *Understand fully how different people perceive the situation.*
- *Analyse data to see if the problem really exists.*
- *Explore the best ideas that competitors have had.*
- *Understand customers' needs in more detail.*
- *Know what has already been tried.*
- *Understand fully any processes, components, services, or technologies that may be of use.*
- *Ensure the benefits of solving the problem will be worth the effort being put into solving it.*

Effective fact-finding will confirm the view of the situation and ensure that all future problem-solving is based on an accurate view of reality.

3. Problem Definition
At this stage, the problem should be reasonably well identified and there should be a good understanding of the facts relating to it.

At this point the exact problem or problems to be solved must be identified.
It is important to solve a problem at the right level. If questions are too broad, there will never be enough resources to answer them effectively. If questions are too narrow, the symptoms of the problem may be solved, rather than the problem itself.

Min Basadur, who created the Simplex process, suggests saying "Why?" to broaden a question, and "What's stopping you?" to narrow a question.

For example:

> If the problem is one of trees dying, ask "Why do I want to keep trees healthy?" This might broaden the question to "How can I maintain the quality of our environment?"
>
> A "What's stopping you?" question here could give the answer "I don't know how to control the disease that is killing the tree."

Big problems are normally made up of many smaller ones. This is the stage at which techniques like drill down can be used to break the problem down to its component parts. The 5 Whys Technique, Cause and Effect Analysis and Root Cause Analysis will also help to get to the root of a problem.

Problem Solving and Decision Making

4. Idea Finding
The next stage is to generate as many problem-solving ideas as possible.

Ways of doing this range from asking other people for their opinions, through programmed creativity tools and lateral thinking techniques, to Brainstorming. Try looking at the problem from other perspectives. A technique like The Reframing Matrix can help with this.

Do not evaluate or criticise ideas during this stage. Instead, just concentrate on generating ideas. Impractical ideas can often trigger good ones! The Random Input technique can be used to help think of some new ideas.

5. Selection and Evaluation
Once a number of possible solutions to the problem have been identified, it is time to select the best one.

The best solution may be obvious. If it is not, then it is important to think through the criteria to be used to select the best idea. Particularly useful techniques include Decision Tree Analysis, Paired Comparison Analysis, and Grid Analysis.

Once an idea is identified, develop it as far as possible. It is then essential to evaluate it to see if it is good enough to be considered worth using. It is important not to let self-confidence get in the way of common sense. If the idea does not offer a big enough benefit, then either try to generate more ideas, or restart the whole process.

Techniques to help do this include:

- **Risk Analysis,** which helps you explore where things could go wrong.
- **Impact Analysis,** which gives you a framework for exploring the full consequences of your decision.
- **Force Field Analysis,** which helps you explore the pressures for and against change.
- **Six Thinking Hats,** which helps you explore your decision using a range of valid decision-making styles.
- **Use of NPVs and IRRs,** which help you ensure that your project is worth running from a financial perspective.

6. Planning
Once an idea is selected, and there is confidence the idea is worthwhile, it is time to plan its implementation.

Action Plans help manage simple projects – these lay out the who, what, when, where, why and how of delivering the work.

For larger projects, it is worth using formal project management techniques. Using these will enable the project to be implemented efficiently, successfully, and within a sensible time frame.

Problem Solving and Decision Making

Where the implementation has an impact on several people or groups of people, it is also worth thinking about change management. Having an appreciation of this will help ensure that people support the project, rather than opposing it or cancelling it.

7. Sell Idea

Up to this stage the work may have been done alone or with a small team. Now the idea must be sold to the people who must support it. These may include managers, investors, or other stakeholders involved with the project.

Selling the project will have to address not only its practicalities, but also things such internal politics, hidden fear of change, and so on.

8. Action

Finally, after all the creativity and preparation comes action!

This is where all the careful work and planning pays off. Again, a large-scale change or project implementation, may warrant brushing up on change management skills to help ensure that the process is implemented smoothly.

Once the action is firmly under way, return to stage 1, Problem Finding, to continue improving the idea. The principles of Kaizen can also be used to work on continuous improvement.

Problem Solving and Decision Making

Data

Data is a collection of facts, such as numbers, words, measurements, observations or even just descriptions of things.

Data can exist in a variety of forms — as numbers or text on pieces of paper, as bits and bytes stored in electronic memory, or as facts stored in a person's mind.

Since the mid-1900s, people have used the word data to mean computer information that is transmitted or stored.

Although the terms "data" and "information" are often used interchangeably, these terms have distinct meanings.

Data is simply facts or figures — bits of information, but not information itself.

A list of dates — data — is meaningless without the information that makes the dates relevant (dates of holiday)

The history of temperature readings all over the world for the past 100 years is data. If this data is organised and analysed to find that global temperature is rising, then it becomes information.

The number of visitors to a website by country is an example of data. Finding out that traffic from the U.K. is increasing while that from Australia is decreasing is meaningful information.

Often data is required to back up a claim or conclusion (information) derived or deduced from it. For example, before a drug is approved by the Government, the manufacturer must conduct clinical trials and present a great deal of data to demonstrate that the drug is safe.

When data is processed, interpreted, organised, structured or presented so as to make them meaningful or useful, they are called information.

Information provides context for data.

Data is employed in scientific research, businesses management (e.g., sales data, revenue, profits, stock price), finance, governance (e.g., crime rates, unemployment rates, literacy rates), and in virtually every other form of human organisational activity (e.g., censuses of the number of homeless people by non-profit organisations).

Data is measured, collected and reported. It can then be analysed and used in graphs, images or other analysis tools. Data as a general concept refers to the fact that some existing information or knowledge is represented or coded in some form suitable for better usage or processing.

Problem Solving and Decision Making

Sourcing Data

Good data is the life blood of any business.

Data is one of the most valuable resources today's businesses have. The more information held about customers, the better their interests, wants and needs can be understood. This enhanced understanding helps meet and exceed customers' expectations and allows communication with them through messaging and products that appeal to them.

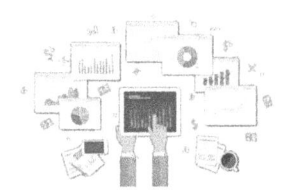

Definition

Data Sourcing (or Data Collection) is the process of extracting data from external or internal systems, which form an organisations IT Infrastructure for diverse purposes of informing business objectives.

Types of Data

Primary Data
The data businesses collect about their customers, is typically first-party data or primary data. First-party data is the information gathered directly from the audience. It could include data gathered from external online sources, data in inhouse systems or non-online data collected from customers through surveys and various other sources.

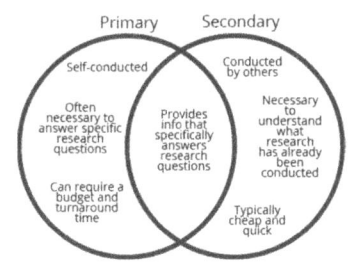

Second party data
Second-party data is the first-party data of another company. Second-party data can be purchased directly from the organisation that collected it or it can be bought in a private marketplace.

Third party data
Third-party data is information a company has pulled together from numerous sources. This kind of data can be bought and sold on a data exchange, and it typically contains a large number of data points.

Problem Solving and Decision Making

It is this thirst for data that has led to the massive increase in computer hacking as criminals try to steal data, which is legally stored by organisation, but which might be of value to others.

Because first-party data comes directly from own data sources, there can be high confidence in its accuracy, as well as its relevance to the business.

Second-party data has many of the same positive attributes as first-party data. It comes directly from the source, so there can be confidence in its accuracy, but it also gives insights which could not be obtained with first-party data. Third-party data offers much more scale than any other type of data, which is its primary benefit.

Different types of data can be useful in different scenarios. It can also be helpful to use different types of data together. First-party data will typically be the foundation of a dataset. If the first-party data is limited, though, it may be supplemented with second-party or third-party data. Adding these other types of data can increase the size of the audience or help reach new audiences.

Sources of Data

Personal data
Personal data is anything that is specific to an individual. It covers their demographics, their location, their email address and other identifying factors. It is usually in the news when it gets leaked (like the Santander scandal) or is being used in a controversial way (when Uber worked out who was having an affair).

Lots of different companies collect personal data (especially social media sites), anytime an email address or credit card details are entered personal data is being given away. Often, that data will be used to provide personalised suggestions to keep the person engaged. Facebook, for example, uses personal information to suggest content based on what other people similar to you like.

In addition, personal data is aggregated (to depersonalise it somewhat) and then sold to other companies, mostly for advertising and competitive research purposes. That is one of the ways targeted ads and content from companies you have never even heard of appear in emails and on social media channels.

Transactional data
Transactional data is anything that requires an action to collect. A click on an ad, making a purchase, visiting certain web page, etc. Pretty much every website will collect transactional data of some kind, either through Google Analytics, another 3rd party system or own internal data capture system.

Transactional data is incredibly important for businesses because it helps them to expose variability and optimise their operations for the highest quality results. By examining large amounts of data, it is possible to uncover hidden patterns and correlations. These patterns can create competitive advantages, and result in business benefits like more effective marketing and increased revenue.

Problem Solving and Decision Making

Web data

Web data is a collective term which refers to any type of data you might pulled from the internet, whether to study for research purposes or otherwise. That might be data on what competitors are selling, published government data, football scores, etc. It is a catchall for anything on the web that is public facing (i.e., not stored in some internal database). Studying this data can be highly informative, especially when communicated well to management.

Web data is important because it is one of the major ways' businesses can access information that is not generated by themselves. When creating quality business models and making important business improvement decisions, businesses need information on what is happening internally and externally within their organisation and what is happening in the wider market.

Web data can be used to monitor competitors, track potential customers, keep track of channel partners, generate leads, build apps, and much more. It is uses are still being discovered as the technology for turning unstructured data into structured data improves.

Web data can be collected by writing web scrapers to collect it, using a scraping tool, or by paying a third party to do the scraping. A web scraper is a computer program that takes a URL as an input and pulls the data out in a structured format.

Sensor data

Sensor data is produced by objects and is often referred to as the Internet of Things. It covers everything from a smartwatch measuring heart rate to a building with external sensors that measure the weather.

So far, sensor data has mostly been used to help optimise processes. For example, AirAsia saved £30-£50 million by using sensors and technology to help reduce operating costs and increase aircraft usage.

By measuring what is happening around them, machines can make smart changes to increase productivity and alert people when they are in need of maintenance.

Big Data

Technically all of the types of data above contribute to Big Data. There is no official size that makes data "big". The term simply represents the increasing amount and the varied types of data that is now being gathered as part of data collection.

As more and more of the world's information moves online and becomes digitised, it means that analysts can start to use it as data. Things like social media, online books, music, videos and the increased number of sensors have all added to the astounding increase in the amount of data that has become available for analysis.

Problem Solving and Decision Making

The thing that differentiates Big Data from the "regular data" analysed earlier is that the tools used to collect, store and analyse it have had to change to accommodate the increase in size and complexity. With the latest tools on the market, there is no longer a reliance on sampling. Instead, datasets can be processed in their entirety and gain a far more complete picture of the world around us.

The importance of data collection

Data collection differs from data mining in that it is a process by which data is gathered and measured. All this must be done before high-quality research can begin and answers to lingering questions can be found. Data collection is usually done with software, and there are many different data collection procedures, strategies, and techniques. Most data collection is centred on electronic data, and since this type of data collection encompasses so much information, it usually crosses into the realm of big data.

It is through data collection that a business or management has the quality information they need to make informed decisions from further analysis, study, and research. Without data collection, companies would stumble around in the dark using outdated methods to make their decisions. Data collection instead allows them to stay on top of trends, provide answers to problems, and analyse new insights to great effect.

Quantitative vs. Qualitative Data

Primary data can be divided into two categories: quantitative and qualitative.

Quantitative data comes in the form of numbers, quantities and values. It describes things in concrete and easily measurable terms. Examples include the number of customers who bought a given product, the rating a customer gave a product out of five stars and the amount of time a visitor spent on your website.

Because quantitative data is numeric and measurable, it lends itself well to analytics. When quantitative data is analysed, it may uncover insights that can help better understand the audience. Because this kind of data deals with numbers, it is very objective and has a reputation for reliability.

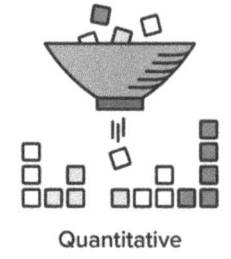

Qualitative   Quantitative

Problem Solving and Decision Making

Data	
Quantitative	Qualitative
Numerical Data – two types	Descriptive data based on observations
Discrete – (Counting)	*Involves the 5 senses:*
Continuous – (Measurement)	*See, Smell, Taste, Hear, Feel*

Qualitative data is descriptive, rather than numeric. It is less concrete and less easily measurable than quantitative data. This data may contain descriptive phrases and opinions. Examples include an online review a customer writes about a product, an answer to an open-ended survey question about what type of videos a customer likes to watch online and the conversation a customer had with a customer service representative.

Qualitative data helps explains the "why" behind the information quantitative data reveals. For this reason, it is useful for supplementing quantitative data, which will form the foundation of your data strategy.

Data Management

Data management is a subset of information management whereby data is managed as a valuable resource.

Specifically, data management refers to the process of creating, obtaining, transforming, sharing, protecting, documenting and preserving data.

The process of data management includes file-naming conventions and documentation of metadata among other things. The process ensures that all data is available, accurate, complete and secure. It also addresses the development and execution of architectures, policies, practices and procedures that manage the full data life cycle

Problem Solving and Decision Making

Managing Data and Information

Once data has been collected it has to be managed. If data were nails, strewn all across the floor, they would soon be swept up and put into a box. Data is much the same. In its raw state it is of very little use, but there is lots of it and it needs controlling. Likewise, information, once created, suddenly becomes valuable, not just to the organisation that created it, but also to its competitors, suppliers, customers and other stakeholders.

Information Management

Information includes both electronic and physical data. For example, this may be in the form of paper records, files and folders or digital databases.

Information management therefore refers to an organisational program or system that manages the processes that controls the structure, processing, delivery and usage of information. Information management is required for business intelligence purposes.

The organisational structure of the information management system, a company has in place, must be capable of managing information through its entire life cycle. This is the case for all sources or formats of data including paper documents and electronic files. This information also needs to be accessible through multiple channels so that those who need access can gain it through the use of mobile phones and laptops no matter where they are in the world.

Problem Solving and Decision Making

Legislation Affecting Data Management

The Data Protection Act 2018

The Data Protection Act 2018 controls how your personal information is used by organisations, businesses or the government. The 2018 Act is the UK's implementation of the General Data Protection Regulation (GDPR). Everyone responsible for using personal data has to follow strict rules called data protection principles. They must make sure the information is:

- *used fairly, lawfully and transparently*
- *used for specified, explicit purposes*
- *used in a way that is adequate, relevant and limited to only what is necessary*
- *accurate and, where necessary, kept up to date*
- *kept for no longer than is necessary*
- *handled in a way that ensures appropriate security, including protection against unlawful or unauthorised processing, access, loss, destruction or damage*

There is stronger legal protection for more sensitive information, such as:

- *race*
- *ethnic background*
- *political opinions*
- *religious beliefs*
- *trade union membership*
- *genetics*
- *biometrics* (where used for identification)
- *health*
- *sexuality or orientation*

There are separate safeguards for personal data relating to criminal convictions and offences.

Rights

Under the Data Protection Act 2018, subjects have the right to find out what information the government and other organisations store about them. These include the right to:

- *be informed about how your data is being used*
- *access personal data*
- *have incorrect data updated*
- *have data erased*
- *stop or restrict the processing of your data*
- *data portability* (allowing you to get and reuse your data for different services)
- *object to how your data is processed in certain circumstances*

There are also rights when an organisation is using your personal data for:

Problem Solving and Decision Making

- *automated decision-making processes (without human involvement)*
- *profiling, for example to predict your behaviour or interests*

The General Data Protection Regulation 2016

GDPR stands for General Data Protection Regulation. The GDPR is a regulation from the Data Protection Act and covers any information related to a person or data subject that can be used to identify them directly or indirectly. It can be anything from a name, a photo and an email address to bank details, social media posts, biometric data and medical information. It also introduces digital rights for individuals.

When it came into effect on May 25, 2018, the GDPR set new standards for data protection, and kickstarted a wave of global privacy laws that forever changed how we use the internet.

Personal data is highly valuable — in fact, it supports a trillion-dollar industry. Companies like Facebook and Google make their profits by selling personal information to advertisers. With this much money at stake, can they be trusted to have your best interests at heart?

The GDPR defines what companies of all sizes can and cannot do with customer information.

Personal Data under GDPR
Personal data is information that can be used to identify an individual. Put simply, it is any private details that an individual would not want to fall into the wrong hands.

These are some examples of personal data:

- *Name*
- *phone number*
- *address*
- *date of birth*
- *bank account*
- *passport number*
- *social media posts*
- *geotagging*
- *health records*
- *race*
- *religious and political opinions*

Think of personal data like a jigsaw. One piece alone might not say much but connected together they reveal a vivid picture of your life.

Breaches under GDPR

Any incident that leads to personal data being lost, stolen, destroyed, or changed is considered a data breach. Unfortunately, breaches happen all the time.

Here are some newsworthy examples from before the GDPR started cracking down:

Problem Solving and Decision Making

- *Almost half the population of the USA had their name, date of birth, and social security number stolen from credit reporting agency Equifax as the result of a data breach.*
- *Political consulting firm Cambridge Analytica secretly took information from 50 million Facebook profiles and gave it to the 2016 Trump campaign.*

Both of these incidents illustrate how data breaches have serious real-world consequences. This is exactly what GDPR and similar laws hope to regulate

Penalties for Violating the GDPR

The GDPR threatens would-be violators with some severe penalties. To make sure companies handle personal data in a legal, ethical way, the fines for noncompliance are:

Up to £17 million or 4% of annual global turnover.

Some big names have already been hit with these noncompliance fines:

- **British Airways** — *£162 million. The UK airline set the record for fines when the booking details of 500,000 customers were stolen in a cyberattack.*
- **Marriott Hotels** — *£87 million. After buying the Starwood Hotels group, Marriott failed to update an old system belonging to the group. This system was hacked, revealing information about 339 million guests.*
- **Google** — *£40 million. Important information was hidden when users set up new Android phones, meaning they did not know what data collection practices they were agreeing to. The Google GDPR fine shows even tech giants are not immune to GDPR enforcement.*

Although smaller businesses would not be hit for such high amounts, they are held to the same standards.

A business owner now has to make sure their operations comply with the GDPR.

The only thing most people will need to do is read the cookie consent banners that now appear on websites and click agree (or not). The GDPR affects everything people do online, but it is mostly working behind the scenes.

Core GDPR Concepts

The following are two of the most common GDPR terms used by security analysts. Understanding them is a vital part of becoming familiar with data protection in general.

Problem Solving and Decision Making

Privacy by Design
Privacy by Design GDPR (PbD) is the name of an approach toward privacy that all businesses should now take when creating products and building websites. PbD involves keeping data collection to a minimum and building security measures into all stages of a product's design.

Consent
Obtaining consent simply means asking users for permission to process their data. Companies must explain their data collection practices in clear and simple language, and then users must explicitly agree to them.

These new standards of consent prohibit the use of sneaky pre-selected settings in apps, as well as pre-checked boxes on websites.

These are some of the main user rights outlined by the GDPR:

- *You are entitled to know exactly how your data is collected and used*
- *You can ask what information has been collected about you (without paying anything)*
- *If there are mistakes in your data, you can request to have them corrected*
- *You can have your data deleted from records (just in case you need to disappear!)*
- *You are allowed to refuse data processing, for example, marketing efforts*
- *Keep in mind that these rights can be limited if they are misused or used excessively.*

Privacy Policies

All businesses are required to have a privacy policy that explains what they do with users' information.

Privacy policies must:

- *Include contact details of the company and its representatives*
- *Describe why the company is collecting the data*
- *Say how long the information will be kept on file*
- *Explain the rights users have*
- *Be written in simple language*
- *Name the recipients of the personal data (if the company shares data with another organisation)*
- *Include contact details for an EU representative and the DPO (if necessary)*

Problem Solving and Decision Making

GDPR - Dos and Don'ts:

Do	*Don't*
Collect information legally and use it fairly	*Mislead users about what you will do with their private details*
Collect as little data as possible	*Collect lots of data just because you can*
Protect data with strong security systems	*Assume data will take care of itself*
Only store data for as long as necessary	*Keep old data you do not need anymore*

Freedom of Information Act 2000

The Freedom of Information Act 2000 provides public access to information held by public authorities.
It does this in two ways:

> *public authorities are obliged to publish certain information about their activities*
> *and*
> *members of the public are entitled to request information from public authorities.*

The Act covers any recorded information that is held by a public authority in England, Wales and Northern Ireland, and by UK-wide public authorities based in Scotland. Information held by Scottish public authorities is covered by Scotland's own Freedom of Information (Scotland) Act 2002.
Public authorities include government departments, local authorities, the NHS, state schools and police forces. However, the Act does not necessarily cover every organisation that receives public money. For example, it does not cover some charities that receive grants and certain private sector organisations that perform public functions.

Recorded information includes printed documents, computer files, letters, emails, photographs, and sound or video recordings.

The Act does not give people access to their own personal data (information about themselves) such as their health records or credit reference file. If a member of the public wants to see information that a public authority holds about them, they should make a data protection subject access request.

Digital Economy Act (2017)

The Digital Economy Act 2017 (the Act) makes provision about electronic communications infrastructure and services, including the creation of a broadband Universal Service Order (USO), to give all premises in the UK a legal right to request a minimum standard of broadband connectivity, expected to be 10 megabits per second (Mbps).

The Act also introduces reform of the Electronic Communications Code and provides greater clarification on data sharing between public bodies.

Problem Solving and Decision Making

The Digital Economy Bill was introduced in the House of Commons on 5 July 2016, completed its parliamentary stages and received Royal Assent, becoming law, on 27 April 2017.

The Bill followed an announcement made in the Queen's Speech to introduce legislation seeking to make the United Kingdom a world leader in the digital economy.

The Act is made up of six parts as follows:

1. *Access to digital services*
2. *Digital infrastructure*
3. *Online pornography*
4. *Intellectual property*
5. *Digital government*
6. *Miscellaneous.*

Problem Solving and Decision Making

Data Quality

Data quality is crucial – it assesses whether information can serve its purpose in a particular context (such as data analysis, for example). So, how is quality determined? There are defined data quality characteristics.

There are five traits that you will find within data quality: accuracy, completeness, reliability, relevance, and timeliness – read on to learn more.

Accuracy
As the name implies, this data quality characteristic means that information is correct. To determine whether data is accurate or not, ask if the information reflects a real-world situation. For example, in the realm of financial services, does a customer really have £1 million in his bank account?

Accuracy is a crucial data quality characteristic because inaccurate information can cause significant problems with severe consequences.

Completeness
"Completeness" refers to how comprehensive the information is. When looking at data completeness, think about whether all of the data needed is available; there may be a need for a customer's first and last name, but the middle initial may be optional.

If information is incomplete, it might be unusable. When sending a mailing out, the customer's last name is needed to ensure the mail goes to the right address – without it, the data is incomplete.

Reliability
In the realm of data quality characteristics, reliability means that a piece of information does not contradict another piece of information in a different source or system. If a person's birthday is January 1st, 1970 in one system, yet it is June 13th, 1973 in another, the information is unreliable.

Reliability is a vital data quality characteristic. When pieces of information contradict themselves, the data cannot be trusted. It could cause a mistake that could cost the organisation money and reputational damage.

Relevance
When looking at data quality characteristics, relevance comes into play because there has to be a good reason as to why the information is being collected in the first place. Consider whether the information is really needed, or whether it is being collected just for the sake of it.

If irrelevant information is being gathered, time as well as money is being wasted. The analyses will not be as valuable.

Problem Solving and Decision Making

Timeliness
Timeliness, as the name implies, refers to how up to date the information is. If it was gathered in the past hour, then it is timely – unless new information has come in that renders previous information useless.

The timeliness of information is an important data quality characteristic because information that is not timely can lead to people making the wrong decisions. In turn, that costs organisations time, money, and reputational damage.

In today's business environment, data quality characteristics ensure that the greatest benefit is derived from the information. When the information does not meet these standards, it is not valuable.

The importance of ensuring that these criteria are met is paramount to obtaining the level of information required to enable effective decision-making. If these are not followed, the results could be catastrophic, unreliable and detrimental to the business. If, for example, a decision was made to develop a new product prior to the information being verified and validated, this may result in unnecessary costs, working time been spent on producing something that in fact is not required, as confirmation of the information gathered may have identified that the product would not be cost-effective.

Gathering Data

When selecting data and information which is to be used in any decision-making process, a manager must ensure the data is collected impartially and in an unbiased manner.

> *The data collected should be relevant and accurate and analysed to come up with conclusions, which can be put forward.*

There are many different techniques for collecting different types of quantitative data, but there is a fundamental process which should be typically followed, no matter which method of data collection is being used using. This process consists of the following five steps.

1. Decide what information to collect
The first step is to identify the details to be collected. Decide what topics the information will cover, who to collect it from and how much data is needed. The goals — what is it hoped to accomplish using the data — will determine the answers to these questions. As an example, it may be decided to collect data about which type of articles are most popular on a website among visitors between the ages of 18 and 34. It may also be decided to gather information about the average age of all of the customers who bought a product from the company within the last month.

2. Set a timeframe for data collection
Next, a plan needs to be formulated for how the data will be collected. In the early stages of the planning process, establish a timeframe for the data collection. Some types of data

Problem Solving and Decision Making

may be gathered continuously. When it comes to transactional data and website visitor data, for example, it may be prudent to set up a method for tracking that data over the long term. If tracking data for a specific campaign, however, track it over a defined period. In these instances, a schedule will be needed for when to start and end the data collection.

3. Determine your data collection method
Choose the data collection method that will make up the core of the data-gathering strategy. To select the right collection method, consider the type of information you want to be collected, the timeframe over which it will be obtained and the other aspects determined previously.

4. Collect the data
Once finalised, implement the data collection strategy and start collecting data. Store and organise the data in a database or on a software package specifically designed for the purpose. Be sure to stick to the plan and check on its progress regularly. It may be useful to create a schedule for when checks on how data collection is proceeding, especially if collecting data continuously. Update the plan as conditions change and new information is obtained.

5. Analyse the data and implement your findings
Once all the data is collected, it is time to analyse it and organise the findings. The analysis phase is crucial because it turns raw data into valuable information that can be used to enhance marketing strategies, products and business decisions. The analytics tools built into data management solutions can also help with this step. Once the patterns and insights in the data have been identified, implement the findings to improve the business.

Data Collection Methods

There are various methods of collecting primary, quantitative data. Some involve directly asking customers for information, some involve monitoring the interactions with customers and others involve observing customers' behaviours. The right one to use depends on the goals and the type of data being collected. Below are some of the most common types of data collection used today.

1. Surveys
Surveys are one way to directly ask customers for information. Use them to collect either quantitative or qualitative data or both. A survey consists of a list of queries respondents can answer in just one or two words and often gives participants a list of responses to choose from. Conduct surveys online, over email, over the phone or in person. One of the easiest methods is to create an online survey hosted on a website or with a third party. Then share a link to that survey on social media, over email and in pop-ups on the website.

2. Online Tracking
A business' website, and apps, are excellent tools for collecting customer data. When someone visits a website, they create as many as 40 pieces of data. Accessing this data

Problem Solving and Decision Making

allows tracking of how many people visited a site, how long they were on it, what they clicked on and more. A website hosting provider may collect this kind of information, and it can also be used by analytics software. Pixels can also be placed on a site, which enables it to place and read cookies to help track user behaviour

3. Transactional data tracking
Whether selling goods in-store, online or both, transactional data can give valuable insights about customers and the business. Transactional records may be stored in a customer relationship management system. That data may come from a web store, a third-party source of data or an in-store point-of-sale system. This information can give insights about how many products are sold, what types of products are most popular, how often people typically purchase from the business and more.

4. Online marketing analytics
Valuable data can also be collected through marketing campaigns, whether they are run on search engines, webpages, email or elsewhere. Information can also be imported from offline marketing campaigns. The software used to place the advertisements will give data about who clicked on the adverts, what times they clicked, what device they used and more.

5. Social media monitoring
Social media is another excellent source of customer data. Look through the follower list to see who follows the organisation and what characteristics they have in common to enhance the understanding of who the target audience should be. Mentions of the brand on social media can also be monitored by regularly searching the brand's name, setting up alerts or using third-party social media monitoring software. Many social media sites will also provide analytics about how the posts perform. Third-party tools may be able to offer even more in-depth insights.

6. Collecting subscription and registration data
Offering customers something in return for providing information about themselves can help gather valuable customer data. This can be done by requiring some basic information from customers or site visitors who want to sign up for an email list, rewards program or another similar program. One benefit of this method is that the leads derived are likely to convert because they have actively demonstrated an interest in the brand. When creating the forms used to collect this information, it is essential to find the right balance in the amount of data asked for. Asking for too much can discourage people from participating, while not asking for enough means the data will not be as useful as it could be.

7. In-store traffic monitoring
In a brick-and-mortar shop, insights can also be gathered from monitoring the foot traffic there. The most straightforward way to do this is with a traffic counter on the door to help keep track of how many people come into the shop throughout the day. This data will reveal what the busiest days and hours are. It may also help give an idea about what is drawing customers to the store at certain times. Installing security systems with motion sensors will help you track customers' movement patterns throughout the shop. The sensor can provide data about which of the shop's departments are most popular.

Problem Solving and Decision Making

Benefits of Collecting Data

Collecting data is valuable because it can be used to make informed decisions. The more relevant, high-quality data available, the more likely decisions will be effective when it comes to marketing, sales, customer service, product development and many other areas of the business. Some specific uses of customer data include the following.

1. Improving understanding of the audience
It can be difficult or impossible to get to know every customer personally, especially in a large business or an online business. The better the understand of the customers, the easier it will be to meet their expectations. Data collection enables this improvement in understanding of who the audience is and disseminate that information throughout the organisation. Through the primary data collection methods described above, the organisation can learn about who the customers are, what they are interested in and what they want from the organisation.

2. Identifying areas for improvement or expansion
Collecting and analysing data helps identify where the company is doing well and where there is room for improvement. It can also reveal opportunities for expanding the business.

Looking at transactional data, for example, can show which of the products are the most popular and which ones do not sell as well. This information might help focus more on the bestsellers and develop other similar products. Customer complaints about a product could also be reviewed to see which aspects are causing problems.

Data is also useful for identifying opportunities for expansion. An e-commerce business may be considering opening a brick-and-mortar store. Customer data will reveal where the customers are and allows the launch of the first store in an area with a high concentration of existing customers. This could then expand to other similar areas.

3. Predicting Future Patterns
Analysing the data can help predict future trends. The data for a new website, for instance, may reveal that DVDs are consistently increasing in popularity, as opposed to other articles. This observation would suggest more resources should be directed into DVDs. It will also enable the prediction of more temporary patterns and react to those accordingly. A clothing store might discover pastel colours are popular during spring and summer, while people gravitate toward darker shades in autumn and winter. Once this is realised, the right colours can be introduced to stores at the right times to boost sales.

Data might show companies with a particular job title often have questions for tech support when it comes time to update their software. Knowing this in advance allows support to be offered proactively, making for an excellent customer experience.

4. Better Personalising Your Content and Messaging
When more is known about customers or site visitors, the messaging sent to them can be tailored to their interests and preferences. This personalisation applies to marketers designing ads, publishers choosing which ads to run and content creators deciding what format to use for their content.

Problem Solving and Decision Making

Using data collection in marketing can help produce promotions that target a given audience. For example: a marketeer looking to advertise a new brand of cereal uses data which shows most people who eat the cereal are in their 50s and 60s, actors in those age ranges can be used in promotions. A publisher is likely to have information about what topics site visitors prefer to read about. Audiences can be grouped based on the characteristics they share and then show visitors with those characteristics content about topics popular with that group. Personalisation can even go further by adjusting the site's experience to the individual's experience. Cookies can be used to determine when someone is revisiting a site or require them to log in to confirm their identity and access their personalised user experience.

Data Analysis

For most businesses and government agencies, lack of data is not a problem. In fact, it is the opposite: there is often too much information available to make a clear decision.

With so much data to sort through, more is needed from the data:

- *Is it the right data for answering your question?*
- *Can accurate conclusions be drawn from that data?*
- *Does the data inform the decision-making process?*

With the right data analysis process and tools, what was once an overwhelming volume of disparate information becomes a simple, clear decision point.

To improve data analysis skills and simplify decision making, execute these five steps in any data analysis process:

Step 1: Define the questions
Questions should be measurable, clear and concise. Design questions to either qualify or disqualify potential solutions to the specific problem or opportunity.

Start with a clearly defined problem:

> *A contractor is experiencing rising costs and is no longer able to submit competitive contract proposals.*

One of many questions to solve this business problem might include: Can the company reduce its staff without compromising quality?

Step 2: Set Clear Measurement Priorities
This step breaks down into two sub-steps: a) Decide what to measure and b) Decide how to measure it.

> *a) Decide what to measure*
> Using the contractor example, consider what kind of data is needed to answer the key question. In this case, it would be the number and cost of current staff and the percentage of time they spend on necessary business functions.

Problem Solving and Decision Making

In answering this question many sub-questions may also need to be answered (e.g., are staff currently under-utilised? If so, what process improvements would help?).

Finally, the decision on what to measure, being sure to include any reasonable objections any stakeholders might have (e.g., If staff are reduced, how would the company respond to surges in demand?).

b) Decide how to measure it
Thinking about how to measure data is just as important, especially before the data collection phase, because the measuring process either backs up or discredits the analysis later on. Key questions to ask for this step include:

- **What is your time frame?** *(e.g., annual versus quarterly costs)*
- **What is your unit of measure?** *(e.g., Pound Sterling versus Euro)*
- **What factors should be included?** *(e.g., just annual salary versus annual salary plus cost of staff benefits)*

Step 3: Collect Data

With the question clearly defined and the measurement priorities set, now it is time to collect the data. As data is collected and organised, remember to keep these important points in mind:

- *Before you collect new data, determine what information could be collected from existing databases or sources on hand. Collect this data first.*
- *Determine a file storing and naming system ahead of time to help all tasked team members collaborate. This process saves time and prevents team members from collecting the same information twice.*
- *If you need to gather data via observation or interviews, then develop an interview template ahead of time to ensure consistency and save time.*
- *Keep your collected data organised in a log with collection dates and add any source notes as you go (including any data normalisation performed). This practice validates your conclusions down the road.*

Step 4: Analyse Data

After the right data has been collected to answer the question from Step 1, it is time for deeper data analysis. Begin by manipulating the data in a number of different ways, such as plotting it out and finding correlations or by creating a pivot table in Excel.

A pivot table lets you sort and filter data by different variables and lets you calculate the mean, maximum, minimum and standard deviation of your data – just be sure to avoid these five pitfalls of statistical data analysis.

As the data is manipulated, the exact data needed may have been captured, but more likely, the original question may need revision or more data may need to be collected. Either way, this initial analysis of trends, correlations, variations and outliers helps to focus the data analysis on better answering the question and any objections others might have.

Problem Solving and Decision Making

During this step, data analysis tools and software are extremely helpful. Visio, Minitab and Stata are all good software packages for advanced statistical data analysis. However, in most cases, nothing quite compares to Microsoft Excel in terms of decision-making tools.

Step 5: Interpret Results

After analysing the data and possibly conducting further research, it is finally time to interpret the results. As the analysis is interpreted, keep in mind that an hypothesis cannot ever be proved true, the hypothesis can only not be rejected. Meaning that no matter how much data is collected, chance could always interfere with the results.
As the results of the data are interpreted, ask these key questions:

- *Does the data answer your original question? How?*
- *Does the data help you defend against any objections? How?*
- *Is there any limitation on your conclusions, are there any angles which have not been considered?*

If the interpretation of the data holds up under all of these questions and considerations, then it is likely a productive conclusion has been reached. The only remaining step is to use the results of the data analysis process to decide the best course of action.

By following these five steps in the data analysis process, better decisions will be made because the choices are backed by data that has been robustly collected and analysed.

With practice, data analysis gets faster and more accurate – meaning better, more informed decisions are made to run the organisation most effectively.

Problem Solving and Decision Making

Critical Analysis of Data

All the information used in the process of decision-making must be critically analysed and validated.

This can be undertaken in several ways including obtaining a second opinion or even a third. Cross-referencing the information provided with other sources can help to validate the information. Asking questions to relevant people, teams or companies is probably the easiest way to do this. Information gathered can be validated and its accuracy ensured by staying in touch with wider aspects of the business or trends and by reading associated journals, press releases, etc.

When selecting data and information it must be gathered in a non-judgemental and unbiased manner.
To ensure this a consistent approach is needed and rules are needed for its collection.

- **Currency of data / information** -how up to date is the data / information?
- **Source of data / information** -how reliable is the source of the data / information?
- **Form of data / information** -is it in a usable format? Can it be readily interrogated?
- **Sufficiency of data / information** -is there enough for the purpose? Is there too little to use?
- **Validity of data information** -is it pertinent to the task? Will it assist in reaching conclusions?
- **Reliability of data/information** -how accurate is the information? Is it misleading (intentional or otherwise)?
- **Speed of data/information** -how long will it take to gather? How long do you have?
- **Cost effectiveness of data/information gathering** -how much (money and time) do you have? Is the cost worth the result?

Other models that can be used to analyse data to support decision-making are:

- **decision trees** - these allow you to map and consider all possible solutions to a decision you need to make
- **paired comparison analysis** - this allows you to compare a limited number of decisions and allocate them in order of importance.
- **grid analysis** - this allows you to compare options using the features or factors you want to consider before deciding
- **root cause analysis** - supports you to find out the root cause of a problem, you can then concentrate on finding out what happened, why it happened and act to reduce the chance of it happening again
- **cause and effect analysis** - this is a type of fishbone diagram that allows you to identify the main facts of the problem and drill down into possible causes. It was first developed in 1960 by Prof Kaoru Ishikawa.

Problem Solving and Decision Making

Ethics and Values

All organisations today spend a huge amount of time, endeavour and money in maintaining, improving and broadcasting their "Brand". Customers will follow a brand and buy from that brand rather than from a competitor. This allegiance is invaluable in business terms. The damage which could be caused by negative reports about a brand can be disastrous.

Because of this, when making decisions, it is vital that organisations consider the impact that any decision may have on their Ethics and Values and therefore, their "Brand".

Here are some criteria that can help ensure appropriate ethical considerations are part of the decisions being made in the organisation:

- **Compliance** - *Does it conform to the company's values and code of ethics? Does it meet (should exceed) legal requirements?*
- **Promote good and reduce harm** - *What solution will be good to the most people while minimising any possible harm?*
- **Responsibility** - *What alternative provides the most responsible response? Does the solution ensure meeting our duties as a good corporate citizen?*
- **Respects and preserves rights** - *Does the option negatively impact an individual's or organisation's rights?*
- **Promotes trust** - *Does the solution lead to honest and open communication? Is it truthful? Is there full disclosure?*
- **Builds reputation** - *Would a headline of your decision generate pride or shame? Does your solution add to or detract with the identity you want for the organisation?*

Making ethical decisions is easier said than done!

Ethics in business decision-making

Ethics define the way an organisation should respond to external environment. Organisational ethics includes various guidelines and principles which decide the way individuals should behave at the workplace.

It also refers to the code of conduct of the individuals working in a particular organisation.

Every organisation runs to earn profits but how it makes money is more important. No organisation should depend on unfair means to earn money. One must understand that money is not the only important thing; pride and honour are more important. An individual's first priority can be to make money but he should not stoop too low just to be able to do that.

Problem Solving and Decision Making

Examples of unethical conduct

- Children below fourteen years of age must not be employed to work in any organisation. Childhood is the best phase of one's life and no child should be deprived of his childhood.
- Employees should not indulge in destruction or manipulation of information to get results. Data Tampering is considered strictly unethical and unprofessional in the corporate world. Remember if one is honest, things will always be in his favour.
- Employees should not pass on company's information to any of the external parties. Do not share any of your organisation's policies and guidelines with others. It is better not to discuss official matters with friends and relatives. Confidential data or information must not be leaked under any circumstances.
- There must be absolute fairness in monetary transactions and all kinds of trading. Never ever cheat your clients.
- Organisations must not discriminate any employee on the grounds of sex, physical appearance, age or family background. Female employees must be treated with respect. Don't ask your female employees to stay back late at work. It is unethical to discriminate employees just because they do not belong to an affluent background. Employees should be judged by their work and nothing else.
- Organisation must not exploit any of the employees. The employees must be paid according to their hard work and efforts. If individuals are working late at night, make sure overtimes are paid. The management must ensure employees get their arrears, bonus, incentives and other reimbursements on time.
- Stealing office property is strictly unethical.
- Organisation must take care of the safety of the employees. Individuals should not be exposed to hazardous conditions.
- Never lie to your customers. It is unprofessional to make false promises to the consumers. The advertisements must give a clear picture of the product. Do not commit anything which your organisation can't offer. It is important to be honest with your customers to expect loyalty from them. It is absolutely unethical to fool the customers.
- The products should not pose a threat to environment and mankind.
- Employees on probation period can be terminated anytime but organisations need to give one month notice before firing the permanent ones. In the same way permanent employees need to serve one month notice before resigning from the current services. Employees can't stop coming to office all of a sudden.

Code of Business Ethics

A organisations ethics are becoming increasingly important as customers and other stakeholders become more attuned to ethical issues both in the workplace and the wider world. Before choosing to use an organisation many people today are inclined to ask the question:

> *"Are organisations conducting their business ethically?"*

In the dictionary, ethics are defined as:

Problem Solving and Decision Making

"the rules and standards governing the conduct of an individual or group".

A code of business ethics often focuses on social issues. It may set out general principles about an organisation's beliefs on matters such as mission, quality, privacy, and the environment. It may delineate procedures that should be used to determine whether a violation of the code of ethics has occurred and, if so, what remedies should be pursued. The effectiveness of such codes of ethics depends on the extent to which management supports and enforces them

Ethical decision making is the process of assessing the moral implications of a course of action.

All decisions have an ethical or moral dimension for a simple reason—they have an effect on others.

Managers and leaders need to be aware of their own ethical and moral beliefs so they can draw on them when they face difficult decisions.

Most ethical decisions exist in a grey area where there is no clear-cut or obvious decision that can be determined solely through quantitative analysis or consideration of objective data or information. Ethical decision making requires judgment and interpretation, the application of a set of values to a set of perceptions and estimates of the consequences of an action. Sometimes ethical decisions involve choosing not between good and bad, but between good and better or between bad and worse.

Making ethical decisions also involves choice about who should be involved in the process and how the decision should be made. For example, if a decision will have a significant impact on the local community, leaders may feel obligated to invite a representative of the community to participate in discussions. Similarly, decisions with a significant ethical dimension may benefit from being made by consensus rather than by decree - to demonstrate that the choice is consistent with an organisation's espoused values.

A Manager's Role in Ethical Conduct

Managers are responsible for upholding the ethical code and helping others to do so as well. Managers hold positions of authority that make them accountable for the ethical conduct of those who report to them. They can fulfil this responsibility by making sure employees are aware of the organisation's ethical code and have the opportunity to ask questions to clarify their understanding.

Managers also monitor the behaviour of employees in accordance with the organisation's expectations of appropriate behaviour. They have a duty to respond quickly and appropriately to minimise the impact of suspected ethical violations. Lastly, managers make themselves

Problem Solving and Decision Making

available as a resource to counsel and assist employees who face ethical dilemmas or who suspect an ethical breach.

Of course, managers are responsible for upholding ethical standards in their own actions and decisions as well. In addition to following the organisation's ethical code, managers may be obligated to follow a separate professional code of ethics, depending on their role, responsibilities, and training. Fiduciary duty is an example that applies to some managerial roles. Someone in this role must put the interests of those to whom he is accountable ahead of any interests and must not profit from his position as a someone in a position of trust unless the principal consents.

Many managers have responsibility for interacting with external stakeholders such as customers, suppliers, government officials, or community representatives. In those encounters, managers may be called on to explain a decision or a planned action in terms of ethical considerations. The stakeholders will be interested to hear how the organisation took ethics into account, and in those cases, it is the manager's duty to speak on the company's behalf.

Additionally, managers may be responsible for creating and/or implementing changes to an organisation's ethical codes or guidelines. These changes may be in response to an internal determination based on the experience of employees; for instance, additional clarification may be needed about what constitutes nepotism or unfair bias in hiring. Alternatively, new regulations, altered public perceptions and concerns, or other external factors may require the organisation to make adjustments.

Ethical Decision-Making Model

When making a major decision for a company, it can be tempting to choose the easiest or most cost-effective course of action -- even if that option is not the best from an ethical standpoint. The PLUS model, a set of questions designed to help make decisions from an ethical point of view, can ensure the decisions are correct and appropriate.

The PLUS model is especially objective because it does not focus on revenue or profit, but rather urges leaders to take a legal and fair approach to a problem.

PLUS Model:

P = **Policies and Procedures** *(Does this decision align with company policies?)*

L = **Legal** *(Does this decision violate any laws or regulations?)*

U = **Universal** *(Is this decision in line with core values and company culture? How does it relate to our organisational values?)*

S = **Self** *(Does it meet my standards of fairness and honesty?)*

Once potential solutions have been considered using these questions as a guide, you are ready to implement the six necessary steps to make your decision.

Problem Solving and Decision Making

Ethical Decision-Making Process

When a difficult problem that threatens the organisation's integrity or beliefs (or could be illegal), these six steps well help to make an ethical decision.

Step One: Define the problem
Use PLUS filters to define the problem, and how it might affect one of the PLUS acronyms. Is it illegal, or does it breach the company's values? Make sure the full scope of the problem has been outlined -- be honest about it, even if there is personal culpability.

Step Two: Seek out resources
It can be difficult, if not impossible, to reach an objective solution alone. To fairly evaluate the problem, seek out all available resources. These resources might be mentors, stakeholders, or even friends and family, but they could also be professional guidelines and organisational policies. Make sure there is full knowledge to understand the extent of the damage.

Step Three: Brainstorm a list of potential solutions
When brainstorming a list of potential solutions to the problem, do not only consider what has been done before. Stay open to new and different ideas and urge other people to share their advice. Consider outside resources, including what other companies have done.

Ultimately, a list of at least three to five potential solutions is ideal. This avoids an either/or situation.

Step Four: Evaluate Those Alternatives
Dive into the list of potential solutions and consider all positive and negative consequences of taking each action. It is important to consider how likely those consequences are to occur, as well. Refer to resources, guidelines, and standards. For instance, it may be decided that one solution has only one negative consequence, but that negative consequence has a high likelihood of happening. Another solution has two negative consequences, but both are extremely unlikely. These are important factors to weigh when making your decision.

Step Five: Make Your Decision, and Implement It
At this stage, all the information needed to make a fair and ethical decision is to hand. If the decision has been made autonomously, it must be shared with the team. Create a proposal outlining why that route has been chosen and what alternatives were considered, so they can understand your steps. Transparency is key. The team needs to understand that appropriate and objective measures were used to find a solution.

Step Six: Evaluate Your Decision
Once the solution is implemented, decide whether the problem was fixed or not. If there are unforeseen consequences, perhaps consider of alternative measures is needed to combat the problem or refer to outside guidance.

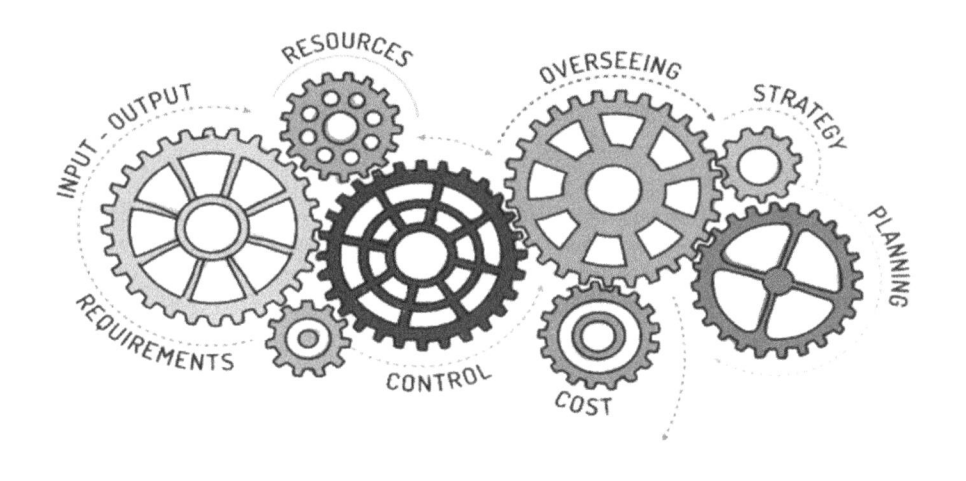

Chapter 6: Operational Management

Operational Management

Operations Management

Every organisation has an operations function, whether or not it is called 'operations' or something else.

The goal or purpose of most organisations involves the production of goods and/or services. To do this, they have to procure resources, convert them into outputs and distribute them to their intended users.

> *The term "operations" encompasses all the activities required to create and deliver an organisation's goods or services to its customers.*

Within large and complex organisations, Operations is usually a major functional area with people specifically appointed to manage all or part of the organisation's operational processes. It is an important functional area because it plays a crucial role in determining how well an organisation satisfies its customers.

In smaller, private-sector organisations, the operations function is usually expressed in terms of profits, growth and competitiveness; in public and voluntary organisations, it is often expressed in terms of providing value for money.

Operations management is concerned with the design, management and improvement of the systems that create the organisation's goods or services. The majority of most organisations' financial and human resources are invested in the activities involved in making products or delivering services. Operations management is therefore critical to organisational success.

> *Operations management involves managing resources including staff, materials, equipment and technology.*

Operations management theory is based on the set practices which organisations use to increase efficiency in production.

People skills, creativity, rational analysis and technological knowledge are all important for success in operations management

Operations managers have direct responsibilities which include managing both the operations process, embracing design, planning, control, performance improvement and operations strategy. Their indirect responsibilities include interacting with those managers in other functional areas within the organisation whose roles have an impact on operations. Such areas include marketing, finance, accounting, personnel and engineering.

Operations managers' responsibilities include:

Operational Management

- **Human resource management** – *the people employed by an organisation either work directly to create a good or service or provide support to those who do. People and the way they are managed are a key resource of all organisations.*
- **Asset management** – *an organisation's buildings, facilities, equipment and stock are directly involved in or support the operations function.*
- **Cost management** – *most of the costs of producing goods or services are directly related to the costs of acquiring resources, transforming them or delivering them to customers. For many organisations in the private sector, driving down costs through efficient operations management gives them a critical competitive edge. For organisations in the not-for-profit sector, the ability to manage costs is no less important.*

Mission and Vision Statements

Most people think of "vision statements" and "mission statements" as being "strategy", but they are only a small part of the strategy story. The mission and vision are simply statements about what the organisation is for and where the executives would like to take it.

> *A Mission Statement defines the organisations business, its objectives and its approach to reach those objectives.*

> *A Vision Statement describes the desired future position of the company.*

> *The difference between a mission statement and a vision statement is that a mission statement focuses on a company's present state while a vision statement focuses on the company's future*

Elements of Mission and Vision Statements are often combined to provide a statement of the company's purposes, goals and values

Mission Statement

A mission statement is a brief description of a company's fundamental purpose. It is a combination of what the business does and how and why it does it, expressed in a way that encapsulates the values that are important to it.

Fred David describes a mission statement in "Strategic Management: Concepts and Cases," as:

> *all mission statements will "broadly describe an organisation's present capabilities, customer focus, activities and business makeup."*

Operational Management

Every business should have a mission statement, both as a way of ensuring that everyone in the organisation is "on the same page" and to serve as a starting point for effective business planning.

The mission statement is often derived from a group effort and writing a mission statement is viewed as a valuable team-building exercise.

Because mission statements are part of an organisations public face, they are also often used in corporate marketing. Many businesses will include them on the "about" page on their website, for instance. Sometimes a company's mission statement even becomes the core of its advertising.

> *It should be remembered that a mission statement is not a vision statement*

Good mission statements can give strategic focus to an organisation and motivate employees to work together toward a common goal. Unfortunately, mission statements often consist of the latest buzzwords or business jargon and have unrealistic or unattainable goals, all of which can negatively affect employee morale. Having a coherent, realistic mission statement is fundamental to engaging employees and fulfilling corporate goals.

This can be achieved by:

- *Gathering employee input when writing the mission statement*
- *Explicitly recognising the talents and contributions of employees in the mission statement*

Examples of Mission Statements

Here are the mission statements of some well-known companies

- **Amazon:** "Our mission is to be Earth's most customer-centric company. This is what unites Amazonians across teams and geographies as we are all striving to delight our customers and make their lives easier, one innovative product, service and idea at a time."
- **Tesla:** "Tesla's mission is to accelerate the world's transition to sustainable energy."
- **Apple:** "Apple designs Macs, the best personal computers in the world, along with OS X, life, iWork and professional software. Apple leads the digital music revolution with its iPods and iTunes online store. Apple has reinvented the mobile phone with its revolutionary iPhone and App Store and is defining the future of mobile media and computing devices with iPad."
- **Virgin Atlantic Airways:** "... to embrace the human spirit and let it fly."

Many of these organisation's mission statements have changed and evolved over the years. It is a good practice to set a mission statement from the start, but consistently review it to ensure it continues to express the organisational purpose as it would be stated today.

Operational Management

Vision Statement

A vision statement is sometimes likened to a picture of a company in the future, but it is so much more than that.

> *The vision statement is the inspiration, the framework for the strategic planning.*

Vision Statement

To be the premier purveyor of the finest coffee in the world.

When writing a vision statement, it defines the dreams and hopes of the business. It describes what it is trying to build and serves as a springboard for future actions.

A vision statement may apply to an entire company or to a single division of that company.

A vision statement is not limited by details. That is why it is important when creating one to let imagination go and dream - and why it is important that a vision statement captures the passion.

> *The vision statement is about dreaming; the mulling over the ways and means to accomplish the vision comes afterwards.*

When Bill Gates first started Microsoft, he envisioned a personal computer in every home and business, not a series of steps for making that happen.

Whilst a vision statement does not say how the dream will be achieved, it does set the direction for business planning. That makes creating one especially compelling for all businesses because the main reason start-up businesses fail is because of poor planning.

Example Vision Statements

- **Amazon** - *Our vision is to be earth's most customer-centric company; to build a place where people can come to find and discover anything they might want to buy online*
- **Harley-Davidson** - *To fulfil dreams through the experiences of motorcycling.*
- **IKEA** - *To create a better everyday life for the many people.*
- **Microsoft** - *To help people around the world realise their full potential.*
- **Starbucks** - *To inspire and nurture the human spirit — one person, one cup and one neighbourhood at a time.*
- **Uber** - *Make transportation as reliable as running water, everywhere, for everyone*

Operational Management

Organisational Strategies

An organisational strategy can address growth or expansion, diversification, acquisition or sustaining its current outputs. The way the strategy is implemented will depend on its direction and this will be determined by the strategy writers.

> *An organisational strategy is the sum of the actions a company intends to take to achieve long-term goals.*

Together, these actions make up a company's strategic plan.

Strategic plans will be produced for a minimum of a year and may extend to 3 and 5 years. They will involve all levels of the organisation in their execution. Senior management create the overarching organisational strategy, while middle and lower management adopt and set goals and plans to fulfil the strategy step by step.

This unified effort can be likened to a journey. The journey starts at the point where we are today and ends at the destination. The route taken to get there will be formulated and the challenges which need to be addressed are the road conditions which must be overcome to complete the sequential legs of the journey, which eventually leads to the ultimate destination.

Strategic plans

There are a variety of models and approaches to strategic planning. Many businesses will include a SWOT analysis or a PESTLE analysis as key elements of their strategic plan.

There will also be implementation schedules, key performance indicators (KPIs') and other accountability measures.

Difference between strategic plans and business plans

Both strategic and business planning documents are essential planning tools for a business. However, depending on business stage and goals, one may be more useful than the other.

> *A strategic plan is for a 3-5-year period and sets out the tasks, the milestones and the steps needed to drive the business forward.*

> *A business plan focuses on a shorter term, usually no more than a year and serves a specific goal – e.g., starting a business, getting funding, or directing operations.*

Operational Management

Strategic planning requires a step back from day-to-day operations and articulating where the business is heading, by setting long-term goals, objectives and priorities for the future. Strategic plans are the result of defining the Organisational Strategy. The strategic plan will be a formalised document that describes the organisations goals and the actions needed to achieve them.

Its primary purpose is to connect three key areas:

- **the mission** - *defining the business' purpose*
- **the vision** - *describing what is to be achieved*
- **the plan** - *outlining how to achieve the ultimate goals*

Strategic plans are necessary to determine the direction for the organisation. It focuses effort and ensures that everyone in the organisation is working towards a common goal. It also helps to:

- *agree actions that will contribute to business growth*
- *align resources for optimal results*
- *prioritise financial needs*
- *build competitive advantage*
- *engage with staff and communicate what needs to be done*

Another significant purpose of strategic planning is to help manage and reduce business risks. Growing a business is inherently risky. Detailed planning will help to:

- *remove uncertainty*
- *analyse potential risks*
- *implement risk control measures*
- *consider how to minimise the impact of risks, should they occur*

Strategic Planning Process

The strategic planning process is the methodology of defining strategy and then cascading it down through the organisation and turning it into a tactical plan.

> *Done well, strategic planning builds strategic alignment into everything the organisation does.*

At every level, managers should be selecting initiatives and investments that support their goals - in other words, the goals become criteria for selecting the right things in which to invest time and resources.

This is often a great opportunity for some bottom-up planning as people lower in the organisation are often the ones who *"know how things work"*. For this to work, however, the

Operational Management

leaders of a group need to be able to clearly articulate the goals and this is one of the common ways an organisation can fail to align its activities to its strategy.

Individual divisions of the organisation will use the mission statement to construct a more detailed plan of action to identify the activities it must undertake and achieve to contribute to the overall achievement of the organisation's mission and thus its vision.

Similarly, business units or departments will repeat this procedure for their own areas of operation down through the teams of that business unit or department and finally, the individuals within those teams. Such a process, therefore, aligns the activities of individuals and allows the setting of key performance indicators (KPI) to ensure the achievement of organisational objectives or goals.

Naturally, this assumes that those heading up the various links, from the individual at the end of the link to those at the head of the link, clearly communicate the objectives and construct an objective plan which ensures those objectives are met. The diagram shows objective linking.

```
Organisational Strategic Objectives
       (from the strategic vision)
                ↓
       Divisional Objectives
                ↓
  Business Unit / Departmental Objectives
                ↓
         Team Objectives
                ↓
       Individual Objectives
```

It becomes apparent that individuals must undertake KPIs' that can be clearly linked to the objectives of the team, which in turn are linked to those of the business unit or department, which in turn are linked to those of the division, which are finally linked to the overall strategic objectives.

Doing this will ensure:

1. that the whole organisation is working towards achievement of objectives that are aligned to the common organisational goal
2. individual members of staff can clearly identify how the achievement of their actions and objectives are contributing to the achievement of the common objective or goal
3. it can define expectations of what must be delivered and how it should be delivered

Operational Management

4. it ensures that all staff are aware of what constitutes high-performance and what they must do to achieve it
5. it can enhance motivation and commitment by recognising achievement and the provision of feedback
6. it provides the basis for personal development planning and improvement plans
7. it allows leaders to monitor their own performance as well as those for whom they are responsible
8. it encourages dialogue about what needs to be done to improve performance by mutual agreement rather than having it imposed from above

Strategic Alignment

Understanding strategic alignment starts with understanding what strategy really is.

> *Strategy - in the context of "strategic alignment" - is the "how".*

For example, a vision/mission statement might say something like: *"We want to be the most profitable widget manufacturer in the world!"*

The key question to be asked before any action is taken to implement this strategic vision is, "How should we do that"?

In the role of a *"widget"* manufacturer, we could ask

> *"Are we going to be the lowest cost provider and take massive market share… or should we be the one that offers the highest level of Widget Service, but does so at a high margin?"*

The "how" statements lead you to strategic goals - the specific targets you have to hit to achieve your vision/mission.

If we decide we are going to be the low-cost, high volume widget maker, that means our strategic goals might be something like:

- *Reduce costs to supply widgets*
- *Increase distribution channels*
- **Manage cash flow** (as volume grows, your organisation will need more cash to hold stock, etc.)

In the real world, you may want to put some specific numbers on these goals, but this "big picture" of what we're trying to achieve (be the most profitable widget company) combined with a high-level statement of how we're going to achieve it (by being low cost, increasing distribution while managing cash) is the "strategy".

Operational Management

Having a strategy on its own, is not enough. In fact, research suggests that having a strategy has no real effect on the performance of a business. It is aligning the activities of the business to the strategies that makes the difference.

Think!

> *deciding you want a cup of coffee (your strategy) is not the same as getting up and making a cup of coffee (aligning your actions to your strategy).*

This gets to the heart of what strategic alignment is.

Most people think of strategic alignment as a noun *("the state of having everything aligned to strategy")*, but it is better to think of strategic alignment as a verb - it is about action.

Definition:

> *Strategic Alignment (verb): The process of aligning an organisation's decisions and actions such that they support the achievement of strategic goals.*

Note that the definition talks about decision-making and actions. Actions typically follow decisions so if your organisation does not have the ability to make well-aligned decisions, they really cannot take well-aligned actions.

Additionally, implicit in the definition, is the fact that strategic alignment involves NOT DOING some of the things that you might currently be doing... things that do not support the realisation of strategic goals

Strategic Projects

At the simplest level, if projects are not directly linked to organisational strategy, there is a huge risk that one can push or pull the other in a direction which is disadvantageous to both, meaning there is no telling where the project or even the organisation may end up

Many factors limit an organisation from performing at its best. The limitations can be removed if employees better understand the strategy, understand the key initiatives and methodologies chosen to achieve it and select the correct performance measures. This way they can more clearly view how what they do contributes to results. Projects are the way to facilitate this.

Projects can be used to ensure that the strategic direction being adopted by the business supports both the strategy and the financial needs of the business

Operational Management

Projects have become an integral part of business management in the 21st century. Project management is rapidly becoming a standard way of implementing strategy in organisations. A typical organisation can accomplish a considerable part of its effort through projects.

Projects today are used for many purposes, not least:

- *deliver organisation's strategy*
- *achieve competitive advantage*
- *drive innovation,*
- *support decision making*
- *enable change.*

Operational Management

Key Performance Indicators (KPIs')

The majority of employees, their leaders and managers, work hard and always strive to perform to the best of their abilities. A frequently asked question, however, is how well are we actually doing?

There needs to be a measure of how effective the hard work has been in delivering the outcomes which are required. Key Performance Indicators (KPIs') can help answer these questions, by quantifying individual and organisational goals and evaluating performance accordingly.

> *A Key Performance Indicator (KPI) is simply a quantifiable metric (measure) that reflects how well an organisation is achieving its stated goals and objectives.*

KPIs' link the organisational vision to individual action. An ideal situation is where KPIs' cascade down through the organisation from level to level.

The organisation can be regarded as a pyramid with the strategic vision at the top, feeding down to specific actions at the bottom. In between will be the KPIs' that have been derived from the strategy, objectives and the Critical Success Factors (CSFs') for the organisation.

CSFs are the areas of activity in which an organisation must perform well in order to be successful. KPIs' are the means by which these CSFs' can be measured.

The actions below the KPIs' are the tasks and projects that you carry out in order to achieve the KPIs'.

KPIs' support the organisation's goals and strategy. They allow people to focus on what matters most and to monitor progress.

Operational Management

Example

Below is an example of how organisational strategy cascades down to an individual team member's goals and KPIs':

- **Organisational Vision:** *to be known for high customer satisfaction and superior service.*
- **Organisational Objective:** *to reduce the number of dissatisfied customers by 25 percent.*
- **Organisational KPI:** *the number of customer complaints that remain unresolved at the end of a week.*
- **Team Member's Goal:** *to increase the number of satisfactory complaint resolutions by 15 percent in this period.*
- **Team Member KPI:** *the weekly percentage difference in complaints handled that result in satisfied customers, as against unsatisfied customers.*

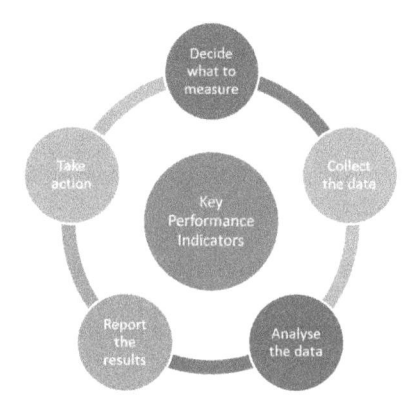

Setting KPIs'

The KPIs' will be different between organisations and across departments, but it is always important to ensure performance metrics are measuring the appropriate activity for each area of the business.

Example:

> Net profit is a standard KPI for an organisation's financial performance. It is easy enough to calculate (total revenue minus total expenses) and the higher it is, the better the organisation is performing. Others may be harder to calculate. A customer satisfaction KPI, for example, may require regular, carefully constructed customer surveys to build the right amount of data. A decision would then have to be made as to what sort of customer satisfaction score represents the benchmark to be achieved.

Operational Management

Note:
It is important not to have too many KPIs': the optimum number for most areas of a business is between four and 10. Make sure there are enough to measure how the team or organisation is performing against the key objectives which have been assigned.

The KPIs' should then be communicated clearly to everyone concerned. Ensure that team members know how each KPI impacts their work and that they know which activities to focus on.

Setting SMART KPIs'

Setting SMART objectives will enable team members to work towards their KPIs' and gives them the support they need to help the team succeed. Spending time and effort to develop SMART objectives for team members ensures everyone has the knowledge and understanding needed to contribute effectively and comfortably to the team and the business.

When a KPI is finalised, it should fulfil all of the SMART criteria.

Example:

> Increase new sign-ups to the newsletter by 25 percent by the end of the second quarter of the financial year.

Ask the following questions to help understand the context and define effective KPIs':

- *What is your organisation's vision? What is the strategy for achieving that vision?*
- *Which metrics will indicate that the organisation is successfully pursuing the vision and strategy?*
- *How many metrics should there be?*
- *What should be the benchmark?*
- *How could the metrics be cheated and how will can this be prevented?*

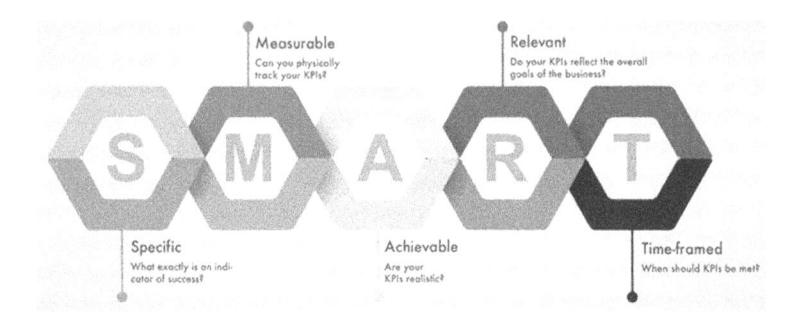

Operational Management

Setting Individual KPIs'

When a goal is set around a desired outcome, the chances of that outcome actually occurring are much higher, simply because you have committed to managing and measuring progress towards it.

When setting goals and KPIs' with individual team members, make sure that they align with the team's overall strategy and KPIs' – which, in turn, align with the overall strategy of the organisation.

Aligning an employee's goal with organisational KPIs' ensures that their daily activities are directly aligned with the goals of the organisation. This is the critical link between employee performance and organisational success.

Implementing KPIs'

Implementing team plans, including operational requirements, are undertaken by open communications, an understanding of the operational aspects of the business and the comprehension of how this is to be achieved.

Decisions must be made as to the most effective ways plans can be implemented and this should include discussions with all those involved. Sharing good practice is a great way of allowing all team members the opportunity to add their own experiences to allow for an effective and relevant way forward to be identified.

Team meetings are an appropriate forum to hold these types of discussions and can be noted and documented to be referred to again in the future.

Resources should also be considered. Resources are not infinite and must be allocated appropriately to gain the most effective results. Resources can include people, machinery and facilities and quite often there will be times when one or the other will be required to be diverted for some reason.

Managing KPIs'

When deciding which KPIs' to use, plan how the data and information needing to be secured will be captured. Net profit requires a different set of data than customer satisfaction for example and requires access to different systems.

Also, establish who will collect the data and how frequently. Sales data can usually be collected daily, whereas KPIs' that require data to be collated from a number of sources might be better measured weekly or monthly. The data will then need to be verified to make sure it is accurate and that it covers all the requirements of the KPI.

A performance dashboard or use a balanced scorecard to measure progress efficiently.

Operational Management

The best places display information regarding KPIs', benchmarking and continuous improvement activities would be in public places that are accessible to everyone along with team boards and the intranet. These should also be displayed to give employees a fuller picture of what is going on, so they buy into the process and take ownership of it. As an operation/departmental manager, you will have your own KPIs' and objectives to achieve and may be reluctant to release any staff or contribute to anything that may increase that burden. Therefore, careful planning and excellent communication is the key to ensuring that all involved are fully aware of the importance of the project and a real need to work in co-operation.

Linking KPIs' to Recognition and Development

When meaningful KPIs' have been established and implemented to measure the performance of the team and of the organisation as a whole, make sure that the appropriate training, support and incentives are in place to enable team members to perform well.

> *Remember! what gets measured, gets done. But what gets rewarded gets done, too!*

When establishing the rewards and recognition policy and practices, make sure that they relate directly to the KPIs' set and that potentially counterproductive behaviours are not being rewarded.

Example:

> When measuring how well people deal with customer complaints, rewarding them for reducing the number of complaints confuses the message you are trying to send.
>
> Intuitively, it may seem that the fewer complaints received, the better the customer service must be. But this may not necessarily be true: there may be fewer complaints because there are fewer customers, or simply because customers are unable to access the support services.

Conversely, if the organisation wants to attract new customers, there may be a KPI that measures how many new customers are gained each week. Depending on the situation, a well-aligned performance system may reward employees based on the number of new customers they personally help to attract.

Operational Management

Business Development tools

Business development tools include among other things quality, analysis and action planning. Business development plans are useful if they identify the desired route the business is to take and the steps included to get there.

As part of the planning process an analysis of the strengths weaknesses opportunities or threats should be undertaken to ensure that all aspects will be addressed, progressed, monitored and reviewed. A SWOT is basically an analytical framework that assesses the business, both internally and externally and will determine what needs to happen to assist the business to achieve its objectives.

Strengths and weaknesses are within the organisation, while opportunities and threats are external. Once completed, the organisation can analyse all aspects of its situation and make clear decisions. It can also help to identify opportunities for the progression of your area of operational control or department and to manage or eliminate threats.

SWOT Analysis

	Strengths	**Weaknesses**
Internal	Strengths are positive characteristics which provide an advantage over the competition. If an organisation fails to monitor its strengths it will not know when these become weaknesses and become a problem for the business	Weaknesses are the inadequate aspects of the business, that if ignored can compromise the organisation. If the business addresses its weaknesses, they can become strengths in the future
	Opportunities	***Threats***
External	Opportunities are favourable conditions in the external market which the organisation can take advantage of. Economic situation, interest rate fall, changes to legislation, etc.	Threats are conditions in the external market which could cause problems for the organisation. These could include changes to legislation, the economic forecast, trends, competitor activity, etc.

A SWOT analysis can help identify any weaknesses in the team and allow remedial action to be taken before they become threats. It also highlights how the team's strengths can be used to open up opportunities. It is also a useful way of finding out how individual team members can best contribute to the ongoing success of the business.

Operational Management

PESTLE

Identifying and assessing factors which are external to the business, but which can have a direct impact on the business operations and functions, can be examined by undertaking a PESTLE analysis. A pestle analysis involves collecting and presenting information about external factors that may have an impact on the business pestle stands for:

Political	this is what is happening or changing in the political backdrop of the business. This includes trade controls, import and export regulations, government agendas and policies, reforms and the political stability in which the organisation operates.
Economic	this is about what is happening in the economy. There is a is their economic decline or growth? What are the current interest rates and other likely to go up or down? Do exchange rates affect the organisation? How does a rising minimum wage affect staffing levels and profits?
Socio-cultural	this covers what is changing in the sociocultural backdrop of the business how are customers buying habits changing? What attitudes and beliefs are affecting their buying habits? How do customers feel about green issues? Are they more health-conscious? How is a population growth rate change in the sociocultural diversity of the customer base affecting how you operate in the business and the product you manufacture? There are many sociocultural aspects of an organisation's operational success and all need to be considered.
Technological	how do you keep up with technological advances? In what ways are customers choosing to interact with you through technology? Are you equipped to respond to those changes? How do you need to update your products and services to maintain a market share?
Legal	this is what happening in changes to the legislation. It can have an impact on employment, access to resources, health and safety management, data management and a long list of other aspects of your organisation. Not abiding by the law can have serious consequences were organisation, so it is imperative to keep it up to date with changes in legislation and more importantly, to successfully implement those changes in your business.
Environmental	this is what is happening the environment and if there any direct consequences of any changes on the organisation. Many of the environmental factors will not have an immediate or direct impact on the organisation itself, but because of these environmental issues, organisations like to see changes in the sociocultural and economic aspects of its operations. Customers respond to knowledge about changes in the environment by purchasing products and services organisation that demonstrate a green conscience, while not in non-environmentally friendly products and services are discarded

Operational Management

Political	Economic	Social Cultural	Technology	Legal	Environmental
• Stability of government • Potential changes to legislation • Global influences	• Economic growth • Employment rates • Inflation rates • Monetary policy • Consumer confidence	• Income distribution • Demographic influences • Lifestyle factors	• International influences • Changes in information technology • Take up rates	• Taxation policies • Employment laws • Industrial regulations • Health and safety	• Regulations and restrictions • Attitudes of customers

Continuous Improvement

Continuous improvement is the idea that business should undertake incremental improvements to their services, products and processes over time. The underlying principles that support continuous improvement are:

1. Make small changes-this is vital because making big changes can be scary, costly and destabilising. Incremental improvements over time reduce the fear factor, keep costs to a minimum and will mean the organisation is continuously improving and not stagnating.
2. Improvements come from employees-they are closer to potential problems and carry out the processing proceeds every day. They should be asked their ideas for improvements.
3. Small changes are inexpensive - employees can implement small changes easily in their day-to-day activities and are well placed to eliminate any unneeded practices.
4. Employees are accountable-they become more invested in their jobs and the outcome of the change because they have come up with their ideas. This increases the chance of more successful changes.
5. Reflective feedback-opening continuous communication during every stage of implementing the change means it is more likely to be successful. This will also keep employees engaged.
6. Measure improvements and repeat them-find out how successful the improvement was and see if it can be implemented elsewhere.

In the marketplace, a business that implements a continuous improvement programme will maintain its competitive edge and compete favourably against its rivals. This is because the program allows it to grow and improve organically over time and in a way that does not interrupt the day-to-day running of the business. These incremental improvements make the business more efficient, keep processes up to date, they reduce waste and lower costs and help to attract more customers due to competitive prices and more innovative products/services.

Operational Management

Total Quality Management (TQM)

A well-known approach to utilise when implementing continuous improvement to quality is the Japanese inspired Total Quality Management (TQM).

TQM can be explained as:

> *"A way of life for an organisation as a whole, committed to total customer satisfaction through a continuous process of improvement and the contribution in improvement of and involvement of people."* Laurie Mullins

To achieve this, the organisation itself must implement, adhere to and monitor its processes and procedures.

The objective of TQM is doing things right the first time over and over again. This saves the organisation the time that is needed to correct poor work and failed product and service implementations (such as warranty repairs). Total Quality Management can be set up separately for an organisation as well as for a set of standards that must be followed- for instance, the International Organisation for Standardisation (ISO) in the ISO 9000 series. Total Quality Management uses strategy, data and communication channels to integrate the required quality principles into the organisation's activities and culture.

Total Quality Management principles

TQM has a number of basic principles which can be converted to the figure below.

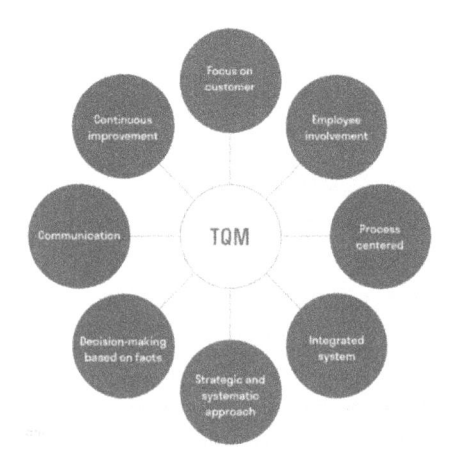

Focus must be on the customer
When using TQM, it is of crucial importance to remember that only customers determine the level of quality. Whatever efforts are made with respect to training employees or improving processes, only customers determine, for example through evaluation or

Operational Management

satisfaction measurement, whether your efforts have contributed to the continuous improvement of product quality and services.

Employee involvement
Employees are an organisation's internal customers. Employee involvement in the development of products or services of an organisation largely determines the quality of these products or services. Ensure that you have created a culture in which employees feel they are involved with the organisation and its products and services.

Process centred
Process thinking and process handling are a fundamental part of total quality management. Processes are the guiding principle and people support these processes based on basis objectives that are linked to the mission, vision and strategy.

Integrated system
Following the principle of Process centred, it is important to have an integrated organisation system that can be modelled for example ISO 9000 or a company quality system for the understanding and handling of the quality of the products or services of an organisation.

Strategic and systematic approach
A strategic plan must embrace the integration and quality development and the development or services of an organisation.

Decision-making based on facts
Decision-making within the organisation must only be based on facts and not on opinions (emotions and personal interests). Data should support this decision-making process.

Communication
A communication strategy must be formulated in such a way that it is in line with the mission, vision and objectives of the organisation. This strategy comprises the stakeholders, the level within the organisation, the communications channels, the measurability of effectiveness, timeliness, etc.

Continuous improvement
By using the right measuring tools and innovative and creative thinking, continuous improvement proposals will be initiated and implemented so that the organisation can develop into a higher level of quality. A supporting Total Quality Management tool that could be used is the Deming cycle (Plan-Do-Check-Act) or the DMAIC process.

Implementing Total Quality Management / TQM

When you implement TQM, you implement a concept. It is not a system that can be implemented but a line of reasoning that must be incorporated into the organisation and its culture.

Practice has proved that there are a number of basic assumptions that contribute to a successful roll-out of TQM within an organisation.

Operational Management

These basic assumptions are:

- *Train senior management on TQM principles and ask for their commitment with respect to its roll-out.*
- *Assess the current culture, customer satisfaction and the quality system.*
- *Senior management determines the desired core values and principles and communicates this within the organisation.*
- *Develop a basic TQM plan using the basic starting principles mentioned above.*
- *Identify and prioritise customer needs and the market and determine the organisation's products and services to meet those needs.*
- *Determine the critical processes that can make a substantial contribution to the products and services.*
- *Create teams that can work on process improvement for example quality circles.*
- *Managers support these teams using planning, resources and by providing time training.*
- *Management integrates the desired changes for improvement in daily processes. After the implementation of improved processes, standardisation takes place.*
- *Evaluate progress continuously and adjust the planning or other issues if necessary.*
- *Stimulate employee involvement. Awareness and feedback lead to an overall improvement of the entire process.*

The cornerstone of TQM is active support and participation of the top management; it is a process, or rather a culture, that can only succeed with the total commitment and encouragement of top management-it is a top-down led process.

Operational Management

Six Sigma

Six Sigma is a set of management tools and techniques designed to improve business by reducing the likelihood of error. It is a data-driven approach which uses statistical methodology for eliminating defects. The resulting increase in performance and decrease in process variation helps lead to a reduction in defects and an improvement in profits, employee morale and quality of products or services. The differing definitions below have been proposed for Six Sigma, but they all share some common threads:

- *The use of teams that are assigned well-defined projects that have a direct impact on the organisation's bottom line.*
- *Training in "statistical thinking" at all levels and providing key people with extensive training in advanced statistics and project management. These key people are designated "Black Belts."*
- *Emphasis on the DMAIC approach to problem solving define, measure, analyse, improve control.*
- *A management environment that supports these initiatives as a business strategy.*

Six Sigma has its foundations in five key principles:

Focus on the customer
This is based on the popular belief that the "customer is the king." The primary goal is to bring maximum benefit to the customer. For this, a business needs to understand its customers, their needs and what drives sales or loyalty. This requires establishing the standard of quality as defined by what the customer or market demands.

Measure the value stream and find your problem
Map the steps in a given process to determine areas of waste. Gather data to discover the specific problem area that is to be addressed or transformed. Have clearly defined goals for data collection, including defining the data to be collected, the reason for the data gathering, insights expected, ensuring the accuracy of measurements and establishing a standardised data collection system. Ascertain if the data is helping to achieve the goals, whether or not the data needs to be refined, or additional information collected. Identify the problem. Ask questions and find the root cause.

Get rid of the junk
Once the problem is identified, make changes to the process to eliminate variation, thus removing defects. Remove the activities in the process that do not add to the customer value. If the value stream does not reveal where the problem lies, tools are used to help discover the outliers and problem areas. Streamline functions to achieve quality control and efficiency. In the end, by taking out the above-mentioned junk, bottlenecks in the process are removed.

Keep the ball rolling
Involve all stakeholders. Adopt a structured process where your team contributes and collaborates their varied expertise for the purposes of problem-solving. Six Sigma processes

Operational Management

can have a great impact on an organisation, so the team has to be proficient in the principles and methodologies used. Hence, specialised training and knowledge are required to reduce the risk of project or re-design failures and ensure that the process performs optimally.

Ensure a flexible and responsive ecosystem
The essence of Six Sigma is business transformation and change. When a faulty or inefficient process is removed, it calls for a change in the work practice and employee approach. A robust culture of flexibility and responsiveness to changes in procedures can ensure a streamlined project implementation. The people and departments involved should be able to adapt to change with ease, so in order to facilitate this, processes should be designed for quick and seamless adoption. Ultimately, the company that has an eye fixed on the data, examines the bottom line periodically and adjusts its processes where necessary, can gain a competitive edge.

Six Sigma Methodology

The two main Six Sigma methodologies are DMAIC and DMADV. Each has its own set of recommended procedures to be implemented for business transformation.

>**DMAIC** is a data-driven method, used to improve existing products or services for better customer satisfaction. It is the acronym for the five phases: D – Define, M – Measure, A – Analyse, I – Improve, C – Control. DMAIC is applied in the manufacturing of a product or delivery of a service.

>**DMADV** is a part of the Design for Six Sigma (DFSS) process, used to design or redesign different processes of product manufacturing or service delivery. The five phases of DMADV are: D – Define, M – Measure, A – Analyse, D – Design, V – Validate. DMADV is employed when existing processes do not meet customer conditions, even after optimisation, or when it is required to develop new processes. It is executed by Six Sigma Green Belts and Six Sigma Black Belts and under the supervision of Six Sigma Master Black Belts.

The two methodologies are used in different business settings and professionals seeking to master these methods and application scenarios would do well to take an online certificate program taught by industry experts.

Although Six Sigma uses various methods to discover deviations and solve problems, the DMAIC is the standard methodology used by Six Sigma practitioners. Six Sigma uses a data-driven management process used for optimising and improving business processes. The underlying framework is a strong customer focus and robust use of data and statistics to draw conclusions.

Operational Management

The Six Sigma Process of the DMAIC method has five phases:

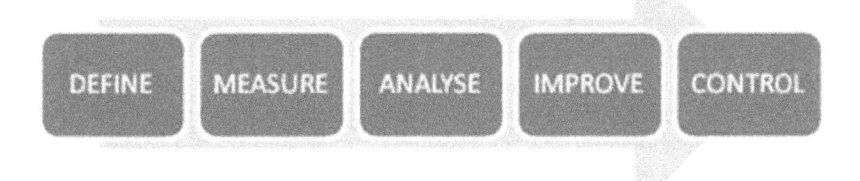

DEFINE → MEASURE → ANALYSE → IMPROVE → CONTROL

Five phases of DMAIC methods

Each of the above phases of business transformation has several steps:

Define
The Six Sigma process begins with a customer-centric approach.

Step 1: The business problem is defined from the customer perspective.
Step 2: Goals are set. What do you want to achieve? What are the resources you will use in achieving the goals?
Step 3: Map the process. Verify with the stakeholders that you are on the right track.

Measure
The second phase is focused on the metrics of the project and the tools used in the measurement. How can you improve? How can you quantify this?

Step 1: Measure your problem in numbers or with supporting data.
Step 2: Define performance yardstick. Fix the limits for "Y."
Step 3: Evaluate the measurement system to be used. Can it help you achieve your outcome?

Analyse
The third phase analyses the process to discover the influencing variables.

Step 1: Determine if your process is efficient and effective. Does the process help achieve what you need?
Step 2: Quantify your goals in numbers. For instance, reduce defective goods by 20%.
Step 3: Identify variations, using historical data.

Improve
This process investigates how the changes in "X" impacts "Y." This phase is where you identify how you can improve the process implementation.

Step 1: Identify possible reasons. Test to identify which of the "X" variables identified in Process III influence "Y."
Step 2: Discover relationships between the variables.

Operational Management

Step 3: Establish process tolerance, defined as the precise values that certain variables can have and still fall within acceptable boundaries, for instance the quality of any given product. Which boundaries need X to hold Y within specifications? What operating conditions can impact the outcome? Process tolerances can be achieved by using tools like robust optimisation and validation set.

Control

In this final phase, you determine that the performance objective identified in the previous phase is well implemented and that the designed improvements are sustainable.

Step 1: Validate the measurement system to be used.
Step 2: Establish process capability. Is the goal being met? For instance, will the goal of reducing defective goods by 20 percent be achieved?
Step 3: Once the previous step is satisfied, implement the process.

Six Sigma Techniques

The Six Sigma methodology also uses a mix of statistical and data analysis tools such as process mapping and design and proven qualitative and quantitative techniques, in order to achieve the desired outcome.

Brainstorming

Brainstorming is the key process of any problem-solving method and is often utilised in the "improve" phase of the DMAIC methodology. It is a necessary process before anyone starts using any tools. Brainstorming involves bouncing ideas and generating creative ways to approach a problem through intensive freewheeling group discussions. A facilitator, who is typically the lead Black Belt or Green Belt, moderates the open session among a group of participants.

Root Cause Analysis/The 5 Whys

This technique helps to get to the root cause of the problems under consideration and is used in the "analyse" phase of the DMAIC cycle.

In the 5 Whys technique, the question "why" is asked again and again, finally leading up to the core issue. Although "five" is the rule of thumb, the actual number of questions can be greater or fewer, whatever it takes in order to gain clarity.

Voice of the Customer

This is the process used to capture the "voice of the customer" or customer feedback by either internal or external means. The technique is aimed at giving the customer the best products and services. It captures the changing needs of the customer through direct and indirect methods. The voice of the customer technique is used in the "define' phase of the DMAIC method, usually to further define the problem to be addressed.

Operational Management

The 5S System
This technique has its roots in the Japanese principle of workplace energies. The 5S System is aimed at removing waste and eliminating bottlenecks from inefficient tools, equipment, or resources in the workplace. The five steps used are Seiri (Sort), Seiton (Set in Order), Seiso (Shine), Seiketsu (Standardise) and Shitsuke (Sustain).

Kaizen (Continuous Improvement)
The Kaizen technique is a powerful strategy that powers a continuous engine for business improvement. It is the practice continuously monitoring, identifying and executing improvements. This is a particularly useful practice for the manufacturing sector. Collective and ongoing improvements ensure a reduction in waste, as well as immediate change whenever the smallest inefficiency is observed.

Benchmarking
Benchmarking is the technique that employs a set standard of measurement. It involves making comparisons with other businesses in order to gain an independent appraisal of the given situation. Benchmarking may involve comparing important processes or departments within a business (internal benchmarking), comparing similar work areas or functions with industry leaders (functional benchmarking), or comparing similar products and services with that of competitors (competitive benchmarking).

Poka-yoke (Mistake Proofing)
This technique's name comes from the Japanese phrase meaning "to avoid errors "and entails preventing the chance of mistakes from occurring. In the poka-yoke technique, employees spot and remove inefficiencies and human errors during the manufacturing process.

Value Stream Mapping
The value stream mapping technique charts the current flow of materials and information, with the purpose of designing a future project. The objective is to remove waste and inefficiencies in the value stream and create leaner operations. It identifies seven different types of waste and three types of waste removal operations.

The Six Sigma Tools

- *Cause and Effect Analysis*
- *Flow Chart*
- *Pareto Chart*
- *Histogram*
- *Check Sheet*
- *Scatter Plot*
- *Control Chart*

Operational Management

Six Sigma Training Levels

The Six Sigma training levels conform to specified training requirement, education criteria, job standards and eligibilities.

White Belt - This is the simplest stage, where:

- Any newcomer can join.
- People work with teams on problem-solving projects.
- The participant is required to understand the basic Six Sigma concepts.

Yellow Belt - Here, the participant:

- Takes part as a project team member.
- Reviews process improvements.
- Gains understanding of the various methodologies and DMAIC.

Green Belt - This level of expertise requires the following criteria:

- Minimum of three years of full-time employment.
- Understand the tools and methodologies used for problem-solving.
- Hands-on experience on projects involving some level of business transformation.
- Guidance for Black Belt projects in data collection and analysis.
- Lead Green Belt projects or teams.

Black Belt - This level includes the following:

- Minimum of three years of full-time employment
- Work experience in a core knowledge area
- Proof of completion of a minimum of two Six Sigma projects
- Demonstration of expertise at applying multivariate metrics to diverse business change settings
- Leading diverse teams in problem-solving projects.
- Training and coaching project teams

Master Black Belt - To reach this level, a candidate must:

- Be in possession of a Black Belt certification
- Have a minimum of five years of full-time employment, or Proof of completion of a minimum of 10 Six Sigma projects
- A proven work portfolio, with certain specific requirements, as given here for instance.
- Have coached and trained Green Belts and Black Belts.
- Develop key metrics and strategies.
- Have worked as an organisation's Six Sigma technologist and internal business transformation advisor.

Operational Management

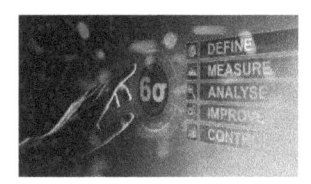

Six Sigma is a long-term commitment. Treating deployment as a process allows objective analysis of all aspects of the process, including project selection and scoping. Utilising lessons learned and incorporating them into subsequent waves of an implementation plan creates a closed feedback loop and real dramatic bottom-line benefits if the organisation invests the time and executive energy necessary to implement Six Sigma as a business strategy!

Kaizen

Kaizen is a compound of two Japanese words that together translate as "good change" or "improvement," but Kaizen has come to mean "continuous improvement" through its association with Lean methodology.

Kai = Change   Zen = Good

Kaizen has its origins in post-World War II Japanese quality circles. These circles or groups of workers focused on preventing defects at Toyota and were developed partly in response to American management and productivity consultants who visited the country, especially W. Edwards Deming, who argued that quality control should be put more directly in the hands of line workers.

Kaizen was brought to the West and popularised by Masaaki Imai via his book Kaizen: The Key to Japan's Competitive Success in 1986.

Kaizen is an approach to creating continuous improvement based on the idea that small, ongoing positive changes can reap major improvements. Typically, it is based on cooperation and commitment and stands in contrast to approaches that use radical changes or top-down edicts to achieve transformation. Kaizen is core to lean manufacturing, or The Toyota Way. It was developed in the manufacturing sector to lower defects, eliminate waste, boost productivity, encourage worker purpose and accountability and promote innovation.

As a broad concept that carries a myriad of interpretations, it has been adopted in many other industries, including healthcare. It can be applied to any area of business and even to personal life. Kaizen can use a number of approaches and tools, such as value stream mapping, which documents, analyses and improves information or material flows required to produce a product or service and Total Quality Management (TQM), a management framework that enlists workers at all levels to focus on quality improvements. Regardless of methodology, in an organisational setting, the successful use of Kaizen rests on gaining support for the approach across the organisation and from the CEO down.

Kaizen is complementary to Six Sigma.

Operational Management

Ten principles of Kaizen

Because executing Kaizen requires enabling the right mindset throughout the company, 10 principles that address the Kaizen mindset are commonly referenced as core to the philosophy. They are:

- Let go of assumptions.
- Be proactive about solving problems.
- Do not accept the status quo.
- Let go of perfectionism and take an attitude of iterative, adaptive change.
- Look for solutions as you find mistakes.
- Create an environment in which everyone feels empowered to contribute.
- Do not accept the obvious issue; instead, ask "why" five times to get to the root cause.
- Cull information and opinions from multiple people.
- Use creativity to find low-cost, small improvements.
- Never stop improving.

How Kaizen works

Kaizen is based on the belief that everything can be improved and nothing is status quo. It also rests on a Respect for People principle. Kaizen involves identifying issues and opportunities, creating solutions and rolling them out -- and then cycling through the process again for other issues or problems that were inadequately addressed. These following seven steps create a cycle for continuous improvement and give a systematic method for executing this process.

Kaizen cycle for continuous improvement:

Get employees involved. Seek the involvement of employees, including gathering their help in identifying issues and problems. Doing so creates buy-in for change. Often, this is organised as specific groups of individuals charged with gathering and relaying information from a wider group of employees.

Find problems. Using widespread feedback from all employees, gather a list of problems and potential opportunities. Create a shortlist if there are many issues.

Create a solution. Encourage employees to offer creative solutions, with all manner of ideas encouraged. Pick a winning solution or solutions from the ideas presented.

Test the solution. Implement the winning solution chosen above, with everyone participating in the rollout. Create pilot programs or take other small steps to test out the solution.

Analyse the results. At various intervals, check progress, with specific plans for who will be the point of contact and how best to keep ground-level workers engaged. Determine how successful the change has been.

Operational Management

Standardise. *If results are positive, adopt the solution throughout the organisation.*

Repeat. *These seven steps should be repeated on an ongoing basis, with new solutions tested where appropriate or new lists of problems tackled.*

Types of Kaizen events

Although the aim of Kaizen is widespread cultural change, events to kick-start Kaizen efforts or focus on a specific set of problems have evolved. In the West, these concentrated efforts to make quick changes to achieve a short-term goal are often the extent of Kaizen efforts. There are numerous names associated with Kaizen events, including:

- *Kaizen blitz*
- *Kaizen burst*
- *Kaizen workshop*
- *Focused improvement workshop*
- *Continuous improvement workshop*
- *Rapid process workshop*

In addition, these can rely on various tools or focus on specific areas, such as 5S, total productive maintenance and value stream mapping.

Kaizen 5S framework

A 5S framework is a critical part of the Kaizen system and establishes an ideal physical workplace.

The 5Ss' focus on creating visual order, organisation, cleanliness and standardisation to improve profitability, efficiency, service and safety.

Below are the original Japanese 5Ss' and their common English translations.

Seiri/Sort (organise) - *Separate necessary workplace items from unnecessary ones and remove unnecessary items.*

Seiton/Set in order (create orderliness) - *Arrange items to allow for easy access in the way that makes the most sense for work.*

Seiso/Shine (cleanliness) - *Keep the workspace clean and tidy.*

Seiketsu/Standardise (standardised cleaning) - *Systematise workplace clean-up best practices.*

Shitsuke/Sustain (discipline) - *Keep the effort going.*

Operational Management

Advantages and disadvantages

While the benefits of Kaizen are many, there are some situations for which it is less suited. Here is a look at some advantages and disadvantages that experts commonly cite.

Advantages:
With its focus on gradual improvement, Kaizen can create a gentler approach to change in contrast to big efforts that may be abandoned due to their tendency to provoke change resistance and abandonment.

- *Kaizen encourages scrutiny of processes so that mistakes and waste can be reduced.*
- *Inspection needs are lessened because errors are reduced.*
- *Employee morale grows because it engenders a sense of value and purposefulness.*
- *Teamwork increases as employees think beyond the specific issues of their department.*
- *Client focus increases as customer requirements awareness is raised.*
- *Systems are in place to ensure improvements are encouraged both short and long term.*

Disadvantages:

- *Companies with cultures of territorialism and closed communication may first need to focus on cultural changes to create a receptive environment.*
- *Short-term Kaizen events may create a burst of excitement that is shallow and short-lived and, therefore, gets abandoned before long.*

Kaizen Users

Toyota is arguably the most famous for its use of Kaizen, but other companies have used the approach successfully. Here are three examples:

> **Lockheed Martin.** *The aerospace company is a well-known proponent of Kaizen. Through the use of Kaizen, it has successfully reduced manufacturing costs, reduced inventory and cut delivery time.*
> **Ford Motor Company.** *When lean devotee Alan Mulally became CEO of Ford in 2006, the automotive giant was on the brink of bankruptcy. Mulally used Kaizen to execute one of the most famous corporate turnarounds in history.*
> **Pixar Animation Studios.** *Pixar has taken a continuous improvement model that reduced risks of expensive movie failure by using quality control checks and iterative processes.*

Operational Management

Lean Production

Lean production is an approach to management that focuses on cutting out waste, whilst ensuring quality. This approach can be applied to all aspects of a business – from design, through production to distribution.

Lean production aims to cut costs by making the business more efficient and responsive to market needs. This approach sets out to cut out or minimise activities that do not add value to the production process, such as holding of stock, repairing faulty product and unnecessary movement of people and product around the business.

Lean production originated in the manufacturing plants of Japan but has now been adopted well beyond large and sophisticated manufacturing activities. The lean approach to managing operations is really about:

- *Doing the simple things well*
- *Doing things better*
- *Involving employees in the continuous process of improvement*
- *...as a result, avoiding waste*

The concept of lean production is an incredibly powerful one for any business that wants to become and/or remain competitive.

Five principles of lean manufacturing

A widely referenced book, Lean Thinking: Banish Waste and Create Wealth in Your Corporation, which was published in 1996, laid out five principles of lean, which many in the field reference as core principles. They are value, the value stream, flow, pull and perfection. These are now used as the basis for lean implementation.

1. Identify value from the customer's perspective.
Value is created by the producer, but it is defined by the customer. In other words, companies need to understand the value the customer places on their products and services, which, in turn, can help them determine how much money the customer is willing to pay.

The company must strive to eliminate waste and cost from its business processes so that the customer's optimal price can be achieved at the highest profit to the company.

2. Map the value stream.
This principle involves recording and analysing the flow of information or materials required to produce a specific product or service with the intent of identifying waste and methods of improvement. The value stream encompasses the product's entire lifecycle, from raw materials through to disposal.

Operational Management

Companies must examine each stage of the cycle for waste -- or muda in Japanese. Anything that does not add value must be eliminated. Lean thinking recommends supply chain alignment as part of this effort.

3. Create flow.
Eliminate functional barriers and identify ways to improve lead time to ensure the processes are smooth from the time an order is received through to delivery. Flow is critical to the elimination of waste. Lean manufacturing relies on preventing interruptions in the production process and enabling a harmonised and integrated set of processes in which activities move in a constant stream.

4. Establish a pull system.
This means you only start new work when there is demand for it. Lean manufacturing uses a pull system instead of a push system.

With a push system, used by manufacturing resource planning (MRP) systems, inventory needs are determined in advance and the product is manufactured to meet that forecast. However, forecasts are typically inaccurate, which can result in swings between too much inventory and not enough, as well as subsequent disrupted schedules and poor customer service.

In contrast to MRP, lean manufacturing is based on a pull system in which nothing is bought or made until there is demand. Pull relies on flexibility and communication.

5. Pursue perfection with continual process improvement, or kaizen.
Lean manufacturing rests on the concept of continually striving for perfection, which entails targeting the root causes of quality issues and ferreting out and eliminating waste across the value stream.

The Eight Wastes of Lean Production

The Toyota Production System laid out seven wastes, or processes and resources, that do not add value for the customer. These seven wastes are:

- *unnecessary transportation*
- *excess stockholding*
- *unnecessary motion of people, equipment or machinery*
- *waiting, whether it is people waiting or idle equipment*
- *over-production of a product*
- *over-processing or putting more time into a product than a customer needs, such as designs that require high-tech machinery for unnecessary features*
- *defects, which require effort and cost for corrections.*

Although not originally included in the Toyota Production system, many lean practitioners point to an eighth waste:

- *Waste of unused talent and ingenuity.*

Operational Management

Lean Manufacturing Tools and Concepts

Lean manufacturing requires a relentless pursuit of reducing waste. Waste is anything that customers do not believe adds value and for which they are not willing to pay. This requires continuous improvement, which lies at the heart of lean manufacturing.

Other important concepts and processes lean relies on include:

Heijunka	*production levelling or smoothing that seeks to produce a continuous flow of production, releasing work to the plant at the required rate and avoiding interruptions.*
Kanban	*a signal -- either physical, such as tag or empty bin, or electronically sent through a system -- used to streamline processes and create just-in-time delivery.*
Jidoka	*A method of providing machines and humans with the ability to detect an abnormality and stop work until it can be corrected.*
Andon	*A visual aid, such as a flashing light, that alerts workers to a problem.*
Poka-yoke	*A mechanism that safeguards against human error, such as an indicator light that turns on if a necessary step was missed, a sign given when a bolt was tightened the correct number of times or a system that blocks a next step until all the previous steps are completed.*
5S	*A set of practices for organising workspaces to create efficient, effective and safe areas for workers and which prevent wasted effort and time. 5S emphasises organisation and cleanliness.*
Cycle time	*How long it takes to produce a part or complete a process.*

Lean vs. Six Sigma

Both lean and Six Sigma seek to eliminate waste. However, the two use different approaches because they see the root cause of waste differently.

In the simplest terms, whereas Lean holds that waste is caused by additional steps, processes and features that a customer does not believe adds value and will not pay for, Six Sigma holds that waste results from process variation. Still, the two approaches are complementary and have been combined as Lean Six Sigma.

Environmental Scanning
Environmental scanning is the process of gathering information about events and their relationships within an organisation's internal and external environments. The basic purpose of environmental scanning is to help management determine the future direction of the organisation. Scanning must identify the threats and opportunities existing in the environment. While strategy formulation, an organisation must take advantage of the opportunities and minimise the threats. A threat for one organisation may be an opportunity for another.

Operational Management

Internal analysis of the environment
This is the first step of environment scanning. Organisations should observe the internal organisational environment. This includes employee interaction with other employees, employee interaction with management, manager interaction with other managers and management interaction with shareholders, access to natural resources, brand awareness, organisational structure, main staff, operational potential, etc. Also, discussions, interviews and surveys can be used to assess the internal environment. Analysis of internal environment helps in identifying strengths and weaknesses of an organisation.

As business becomes more competitive and there are rapid changes in the external environment, information from external environment adds crucial elements to the effectiveness of long-term plans. As environment is dynamic, it becomes essential to identify competitors' moves and actions.

Organisations have also to update the core competencies and internal environment as per external environment. Environmental factors are infinite; hence, organisation should be agile and virile to accept and adjust to the environmental changes. For instance - Monitoring might indicate that an original forecast of the prices of the raw materials that are involved in the product are no longer credible, which could imply the requirement for more focused scanning, forecasting and analysis to create a more trustworthy prediction about the input costs. In a similar manner, there can be changes in factors such as competitor's activities, technology, market tastes and preferences.

While in external analysis, three correlated environments should be studied and analysed

- *immediate / industry environment*
- *national environment*
- *broader socio-economic environment / macro-environment*

Industry Environment
Examining the industry environment needs an appraisal of the competitive structure of the organisation's industry, including the competitive position of a particular organisation and its main rivals. Also, an assessment of the nature, stage, dynamics and history of the industry is essential. It also implies evaluating the effect of globalisation on competition within the industry.

National Environment
Analysing the national environment needs an appraisal of whether the national framework helps in achieving competitive advantage in the globalised environment.

Macro-environment
Analysis of macro-environment includes exploring macro-economic, social, government, legal, technological and international factors that may influence the environment. The analysis of organisation's external environment reveals opportunities and threats for an organisation.

Operational Management

This type of analysis is best suited to the PEST Analysis Tool

PEST analysis (political, economic, socio-cultural and technological) describes a framework of macro-environmental factors used in the environmental scanning component of strategic management. It is part of an external analysis when conducting a strategic analysis or doing market research and gives an overview of the different macro-environmental factors to be taken into consideration. It is a strategic tool for understanding market growth or decline, business position, potential and direction for operations.

Political	*Economic*
<ul><li>ecological/environmental issues</li><li>current legislation home market</li><li>future legislation</li><li>international legislation</li><li>regulatory bodies and processes</li><li>government policies</li><li>government term and change</li><li>trading policies</li><li>funding, grants and initiatives</li><li>home market lobbying/pressure groups</li><li>international pressure groups</li><li>wars and conflicts</li></ul>	<ul><li>home economy situation</li><li>home economy trends</li><li>overseas economies and trends</li><li>general taxation issues</li><li>taxation specific to product/services</li><li>seasonality/weather issues</li><li>market and trade cycles</li><li>specific industry factors</li><li>market routes and distribution trends</li><li>customer/end-user drivers</li><li>interest and exchange rates</li><li>international trade/monetary issues</li></ul>
Social	*Technological*
<ul><li>lifestyle trends</li><li>demographics</li><li>consumer attitudes and opinions</li><li>media views</li><li>law changes affecting social factors</li><li>brand, company, technology image</li><li>consumer buying patterns</li><li>fashion and role models</li><li>major events and influences</li><li>buying access and trends</li><li>ethnic/religious factors</li><li>advertising and publicity</li><li>ethical issues</li></ul>	<ul><li>competing technology development</li><li>research funding</li><li>associated/dependent technologies</li><li>replacement technology/solutions</li><li>maturity of technology</li><li>manufacturing maturity and capacity</li><li>information and communications</li><li>consumer buying mechanisms/technology</li><li>technology legislation</li><li>innovation potential</li><li>technology access, licencing, patents</li><li>intellectual property issues</li><li>global communications</li></ul>

Operational Management

Total Productive Maintenance (TPM)

Almost all industrial production processes are carried out with the aid of machines, as a result of which each production-oriented organisation is largely dependent on its machinery. When a breakdown or a long-term disruption occurs of machines, equipment or important tools, this will automatically have far-reaching consequences for the total production.

Total productive maintenance (TPM) is a method of maintaining and improving the integrity of production and quality systems through the machines, equipment, employees and the supporting processes. TPM can be of great value and its target is to improve core business processes. The phrase TPM was first used in 1961 by the Japanese company Denso. This supplier to the automotive industry, carried out an improvement project with continuous improvement as their starting point and they introduced autonomous and preventive maintenance to machines. TPM is especially meant for companies with a lot of machines that involve high maintenance costs.

Productivity improvement
TPM is not just about maintaining productivity but also about the maintenance of machines and the prevention of possible breakdowns. TPM is about productivity improvement and optimisation of machine availability through which machines operate at their optimal level.

Everyone within the organisation has to be aware of the hidden losses with respect to machine failure or the time needed for machine repair. Also, when a machine cannot run at full speed or produces inferior products, this is considered to be a loss-making activity for the organisation.

The aim is to have an Overall Equipment Effectiveness (OEE) score of 100% and this represents perfect production. In that case, machines always work at full speed and deliver products of perfect quality.

Preventive maintenance concept
Running machines until they break down is not an option. Curative maintenance is characterised by waiting for a breakdown to happen which will consequently be repaired. Especially when productions need to continue round the clock, this type of maintenance is far too costly. TPM puts machinery at the heart of the organisation and does not just safeguard production continuously but improves it where possible. TPM focuses on productivity improvement and its primary purpose is to maximise availability of machines.

Everyone is responsible
The starting point of TPM is that everyone is responsible for the day-to day maintenance of the machines. Employee participation in improvement proposals and maintenance are key features within TPM, so that they can jointly improve the machine efficiency, step-by-step. Maintenance therefore also means 'improvement'. Machines are purchased for their intended purpose only. After that, it is possible to expose and eliminate hidden defects in the machines.

Operational Management

Multi-disciplinary teams
Everyone, from operator to maintenance engineer, should make joint efforts to improve the OEE. This can be achieved by forming small multidisciplinary teams. This can be achieved by giving attention to autonomous maintenance, preventive maintenance, training of the employees involved, security and standardisation of work processes, the goal is Zero Defects: zero errors, zero losses and zero work-related accidents. By using such multidisciplinary teams, the availability of machines will improve greatly.

TPM focuses on the effective and efficient use of production means and aims at involvement of all departments. The small multidisciplinary teams work together from seven different TPM pillars, supported by 5S, to improve equipment reliability and increase productivity.

These basic seven pillars are:

- *Autonomous maintenance*
- *Kobetsu Kaizen (Focused Improvement)*
- *Planned Maintenance*
- *Quality maintenance*
- *Training and Education*
- *Office TPM*
- *Safety Health Environment (SHE)*

Continuous improvement
TPM will improve productivity by 70% and reduce complaints by approximately 60%. In addition to measuring OEE, TPM also focuses on maintenance backlog which is also referred to as Total Clean Out (TCO). After this, a start can be made with the continuous improvement cycles. Each multidisciplinary team tackles one specific problem that limits the OEE, therefore the continuous improvement cycle can be carried out very effectively. The project that this small team carries out is called Small Group Activity (SGA). In such an SGA project team there are both machine operators and mechanics as well as quality inspectors and logistics managers. The whole group is responsible for the functioning of a specific machine.

Perfection
Like other process improvement methods, TPM has grown into a general process management method, which can be applied broadly to strive for machine perfection. In addition to machine availability, other factors play a role such as logistical and human aspects. Therefore, the strong involvement of employees across different disciplines forms an important part of TPM. Everyone is involved from start to finish. This makes TPM a useful method that monitors complex and/or expensive machines; it prevents maintenance costs from becoming too high and it ensures that production does not stagnate.

Set up Reduction Techniques
Set up reduction techniques are used to minimise the time during which machines are not working as they need to be changed from performing one task to another. The down time is

Operational Management

an unnecessary cost to the business and a waste which the organisation cannot afford. TPM, set up reduction techniques and the 5s all serve to make the processes safer, more efficient and standardised.

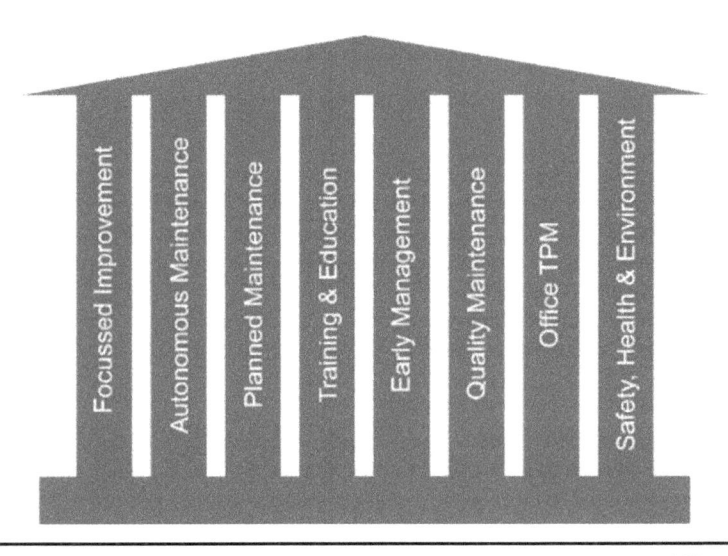

- Focussed Improvement
- Autonomous Maintenance
- Planned Maintenance
- Training & Education
- Early Management
- Quality Maintenance
- Office TPM
- Safety, Health & Environment

Operational Management

Operational Business Planning

Turning strategy into an operational plan is not about doing more things right – it is about doing more of the right things. In contrast to strategic planning, the goal of an operational plan is to see how you will execute on your strategy month by month, week by week. Since you work in a vacuum, this means you will need to coordinate people, time and budgets across teams (and maybe across departments, too).

An actionable operational plan answers questions like:

- *What milestones do we need to hit?*
- *Who will work on what?*
- *Where might we run into bottlenecks and how can we avoid them?*
- *How will we define success?*
- *What early indicators will tell us we are on the right track?*

Once an actionable plan has been drafted, gather and incorporate feedback from the core team involved, as well as stakeholders. Do not get discouraged if you go through a few iterations before landing on a plan everyone can get on board with.

Resource Management

Resource management is the process by which businesses manage their various resources effectively. Those resources can be intangible – people and time – and tangible – equipment, materials and finances.

It involves planning so that the right resources are assigned to the right tasks. Managing resources involves schedules and budgets for people, projects, equipment and supplies.

While it is often used in reference to project management, it applies to many other areas of business management. A small business, in particular, will pay attention to resource management in a number of areas, including:

- **Finances** – *Can it meet current expenses or afford to invest in new equipment or staff training?*
- **Staffing** – *Does it have the right people for the work at hand? Will it need to hire if it gets that new client and if so, what skills will those people need to have?*
- **Physical space** – *Is the company's office or manufacturing space configured so that other resources can be managed for maximum efficiency?*
- **Equipment** – *Does it have the tools needed to do what is required?*
- **Technology** – *What does the business need to succeed and should financial resources be reallocated to fund what is missing?*

Operational Management

Advantages of Resource Management

Avoids unforeseen hiccups
By understanding your resources upfront and planning how to use them, you can troubleshoot gaps or problems before they happen.

Prevents burnout
Effective resource management allows you to avoid "overallocation" or "dependency" of resources by gaining insight into your team's workload.

Provides a safety net
If a project was not successful due to lack of resources (it happens). Resource planning and management establishes that you did everything you could with what you had.
Builds transparency: Other teams can gain visibility into your team's bandwidth and plan accordingly if your team is at maximum capacity or available to take on new projects.

Measures efficiency
With a high-level understanding of what is needed to manage and execute an upcoming project, you can effectively plan and measure ROI.

Resource management techniques

1. Resource Allocation
Resource allocation helps you get the most from your available resources. Based on team members' skills and capacity, resource allocation is the process of tackling problems using the resources you have at your disposal in the most efficient manner possible. To get a clear view into allocation, managers will often use resource allocation reports. These can give anywhere from a high-level view to a detailed run down of resource availability — helping avoid schedule delays and going over budget. The better the reporting capabilities at your disposal, the more transparency and efficiency you will have over managing resources.

2. Resource Levelling
Another type of resource management is called resource levelling. This technique aims to discover underused or inefficiently used resources within the organisation and work them to your advantage. An example of resource levelling is having a content writer who has experience in graphic design help out the design team by taking on small content tasks that require design work. If a team member can flex their design skills, the design team will not need to hire a freelancer if they suddenly get flooded with design requests

3. Resource Forecasting
Having a resource management plan is critical to optimising people, materials and budget efficiency. Resource forecasting allows you to predict your future resource requirements before a project begins. During the planning stages of a project, resource forecasting determines the project's scope, possible constraints, unforeseen costs and potential risks.

Operational Management

Developing Sales and Marketing Plans

A proper sales and marketing strategy involves more than just running some ads and cold calling a list of prospects. Developing the right strategy is a process that requires research to discover who your prime sales prospects are, what motivates their purchasing and how your firm fits in the marketplace. The data your research provides is what will drive your sales and marketing strategy. With the right plan, growth and profitability are predictable and controllable.

Effective sales and marketing require talent, expertise, effort and consistency. If that does not exist inside your organisation, then it is important that you find an outside resource that can help you develop and implement your strategy.

Developing Strategy

> *See the marketplace and prospects as they really are—not how you would like them to be.*

The best strategies consider the marketplace as it really is, not the way we think it is or wish it were. The same holds true for potential clients—we may think we know what they want, but reality may be quite different. In the absence of objective information, it is too easy to fall into a pattern of wishful thinking.

The strategy should start by taking an objective look at the target client and the marketplace in which the organisation operates. Do not make the mistake of focusing at first on the services it offers or what you think the target audience might want. Do the research necessary to understand what the ideal client really wants or needs and tailor your offerings accordingly.

> *Research has revealed that organisations which conduct regular research on their target client groups grow faster and are more profitable than those who do not.*

Done correctly, this research will give a clear idea of client needs and priorities, their buying process, the competitive landscape, how the organisation's brand is perceived and the real benefits clients receive from working with it. This knowledge can dramatically reduce risk and lead to a much better strategy.

Questions need to be asked and answered in relation to the organisation. These questions might include:

- *What does the organisation want to accomplish?*
- *What valuable product or service does the organisation have that the target client wants?*

Operational Management

- *Does the organisation want to add new or different products or services or expand into new markets?*
- *Is the organisation interested in growth? If so, what kind and how much?*

Answers to questions like these provide the business context for the sales and marketing strategy. They reveal what the strategy will need to accomplish and how it should be evaluated as it is implemented.

Internal and external research helps ground the plan in reality and makes success more likely.

Assess current resources.
The best sales and marketing strategy in the world is useless if the resources to successfully execute it are not available. What sort of talent is already on board? What level of training do they have? Do the sales team have the skills and knowledge they need? Do the marketing staff understand the services the organisation offers?

How about tools? Do you have the marketing infrastructure you need to pull off an inbound strategy? How about sales tools such as marketing collateral or case study videos?

Answering questions like these will give a real insight into what is both possible and practical. Without this information, strategies are often under-resourced or simply not feasible because they are not based in reality.

Use a strategy that aligns with the organisation's abilities.
After researching the target client and marketplace, determining what the organisation's strategy seeks to accomplish and assessing its resources, it is time to settle on how to implement the strategy:

Are you a sole proprietor? If you are, then you will most likely employ the "seller-doer" model in which you are the brand—selling your hands-on expertise and its value, while building a personal rapport and trust with the client.

Does the organisation have a dedicated sales staff selling services performed by others who are the experts? If so, the "seller-expert" model aligns better with the business to make the visible experts the leaders in the marketplace.

- *How will you position your firm in the marketplace?*
- *What are your key messages?*
- *Will you use inbound or outbound marketing or both?*

Operational Management

Developing an implementation plan

A good sales and marketing strategy is not a one-time thing. It requires ongoing commitment, effort and follow-up to analyse its effectiveness. An implementation plan outlines everything needed to make the strategy a reality. Some key considerations include:

- *Strategy implementation schedule, budget and responsibilities*
- *Talent—either internal or outsourced*
- *Sales and marketing tools, such as sales collateral, videos and webinars*
- *Infrastructure, such as a customer relationship management (CRM) or marketing automation system*
- *Training, if needed*
- *Marketing calendar for scheduling and coordinating advertising and marketing activities*
- *Metrics that will enable you to evaluate and adjust your strategy*

Sales and marketing plans are a vital part of any business strategy as they are needed to boost profits and gain ground on your competitors. A good way to start is by breaking down the process into discrete, manageable elements. You end up with a checklist that can be reviewed to prioritise areas needing improvement and serve as the groundwork for an effective marketing strategy.

1) Markets
Research current and future markets to learn why the customers buy from the organisation and what it could offer to attract more customers. Identify ways to sell more to the most profitable customers and if there are bulk, institutional, industrial, or corporate markets beyond normal retail that are being ignored. This data can help determine if new features or services will attract new customers or if people will pay more for them.

To collect information, study what competitors are doing and collect information about customers. Use surveys to gather information and establish customer loyalty programs that require participants to register by providing some basic information about themselves. These details can help figure out what demographics you are attracting—or failing to attract.

2) Competition
Know who your competitors are and what they are up to. What is the overall market trend and how are you holding up in terms of market share and profit position? How do you rank against competitors? What substitutes are there to your products and how much of a threat are they?

Use competitive intelligence to maintain and enhance your business's market share. This involves researching what your competitors offer, their price points and what their marketing strategies say about the demographics they are targeting.

Operational Management

3) Distribution
Identify ways to get your products or services to new outlets profitably. This could involve increasing your web sales, expanding delivery options, contracting with additional retail outlets to carry your products and more. You might even be able to find mutually beneficial ways to collaborate with other businesses. For example, if you are an event photographer, you could work with a florist or a caterer to offer purchasing options that include both of your services. Such an arrangement allows both parties to expand their client bases.

4) Supply Chain
Research suppliers thoroughly and have multiple options available, when possible, to avoid being at the mercy of wholesalers who might increase prices for raw materials or product components. Manage supplies more effectively by using multiple wholesalers to keep costs in check. Always be on the lookout for new suppliers who might be willing to offer deals to gain your business.

When shopping around for wholesalers, it is also worth checking if prefabricated items might represent cost savings over doing it yourself.

5) Positioning
It is important to know where you fit in the market and knowing your competition is a big part of this. You might have a larger operation that you hope can be all things to all people, but it is more likely that you will be zeroing in on a specific demographic, such as those seeking premium quality items or services, those seeking discounted products or services, or something in between.

If you are a low-priced pizza shop struggling in a town full of low-priced pizza shops, you might find that you will be able to improve your market share by targeting those willing to pay a premium for top-quality ingredients or toppings.

6) Promotion
Do a better job of reaching your potential customers by figuring out where your potential customers are at. If you are trying to reach an audience through social media, for example, it is good to know which age group is using which platforms.

A 2019 Pew Research Centre survey showed that adults are nearly twice as likely to be on Facebook than on Instagram. However, when looking only at those aged 18-24, the gap narrows significantly with 71% on Instagram and 80% on Facebook. Using that data as an example, it is wise to make you sure you do not forget about Instagram if you are trying to reach a younger audience.

7) Pricing
Review your pricing strategy to be sure it makes sense for everything you offer. Consumer demand, product availability and other external factors all can play a role in how much you should be charging for the goods and services you are selling.

If you ran an ice cream shop in a town that draws a lot of tourists during the summer months. When demand is high and more customers are entering the

Operational Management

store, it is fair to charge a premium for the items on the menu. However, during the colder months when the tourist crowd is gone, the menu should be updated and offer winter-themed items at discount prices to keep traffic heavy.

8) Customer Service
The first step to providing good customer service is understanding the kind of service your customers want. If you run a convenience store where people stop in quickly to grab a soft drink or a power bar, they are simply looking for a friendly cashier to take care of their transaction quickly and without hassle.

However, something like a full-service restaurant or a retail establishment that sells specialty products will draw people who are looking to be waited on or have their questions answered.

It is also important to seek feedback. Provide ways for customers to review your business. If you have a customer loyalty program, regularly contact customers who have not made purchases in a while to offer discounts or inquire about why they have not visited your business recently.

9) Financing
Review your capital structure regularly or have your accountant do it for you to make sure you are handling your assets and liabilities in the most cost-effective way. If you have achieved some success, are viewed as a stable business in the community and have a solid reputation, you may be able to attract angel investors or venture capitalists to assist with expanding your business.

10) Consistent Strategies
Building customer loyalty and increasing sales to existing customers should be a constant focus of your operation. Bringing people in the door sometimes requires different approaches based on your needs at the time. For example, if the spring months of March, April and May typically are slow for your business, it is a good idea to schedule events during those months designed to bring potential customers in the door.

Do not limit yourself to strategies built around sales. Consider holding workshops or training sessions centred around the products or services you provide to draw attention to your brand. Let the sales come naturally from that boost of attention.

An effective sales and marketing strategy is a major element of an overall business strategy. It requires a major commitment, which is why, in larger organisations, it is important that senior management fully buy into the strategy. No strategy will be successful without full management support. But with a proper investment of time, money and effort, your carefully developed and implemented sales and marketing strategy will yield big results.

Operational Management

Management Systems and Processes

A management system is a set of policies, processes and procedures used by an organisation to ensure that it can fulfil the tasks required to achieve its objectives. These objectives cover many aspects of the organisation's operations (including financial success, safe operation, product quality, client relationships, legislative and regulatory conformance and worker management).

For instance, an environmental management system enables organisations to improve their environmental performance and an occupational health and safety management system (OHSMS) enables an organisation to control its occupational health and safety risks, etc.

Many parts of the management system are common to a range of objectives, but others may be more specific.

Elements may include:

- *Leadership Involvement and Responsibility*
- *Identification and Compliance with Legislation and Industry Standards*
- *Employee Selection, Placement and Competency Assurance*
- *Workforce Involvement*
- *Communication with Stakeholders (others peripherally impacted by operations)*
- *Identification and Assessment of potential failures and other hazards*
- *Documentation, Records and Knowledge Management*
- *Documented Procedures*
- *Project Monitoring, Status and Handover*
- *Management of Interfaces*
- *Standards and Practices*
- *Management of Change and Project Management*
- *Operational Readiness and Start-up*
- *Emergency Preparedness*
- *Inspection and Maintenance of facilities*
- *Management of Critical systems*
- *Work Control, Permit to Work and Task Risk Management*
- *Contractor/Vendor Selection and Management*
- *Incident Reporting and Investigation*
- *Audit, Assurance and Management System review and Intervention*

A simplification of the main aspects of a management system is the 4-element "Plan, Do, Check, Act" approach. A complete management system covers every aspect of management and focuses on supporting the performance management to achieve the objectives. The management system should be subject to continuous improvement as the organisation learns.

Operational Management

PDCA (Plan-Do-Check-Act)

> *PDCA is a repetitive four-stage model for continuous improvement.*

PDCA, sometimes called PDSA, the "Deming Wheel," or "Deming Cycle," was developed by renowned management consultant Dr William Edwards Deming in the 1950s. Deming himself called it the "Shewhart Cycle," as his model was based on an idea from his mentor, Walter Shewhart.

Deming wanted to create a way of identifying what caused products to fail to meet customers' expectations. His solution helps businesses to develop hypotheses about what needs to change and then test these in a continuous feedback loop.

The four phases are:

Plan: *identify and analyse the problem or opportunity, develop hypotheses about what the issues may be and decide which one to test.*

Do: *test the potential solution, ideally on a small scale and measure the results.*

Check/Study: *study the result, measure effectiveness and decide whether the hypothesis is supported or not.*

Act: *if the solution was successful, implement it.*

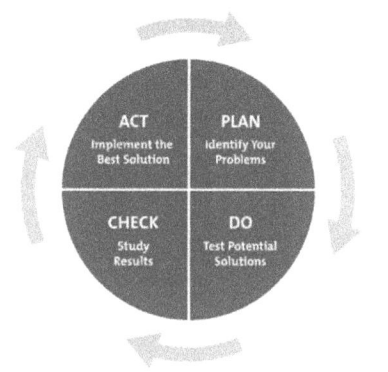

The PDCA cycle helps you to solve problems and implement solutions in a rigorous, methodical way.

Follow these four steps to ensure that you get the highest quality results.

1. Plan
First, identify and understand the problem, or the opportunity to be taken advantage of. Using the first six steps of the Simplex Process can help, by guiding through a process of exploring information, defining the problem, generating and screening ideas and developing an implementation plan.

At the final part of this stage, state quantitatively what the expectations are, if the idea is successful and the problem is resolved. This will be reassessed at the Check stage.

Operational Management

2. Do
Once a potential solution has been identified, test it with a small-scale pilot project. This will enable an assessment whether the proposed changes achieve the desired outcome, with minimal disruption to the rest of the operation if they do not. For example, a trial could be organised within a department, in a limited geographical area, or with a particular demographic.

3. Check
At this stage, the pilot project's results are analysed against the expectations that defined in Step 1 to assess whether the idea has worked or not. If it has not worked, return to Step 1. If it has worked, proceed to Step 4.

Where results are inconclusive, it may be decided to try out more changes and repeat the Do and Check phases – do not settle for a less-than-satisfactory solution.

Move on to the final phase (Act) only when genuinely satisfied with the trial's outcome.

4. Act
This is where the solution is implemented. Remember that PDCA / PDSA is a loop, not a process with a beginning and an end. This means that the improved process or product becomes the new baseline and the search continues looking for ways to make it even better for the organisation or customers.

The PDCA cycle encourages a commitment to continuous improvement.

Think about this scenario:

The customer satisfaction score on a popular business ratings website has dropped. Recent comments suggest that customers are complaining about late delivery and that products are being damaged in transit.

A small pilot project over a month, using a new supplier to deliver products to a small sample of customers could be implemented quickly.

The results identify that the feedback from these customers is positive. As a result, the new supplier is used for all further orders.

This completes one loop around the PDCA Cycle.

Operational Management

When to use PDCA

The PDCA framework can improve any process or product by breaking it into smaller steps. It is particularly effective for:

- *Helping to improve processes.*
- *Exploring a range of solutions to problems and piloting them in a controlled way before selecting one for implementation.*
- *Avoiding wastage of resources by rolling out an ineffective solution on a wide scale.*

You can use the model in all sorts of business environments, from new product development, project and change management to product lifecycle and supply chain management.

Pros and Cons of PDCA

The model is a simple, yet powerful way to resolve new and recurring issues in any industry, department or process. Its iterative approach allows you and your team to test solutions and assess results in a waste-reducing cycle.

It instils a commitment to continuous improvement, however small and can improve efficiency and productivity in a controlled way, without the risks of making large scale, untested changes to your processes.

However, going through the PDCA cycle can be much slower than a straightforward, "gung-ho" implementation. So, it might not be the appropriate approach for dealing with an urgent problem or emergency.

It also requires significant "buy-in" from team members and offers fewer opportunities for radical innovation, if that is what your organisation needs.

Operational Management

Contingency Planning and Risk Management

The aim of contingency planning is to minimise the impact of a significant foreseeable event and to plan for how the business will resume normal operations after the event.

Contingency planning involves:

- *Preparing for predictable and quantifiable problems*
- *Preparing for unexpected and unwelcome events*

Contingency Planning
Contingency planning is one of the three approaches a business can take to manage risk. These are:

> **Risk management:** *identifying and dealing with the risks threatening a business*
> **Contingency planning:** *planning for unforeseen events*
> **Crisis management:** *handling potentially dangerous events for a business*

The process of contingency planning involves:

- *Identifying what and how things can and might go wrong*
- *Understanding the potential effects if things go wrong*
- *Devising plans to cope with the threats*
- *Putting in place strategies to deal with the risks before they happen*

Almost by definition, contingency planning should focus on the most important risks; those that have the potential for significant business disruption or damage. Risks vary in terms of their significance to the business. Contingency planning is not required for every eventuality. However, risks of strategic significance cannot be ignored

Risk
Risk can be:

- *The possibility of loss or business damage*
- *A threat that may prevent or hinder the ability to achieve business objectives*
- *The chance that a hoped-for outcome will not occur (e.g., customers do not respond well to a new product launch)*

Risk is ever-present in business and there are a variety of possible responses to it:

- *Ignore it (wait and see)*
- *Share/deflect the risk (e.g., take-out insurance)*
- *Make contingency plans - prepare for it*
- *race risk as an opportunity- particularly if it also affects other competitors*

Operational Management

Some examples of how action can be taken to reduce risk include:

Marketing

- Avoid over-reliance on customers or products
- Develop multiple distribution channels
- Test marketing for new products

Operations

- Hold spare capacity
- Rigorous quality assurance & control procedures & culture

Finance

- Insurance against bad debts
- Investment appraisal techniques

People

- Key man insurance – protect against loss of key staff
- Rigorous recruitment & selection procedures changes.

Operational Management

Initiate and Manage Change

"What is change management?" This is a question you may have heard from colleagues or co-workers in passing or in formal presentations. While many of us know intuitively what change management is, we have a hard time conveying to others what we really mean.

In thinking about how to define change management, it is important to provide context related to two other concepts: the change itself and project management. Change management and project management are two critical disciplines that are applied to a variety of organisational changes to improve the likelihood of success and return on investment.

When you introduce a change to the organisation, you are ultimately going to be impacting one or more of the following:

- *Processes*
- *Systems*
- *Organisation structure*
- *Job roles*

While there are numerous approaches and tools that can be used to improve the organisation, all of them ultimately prescribe adjustments to one or more of the four parts of the organisation listed above. Change typically results as a reaction to specific problems or opportunities the organisation is facing based on internal or external stimuli.

While the notion of becoming "more competitive" or "closer to the customer" or "more efficient" can be the motivation to change, at some point these goals must be transformed into the specific impacts on processes, systems, organisation structures or job roles. This is the process of defining the change.

It should be recognised there are 2 types of organisational change; imposed and self-generated, both of which are influenced internally and externally to the organisation. To implement a coaching or mentoring scheme to bring about organisational change, the desired outcomes must be identified, even if they are obvious.

Projects are often used as a means of achieving change and it must be recognised that change means that many things will be unfamiliar, uncertain and ambiguous. Managing projects and managing change is therefore quite different from managing systems.

The system once in place, is familiar, establishes patterns of work and interaction and generate its own momentum; it is by its very nature long-term. The project, on the other hand, is new and temporary, information may be uncertain, the authority to control may have to be indirect and exactly who is in charge may be ambiguous. Thus, project managers also need to understand their project environment and not just the technical requirements and objectives that appear on the project documents. The forces that prompted the project, the people that will make the project happen and the forces that will support and obstruct the project must be understood.

To avoid conflict when implementing any type of change, it is essential to ensure that all people involved understand the reasons behind the changes. As an operations or

Operational Management

departmental manager, you will need to be able to avoid conflict, which can be achieved by ensuring that clear lines of communication and authority are always identified.

There are several things should be considered when conflict or barriers are being displayed. The effective manager should be prepared and have adequate information to hand to be able to provide a full picture of the situation, together with the perceived benefits and advantages.

You should be able to consider the impact the change will have on team members:

- empathise with them and be prepared to provide alternatives if required
- ensure that discussions made that may lead to conflict are held in an appropriate location and in a positive atmosphere
- ensure that the concerns or barriers presented by team members are taken seriously and listen attentively
- do not dictate to them, instead, encourage the team to expand on its thoughts
- asked them how they think the situation could be overcome or resolve to take the ideas on board
- if you are unable to comply with them, explain why and ensure your explanation is understood

Defining Change Management and Project Management

It is not enough to merely prescribe the change and expect it to happen; creating change within an organisation takes hard work and an understanding of what must actually take place to make the change happen.

Change Management

Change management is the process, tools and techniques to manage the people side of change to achieve the required business outcome.

Change management incorporates the organisational tools that can be utilised to help individuals make successful personal transitions resulting in the adoption and realisation of change.

Change management supports moving an organisation from a current state (how things are done today), through a transition state to a desired future state (the new processes, systems, organisation structures or job roles defined by the change). Change management focuses on the people impacted by the change.

Operational Management

Any change to processes, systems, organisation structures and/or job roles will have a technical side and a people side.

The goal of change management is to help each individual impacted by the change to make a successful transition, given what is required by the solution.

The Change Curve

The Change Curve is based on a model originally developed in the 1960s by Elisabeth Kubler-Ross to explain the grieving process. Since then, it has been widely utilised as a method of helping people understand their reactions to significant change or upheaval. Kubler-Ross proposed that a terminally ill patient would progress through five stages of grief when informed of their illness. She further proposed that this model could be applied to any dramatic life changing situation and, by the 1980s, the Change Curve was a firm fixture in change management circles.

The curve and its associated emotions can be used to predict how performance is likely to be affected by the announcement and subsequent implementation of a significant change.

The original five stages of grief – denial, anger, bargaining, depression and acceptance – have adapted over the years.
There are numerous versions of the curve in existence. However, the majority of them are consistent in their use of the following basic emotions, which are often grouped into three distinct transitional stages.

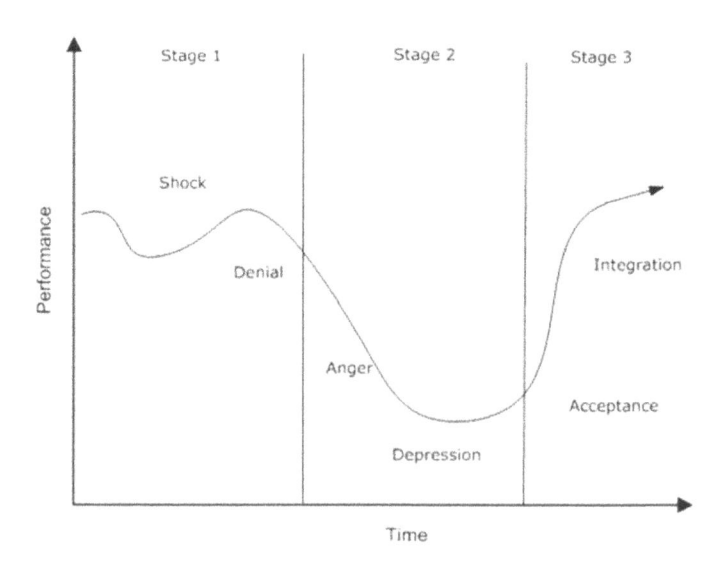

Stage 1 – Shock and denial
The first reaction to change is usually shock. This initial shock, while frequently short lived, can result in a temporary slowdown and loss of productivity.

Operational Management

Performance tends to dip sharply, individuals who are normally clear and decisive seek more guidance and reassurance and agreed deadlines can be missed.

The shock is often due to:

- *lack of information*
- *fear of the unknown*
- *fear of looking stupid or doing something wrong*

After the initial shock has passed, it is common for individuals to experience denial. At this point focus tends to remain in the past. There is likely to be a feeling that as everything was OK as it was, why does there need to be a change?

Common feelings include:

- *being comfortable with the status quo*
- *feeling threatened*
- *fear of failure*

Individuals who have not previously experienced major change can be particularly affected by this first stage. It is common for people to convince themselves that the change is not actually going to happen, or if it does, that it will not affect them. Performance often returns to the levels seen before the dip experienced during the initial shock of the change.

People carry on as they always have and may deny having received communication about the changes and may well make excuses to avoid taking part in forward planning.

At this stage, communication is key. Reiterating what the actual change is, the effects it may have and providing as much reassurance as possible, will all help to support individuals experiencing these feelings.

Stage 2 – Anger and depression
After the feelings of shock and denial, anger is often the next stage. A scapegoat, in the shape of an organisation, group or individual, is commonly found.

Focussing the blame on someone or something allows a continuation of the denial by providing another focus for the fears and anxieties the potential impact is causing.

Common feelings include:

- *suspicion*
- *scepticism*
- *frustration*

The lowest point of the curve comes when the anger begins to wear off and the realisation that the change is genuine hits. It is common for morale to be low and for self-doubt and

Operational Management

anxiety levels to peak. Feelings during this stage can be hard to express and depression is possible as the impact of what has been lost is acknowledged. This period can be associated with:

- *apathy*
- *isolation*
- *remoteness*

At this point performance is at its lowest. There is a tendency to fixate on small issues or problems, often to the detriment of day-to-day tasks. Individuals may continue to perform tasks in the same way as before, even if this is no longer appropriate behaviour.

People will be reassured by the knowledge that others are experiencing the same feelings. Providing managers, teams and individuals with information about the Change Curve underlines that the emotions are usual and shared and this can help to develop a more stable platform from which to move into the final stage.

Stage 3 –Acceptance and integration
After the darker emotions of the second stage, a more optimistic and enthusiastic mood begins to emerge. Individuals accept that change is inevitable and begin to work with the changes rather than against them.

Now come thoughts of:

- *exciting new opportunities*
- *relief that the change has been survived*
- *impatience for the change to be complete*

The final steps involve integration. The focus is firmly on the future and there is a sense that real progress can now be made. By the time everyone reaches this stage, the changed situation has firmly replaced the original and becomes the new reality.

The primary feelings now include:

- *acceptance*
- *hope*
- *trust*

During the early part of this stage, energy and productivity remain low, but slowly begin to show signs of recovery. Everyone will have lots of questions and be curious about possibilities and opportunities. Normal topics of conversation resume and a wry humour is often used when referring to behaviour earlier in the process.

Individuals will respond well to being given specific tasks or responsibilities; however, communication remains key. Regular progress reports and praise help to cement the more buoyant mood. It is not uncommon for there to be a return to an earlier stage if the level of support suddenly drops.

Operational Management

Individual reactions

Each person reacts individually to change and not all will experience every phase. Some people may spend a lot of time in stages 1 and 2, whilst others who are more accustomed to change may move fairly swiftly into stage 3. Although it is generally acknowledged that moving from stage 1 through stage 2 and finally to stage 3 is most common, there is no right or wrong sequence. Several people going through the same change at the same time are likely to travel at their own speed and will reach each stage at different times.

Summary

Managing change within the team will entail the sharing of information and perhaps asking for ideas as to how the relevant change can be managed or implemented. If it is a change in a process, for example, encouraging team members to come forward with their own ideas should be considered.

A quality circle may be formed and can be a more formal approach to the generation of ideas, although adding quality to the standing agenda for a team meeting can often produce effective results for ideas of how to change.

A quality circle is a participatory management technique within the framework of an organisation wide quality system, which small teams of usually 6 to 12 employees voluntarily form to define and solve the quality or performance-related problem.

Discussing the change in detail, the reason for it, the benefits from its implementation and the resources and costings involved, will engage with the team members and provide them with their understanding of why this must happen. Through engagement, the team is more likely to feel empowered and valued and hence any changes made will be transitioned to smoothly

When plans and priorities change, the team members need to be flexible in their approach and attitude to be to confront those changes and adapt accordingly however on certain occasions, there will be issues that are beyond your control that impact on their ability to amend priorities and plans.

These constraints may include:

- **Cost** - *are there any additional costs that will be incurred from making these amendments and if so, how will they be met? Are these cost hard costs for any tangible resources required or do they include the cost of the time it would take to?*
- **Time** - *can the plan be executed in the given timeframe or are extensions required? What will be the implications of the business of extensions are required?*
- **Support** - *is the relevant support available to ensure the plan/priority can be met and achieved? At what cost?*
- **Competence** - *is there sufficient capacity and capability within the available resources to ensure the amendments can be considered?*

Operational Management

Effective Change Management

Most organisations today are in a constant state of flux as they respond to the fast-moving external business environment, local and global economies and technological advancement. This means that workplace processes, systems and strategies must continuously change and evolve for an organisation to remain competitive.

Change affects your most important asset, your people. Losing employees is costly due to the associated recruitment costs and the time involved getting new employees up to speed. Each time an employee walks out of the door, essential, intimate, knowledge of the business leaves with them. A change management plan can support a smooth transition and ensure your employees are guided through the change journey. The harsh fact is that approximately 70 percent of change initiatives fail due to negative employee attitudes and unproductive management behaviour.

1. Clearly define the change and align it to business goals.
It might seem obvious, but many organisations miss this first vital step. It is one thing to articulate the change required and entirely another to conduct a critical review against organisational objectives and performance goals to ensure the change will carry your business in the right direction strategically, financially and ethically. This step can also assist you to determine the value of the change, which will quantify the effort and inputs you should invest.

Key questions:

- *What do we need to change?*
- *Why is this change required?*

2. Determine impacts and those affected.
Once you know exactly what you wish to achieve and why, you should then determine the impacts of the change at various organisational levels. Review the effect on each business unit and how it cascades through the organisational structure to the individual. This information will start to form the blueprint for where training and support is needed the most to mitigate the impacts.

Key questions:

- *What are the impacts of the change?*
- *Who will the change affect the most?*
- *How will the change be received?*

3. Develop a communication strategy.
Although all employees should be taken on the change journey, the first two steps will have highlighted those employees you absolutely must communicate the change to. Determine the most effective means of communication for the group or individual that will bring them on board. The communication strategy should include a timeline for how the

Operational Management

change will be incrementally communicated, key messages and the communication channels and mediums you plan to use.

Key questions:

- *How will the change be communicated?*
- *How will feedback be managed?*

4. Provide effective training.
With the change message out in the open, it is important that your people know they will receive training, structured or informal, to teach the skills and knowledge required to operate efficiently as the change is rolled out. Training could include a suite of micro-learning online modules, or a blended learning approach incorporating face-to-face training sessions or on-the-job coaching and mentoring.

Key questions:

- *What behaviours and skills are required to achieve business results?*
- *What training delivery methods will be most effective?*

5. Implement a support structure.
Providing a support structure is essential to assist employees to adjust to the change emotionally and practically and to build proficiency of behaviours and technical skills needed to achieve desired business results. Some change can result in redundancies or restructures, so you could consider providing support such as counselling services to help people navigate the situation. To help employees adjust to changes to how a role is performed, a mentorship or an open-door policy with management to ask questions as they arise could be set up.

Key questions:

- *Where is support most required?*
- *What types of support will be most effective?*

6. Measure the change process.
Throughout the change management process, a structure should be put in place to measure the business impact of the changes and ensure that continued reinforcement opportunities exist to build proficiencies. You should also evaluate your change management plan to determine its effectiveness and document any lessons learned.

Key questions:

- *Did the change assist in achieving business goals?*
- *Was the change management process successful?*
- *What could have been done differently?*

Operational Management

Open Communication

Another key to successful change management is to ensure there is open communication throughout the business.

Operating on a need-to-know basis is a costly choice for any businesses. Business needs the complete commitment and participation of all its employees. Creating an atmosphere of open communication contributes to a more vibrant, creative workforce where all employees have a deep understanding of the goals of the business and what needs to be done to accomplish those goals. Open communication gives everyone equal participation in the success of the business.

1. Start with commitment from the top.
Ensure that all managers are committed to open communication. Be visible and available to employees. Evaluate the systems of communication and ensure that processes are in place that allow for vital information to be communicated regularly throughout the business.

2. Keep your message positive.
Motivate employees by pointing out accomplishments and exemplary work. State messages in terms of what needs to be done and what is being done well rather than what should not be done or what is being done poorly.

3. Make your communication process transparent.
Hold open-ended meetings that give each team member the opportunity to share concerns, accomplishments and ideas. Set clear expectations for all work tasks and what you expect employee behaviour to be. Avoid springing surprises on your employees when it comes to what they are expected to do.

4. Take inventory of the diversity of employees in your workplace.
Analyse how different groups of employees receive information. Avoid using slang or jargon that might not be understood by subcultures within your workplace. Provide employees with mentors if they lack communication skills common to the greater group -- for example, international workers may be unfamiliar with communication techniques.

5. Establish a grievance system through which employees can make complaints in a protected manner.
Give complaints serious consideration when warranted and always let employees know that they have been heard. Act on complaints and communicate those actions to all involved parties.

Encourage Open Communication
Many organisations today champion a culture of honest and open communication, but unfortunately most of them do not get down to actually creating it. You have to walk the talk if you truly want managers and employees to share ideas and opinions.

Level 5: Operations / Departmental Manager

Operational Management

Many employees are reluctant to disagree with their company's leadership and management out of fear of retribution. Many companies have a forced, "happy" culture that names "open communication" as a corporate value while managers actively and/or passively discourage dissenting opinions.

As a result, employees will avoid voicing their concerns at all costs and prefer to continue doing things as instructed by their bosses even when they suspect (or know) that there is a better way.

Most organisations have room for improvement when it comes to encouraging open communication. Employees often struggle to open up and speak freely when communicating with their managers and some of the most common reasons why they feel this way are:

- *never bother to ask for employees' thoughts, views and opinions*
- *not listening, responding, or taking any action based on employee input*
- *not stopping to look at the employee and acknowledge what they are saying*
- *condescendingly discounting employees' ideas, views and concerns*
- *getting mad and/or confrontational thus inspiring fear of retaliation*

Employees are much more likely to believe the communications environment they actually experience in their day-to-day work at the office no matter how glossy the "openness and honesty" posters that they see in reception are.

This means the organisation must create an environment where managers clearly know the company values communication and employees feel comfortable speaking up.

Opening up communication takes commitment and intentional effort, but the results are totally worth it.

Acknowledge that your employees' views are important
The first step in opening up communication is to admit to that staff members have a unique and yet very important viewpoint of what is going in the organisation and industry as a whole.

Free sign up
Employees are right on the front line of customer service, so they are always the first to notice the future needs and demands of customers. When time and energy is spent to gather their thoughts and observations, it increases the organisation's chances of staying agile and innovative.

Ask your employees for input
Unfortunately, many managers often respond to an employee's interest in providing input by saying they do not have the time for it.

Managers must make time to ask employees for suggestions.

Operational Management

This may sound simple and obvious, but it is important to communicate unambiguously that management, in fact, wants to hear from employees: ideas, concerns as well as questions.

Listen to your employees reflectively
Encourage managers to clearly show that they have heard employees' opinions. One way to do this is to pause a bit before replying and perhaps repeat back to the employee what they said instead of rapidly firing back own opinions without any indication that they have been heard or their view considered.

Show employees that you are not just hearing what they are saying, but that the emotions behind it are recognised and understood. Tell them the particular emotions being detected in their tone or body language but do not discount or invalidate them, but rather affirm and validate them.

Reflect by saying "I hear the concern in your voice," instead of "There's no need to be concerned" or "I can see how agitated you are by this," instead of "You need to relax."

Engage your employees on a personal level
Greet employees when you see them. You do not have to know every employee's name (no one expects you to), but a simple, "Good morning!" or "Beautiful day, isn't it?" helps create a more relaxed and comfortable environment in which employees can feel confident enough to be more open.

Try to get to know employees beyond their role in the company. Ask what they did over the weekend, how their children or parents are doing or how their favourite sports team is doing. Showing interest in employees communicates that they are valued beyond their work — as human beings.

Be respectful to your employees
When employees come to you with problems or suggestions, make it clear they have your full attention; stop what you are doing, look them straight in the eye, listen and ask questions about what they are saying.

Do not give employees the impression that they are not important by not acknowledging them, continuing to type, checking email, taking phone calls or rummaging through your files.

Acknowledge your employees' input
Managers do not have to act on every suggestion. Employees understand that not every idea is appropriate or realistic, but they just want to know that their ideas were heard and considered.

Even if you cannot act on it, sharing your employees' input in the next company publication, for example goes a long way. They key is to show your employees that their opinions are heard and respected.

Recognise your employees

Operational Management

When employees say they want more recognition, company leadership often assumes they are talking about money – that they want a bonus or raise. In fact, they are most often talking about two simple words, "Thank you."

Expressing gratitude employees for taking the lead on a project, staying late or putting in extra time goes a long way toward encouraging open communication in your company.

Make a schedule and stick to it
Schedule regular times for small meetings with employees and honour those commitments. Employees often complain about managers announcing a series of bi-weekly staff meetings, holding the first few and then becoming "too busy" for any further sessions.

Do not suggest a schedule that will be unrealistic – you are better off arranging for fortnightly meetings that you can actually consistently honour.

Describe instead of judging
When discussing an employee's behaviour or a decision they made, avoid judging their behaviour or the reasoning behind their decision. Instead, describe what you observed.

For example, "I noticed status reports have been a few days late for three weeks now," instead of, "You've become lazy and don't seem to care about your work." The former leaves room for the employee to explain themselves and/or commit to improving while the latter simply pushes them to disengage and feel ashamed or agitated.

Do not shy away from problems
Should a problem arise in the workplace or an employee's performance weaken, have the courage to see the situation for what it really is and address it in its nascent stages before it grows too big to handle instead of shying away from it or pretending it does not exist.

Furthermore, when you avoid facing the performance issue everyone else on the team knows you are not capable of holding people accountable, which in turn undermines their trust and confidence in you.

Encouraging honest and open communication takes more than just talking about it in your mission statement and press releases. It requires putting in place active measures that foster an open exchange of information and ideas among employees at every level of your organisation.

Operational Management

Data Protection

Data protection is about ensuring people can trust you to use their data fairly and responsibly. If you collect information about individuals for any reason other than your own personal, family or household purposes, you need to comply.

Data protection is the fair and proper use of information about people. It is part of the fundamental right to privacy – but on a more practical level, it is really about building trust between people and organisations. It is about treating people fairly and openly, recognising their right to have control over their own identity and their interactions with others and striking a balance with the wider interests of society.

It is also about removing unnecessary barriers to trade and co-operation. It exists in part because of international treaties for common standards that enable the free flow of data across borders. The UK has been actively involved in developing these standards.

Data protection is essential to innovation. Good practice in data protection is vital to ensure public trust in, engagement with and support for innovative uses of data in both the public and private sectors.

The UK data protection regime is set out in the DPA 2018 and the GDPR (which also forms part of UK law).

The Data Protection Act 2018 is split into a number of different parts, which apply in different situations and perform different functions. It sets out four separate data protection regimes:

Part 2 Chapter 2: General processing (GDPR)
Part 2 Chapter 3: General processing (applied GDPR)
Part 3: Law enforcement processing
Part 4: Intelligence services processing

It sits alongside the GDPR and tailors how the GDPR applies in the UK - for example by providing exemptions. It also sets out separate data protection rules for law enforcement authorities, extends data protection to some other areas such as national security and defence and sets out the Information Commissioner's functions and powers.

GDPR is the General Data Protection Regulation (EU) 2016/679. It sets out the key principles, rights and obligations for most processing of personal data – but it does not apply to processing for law enforcement purposes, or to areas outside EU law such as national security or defence.

The GDPR came into effect on 25 May 2018. As a European Regulation, it has direct effect in UK law and automatically applies in the UK until we leave the EU (or until the end of any agreed transition period, if we
Identifying the correct regime is important, as although the overall principles are similar, there are some key differences. You will need to be able to demonstrate that you are applying the correct regime.
Most organisations fall under the general processing regime.

Operational Management

The Seven Principles of GDPR

The GDPR sets out seven principles for the lawful processing of personal data. Processing includes the collection, organisation, structuring, storage, alteration, consultation, use, communication, combination, restriction, erasure or destruction of personal data. Broadly, the seven principles are:

- *Lawfulness, fairness and transparency*
- *Purpose limitation*
- *Data minimisation*
- *Accuracy*
- *Storage limitation*
- *Integrity and confidentiality (security)*
- *Accountability*

The principles are at the centre of the GDPR; they are the guiding principles of the regulation and compliant processing.

Data controllers are responsible for complying with the principles and letter of the regulation. Data Controllers are also accountable for their processing and must demonstrate their compliance. This is set out in the new accountability principle.

Lawfulness, transparency and fairness are the key ingredients to the first principle of data processing in the General Data Protection Regulation (GDPR): "Personal data shall be processed lawfully, fairly and in a transparent manner in relation to the data subject."

Each of these elements deserves special attention, but here, we want to look specifically at the "lawful" requirement, exploring the six lawful bases for processing personal data under the GDPR:

Consent:	*The data subject has freely given consent for their information to be processed for a specific purpose.*
Contract:	*Processing is necessary due to the fulfilment of a contract.*
Legal Obligation:	*Processing is necessary to comply with the law.*
Vital Interest:	*Processing is necessary to save or protect an individual's life.*
Public Tasks:	*Processing is necessary to perform a public interest in official functions. (Primarily applies to governmental agencies/entities.)*
Legitimate Interests:	*Processing is necessary to the legitimate interests of an organisation or a third-party affiliate.*

Lawful basis is not to be trifled with – it is the foundation for data processing under the GDPR. The GDPR requires every organisation (government, non-profit, commercial, etc.) to have a lawful basis for each and every instance of data processing. Those who do not properly identify a lawful basis that corresponds to each processing activity will be in violation of the regulation.

Operational Management

Rights of the Individual

The GDPR provides the following rights for individuals:

The right to be informed
The right of access
The right to rectification
The right to erasure
The right to restrict processing
The right to data portability
The right to object
Rights in relation to automated decision making and profiling.

Obligations

- Individuals have the right to be informed about the collection and use of their personal data. This is a key transparency requirement under the GDPR.
- You must provide individuals with information including: your purposes for processing their personal data, your retention periods for that personal data and who it will be shared with. This is called 'privacy information'.
- You must provide privacy information to individuals at the time you collect their personal data from them.
- If you obtain personal data from other sources, you must provide individuals with privacy information within a reasonable period of obtaining the data and no later than one month.
- There are a few circumstances when you do not need to provide people with privacy information, such as if an individual already has the information or if it would involve a disproportionate effort to provide it to them.
- The information you provide to people must be concise, transparent, intelligible, easily accessible and it must use clear and plain language.
- It is often most effective to provide privacy information to people using a combination of different techniques including layering, dashboards and just-in-time notices.
- User testing is a good way to get feedback on how effective the delivery of your privacy information is.
- You must regularly review and where necessary, update your privacy information. You must bring any new uses of an individual's personal data to their attention before you start the processing.
- Getting the right to be informed correct can help you to comply with other aspects of the GDPR and build trust with people but getting it wrong can leave you open to fines and lead to reputational damage.

Operational Management

Data Security

Data Security is the term used to describe the process of protecting files, databases and accounts which are stored on a computer network by adopting and implementing a set of controls, tools and techniques that identifies the importance of the data, its sensitivity, the needs of regulatory compliance and applying appropriate policies, processes and tools to secure those resources.

Data security is not the only method used to reduce the risk that comes with storing data of different kinds.

Implicit in the security process is confidentiality, integrity and availability. These three elements are collectively known as the CIA triad. It forms a model and a guide for organisations to protect sensitive data protected from unauthorised access and data theft.

- *Confidentiality ensures that data is accessed only by authorised individuals*
- *Integrity ensures that information is reliable as well as accurate*
- *Availability ensures that data is both available and accessible to satisfy business needs.*

There are a few data security considerations which should be considered:

- **Where is the sensitive data located?** *Data cannot be protected if its storage location is unknown.*
- **Who has access to the data?** *Uncontrolled access and irregular access reviews leaves organisations at risk of data abuse, theft or misuse. Knowing who has access to the data at all times is one of the most vital data security considerations to have.*
- **Has continuous monitoring and real-time alerting on data been implemented?** *Continuous monitoring and real-time alerting are important not just for compliance with regulations, but will detect unusual file activity, suspicious accounts and adverse computer behaviour before it is too late.*

Data Security Technologies

The following are data security technologies used to prevent breaches, reduce risk and sustain protections.

Data Auditing
Today, it is not *if* a security breach occurs, but **when** a security breach will occur. When forensics get involved in investigating the root cause of a breach, having a data auditing solution in place to capture and report on who has access to control and make changes to data, who has had access to sensitive data, and when it was accessed, are vital to the investigation process.

With proper data auditing solutions, IT administrators can gain the visibility necessary to prevent unauthorised changes and potential breaches.

Operational Management

Data Real-Time Alerts
Typically, it takes organisations several months (or 206 days) to discover a breach. They often find out about breaches through their customers or third parties rather than their own IT departments. By monitoring data activity and suspicious behaviour in real-time, security breaches that lead to the destruction, loss, alteration, unauthorised disclosure of, or access to personal data can be identified and mitigated far more quickly.

Data Risk Assessment
Data risk assessments help organisations to identify the most vulnerable sensitive data and offer appropriate steps to prioritise and fix serious security risks. The process starts by identifying accessible sensitive, stale data and/or inconsistent permissions. Risk assessments summarise important findings, expose the vulnerabilities of the data and provide a means of identifying appropriate remediation.

Data Minimisation
The last ten years has seen a shift in the perception of data. Previously, having more data was almost always better than less. The more data held – the more could be done with it. Today, data has become a liability. The threat of a data breach and the cost of regulatory fines reinforce the notion that collecting anything beyond the minimum amount of sensitive data is extremely dangerous.

Purge Stale Data
Data that is not stored is data that cannot be compromised. Systems should be put in place that track file access and automatically archive unused files. It is quite likely that any organisation of significant size will have multiple forgotten computers and servers containing sensitive data that are being retained for no good reason.

Operational Management

Information Management

In the 1970s, information management began to emerge from data management as virtual media began to overtake physical media (punch cards, magnetic tapes, paper, etc.). As PCs started to replace mainframes as the primary computing platform in the 80 sand as networked systems came to prominence in the 90s, information management came into its own.

An Information Management Process is the method an organisation uses to:

- *Acquire or retrieve information*
- *Organise information*
- *Maintain information*

Data management holds a key role in the Information Management Process as ensuring the accuracy of the data you capture and hold is vital if you are to extract value from it.

The information an organisation holds will be complex and come from a variety of different sources, for example - customer data from dealing with queries online or over the phone, employee details and contact details for target prospects. Managing this data consistently across multiple departments can be a challenge. With an effective information Management Process in place, you will:

- *Extract real value from the data you hold as it enables effective data profiling*
- *Adhere to data regulation and compliance rules and laws (such as GDPR)*
- *Store data in one central place enabling organisation and easy retrieval for analysis*

A good Information Management Process will enable you to recognise the value of your organisation's data and identify gaps or problems with your data quality. In order to maintain this process, you should utilise the correct data quality tools and software to make sure the data you hold and capture is always business relevant.

Information management is the collection, storage, dissemination, archiving and destruction of information. It enables teams and stakeholders to use their time, resource and expertise effectively to make decisions and to fulfil their roles.

What Information Management is not

Information Management is often confused with content management or knowledge management. While all three processes are related and there is some overlap, they do have some differences. Content management deals with data (blocks of text, images, videos and more) a website uses and the covers to organise and display the data (e.g., XML tags or HTML coding). Knowledge management is similar to library science and deals with information for training and education, as well as knowledge and expertise transfer and passing on lessons learned.

Operational Management

Information, as we know it today, includes both electronic and physical information. The organisational structure must be capable of managing this information throughout the information lifecycle regardless of source or format (data, paper documents, electronic documents, audio, video, etc.) for delivery through multiple channels that may include cell phones and web interfaces.

Given these criteria, we can then say that the focus of Information Management is the ability of organisations to capture, manage, preserve, store and deliver the right information to the right people at the right time.

The information management process starts with data collection and creation and its conversion to information.

Information assets are corporate assets. This principle should be acknowledged or agreed upon across the organisation otherwise any business case and support for Information Management will be weak.

Information must be made available and shared. Of course, not all information is open to anyone, but in principle the sharing of information helps the use and exploitation of corporate knowledge.

Information the organisation needs to keep is managed and retained corporately. In other words, the retention and archiving, of information. If you save a document today, you expect it to be secured and still available to you tomorrow.

Information management is a corporate responsibility that needs to be addressed and followed from the upper most senior levels of management to the front-line worker. Organisations must be held and must hold its employees accountable to capture, manage, store, share, preserve and deliver information appropriately and responsibly. Part of that responsibility lies in training the organisation to become familiar with the policies, processes, technologies and best practices in Information Management.

Information management has four main components.

> **People:** *Not only those involved in Information Management, but also the creators and users of data and information.*
> **Policies and Processes:** *The rules that determine who has access to what, steps for how to store and secure information must be stored and secured and timeframes for archiving or deleting.*
> **Technology:** *The physical items (computers, filing cabinets, etc.) that store data and information and any software used.*
> **Data and Information:** *What the rest of the components use.*

Operational Management

Principles of Information Management

There are many information management principles. A well-known set is the Information Management Body of Knowledge (IMBOK), which is a framework that breaks down management skills into six knowledge areas and four process areas.

The knowledge areas include the following:

Information Technology (IT): Hardware and software
Information Systems: IT built into a system that meets business needs and policies
Business Information: Created by analysing and contextualising data using tools such as the information system
Business Processes: How to evaluate and use the business information to make decisions
Business Benefit: The desired advantage the business information will provide
Business Strategy: The master plan that gives a company a direction. Ideally, decisions made through the business processes, which are based on business information, will guide the strategy and lead to the realisation of the business benefits.

The IMBOK process areas are:

Projects: Adding new capacity, software and hardware to information systems
Business Change: Evaluating information to drive improvements in processes
Business Operations: The day-to-day of a business. These will guide improvements based on updates to processes and will hopefully increase benefits.
Performance Management: Trying to ensure operations are running at peak capacity

Data as a Product
In the same way a company produces something like nuts and bolts, one company department (like IT) can produce data that other departments (like finance or marketing) or another business treat like a product or service. With this frame of mind, the providing entity will see the receiving entity as a customer and therefore may be more responsive to their needs.

Information Management Strategies
Information management strategies are plans that guide a company to keep its Information Management practices in sync, improve its processes and prepare for the future. These plans can include the following information:

- Current status
- Goals for the future
- Concrete steps to achieve those goals
- Plans to acquire new resources
- Processes and policies for interacting with business departments
- Assigning responsibility for implementing and reporting each

Operational Management

Data & Information

The words data and information are often used interchangeably, but there is an important distinction, especially in the world of information management. Data are raw facts. Information is data that has been processed, structured, interpreted and organised, so that it can inform decisions and plans. Companies can get data from many sources, including the following:

> **Legacy Systems:** Used for data that has been piling up for a long time. A company's legacy systems (e.g., learning management, employee records, financial history) all contain useful data that can be tapped.
>
> **Data Creation:** Transactions, manufacturing, making payments, purchasing and employee reviews (to name a few) all create data. For a retailer, the data could be how many hammer and saw sales their point-of-sale system tracked. For a manufacturer, it could be the number of computer monitors that were assembled. For a delivery company, it could be the time a package was dropped off at a designated location.
>
> **Data Collection:** Data that comes from external sources, such as weather trends, news reports, road closure notices, or hiring trends. This kind of data can be purchased or collected for free.

Data can be in two forms

Data can be classified into two categories; these are qualitative data and quantitative data. Qualitative data is based on a judgement such as feedback given after using a service and Quantitative data is captured as a result of some form of measure.

Quantitative Data

Quantitative data is easier to define and identify than qualitative data.

Quantitative data is always numerical and is analysed using mathematical and statistical methods. If there are no numbers involved, then it is not quantitative data.

Some phenomena obviously lend themselves to quantitative analysis because they are already available as numbers. Examples include changes in achievement at various stages of education, or the increase in number of senior managers holding management degrees. However, even phenomena that are not obviously numerical in nature can be examined using quantitative methods.

Example: turning opinions into numbers

> If you wish to carry out statistical analysis of the opinions of a group of people about a particular issue or element of their lives, you can ask them to express their relative agreement with statements and answer on a five- or seven-point scale, where 1 is strongly disagree, 2 is disagree, 3 is neutral, 4 is agree and 5 is strongly agree (the seven-point scale adds slightly agree/disagree).

Such scales are called Likert scales and enable statements of opinion to be directly translated into numerical data. The development of Likert scales and similar techniques

Operational Management

mean that most phenomena can be studied using quantitative techniques. This is particularly useful if you are in an environment where numbers are highly valued and numerical data is considered the 'gold standard'.

However, it is important to note that quantitative methods are not necessarily the most suitable methods for investigation. They are unlikely to be very helpful when you want to understand the detailed reasons for particular behaviour in depth. It is also possible that assigning numbers to fairly abstract constructs such as personal opinions risks making them spuriously precise.

Sources of Quantitative Data
The most common sources of quantitative data include:

- *Surveys,* whether conducted online, by phone or in person. These rely on the same questions being asked in the same way to a large number of people
- *Observations,* which may either involve counting the number of times that a particular phenomenon occurs, such as how often a particular word is used in interviews, or coding observational data to translate it into numbers
- *Secondary data,* such as company accounts.

Analysing Quantitative Data
There are a wide range of statistical techniques available to analyse quantitative data, from simple graphs to show the data through tests of correlations between two or more items, to statistical significance. Other techniques include cluster analysis, useful for identifying relationships between groups of subjects where there is no obvious hypothesis and hypothesis testing, to identify whether there are genuine differences between groups.

Qualitative Data
Qualitative data is any data which does not involve numbers or numerical data. It often involves words or language but may also use pictures or photographs and observations.

Almost any phenomenon can be examined in a qualitative way and it is often the preferred method of investigation in the UK and the rest of Europe; US studies tend to use quantitative methods, although this distinction is by no means absolute.

Qualitative analysis results in rich data that gives an in-depth picture and it is particularly useful for exploring how and why things have happened.

However, there are some pitfalls to qualitative research, such as:

- If respondents do not see a value for them in the research, they may provide inaccurate or false information. They may also say what they think the researcher wishes to hear. Qualitative researchers therefore need to take the time to build relationships with their research subjects and always be aware of this potential.
- Although ethics are an issue for any type of research, there may be particular difficulties with qualitative research because the researcher may be party to confidential

Operational Management

information. It is important always to bear in mind that you must do no harm to the data subjects.
- It is generally harder for qualitative researchers to remain apart from their work. By the nature of their study, they are involved with people. It is therefore helpful to develop habits of reflecting on your part in the work and how this may affect the research.

Sources of Qualitative Data

Although qualitative data is much more general than quantitative, there are still a number of common techniques for gathering it. These include:

- **Interviews,** which may be structured, semi-structured or unstructured
- **Focus groups,** which involve multiple participants discussing an issue
- **'Postcards',** or small-scale written questionnaires that ask, for example, three or four focused questions of participants but allow them space to write in their own words
- **Secondary data,** including diaries, written accounts of past events and company reports
- **Observations,** which may be on site, or under 'laboratory conditions', for example, where participants are asked to role-play a situation to show what they might do.

Analysing Qualitative Data

Because qualitative data is drawn from a wide variety of sources, it can be radically different in scope.

There are, therefore, a wide variety of methods for analysing them, many of which involve structuring and coding the data into groups and themes. There are also a variety of computer packages to support qualitative data analysis. The best way to work out which ones are right for the research is to discuss it with academic colleagues and line managers.

Finally, it is important to emphasise that there is no right and wrong answer to which methods you choose. Sometimes you may wish to use one single method, whether quantitative or qualitative and sometimes you may want to use several, whether all one type or a mixture. It is your data and only you can decide which methods will suit both your investigation and your skills, even though you may wish to seek advice from others.

Operational Management

Data Collection

When any sort of data is collected, especially quantitative data, whether observational, through surveys or from secondary data, you need to decide which data to collect and from whom.

This is called the sample.

There are a variety of ways to select your sample and to make sure that it gives you results that will be reliable and credible.

The difference between population and sample

Ideally, research would collect information from every single member of the population that you are studying. However, most of the time that would take too long and so you have to select a suitable sample: a subset of the population.

The idea behind selecting a sample is to be able to generalise your findings to the whole population, which means that the sample must be:

> **Representative of the population.** *In other words, it should contain similar proportions of subgroups as the whole population and not exclude any particular groups, either by method of sampling or by design, or by who chooses to respond.*
>
> **Large enough to give you enough information to avoid errors.** *It does not need to be a specific proportion of your population, but it does need to be at least a certain size so that you know that your answers are likely to be broadly correct.*
>
> **If your sample is not representative, you can introduce bias into the study.** *If it is not large enough, the study will be imprecise.*

However, if you get the relationship between sample and population right, then you can draw strong conclusions about the nature of the population.

How Data Becomes Information

Data becomes information by interpretation, analysis, contextualisation, processing and other Information Management activities.

> *Example:*
>
> A driver's record of how many gallons of petrol they purchase is data. That same driver calculating their mileage makes it information. If they chart their mileage by weather conditions or city versus motorway driving, it is richer information.
>
> In a business context, the number of pairs of shoes sold and the price paid per pair is data. Charting sales by store, comparing sales numbers to the previous period, or tracking how many customers used a coupon makes it information.

Operational Management

While there are many ways of conceptualising the way data becomes information, a well-known concept is the portfolio model created by Andy Bytheway, a Professor of Computer Science at University of the Western Cape in South Africa. This model posits two axes:

- **Source: Internal vs. External -** *Whether data comes from within an organisation (sales figures, email) or outside (news reports, hourly road conditions).*
- **Structure: Structured versus Unstructured** - *Whether data has been analysed or put in context or is just a collection of facts.*

The most valuable quadrant is internal structured. This information has been vetted, processed, put in context and provides the best basis for business operational decision making.

Data and Information Value

Data and information are corporate assets that are created or gathered by a company. Because they can make the business more valuable, they need protection. Unlike computers or buildings, data and information are intangible, so it is often difficult to assign a real value.

- **Collect and Create Data:** *The data has value as a resource.*
- **Process Data:** *The value is in the ability to combine, contextualise, etc.*
- **Generate Information:** *The diverse patterns and connections that become visible are the value created in this step.*
- **Apply Knowledge:** *The value comes from using what has been created to make changes to operations, processes, etc*

The Digital Workplace

The impact of COVID will not be fully understood or measured for some time, however, it has turned the world of work and Information Technology on its head. Gone are the days when the workplace was merely a physical space employees occupied during regular office hours. With huge numbers of employees now working from home, todays always connected, instant access environment has blurred the lines between the physical office and the place where work actually happens. This has only been possible with the use of IT systems.

As the distinction between professional and personal life dissolves and the workplace becomes truly digital, employees are communicating and collaborating in unprecedented ways. To enable knowledge sharing across the organisation, they want the ability to forge productive business relationships beyond natural work groups.

To meet this changing work experience, leading organisations have begun to evolve and implement the digital workplace. By integrating the technologies that employees use (from e-mail, instant messaging and enterprise social media tools to HR applications and virtual meeting tools), the digital workplace breaks down communication barriers fostering efficiency, innovation and growth. The key to success, however, lies in the effective implementation of a digital workplace strategy capable of driving true cultural change.

Operational Management

While the workplace began transforming as far back as the agricultural and industrial revolutions, COVID has accelerated the widespread proliferation of information technology changing forever the ways in which employees connect, collaborate and communicate.

This change has developed over the last 30 years due to the emergence of three fundamental trends, but more recently accelerated at an unthinkable pace due to the pandemic.

- **Ageing workforce:** *as the baby boomers continue to retire, they are taking key knowledge with them, increasing the need to capture their knowledge.*
- **Information overload:** *information is still growing at exponential rates and employees cannot find what they need, even with technology advances.*
- **The need for speed:** *with the rapid pace of today's work environment, employees increasingly need to work faster and collaborate more effectively to get their jobs done.*

The digital workplace should be considered the natural evolution of the workplace. It comprises all the technological aspects of the working environment.

It encompasses all the technologies used to get work done in today's workplace – both the ones in operation and the ones yet to be implemented. It ranges from your HR applications and core business applications to e-mail, instant messaging and enterprise social media tools and virtual meeting tools.

Because most organisations already use many of these components, the digital workplace does not need to be built from the ground up. Staff already respond to e-mails from smartphones, record their expenses online or digitally enter a sales lead, many organisations are already on the verge of becoming a truly digital workplace.

Even where new technologies are required, the benefits increasingly outweigh the costs. As the workplace continues to evolve and employee expectations shift, organisations that do not embrace the digital workplace risk falling behind.

Benefits of a Digital Workplace
If the risks of inaction are not sufficient motivators, the benefits of adopting a digital workplace make it a compelling business case. Benefits include:

- **Employee attraction:** *64% of employees would opt for a lower paying job if they could work away from the office.*
- **Employee productivity**: *organisations with strong online social networks are 7% more productive than those without.*
- **Employee satisfaction:** *organisations that installed social media tools internally found a median 20% increase in employee satisfaction*.
- **Employee retention:** *when employee engagement increases, there is a corresponding increase in employee retention by up to 87%.*
- **Communication tools:** *information workers prefer newer communication tools, particularly instant messaging, over more traditional ones like e-mail or team workspaces.*

Operational Management

Employees must be provided with the tools they require to collaborate, communicate and connect with each other. Any Information system strategy must avoid siloed implementation and departmental ownership. There should be a clear roadmap to ensure the digital workplace delivers measurable business value while mitigating risks and adhering to compliance requirements.

The Digital Workplace Framework
The digital workplace framework includes four layers covering the following components:

Use: collaborate, communicate, connect
The digital workplace is all about the employees' ability to do their job by collaborating, communicating and connecting with others. The goal is to forge productive business relationships within and beyond natural work groups and to enable knowledge sharing across the organisation.

Technology: the digital toolbox
Technology enables the digital workplace. Each organisation already has a digital workplace toolbox with different tools. Depending on the industry and business needs, the tools needed to support the digital workplace will vary. The key is to adopt the right tools for employees to do their jobs.

Control: governance, risk and compliance
The effective use of technology in the digital workplace is underpinned by appropriate controls. This means the digital workplace must be supported by appropriate governance structures and management processes. Information flow and use must also comply with the organisation's policies and industry regulations.

Business drivers: measurable business value
As with any core initiative, it is essential for business needs to drive the digital workplace. To deliver the necessary benefits, the direction of the organisation should guide the direction of the digital workplace.

The implications of organisational culture
It is no secret that an organisation's culture guides the way employees behave and work. People and culture lie at the heart of organisational performance and typically drive both success and failure. This means the culture ultimately determines how and to what extent employees prioritise the digital workplace to connect, communicate and collaborate.

The key is to understand how employees prefer to work. A change management plan and digital workplace strategy that aligns to the organisations working culture can then be developed.
By fostering this type of cultural change and unifying your technology components, a digital workplace can help improve:

- **Collaboration:** to solve business problems and operate productively, organisations need the ability to manage knowledge across the enterprise with online, seamless, integrated and intuitive collaboration tools that enhance your employees' ability to work together.
- **Communications:** as information continues to grow at an unprecedented rate, more tools exist that enable people to create their own content, rather than simply consuming

Operational Management

existing content. To ensure the right information reaches the right audience, employees need tools that support two-way communication and the personalisation of content.

- **Connections:** *self-sufficiency no longer guarantees effectiveness. Employees need tools that allow them to connect across the organisation, leverage intellectual property and gain insight from one another. The digital workplace delivers on these goals by fostering a stronger sense of culture and community within the workplace.*

The Digital Workplace Toolbox

In most organisations, the digital workplace toolbox can be broadly defined in eight categories to support the ways in which you communicate, collaborate, connect and deliver day-to-day services. Too often, organisations implement these tools in silos without the benefit of a holistic digital workplace strategy.

Take the time to create a digital workplace strategy that clearly articulates the business focus and can guide the development of the digital toolbox. By assessing capabilities in each category, it is possible to identify focus areas and refer to the organisation's culture and business requirements to identify the tools most needed.

The digital workplace gives employees the tools they need to improve their communication, collaboration and connections with each other. Implemented effectively, it also allows organisations to mitigate common risks, adhere to their regulatory compliance mandates and ultimately realise enhanced business value.

> *Employees will not wait! They will find a way to do what they need*

Technology has grown to become an immense part of our personal lives and has reshaped the average workplace. People are interested in getting the most current technology whether it be the newest smartphone or latest car model. If we constantly want to update our personal technology, why should we not want to modernise our professional technology as well? Technology in the workplace is important to keep an organisation running smoothly and efficiently.

Operational Management

Messaging	Productivity	Collaboration	Communication
Provides a fast way to communicate with colleagues	Enables workers to get their jobs done efficiently	Enable employees to work with each other and with partners	Supports information sharing and internal publishing
E-mail Instant messaging Micro Blogging Mobile messaging	Word processors Spreadsheet software Presentation Software Calculator	Team rooms Communities Wikis Web conferencing	Portals/intranet Blogs Personalised Homepage
Business applications	**Crowd sourcing**	**Connectivity**	**Mobility**
Enable employees to access self-service applications online	Enables organisation to gather ideas, inputs and thoughts from employees	Helps locate experts and colleagues across the organisation	Enables access of tools away from the physical office or workplace
Expense claims HR systems ERP CRM	Ideas platform Polling Survey Forums	Employee directory Organisation chart Rich profile	PC/laptop Mobile/smart phone Home office Remote scanners

Below are 7 reasons to keep technology up to date at the workplace.

Staying Innovative
An innovative workplace is on the cutting edge of technology, design and business practices. With a little creativity, better ways to design products, connect with customers, market the business and develop promotions can all be identified. Thinking outside the box, might find an answer to a problem that no one else thought of before. Because these innovations are unique, businesses', potential customers and employees will take notice and go to this business instead of another.

Computational Accuracy
Small discrepancies in an organisation can bring about large amounts of uncertainty. Modern spreadsheets like Excel, with its hundreds of computational formulas, help ensure accuracy. Accounting programs allow you to accurately manage stock, make and record sales, manage and pay bills and handle payroll. Now, data can be regularly maintained in a software program and keep detailed records without errors.

Industry Efficient
Whatever product or service on offer, the business must compete. The competitors use technology, so you need to as well. Having the latest technology allows the organisation to stay competitive and provide the best quality service or products as possible.

Operational Management

Communicate Better, Collaborate More
Technology has given us a level of communication never seen before. We can literally connect with any one of our employees, leaders and co-workers anytime, anywhere. The influx of new technology in the workplace has affected how employees communicate, collaborate and work more efficiently. In fact, with many employees believing that face-to-face meetings will be obsolete soon, the norms of office communication could be the next major change impacting the workplace.

Security and Safety
The security of company information can be severely compromised without the implementation of proper channels of technology and software. A company should implement innovative technology as a safe haven against such breaches of security. Stealing critical and important information was easy in the past, but now with the use of technology, the threat of data thefts and leaks is nearly impossible.

Maintain Organisation
Technology helps in keeping the business fully organised. Systems like Project Management Software helps in building, delegating, reviewing and assessing a task. Employers and managers can easily supervise workplace activities that help in keeping everything on track. It fixes the responsibility, accountability and timed delivery of tasks assigned to people.

Increase Productivity
It is important to study and utilise different hardware and software solutions that can improve employee productivity. Businesses nowadays rely on many tools to overcome challenges of executing on strategy every day. It enables managers to track progress more easily during every phase of goal completion and offer immediate reinforcement or coaching to keep performance and deadlines on track.

The workplace is transforming fast and so are the needs of today's workforce as they experience the rapid evolution of technology. It is important to understand the integral and beneficial aspects of technology in the workplace to have a successful business.

Chapter 7: Leading People

Leading People

Leadership

Leadership definitions and descriptions vary enormously and examples of leadership can be extremely diverse too.

Business directory.com states that leadership is:

> *"the activity of leading a group of people or an organisation or the ability to do this"*

There are many more definitions, but leadership is about the ability to get other people to do something willingly.

Leaders do not exist without followers.

- We lead when we manage a football team or teach a classroom of children.
- We lead our children as parents
- We lead when we organise anything.
- We lead when we manage projects or develop a new business.
- We lead the moment we take the first supervisory responsibility at work
- We may lead even before we assume official responsibility to do anything.

A vicar or preacher leads a congregation. A writer or visionary may lead when he or she puts pen to paper and creates a book, or poem, or article which inspires and moves others to new thoughts and actions. A monarch and a president are both leaders. A ruthless dictator is a leader. So was Mother Theresa and so was Mahatma Gandhi.

We can find leadership in every sort of work and play and in every sort of adventure and project, regardless of scale and regardless of financial or official authority.

Given the many ways in which leadership operates, it is no surprise that leadership is so difficult to define and describe.

Understanding Leadership

Many people consider leadership to be an essentially work-based characteristic. However, leadership roles are all around us and not just in work environments.

Ideally, leaders become leaders because they have credibility and because people want to follow them. Using this definition; it becomes clear that leadership skills can be applied to any situation where you are required to take the lead, professionally, socially and at home in family settings.

Examples of situations where leadership might be called for, but which you might not immediately associate with that, include:

Leading People

Planning and organising a big family get-together, *for example, to celebrate a wedding anniversary or important birthday*
Responding to an illness or death in the family *and taking steps to organise care or make other arrangements*
Making decisions about moving house, or children's schooling.

In other words, leaders are not always appointed and leadership skills may be needed in many circumstances.

An oft cited quotation is:

> *"some are born leaders, some achieve leadership and some have leadership thrust upon them".*

But what exactly is a leader? - A leader can be defined as:

> *'a person who leads or commands a group, organisation or country'.*

This definition is broad and could include both formal and informal roles—that is, both appointed leaders and those who emerge spontaneously in response to events.

In recent years, considerable evidence has emerged that the strongest organisations and groups tend to permit and actively encourage each member of the group or organisation to take the lead at the appropriate point. In contrast, organisations and families with particularly controlling leaders, tend to be fairly dysfunctional.

Leadership, therefore, is in practice, fairly fluid: leaders are made by circumstances. The crucial issue is whether people are prepared to follow them at the right moment.
People also struggle with the concept of how being a leader is different from being a manager. You may have heard the idea that 'leaders do the right thing and managers do things right'.

This is a fairly delicate distinction and many leaders are also managers (and vice versa). Perhaps the key difference is that leaders are expected to create and communicate a compelling vision, often associated with change. Managers, on the other hand, are perhaps more often associated with maintaining the status quo.

Leadership vs. Management

It is important to know and understand that there are clear differences between management and leadership. One major difference between leadership and management, is that leadership always involves leading people, whereas management need only be concerned with responsibility for things such as money, IT equipment, etc.

Leading People

Of course, many management roles have substantial people-management responsibilities, but the fact that management does not necessarily include responsibility for people; whereas leadership always does, is a big difference.

Likewise, good leadership always includes responsibility for managing.
When managing, many of the management duties may be delegated through others, but the leader is responsible for ensuring there is appropriate and effective management for the situation or group concerned. The opposite is not the case.

Management could be regarded as a function or responsibility within leadership, but not vice-versa.

Leadership is actually a much bigger and deeper role than management - a useful way to understand the differences between leadership and management is to consider some typical responsibilities of leading and managing and to determine whether each is more a function of leading, or of managing.

Typical Responsibilities	
Management	*Leadership*
1. Implementing tactical actions 2. Detailed budgeting 3. Measuring and reporting performance 4. Applying rules and policies 5. Implementing disciplinary rules 6. Organising people and tasks within structures 7. Recruiting people for jobs 8. Checking and managing ethics and morals 9. Developing people 10. Problem-solving 11. Planning 12. Improving productivity and efficiency 13. Motivating and encouraging others 14. Delegating and training	1. Creating new visions and aims 2. Establishing organisational financial targets 3. Deciding what needs measuring and reporting 4. Making new rules and policies 5. Making disciplinary rules 6. Deciding structures, hierarchies and workgroups 7. Creating new job roles 8. Establishing ethical and moral positions 9. Developing the organisation 10. Problem-anticipation 11. Visualising 12. Conceiving new opportunities 13. Inspiring and empowering others 14. Planning and organising succession 15. All management responsibilities, including all listed left

When a manager does things which appear in the leadership list, then they are leading, as well as managing.

James Scouller has an additional and helpful viewpoint on the distinction between leadership and management: He says:

Leading People

"Leadership is more about change, inspiration, setting the purpose and direction and building the enthusiasm, unity and 'staying-power' for the journey ahead. Management is less about change and more about stability and making the best use of resources to get things done...

But here is the key point:

...... leadership and management are not separate. They are not necessarily done by different people. It is not a case of, 'You are either a manager or a leader'. Leadership and management overlap..." (From The Three Levels of Leadership, J Scouller, 2011)

Leadership vs. Management Model

Traditionally, management is described as:

> *the identification and agreement of goals, obtaining the necessary resources, designing, organising, directing and controlling activities and providing motivation and reward to the individuals completing the required work.*

On the other hand, leadership is described as:

> *the process of seeing beyond identified constraints and instead, breaking out in new directions, bringing down boundaries, using innovation, taking risks and changing the mindset of others to precipitate change and develop.*

Peter Farey (1993) developed this by identifying two additional dimensions in which Leaders and Managers can operate. He proposed that leaders can either be:

- *The individual at the front, doing what they do best - succeeding at a task.*
- *Someone who can inspire followers - people.*

Farey went on to develop a Leadership / Management model in which he compared the Task vs People, to develop another perspective from which to compare the two roles and the different styles or approaches by those who hold the roles.

The model represents the attitudes and the behaviours exhibited by those in the roles. Attitude refers to whether the leader tends to lean towards specific points on the four axes which are identified as Leadership, Management, Tasks and People. The criteria listed in each of the quadrants are the leadership behaviours they tend to exhibit.

Leading People

- **Those who identify in the upper two quadrants are the leaders-** *individuals exhibit a tendency for new, radical ideas. They want to be seen as unique and revolutionary, challenging the pre-existing constraints and mechanisms for change.*
- **Those who identify in the lower two quadrants are the managers** – *focussed on developing what already exists to achieve results. Continuity of operation is the primary focus to maintain efficiency and productivity in all activities undertaken by them and their team.*

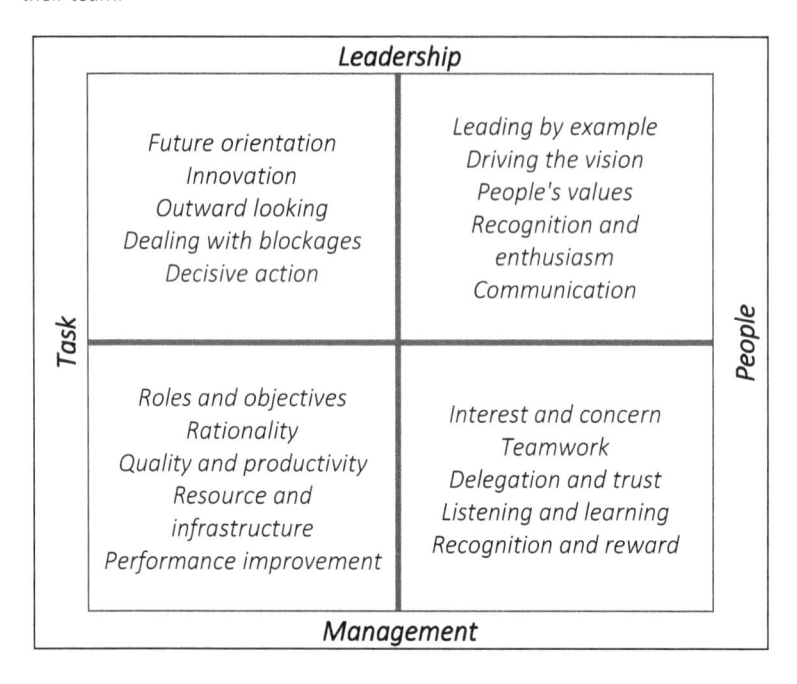

	Leadership	
Task	Future orientation Innovation Outward looking Dealing with blockages Decisive action	Leading by example Driving the vision People's values Recognition and enthusiasm Communication
	Roles and objectives Rationality Quality and productivity Resource and infrastructure Performance improvement	Interest and concern Teamwork Delegation and trust Listening and learning Recognition and reward
	Management	**People**

The quadrants to the left of the centre line are the Task oriented Managers and Leaders whilst those to the right of the centre line are the People oriented leaders and managers.

- **Task oriented Leaders and Managers are primarily concerned with production and output** – *where results are measured against success on achieving deadlines and overcoming constraints.*

- **People oriented Leaders and Managers are focussed on those who deliver the production and output** – *they look to use their relationship with the team to motivate them to achieve targets.*

Depending on which quadrant the individual tends towards, each has its own unique traits and behaviours. These may well be suited to individual situations, but will not satisfy every situation. Although there is a tendency towards a particular quadrant, it is important that they are considered interchangeable, to satisfy the demands of each situation and the needs of the team members involved.

Level 5: Operations / Departmental Manager

Leading People

People Leadership

People Leadership utilises the concept inspiring people to succeed. The more a manager/leader engages with team members on an individual level – understanding their needs, wants and motivations - the more motivated they will be to succeed. This increased motivation is the energy which drives a team to achieve new heights.

People Leadership is directly related to the charisma exhibited by the manager/leader. By reflecting on leaders from the past, it is not difficult to identify individuals who, simply by using their personality, created a sense of following – people want to work for them. Unfortunately, in the wrong hands, this can be catastrophic. It is also possible for the manager/leader to overdo the hype to a point where it has the absolute opposite effect.

By using their personality, a manager/leader can build a strong rapport with team members to build motivation and this will always be more successful than if there is no rapport.

This may not be a natural trait - though it often is - manager/leaders need to learn how to bring the best out in others by first bringing the best out of themselves.

Task Leadership

Task Leadership is regarded as being the entrepreneurial facet of management.

There will often be different behaviours depending on whether the individual is a Task Leader or a Task Manager

People Leadership focusses on the engagement, development and motivation of team members, whereas Task Leadership focusses on defeating the challenges and obstacles at all costs to achieve success.

- *The Task Leader wishes to search for novel, innovative, solutions; whereas Task Managers strive only to improve those solutions, objects and processes which already exist.*

- *The Task Leader is willing to challenge things which are currently the "norm" or are within policy, whilst the Task Manager tends to operate within external constraints and policy limits.*

- *Task Managers are focussed exclusively on issues within their own area of work, their own team, or their own departments; whilst Task Leaders constantly monitor forces, influences and innovation which are external to their own area of responsibility.*

- *Task Leaders look to the future and Task Managers focus only on the present.*

Each individual Task Leader/Manager must control their tendency towards each area. Insufficient Task Leadership will inhibit change and things will remain the same. Too much

Leading People

Task Leadership and an obsession with winning can develop – to a point where other departments, teams and managers within the organisation become competitors and will not receive any support or opportunities to collaborate for the good of the organisation.

Leadership Styles

Whilst there are many different leadership styles, everyone has a default leadership style that comes most naturally to them. Leadership styles determine how someone uses their power and authority to lead others. The default leadership style is the way which feels most comfortable when leading others to achieve the vision. Understanding the default style will enable the common pitfalls of that particular style to be anticipated and avoided.

The best leaders are able to adjust their style based on the situation they find themselves in, for example, turning around a failing organisation might require a more forthright approach than being asked to grow an already successful organisation.

Autocratic Leadership

Autocratic leadership is centred around and focused on the leader. With this style of leadership, all of the decision-making resides with the leader and decisions are made by the leader without consulting subordinates.

An autocratic leader will reach a decision themselves, communicate it with their team and expect the team to execute, with no questions asked. With autocratic leadership, authority is in the hands of a single person, the leader. Examples of autocratic leaders include Donald Trump and Martha Stewart.

Advantages

- *Decision making is fast.* With no consultation required the leader can make quick decisions.
- *Improves performance in certain situations.* Managers are motivated to perform due to a "leader is watching" feeling.
- *Less stress in certain circumstances.* For managers and other subordinates, it can result in less stress as the leader is shouldering all responsibility for outcomes.

Disadvantages

- *Frustrating for subordinates.* Communication is one way which can be frustrating for subordinates.
- *Fear and resentment are common* as people do not like being bossed about and criticised more often than praised.
- *A paralysed organisation.* The organisation is paralysed when the leader is not present, as the entire organisation is dependent on the leader for instructions.
- *New Opportunities Missed.* Unless the leader keeps pace with new trends as time goes on, new opportunities could be missed. Additionally, the lack of flexibility in autocratic leadership does not lend itself to planning for long-term initiatives.

Leading People

- **Communication Breakdown.** Because directives flow downwards from the leader to the subordinates, misunderstandings and confusion can arise because of the lack of feedback that is allowed from subordinates.

When to Use
- **When quick decisions are needed.** Autocratic leadership works best in situations where quick decisions are needed, such as turning around a failing organisation.
- **When close supervision is required.** Autocratic leadership can work well when existing management is too lenient and workers are not pulling their weight. The autocrat will issue directives to be followed and the activities performed as a result of these directives will be closely followed.
- **When workflows need to be streamlined quickly.** Autocratic leadership works well when things just need to get done and this style enables subordinates to get things done without worrying about the bigger picture. This explains why autocratic leadership is very common in the military.

Democratic Leadership

Democratic leadership (often called participative leadership) is focused on the leader's team and is characterised by decision making being shared across the team. In stark contrast to the autocratic leadership style, ideas are shared freely and open discussion is encouraged.

Although discussion is encouraged it is the role of the leader to guide and direct these discussions and ultimately decide which way to proceed. Democratic leaders expect their subordinates to have in-depth valuable experience and to be self-confident.

Examples of democratic leaders include John F. Kennedy and Larry Page.

Advantages
- **Decreased risk of catastrophic failure.** As decisions are made with the involvement of the entire group, it provides a group check resulting in it being less likely for the leader to make a disastrous decision.
- **Good working environment.** Subordinates at all levels can feel engaged and take on the responsibility to challenge themselves because they are involved in decision making and it is this sense of engagement that can lead to the creation of a good working environment and increased job satisfaction.
- **High-performance teams.** Subordinates are encouraged to solve problems under their own initiative, which in turn can create a higher performing team. This higher performance, in turn, leads to greater productivity.

Disadvantages
- **Slow decision making.** Involving subordinates in decision making can dramatically slow down decision making. This can be a real problem in situations where the organisation needs to be turned around urgently, or where maintaining first mover advantage is necessary.
- **Over-dependence on the team.** A danger of the democratic leadership style is that the leader can become overly dependent on the group or hidden within the group, allowing the group to make the decisions. This can result in decisions being made

Leading People

   which drift the organisation towards its strategic goal rather than rapidly and purposely moving towards its goal.
- **Collaboration burden.** Leaders can become overly burdened with the overhead of ensuring experts meet and collaborate that they take their focus off key metrics and the urgent need to move towards the strategic vision.

When to Use
- **When subordinates are experts.** Democratic leadership styles work well when working with subject domain experts, for example, technology experts or pharmaceutical experts.
- **When subordinates are professionals.** For an experienced and professional team, a democratic leadership style can bring out the best in them, by building on their existing strengths and talents rather than just expecting them to perform.
- **When it is necessary to create ownership.** *By* involving the team in decision making and planning, you implicitly create buy-in to both the decision and the plan. This makes team members much more committed to the plan and much more likely to overcome or workaround barriers to execution as they arise.

Transformational Leadership

A Transformational leader is one who models the behaviour they expect to see, sets clear goals and has high expectations, whilst at the same time supporting and emotionally guiding subordinates to achieve.

At the very foundation of transformational leadership is the consistent promotion of a compelling vision, along with a set of values to live and work by. Transformational leaders create a culture of no-blame where the focus is on the problem at hand and how to solve it and not who is responsible for creating the problem.

Examples of transformational leaders include Peter Drucker and Barack Obama.

Transformational leaders are sometimes known as the "quiet leaders", known for possessing a willingness to lead by example. They often do not make detailed strategic plans, but instead, facilitate conversations between key people both within and outside of their organisation to achieve this end.

You can think of transformational leaders as having four key characteristics:

1. *They know their followers and demonstrate concern and empathy for them.*
2. *They encourage their followers to think for themselves*
3. *They motivate their followers to perform to their potential by inspiring them.*
4. *They model the behaviour they expect from others and are thus great role models.*

Leading People

Advantages
- ***Balanced goals.*** Transformational leaders balance the need for short-term and long-term goals.
- ***Trust.*** Subordinates feel supported and deeply trust their leader because they behave with integrity and build strong coalitions.
- ***Vision focused communication.*** Transformational leaders are very focused on the long-term strategic vision and by communicating the vision regularly with passion and clarity, they keep everyone on-side and motivated to reach it.

Disadvantages
- ***Can be ineffective in the beginning.*** Transformational leadership is built on trust. Thus, transformational leaders can be ineffective at the start of their leadership journey as they have yet to obtain the trust of their team or build strong collaborations.
- ***Not detail orientated.*** Whilst transformational leaders are characterised by inspiring others, they can struggle with the detail of day-to-day implementation.

When to Use
- ***When it is necessary an inspiring long-term vision of the future.*** Transformational leadership works when you have a strong vision of the future and are willing to work within the system and bring diverse people together to make it happen.
- ***When the right to lead has been earned.*** Transformational leadership is often not appropriate when you are new to an organisation and both your leadership is unproven and you've yet to build the necessary trust of your team.
- ***When an urgent short-term focus is not necessary.*** Because transformational leadership focuses so much on a vision for the future it is not appropriate when all the focus needs to be on the short term.

Laissez-Faire Leadership

Laissez-faire leadership is where the leader does not actually lead the team but instead allows the team to entirely self-direct. This style of leadership is also known as the "hands-off" style and in contrast to the other leadership styles we have looked at all authority is given to subordinates including goal setting, problem-solving and decision making. From the leader's perspective, the key to success is to build a really strong team and then stay out of their way.

A common question people ask upon learning about laissez-faire leadership is "what does a laissez-faire leader do?". Well, this will differ from leader to leader but typically they are more concerned with the creation and articulation of their compelling vision. They are also typically concerned with which steps to take to help achieve the vision. It is then obviously left to the team to work out how to achieve a particular step. Examples of laissez-faire leaders include Warren Buffett; due to the hands-off approach he takes in the companies he owns and Andrew Mellon.

A Laissez-faire leadership style typically works best near the top of the organisational tree where senior leaders appoint other senior leaders to run their respective departments and let them get on with it.

Leading People

Advantages
- **Creates personal responsibility.** Laissez-faire leadership styles challenge subordinates to take personal responsibility for their work and the outcomes of their work.
- **Supports fast course corrections.** Motivated people working autonomously are typically able to overcome roadblocks and adjust course far more quickly than when they need to seek approval.
- **Supports higher retention.** When successful it can result in higher retention as motivated professionals and experts thrive in their work environment which supports autonomous decision making.

Disadvantages
- **Lack of accountability.** There is nobody accountable to take the credit in cases of success, or to take the blame in cases of failure.
- **Higher stress levels.** Subordinates can suffer from high levels of stress if they feel unsupported by their leader or unsure of their capabilities.
- **Missed deadlines.** Self-organising teams without oversight or direction are prone to miss deadlines.

When to Use
- **When working with creative experts.** Use with creative professionals who have solid skills and lots of experience in their jobs.
- **When people are proven.** When a team has a proven track record of high performance and achievement on certain types of project.
- **When a team is driven.** When a team is motivated and driven to succeed on their own and are comfortable working without supervision.

Leading People

Making Sense of Leadership Styles

There are many other leadership styles in addition to the ones we have described, including amongst others:

- *Strategic leadership*
- *Affiliative leadership*
- *Coaching leadership*
- *Bureaucratic leadership*
- *Cross-cultural leadership*
- *Servant Leadership*

To make matters more complex, no two leaders will be exactly the same and may, in fact, have characteristics borrowed from other leadership styles to suit their needs.

The following diagram can be really helpful in thinking about where different leadership styles have their main areas of focus.

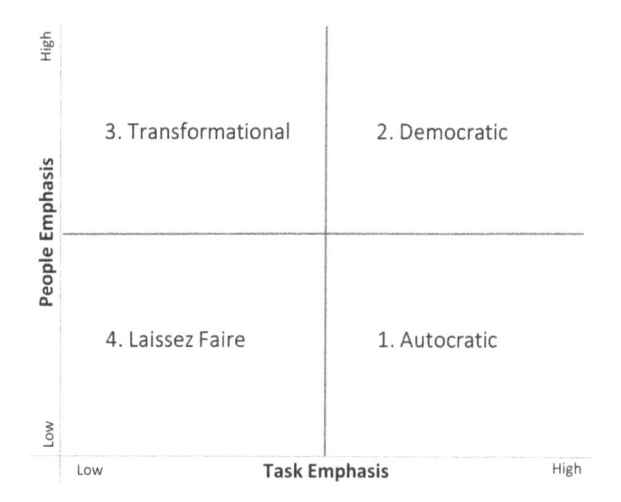

	Low Task Emphasis	High Task Emphasis
High People Emphasis	3. Transformational	2. Democratic
Low People Emphasis	4. Laissez Faire	1. Autocratic

This framework can be used to think about any leadership styles you encounter.

- **Autocratic leaders** have a high task emphasis and low people emphasis.
- **Democratic leaders** have a high task emphasis as well as a high people emphasis.
- **Transformational leaders** have a low task emphasis and high people emphasis
- **Laissez-faire leaders** have a low task emphasis and low people emphasis

There is a reason the boxes in the diagram are labelled 1 to 4 and it has to do with subordinates. The higher the skill level of our subordinates the higher the box number and the more appropriate that style of leadership is for those subordinates, so autocratic leadership is good for people with a very low skill level, whereas laissez-faire leadership works for people with a very high degree of skill. Essentially, the leader's behaviour should change according to which quadrant the followers' capabilities fall.

Leading People

Another point to note from this diagram is that the abilities of the leader, both in terms of soft and hard skills, must increase as we move from box 1 to 4.

Leadership Skills

The question of what makes a good leader is widely debated. It is clear that the ability to lead effectively relies on a number of key skills, but also that different leaders have very different characteristics and styles.

One of the most important aspects of leadership is that not every leader is the same. Of course, we have all heard jokes about 'mushroom' leadership (keep them in the dark and feed them B*****t!) and 'seagulls' (swoop in, squawk and drop unpleasant things on people) but jokes aside, there are many different styles of leadership.

Different leadership styles are appropriate for different people and different circumstances and the best leaders learn to use a wide variety of styles. There is, in fact, no one right way to lead in all circumstances and one of the main characteristics of good leaders is their flexibility and ability to adapt to changing circumstances.

Leadership skills are highly sought after by employers as they involve dealing with people in such a way as to motivate, enthuse and build respect. Whether or not leadership itself can be taught, there is no question that there are a number of core skills that most good leaders have. These skills can be learnt like any others.

Strategic Thinking	Planning And Delivery	People Management
Developing a vision of where you want to be	Planning how to achieve your vision and dealing with challenges along the way	Finding the right people and motivating them to work towards your vision
Change Management	Communication	Persuasion And Influence
Recognising, responding and managing changes to your vision and plans	Working on the best ways to communicate your vision to others and listening to ideas	Encouraging others to help you achieve your vision by demonstrating its advantages

There are a number of broad skill areas that are particularly important for leaders. These include strategic thinking, planning and delivery, people management, change management, communication and persuasion and influencing.

1. Strategic Thinking Skills

Perhaps the most important skill a leader needs—and what really distinguishes leaders from managers—is to be able to think strategically.

This means, in simple terms, having an idea or vision of where you want to be and working to achieve that.

Leading People

The best strategic thinkers see the big picture and are not distracted by side issues or minor details. All their decisions are likely to be broadly based on their answer to the question

does this take me closer to where I want to be?

As well as being able to create a compelling vision, they must also be able to communicate it effectively with their followers, which is partly why communication skills are also vital to leaders.

Creating a vision is not simply a matter of having an idea.

Good strategic thinking must be based on evidence and that means being able to gather and analyse information from a wide range of sources. This is not purely about numbers, but also about knowing and understanding your market and your customers and most important of all - using that information to support strategic decisions.

2. Planning and Delivery Skills

While it is important to be personally organised and motivated as a leader it is perhaps even more important to be able to plan and deliver for the organisation.

These are also key management skills, but the best leaders will also be able to use these.

The best vision in the world is no good without the plan to turn it into reality.

Alongside strategic thinking are organising and action planning, both essential for delivery of both vision and strategy. Project Management and Project Planning are also helpful skills for both managers and leaders. Good risk management is also important to help avoid things going wrong and manage when they do.

Good leaders often have very strong facilitation skills, to manage groups effectively.

Leaders also need to be able to make effective decisions in support of their strategy delivery and to solve problems.

With a positive attitude, problems can become opportunities and learning experiences and a leader can gain much information from a problem resolved.

3. People Management Skills

Without followers, there are no leaders. Leaders therefore need skills in working with others on a one-to-one and group basis and a range of tools to deal with a wide range of situations. In particular, leaders are expected to motivate and encourage their followers, both directly and by creating a motivational environment.

Leading People

One of the first skills that new leaders need to master is how to delegate. This is a difficult skill for many people but, done well, delegation can give team members responsibility, a taste of leadership themselves and motivate them.

There are further challenges to delegating work within a team, including balancing workloads and ensuring that everyone is given opportunities to help them develop.

Leaders and managers both need to understand how to build and manage a team. They need to know how to recruit effectively and bring people 'on board' through induction processes. They also need to understand the importance of performance management, both on a regular basis and to manage poor performance.

4. Change Management and Innovation Skills
Change management may seem like an odd companion to people management and communication, but leadership is particularly important at times of change.

A leader needs to understand change management in order to lead an organisation through the process.

> *Change management requires the creation and communication of a compelling vision.*

It also requires the change to be driven forward firmly and sound leadership to make it 'stick', if the organisation is not to revert back to old practices within a very short period.

One particular element of change management is innovation. Good leaders know how to innovate and also how to encourage innovation in others.

5. Communication Skills
While communication skills are important for everyone, leaders and managers perhaps need them even more. These skills are general interpersonal skills, not specific to leadership, but successful leaders tend to show high levels of skill when communicating.

Good leaders tend to be extremely good listeners, able to listen actively and elicit information by good questioning. They are also likely to show high levels of assertiveness, which enables them to make their point firmly but without aggression. They know how to build rapport quickly and effectively, to develop good, strong relationships with others, whether peers or subordinates. These skills come together to help to build charisma, that quality of 'brightness' which makes people want to follow a leader.

Leaders also need to know how to give others positive feedback on personal performance in a way that will be constructive rather than destructive and also hear others' opinions of them. They are usually very good at effective speaking, equally skilled at getting their point across in a formal presentation, a board meeting, in an informal meeting or a casual corridor conversation. They will also have honed their ability to communicate in difficult situations, usually by practice over time.

Leading People

6. Persuasion and Influencing Skills
Finally, one particular area of communicating that is especially important for leaders is being able to persuade and influence others.

Good leaders use a range of tools.

Leaders also need tools to help them understand the way that others behave and create positive interactions. As a first step, it may be helpful to understand more about emotional intelligence - another vital quality for leaders to possess - but there are a number of other tools that may also be useful, including Transactional Analysis and Myers-Briggs Type Indicators.

Developing Leadership

Many people wonder if leadership can really be taught. People with vested interests (academics and those offering leadership training or literature of some sort) are convinced that it can. Many successful leaders, however, have never had any formal training. For them, leadership is a state of mind and it is their personalities and traits that make them successful leaders. There is, clearly, a balance to be struck between these two positions.

There is no question that some people are more drawn towards leadership roles than others. However, it would be nonsense to suggest—although this has been mooted in the past—that only people with certain physical or personal traits could lead. For example, it has clearly been proven that being male, or being tall, does not of itself make someone a better leader, although many leaders are both male and tall.

It seems most likely that leadership requires certain skills. Some people will acquire these skills more easily than others.

One can, of course, learn about effective leadership skills and practices but being able to implement them may require a completely different set of skills and attitudes.

The question *"Can leadership be taught?"* has no simple answer and one needs to keep an open mind on the subject and research information about the skills a good leader needs.

Communication

Effective leadership requires knowledge of how to communicate with all elements of the organisation, including employees, managers, customers and investors. Each group may require a different communication style and leadership style. Leaders must be able to adapt based on the group they are communicating with at the time.

Effective communication skills are an important aspect of any leader's portfolio of skills and experience.

Leading People

1. Listening
An important aspect of communication is the ability to listen. Active listening should always be a goal, with the leader focusing on both the verbal and non-verbal language being used by themselves and the speaker and ignoring outside interruptions, including the leader's own wandering thoughts or possible responses.

Active listeners also refrain from interrupting, giving the speaker time to finish and show they are listening by doing things like nodding or smiling and subsequently paraphrasing back to the listener to verify their understanding.

> *Professional listening skills include listening for the message, listening for any emotions behind the message and considering relevant questions about the message.*

Listening for the message means hearing the facts accurately, without prejudgment or being distracted by other thoughts. It is also important to listen for any unusually strong stresses in the sentences or other signs of emotion.

2. Complimenting
People work for more than pay; they want to be noticed and praised for their work. Compliments are most effective if they are specific to the situation and in writing, so they can be re-read. For example:

> "You stayed late to finish that report for our client and made sure every aspect of the project was to his specifications. Thank you for your attention to detail and pride in your work!"

> "I noticed you took extra time to make sure the new employee had a great first day. She was very excited about the company and her new job at the end of the day!"

Use this technique on the leaders, managers or supervisors, to show them how to do it for their direct reports.

3. Delegating Tasks Clearly
Think of the "who," "what," "when," "where," "why" and "how" when explaining what needs to be done. Explaining the reason (the "why") is especially vital, particularly in regard to deadlines.

Employees may not realise that their job is only part of a series of tasks for a big project. People like to know the reasons they are doing something. Establish toolbox meetings to discuss progress.

4. Managing Meetings
What is a "good" meeting, from the point of view of the leader, meeting participants and the organisation?

Leading People

Multiply the estimated hourly pay of each person invited to the meeting by the length of the meeting and decide if the meeting is worth this cost. Would an e-mail do just as well to convey information?

If the purpose of the meeting is to share information, ask talkative attendees closed questions (yes or no answers). Via email, ask open-ended questions (such as, "What are your thoughts on …") to encourage quieter attendees to share their ideas ahead of time, or ask them at the meeting itself.

Introverted employees may have great ideas but be reluctant to talk in a meeting.

5. Positive Verbal and Non-Verbal Communication
Verbal communication is the most obvious form of communication. However, research has shown people pay much less attention to the words that are said and much more attention to the actions and nonverbal cues that accompany those words.

Nonverbal cues include facial expressions, use of hand motions, body posture and eye movements. Leaders should strive to always match their nonverbal cues to their words; when they do so, they are more believable and trustworthy.

Employees closely observe leaders. Even if there is bad news, when being observed by any employees, act positively. The employee grapevine is amazingly fast!

Smile and say "hello" to each employee you see.

6. Adapting Styles to the Audience
A good leader adapts their communication style depending on the audience. When speaking to employees, they may need to have a much more directive style than when they are delivering a presentation to stakeholders or speaking to customers. Leaders should identify the audience and their characteristics and interests, then adjust their communication style based on what the audience needs and what will encourage them to react to meet the goals of the communication.

7. Leading by Example
Leaders and business managers should realise employees will look to them as a model of how they should behave under certain circumstances.

Employees tend to emulate how they see leaders acting and communicating. If employees see a leader using an active listening style and empathetic tone with customers, they are more likely to do the same. When leaders are open to the ideas of others and praise often, employees will tend to follow suit. When speaking, leaders should consider whether they would want their employees to speak in the same way to the same audience. If not, the leader should adjust their communication style.

Leading People

An Effective Leader

One might expect to see certain traits or characteristics in the leaders who are considered to be effective. Some characteristics are more important than others, depending on people's values as followers or even the situations that they are in.

The leadership style adopted will depend on the urgency of the task, as well as on the needs, levels of experience and skill set of the team.

Leaders need to be trustworthy, honest and relied upon by team members. They can be counted on to follow through on their commitments. They stick to their principles and maintain professional standards of conduct. Team members trust, respect and believe in leaders who possess integrity

Effective leaders are strong communicators - they will communicate well with a wide range of people and in different situations, using different communication methods that are suited to the situation. They give clear directions and can support your ideas and opinions with facts. They are good listeners and demonstrate interest in the people around them. They can connect with members of the team and external stakeholders to build and maintain healthy working relationships.

Effective leaders are also resourceful - they demonstrate initiative, especially difficult situations. They keep up to date with new developments and influences and are aware of any new policies and procedures that are in place. They are adaptable, responding appropriately to the changing needs of the organisation and the individual team members while keeping their eye on the goals that must be achieved.

Effective leaders are also accountable for their actions - they accept responsibility for failures and poor performance and mistakes as well as success and good performance, not only their own, but the wider teams as well. Effective leaders do not pass on blame and they give full credit to team members for their success, ensuring that they recognise their achievements and contributions

Effective leaders are good problem solvers - they properly evaluate different options before making decisions and base their judgements on facts and information rather than hearsay or emotion. They take a proactive approach to problem solving. They do not simply react to different issues that arise but try to anticipate potential challenges or threats, implementing solutions is necessary. Leaders who can think and plan beforehand and are enthusiastic, have the edge.

Effective leaders have a positive attitude – they inspire confidence in others, they have a can-do attitude and demonstrate a desire and commitment to achieve. They overcome resistance in conflicts and do not quit when the going gets tough. They are persistent, staying with and solving problems, while encouraging and motivating their teams to achieve too. They will help to cultivate the lift or buzz that comes with success. Effective leaders are well organised and able to delegate. They bring order to chaos. They know they work better in a well-managed team and delegate the workload according to the team members abilities. They plan the workload well, are good at managing their own time and prioritise tasks accordingly.

Leading People

Models' vs Philosophies vs Styles

Leadership can and necessarily should, be approached from a variety of standpoints. A helpful way to understand leadership is by exploring leadership thinking and theories using these three main conceptual viewpoints:

1. *Leadership Models*
2. *Leadership Philosophies*
3. *Leadership Styles*

These three groups are different ways of looking at leadership or different aspects of leadership.

These different aspects can cause confusion when attempting to understand what leadership is - especially if only one aspect is used to consider the subject.

For example:
> *One person may be seeing leadership from a 'style' standpoint while another may be thinking about leadership 'philosophy'. The two people might hold similar or overlapping views and yet because the standpoints are different (and usually, therefore, the terminology and reference points are different too), it can seem that there is conflict about what leadership is, when actually there may be close agreement.*
>
> *Therefore, two people may disagree about something, purely because they are approaching it from a different standpoint when actually, they may be seeing the same thing, or two things which substantially overlap.*

In addition to providing a helpful theory structure, using the three groups also helps to show that lots of leadership thinking is overlapping and compatible, when it might otherwise seem conflicting and wildly diverse. Below are definitions of the three categories: models, philosophies and styles.

Leadership ideas can be:

- **models** - *learned/taught/applied in a very practical sense*
- **philosophies** - *about attitude and where power comes*
- **styles** - *interesting as typical leadership behaviours - helpful in understanding leadership generally and to a lesser degree may be facets within leadership models.*

Leading People

Definition of leadership models	Definition of leadership philosophies	Definition of leadership styles
A leadership model contains theories or ideas on how to lead effectively and/or become a better leader. **Action-Centred Leadership** is an example of a model.	A leadership philosophy contains values-based ideas of how a leader should be and act and the sources of a leader's power. **Servant Leadership** is an example of a leadership philosophy.	A leadership style is a classification or description of the main ways in which real-life leaders behave. **Transformational Leadership** is an example of a leadership style.
A leadership model is a structure which contains either processes or logic or a framework, which can be used or applied like a tool, in performing, understanding and teaching leadership. A model is often also shown in some sort of diagram format. There may also be a sense of mechanics or engineering, with inter-related and linked moving parts. In some cases, a leadership model may contain measurable elements, sometimes entailing complex relative factors and may also enable a reasonably consistent measurement or indication of standard, for example, effective versus ineffective leadership.	Any philosophy is a way of thinking and behaving. It is a set of values and beliefs. A philosophy is a series of reference points or a foundation upon which processes, decisions, actions, plans, etc., can be built, developed and applied. A leadership philosophy connects leadership with humanity and morality and ethics. A leadership philosophy will at some point be influenced by beliefs about human nature and society and perhaps religion, or universal truth and a sense of fairness and natural justice.	A leadership style is a narrower and more specific category than a model or a philosophy. In fact, many leadership styles are contained within leadership models as components of the model. A style is a distinct way of behaving. A leadership style tends to contain and is influenced strongly by the purpose or aim of the leadership. A leadership style may also be strongly influenced and perhaps determined by the personality of the leader and/or the personality or capability of the followers or group being led and/or of the situation in which the leader is leading the people.

A leadership model then provides a process or framework for learning, applying and adapting leadership for given groups, organisations, or situations.

A leadership philosophy is a way of thinking and behaving in leadership - its aims and means - according to values and beliefs.

A leadership style is a narrow and specific behaviour compared to a model or philosophy. The leadership style may be strongly influenced by the leader's personality, the aims of the leader and relationship with followers.

Leading People

	Summary	More Detail
Leadership Models	Leadership models aim to teach us how to be successful or effective as leaders. They show us the keys to effective leadership. Models often contain different leadership styles and enable 'switching' between them.	Leadership models tend to contain or enable processes and measurable standards and a 'switching' capability in response to different circumstances. Models may be supported by diagrams and graphs. A model may be influenced by or underpinned by a philosophy.
Leadership Philosophies	Leadership philosophies examine the sources of a leader's power and offer a value laden view of the aims that leaders should pursue and how they should go about them. Leadership philosophies focus on what kind of leadership one should offer. A leadership philosophy is usually more difficult to learn and apply than a model as it is dependent on values not technique.	Leadership philosophies tend more than the other categories to be based on a life code or moral position. A philosophy - since it is expressed mainly through ideas and words, rather than processes and structured elements - is usually more difficult (than a model) to explain, transfer, teach, apply, or to develop into a measurable set of rules or instructions. A philosophy may underpin a model and may also underpin a style. A philosophy also involves far more and deeper references to society, politics, civilisation, etc., than models or styles.
Leadership Styles	Leadership styles are essentially descriptive. They are observed classifications of leadership behaviours. They aim to describe the real-life forms of leadership we see around us. Unlike leadership philosophies, they offer no guidance on the kind of leadership that leaders should offer – they merely reflect what is out there.	A leadership style is a narrow and specific behaviour compared to the other two categories. Leadership styles tend to be determined or strongly influenced by the leader's personality and the aim of the leadership. A leadership style is also strongly influenced by the purpose for which leadership is needed or has been established. A style may be suggested or dictated by a model and to a lesser degree also by a philosophy.

Leading People

Leadership Theories

The leadership style you adopt at any given time will depend on the urgency of the task as well as the needs levels of experience and skill set of the team.

It is recognised that there are several specific leadership styles and models that can be identified in that each manager may show a preference for a particular style or a number of styles. It would be professional to believe that a manager should be flexible in their approach to the management of individuals and communication is the key to that flexibility.

Blake and Mouton's Managerial Grid

Building on the work of the researchers at these Universities, Robert Blake and Jane Mouton (1960s) proposed a graphic portrayal of leadership styles through a managerial grid (sometimes called leadership grid). The grid depicted two dimensions of leader behaviour, concern for people (accommodating people's needs and giving them priority) on y-axis and concern for production (keeping tight schedules) on x-axis, with each dimension ranging from low (1) to high (9), thus creating 81 different positions in which the leader's style may fall.

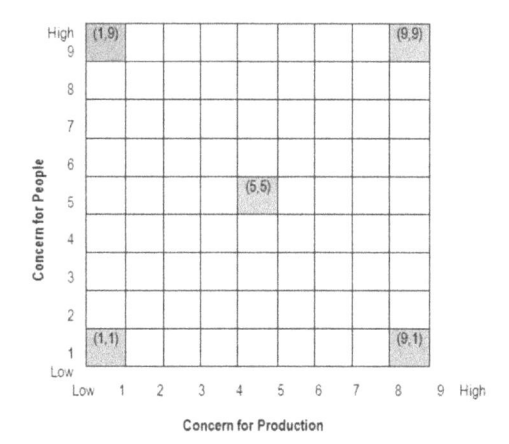

The five resulting leadership styles are as follows:

1. ***Impoverished Management (1, 1):*** *Managers with this approach are low on both the dimensions and exercise minimum effort to get the work done from subordinates. The leader has low concern for employee satisfaction and work deadlines and as a result disharmony and disorganisation prevail within the organisation. The leaders are termed ineffective wherein their action is merely aimed at preserving job and seniority.*

Leading People

2. **Task management (9, 1):** *Also called dictatorial or perish style. Here leaders are more concerned about production and have less concern for people. The style is based on theory X of McGregor. The employees' needs are not taken care of and they are simply a means to an end. The leader believes that efficiency can result only through proper organisation of work systems and through elimination of people wherever possible. Such a style can definitely increase the output of organisation in short run but due to the strict policies and procedures, high labour turnover is inevitable.*

3. **Middle-of-the-Road (5, 5):** *This is basically a compromising style wherein the leader tries to maintain a balance between goals of company and the needs of people. The leader does not push the boundaries of achievement resulting in average performance for organisation. Here neither employee nor production needs are fully met.*

4. **Country Club (1, 9):** *This is a collegial style characterised by low task and high people orientation where the leader gives thoughtful attention to the needs of people thus providing them with a friendly and comfortable environment. The leader feels that such a treatment with employees will lead to self-motivation and will find people working hard on their own. However, a low focus on tasks can hamper production and lead to questionable results.*

5. **Team Management (9, 9):** *Characterised by high people and task focus, the style is based on the theory Y of McGregor and has been termed as most effective style according to Blake and Mouton. The leader feels that empowerment, commitment, trust and respect are the key elements in creating a team atmosphere which will automatically result in high employee satisfaction and production.*

Advantages of the Managerial Grid
The Managerial or Leadership Grid is used to help managers analyse their own leadership styles through a technique known as grid training. This is done by administering a questionnaire that helps managers identify how they stand with respect to their concern for production and people. The training is aimed at basically helping leaders reach to the ideal state of 9, 9.

Limitations of the Managerial Grid
The model ignores the importance of internal and external limits, matter and scenario. Also, there are some more aspects of leadership that can be covered but are not.

Leading People

Daniel Goleman - Six Leadership Styles

Daniel Goleman, in his article "Leadership That Gets Results", has identified six different leadership styles and he believes that good leaders will adopt one of these six styles to meet the needs of different situations.

> *"Coercive leaders demand immediate compliance. Authoritative leaders mobilise people toward a vision. Affiliative leaders create emotional bonds and harmony. Democratic leaders build consensus through participation. Pacesetting leaders expect excellence and self-direction. Coaching leaders develop people for the future."* –
> Daniel Goleman.

None of the six leadership styles posited by Daniel Goleman are right or wrong – each may be appropriate depending on the specific context. Whilst one of the more empathetic styles is most likely to be needed to build long-term commitment, there will be occasions when a commanding style may need to be called upon, for example, when a rapid and decisive response is required.

1. Coercive leadership is the least effective in most situations. The leader's extreme top-down decision-making kills new ideas. People feel disrespected. Their sense of responsibility evaporates. Unable to act on their own initiative, they lose their sense of ownership and feel little accountability for their performance. The coercive style should be used only with extreme caution and in the few situations when it is absolutely imperative, such as during a turnaround or when a hostile takeover is looming.

2. The authoritative leader motivates people by making it clear to them how their work fits into a larger vision for the organisation. When the leader gives performance feedback, the main criterion is whether or not that performance furthers the vision. The standards for success are clear to all. Authoritative leaders give people the freedom to innovate, experiment and take calculated risks. The authoritative style tends to work well in many business situations but fails, when the team consists of experts or peers who are more experienced than the leader.

3. The affiliative leader strives to keep employees happy, to create harmony and to increase loyalty by building strong emotional bonds. Affiliative leaders give people the freedom to do their job in the way they think is most effective. Affiliative leaders are likely to take their direct reports out for a meal or a drink, to see how they are doing. They will take out the time to celebrate a group accomplishment. They are natural relationship builders. The affiliative style is effective in many situations, but it is particularly suitable when trying to build team harmony, increase morale, improve communication, or repair broken trust. One problem with the affiliative style is that because of its exclusive focus on praise, employees may perceive that mediocrity is tolerated. And because affiliative leaders rarely offer constructive advice on how to improve, employees must figure out how to do so on their own.

Leading People

4. Democratic leaders increase flexibility and responsibility by letting workers themselves have a say in decisions that affect their goals and how they do their work. By listening to employees' concerns, the democratic leaders learn what to do to keep morale high. People have a say in setting their goals and performance evaluation criteria. So, they tend to be very realistic about what can and cannot be accomplished. But the democratic style can lead to endless meetings and postponement of crucial decisions in the hope that sufficient discussion and debate will eventually yield a great outcome. The democratic style does not make sense when employees are not competent or informed enough to offer sound advice. Such an approach also does not make sense during a crisis.

5. Pacesetting leaders set extremely high-performance standards, are obsessive about doing things better and faster and demand the same from everyone around them. If poor performers do not rise to the occasion, these leaders do not hesitate to replace them with people who can. The pacesetter's demands for excellence can overwhelm employees and their morale drops. Such leaders also give no feedback on how people are doing. They jump in to take over when they think people are lagging. When they leave, people feel directionless as they are so used to "the expert" setting the rules.

6. Coaching leaders help employees identify their unique strengths and weaknesses and consider their personal and career aspirations. They encourage employees to establish long-term development goals and help them conceptualise a plan for attaining them. Coaching leaders excel at delegating, give employees challenging assignments, are willing to put up with short-term failure and focus primarily on personal development. When employees know their boss watches them and cares about what they do, they feel free to experiment. People know what is expected of them and how their work fits into a larger vision or strategy.

The coaching style works particularly well when employees are already aware of their weaknesses and would like to improve their performance. By contrast, the coaching style makes little sense when employees, for whatever reason, are resistant to learning or changing their ways. And it fails if the leader is inept at coaching.

Leading People

The Six Leadership Styles (Goleman)						
	Commanding	Visionary	Affiliative	Democratic	Pacesetting	Coaching
The Leader's Modus Operandi	Demands immediate compliance	Mobilises people towards a vision	Creates harmony and builds emotional bonds	Forges consensus through participation	Sets high standards for performance	Develops people for the future
The style in a phrase	"Do as I say."	"Come with me."	"People come first."	"What do you think?"	"Do at my pace."	"Try this."
Underlying emotional intelligence competencies	Drive to achieve, initiative, self-control	Self-confidence, empathy, change catalyst	Empathy, building relationships, communication	Collaboration, team leadership, communication	Conscientious, drive to achieve, initiative	Developing others, empathy, self-awareness
When the style works best	In a crisis, to kick start a turnaround, or with problem employees	When changes require a new vision, or when a clear direction needed	To heal rifts in a team or to motivate people during stressful circumstances	To build buy-in or consensus, or to get input from valuable employees	To get quick results from a highly motivated and competent team	To help an employee improve performances or develop long-term strengths

The most effective leaders switch flexibly from one style to another, depending on the circumstances.

> *"The best leaders don't know just one style of leadership – they are skilled at several and have the flexibility to switch between styles as the circumstances dictate."*
> – Daniel Goleman.

In practice, each of the six styles has its place and the object of leadership development is to give the leader the necessary versatility skills to choose the appropriate style for each situation and be able to switch between them whilst staying authentic and true to their values and principles.

> *"The business environment is continually changing and a leader must respond in kind. Hour to hour, day to day, week to week, executives must play their leadership styles like a pro – using the right one at just the right time and in the right measure. The payoff is in the results."* – Daniel Goleman.

Leading People

Fred Fiedler - Contingency Theory of Leadership

Fred Fiedler's Contingency Model was the third notable situational model of leadership to emerge. This model appeared first in Fiedler's 1967 book, A Theory of Leadership Effectiveness.

The essence of Fiedler's theory is that a leader's effectiveness depends on a combination of two forces:

- *the leader's leadership style*
  and
- *'Situational favourableness'.*

Fiedler called this combination (of leadership style and 'situational favourableness'):

Situational Contingency.
Fiedler's Contingency Theory of Leadership states that effectiveness as a leader is determined by how well the leadership style matches the situation.

Fiedler's Contingency Theory is not the only contingency theory. Contingency theory is a general theory which says that there is no one singular best way to structure an organisation and lead the team.
Instead, the best way to do this will be contingent on the situation. So, contingency theories examine how best to run the team or organisation given different situations. Another way to say this is that:

the best leadership style will be contingent on the situation.

1. Leadership Style
The first step in using the model is to determine your natural leadership style. To do this, Fiedler developed a scale called the Least Preferred Co-worker (LPC).

To score yourself on this scale you have to describe the co-worker with whom you least prefer to work. Ask the question: What do you think about those people you least prefer working with?

According to the model, the more favourably you rate the person you least prefer to work with, the more relationship oriented you are. The less favourably you rated the person you least like working with, the more task-oriented you are. In other words:

High LPC = Relationship- oriented leader
Low LPC = Task-oriented leader

Leading People

Task-oriented leaders tend to be good at organising teams and projects and getting things done. Relationship-oriented leaders tend to be good at building good relationships and managing conflict to get things done.

2. Situational Favourableness

The next step is to understand the favourableness of the situation you face. This is determined
by how much control over the situation you have as a leader (situational control).

Determining situational favourableness is done by examining the following three factors:

a. **Leader-Member Relations.**
   This factor measures how much your team trusts you. Greater trust increases the favourableness of the situation and less trust reduces it.

b. **Task Structure**
   This factor measures the tasks that need to be performed. Are they clear and precise or vague? Vague tasks decrease the favourableness of the situation and concrete and clear tasks, increase it.

c. **Position Power**
   This is determined by your authority, meaning the power you have to reward or punish your subordinates. As you might expect, having more power increases the situational favourableness.

Leadership Style	Situational Favourableness
Fiedler described two basic leadership styles - task-orientated and relationship-orientated: • Task-orientated leaders have a strong bias towards getting the job done without worrying about their rapport or bond with their followers. They can of course run the risk of failing to deliver if they do not engage enough with the people around them. • Relationship-orientated leaders care much more about emotional engagement with the people they work with, but sometimes to the detriment of the task and results. Fiedler said neither style is inherently superior. However, he asserted that certain leadership challenges suit one style or the other better.	Fiedler defined three factors determining the favourableness of the situation: • How much trust, respect and confidence exists leader and followers. • How precisely the task is defined and how much freedom the leader gives to the followers. • How much the followers accept the leader's power. Fiedler believed the situation is favourable when: • There is high mutual trust, respect and confidence between leader and followers. • The task is clear and controllable. • The followers accept the leader's power. The situation is unfavourable if the opposite is true on all three points

Leading People

The diagram below illustrates this point.

situation favourableness		most effective orientation (style)
high	=	task-oriented leader
high	=	relationship-oriented leader
low	=	task-oriented leader

Effectiveness

Fiedler said that task-orientated leaders are most effective when facing a situation that is either extremely favourable or extremely unfavourable. In other words:

- *when there is enormous trust, respect and confidence,*
- *when the task is very clear and*
- *when followers accept the leader's power without question*

and also, when the opposite is true, i.e. -

- *when trust and respect do not exist,*
- *when the challenge people face is vague and undefined*
- *when the atmosphere is anarchic or even rebellious* (for example, an emergency or crisis)

Fiedler concluded that relationship-orientated leaders are most effective in less extreme circumstances. That is, in situations that are neither favourable or unfavourable, or situations that are only moderately favourable or moderately unfavourable.

Fiedler's theory took a significant and firm view about personality: He said that a leader's style reflected their personality, *(which he assessed in his research using a psychometric instrument).*

Fiedler's view about personality - and indeed the common notion of the times – was that individual personality is fixed and does not change during a leader's life/career. Consequently, Fiedler's theory placed great emphasis on 'matching' leaders to situations, according to the perceived style of the leader and the situation faced (by the organisation).

Fiedler's Contingency Model is therefore a somewhat limited model for effective leadership. Notably it is not a useful guide for helping people become better leaders; nor is it an efficient or necessarily flexible model for modern leadership in organisations, given the dynamic variety of situations which nowadays arise. A further implication of Fiedler's theory is potentially to require the replacement of leaders whose styles do not match situations, which from several viewpoints (legal, practical, ethical, etc) would be simply unworkable in modern organisations.

Nevertheless, despite its limitations, Fiedler's theory was an important contribution to leadership thinking, especially in reinforcing the now generally accepted views that:

Leading People

- There is no single ideal way of behaving as a leader and
- Matching leadership behaviour (or style) to circumstances (or situations) – or vice-versa - is significant in effective leadership.

Personality
Fiedler's theory also encourages us to consider the leader's personality and the leader's behaviour from these angles:

- the extent to which (a leader's) personality is fixed and
- the extent to which (a leader's) personality controls (a leader's) behaviour.

Clearly, if a model such as this is to be of great value, then these questions need to be clarified rather more than they have been to date, which is not easy given the complexity of human nature.

Summary
We are left to conclude somewhat conditionally, that if personality is fixed (which generally it is) and personality controls behaviour, (which generally it seems to) then…the notion of:

- 'matching behaviour to the circumstances'

    probably equates unavoidably to:

- 'matching the person to the circumstances',

Which is usually not a viable approach to leadership and leadership development within modern organisations.

We live in an increasingly virtual world which allows lots of inter-changeability (like 'matrix management' for example - where followers may have two different bosses for two different sets of responsibilities, such as local markets vs international markets), but most indications are that frequently changing leaders in order to match fixed leadership behaviours to corresponding and suitable situations is less efficient and effective than organisations having leaders who can adapt freely outside of and despite, individual personality constraints.

Using Fiedler's Contingency Model
To use Fiedler's Contingency Theory of Leadership, follow these steps.

Step 1. Identify your Leadership Style
The first step is to determine your preferred leadership style using the LPC scale.
You can use the following table to score yourself on the LPC scale. Fill in your answers keeping in mind the one person that you least like to work with.

Leading People

Negative	Score								Positive
Unpleasant	1	2	3	4	5	6	7	8	Pleasant
Rejecting	1	2	3	4	5	6	7	8	Accepting
Tense	1	2	3	4	5	6	7	8	Relaxed
Cold	1	2	3	4	5	6	7	8	Warm
Boring	1	2	3	4	5	6	7	8	Interesting
Backbiting	1	2	3	4	5	6	7	8	Loyal
Uncooperative	1	2	3	4	5	6	7	8	Co-operative
Hostile	1	2	3	4	5	6	7	8	Supportive
Guarded	1	2	3	4	5	6	7	8	Open
Insincere	1	2	3	4	5	6	7	8	Sincere
Unkind	1	2	3	4	5	6	7	8	Kind
Inconsiderate	1	2	3	4	5	6	7	8	Considerate
Untrustworthy	1	2	3	4	5	6	7	8	Trustworthy
Gloomy	1	2	3	4	5	6	7	8	Cheerful
Quarrelsome	1	2	3	4	5	6	7	8	Harmonious

You can now calculate your LPC score by totalling all the numbers you circled. You can interpret your score as follows:

> ***73 and above:*** *You are a relationship-oriented leader.*
> ***54 and below:*** *You are a task-oriented leader.*
> ***Between 55 and 72:*** *You are a mixture of both and it is up to you to determine which style suits you the best.*

Step 2: Understand your Situation
To understand the situation you are facing, answer the following questions:

- Is trust with your team high or low (member relations)?
- Are tasks vague or clear-cut and well understood (task structure)?
- Is your authority low or high (position power)?

The easiest way to do this is to score each answer from 1 to 10, with 10 representing the highest value.

Step 3: Find the Right Leadership Style
Now that we understand how we like to lead and we understand the situation we are facing, we are in a position to determine if we have the right style for the situation we are facing.

Leading People

Advantages and Disadvantages

The advantages of Fiedler's Contingency Theory of Leadership are:

- It provides a simple rule of thumb for identifying which leaders are best for which situations.
- Unlike many other leadership theories, it takes the situation into account in determining the effectiveness of a leader.
- Both the LPC and the situational factors are easy to measure.

The disadvantages of Fiedler's Contingency of Leadership are:

- It is not flexible at all. If your leadership style does not match the situation, that is it. Game over. You need to be replaced. There is nothing you can do to change the situation.
- The LPC scale is subjective and so it is possible to incorrectly assess your own leadership style.
- If you happen to fall in the middle of the LPC scale, then there is no guidance as to which kind of leader you might be.
- Your assessment of the situation is subjective. This means you may incorrectly assess the situation and consequently, you may incorrectly determine what kind of leader is required.

Summary
Fiedler's Contingency Theory of Leadership states that your effectiveness as a leader is determined by how well your leadership style matches the situation.

The theory is based on the premise that each of us has one and only one leadership style which can be scored on the Least Preferred Co-worker (LPC) scale. Using this LPC scale you are either a relationship-oriented leader or a task-oriented leader.

According to Fiedler, task-oriented leaders get the best results when faced with strongly favourable or strongly unfavourable situations. In situations of mixed favourableness then relationship-oriented leaders get the best results.

It is important to realise that in Fiedler's Contingency Theory your leadership style is fixed. You cannot change your style to suit the situation. Instead, you must put leaders into situations that match their style.

This puts the theory at odds with more modern contingency theories such as situational leadership.
There are two important factors in Fiedler's Contingency Theory: leadership style and situational favourableness.

Leading People

Tannenbaum and Schmidt Continuum

The Leadership Continuum was developed by Robert Tannenbaum and Warren Schmidt in their 1958 article, "How to Choose a Leadership Pattern".

The Tannenbaum-Schmidt Leadership Continuum is a model showing the relationship between the level of authority you use as a leader and the freedom this allows your team. At one end of the continuum are managers who simply tell their employees what to do. At the other end of the continuum are managers who are completely hands off.

This is a positive way for both teams and managers to develop. As a manager, one of your responsibilities is to develop your team. You should delegate and ask a team to make its own decisions to varying degrees according to their abilities. There is a rising scale of levels of delegated freedom that you can use when working with your team. The Tannenbaum and Schmidt Continuum is often shown as a simple graph:

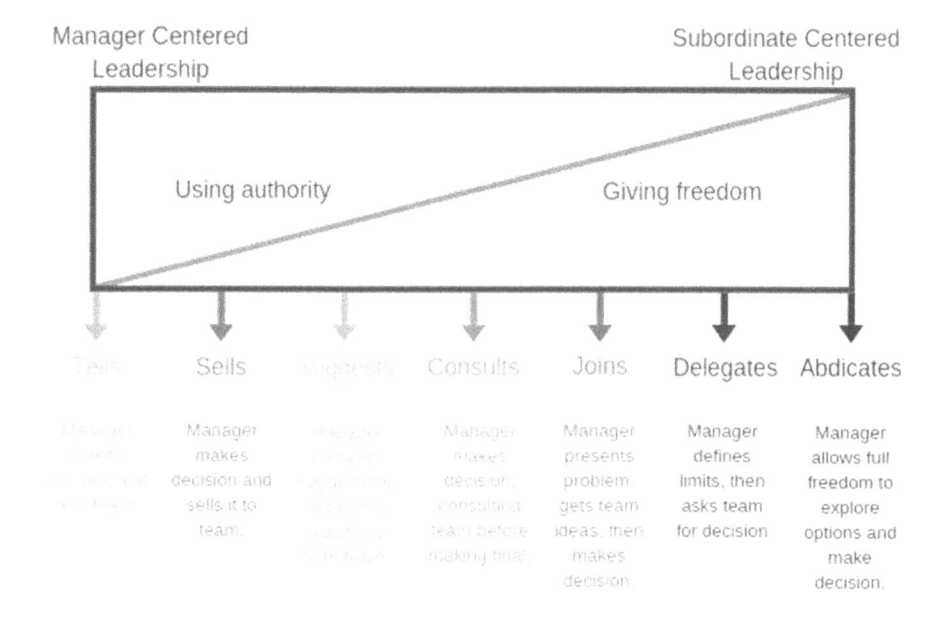

Tells	Sells	Suggests	Consults	Joins	Delegates	Abbdicates
Manager makes decision and tells team.	Manager makes decision and sells it to team.	Manager suggests decision and invites questions.	Manager makes decision, consults team before making final.	Manager presents problem, gets team ideas, then makes decision.	Manager defines limits, then asks team for decision.	Manager allows full freedom to explore options and make decision.

As you move from one end of the continuum to the other, the level of freedom you give your team will increase and your use of authority will decrease. Most managers and leaders will lie somewhere in the middle between these two extremes.

Over time, a leader should aim to take the team from one end to the other, up the scale, at which point you should also aim to have developed one or a number of potential successors from within your team to take over from you. This process can take a year or two, or even longer, so be patient, explain what you are doing and be aware constantly of how your team is responding and developing.

Leading People

Continuum Extremes
Before getting into the details of the points along the continuum, it is important to understand the extremes that mark each end. On one end of the spectrum, we find Manager-Oriented Leadership.

This means that the leader acts mostly like a dictator, telling the team members what to do and leaving very little (or no) room for negotiation. Most commonly, this is a strategy employed by leaders who are dealing with an inexperienced team, or a tight deadline that they have to meet. However, even the strictest leader will typically leave at least a little room for discussion and collaboration.

At the other end is what is called Team-Oriented Leadership. As you might imagine, this is a leader who provide their team with plenty of flexibility and encourages collaboration and the sharing of ideas. Usually, this sort of latitude will only be afforded to a team that has a high level of experience and acumen in a given area. This kind of leader must have a great deal of trust in their team in order to trust them with such freedom.

Within those extremes, the Tannenbaum-Schmidt Leadership Continuum highlights seven points along the way which can be used to describe various leadership styles.

When examining and applying the Tannenbaum and Schmidt principles, it is extremely important to remember; irrespective of the amount of responsibility and freedom delegated by a manager to a team, the manager retains accountability for any catastrophic problems that result. Delegating freedom and decision-making responsibility to a team absolutely does not absolve the manager of accountability.

That is why delegating, whether to teams or individuals, requires a very grown-up manager. If everything goes well, the team must get the credit; if it all goes horribly wrong, the manager must take the blame. This is entirely fair, because the manager is ultimately responsible for judging the seriousness of any given situation - including the risks entailed - and the level of freedom that can safely be granted to the team to deal with it. This is not actually part of the Tannenbaum and Schmidt Continuum, but it is vital to apply this philosophy, or the model will definitely be weakened, or at worse completely back-fire.

Using the Tannenbaum-Schmidt Leadership Continuum is an excellent way to understand the various approaches that leaders can take to managing their teams. Since it is more nuanced than many other leadership theories, a wider variety of leaders will find this tool to be a useful one. As you prepare to lead a new team, or work on improving the performance of your current team, consider the various styles represented within this model.

Step 1: The Manager decides and announces the decision.
The manager reviews options in light of aims, issues, priorities, timescale, etc., then decides the action and informs the team of the decision. The manager will probably have considered how the team will react, but the team plays no active part in making the decision. The team may well perceive that the manager has not considered the team's welfare at all. This is seen by the team as a purely task-based decision, which is generally a characteristic of X-Theory management style.

Leading People

Step 2: The manager decides and then 'sells' the decision to the group.
The manager makes the decision as in 1 above and then explains reasons for the decision to the team, particularly the positive benefits that the team will enjoy from the decision. In so doing the manager is seen by the team to recognise the team's importance and to have some concern for the team.

Step 3: The manager presents the decision with background ideas and invites questions.
The manager presents the decision along with some of the background which led to the decision. The team is invited to ask questions and discuss with the manager the rationale behind the decision, which enables the team to understand and accept or agree with the decision more easily than in 1 and 2 above. This more participative and involving approach enables the team to appreciate the issues and reasons for the decision and the implications of all the options. This will have a more motivational approach than 1 or 2 because of the higher level of team involvement and discussion.

Step 4: The manager suggests a provisional decision and invites discussion about it.
The manager discusses and reviews the provisional decision with the team on the basis that the manager will take on board the views and then finally decide. This enables the team to have some real influence over the shape of the manager's final decision. This also acknowledges that the team has something to contribute to the decision-making process, which is more involving and therefore motivating than the previous level.

Step 5: The manager presents the situation or problem, gets suggestions, then decides.
The manager presents the situation and maybe some options, to the team. The team is encouraged and expected to offer ideas and additional options and discuss implications of each possible course of action. The manager then decides which option to take. This level is one of high and specific involvement for the team and is appropriate particularly when the team has more detailed knowledge or experience of the issues than the manager. Being high-involvement and high-influence for the team this level provides more motivation and freedom than any previous level.

Step 6: The manager explains the situation, defines the parameters and asks the team to decide.
At this level, the manager has effectively delegated responsibility for the decision to the team, albeit within the manager's stated limits. The manager may or may not choose to be a part of the team which decides. While this level appears to give a huge responsibility to the team, the manager can control the risk and outcomes to an extent, according to the constraints that he stipulates. This level is more motivational than any previous and requires a mature team for any serious situation or problem. (Remember that the team must get the credit for all the positive outcomes from the decision, while the manager remains accountable for any resulting problems or disasters. This is not strictly included in the original Tannenbaum and Schmidt definitions, so it needs pointing out because it is such an important aspect of delegating and motivating and leadership.)

Step 7: The manager allows the team to identify the problem, develop the options and decide on the action, within the manager's received limits.

Leading People

This is obviously an extreme level of freedom, whereby the team is effectively doing what the manager did in level 1. The team is given responsibility for identifying and analysing the situation or problem; the process for resolving it; developing and assessing options; evaluating implications and then deciding on and implementing a course of action.

The manager also states in advance that they will support the decision and help the team implement it. The manager may or may not be part of the team and if so then they have no more authority than anyone else in the team. The only constraints and parameters for the team are the ones that the manager had imposed on him from above. *(Again, the manager retains accountability for any resulting disasters, while the team must get the credit for all successes.)*

This level is potentially the most motivational of all, but also potentially the most disastrous. Not surprisingly the team must be mature and competent and capable of acting at what is a genuinely strategic decision-making level.

Advantages and Disadvantages
The advantages of the Tannenbaum-Schmidt Leadership Continuum include:

- *As a leader, it gives you a range of ways in which to involve and interact with your team.*
- *Allows you to understand how your approach should change over time as the situation changes.*
- *Allows experimentation. You can try giving more responsibility to your team, but if that does not work and the team is not ready, you can take a step back.*
- *It provides an incremental way to increase or reduce your team's involvement in decision making.*
- *The disadvantages of the Tannenbaum-Schmidt Leadership Continuum include that it:*
    - *Only examines the process of giving a task to the team, not what happens next.*
    - *Ignores soft factors such as cultural norms and office politics.*
    - *Does not provide a mechanism to determine what is the right approach from the continuum for the team. It leaves that up to the leader.*

Leading People

Hersey and Blanchard's Situational Leader

Paul Hersey and Ken Blanchard first published their Situational Leadership® Model in their 1982 book, Management of Organisational Behaviour: Utilising Human Resources.

The concept has become perhaps the best known of all the Situational/Contingency models.

The Situational Leadership® model is sophisticated. Its notable features are briefly that the model:

- *Focuses on followers, rather than wider workplace circumstances.*
- *Asserts that leaders should change their behaviour according to the type of followers.*
- *Proposes a 'continuum' or progression of leadership adaptation in response to the development of followers.*

Given the Situational Leadership®, it is useful to note that Hersey and Blanchard used the word 'situational' chiefly to suggest adaptability, more than the situation in which people operate.

In fact, Situational Leadership® focuses firmly on the follower(s), rather than the wider situation and workplace circumstances and the model particularly asserts that a group's performance depends mostly on how followers respond to the leader.

Situational Leadership® theory is commonly shown as classifying followers according to a 2x2 matrix, using the highs and lows of two criteria, thereby giving four types of follower groups. The term 'follower' may be interpreted to apply to an entire group for situations in which members possess similar levels of capability and experience. The criteria of the followers are:

1. *Competence*
2. *Confidence and commitment*

    Alternatively:

1. *Ability*
2. *Willingness*

Logically the four group types are:

1. *Low Competence/Low Confidence and commitment*
2. *Low Competence/High Confidence and commitment*
3. *High Competence/Low Confidence and commitment*
4. *High Competence/High Confidence and commitment*

Leading People

or more simply:

1. *Unable and Unwilling*
2. *Unable but Willing*
3. *Able but Unwilling*
4. *Able and Willing*

Extending the logic of this, Hersey and Blanchard further described and presented these four follower 'situations' as requiring relatively high or low leadership emphasis on the Task and the Relationship.
Example:

- *a high task emphasis equates to giving very clear guidance to followers as to aims and methods.*
- *a low task emphasis equates to giving followers freedom in deciding methods and perhaps even aims.*
- *a high Relationship emphasis equates to working closely and sensitively with followers.*
- *a low Relationship emphasis equates to detachment or remoteness and either a trust in people's emotional robustness, or a disregard for emotional reactions. This 'low relationship' aspect is also called 'separated'.*

- **High Task means followers have Low Ability.**
- **Low Task means followers have High Ability.**
- **High Relationship means followers are Willing.**
- **Low Relationship means followers are Unwilling.**
  (Note that 'Unwilling' may be because of lack of confidence and/or because the aims/goals are not accepted. It is possible for a group of followers to be good at their jobs, but not committed to the aims/task.)

The high/low Task/Relationship dimensions feature strongly in the diagrams and applications that Hersey and Blanchard developed around the Situational Leadership® theory.

The logic can be represented helpfully as a simple practical concise 'leadership styles guide', as below, including the continuum, by which the leader changes styles in response to the growing / different maturity of followers.

Leading People

Follower 'Situation'	Leadership Style Emphasis	H & B Terminology	Description	Continuum
Unable and Unwilling	high task - low relationship	Telling	instruction, direction, autocratic	M1
Unable but Willing	high task - high relationship	Selling	persuasion, encouragement, incentive	M2
Able but Unwilling	low task - high relationship	Participating	involvement, consultation, teamwork	M3
Able and Willing	low task - low relationship	Delegating	trust, empowerment, responsibility	M4

The model also proposes a 'continuum' or progression of leadership adaptation in response to the typical development of followers.

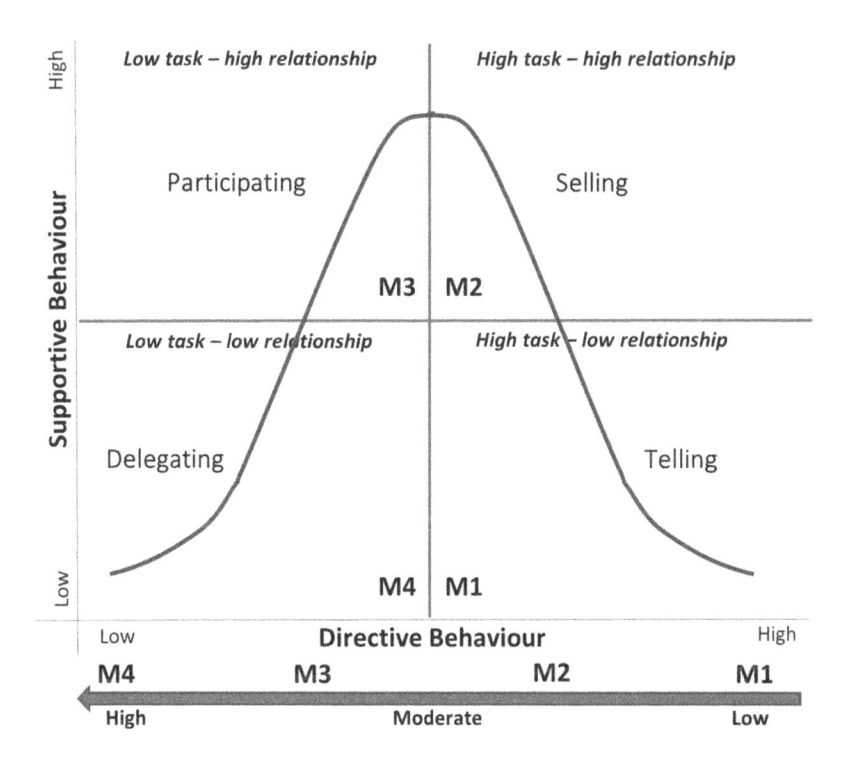

Hersey and Blanchard used the word 'maturity' in referring to the continuum of follower development, requiring and enabling a leader to change leadership style through the stages outlined above. Here 'maturity' entails experience, skills, confidence, commitment, etc - a

Leading People

combination of the two main 'follower' criteria, namely Ability and Willingness (Competence and Confidence/Commitment), which we can also interpret to be the follower's ability to self-manage or self-lead.

According to Paul Hersey and Ken Blanchard the leader will have to adapt his style to match the level of maturity of the employee. As their maturity increases, the independence of the employee also increases.

Consequently, four leadership styles are created within situational leadership.

M1: Telling (Directing)
At this level, the leader must deal with employees that are not competent and (still) unmotivated. This may have different causes. New and/or inexperienced employees are not capable enough to carry out tasks independently. It may be experienced as threatening when an employee is not competent enough to perform a task. This might cause him to postpone the task or do this unwillingly. Good instruction and monitoring of the entire work process would be the best style of leadership in this situation. This is also sometimes referred to as task-oriented leadership with little or no concern for human relationships and support.

The employee will receive a lot of direction from the leader when it comes to the tasks they have to fulfil. Not just the final objective is made clear, but also the steps that must be taken along the way. That is why he needs specific instructions in the form of composed tasks. The leader makes the final decisions. It helps to compliment the employee about progress he is making and not overburdening him with too much information at once. It is a good idea for a leader to have the employee repeat in his own words what he is supposed to do. That way, it becomes clear if the instructions have been correctly understood.

M2: Selling (Coaching)
At this level, the employees have a desire to work independently but they are not capable of doing this yet. They are employees who have not reached full maturity and are hindered by circumstances for example a change or a reform of the organisation. This employee wants to set to work enthusiastically but he cannot work independently because of his lack of skills and knowledge. A situation like this might make an employee insecure. By explaining his decision-making and by listening to the employee and giving him undivided attention, the leader is guiding him. This style can be compared to the consultative leadership style.

This leadership style is also called selling for a reason; the leader has to 'sell' the tasks to the employee and convince him that he is able to do them. Specific instructions are important here, as are communication at a level of equals. The leader makes the decisions, but it is good if the employee asks questions and wants to know the purpose of the task. When the employee shows progress, he should be complimented to make him feel confident about his skills.

M3: Participating (Supporting)
At this level, the employees are capable but (temporarily) unwilling. They are qualified workers but because of the number of tasks, they might get the idea that they are being

Leading People

inundated with work. This can make them insecure and reluctant. To take away this insecurity, it is important that the leader confers with the employees and supports them in their work. By having employees participate in the decision-making process, acceptance will increase and the employees will be able to work independently again. It is also possible that a mistake has been made for which the employee blames himself. This can make him stagnate and lose confidence. That is why support from the leader is important.

The employee needs to be stimulated and must get back the confidence to make decisions independently again. It is a good idea for the leader to give that confidence to the employee and remind him of other tasks and projects that he did do well in the past. This type of employee can benefit from some calm, face-to-face brainstorming or sparring about a question or an issue. That increases his confidence and makes his superior someone he can talk to. The employee is allowed to take some risks and trust in his own abilities.

M4: Delegating

At this level the employees can and want to carry out their tasks independently, they have a high level of task maturity, as a result of which they need less support. Employees inform the leader about their progress of their own accord and at the same time they indicate when problems present themselves or when the work is stagnating. They become motivated because of their independence and as a result a leader does not have to consult with them continuously.

Delegating may seem easy, but it rarely is in practice. It is a good idea for a leader to discuss the final goal with the employee, when the task must be (deadline) and how he plans to carry it out. It is possible to plan evaluation moments in order to monitor progress and check if everything is going according to plan. The leader must realise that delegating involves keeping distance; the employee is responsible for the decisions. If things go well, compliments are in order. Boosting confidence and letting go are the foundational techniques of delegating.

Through situational leadership, leadership behaviour is immediately adjusted to the employee's behaviour. According to Hershey and Blanchard the main factors are independence and suitability. Based on these two factors, they directly link four situational leadership styles. It should be noted that a leader must be willing to be very flexible with respect to his employees. In addition, employees will always develop themselves in the (positive) direction of delegating (M4).

Hersey and Blanchard clearly mapped a progression of changing leadership styles in response to the tendency for people's maturity to increase over time.

This aspect aligns somewhat with the Tannenbaum and Schmidt Continuum model, specifically limited to where both models can apply to group maturity/capability development. That is, under certain circumstances, a leader adapts his/her behaviour progressively, in response to followers' growing maturity/capability, usually over many months, potentially from the inception or inheritance of a new team, ultimately to when the team can self-manage, perhaps even (and some would say ideally) to be led by a new leader who has emerged from the team to succeed the departing leader.

Leading People

Hersey and Blanchard's 2x2 matrix, or four-square grid, has become a much-referenced tool and proprietary training method, for teaching and applying the Situational Leadership® model, notably matching the four leadership behaviours/styles to corresponding follower situations (or to 'entire group' situations, subject to the provisions already explained, that followers must possess similar levels of ability and experience as each other):

		Task / Ability	
		Low	High
Relationship / Willingness	High	**Participating** (Supporting) M3	**Selling** (Coaching) M2
	Low	**Delegating** M4	**Telling** (Directing) M1

Here are Hersey and Blanchard's matched sets of four follower types with four corresponding leadership styles, in order of the suggested continuum or progression coinciding with increasing follower maturity:

	Follower type	Leadership Style or Behaviour
1	Follower lacks experience or skill and confidence to do the task and may also lack willingness.	**Telling** - Leader gives precise firm instructions and deadlines and closely monitors progress.
2	Follower lacks the ability, perhaps due to lack of experience, but is enthusiastic for the work.	**Selling** - Leader explains goals, tasks, methods and reasons and remains available to give support.
3	Follower is capable and experienced but lacks confidence or commitment and may question the goal or task.	**Participating** - Leader works with follower(s), involved with group, seeks input and encourages efforts.
4	Follower is capable, experienced, confident and committed to the goals.	**Delegating** - Leader gives responsibility to followers for setting goals, planning and execution.

Leading People

Vroom Yetton Jago Decision Model

The Vroom Yetton Jago Decision Model was originally developed by Victor Vroom and Phillip Yetton in 1973 and it was expanded 15 years later by supplementations from Arthur Jago.

The Vroom Yetton Jago Decision Model is a model for decision-making that is based on situational leadership. The model can be used by everyone, irrespective of rank or position and helps to choose the right management style in various decision situations. In some business situations, it is better that the leader takes all the decisions, whereas in other situations it is better if the group has a say.

The Vroom Yetton Jago Decision Model helps to choose the right style by having the user answer a series of questions with either yes or no. This series of questions is presented in the form of a decision matrix. After answering the questions, the user immediately sees what method best suits the situation concerned.

According to the model, three specific factors have direct influence on the method for decision making: quality, collaboration and time. The series of questions creates clarity regarding the influence of these factors in the decision situation. Subsequently, the model displays how the leader should make the decision: independently, together with the group or after obtaining advice. There are five different situations in total in which a different approach is desired and effective.

Three Factors in Decision-making
When a decision must be made, the desired management style and the degree of participation of team members are influenced by three important factors. The Vroom Yetton Jago Decision Model therefore demands proper thought before answering the series of questions. By considering the three specific factors, better insight is formed about the decision to be made. The following three factors are important in each decision situation:

The Quality of the Decision
The quality of the decision to be taken is about how much impact the decision will have and how important it is to find the right solution. The higher the decision's quality, the more people must be involved in the decision process.

Involvement and Collaboration
Involvement and collaboration concerns the question of how important it is that everyone agrees to the decision in a team. Depending on how important this is, the degree of participation must be raised or lowered.

Time Constraints
How much time is there to take decision? If there's little time, a fast, autocratic approach might be more desirable, as there is no time to lose in certain situations. If there is a lot of time, there are more options to involve more team players in the decision process.

The way in which these factors influence the situation helps the user to determine what the best leadership style and decision method are.

Leading People

Five Decision-making Styles
The Vroom Yetton Jago Decision Model distinguishes between three leadership styles and five different decision processes:

Autocratic I (A1)
In this decision process, the leader uses the available information to make a decision independently. The opinion of team members or external parties is not consulted in this case. Although the decision itself is not dependent upon the team members and their opinion does not matter, it is important that the decision is communicated openly and clearly towards the team.

Autocratic II (A2)
Here too, the leader independently makes the decision, but the difference with autocratic style 1 is that the leader has a bit more time and gathers information from team members or external parties. The team members do not know why information is requested from them and do not think about the situation, alternative or eventual choice.

Consultative I (C1)
The leader adopts a consulting role and actively takes the lead to have team members individually give their opinion about the situation, the problem and the decision to be made. Here, the team's involvement is higher than in the autocratic decision-making style. However, the decision is still made by the leader; he can choose to disregard the team's opinion and input when these have not changed his outlook on the situation.

Consultative II (C2)
Where the leader requests the individual opinions from the team members in the first consulting style, he brings the team together in a group meeting for a discussion in the second. Ideas and suggestions are asked for in this meeting. Here, the leader shares the problem and the situation with the group, but eventually, the leader is still the one to individually make the decision.

Group II (G2)
The group as a whole makes the decision. The leader presents the situation and the problem to the group, identifies alternatives and makes a consensus decision. The leader purely plays the role of facilitator and accepts the decision of the group without considering his own opinion or vision.

In order to determine which of these styles and processes is most suitable, considering the three factors, the decision tree from the Vroom-Yetton-Jago Decision Model must be completed.

Determining the Right Decision Style
Vroom, Yetton and Jago developed eight questions that must be answered with yes or no to arrive at the right decision style. All the questions have a certain theme. These themes are represented by the abbreviations in the model. The eight questions must be answered in the order below by the leader so as to determine the right leadership style and decision method.

Leading People

1. Is the quality of the decision very important? Are the consequences of possible failure significant? – QR (quality requirement)
2. Is a successful result dependent upon the team members? – CR (commitment requirement)
3. Does the leader have sufficient information to make an important decision alone? – LI (leader's information)
4. Has the problem been defined and structured properly so it can be easily understood what needs to be done and what a good solution might be? - ST (problem structure)
5. When a leader makes the decision himself, is it likely to assume that the team is sufficiently involved and motivated and will accept the decision? – CP (commitment probability)
6. Are the goals of the team consistent with the goals of the organisation that have been set to define a successful solution? – GC (goal congruence)
7. If the team has to make a decision, are conflicts expected about the decision to be made and solution? – CO (subordinate Conflicts)
8. Do the team members and other external parties have sufficient information to make an important decision? – SI (subordinate information)

Use the visualisation of the model to answer the questions step by step and arrive at the right style of decision-making. All the way to the right in the image of the model, an arrow is used to indicate which decision method is most suitable for the situation.

Advantages and Disadvantages

The main advantage of the Vroom, Yetton, Jago Decision Model is that it can flexibly be used in many situations. The capacity to organise the decision process is a quality of the model many a leader could use to their advantage. Each situation demands a different approach and practically every situation can be considered with this model.

On the other hand, the model also has several shortcomings. For instance, the personal factors and characteristics of the leader are not considered and the questions in the model might not be specific enough to determine the ideal decision method.

Additionally, users of the model also indicate that they have doubts regarding the Vroom Yetton Jago Decision Model's effectiveness to determine the decision strategy for important decisions the outcomes of which influence a large team.

Leading People

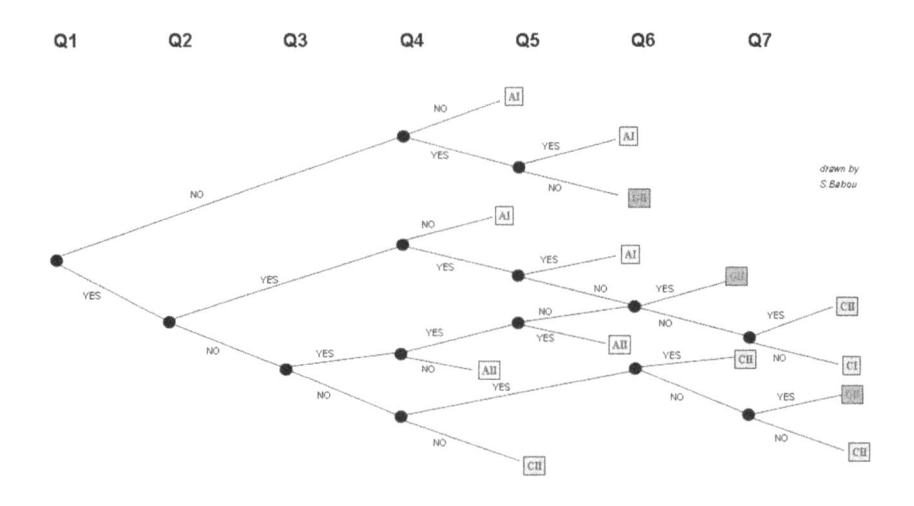

House's Path-Goal Leadership Theory

The theory was developed by Robert House and has its roots in the expectancy theory of motivation. The theory is based on the premise that an employee's perception of expectancies between his effort and performance is greatly affected by a leader's behaviour.

The leaders help group members in attaining rewards by clarifying the paths to goals and removing obstacles to performance. They do so by providing the information, support and other resources which are required by employees to complete the task.

House's theory advocates servant leadership. As per servant leadership theory, leadership is not viewed as a position of power. Rather, leaders act as coaches and facilitators to their subordinates. According to House's path-goal theory, a leader's effectiveness depends on several employee and environmental contingent factors and certain leadership styles.

These are explained below:

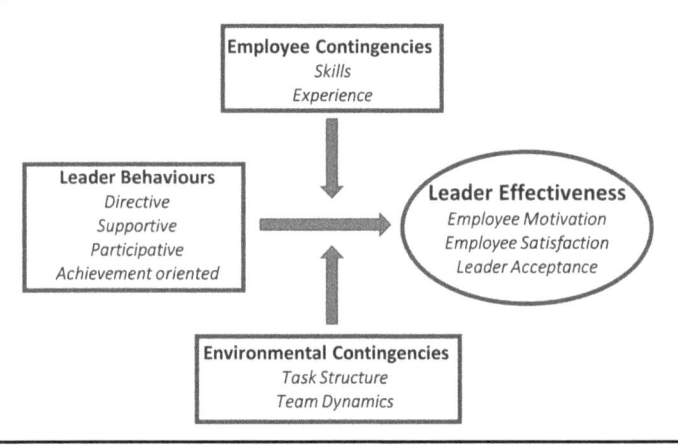

Level 5: Operations / Departmental Manager

Leading People

Leadership Styles
The four leadership styles are:

- *Directive:* Here the leader provides guidelines, lets subordinates know what is expected of them, sets performance standards for them and controls behaviour when performance standards are not met. He makes judicious use of rewards and disciplinary action. The style is the same as task-oriented one.
- *Supportive:* The leader is friendly towards subordinates and displays personal concern for their needs, welfare and well-being. This style is the same as people-oriented leadership.
- *Participative:* The leader believes in group decision-making and shares information with subordinates. He consults his subordinates on important decisions related to work, task goals and paths to resolve goals.
- *Achievement-oriented:* The leader sets challenging goals and encourages employees to reach their peak performance. The leader believes that employees are responsible enough to accomplish challenging goals.

According to the theory, these leadership styles are not mutually exclusive and leaders are capable of selecting more than one kind of a style suited for a particular situation.

Contingencies
The theory states that each of these styles will be effective in some situations but not in others. It further states that the relationship between a leader's style and effectiveness is dependent on the following variables:

- *Employee characteristics:* These include factors such as employees' needs, locus of control, experience, perceived ability, satisfaction, willingness to leave the organisation and anxiety. For example, if followers are high inability, a directive style of leadership may be unnecessary; instead, a supportive approach may be preferable.

- *Characteristics of work environment:* These include factors such as task structure and team dynamics that are outside the control of the employee. For example, for employees performing simple and routine tasks, a supportive style is much effective than a directive one. Similarly, the participative style works much better for non-routine tasks than routine ones.

When team cohesion is low, a supportive leadership style must be used whereas in a situation where performance-oriented team norms exist, a directive style or possibly an achievement-oriented style works better. Leaders should apply directive style to counteract team norms that oppose the team's formal objectives.

The theory has been subjected to empirical testing in several studies and has received considerable research support. This theory consistently reminds the leaders that their main role as a leader is to assist the subordinates in defining their goals and then to assist them in

Leading People

accomplishing those goals in the most efficient and effective manner. This theory gives a guide map to the leaders about how to increase subordinate's satisfaction and performance level.

John Adair's Action-Centred Leadership

John Adair, born 1934, British, developed his Action Centred Leadership model while lecturing at Sandhurst Royal Military Academy and as assistant director and head of leadership department at The Industrial Society. This was during the 1960s and 70s, so in terms of management theories, Adair's work is relatively recent.

His work certainly encompasses and endorses much of the previous thinking on human needs and motivation by Maslow, Herzberg and Fayol and his theory adds an elegant and simple additional organisational dimension to these earlier works. Very importantly, Adair was probably the first to demonstrate that leadership is a trainable, transferable skill, rather than it being an exclusively inborn ability.

The Action Centred Leadership model is Adair's best-known work, in which the three elements - Achieving the Task, Developing the Team and Developing Individuals - are mutually dependent, as well as being separately essential to the overall leadership role.

John Adair's action-centred leadership task-team-individual model adapts extremely well for the demands of modern business management. When using it in your own environment think about the aspects of performance necessary for success in your own situation and incorporate local relevant factors into the model to create your own interpretation. This will give you a very useful management framework:

Managerial Responsibilities: The Task

- identify aims and vision for the group, purpose and direction - define the activity (the task)
- identify resources, people, processes, systems and tools (inc. financials, communications, IT)
- create the plan to achieve the task - deliverables, measures, timescales, strategy and tactics

Leading People

- establish responsibilities, objectives, accountabilities and measures, by agreement and delegation
- set standards, quality, time and reporting parameters
- control and maintain activities against parameters
- monitor and maintain overall performance against plan
- report on progress towards the group's aim
- review, re-assess, adjust plan, methods and targets as necessary

Managerial Responsibilities: **The Group**

- establish, agree and communicate standards of performance and behaviour
- establish style, culture, approach of the group - soft skill elements
- monitor and maintain discipline, ethics, integrity and focus on objectives
- anticipate and resolve group conflict, struggles or disagreements
- assess and change as necessary the balance and composition of the group
- develop team-working, cooperation, morale and team-spirit
- develop the collective maturity and capability of the group - progressively increase group freedom and authority
- encourage the team towards objectives and aims - motivate the group and provide a collective sense of purpose
- identify, develop and agree team- and project-leadership roles within group
- enable, facilitate and ensure effective internal and external group communications
- identify and meet group training needs
- give feedback to the group on overall progress; consult with and seek feedback and input from the group

Managerial Responsibilities: **The Individuals**

- understand the team members as individuals - personality, skills, strengths, needs, aims and fears
- assist and support individuals - plans, problems, challenges, highs and lows
- identify and agree appropriate individual responsibilities and objectives
- give recognition and praise to individuals - acknowledge effort and good work
- where appropriate reward individuals with extra responsibility, advancement and status
- identify, develop and utilise each individual's capabilities and strengths
- train and develop individual team members
- develop individual freedom and authority

Core Functions

Adair set out these core functions of leadership and says they are vital to the Action Centered Leadership model:

- ***Planning*** - seeking information, defining tasks, setting aims
- ***Initiating*** - briefing, task allocation, setting standards

Leading People

- **Controlling** - maintaining standards, ensuring progress, ongoing decision-making
- **Supporting** - individuals' contributions, encouraging, team spirit, reconciling, morale
- **Informing** - clarifying tasks and plans, updating, receiving feedback and interpreting
- **Evaluating** - feasibility of ideas, performance, enabling self-assessment

The Action Centred Leadership model, therefore, does not stand alone, it must be part of an integrated approach to managing and leading and also which should include a strong emphasis on applying these principles through training.

Adair also promotes a '50:50 rule' which he applies to various situations involving two possible influencers, e.g., the view that 50% of motivation lies with the individual and 50% comes from external factors, among them leadership from another. This contradicts most of the motivation gurus who assert that most motivation is from within the individual. He also suggests that 50% of team building success comes from the team and 50% from the leader.

The 3-D Leadership Model – Bill Reddin

Prof Bill Reddin identified 2 fundamental dimensions relating to leadership.

> **Task orientation:** being the extent to which the manager directs both the personal and subordinate's efforts through planning, organising and control
> **Relationship orientation**: is being dependent on the manager's personal job relationship is characterised by the consideration of subordinates' feelings, mutual trust and encouragement.

The combination of task orientation and relationship orientation determines a manager's basic type of behaviour and these are identified as the following which form the basis of the 3-D leadership model

> **Integrated type -** high relationship orientation/l task orientation
> **related type -** high relationship orientation low task orientation
> **dedicated type** - low relationship orientation/hi task orientation
> **separated type** - low relationship orientation/low task orientation

Reddin added to his model to include 8 further styles identifying four he labelled as being appropriate four as inappropriate, measuring the level of effectiveness of each style. This was represented as a grid, naming it the 3-D theory of managerial effectiveness.

Leading People

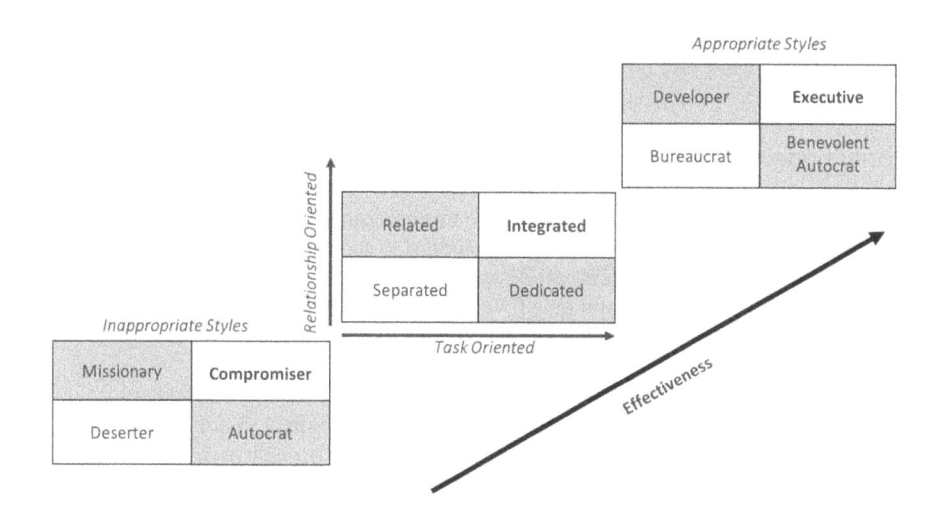

The eight additional management styles at the more or less effective ends of this grid are described below:

More effective styles

Bureaucratic -low concerns about the task in the relationship, interested mainly in the rules and procedures to control the situation, possibly conscientious

Benevolent autocrat -high concern for the task, low conserve relationships, know what they want to achieve and how to achieve it without causing undue resentment

Developer - high conserve relationships, low concerns a task, as implicit trust in people is concerned mainly with developing them as individuals

Executive - high consent of both the task and relationships a good motivator, sets high standards, treats people as individuals and favours team working and management

Less effective styles

Deserter - low concerns about the task and relationships in a situation where such behaviour is inappropriate, lacks involvement and is negative

Autocrat - high concern for the task of low conserve relationships of a situation where such behaviour is inappropriate, lacks confidence in others, unpleasant and interested only in the task at hand

Missionary - high conserve relationships and low conserve the task where such behaviour is inappropriate, interested mainly preserving harmony in the work environment

Compromiser - high conserve about the task and relationship in a situation requiring high concerns and neither author only one, poor decision-making, easily influenced by pressures out of the situation, avoids immediate problems at the expense of maximising long-term output

Leading People

Reddin stated that the manager must be adaptable in style of behaviour, which is applied, which will determine their effectiveness in achieving the required outputs. This is known as situational leadership but is also referred to as style travelling.

Transformational Leadership

Transformational Leadership is a style first described by American historian and political scientist James MacGregor Burns in his 1978 book Leadership and expanded on during the 1980s by fellow scholar Bernard M. Bass. MacGregor had studied various political leaders, including both Franklin D. Roosevelt and John F. Kennedy and it is during this period he developed his leadership theories, including Transformational and Transactional Leadership.

It is a style which is utilised by leaders possessing specific traits, who look to work alongside their team members to identify change and develop the next action steps. But most importantly, they transform others - developing and empowering their individual followers to become leaders in and of themselves.

Transformational Leadership was utilised by notable historical figures such as Mahatma Gandhi and Nelson Mandela and is thus also often associated with the Servant Leadership philosophy. It is also particularly used in Change Management and Strategic Planning to develop and deliver a specific vision for the team or the organisation, or to change the culture of the company.

Traits of a Transformational Leader
These types of leaders are often referred to as role models and mentors due to the empowering position they hold in creating a diverse environment, open to ideas and innovations. Their followers hold a level of trust in them and they are quick to recognise the achievements of others to build confidence. Though they are open to new concepts and ideas, they encourage a culture of thinking which matches thoughts with the goals, values and beliefs of the organisation.

According to Bernard M. Bass in his 1985 book Leadership and Performance Beyond Expectations, transformational leaders:

- *Act with integrity and fairness*
- *Set clear goals for individuals and the team*
- *Encourage others*
- *Provide individual support and recognition*
- *Raise the morale and motivation of others*
- *Steers individuals away from their self-interest and towards selflessness*
- *Inspire others to strive for the improbable*

Though these are important traits and actions of a transformational leader, there is a simple pathway by which everyone can integrate the style into their leadership or change management techniques.

Leading People

Becoming a Transformational Leader

Transformational Leadership is often associated with the Servant Leadership philosophy. This is because Transformational Leadership involves working closely alongside members of the team, inspiring and motivating them and using others to help identify the need for change, creating a specific vision to drive change and execute it as a cohesive team.

Like all leadership styles, one of the key aims is to drive motivation amongst team members. Transformational Leadership does this by operating a number of mechanisms, including; connecting the follower's sense of identity to that of the task and the organisation as a whole, acting as a role model and setting the standards for the project, allowing followers greater independence and responsibility for tasks and assigning tasks which are suited to specific followers' strengths and weaknesses.

MacGregor and Bass' thoughts have been broken down into 5 simple steps to follow when trying to become a transformational leader. These are:

1. Identify the strengths and weaknesses of team members

Like Hersey and Blanchard's Situational Leadership, or Tannenbaum and Schmidt's Behavioural Continuum, it is crucial to this style that the strengths and weaknesses of each and every individual team member is fully understood. It is often the case that this is only something which can be developed over time and as the relationship between the leader and their team members develops, but it is important to be proactive and openly get to know everyone who you are responsible for. Tasks and visions can only be correctly implemented if individual team members are operating in roles which are suited to their experience and capabilities and will also allow them to remain motivated and to develop a sense of trust in the leader.

2. Develop an inspiring and motivational vision for the future

It is important to involve the team and jointly develop a vision for the future which instils a sense of optimism and motivates all members of the team. This vision should integrate the culture of the team and organisation and the values that are desired. This will always be dependent on the resources and individuals available, so it is crucial that the team and organisation are fully understood.

3. Motivate each individual and get them to buy into the vision

When developing the vision for the future, you should have been considering the values and beliefs of your team members; including what they see for their personal future and the future of the organisation. For this stage, you can utilise business storytelling as a way to make it clear what your vision is and how it is going to help the organisation and its consumers, as well as the team themselves. It is important that you understand the various motivational models and techniques in order to encourage employee buy-in.

4. Manage and involve yourself in the delivery of the vision

It is important for a transformational leader that they involve and integrate themselves in the delivery of the vision. Transformational leaders will be able to combine appropriate project management techniques with superb change management skills to ensure successful delivery. Roles will be communicated well and in accordance with all of the strengths and weaknesses of team members. Any individuals who require support will be offered help with their progress throughout the process.

Leading People

When allocating roles, make sure it is clear how these fit in with the plans and with the overall organisational objectives - everyone needs to buy into their position within the team. Any individual goals set should be set using a carefully thought-out model such as SMART (Specific, Measurable, Accurate, Realistic, Timely). It is important to remain focussed and motivational during the entire process - it is easy for effort levels to drop off. Always ensure availability and be open to questions, discussion or offering help to those who need it.

5. Continue to develop stronger relationships with your team members

A leader is only as strong as their team. It is crucial that any leader looks to develop and retain the trust and attention of all individuals amongst them. Leadership is a long-term process: it requires constant attention to facilitate the continual development of leader and team and the relationship between the two. Construct regular meetings to get a grasp of individual developmental needs and how they are finding any ongoing tasks or projects. Ask what they would like to achieve over the next year or years and try to figure out how they can be helped to achieve it. Offer coaching sessions if that would help them to improve personally or professionally. However, most important is to be honest with everyone. Nothing develops trust more quickly and effectively than honesty.

4 I's of Transformational Leadership

In Bass' interpretation, he identified four separate elements that make up a Transformational Leader, which became known as the 4 I's. They were:

1. *Idealised Influence*
2. *Intellectual Stimulation*
3. *Inspirational Motivation*
4. *Individualised Consideration*

These 4 elements, in Bass' view, were crucial if a leader wished to inspire, nurture and develop their followers. Leaders would use these to create an open, communicative and diverse culture, allowing followers to freely share ideas and therefore to empower them on an individual level.

Transformational leaders are often described as mentors and role models as they lead by example, encouraging an environment where innovative thinking is aligned with the values, beliefs and objectives of the organisation and individuals are openly recognised for their contributions and for going above-and-beyond the norm expected of them.

Summary

Transformational Leadership is an important style for driving change within an organisation or group. Though it favours individuals of specific personality traits or experiences, it can be utilised by anyone who understands when and how.

Key action points:

Leading People

1. *Identify strengths and weaknesses*
2. *Develop an inspiring vision for the future*
3. *Motivate everyone to buy into the vision*
4. *Manage and involve yourself in delivery*
5. *Reinforce your relationships with the team*

Transactional Leadership

Transactional Leadership is a theory or style first discussed by sociologist Max Weber in 1947 and later expanded upon by Bernard M. Bass, who also played a leading role in the development of Transformational Leadership.

Transactional Leadership is also often known as Managerial Leadership, due to its objective focus on supervision, organisation and group performance. The basic assumptions of Transactional Leadership are:

- *People perform at their best when the chain of command is definite and clear.*
- *Rewards and punishments motivate workers.*
- *Obeying the instructions and commands of the leader is the primary goal of the followers.*
- *Subordinates require careful monitoring to ensure that expectations are met.*

It is based around the simple behavioural tenet of motivators. Unlike models such as Transformational Leadership, which target individual development and freedom as a motivator, the main focus of transactional leaders is on specific tasks, using rewards and punishments as incentives and motivation.

When employees are successful, they are rewarded; and when they are unsuccessful, they are reprimanded. It is popular in environments such as sports teams and proves an incredibly powerful motivator for players from game-to-game. Also, unlike Transformational Leadership, Transactional Leadership focusses on maintaining the status quo, rather than trying to shift the values or culture of the organisation. Leaders do not sell changes to their subordinates, instead, they dictate and assign tasks.

Rewards and Punishments
Transactional leaders view the relationship between employee and leader as an exchange. One offers the other something (e.g., a task) for something in return (e.g., a reward). Rules, procedures and standards are crucial to Transactional Leadership, as any deviation from any of these must result in a punishment. Equally, good performance will be rewarded.

Transactional leaders clearly define organisational and individual objectives
Tasks and objectives are the focus of any Transactional Leader - the process is entirely about getting results. Transactional leaders will carefully monitor and track the progress of their employees. Carefully constructed performance management systems are crucial to ensure that employees are being rewarded or punished appropriately for their output and

Leading People

for their accordance with the rules and standards of the organisation. Rewards and punishments are at the discretion of the leader but must be standardised across employee performance.

Applicability
Transactional Analysis is not about driving or developing new, pioneering visions for the future. Instead, the systematic and objective nature of it is suited to maintaining the status quo. Individuals are not encouraged to go above or beyond their role, just to perform their assigned tasks efficiently and successfully. These leaders are good at setting expectations and are often expected to clearly communicate roles and feedback on future and previous tasks in order to improve employee productivity.

Transactional Leadership is most suitable when problems are simple and well-defined
Transactional Analysis does not encourage employees to look for new solutions to problems. Instead, they are encouraged to enact already-tested answers to regular, well-defined issues. It is often suitable in 'crisis situations' where everyone is required to complete their allocated tasks and it is the leader or manager's role to maintain the status quo and to keep the ship afloat. As the model is designed only to maintain the integrity and performance of the group, it is often considered limited to helping individuals (both employee and leader) to achieve their full potential.

Transformational vs Transactional Leadership

James MacGregor Burns, who studied political leaders like Roosevelt and Kennedy, first described these two distinct styles of leadership in his 1978 book, Leadership. He used the word 'transforming' rather than 'transformational'. Both terms are used here and they mean the same. Below are the descriptions and differences of the two styles:

Transforming Leadership	*Transactional Leadership*
Where the leader taps into his followers' higher needs and values, inspires them with new possibilities that have strong appeal and raises their level of confidence, conviction and desire to achieve a common, moral purpose.	Where the leader causes a follower to act in a certain way in return for something the follower wants to have (or avoid). For example, by offering higher pay in return for increased productivity; or tax cuts in exchange for votes.

Many political leaders demonstrate the transactional style. Mahatma Gandhi was an exemplar of someone who leads using the transforming or transformational style. The transformational leadership style therefore can have an overlap with the servant leader leadership philosophy.

There are three main differences between the two styles of transformational and transactional leadership.

1. *The first involves purpose*
2. *The second involves morality*
3. *The third involves the timescale or time horizon*

Leading People

Differences between Transformational and Transactional Leadership styles

Purpose		Morality		Timescale	
transforming	transactional	transforming	transactional	transforming	transactional
A shared higher, more stretching purpose is central to transformational leadership.	No shared purpose binds follower and leader, other than perhaps maintaining the status quo.	Burns said there is always a moral aspect to transforming leadership. *	There is no explicit moral side to transactional leadership - the leader's aims may be moral or immoral.	Transforming leadership centres on longer-term, more difficult (often more inspiring) aims.	Transactional leadership usually focuses on leaders' and followers' shorter-term needs.

* Although Hitler transformed Germany in the 1930s, under Burns' definition he would not be a transforming leader. Some scholars have used the term 'pseudo-transformational leaders' for those who pursue immoral aims.

While the defining feature of transactional leadership is a two-way exchange ("I'll give you this if you give me that"), the main features of transforming leadership are inspiration, mobilisation and moral purpose. Indeed, MacGregor Burns summarised transforming leadership:

> *"Such leadership occurs when one or more persons engage with others in such a way that leaders and followers raise one another to higher levels of motivation and morality."*

When he talked about morality, he meant leadership that:

> *"...can produce social change that will satisfy followers' authentic needs."*

Of the two styles, transforming leadership is more likely to achieve major change than transactional leadership - mainly because, by definition, the former goes after more ambitious goals.

Management by Walking About

Management by Walking About (MBWA) basically refers to managers spending some part of their time listening to problems and ideas of their staff, while wandering around an office or plant. The use of management by walking about can also instil a level of confidence in the team members that their manager will be aware of any issues that perhaps they do not want to openly discuss. Such issues are then dealt with appropriately, this may lead to an increased level of trust being developed.

MBWA might imply an aimless meander around the office, but it is a deliberate and genuine strategy for staying abreast of people's work, interests and ideas. It requires a range of skills, including active listening, observation, recognition and appraisal.

Leading People

MBWA also brings participation, spontaneity and informality to the idea of open-door management. It takes managers into their teams' workplaces to engage with the people and processes that keep companies running, to listen to ideas, to collect information and to resolve problems.

By managing by example, an environment of empathy, respect, trust and honesty can be established hopefully will filter to all teams and team members. Each member of the team can have the confidence of the manager is going to listen to them, be approachable, open to ideas and empathetic to any issues that they may experience. This could lead to many of the team members demonstrating a high level of flexibility. By being very open and honest with the teams an appropriate environment can be created that will lend itself to the team members returning the openness and honesty and a willingness to achieve and engage will be demonstrated during meetings with individual team members.

What MBWA can achieve

MBWA can produce a huge range of results. It can help you to be more approachable. People are often reluctant to speak with their managers because they feel intimidated, or they think that they will not care. But when team members see a leader as a person as well as a manager, they will trust them and be more willing to share ideas and issues with them.

Communication
Frequent, natural and trusting communication can be infectious and it can encourage people to work together as a team. With better communication and an improved sense of what is happening in a team, it will allow problems to be identified before they happen and place the leader in a better position to coach their team to avoid them.

Performance
Business knowledge, commercial awareness and problem-solving opportunities can all take leaps forward when better connected with the "front line." It will improve understanding of the functions, people and processes at work there and will boost people's company and industry knowledge. Everyone is better equipped to perform their roles when they have the right information and they are energised by an improved flow of ideas.

Motivation
Morale will get a lift from MBWA, too. Casual exchanges and opportunities to be heard help people to feel more motivated, more inspired and more connected. Furthermore, it will boost accountability and productivity, as any actions agreed with will get done because there is regular interaction.

Dangers to avoid

> *"Wandering about" may seem easy to do and harmless enough, but it is important to do it right.*

Research has shown that simply being physically present with team members is not enough. It is the post-walkabout actions that are taken and the problems that are solved that will

Leading People

determine the success of an MBWA strategy. If the right balance is not achieved, it can result in doing more harm than good.

Do not do MBWA out of a sense of obligation – this will not work very well. There must be a motivation to get to know the staff and operations and a commitment to following up on people's concerns and to seeking continuous improvement.

A big benefit of MBWA is that people can be open with you, but ignoring a negative comment or failing to follow up when you promised, it may be perceived as defensive or as someone who does not keep their word.

Gauging the level of trust within your environment is important because, if there is no trust, MBWA could make team members think it is a way of interfering or spying. It is also important to consider the team members' preferences and tailor the approach to these. For example, one team member may be happy to receive suggestions for improvements within earshot of co-workers, but another might be embarrassed by it, or even get angry about it.

How to use MBWA
The biggest challenge when implementing MBWA is to overcome the habit of being "too busy," and to start walking around.

Relax
People will sense when a leaders is relaxed and will respond accordingly. Stiff discussions held in formal spaces will lead to rigid responses, so keep team members at ease with relaxed and unstructured conversations. Hold these conversations where people will likely feel relaxed, such as at their desks or in a neutral place, rather than in the leaders office.

Monitor body language and dress. Turning up on a production line wearing a crisp pinstriped suit, will distance the leader from the people and put them off talking to them.

Listen and observe more than talk
Take care to sound inquisitive rather than intrusive. Ask people what they are working on, how comfortable they feel doing their jobs, what they find difficult, whether they see how their work contributes to "the big picture," and so on. Ask for ideas about how to make things better.

Actively listen to the team members' replies. Give them undivided attention. When they recognise there is interest in what they have to say, they will be more open and receptive and this will build rapport.

When talking, be open and truthful. If an answer to someone's question is not known, find it out afterward and follow up. If something cannot be shared, say so. Telling half-truths can break down trust and trust is crucial for successful MBWA.

Try doing the team members' work, to experience what they experience and to understand the issues that they face.

Be inclusive

Leading People

Do not favour one department or team more than another, or people may feel left out. Instead, spread attention evenly. Anyone can have great ideas or need support, so talk to everybody, regardless of their job title or position. If people work remotely, make the effort to get in touch with them. If they work the night shift, stay late to talk to them.

Recognise good work
Always look for successes rather than failures and, if you see something good, compliment the person. This is an effective and simple way to show your gratitude and to boost morale.

Spread the word
Share good news and reinstall company goals, values and vision within the team. Tell people how the aims for the team fit with the big picture. The MBWA is an opportunity to share information that helps everyone to understand and do their jobs better.

Embrace "chat"
Effective organisations are not all about work. MBWA allows the opportunity to strike a balance between people's work and their personal lives and to enjoy the lighter side of the job. Enjoying a joke or two, chatting with team members about their hobbies and finding out their kids' names helps to build relationships.

There is no need to befriend them on Facebook or play pool after work, but it can be surprising how good it feels to relate with colleagues on a personal level.

Do not overdo it
Do not leave people feeling that they are being spied on. Wander around often enough to get a good feel for what is going on – to make it a key part of the management strategy – but not so often that it feels like a distraction. Try not to do it at the same time each day: be spontaneous and unplanned, frequent but random.

Review your conversations
A presence alone is not enough to impact on frontline staff performance. Be sure to review the things learned – both the good and bad – and act accordingly

Leading People

Summary of Leadership Styles

This list below contains a brief summary of the different leadership styles which are common among leadership theory.

Autocratic Leadership
Autocratic leadership is an extreme form of transactional leadership, where leaders have a lot of power over their people. Staff and team members have little opportunity to make suggestions, even if these would be in the team's or the organisation's best interest.

The benefit of autocratic leadership is that it is incredibly efficient. Decisions are made quickly and work gets done efficiently. The downside is that most people resent being treated this way. Therefore, autocratic leadership can often lead to high levels of absenteeism and high staff turnover. However, the style can be effective for some routine and unskilled jobs: in these situations, the advantages of control may outweigh the disadvantages.

Autocratic leadership is often best used in crises when decisions must be made quickly and without dissent. For instance, the military often uses an autocratic leadership style; top commanders are responsible for quickly making complex decisions, which allows troops to focus their attention and energy on performing their allotted tasks and missions.

Bureaucratic Leadership
Bureaucratic leaders work "by the book." They follow rules rigorously and ensure that their people follow procedures precisely. This is an appropriate leadership style for work involving serious safety risks (such as working with machinery, with toxic substances, or at dangerous heights) or where large sums of money are involved. Bureaucratic leadership is also useful in organisations where employees do routine tasks (as in manufacturing).

The downside of this leadership style is that it is ineffective in teams and organisations that rely on flexibility, creativity, or innovation.

Much of the time, bureaucratic leaders achieve their position because of their ability to conform to and uphold rules, not because of their qualifications or expertise. This can cause resentment when team members do not value their expertise or advice.

Charismatic Leadership
A charismatic leadership style can resemble transformational leadership because these leaders inspire enthusiasm in their teams and are energetic in motivating others to move forward. This ability to create excitement and commitment is an enormous benefit.

The difference between charismatic leaders and transformational leaders lies in their intention.
Transformational leaders want to transform their teams and organisations. Charismatic leaders are often focused on themselves and may not want to change anything.

The downside to charismatic leaders is that they can believe more in themselves than in their teams. This can create the risk that a project or even an entire organisation might collapse if the leader leaves. A charismatic leader might believe that they can do no wrong, even when others are warning them about the path they are on; and this feeling of invincibility can ruin a

Leading People

team or an organisation. Also, in the followers' eyes, success is directly connected to the presence of the charismatic leader. As such, charismatic leadership carries great responsibility and it needs a long-term commitment from the leader.

Democratic/Participative Leadership

Democratic leaders make the final decisions, but they include team members in the decision-making process. They encourage creativity and team members are often highly engaged in projects and decisions. There are many benefits of democratic leadership. Team members tend to have high job satisfaction and are productive because they are more involved in decisions. This style also helps develop people's skills. Team members feel in control of their destiny, so they are motivated to work hard by more than just a financial reward.

Because participation takes time, this approach can slow decision-making, but the result is often good. The approach can be most suitable when working as a team is essential and when quality is more important than efficiency or productivity.

The downside of democratic leadership is that it can often hinder situations where speed or efficiency is essential. For instance, during a crisis, a team can waste valuable time gathering people's input. Another downside is that some team members might not have the knowledge or expertise to provide high quality input.

Laissez-Faire Leadership

This French phrase means "leave it be," and it describes leaders who allow their people to work on their own. This type of leadership can also occur naturally when managers do not have sufficient control over their work and their people.

Laissez-faire leaders may give their teams complete freedom to do their work and set their own deadlines.
They provide team support with resources and advice, if needed, but otherwise do not get involved. This leadership style can be effective if the leader monitors performance and gives feedback to team members regularly. It is most likely to be effective when individual team members are experienced, skilled, self-starters.

The main benefit of laissez-faire leadership is that giving team members so much autonomy can lead to high job satisfaction and increased productivity.

The downside is that it can be damaging if team members do not manage their time well or if they do not have the knowledge, skills, or motivation to do their work effectively.

People-Oriented/Relations-Oriented Leadership

With people-oriented leadership, leaders are totally focused on organising, supporting and developing the people on their teams. This is a participatory style and tends to encourage good teamwork and creative collaboration. This is the opposite of task-oriented leadership.

People-oriented leaders treat everyone on the team equally. They are friendly and approachable; they pay attention to the welfare of everyone in the group and they make themselves available whenever team members need help or advice.

Leading People

The benefit of this leadership style is that people-oriented leaders create teams that everyone wants to be part of. Team members are often more productive and willing to take risks because they know that the leader will provide support if they need it.

The downside is that some leaders can take this approach too far; they may put the development of their team above tasks or project directives.

Servant Leadership
This term, created by Robert Greenleaf in the 1970s, describes a leader often not formally recognised as such. When someone at any level within an organisation leads simply by meeting the needs of the team, he or she can be described as a "servant leader."

Servant leaders often lead by example. They have high integrity and lead with generosity. In many ways, servant leadership is a form of democratic leadership because the whole team tends to be involved in decision making. However, servant leaders often "lead from behind," preferring to stay out of the limelight and letting their team accept recognition for their hard work.

Supporters of the servant leadership model suggest that it is a good way to move ahead in a world where values are increasingly important and where servant leaders can achieve power because of their values, ideals and ethics. This is an approach that can help to create a positive corporate culture and can lead to high morale among team members.

However, other people believe that in competitive leadership situations, people who practice servant leadership can find themselves left behind by leaders using other leadership styles. This leadership style also takes time to apply correctly: it is ill-suited in situations where you have to make quick decisions or meet tight deadlines.

Although you can use servant leadership in many situations, it is often most practical in politics, or in positions where leaders are elected to serve a team, committee, organisation, or community.

Task-Oriented Leadership
Task-oriented leaders focus only on getting the job done and can be autocratic. They actively define the work and the roles required, put structures in place and plan, organise and monitor work. These leaders also perform other key tasks, such as creating and maintaining standards for performance.

The benefit of task-oriented leadership is that it ensures that deadlines are met and it is especially useful for team members who do not manage their time well.

However, because task-oriented leaders do not tend to think much about their team's well-being, this approach can suffer many of the flaws of autocratic leadership, including causing motivation and retention problems.

Transactional Leadership
This leadership style starts with the idea that team members agree to obey their leader when they accept a job. The "transaction" usually involves the organisation paying team members in

Leading People

return for their effort and compliance. The leader has a right to "punish" team members if their work does not meet an appropriate standard.

Although this might sound controlling and paternalistic, transactional leadership offers some benefits. For one, this leadership style clarifies everyone's roles and responsibilities. Another benefit is that, because transactional leadership judges team members on performance, people who are ambitious or who are motivated by external rewards – including compensation – often thrive.

The downside of this leadership style is that team members can do little to improve their job satisfaction. It can feel stifling and it can lead to high staff turnover.

Transactional leadership is really a type of management, not a true leadership style, because the focus is on short-term tasks. It has serious limitations for knowledge-based or creative work. However, it can be effective in other situations.

Transformational Leadership
Transformation leadership is often the best leadership style to use in business situations.

Transformational leaders are inspiring because they expect the best from everyone on their team as well as themselves. This leads to high productivity and engagement from everyone in their team.

The downside of transformational leadership is that while the leader's enthusiasm is passed onto the team, he or she can need to be supported by "detail people."
That is why, in many organisations, both transactional and transformational leadership styles are useful. Transactional leaders (or managers) ensure that routine work is done reliably, while transformational leaders look after initiatives that add new value.

It is also important to use other leadership styles when necessary – this will depend on the people you are leading and the situation that you are in.

Leading People

Organisational Culture

Organisational culture can be defined as the way you do things; the values, beliefs and codes of practice or policies that determine the culture of an organisation.

Companies often confuse leadership styles with corporate culture. While the corporate culture of a company often can be influenced by its leadership (the smaller the company, the more likely this is to be true), following the culture is how things get done.

The values, customs, traditions and meanings practiced by the company, combined with its processes and systems, constitute a corporate culture. Within that framework, individual leadership style influences the motivation of individuals and departments.

There are several management specialists who have written about organisational culture, including Tom Peters, who focused on culture as being a differentiator of successful organisations. Together with Robert Waterman, he developed the McKinsey 7-S framework and identify the key values that need to be in place for successful culture.

strategy: *the overall organisational plan*
structure: *the reporting structure of the organisation*
systems: *the procedures and processes to be followed to complete everyday tasks*
shared values: *the core values of the company that come across in the organisational culture work ethic*
style: *the leadership style used*
staff: *the employees of the organisation of their capabilities.*
skills: *the skills and competence of the employees*

Three Levels of Organisational Culture – Edgar Schein

Theorist Edgar Schein in his Three Levels of Organisational Culture, believes that the culture grows slowly over time based on the experiences and challenges faced.

Artefacts *are the things that can be seen in the organisation such as facilities furniture in appearance or dress code. This could be informal where employees can wear what they like, are laid-back and the culture is weak. A more formal culture would have a smart dress code, to encourage respect would be stricter on deadlines.*

Values *are based on the strategies and goals of the organisation; the way that employees think about the organisation affects its culture. They form the rules how team members behave.*

Leading People

Assumed values are deeper values that are often hidden, then not tangible concept, but are important in defining the culture of the organisation and form the basis of unconscious behaviour.

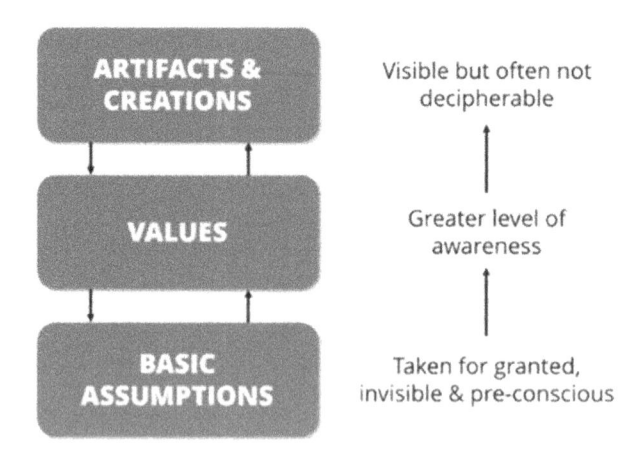

```
ARTIFACTS & CREATIONS      Visible but often not decipherable
         ↕                              ↑
       VALUES                 Greater level of awareness
         ↕                              ↑
  BASIC ASSUMPTIONS        Taken for granted, invisible & pre-conscious
```

Four Cultures Theory – Charles Handy

Charles Handy best for known his Four Cultures Theory, also known as the Gods of Management Theory.

This theory explores classifications of business structures and organisation based upon the functions and roles of the individual. Each culture defines the origin of power within that particular organisation and how that affects the success of other employees and the business.

Below is information on each of the four God-like cultures as well as information on other management theories and thoughts developed by Charles Handy.

Zeus Culture
Zeus Culture, also known as Club Culture or Power Culture, is the first in Handy's Gods of Management Theory. In this business culture, the power is centralised around one person, the boss.

Apollo Culture
The Apollo (Role) Culture has a hierarchy of power distribution among employees and has a primary focus on order and efficiency. The culture generally ignores change on initial onset and, rather, attempts to rely upon the already established routines. Life insurance companies are a prime example of an Apollo Culture

Athena Culture
The Athena, or Task, Culture distributes power to employees based upon their ability to perform the task necessary at a given time. Everything within this business structure revolves around the work/tasks. Individuals tend to receive a bit of independence within this business culture.

Leading People

Dionysius Culture

The Dionysius Culture, also known as Person Culture, is existential in nature (and often also called Existential Culture). The focus of these businesses is the success of the employees, rather than the company. Employees view themselves as specialists, temporarily loaning their skills and services to the corporation.

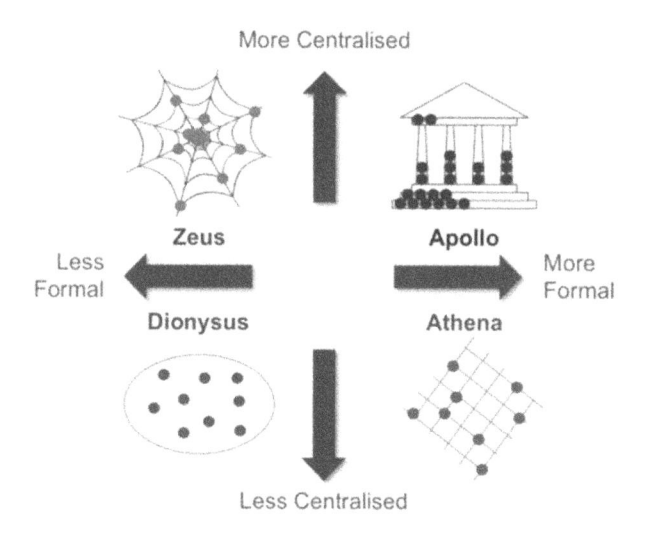

Cultural Web Model - Johnson and Scholes'

Strategy and development in an organisation are influenced heavily by the culture and environment. This is often positive, but it can also act as a hinderance, or even a barrier to growth and success. When trying to drive change, managers and other figures of responsibility may find it difficult to break out of the systems, structures and routines embedded in the company's culture and politics or individual relationships often play a huge role in deciding strategy.

Published by authors and academics in the fields of business, leadership and management, Kevan Scholes and Gerry Johnson in 1992, the Cultural Web is a useful tool for analysing and altering assumptions surrounding the culture of a company. It can be used to highlight specific practices and beliefs and to subsequently align them with your company's preferred culture and strategy.

The Elements

Johnson and Scholes identified six distinct but interrelated elements which contribute to what they called the "paradigm", equivalent to the pattern of the work environment, or the values of the organisation. They suggested that each may be examined and analysed individually to gain a clearer picture of the wider cultural issues of an organisation. The six contributing elements (with example questions used to examine the organisation at hand) are as follows:

Leading People

1. Stories and Myths
These are the previous events – both accurate and not – which are discussed by individuals within and outside the company. Which events and people are remembered by the company indicates what the company values and what it chooses to immortalise through stories.

- *What form of company reputation is communicated between customers and stakeholders?*
- *What stories do people tell new employees about the company?*
- *What do people know about the history of the organisation?*
- *What do these stories say about the culture of the business?*

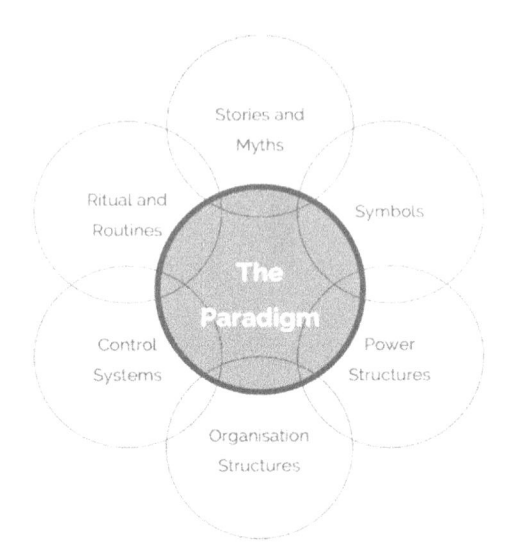

2. Rituals and Routines
This refers to the daily actions and behaviours of individuals within the organisation. Routines indicate what is expected of employees on a day-to-day basis and what has been either directly or indirectly approved by those in managerial positions.

- *What do employees expect when they arrive each day?*
- *What experience do customers expect from the organisation?*
- *What would be obvious if it were removed from routines?*
- *What do these rituals and routines say about organisational beliefs?*

3. Symbols
This is the visual representation of the company; how they appear to both employees and individuals on the outside. It includes logos, office spaces, dress codes and sometimes advertisements.

Leading People

- *What kind of image is associated with the company from the outside?*
- *How do employees and managers view the organisation?*
- *Are there any company-specific designs or jargon used?*
- *How does the organisation advertise itself?*

4. Control Systems

These are the systems and pathways by which the organisation is controlled. This can refer to many things, including financial management, individual performance-based rewards (both measurement and distribution) and quality-control structures.

- *Which processes are strongly and weakly controlled?*
- *In general, is the company loosely or tightly controlled?*
- *Are employees rewarded or punished for performance?*
- *What reports and processes are used to keep control of finance, etc?*

5. Organisation Structures

This refers to both the hierarchy and structure designated by the organisation. Alongside this, Johnson and Scholes also use it to refer to the unwritten power and influence that some members may exert, which also indicate whose contributions to the organisation are most valued by those above them.

- *How hierarchical is the organisation?*
- *Is responsibility and influence distributed in a formal or informal way?*
- *Where are the official lines of authority?*
- *Are there any unofficial lines of authority?*

6. Power Structures

This is the genuine power structures and responsible individuals within the organisation. It may refer to a few executives, the CEO, board members, or an entire managerial division. These individuals are those who hold the greatest influence over decisions and generally have the final say on major actions or changes.

- *Who holds the power within the organisation?*
- *Who makes decisions on behalf of the company?*
- *What are the beliefs and culture of those as the top of the business?*
- *How is power used within the organisation?*

Leading People

Using the Cultural Web to Effect Change

As above, the first step of changing the culture of the organisation is to analyse elements of the Cultural Web as they are in the present. The next step is to repeat the process, examining each element, but this time considering what one would like the culture, beliefs and systems to be. This can then subsequently be compared with the ideal culture and the differences between the two can be used to develop achievable steps towards change within the company. One will likely only then realise the true strengths and weaknesses of the organisation's current culture, what the various hinderances are to growth and how to go about changing specific elements to develop and achieve success.

A new strategy can evolve from this by looking at introducing new beliefs and prioritising positive reinforcement of current, successful ones. Hopefully, by integrating this system of analysis, managers can find themselves able to break free of ritual and belief systems within a company to achieve real change and innovation

Cultural Dimensions - Geert Hofstede

Cultures around the world are getting more and more interconnected and the business world is becoming increasingly global. For managers, this means they should be able to work with a large variety of people from different countries and cultural backgrounds. However, since most people are so strongly immersed in their own culture, they often fail to see how it affects their patterns of thinking or their behaviour. To overcome this, researchers suggested some kind of tools or mechanisms with which to compare countries on cultural similarities and differences.

A number of attempts have been made to combine these cultural differences across borders (e.g., the GLOBE study, Trompenaars' cultural dimensions and Hall's cultural dimensions). However, the most used and best-known framework for cultural differences is Geert Hofstede's Cultural Dimensions. Over the years, his study led to six cultural dimensions on which countries can be ranked:

- *Power Distance*
- *Individualism/Collectivism*
- *Masculinity/Femininity*
- *Uncertainty Avoidance*
- *Long-term/Short-term Orientation and*
- *Restraint/Indulgence.*

Leading People

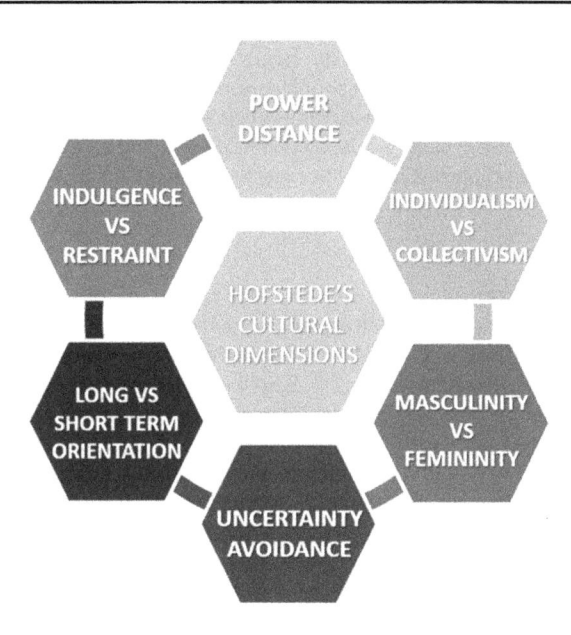

Each dimension is explained below:

Power Distance
This dimension expresses the degree to which the less powerful members of a society accept and expect that power is distributed unequally: beliefs about the appropriate distribution of power in society. The fundamental issue here is how a society handles inequalities among people. People in societies exhibiting a large degree of Power Distance accept a hierarchical order in which everybody has a place and which needs no further justification. In societies with low Power Distance, people strive to equalise the distribution of power and demand justification for inequalities of power. China and Saudi Arabia are countries with a high Power Distance index.

Individualism
The Individualism/Collectivism dimension is about the relative importance of individual versus group interests. The high side of this dimension, called individualism, can be defined as a preference for a loosely knit social framework in which individuals are expected to take care of only themselves and their immediate families. Its opposite, collectivism, represents a preference for a tightly knit framework in society in which individuals can expect their relatives or members of a particular in-group to look after them in exchange for unquestioning loyalty. A society's position on this dimension is reflected in whether people's self-image is defined in terms of "I" or "we." The USA is considered as one of the most individualistic countries in the world.

Masculinity
The Masculinity/Femininity dimension is about what values are considered more important in a society. The Masculine side of this dimension represents a preference in society for

Leading People

achievement, heroism, assertiveness and material rewards for success. Society at large is more competitive. Its opposite, femininity, stands for a preference for cooperation, modesty, caring for the weak and quality of life. Society at large is more consensus oriented. In the business context Masculinity versus Femininity is sometimes also related to as "tough versus tender" cultures. Japan is considered to be a very masculine country, whereas Scandinavian countries such as Norway and Sweden are considered highly feminine.

Uncertainty Avoidance

The Uncertainty Avoidance dimension expresses the degree to which the members of a society feel uncomfortable with uncertainty and ambiguity. In addition, its impact on rule making is considered. The fundamental issue here is how a society deals with the fact that the future can never be known: should we try to control the future or just let it happen? Countries exhibiting a high Uncertainty Avoidance maintain rigid codes of belief and behaviour and are intolerant of unorthodox behaviour and ideas. These countries often need many rules to constrain uncertainty. Countries with a low Uncertainty Avoidance index maintain a more relaxed attitude in which practice counts more than principles, tolerance for ambiguity is accepted and the need for rules to constrain uncertainty is minimal. South American countries such as Chile, Peru and Argentina are highly uncertainty avoiding countries.

Time Orientation

Every society has to maintain some links with its own past while dealing with the challenges of the present and the future. Societies prioritize these two existential goals differently. Countries that score low on this dimension, for example, prefer to maintain time-honoured traditions and norms while viewing societal change with suspicion. They are past and present oriented and value traditions and social obligations. Countries with cultures that scores high on this dimension on the other hand take a more pragmatic approach: they are future oriented and encourage thrift and efforts in modern education as a way to prepare for the future. Asian countries such as China and Japan are known for their long-term orientation. Morocco is a short-term oriented country.

Indulgence

The Indulgence dimension is a relatively new dimension to the model. This dimension is defined as the extent to which people try to control their desires and impulses, based on the way they were raised. Relatively weak control is called Indulgence and relatively strong control is called Restraint. Cultures can, therefore, be described as Indulgent or Restrained. Indulgence stands for a society that allows relatively free gratification of basic and natural human drives related to enjoying life and having fun. Restraint stands for a society that suppresses gratification of needs and regulates it by means of strict social norms.

Leading People

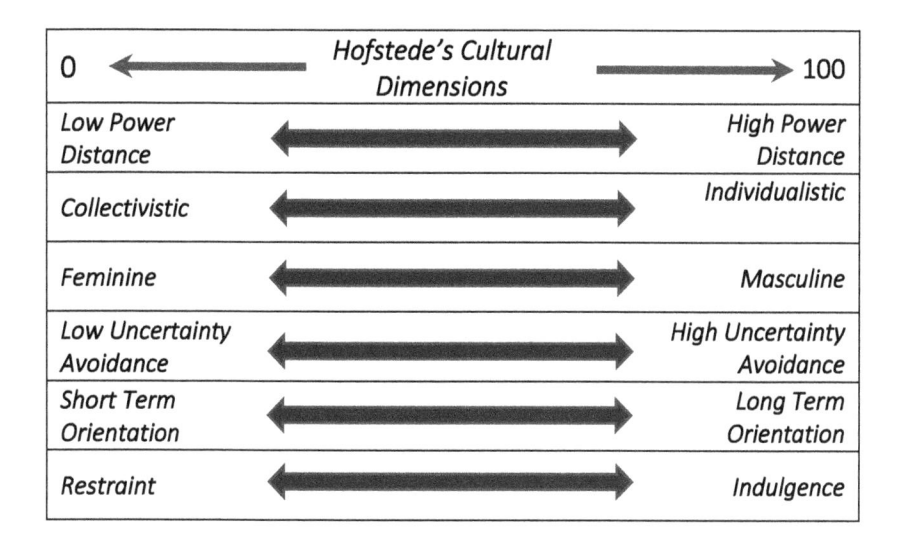

0 ←	Hofstede's Cultural Dimensions	→ 100
Low Power Distance	⟷	High Power Distance
Collectivistic	⟷	Individualistic
Feminine	⟷	Masculine
Low Uncertainty Avoidance	⟷	High Uncertainty Avoidance
Short Term Orientation	⟷	Long Term Orientation
Restraint	⟷	Indulgence

Issues with Organisational Culture

Collective Behaviour and Shared Values

The tangible elements of a corporate culture can include a company's routines, stories and symbols; its outward facing Organisational structure and its hidden power structure. Culture can include what it says outwardly, but also what the company really means when it says it.

While it is common practice for companies to share their vision and mission with employees, this does not mean that all do an equal job of explaining what they mean. Some corporate cultures can be outward-looking and open, sharing much more about how they plan to reach their goals. Others are more secretive and operate on a need-to-know basis.

Formal or Informal Culture

Corporate culture is unique to each company. Two companies in the same industry can have very different cultures.

Both IBM and Sun Microsystems manufacture computers and software. One is known as Big Blue, complete with a white-shirt-and-tie image. The other is California casual. One's historically regimented organisation and sheer scale gets the job done, while the other's entrepreneurial, innovative solutions regularly amaze its customers. Both have been highly successful because each company and its employees share an energy of related values and common business behaviours.

Corporate Culture as an obstacle

A company that says it values its people, then lays them off and has them and their belongings escorted off the premises by guards, is not nearly as sensitive to the feelings of its staff as it would have people believe.

Leading People

Defining the culture of a new company and identifying how to fit into that culture is one of the most difficult things for an executive to do. Sometimes that is because the company states publicly that it is one kind of company but acts internally in a way that belies its words.

A new manager might be told that the company strongly endorses a team approach to process improvement. However, he quickly discovers that any suggestions are ignored or put down. Or the company might say that it promotes from within, but any time a senior position opens up, the job goes to an outside recruit.

Meshing Leadership Styles with Corporate Culture
Strong leadership is required to align a corporate culture with an organisation's strategy, especially if that strategy is a significant shift from the way things have been done. Risk-averse companies that set the goal to become innovative and nimble have to be taught an entrepreneurial culture.

Entrepreneurial in a Command-and-Control company
The primary leadership style in our society is what is called "command-and-control." It is accepted because it is efficient. Once workers learn skills, they generally repeat them and over time can come to resist change. This style is prevalent in large companies.
The opposite style, "leadership by worker responsibility," motivates people to thrive on challenge and change. This is precisely the environment cultivated in start-up and entrepreneurial environments.

While it is possible to be an entrepreneurial, mid-level leader within a regimented environment, it is not easy. To survive, the leader adopts a dual style: managing up as a line-skill manager and managing down as a motivational challenger, encouraging risk-taking and new skill acquisition.

Leading by Motivation
A good leader uses more than one leadership style, depending on individual situations. Staff assessment is necessary to identify what style best motivates each worker. One employee might be completely self-motivated and independent and need minimal supervision. He is motivated by opportunities to be creative and can be highly productive. Another employee longs to find solutions and make decisions, is team-motivated and thrives on democratic discussion, change and responsibility.

Still others might be motivated by goals and opportunity, by rewards and material prompts, or recognition and social status. Managing these employees requires skill in creating a work environment that provides enough motivational "honey"

Leading People

Leading High-Performing Teams

A high-performance team is a group of people who work together for a common goal and are able to achieve extraordinary results. High performance teams are created on a solid foundation of:

- *building productive communication,*
- *creating innovative solutions and*
- *delivering great performance.*

In other words, high performance teams are equipped with a high-performance team culture.

One of the areas an operational departmental manager's main focus should be on is developing teams that can work at the highest performance levels. You should help support individuals to develop by giving them the motivation they need to achieve the desired results. A high performing team is defined as a group of individuals in different roles work together towards a common goal. They have the necessary talents and skills to collaborate and the innovative high levels to produce excellent results. There are several key features of high performing teams that you need to consider:

- *the businesses vision and values need to be communicated and understood*
- *team members roles must reflect individual skills and responsibilities must be clearly defined*
- *team members should be given autonomy, responsibility and accountability*
- *communication systems within and between teams should be effective and managed appropriately*
- *team members should support each other by communicating, giving feedback and making joint decisions*
- *team members should be encouraged to use their talents and strengths, which will increase motivation and therefore performance*
- *team members must be able to trust each other, with which develops team bonds and loyalty*
- *conflict should be handled effectively; this can create a positive culture where team members are able to discuss their differences of opinion and come to a consensus*
- *review of goal should be carried out regularly, outputs need to be evaluated and plans amended to ensure success*
- *achievements and successes should be shared and celebrated*
- *teams need to be adaptable and able to respond quickly to changes, adapting plans and working together to achieve outcomes*
- *teams need to have a strong sense of identity and belonging, this will ensure that a team is motivated and energetic and values and behaviours will be instilled in all team members*
- *individual team members will represent the same both internally and externally*

Leading People

Building a High-Performing Team

Teams do not simply happen. Indeed, teams are much more than groups of people. They occur when there are common goals, values and behaviours. And every leader has a part to play in building teams. Here are my top tips for building high performance teams.

1. Model Excellence
You have probably heard the phrase: Behaviour breeds behaviour. This saying is illustrated by a simple model called the Betari Box.
The Betari Box helps understand how our attitudes and behaviours directly affect the attitudes and behaviours of others.

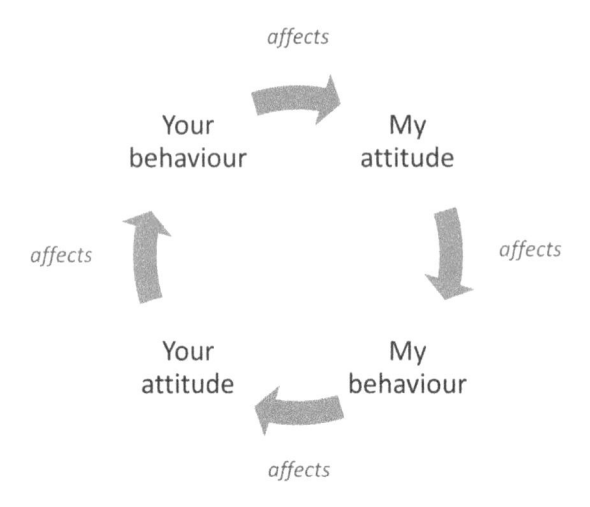

affects

Your behaviour → My attitude

affects ↑ ↓ *affects*

Your attitude ← My behaviour

affects

When we are stuck in a cycle — mistrust, not taking responsibility, positive attitude and so on — it is up to the team leader to break the cycle and change attitudes.

Inevitably this has a positive impact on those around us. When we take charge and change our behaviour our team is more likely to follow our lead.

2. Open and Honest Communication
A hallmark of the high-performance team is a high level of open, honest, robust and transparent communication. High performance teams increase trust by building a culture of partnership and shared values.
This starts with open and honest communication.

> *When honesty and transparency are lacking there can be no trust.*

Without trust teams fail to solve problems or make decisions. Without trust teams are crippled by conflict.

Leading People

3. A Supportive Environment
High Performance teams meet regularly and discuss progress, concerns and ideas for improvement.

Likewise, the team leader meets the individual to talk about their objectives, development and performance. The high-performance team supports its members by:

- *accepting difference and diversity,*
- *encouraging each other's strengths and*
- *supporting its members at times of personal or professional challenge.*

4. Understand the Expertise
Know your team's strengths and talents.

Motivation and positive attitude is more valuable to high performance teams than experience and negative character. The high-performance team motivates and coaches the individual. It helps and develops the less experience colleague. Moreover, the team listens to everyone and creates a sense of belonging. The team understands what each player has to offer and how they help achieve shared business objectives.

5. Celebrate Success
Share good news. Make noise about successes.

Let everyone know when the team or a team member does something exceptional.

And finally, ... encourage extracurricular activities for team members to forge close-knit relationships and build high levels of mutual trust and friendship

Developing a High Performing Team

The following is a less detailed but fuller list of what leaders should do to get people to work together to attain organisational goals.

1. ***Define a very clear picture of the future—a vision for the team.*** This is crucial because teams search desperately for specific targets. Consider the old expression: "If you don't know where you are going, any road will get you there." Journeys without a clear destination leave groups feeling flat and lost. Keeping teams informed on where they are headed and how best to get there means leaders must be prepared to acknowledge and adapt to changes in operational conditions and even objectives. Leaders cannot sit back and watch, but instead must create and recreate the vision and team spirit that stops people from losing heart and becoming lost.

2. ***Be genuine, even if it means lowering your guard.*** Leaders who create "click" have an uncanny sense about how and when to express their inner selves. They will even reveal their own vulnerabilities at the right time to gain the respect of those around

Leading People

them. They are not so concerned about projecting a perfect image: they know that high-impact leaders get results by laughing at their own flaws. They do not play make-believe, knowing it is more important "to be" than to "seem to be."

3. *Ask good questions.* They use inquiry and advocacy in such a way as to keep them abreast of what is really going on. They seem to use a simple formula of the 70-20-10 rule in conversations: 70 percent listening, 20 percent enquiring with just the right amount of advocacy and 10 percent tracking (i.e., summarising and synthesising information and providing possible courses of action).

4. *Talk about things—even the hard things.* A leader who gets their team to click is not afraid to talk about the tough stuff. They find ways to have the difficult conversations in the knowledge that burying problems does not make them go away. They also know that if they, as leader, do not talk about things, no-one will and, pretty soon, a culture will develop in which too many things are left unsaid. (I can always tell when teams are dysfunctional by measuring the amount of stuff not talked about, or what I call the "let's not go there" issues.)

5. *Follow through on commitments.* Leaders of high-performing teams find ways to build trust and maintain it, especially by making teams hold to their commitments and keeping the team's view of its goals clear. However, they also know how to distinguish professional trust from blind loyalty.

6. *Let others speak first.* In high-performing teams, members see themselves as equal in terms of communication. Leaders should therefore encourage this by putting the other person's need to express his or her agenda ahead of their own.

7. *Listen.* High-performing teams are comprised of people who have mastered the art of listening without fear, of allowing others to speak without reacting strongly or negatively to what is being said, or what they anticipate will be said. The leader fosters and honours this attribute within the team by quickly putting a stop to bad conversational behaviour that cuts other people off and implies that their ideas are not valued. The leader knows that achieving higher levels of innovation requires team members to be unafraid to express unusual ideas and advocate experimental processes. They emphasise this by publicly thanking those who take risks—and by making sure that sharpshooters put their guns away.

8. *Face up to non-performing players.* This brings us to a very important characteristic of high performing teams, which is that their leaders do not tolerate players who pull the team apart. Interestingly, experienced leaders frequently maintain unity and discipline through third parties in the form of people we call "passionate champions." A leader may surround him- or herself with several passionate champions, who have established an understanding and close working *relationship with one another and who are totally focused on and committed to, the team's objectives. They are capable of getting the job done—and not afraid to remove people who are failing to help them do so.*

9. *Have fun, but never at others' expense.* High-impact leaders steer clear of sarcasm: they always take the high road. If they poke fun at someone, it is usually themselves. They have learned the lesson that reckless humour can be misinterpreted and backfire.

Leading People

They know that critics of the organisation can turn inappropriate remarks back on a leader who makes them.

10. **Be confident and dependable.** *Somehow, over and above the daily struggle, leaders who get teams to click project confidence. They do this by preparing their conversations and not backing away from, or skimming over, real issues and problems, even difficult or confrontational ones. They always address "What's up?" and "What's so?" in the organisation. They do not try to be spin doctors because they know that, ultimately, this does not work. Rather, they are known as straight shooters–people who play hard, fight fair and never, never give up. At the end of the day, team members know that, whatever happens, their leader will be left standing. This gives them confidence that they will be standing, too. They also know that, should things get really bad, their leader will not desert them or try to shift the blame, but seek to protect them, even if it means standing in the line of fire.*

Leading Remote or Multiple Teams

Dealing with multiple teams or people who may not be in close proximity, creates a whole new challenge from managers. Not only in the number of employees they may have responsibility for, but also ensuring that the locations culture and requirements are considered. It would suggest that this role would fall to a regional manager who will then have team leaders or managers to help carry out their managerial responsibilities.

Where this is the case, it would be logical to ensure that policies and practices remain consistent across locations as far as practical. It should also be recognised that there will be some occasions where the regional requirements regarding working arrangements and purposes may be different, however, having an employee handbook that is consistent across all locations will set the tone.

It is important as a manager of several locations to maintain a regular presence across all sites. This does not have to be physical visits, which might prove inefficient or costly, in some cases, but might consist of videoconferencing, telephone calls on a regular basis, especially with team departmental managers to ensure awareness of any progress and issues that may be arising. This will also demonstrate your team leaders and managers that your visible and available for support if required.

Managers with multiple teams and locations will need to be much more adept at delegating and ensure a level of trust is placed in those reporting to them. Defined lines of communication, which are open, must be implemented across all sites and all teams to ensure the information flows effective, even if and to simulate disseminated simultaneously

Qualities of an effective remote team manager paragraph the following qualities are essential for managers or managing remote teams and locations

Positivity - you need to be a brand ambassador across all teams and individuals, sharing and celebrating success. Having a positive and consistent approach will motivate team leaders and members to achieve and promote the brand.

Leading People

Encouragement - ensuring that each team or location has common procedures and guidelines clear lines of communication and team members are valued equally will promote a culture where there motivated and encouraged to succeed

Approachability - an effective manager must be approachable and this is especially important when managing remote teams. You need to establish how you going to make yourself available and consider whether you can promote an open-door policy.

Constructive and proactive - an effective manager will think ahead and plan for foreseeable events having good contingency plans in place will support teams to deal with issues as they arise and it is important that they do so efficiently, especially when working in remote locations where your support may not be immediately available.

Empathy - you need to be aware of how remote team members may feel, especially those working in isolation from others. You will need to manage the psychological impact of remote working, involve all team members in discussions and maintain contact at least once a week, more often if necessary
understand team dine manner dynamics-consideration needs to be made as to how different teams and team members interact with each other when remote working. Effective structures for communication between and within teams will need to be in place, this will help to prevent teams from becoming isolated and reducing consistency and conflicts from arising.

Effective communicator - as a remote team manager you will need to communicate effectively using active listening and respond appropriately and in a timely manner. Team leaders and supervisors should be trained to and empowered to use their own effective communication skills.

In addition to these qualities there are some points that you will need to consider when leading remote teams and team leaders

- *establish a common vision and goals across and within teams*
- *use coaching and mentoring or implement body systems where practicable. This can be face-to-face periodically or by Webcam or social media in line with policies and procedures.*
- *establish clear expectations by setting monitoring and reviewing clear objectives*
- *arrange regular meetings it is good to bring everyone together once or twice during the year, this could be an annual conference or team building days.*
- *establish your availability, this could be set times during the day when you are available for team leaders and members to contact you. Inform teams of the times when you cannot be disturbed unless in an emergency.*
- *delegate responsibilities and empower team leaders*
- *maximise the use of technology using internal intranet, conference calling, email, e-learning and online training.*

Leading People

- *remember to meet face-to-face, for example one-to-one meetings, supervisions are and annual appraisals or performance reviews.*
- *trusting your team and team members to get work task done and to meet deadlines. If you believe in the abilities of individuals and give autonomy to people rather micromanaging them, you will enjoy loyalty.*

Leading Virtual Teams

In the past, new managers often had the luxury of cutting their teeth on traditional co-located teams: groups of people, sitting down the corridor from one another, who met up in conference rooms to thrash out what they were trying to achieve and how to get there.

A virtual team is a group of people that work together on common goals and projects but do not sit together and so communicate electronically rather than face-to-face – although they may occasionally meet in person. Virtual team members are sometimes homeworkers located in nearby towns but often they are based in offices across borders and continents. Virtual team working is notoriously challenging and it is often quoted that 50% of virtual teams fail to meet their objectives – and even when virtual teams do meet their objectives they very often do not want to work together again.

Unfortunately, in today's increasingly global work environment that luxury is often denied. Many first-time managers find themselves assigned to a team of subordinates scattered far and wide. You might assume that if you have led teams before you will be able to manage a virtual team without any problem, but it takes a highly skilled team leader to be able to build, manage and maintain a successful virtual team. You will need all those skills you developed when managing face-to-face teams – and a whole lot more.

The absence of those informal opportunities to collaborate or those water cooler moments where colleagues share a joke and build rapport means that it is much harder to build trust and create a sense of common purpose and engagement in virtual teams. The virtual manager needs to dedicate more time, energy and resources to establishing good relationships throughout the team, not only between themselves and the rest of the team but also between colleagues.

Challenges
Managing a distributed team can feel overwhelming as it requires you to navigate many different types of distance: geographic, temporal, cultural, linguistic and configurational (the relative number of members in each location). Every one of these dimensions affects team dynamics and, therefore, has an impact on effectiveness and performance as well. Daunting as that may seem, there is good news in the form of a large and ever-increasing body of research and best practice on how to increase your odds of success. But first, it is important to understand which aspects of team dynamics are and are not, affected by distance.

Leading People

The Effects of Distance
While all of the different types of distance listed above affect us, they do so primarily through two core mechanisms: shared identity and shared context. Understanding these will help you develop a much more targeted plan of attack for managing from afar.

Firstly, distance affects how you feel about people. Dealing with the types of distance listed above (often grouped together and labelled "locational") triggers a sense of "social distance" – no sense of shared identity, or a feeling of "us vs. them." A lack of a shared identity has a far stronger impact on team dynamics than any of the types of distance individually.

It has been shown that unshared identity arising from social distance increases coordination problems and reduces group cognition in the form of transactive memory. When teams function with high levels of transactive memory, they know where different knowledge is held in the team and how to access it.

Secondly, distance affects what you know about people. Catherine Cramton refers to this concept as "the mutual knowledge problem," put simply, it means that you do not know what they know – and vice versa.

Why does this matter? Because a shared sense of context, a shared understanding of not only what you do but how you do it and why, is a key driver of your ability to coordinate and collaborate. Teams with a shared understanding are more efficient. They do not waste time ensuring everyone is on the same page and they have fewer issues with miscommunication.

Taken together, this means that when assessing the effects of distance on your team, you need to keep in mind both how you feel and what you know, about your distant colleagues.

Though it may come as a bit of a surprise, distance does not change the fundamental rules of the game. A global virtual team is first and foremost a team — just because yours is distributed does not mean you should discard the prevailing wisdom about how the most effective teams operate. You need to arm yourself with a good model of team effectiveness and use it to assess and improve team dynamics and processes. A model provides structure and will help you organise your efforts as you tackle management for the first time. This is especially important for those who are dealing with the added complexities of distance.

Managing the Effects of Distance
First things first: do not panic. Remember that global, virtual, distributed teams are composed of people just like any other team. The more you and your team members can keep this in mind, the better your results will be. As the manager, encourage everyone to engage in some perspective taking: think about how you would behave if your roles were reversed. This is a small way of reminding your team that collaboration is not magic, but it does take some effort.

Second, remember the basics. Arm yourself with a well-tested model of team effectiveness and use it to help structure your thinking. There are, of course, many models out there. J. Richard Hackman's Team Effectiveness Model is an excellent starting point. It is based on a massive amount of rigorous research across a wide range of teams. This model stresses the importance of the team goal. Building on Hackman's work, research shows that if you do only one thing, ensure that the team's goal is clear, challenging, consequential and commonly held as this yields the biggest benefit. This holds true whether your subordinates are down the hall

Leading People

or around the globe. In the end, being mindful about your team process is more important than which particular model you choose. Take that model and use it to assess how you have done, where you stand and where you are going.

Third, think (and talk) about how to overcome the negative effects that a lack of shared identity and shared context can have. To help your team combat "us-vs.-them" thinking, reinforce what is shared: the team's purpose. All teams are designed to achieve something and if the team is designed well, team members depend on one another to accomplish their goal. Remind your team that you are all working to the same end and that you need each other to get there. Doing so at the outset and intermittently throughout the project will help you build a strong sense of shared identity.

A shared understanding comes from sharing information. Team members working at a distance need to try to understand what is happening in each person's local context. Importantly, that includes information not only about the work being done but also about the environment in which people are working (e.g., structural changes, office politics, even personal life events). All of these affect the psychology of your dispersed colleagues and, therefore, how they react to you and the rest of the team.

One last note — it is easy to get fixated on either information or interpersonal dynamics to the exclusion of the other but that paints an incomplete picture. You need to consider the effects of both and how they reinforce one another. Always encourage team managers to have regularly scheduled check-ins not just to measure progress towards the team's goal but to discuss both its context (what it knows) and identity (who it is).

Transparent Communication

> *"The single biggest problem with communication is the illusion that it has taken place."* George Bernard Shaw

Excellent communication skills are essential for virtual team leaders who do not have the luxury of face-to-face communication but instead have to rely much more on text or voice only communication.

Without the benefits of non-verbal clues, it can be much harder to interpret the real intention of what is being said and know what the speaker is really thinking. As a virtual team manager, you must ensure that your communication is clear and unambiguous and that you make sure not only that you fully understand your team but that you are understood yourself.

Here are some tips for virtual communication:

- Communicate regularly and frequently but do not overload your team with information. Very long emails or online meetings should be avoided
- Make time for regular one-to-one communication with individual team members as well as group emails and meetings. Picking up the phone to see how someone is doing is usually appreciated and is certainly the best method if you have something sensitive to discuss
- Paraphrase and summarise when you are giving complicated instructions and check back that you have been understood

Leading People

- Particularly with new team members be wary of using jargon or acronyms that they may not understand
- Listen attentively and be ready to read between the lines. Ask the right questions to check that you have understood

Patience
Working virtually is challenging. Technology can let you down, response times may be longer if you are working across time zones and a lack of face-to-face communication can make it so much harder to interpret the real message.

You may also have language and cultural barriers to manage. Particularly in the early stages of your virtual team, you are going to have to flex your patience muscle: things will take longer, interpersonal irritations and upsets may well occur, people will not always say what they really think, meetings will not always go to plan and you will need to remain positive and focused on achieving your goals. You are likely to need a lot of patience!

Rapport-Building
Virtual teams risk losing the human element of the workplace and so their leaders need to be highly skilled in building relationships and creating good rapport with their team members.

Make sure you allow time for the team to get to know a little more about each other's personal lives and factor in a few minutes small talk at the start of meetings – and do not be afraid to share a joke. Remember that your team are human beings so from time to time check in on how they are feeling as well as what they are doing and engage sensitively when a team member is experiencing personal or professional challenges.

A regular quarterly or even annual face-to-face meeting will help enormously to build positive team relationships. And do make sure you use any face-to-face time wisely and focus on team-building activities rather than on updates and reporting that can just as easily be done at a distance.

Results-Focus
Of course, all team leaders need to focus on results but one of the challenges of managing a virtual team is that you cannot see what people are doing or monitor their performance in the same way and so you can only really manage, measure and reward based on outcomes and results. When managing virtual teams, it is crucial to have clear individual accountabilities in place with agreed methods of monitoring and measuring performance.

Intercultural Skills

> *"Tolerance, intercultural dialogue and respect for diversity are more essential than ever in a world where people are becoming more and more closely interconnected."* - Kofi Annan

If you manage a virtual team the chances are that it is also an international team with members located across cultures and time zones. This means you will need to navigate values,

Leading People

communication styles and working preferences that may be at odds with your own or with other team members'.

Virtual team leaders need to manage multiple perspectives and decode different cross-cultural styles so that they can get the best from their individual team members and also maximise the diversity of the team as a whole. Be prepared to listen and learn about other cultural norms and move beyond nationality stereotypes. If colleagues in one location never seem to deliver on time, do not jump to conclusions but consider how milestones and deadlines are managed, how much support they are getting and if instructions are clear and accessible. If another colleague rarely contributes during online meetings, think about how the meeting is managed, if more materials could be circulated ahead of the meeting and whether they need additional language support – and make sure you make time to speak to them one-to-one.

Technology Skills

> *"The more elaborate our communication the less we collaborate."* - Joseph Priestly

Virtual teams rely on technology to interact with each other and share information and as the team manager you need to lead by example and demonstrate excellent technical skills.
You want to be able to select the right tools and platforms for your team and match each task or interaction type to the most appropriate mode of communication. And it goes without saying that you should be a competent user and be able to stay calm and trouble-shoot when technology lets you down.

Select a relatively small number of tools that can be used regularly and consistently but also be aware of how individual team members prefer to communicate. You might find you get a faster response from some colleagues by using an Instant Chat function while others prefer the human contact of a quick Skype call.

Challenges for Virtual Team Members

These can include:

Poor and infrequent communication
It can hinder innovation, effectiveness and decision making. Moreover, not being in regular contact can prevent team members from creating working friendships and can leave them feeling isolated. They may not see how their work and projects fit as a whole and become demotivated and despondent. Team leaders can create interdependent tasks and encourage partnerships within the team—but it is also every team member's responsibility to increase everyday interactions.

Lack of trust
Because virtual team members rarely work at the same time, they cannot see what others are doing and they do not get immediate responses. These problems can be averted by setting clear goals and expectations, as well as creating awareness of the contribution and achievements of every team member.

Leading People

Diverse multicultural teams
They often comprise people with conflicting customs, work habits and values. Members prefer their own way of working and leaders must find common grounds to manage them. To minimise conflicts, all team members should agree on the fact that common, acceptable work ethics and team customs foster cultural understanding.

Loss of team spirit
Virtual teams can be more effective, cohesive and engaged through shared leadership. The team's leaders should create a clear direction for the other members, ensuring everyone accepts a common goal and vision.

Physical distance
It can foster cold, distant relationships among members—posing risks for the team's competence and cohesion. Members feel unable to ask questions and there are difficulties with the delegation. So, team leaders should pay individual attention to each member to create a sense of commitment and project ownership.

Time zone differences
Use collaboration tools in order to help you minimise the time overlap between members. This will also result in the reduction of virtual meetings.

An over-lengthy daily routine
It reduces worker concentration and motivation. Team members can feel exhausted if they are required to stay at their computers for many hours at a time to correspond with colleagues operating in different time zones. Encourage team members to work 'normal length' days, even if they are not 'nine-to-five'.

Personal life and work-life imbalance
Virtual team members often work in the same physical space where they go about their personal lives. So, work can affect team members' personal life— and the other way around. Harmonising personal life and work life is crucial to the success of any virtual work.

Lack of clarity, direction and priorities
The hardest part of establishing a specific goal is maintaining it and keeping everyone focused. Overcoming this challenge for virtual teams requires planning, dedication, foresight, hard work—and getting all team members to engage with each other.

Virtual team working is becoming increasingly common, yet many teams struggle to perform effectively.

Virtual team managers need to consider how they adapt and expand their skills to adjust to the lack of human interaction – they need additional skills, but they also need to be aware of how and when they use the skills they have.

> *Successful virtual leaders and project managers are going to be in demand!*

Leading People

Motivating Teams

There are several theories and models of motivation, including that of Frederick Hertzberg who published is to factor content theory in 1959 which explains the factors of an individual's motivation. The 2 factors identified in this theory are the hygiene factors which can demotivate or cause dissatisfaction when not present and the motivation factor which often motivates or creates satisfaction and rarely causes dissatisfaction.

Hygiene factors include:
- *policies*
- *supervision*
- *relationships*
- *working conditions*
- *salary*

Motivators include:
- *achievement*
- *recognition*
- *the work itself*
- *responsibility*
- *advancement*
- *growth*

It is obvious therefore that satisfaction and dissatisfaction in the workplace are not simply opposing reactions to the same issues but are very definitely different aspects altogether. By understanding how staff are motivated and the types of issues that are satisfying to individuals, managers and companies can ensure that the basic needs and requirements of staff are met to ensure their happy and productive.

Frederick Winslow Taylor believe that individuals were motivated only by money and while this may have been true some time ago, it is now widely recognised that people can come to work from more than the money. Elton Mayo believed that staff were motivated more by having their social needs met while at work and therefore responded more positively to several factors including better communication, greater management involvement and working within groups or teams.

One of the best-known and still valid theories of motivation that is widely used is as the basis for these theories that followed belongs to Maslow his hierarchy of human needs theory Maslow's basic proposition is that people are wanting individuals they always want more on what they want depends on what they already have; he suggested that people's needs are arranged in a series of levels or a hierarchy of importance. While Maslow identified 8 needs the hierarchy is usually shown as raging through 5 main levels from the lowest psychological needs to the high self-actualisation

As an operations/departmental manager, you will always be looking out for opportunities and ways to motivate your team. Some individuals are highly self-motivated, but most team members require motivation from time to time. As a leader, you need to ensure that your team stays motivated and you are on track to reach your organisational goals. You can do this in several ways including:

Leading People

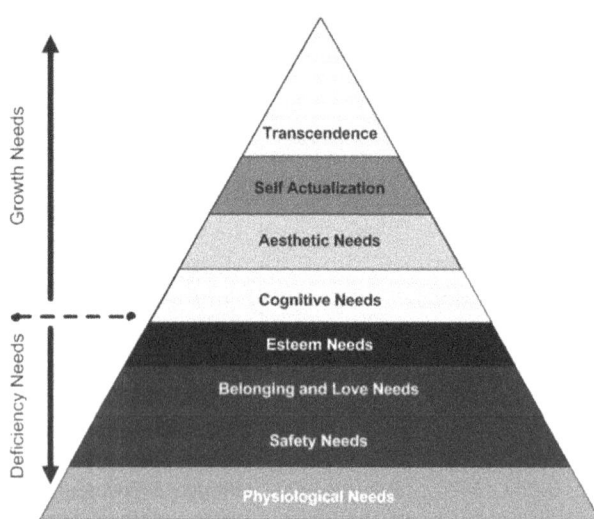

MASLOW'S MOTIVATION MODEL

(Pyramid from top to bottom: Transcendence, Self Actualization, Aesthetic Needs, Cognitive Needs, Esteem Needs, Belonging and Love Needs, Safety Needs, Physiological Needs. Growth Needs on upper portion, Deficiency Needs on lower portion.)

- *By recognising the efforts of employees for a job well done.* Simply say well done to team members or thank you goes a long way to making them feel appreciated and giving them a sense of achievement. Awarding an accolade such as an employee of the month is an effective way of recognising efforts and achievements publicly.
- *Give praise wherever possible as a leader you should exude self-confidence and integrity and recognise the efforts of your team members rightly.* If a job is being well performed, do not estate congratulate the team member-been appreciated boost morale considerably.
- *By offering rewards.* This can be financial rewards, such as pay rise, but it could also be time for prizes.
- *By offering promotion or additional responsibilities.* Some people are motivated by the progress they are making and encouraged by the prospect of a promotion and additional, interesting challenges.
- *By offering development opportunities, such as coaching or external training.* This adds to a person sense of achievement because they feel they are making progress in their careers.
- *By celebrating the teams amazing achievements*, for example, by organising the celebration

Leading People

Improving performance

To promote motivation and improve performance in your team, you should use constructive feedback mechanisms, which provide individuals orbiting with feedback on their current performance and progress towards the achievement of set objectives.

Constructive feedback is defined as an assessment of a person's performance that is used as a basis for improvement and has always intended to have a useful benefit or purpose.

Feedback is vital at every stage of an employee's development. It not only provides individuals with a regular update on the progress but also provides the opportunity for review and amendments to be made if required. There are many ways in which feedback can be provided each with their own advantages and disadvantages the following table provides a few examples:

You may wish to use feedback models such as 360° feedback this will give you greater insight into how well your team members are performing by asking for a range of people for feedback

With 360° feedback you would ask team members to complete a questionnaire describing various aspects of your performance. These aspects of eraser from high to low and you should complete a questionnaire for yourself to so you can compare the results and these areas could include

Teamwork
- *collaborates with the team collaborates with other departments*
- *motivation empowers others as a positive attitude provides positive feedback*

Communication and listening skills
- *questioning*
- *verbal*
- *written body language*

Vision and mission of the organisation
- *worst of the standard and quality expected by the organisation*
- *communicates its vision and mission to others*

Problem-solving
- *users own initiative*
- *makes plans to solve problems*
- *communicate solutions effectively*

Leading People

	Advantages	Disadvantages	Best used
appraisal meetings	Structured and planned Allow for open communication Formal record of meeting Allows staff time to think about responses	Can be dictatorial – one-way communication Allow staff time to think about responses Formal and can be intimidating to some	Annually when records need to be updated Staff become familiar with the system and accept the rationale
midyear review meetings	Allow for reviews and amendments as required Supportive Written record of discussions	Can be hurried or forgotten Can include 1-way communication May be used to identify blame	Midyear preview to update progress and review amendments
team meetings	Group discussion Written record of discussions Sharing of ideas Increased confidence Structured	Some staff may not participate Discussions may become irrelevant Digression may take place	Regularly to ensure the sharing of ideas and passing of information when all team members need to be aware
one-to-one meetings	Structured Planned in advance Allows for in-depth discussions Immediate feedback	Not always at appropriate times Team members may prefer a group setting	Regularly and ad hoc as required Allows for Hot feedback
MBWA	Informal setting Team members more likely to share information Keeps the manager in touch with staff and issues that would otherwise be hidden	Informal – not always a record of discussions Time constraints	Regularly to ensure communication stays open between staff and management

Leading People

Leadership Skills common in high performing teams

The role of a manager is not always smooth sailing. Whereas at the beginning of your career it is likely that you were purely responsible for your work alone, it is now your duty to inspire, lead and motivate your team to accomplish a set of goals for the organisation. Not everyone is going to be easy to work with and ensuring everything is running without a hitch can often prove a challenge.
From innovation to effective communication, a true leader is a step above the average manager, bringing an injection of motivation and insight into their role that not everyone has the ability to harness.

Here are a few of the leadership skills needed to stand out and lead a team to consistent long-term success:

Communication
Becoming a strong leader means mastering the art of communication. To reach the level of manager, you will have no doubt demonstrated some level of talent for this; but to set yourself apart as a leader, you need to make sure truly impactful communication is at the heart of everything you do.

Strong team leadership requires not just regular, but shrewd communication. While transparency on developments within the company is valuable for team morale and development, a lot can be said for possessing astute judgement about what you share to keep morale buoyed and your team driven towards success.

Approachability and Availability
As an integral part of your team, you need to be an ever-present member of the team, a presence at the very heart of everything they do.

Depending on the demands of the job, there will always be instances when you are not physically around, but it is imperative your team knows you are available and approachable so they know they can come to you when it matters. Set up regular one-on-one is and catch ups with your team, invest real time in their development and more than anything, nurture a culture of openness and approachability that fosters trust and respect throughout the team.

Showing Consistency
Everyone has their bad days - days when they feel tired, unmotivated, distracted or less than 100%. Apart from the true leader, of course.

Your team relies on you to be measured and consistent in your role. It means expressly setting a standard that your team can trust and lean on. That includes everything from the way you address disciplinary matters through to backing them up on internal issues. Your team needs to know that they can trust you and know what to expect from you to get the best out of their performance.

Organisation
Your team will look to you to be the person who is on the ball at all times.

Leading People

From meetings to workloads and, team projects, you need to know what is going on, who is doing what and how to approach the next steps before anyone else does. Not only that, but if operations run smoothly and everyone knows their responsibilities, then you also need to create solid guidelines for others to follow. This then makes another key aspect of team leadership easier to introduce delegation.

Delegation

Delegation is one of those tasks that anyone can do. But effective and impactful delegation is an art and one that only the most effective team leaders can learn to master. Delegating work does not mean passing on the stuff you do not want to do - it is about lightening your own workload, making sure the right people are on with the right tasks and empowering team members at the same time. Becoming a leader at work means you have time pressures in other areas, so even if your natural inclination is to take on everything placed in front of you, it is just not possible, nor beneficial, to you or your team. By delegating new work to others, you give them the opportunity to expand their portfolio, gain new experiences and grow.

As you delegate, aim to lead from the front. By coaching others through new tasks and experiences, sharing opportunities within your team and working hard yourself, you will enhance your position as a true leader and help your team become more productive and effective along the way. When working remotely, managers can be faced with challenges in adapting to this new way to delegate and manage their teams. Thanks to technology such as Zoom and Microsoft Teams, you can keep up with the fast-paced climate via effective virtual communications, through video calling and webinars. Virtual training could be an essential part of your leadership skills, to allow your teams to be fully equipped with the latest techniques and behaviours to excel; even more so when it comes to delivering against sales targets.

Confident and Knowledgeable

As a team leader, you need to command an impressive level of knowledge and, carry that off with confidence. The two properties are linked - if you know your stuff when it comes to your industry, you will feel confident in your performance and your expertise will influence your team. It goes without saying that any credible leader needs to be respected by his or her team; if that respect is missing, it can seriously hamper your chances of being a good team leader.

Be decisive

A good leader needs to be able to assert their authority and make important decisions for the team. There is no space for flakiness in a leadership role, so it is crucial that you stick to your guns and go with what you feel is best the business.

Innovate and Inspire

One of the key things that sets inspiring leaders apart from managers is the ability to innovate.

By bringing new ideas to processes and looking out for new ways to improve the way your team works, you lead by example and encourage others to find new ways to get tasks done. You will also inspire those around you to work harder and instil a practice of looking for constant improvement and development opportunities, the driving force of success.

Leading People

Set a good example
Your staff will look to you for guidance and inspiration, so it is essential that you set a good example to gain their respect. If you expect them to behave professionally and commit to their work, it is vital that you do so yourself. Make sure that you are doing your job, continuing to develop your career and support your team in doing so too.

Build positive working relationships
It is important to get to know members of your team individually, not only on a professional level but on a more personal level too. When you put the effort in to get to know a bit more about how your colleagues are doing and what they are interested in, it will build a much better rapport among the team.

Acknowledge good work
Do not be one of these bosses who only gives feedback when you have got something to criticise! By providing your staff with positive feedback it will help to build their confidence and encourage them to get more involved in the future, so it is vital that you acknowledge their achievements and the effort that they are putting in. Encourage creativity and ensure that everyone is clear about what is expected of them.

Be real
Your team does not expect you to be superhuman, so if you are feeling the pressure and need a helping hand, do not be afraid to admit it and if you make a mistake, own up! By showing the human side of yourself and allowing your staff to get to know you a bit better, your team will feel more relaxed and comfortable approaching you.

Manage conflict
When there is conflict in the workplace, it should not be ignored. Turning a blind eye could lead to a negative atmosphere, which could have implications for staff productivity and communication among the team may suffer. When an issue arises, it is crucial that it is addressed straight away before it builds.

Leadership may be very different from management, but it is also something that can be learnt and developed over time.

Leading and Managing Change

Fundamentally there is a requirement for managers to ensure that the culture and operations of the organisation are aligned. It is also important to take constant care of customers and ensure that the organisation achieves innovation in response to market changes and technological obsolescence.

Technological obsolescence is defined as the time when the technical product or services are no longer needed or wanted even though it could still be working order. It generally occurs when a new product is being created to replace an earlier version.

Hewlett-Packard Corporation identified 6 individual areas where a manager must be seen to be active these are:

Leading People

- *Taking the role of protector and promoter of the organisational values*
- *Demonstrating these values through appropriate leadership*
- *Having knowledge of the most mundane routine activities and the individuals carrying out those activities*
- *Being seen walking about the organisation, promoting and protecting its values*
- *Communicating with and being highly visible towards both staff and stakeholders*
- *Ensuring that all other people practice this process from the very top organisation to the bottom*

None of the above can be effectively conducted without the manager wondering or walking around the organisation, gauging the feelings, understand the day-to-day difficult and solutions faced by the staff and communicating, however unpleasant, the content of the discussion, with all employees being out.

Being able to and willing to listen and observe first-hand will invariably produce a much more accurate picture of the environment and culture than receiving 2nd or 3rd hand information. As a result, any decisions made, are much more likely to be the correct decisions.

As a result of monitoring activities in your role of a manager, you may identify things that you want to change or improve

Continuous improvement and change are essential for the culture of the business and its success. For example, changes in legislation or in the economy will have an impact on the business and solutions may need to be implemented to ensure that the vision and values reflect these changes. This ultimately has an impact on organisational culture. The opposite is also true, in that the culture of the organisation can have an impact on how changes managed and received by team members. They may be resistant to change for the following reasons:

- *lack of trust*
- *lack of understanding*
- *fear and uncertainty*
- *having their own agenda*
- *differing goals and views*
- *traditional values and culture*

with careful management most cultural barriers can be overcome by:

- *effective communication*
- *training*
- *allaying fears and concerns*
- *encouraging participation and team members involvement*
- *supporting team members through changes*
- *negotiating obtaining agreement*
- *encouraging incremental change*

Leading People

Adapting a leadership style to different personalities

Once upon a time, there was a young engineer. He spent his work hours in an enclosed cubicle at an office where personal computers and scientific calculators were designed. He liked to work alone, preferring solitude over committees and team meetings.

His name was Steve Wozniak. He was an introvert. He invented the first Apple computer. Here is the crazy part of this story:

> Wozniak's managers at the time did not recognise the magnitude of what their employee had been able to create while working in relative solitude. The leaders at Hewlett-Packard turned down his prototype five times before he formed a business relationship with Steve Jobs instead.

As managers, it is so important to be tuned in to our employees' personalities. Whether they are working on the next great technical innovation or simply working toward your company's next big goal, people tend to thrive when team culture bends to fit different communication styles and recognises the unique contributions of individual members—instead of forcing everyone to fit into the same mould.

Right now, you might not be aware of your employees' disparate needs for productivity and performance. You might even fear overlooking a Steve Wozniak in your midst. If you are feeling a little unsettled about your own leadership style in the midst of myriad employee personalities, do not panic. There are ways to channel your inner chameleon and adapt to the distinct needs of each type.

Employee personalities and the complexities of team dynamics

Not long ago, there were introverted employees and extroverted employees. Everyone was separated by office walls or cubicles located in the same office.

Now there are outgoing extroverts working in isolated remote locations, silent introverts being asked to stand up and tell everyone what they are doing and ambiverts who…wait, what is an "ambivert?"

Think about the various personalities in your team. This will help you identify when the communication style you use to great effect with one employee is actually detrimental to the productivity of another. You might even discover some untapped strengths that will help you realise the powerful potential of personality-based leadership.
For example, many leaders are not aware that:

> Passive employees are often best led by extroverted managers. A study from Harvard, the Wharton Business School and the University of North Carolina at Chapel Hill shows how extrovert leadership characteristics—bold, assertive, talkative and energetic—can be an advantage when a team consists of passive employees.

Leading People

Researchers Adam Grant, Dave Hofmann and Francesca Gino compared the profitability of 57 different stores within the same U.S. pizza delivery chain. In stores with less assertive employees, those led by extroverts achieved 16% higher profits than those led by introverts. By comparison, stores with proactive employees led by extroverts showed 14% lower profits.

Teams rarely consist of just one personality type. While certain industries may attract one type over another, most teams will have a mix of all three. As a manager, you have your own personal preferences for communication and collaboration—which may not always naturally align with the dispositions of people you are leading.

So… How should an introverted manager handle a whirlwind of knocks on the door when all he wants is a quiet place to think? Likewise, how can an extroverted manager get things done when surrounded by quiet thinkers who do not share their love of out loud brainstorming?

How to Lead an Introverted Team Member
On one end of the Myers-Briggs personality spectrum is the reflective and reserved introvert. In work settings, introverts tend to:

- *Think and plan ahead*
- *Focus on one task or issue at a time*
- *Draw energy from inner reflection*

They are generally uncomfortable with:

- *On-the-spot brainstorming*
- *Loud, open office spaces*
- *Meetings that lack purposes and agendas*

When leading introverts, it is a good idea to:

- *Send a meeting agenda ahead of time so introverted employees can ponder on things and join the conversation with thought-out contributions.*
- *Avoid spontaneous brainstorming sessions in favour of pre-planned discussions, which will give your introverts ample time to process information and prepare.*
- *Offer quiet, closed-door spaces for inner reflection and silent brainstorming. Or, better yet, give your staff the freedom to work remotely as often as needed.*

How to lead an extroverted team member
Extroverts are outgoing and draw energy from social interactions. In direct contrast to their introverted counterparts, extroverted employees tend to:

- *Talk first and think later*
- *Multitask and brainstorm out loud*
- *Thrive in group settings and open office concepts*

Leading People

They are generally uncomfortable with:

- *Solitary tasks*
- *Quiet, enclosed spaces with few interruptions*
- *Meetings with too much structure*

To effectively lead extroverts, you can:

- *Make time for face-to-face conversations, especially if you rely on online stand-ups to minimise meetings and foster communication.*
- *Work team building activities into your routine or, better yet, hand over the reins to your extroverted team members when it is time to plan social gatherings.*
- *Provide opportunities for out-loud thinking, whether it is an optional group brainstorm, or an office area dedicated to impromptu debates and discussions.*

How to lead an ambivert team member

Ambiverts fall in the middle of the personality spectrum. You can recognise ambivert employees by their tendencies to:

- *Move comfortably from isolation to group settings*
- *Toggle back and forth between initiating and reacting to ideas*
- *Adapt to the communication styles around them*
- *You would have to work pretty hard to make an ambivert uncomfortable.*

When leading ambiverts, try to:

- *Remain flexible. For example, an ambivert who works remotely may want to take advantage of employee benefits that let him work from a home office and a coworking space.*
- *Mix things up so ambiverts have equal opportunities to be stimulated by group settings and recharge with alone time to think.*

Adapting to multiple styles

As team leader, it is your job to adapt to each individual while simultaneously helping everyone work more effectively together. Encouraging your staff to celebrate differences can help everyone stay in sync and reach goals faster.

> *For instance, you might choose to adopt Jeff Bezos' strategy for levelling the playing field at meetings by starting with silent reading and thinking. Or, if that*

Leading People

is too much for you, require participants to set aside 15-30 minutes on their own time to prepare ahead. You will give introverts time to formulate and share thoughts confidently, motivate extroverts to reflect and listen and provide ambiverts with an opportunity to do both.

You can also structure meetings to accommodate different personalities. Keep them short and on-task, then host optional 15-minute brainstorm sessions for the extroverts when they are over. For the introverts, you can offer a suitable feed for follow up ideas.

The key to maximising your team's talents is to identify the zone of stimulation that is right for each individual. Some employees will prefer quiet; others may thrive in open-office concepts. Some need reflective time be creative; others are energised by group activities. Once you understand the innate needs of each personality type, it is possible to open up a whole new world of productivity.

Effective Delegation

Effective leaders are well organised and able to delegate. They bring order to chaos. They know they work better in a well-managed team and delegate the workload according to team members abilities. They plan the workload well, are good at managing their own time and prioritise task accordingly it should direct

It should be recognised that delegation does not always come easy. There are a few negatives that can be attributed to delegating and therefore some managers will talk themselves out of it before attempting to delegate effectively.

There may be a feeling of the need to control everything for it to be done right, that they have to be the ones to do it. It may be perceived that it can be more effective with regard to time management to do the task rather than to train, coach, show or explain to someone else out to do it. There may also be a trust issue to be considered. Do you trust the person is taking on this task or responsibility? While these hurdles may appear valid and significant, a well-planned approach that follows a logical structure can assist alleviate them.

Knowing what to delegate must be the first consideration. It should be accepted that some Tasks can be delegated while others should not be.

Delegation depends on the relationship with the individual. For a successful relationship to be built, several criteria need to be met by the individual, including:

Do they have the necessary skills?
Are they trustworthy?
Do they have the required capacity?
Do they have a positive performance history?

When these aspects are met the person in question would be a prime candidate for task to be delegated to.

Leading People

Clear instruction and documentation. Detailed information should be provided minimise any risk of miscommunication or lack of understanding

Review and monitor progress of the task on a regular basis. This could be daily, weekly or even hourly, depending on the nature of the task. Ongoing communications are required in as the business responsibilities change; delegation needs will also change.

Workload should be examined on a regular basis. The individual's capacity and capability should be considered, ensuring delegation does not overload them and that their work performance remains at a high level.

Successful delegation relies on having the above in place or these points can be incorporated into easy steps as follows.

1. decide on defined the activity
2. select the activity or team to delegate the activity to
3. assess the capabilities of the individual or team to complete the activity
4. explain the rationale for the activity
5. state the desired outcomes of the activity
6. plan and sauce resources
7. agree on an action plan and deadlines
8. established lines of communication support
9. decide the feedback mechanisms and went to review results

A good tool to use for effective delegation is an extension of SMART and utilising SMARTER goals associated with delegated activities, can keep them on track. This stands for specific measurable agreed realistic time bound ethical and recorded
The addition of ethical will ensure that the activities that are undertaken in line with the culture of the business and the fact that the goals are recorded can make the delegated task easy to track and monitor.

Tannenbaum and Schmidt developed a leadership theory that concentrates on delegation, outlining 7 levels of delegation and freedom. The 7 levels are:

1. The manager makes the decision informs the staff
2. The manager sells the decision to the team
3. The manager presents ideas and invites team to discussion us questions
4. The manager presents a provisional decision that is subject to change
5. The manager presents the problems, asks for suggestions, then makes a decision
6. The manager asked the teams to make the decision from the options given, based on set limits
7. The manager allows a team to develop the options and make the decisions based on the limitations set

Leading People

As an operation/departmental manager, you should be able to explain the organisation's vision and goals to your team members and others, including how these apply to them.

Communicating with a Team

Leadership is important in any organisation. Effective leadership ensures that the organisation has an established vision and that this is clearly communicated to the teams within the organisation.

> *Your skills in communication have a significant impact on performance at an organisational and team level.*

Team members will rely on their manager to keep them informed, answer their questions and support them in achieving the objectives that come from the organisation strategy, which informs the purpose of the team.

Poor leadership and communication can have a negative impact on a team's performance. As a manager, you are only as good as the team perceives you to be. Being connected is a necessity to rule out misconceptions and be clear in your dealings. When communicating the organisation's strategy and the team's purpose, information should include the individual and team objectives, responsibilities and priorities. Team members need to know of any specific objectives, the rationale behind them as well as how they can be achieved and how they fit into the strategy. Everyone will need to be made aware of who has responsibility for the completing the objective, for reviewing it and the timeframe in which it must be achieved.

The purpose of the team should align with specific job roles specifications. Any plan should be structured, defined and documentation provided that can be referred to on a regular basis. It should be flexible and reviewed an ongoing basis to ensure additional support can be provided as required or the objective is amended appropriately, in line with the service or the organisation's, requirements.

Effective communication should be maintained throughout the process of sharing the strategy and team purpose and when setting and working towards achieving objectives. There are several different ways that information can be communicated and conveyed to the relevant parties. However, the method chosen must be appropriate and relevant. This will vary according to the nature of the information and who needs to be in receipt of it, as well as the urgency to disseminate the details,
Example:

> *Communicating information that has an immediate impact could be disseminated via email rather than waiting until a group of people can be brought together.*

A selection of different communication methods can be found in the following table together with their advantages and disadvantages and when they are best used.

Leading People

Being knowledgeable about the organisation strategy and purpose of the team is very important and the way it is communicated is crucial in passing on this knowledge. It will be necessary to adapt how this is explained depending on the audience.

Team members will typically be a mixture of experienced individuals who will already have knowledge of the strategy and purpose and will be familiar with the terminology used in the business and inexperienced individuals who have little knowledge. Avoiding jargon or abbreviations that not everyone will understand is a necessity. New employees should also be invited to ask questions and providing explanations and additional resources may help them.

Method	Advantages	Disadvantages	Best Used for
Oral Presentation	Audience is captive Immediate clarification Allows Q&A Body language can be monitored Same message at the same time	Takes time to arrange Some delegates my not be able to attend Some delegates may be intimidated by large groups	When immediate feedback is required When briefing teams and information needs to be passed simultaneously
Written Presentation	Can be read more than once Provides a written record	May not be received Information is subject to misinterpretation	When a written response is required When time is not a constraint A formal record is required
Email	When an audit trail is needed Blanket mailing is available	May be sent to junk or spam Not all recipients may be able to access it	When large numbers of people need to be notified
Notice board	Prominent location so widely seen Bush telegraph will pass on message	May not be seen by all Message open to misinterpretation	Message is not critical – not tracked
Internal memos	When a written record is required	May not be received by all Open to misinterpretation	When sending confidential information to internal staff
Brief others and delegate tasks	Staff development Career progression Confidence building	Information may be misinterpreted by sender or receiver Delegates lack the confidence to deliver the message	To offer personal / professional development

Leading People

Improving Leadership

It is vital that every leader and manager does not ignore the fact that there is always scope to improve their Leadership Skills. Consider some of the following suggestions and try to implement or develop these within the existing leadership style.

Be transparent
It is important to be transparent with Stakeholders right across the organisation. Transparency makes teams more accountable, happier, motivated and creative. Transparent workplaces help develop mutual respect between team members and their leaders. Open and consistent communication, combined with transparency help team members feel secure in their positions and they are happy to contribute their ideas and suggestions for improvement and change which in turn, enhances creativity.

Maintain communications
Open communications create an environment where team leaders are able to provide open, honest and constructive feedback to team members who also feel confident to express their concerns to one another. Where team members are working remotely, Teams, Zoom, et al. provide an opportunity to enjoy some face-to-face contact is achieved. If a distributed team is working across time zones and it is necessary to set up a standing appointment for calls, it is important to find a time which works for everyone involved. By not always holding calls at inconvenient times for the remote team member, they will be more open (and awake) to communicate honestly and accurately.

Provide valuable feedback
Providing feedback is one of the best ways to support team members and help them to develop professionally and personally.

Regular, planned, opportunities should be set aside to simply catch up even if there is no feedback to give. Any areas of work which could be improved could be discussed and provide an opportunity to express how team members are progressing and could develop further.   Delivering feedback can be challenging, but it is an essential part of team management leadership. These conversations can be difficult, but they are important and necessary for the development of team members and the success of the wider team.

Collaboration
Team members should be encouraged to collaborate. The team will have a diverse set of skills and by ensuring that all of these skills are drawn upon by the whole team, the collaboration will increase creativity. Cloud drives encourage collaboration by allowing real-time updates on shared documents. Online mind mapping is another effective tool to which team members can contribute ideas as they happen. This has been found to boost creative thinking, as it engages everyone's minds in processing and creating new ideas and concepts by using visual, spatial and kinaesthetic senses to increasing creativity.

Trust the team to do their job
Effective team management should not mean micro-management. Organisations recruit competent staff to work in specialist areas, like programming and they are best left alone to do their job.

Leading People

By take a back seat in the process you to remain in the loop with how the task is progressing and are also part of related discussions, but only stepping in to provide support when needed.

Prevent burn-out
As a team leader, you set the boundaries of work, play and relaxation. It is the responsibility of the employer to draw the line about when and where team members should be switching off from work entirely. Planned legislation requires that employers cannot require team members to check emails after working hours.

The effective leader should encourage team members to set themselves some working limits, to sleep well and avoid burn-out.

Supporting the Management of Change within the Organisation

To manage change effectively, it is vitally important you understand the reasons behind the change. This is true whether it is something that you have been instructed to do or an incremental change you want to make.

Preparations should include consideration of why the change is going to be made, and it is important to assess and anticipate the potential impact and possible reaction of team members.

> *A manager's role is one of communicating, facilitating and enabling the change to happen.*

This needs to be done in a way that brings team members and colleagues on board. Initial meeting should be face-to-face and team member should be allowed to ask questions, voice their concerns and make suggestions. You will need to identify those who may take change badly or will be negative from the outset and it may be prudent to involve such individuals, drawing on their skills and experience.

John P Cotter developed a model for change management. His 8 steps to successful change are listed below and can be used to demonstrate support for the team.

1. **Increase urgency-ensure object is achievable and motivate team members**
2. **Build the guiding team-use team members are committed to the change and have the right skills**
3. **Get the vision right-involve the team in establishing a plan to meet the vision use their creativity to drive it forward**
   - *Communicate for buying-use clear and concise communication, use technology were appropriate and get team members involved*
   - *Empower actions-consider any obstacles and remove them, recognise achievement and reward progress and encourage constructive feedback*

Leading People

- *Create short-term wins-set short-term, achievable goals, which are manageable and finish one before moving on to the next*
- *Do not let up-monitor progress and report on the achievement of short-term goals, highlight future goals and make progress visible*
- *Make change stick-highlight and reinforce successful change, use opportunist promotional recruitment.*

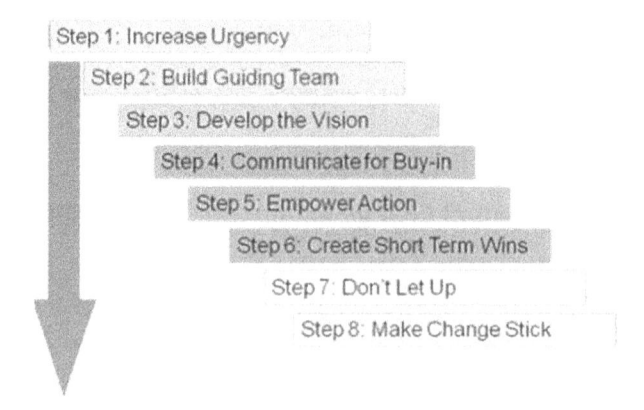

Step 1: Increase Urgency
Step 2: Build Guiding Team
Step 3: Develop the Vision
Step 4: Communicate for Buy-in
Step 5: Empower Action
Step 6: Create Short Term Wins
Step 7: Don't Let Up
Step 8: Make Change Stick

Supporting Development through Coaching and Mentoring

The team's ongoing development is crucial to the success of the business. A manager should be able to demonstrate that they support their team through coaching and mentoring and by promoting positive attitudes and behaviours.

By personally and professionally developing team members, they will feel valued and engaged in the process, display increase motivation and achieve a sense of self-worth which will increase job satisfaction and enable them to complete their role more effectively and efficiently.

This will also help lift team morale and performance as well as improved attitudes which could in turn have a positive impact on behaviours and improve prospects for internal promotion, if desired. The key to self-development is to ensure that the plan is structured and compiled using a personal development plan.

Coaching and mentoring activities are excellent method for supporting high-performance working

Coaching is a method of directing, instructing and training a person or a group of people, with the aim of achieving goals or developing specific skills.
Mentoring is an employee training system under which a senior or more experienced individual, the mentor, is assigned to act as an adviser, counsel or guide to a junior or trainee.

Leading People

The mentor is responsible for providing support to and feedback on the individual in their charge

The coach will often be a more senior experience colleague, ideally displaying excellent interpersonal skills.

Coaching members of your team can have many benefits, not only on the team's performance, but also for their colleagues in the organisation.

Coaching your team members can

- *Build on existing skills of the team members*
- *develop new skills specific to a role or task*
- *improving individual or the team's performance*
- *contribute to the success of the business*
- *increase employee's loyalty to the organisation*
- *ensure team member feels supported and valued*
- *contribute quality*
- *provide fast on-the-job training*

To implement a coaching programme within an organisation, there are key elements that need to be considered including:

- *identify the reason for the program*
- *understand the requirements*
- *the approach to be taken*
- *development of action plans*
- *review*

Armstrong identified 4 principles to successful coaching

1. **controlled delegation of developmental tasks** - *do not leave the responsibility to the individual, as a coach you should be as specific as possible at a should be detailed and understood.*
2. **use of all situations as a learning environment** - *an effective coach will recognise learning opportunities and utilise these to the benefit of the individual.*
3. **effective guidance on specific tasks -** *the individual needs to receive specific details on what is to be achieved not necessarily the how. A good coach will set flexible parameters to be followed.*
4. **provision of feedback on specific tasks** - *it should be accepted that feedback will be provided promptly and constructively.*

The implementation of a successful coaching program can be a cost-effective approach to staff development, utilising the skills and experience available within a department, team or division. It enables organisations to focus on specific individuals and identified areas of need.

Leading People

The requirement to recruit new employees can be reduced and staff morale and motivation improve, leading to a reduction in turnover costs.
However, this can only be achieved when all levels of the management structure have bought into the program, are aware of the benefits and supportive of those staff involved. The focus of the programme should be on one-to-one relationships and just as it is important for a trainee to receive appropriate coaching to develop their skills, the coach should also receive the appropriate training, supervision, support and guidance to be effective.

Whereas coaching is a task and skill specific, it should be acknowledged that it is no substitute for formal training but serves as a supplement to this and the many other training and learning opportunities available.

Mentoring programs are often implemented to provide support and guidance to individuals considering longer term development or career progression. Mentoring should not be provided by an individual's line manager and mentor's will usually be more senior members of staff.

Both coaches and mentors need to be skilled in providing constructive feedback and have the ability to motivate and inspire. When coaches and mentors are being paired with employees, consideration must be given to the personalities involved; do they get on well, will they gel? To maximise possibilities for success and reduced negativity, compatibility has to be found. For these partnerships to progress, availability also has to be considered. Where are the benefits in being coached by an individual who is not available when you are? When these partnerships have been identified, clarification should be provided by both parties confirming that each is clear on the expectations of the other, as well as any boundaries or restraints that can be identified on what will or will not be done on behalf of the other.

This not only avoids confusion, but also minimises disappointment when previously unspoken expectations are not met.

> *The basis for success within the relationship must be that of trust and there is no exception, without it the program and its stated objectives is highly likely to fail.*

A coaching or mentoring contract should be agreed, which provides clear and concise roles and responsibility to both parties. At the same time, it can be utilised to include a timetable for the meetings or sessions, the types of lines of communication that are available and any boundaries or borders identified.

It must be recognised that confidentiality within the partnership is an important aspect of its success and must be adhered to always. All aspects of discussions between coach and trainee or mentor and mentee, will remain confidential unless both parties agree to its disclosure. However, it must be recognised any information disclosed with either legal or financial imprecations to the organisation may not be contained within the clause of confidentiality.

When a promising relationship has been instigated, work must be ongoing to ensure this is built on effectively. Mutual trust and respect are earned and in maintaining this, promises must be kept and objectives met appropriately. Regular reviews of progress are a good way of

Leading People

maintaining the relationship positively, as is that of ensuring future objectives and action planning is agreed.

> *Maintenance of open lines of communication is paramount to ensuring the relationship can grow positively and by making sure availability is structured and met and commitment will be demonstrated by all concerned.*

It must be acknowledged that some people just do not get on or do not get the best from each other and this must be addressed. The contract can include the steps that should be taken in such circumstances and the outgoing coach or mentor should be instrumental in ensuring an alternative individual is identified and an effective handover provided.
When preparing a coaching plan from member staff consideration needs to be given to:

What is to be achieved?
An objective needs to be identified in this can vary from being something quite minor and easily achievable in a minimum number of sessions, to something quite sizeable that may take a longer period with a high number of meetings or sessions range. Larger objectives may need to be broken down into smaller achievable targets.

Who will be identified as the coach?
Identification densification of the appropriate person to act as a coach needs to be clarified as early as possible in the planning of the programme, considering aspects identified previously, including availability. It is accepted the immediate supervisors or line managers lend themselves to be very effective coaches as do more experienced peers.

What learning method should be considered
Due consideration is required to the preferred learning styles of the trainee and where possible we should be incorporated in the plan. Identification of the coach of the preferred learning style should be undertaken before the plan is developed and finalised to increase the appropriateness of the plan itself and how the objectives will be achieved.

How does a trainee prefer to receive information?
The methods of sending receiving information should be established at the beginning the process and could be carried out face-to-face or remotely for example, using email or conference calls

What form will the coaching take?
Coaching can be formal or informal. Formal culture will be structured and planned in informal coaching is very structure may be opportunistic. It may be used alongside training in conjunction with mentoring and can enhance businesses internal learning programme or could be provided by an external training organisation, or a mix of both. It is important that the trainee knows what form of coaching will take the planning stage.

What timetable will be set
The timetable will be agreed upon on the to the individual, the business, the availability of the coach. The length of the programme will depend on the objectives set, which means that it could be short-term, for example, when learning a skill, or longer term, for example

Leading People

when undertaking a reduction program. It is important that the timetable is monitored, reviewed and amended as necessary throughout the life of the coaching programme.

How will it be reviewed and evaluated

The final stage of any coaching or mentoring plan must be the review and evaluation stage. Discussions need to be held to identify whether the initial objectives/outcomes of be met and to the agreed acceptable standards. The review should be a two-way discussion with not only the coach identify what the trainee is achieved, but also the trainee be encouraged to identify what the coach did well, did not do well and/or how improvements the process could be made.

Formal evaluation can take place that may include a 3rd member staff be requested to observe either discussions or actual outcomes. Evaluation forms could be utilised, which would be completed and areas of development identified. Evaluation can also take the form of testing to identify the member staff knowledge and measure the success of the training. Kirkpatrick's four level training evaluation model takes this further and includes workplace behaviours, looking at how the coaching/learning is affected work environment. At an organisational level, he says the impact of coaching/learning on the organisation should also be considered. The model includes:

1. **reaction**-how did the learners react to the training or coaching?
2. **learning**-has their knowledge increased as result of the training/coaching?
3. **behaviour**-have they changed their behaviour as a result of the training/coaching?
4. **results**-analyse the results, have the desired outcomes been achieved?

What will be the next steps?

The review of the plan should also identify the next steps if the current objective has been successfully met this may be moving on to another area of development, or that the trainee is now able to move onto a more structured form of professional development or training programme. If the initial objectives or task has been met in full then the review will address this and the new plan will be devised, learning from the one just completed. These next steps can be identified as part of individuals appraisal or object is for the future.

Both coaching and mentoring will rely on other processes been in place the individual, for example, work shadowing, one-to-one training, setting the green goals and personal development plans.

Leading People

Coaching and Mentoring Models

OSCAR Model

The OSCAR coaching model was originally described by Karen Whittleworth and Andrew Gilbert in 2002. The aim of the authors was to develop a model that built upon and enhanced the existing GROW model (1990s), with the intention to provide those in managerial positions with the ability to adopt a developmental coaching style, to the benefit of their company and team.

The model is built around five contributing factors:

Outcome	Situation	Choices	Actions	Review
Determine the outcome and goals of the session	Clarify the individuals current situation and feelings	Generate choices and consider the consequences	Determine the next immediate steps in their chosen process	Develop a plan to return back and review the process

The model operates under the notion that if these factors are satisfied, understood and applied by the coach then the long-term result of their interaction with the employee will be achieving the *'outcome'*, whereby demonstrating effective coaching.

The OSCAR model can be applied in almost any personal development scenario; however, it is argued that it is most effective when used when working towards long term *'outcomes'*, as the framework provides impetus for the implementation of attainable milestones through the *'actions'* aspect.

Example:

> an employee may approach the coach for advice on becoming a stronger team leader when taking part in team-based tasks.

Firstly, the coach and the employee should discuss the issue at hand (the primary topic of the meeting) and work together to identify the desired outcome of the session and the long-term goals of the individual.

In the case of the example above, this would likely be to develop the ability to take charge and be heard in team-based scenarios. In a less specific scenario, here are a few sample questions that the manager or coach may ask the individual to encourage discussion:

- *What is it you would like to achieve from this session?*
- *What is your long-term goal?*
- *Once you have reached your goal – what does it look like? What does it feel like?*

Leading People

The second step would be to ascertain the current skill/ability/knowledge level of the team member and encourage discussion as to why they are at that level. The aim of questioning and discussion here is to raise the mentee's understanding and awareness of their own situation.

Also discussed during this section of the process are the feelings of the individual and how they feel their current situation is impacting their lives and those of their peers.

- *How do you currently feel about your situation?*
- *Where are you at now in terms of your goals?*
- *What has been happening in your work and life recently?*
- *How do you think others feel about your current situation?*

Following this, the coach will help the team member to identify all the potential avenues for attaining the 'outcome'. For example, perhaps undertaking a training course of some sort. For all the brainstormed choices discussed, the consequences and ramifications of each will be considered, allowing the individual to discard less practical or excessively difficult avenues and work towards a single viable route to their long-term goals.

- *What current options for action are available to you?*
- *What are the consequences of any potential choices?*
- *What would be the impacts on other people?*
- *Which of your options has the best consequences for you and for others?*

The next step is to identify where improvements can be made and how to make them. The focus of actions is the immediate and attainable targets that the mentee can work towards. SMART (specific, measurable, accurate, realistic and timely) can serve as a checklist for any of the actions designed during this period of the session. All actions should be motivational enough that the individual will strive and work towards them, but not so far from their current situation that they will find the task impossible and therefore lose motivation. All actions should have distinct – though realistic – deadlines so that the individual is motivated to work and has points at which they can measure progress. An example of action could be signing up for a training course or identifying a course that would most suit the team member. In addition to this, any support that may be required during the process should be identified.

- *What immediate actions will you take?*
- *When are you going to take those actions?*
- *Who is going to provide the support for you throughout the process?*
- *How motivated are you to take these actions?*

Finally, in the review stage the coach and learner will arrange to hold regular meetings to ensure that the team member is on track and to offer any assistance, should it be required. These meetings and review checkpoints can be based upon the deadlines for tasks set in the action section of the process. If it is found that the individual is no longer on track for sections of their action plan, perhaps the long-term and short-term goals should be re-assessed using the OSCAR process once more.

Leading People

- *How do you plan to review your progress?*
- *When is it suitable for us to review progress?*
- *Have your actions been moving you towards your goal?*
- *Are you still motivated to take said actions?*

The OSCAR model is useful for coaches that choose to adopt less autocratic approaches to leading and coaching, as it allows them to provide support whilst giving the employee space to take charge of their own action plan. By integrating the model, the coach or manager can regularly check that their team member is on track and working towards achieving their goals, whilst providing a safety net should the team member become overwhelmed or unable to complete certain tasks.

As a result, the primary use of OSCAR is to encourage employee development over both the short and long-term. It is particularly useful for coaches that do not have large amounts of time to personally supervise and guide each employee to their outcome, as it allows the coach to provide support whilst encouraging the employee to take the lead on their own development.

GROW Model

The GROW Model is probably the most widely utilised goal-setting and problem-solving model in the UK, perhaps the world. It provides a simple and methodical, yet-powerful framework of four main stages of a coaching or mentoring session. Though no-one can claim to be the sole inventor of the model, thought leaders and writers Alan Fine and Graham Alexander, along with former racing car champion John Whitmore made large contributions to the contemporary model, which was largely developed during the 1980s and 1990s.

The acronym **GROW** stands for:

- *Goal*
- *Reality*
- *Opportunity*
- *Will/Wrap-up/What*

These four words and phrases correspond to the four main stages of a coaching or mentoring session.

Goal
During the first stage of the process, the goal is the priority. Once a topic for discussion is agreed, specific outcomes and objectives should be discussed by the coach/mentor and the client/mentee/pupil. These may be short term goals, or – when appropriate and a clear path to the outcome can be agreed – they may be long term aims. Goals should be SMART: Specific, Measurable, Accurate, Realistic and Timely. The goal should also be inspirational and positive, whilst being challenging and requiring them to stretch themselves and their abilities to achieve it.

Example questions for a coach:

Leading People

- *What do you want?*
- *What does that look like?*
- *What will people be saying to you?*
- *How will you feel once this is achieved?*
- *What is different?*

Reality
During the second stage of the process, both coach and mentee outline and discuss the current reality of the situation using a variety of different methods and techniques. The coach may invite the client to assess their own situation before offering their own advice or specific feedback on the current scenario and obstacles faced. The focus should be on the client and the coach should be looking to identify potential in the situation, rather than problems. They should examine any assumptions made by the client with regards to their reality and outlook on future goals and discard any history or events that are irrelevant to the goals at hand.

Example questions:

- *What is happening right now?*
- *How far are you from an ideal situation?*
- *How do you feel about your current situation?*
- *What is the impact on you and your life?*
- *What is standing in the way of your goal?*

Opportunity
Once reality and all obstacles to current goals have been discussed and irrelevant 'pseudo-obstacles' discarded, the options as to how to overcome current issues preventing progress should be examined. At first, the full range of options should be put-forward and discussed, predominantly inviting suggestions from the client. Any suggestions posited by the coach or mentor should be offered carefully and with consideration of the client's overall position. By the end of stage 3, the coach should ensure that at least some choices have been made with regards to overcoming obstacles and there is significantly less ambiguity surrounding immediate actions.

Example questions:

- *What could you have?*
- *What ideas do you have?*
- *What actions have worked for you in the past?*
- *Who could help you to achieve your goals?*
- *What information do you need and how could you acquire it?*

Will/Wrap-up/What next? /Way Forward
The final stage of the process is when the client commits to decisive actions in order to move towards their goal. A plan is drawn up, with the coach guiding the ideas discussed by

Leading People

the mentee – including specific guidelines and timings in order to make achievable progress. Any potential obstacles that may be encountered during the process are identified and subsequent solutions are considered, including an outline of the support required throughout. Both mentor and mentee should remain flexible throughout the entire process and goals/actions may need to be altered to react to both positive and negative events.

Example questions:

- *What will you do to achieve your goals?*
- *How and when will you do it?*
- *Who will you talk to throughout?*
- *Are there any other measures you need to put into place?*
- *How committed are you to this action?*

ACHIEVE Model

ACHIEVE is a coaching and mentoring model developed by The Coaching Centre (Dembkowski and Eldridge, 2003), building upon the foundations of the **GROW** model, inspired by leading thinkers such as Alan Fine, Graham Alexander and John Whitmore. It is posited as a methodical and systematic framework for coaching, but with added flexibility and feedback-reactivity compared with GROW. It was observed that leading executive coaches intuitively went above the framework outlined by GROW, so a new cyclical ACHIEVE model was formulated to accommodate this responsive plasticity and to attain measurable and sustainable results for their clients. This model is intended to increase trust between client and coach by increasing understanding of the methods involved in goal-setting and problem-solving.

The seven stages of the ACHIEVE model are:

- *Assess current situation*
- *Creative brainstorming*
- *Hone goals*
- *Initiate option generation*
- *Evaluate options*
- *Valid action programme design*
- *Encourage momentum*

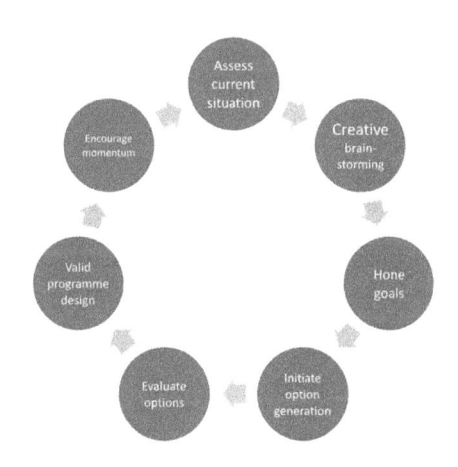

Assess the current situation
During the first stage of the process, the client or mentee is encouraged to think deeply about their current situation. Increased self-awareness of their state and surroundings allows the mentee to reflect on their current issues and goals and to contextualise any

Leading People

future actions. It also increases understanding of how the current situation came about, which actions they took to reach this point and how they initiated emotional responses in others.

Creative brainstorming
This stage is designed to broaden the mentees perspectives and develops the foundation for behavioural change and creative solutions to current challenges. Sometimes, individuals' perspectives can narrow when under stress – resulting in "tunnel vision" – the goal of the brainstorming stage is to open their mind and examine solutions that were not previously visible to the mentee. Mentees are moved towards a broader perspective and removes them from repetitive, unhelpful cycles of behaviour. Creative brainstorming is the foundation for goal setting and action-planning.

Hone goals
In stage three, the mentee develops specific goals from alternative solutions and suggestions which evolved during stage two. **SMART** *(specific, measurable, accurate, realistic, timely)* goals are developed and refined here by feedback between coach and client. Often, individuals struggle to identify what they do want – rather, the focus is on what they do not wish to happen. It is the aim of the coach to ensure that this negative thinking does not occur and instead the emphasis is on achievable goal formation.

Initiate option generation
At this stage in the process, the immediate steps in order to achieve the goals must be considered. The client should be aided in developing an array of possible options, rather than focusing on finding a single "right" way to act. Indeed, the volume of options at this stage should outweigh any focus on the quality or achievability of a single action.

Evaluate options
At step five, the actions and options generated during the previous stage will be assessed, scrutinised and prioritised. The coach begins to guide the client towards a focus, or small number of foci. It is crucial that aims are well-defined, in order to make goals appear within reach to the mentee. Though the coach may be purely executive, they may encourage that the client also applies these steps to their private lives – an aspect often not considered or analysed methodically by the mentee.

Valid action programme design
The aim of stage 6 is to put the options into action. Pragmatic approaches will be developed to break down overall goals into smaller chunks. This is when the client/mentee will commit to the plan via achievable steps of action with clear deadlines, often in writing or illustrated form. The challenge is often applying newly developed knowledge and skills from coaching and training into a workplace or other scenario and it is the job of the mentor to guide their mentee into such a position where they have the confidence to apply themselves.

Encourage momentum
The final stage of ACHIEVE is to encourage momentum – both towards goals – and between coaching sessions. Until goals have been met, it is often difficult for individuals to remain motivated and it is therefore the role of the coach to maintain encouragement and keep achievable goals within sight. The smallest steps and achievements must be met with

Leading People

encouragement and a sense of fulfilment. Small, sustainable goals and changes are the way to remain on the path towards a far larger, more distant aim.

……………………Repeat

The ACHIEVE process is flexible and repetitive, once goals have been reached – or perhaps a sustained plateau of little progress occurs – it may be suitable to begin to reassess the current situation at stage 1 and plan new steps and pathways as to how to rebuild momentum towards the final goal

STEPPPA Model

STEPPPA (2003) is a coaching and mentoring model developed by world-renowned coach and instructor, Dr. Angus McLeod. It acts as a process by which the context and emotion of a situation or issue can be used to define and act towards new goals. STEPPPA is primarily utilised as a technique when there are difficult emotions in play which need to be overcome. It acts as a framework to assist coaches both during coaching sessions and afterwards to reflect upon coaching practice. The questions and prompts which should be utilised during STEPPPA coaching practice are organised acronymically into the following framework:

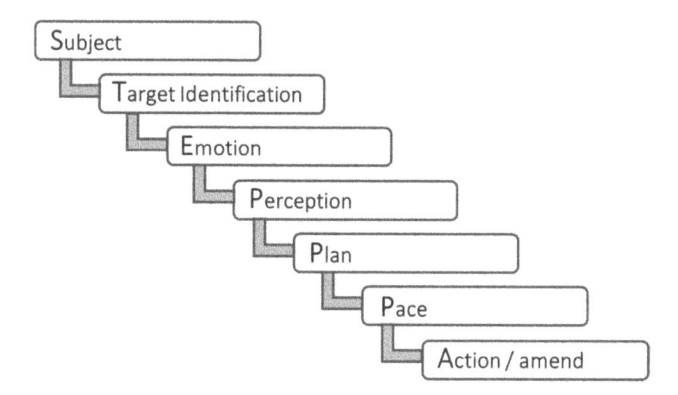

- **S**ubject
- **T**arget Identification
- **E**motion
- **P**erception
- **P**lan
- **P**ace
- **A**ction / amend

The starting point of the coaching session will be to identify and understand the subject and context of the discussion. Generally, the client will be encouraged to initiate the discussion and bring up the topic for discussion. It will be the role of the coach to support the client by separating any emotions which may cloud the discussion and hinder the development of any future goals set. It may take some time and prompting for the coach to fully unravel the extent and context of the subject and patience is required.

Example questions:

- *What would you like to discuss?*
- *Is there an area you would like to focus on?*

Leading People

Target Identification
At this stage in the process, the learner is encouraged to establish an attainable target or outcome, following the **SMART** *(Specific, Measurable, Accurate, Realistic and Timely)* template for goal setting. If a goal cannot be immediately formed, then the coach should gently question the client and guide them towards a desired outcome. The target must be motivational enough for the client to wish to reach for it, but not so far that it is unachievable. The wider context and impact of such new goals should also be considered. If a SMART target cannot be set during this period, the process can continue, but target identification should be reintroduced following the perception section in order to be able to develop a plan for such. Example questions:

- *What would you like to be the outcome of this session?*
- *What are your long-term goals?*
- *When do you plan to achieve your current goals?*

Emotion
No decision is entirely objective - emotions are one of our most important motivators, yet are often neglected by mentors when it comes to aiding their mentees make important decisions. Sometimes emotions will aid oneself in the drive towards a goal but often they can also act as a hinderance, blocking perfectly attainable targets. With a target or area for the subject to aim for, it must be considered whether emotions ae going to act restrictively, or as a motivator en route to these goals. If the envisaged emotions are restricting or damaging, it should be considered whether or not the targets which have been set will be worth it. Pathways should be set out by which the individual can work to overcome any current or potential negative emotions. It should be concluded whether the client has the emotional motivation to achieve any of the targets previously discussed. Often, professional coaches will require additional training to be suited to interpreting and dealing with the expression of emotions.

Example questions:

- *How much do you want your goal – on a scale of 1 to 10?*
- *If you achieve your goal – how will you feel? How will it look?*
- *How motivated are you to reach this goal?*
- *What would make you more motivated?*
- *What is it exactly that excites you about this goal?*
- *How will you know when you have achieved your goals?*

Perception
Perception refers to the understanding of the wider context of the mentee's situation and goals – how it will impact the grand scheme of things, how it will impact other people's emotions and goals and how it will open doors for the next stage of progress. Once both coach and learner's perspectives have been opened to the wider picture, it is much simpler to explore the various options available to the individual. The coach should not look to decide anything for their client, instead they should purely look to guide the individual down a single pathway towards a SMART goal, whilst allowing them to continue to make their own decisions.

Leading People

Example questions:

- *What do you feel about the current situation?*
- *What have you already tried?*
- *What problems still remain?*
- *Is your target definitely what you need at the moment?*
- *What choices are you currently making? What other choices are there?*
- *What are your impacts on other people? What are the future impacts?*
- *How could you play to your strengths?*
- *What could you do if resources (time, money, etc.) were not a limitation?*

Plan

Once a target and overall path is initially decided upon, it is necessary to develop and systematically organise the first steps along said path. Once again, the coach should purely provide support whilst allowing the individual to keep control of their own decisions and actions. The plan should follow a series of steps which are entirely mapped out and under the individual's control, with no ambiguity or difficult choices to be made along the route – instead, all decisions should be made now, before the plan is put into action. They should have clear guidelines and processes set in order for them to be able to check on their progress at regular stages along the route. The coach should offer potential amendments to these carefully laid out plans in order to further aid the individual in finding the most appropriate route to their goals.

Example questions:

- *What feels like the natural next step in the process?*
- *What will that open doors for you to do?*
- *How will the options you have chosen, move you closer to your goals?*
- *Look back once you have achieved your goals – what were the steps?*

Pace

The pace of the plan should be decided through setting timescales and deadlines for the completion of each individual task within. Short-term goals and timescales maintain commitment from the mentee, as minor goals and targets are always attainable and within their sights. These timescales should also however be realistic, not unnecessarily short. Deadlines should be used as milestones for progress and also to act as brief respites when the effects of previous actions can be reviewed.

Example questions:

- *When will you take each of these steps?*
- *What is the timeline for your progress?*
- *How will you review and measure progress?*
- *What support might you require?*
- *Are these deadlines realistic?*

Leading People

Action/Amend
The entire STEPPPA process should be reviewed, including each individual decision that has been made. This is when it should be considered whether there are any further steps that need to be made to make the goals more attainable for the mentee, or whether any action is inappropriate on further reconsideration. If so, stages of this process may need to be repeated in order to gain full commitment from the individual.

Example questions:

- *What have you learnt from the session?*
- *What may need to be adjusted?*
- *What possible barriers may you reach during your first stage?*
- *Is your plan sensible?*

The aim is that the subject will leave the coaching session with an idea of their current situation, long and mid-term goals, the effect of their own emotions on motivation and how to improve their drive, a greater perception of their actions on themselves and the world around them and a carefully devised plan of action with clearly defined steps and measurable goals. This should allow them to retain their motivation throughout a manageable process towards their long-term goals.

Heron's Six Categories of Intervention

The Six Categories of Intervention were formulated by John Heron and initially described in 1975 with the intention of providing leaders and managers with a more adaptive and flexible approach to assisting their staff and team members with work or personal growth.

The Six Categories can be split down-the-middle into two major sub-groups: 'Authoritative' and 'Facilitative'. These sub-groups are designed in such a way as to allow the manager to easily choose the intervention that fits their leadership style or philosophy, or which intervention best suits the situation or the target individual at hand.

Leading People

| Heron's Six Categories of Intervention ||
Facilitative	Authoritative
Cathartic: If a team member has hit a wall with their work, this approach is used to help allow them to express their thoughts and feelings and to tackle those themselves. Look to understand their situation from their perspective.	**Prescriptive:** The simplest of all the techniques-this involves telling the individual directly what is required and how to achieve it. Generally utilised with inexperience individuals or when under time constraints.
Catalytic: This is likely the most commonly used approach will stop it involves providing support urine individual self-discovery for the team member. Decisions and path should be supported but control remains with the individual.	**Informative:** The approach involves passing on information or experience about a given task or challenge, without directly controlling the individual. Generally utilised with productive but inexperienced individuals.
Supportive: This approach focuses on building the confidence of the individual. The leadership highlight their achievements and value to the company and encourage them to find confidence in their personal abilities.	**Confronting:** This most aggressive at all the approaches considered. This should be used in a positive manner; however, they will directly address issues and ask the individual to consider whether their method is correct.

Authoritative Style
The first of the two sub-groups, the Authoritative style is indicative of an autocratic or 'hands-on' leader and is most suited to managers who prefer to take charge of each project and control individual team members. The three different authoritative approaches are as follows:

Prescriptive
The most straightforward approach - this involves describing in clear terms to the employee what is required of them and how to do it. This approach is generally utilised when time is of the essence or is targeted at inexperienced staff. However, it also often characterises a lack of trust between manager and team member.

Informative
This approach involves passing on personal experience at performing a certain task to a less experienced member of staff, to aid them in completing the assignment efficiently and effectively. This technique is generally used to provide aid on tasks of which the team member is familiar, or is within their skill set – however, they are not quite proficient enough to be fully independent as of yet.

Confronting
This is the most aggressive of the three authoritative approaches. It involves questioning the employees' approach to the task in order to encourage them to consider other options, or to view the task in a different light. This method is best utilised when trying to encourage the employee to think independently, whilst still being overseen by the manager.

Leading People

Facilitative Style
The Facilitative style is typical of *laissez-faire* managers that understand the strengths and weaknesses of their individual team members and know that they can rely on each individual to handle their tasks efficiently and to a high standard. The different facilitative approaches are as follows.

Cathartic
This approach is usually considered when a proficient team member is beginning to slow in productivity or performance. It aims to allow and encourage the individual to express their emotions and frustrations with the task or situation, so that the issue can be identified. Once identified, the individual and the manager can work together to find and discuss a constructive solution.

Catalytic
The aim of this approach is to aid an employee with reflecting on their own abilities. Its purpose is to enable them to find their own weaknesses, which they can subsequently improve upon. In addition, it helps them to recognise and understand their strengths. By doing this, the employee can see their work from an objective viewpoint and can subsequently work to develop and resolve any knowledge or performance issues they may have had.

Supportive
This approach aims to build employee confidence and self-esteem. This is done by identifying and pointing out the individual's strengths, through their qualifications, contributions, achievements and general qualities. It may also be reinforced to the individual their value to the team and the company as a whole. The outcome of this approach is to enable the employee to tackle a challenge with renewed confidence.

Heron's Six Categories of Intervention can be applied to the majority of employee-based business issues. A general and unspecific example of one category would be a manager taking an informative approach with a member of staff that has recently taken on more responsibility, as the manager has already experienced the obstacles that the staff member will be experiencing. Another example is: if an experienced member of staff is falling behind in productivity and their confidence is being affected as a result, the manager would potentially opt for a supportive and cathartic intervention. This is so that the team member can express their frustrations, whilst being reassured that the manager believes in and supports them. However, the approach that may be taken is also dependent on the skills, knowledge, personality and leadership style of the manager and therefore may not always be this flexible.

Using or considering Heron's Six Categories of Intervention allows the manager to be flexible and through analysis of each unique case, they are able to identify and utilise the most suitable intervention technique for each member of staff and individual situation to maximise productivity and raise job satisfaction.

Furthermore, by being able to apply a plethora of differing approaches, the manager becomes more aware of how best to tackle certain situations and issues that each member of staff may face. This approach also brings the added benefit of flexibility - not only are each of the interventions suitable to their own specific problems - but they can be combined for more

Leading People

complex issues and this makes the approach highly effective for managers struggling with a wide range of issues across their team or is leading a group of varying skill sets and experiences.

CLEAR Model

The CLEAR model was formulated in the early 1980's by Professor of Leadership, Peter Hawkins, of *Bath Consultancy Group*. Though it preceded the popular GROW model which developed during the 1990s, it is still considered a functional alternative for managers and coaches. CLEAR operates under the idea that in order to achieve maximum workplace performance, it is no longer enough to be just a manager – directing and orchestrating actions – you must often intervene in the processes of staff and act as a catalyst, or a guide to their development. The model places strong emphasis on the need for coaching and mentoring in today's fast and competitive business environment to promote employee growth.

he primary focus of the CLEAR model is to create employees that are committed to team plans and are happy to contribute to shared goals, rather than simply complying to managerial demands. The learner's situation can be assessed as a whole, or each problem they have can be examined individually and then the process repeated iteratively. The CLEAR model is comprised of five key stages, which are as follows:

- **Contract.** this stage focusses on establishing desired outcomes – both individual and shared – and revealing how the coach and the process can be tailored to be most valuable to the individual's needs. The main goal of this stage is to clarify the general scope of the session and to outline the coaching process in order to avoid confusion and misunderstanding. Logistical issues should be tackled, including the frequency, duration and location of meetings, in order to create an organised and trackable schedule for the process.

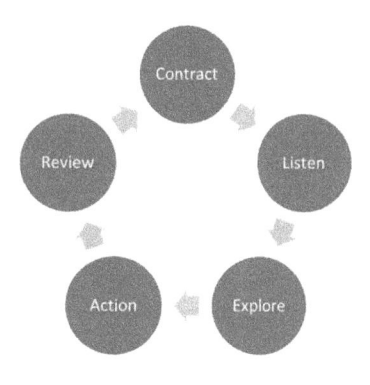

- **Listen.** This stage puts emphasis on the coach having the employee share their reality, their thoughts and feelings. The key aspects here are 'active listening' and 'contract'-focused, catalytic questions that aim to allow the coach and individual to truly understand the situation. This step is crucial, as it allows the individual to challenge their own assumptions and motivations surrounding their behaviour.

The coach should not intervene overly during this period; instead, they need only encourage and guide the conversation towards the topics and issues at hand. The four levels of listening should here be utilised:

  - *Attentive:* The coach should provide full and undivided attention to the individual.
  - *Accurate:* The coach should be able to interpret and understand what the individual has said, so that they would be able to paraphrase the discussion.

Leading People

- **Empathetic:** *The coach should be able to show that they understand the underlying emotions of the conversation, not purely the surface-level*
- **Pure:** *The coach should be able to understand, interpret and express further than what has been said by the learner.*

- **Explore.** Once the individual has outlined their current situation, the coach should act slightly more pro-actively to probe further about the depth and context of the situation. This step aims to enable the employee to develop an emotional connection to their behavioural change. More catalytic questions should be utilised to examine how the employee is emotionally and professionally affected by their current situation and how future actions would impact them. Often in this step, an individual will have an epiphany, or a small 'light-bulb' moment, in which they will realise something which has been preventing them reaching their goals. This step also involves the initial determination of potential interventions and exploration of their effectiveness.

- **Action.** The focus of this stage is to get the employee to commit to the required changes with the intent of internalising their new outlook. The employee should lead the route to action by truly considering each potential option for their next step and its impact on them, personally and professionally. Once again, the model suggests taking a slightly-backseat, question-focused approach that promotes consideration. This is done with questions that use 'who' 'what' 'where' 'when' and 'how' to enable the employee to put consideration into their rationale for each decision and how their action plan will make them feel in perhaps a few months' time. The coach should also offer support or help to organise potential support pathways throughout the action process.

- **Review.** This stage is as much about following up on employee progress as it is about feedback on the manager's coaching ability. It is important to ensure that the employee is on track to reaching their goal whilst asking how the coach can improve their style to provide more support. Feedback should be encouraged from the employee – what they found beneficial, what they struggled with and what they would change in future coaching sessions. The set of action steps should be reviewed and examined, to confirm that the most suitable and practical plan has been developed. Failure to reach several of their newly developed goals (perhaps gathered at a future coaching session) may require the process to begin again, with a re-assessment of the individual's new position.

The CLEAR model is primarily used for goal-focused coaching, whereby the coach supports and enables an employee to make changes to their beliefs and behaviours to facilitate their personal and professional growth. It can be applied to situations in which an employee wants to or recognises that they need to make a change to enable them to become more effective at a specific role or task. An example of this would be if an employee recognised that they were finding it hard to gain support for their ideas, as they can be over-bearing in team meetings.

By using the CLEAR model, the coach can enable the employee to identify the areas that require attention as well as the strategies required to remedy these areas. All this personal

Leading People

growth is also overseen from distance by the coach thereby allowing the employee to receive support when they need it whilst still retaining the space to focus on themselves.

The CLEAR model is useful for individuals with managerial responsibilities who also see themselves as personable, aspiring coaches and who are still refining their style, as it allows for feedback for them whilst also providing a platform that encourages employee growth. It can be applied to many scenarios and does not rely solely on the employee noticing that they need to make a change it can also be implemented in situations where the manager intervenes as they believe that there are improvements to be made. Finally, the model is flexible and can be used to promote both long-term and short-term growth both to employees and the managers own coaching style.

Cognitive Behavioural Coaching

Cognitive behavioural coaching (CBC) is a corporate and personal coaching technique used to enable those restricted by emotional or psychological barriers to reach their goals. It was derived and developed from two separate source techniques – firstly, Cognitive Behavioural Therapy (CBT), which was outlined in its contemporary form by psychiatrist and professor, Aaron Temkin Beck.

It was a concept interwoven with his earlier-described concept of 'automatic thoughts', the emotion-filled contemplations that would materialise in an individual's mind when asked an emotive question. He discovered that by learning and developing the ability to identify and report such responses, one was able to overcome the difficulties associated with automatic thought. Secondly and to a lesser extent, Rational Emotive Behavioural Therapy (REBT), the work of Albert Ellis. Both have been used increasingly over the past 40 years – though, particularly CBT – to treat trauma and mental health issues such as depression and agoraphobia.

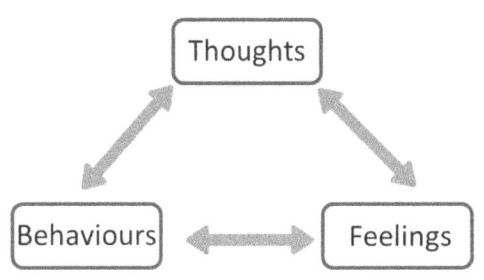

The effective principle of CBC is this: what we think about a situation, affects how we feel about it. As we can control what we think of things, we can therefore subsequently control our feelings. The tools and methodology used in CBT can equally be applied to non-clinical scenarios, such as dealing with lack of motivation, confidence issues and general personal or professional skill development. With regards to leadership and business, CBC was developed with the intention of aiding individuals in overcoming functional weaknesses or mental obstacles within the workplace.

Leading People

Breaking down emotional barriers

The aim of CBC is to identify the root of an issue that may be preventing an individual reaching their full potential. It differs from other coaching frameworks such as GROW in that it focusses on emotional or psychological barriers, rather than purely practical knowledge, skill or strategic shortcomings. The primary belief of CBC is that abnormalities and deficiencies stem from faulty cognition, or inaccurate interpretations of the world around us. When the cause of the issue is identified, the next priority is to ascertain which action/actions should be undertaken to take control of the issue and to address it, by altering the individual's belief systems regarding the event or situation. Although similar to CBT, this form of coaching is primarily focused on the workplace and the individual's ability to perform. CBC focusses on the notion that our reactions are the driving factor behind our beliefs concerning such *events*, rather than our reactions being directly caused by the event.

By focusing on and isolating the negative thoughts and beliefs surrounding *events*, it becomes possible to utilise alternative behaviours and viewpoints to ultimately alter our negative beliefs surrounding the *event*. These alternative viewpoints and behaviours can in turn be reinforced by positive feedback from managers and colleagues, creating a 'new self' through discarding old beliefs. This is why CBC operates in many cases under the notion that if someone can talk themselves into ineffectiveness, they are also able to talk themselves out of it. This ability subsequently allows, in theory, the individual to reach their true potential within the workplace.

It is suggested that CBC covers a broad range of issues and can effectively be used to resolve indecisiveness, procrastination, impatience, self-confidence and assertiveness, to name but a few examples. This means that it can be applied in the workplace to fine-tune team members that are struggling with certain aspects of their jobs. For example, CBC can be used for 'stage-fright' (performance anxiety) - if an individual believes that the *event* of public speaking is going to result in a bad outcome, then they will avoid it or shut themselves off. In this case, one would have to address the belief system surrounding the individual's perception of public speaking through discussion. When the core cause is identified, alternative views and behaviours can be proposed to the individual. By doing this, the belief system can be slowly eroded and rebuilt with positive beliefs, which - in theory - will enable the individual to expose themselves to public speaking and thus, over time, become accustomed to the experience and effective at it, resulting in personal growth and a more effective team member.

Leading People

ABCDE Model

The ABCDE Model (Neenan and Dryden, 2000) is a framework for using CBC.

- Activating Event
- Beliefs
- Consequences
- Disputes
- Effects

Activating Event or Adversity – *the process begins by identifying the event which causes or triggers mental or psychological stress, or other negative emotional shifts. These are not always significant – people can be greatly affected by superficially trivial events or words. Recognising the issue is sometimes difficult but is an important first step in rectifying its effects. If it is a particularly traumatic event, a coach may have to use a delicate touch to encourage discussion of the affected individual's memories of such.*

Beliefs – *these are the systems which have facilitated the individual's response to the prior stimuli. These are often negative, limiting beliefs and challenging these restrictions is a crucial step in recovery. During this stage, one may begin to examine the logic surrounding these belief systems and why they have developed in the first place. Individuals must be able to remove harmful "self-talk", particularly those which convey a pessimistic output towards one's skills, knowledge or abilities.*

Consequences: Emotional, Psychological – *these are the consequences of one's belief systems on their actions. Believing you are going to be bad at a certain task is often self-fulfilling and the lack of confidence will not allow you to perform under your own pressure. Public speaking is a prime example – if one believes that they are going to perform a terrible speech, then the likelihood is that their oratory skills will suffer even more as a result.*

Disputes: Challenging Self-Defeating Beliefs – *this is when one's harmful belief systems truly begin to be approached and subsequently repaired or destroyed. It is suggested that there are three disputes that one may take up with their beliefs: Empirical: What is the basis for these beliefs? Functional: Are there beliefs an aid in working towards another, possibly unconscious goal? Logical: Does the belief make sense, or is it part of another underlying belief system? If the beliefs do not hold true to any of these disputes, it makes it a lot simpler to remove them from one's mental processes.*

Effects – *The impacts of altering or removing the pre-existing harmful belief system. This is when new habits and patterns are formed and previous mental processes are deconstructed and reconstructed as to have positive outputs. These often work in positive feedback loops – greater results encourage more self-belief and further impressive outputs follow.*

Leading People

Barriers to Organisational Learning

There are many reasons given by organisation why they do not bother to train and develop staff. The following are, perhaps, the most common reasons given why organisations fail to develop their team to perform at higher levels.

Employee resistance to change
Resistance to change is a common barrier to organisational learning. People who have been at their jobs for a long time and are set in their ways often do not want to learn new processes.

But resistance to change does not only occur among the most tenured of employees. No, this kind of mentality can arise among anyone who does not want to step away from the comfort of familiar processes and systems.

For an organisation to advance, change must be ongoing. As an organisation adapts to dynamic markets, internal processes, knowledge and use of technology will need to keep up.
To prevent resistance to change, explanations must be given to employees why the change is necessary and how it will benefit them. Reasons should be creative and try to understand on a deeper level what is getting under employees' skin.

Ignoring the elephant in the room
What elephant are we referring to? That of the unpleasant aspects of organisational learning. These sensitive topics will vary depending on the change to be implemented, but they could be a new process, eliminating a technology platform the team is used to, or disruption to workflow.

It is important to directly communicate the potential pitfalls and challenges that employees might encounter from the outset. Ignoring these concerns will erode trust and potentially create more resistance to proposed changes. Transparency and direct communication will make it easier in the future to institute change and new learning requirements for your organisation.

"What if...... and I know this sounds crazy, ...we actually talked to the employees."

Leading People

Lack of leadership training
Leadership development is critical to organisational learning.

Communication, change management and support skills required to guide organisational learning must be taught and encouraged.

Inadequate leadership training leads to poorly run teams and chaos during periods of change. If a supervisor or manager is not engaged with a new process or training, they are supposed to lead, employees will most likely tune out. If organisational learning is not prioritised from the top-bottom, it will not succeed, thus undermining the organisation as a whole.

On the other hand, leaders who are equipped to guide learning efforts will boost the morale and confidence of their teams.

Continuous training and development is the key to ensuring your managers can guide change and learning efforts effectively.

Disregard of team success
Sometimes, it is difficult to see how organisational learning programs fit in with an individual's personal goals.
Learning often takes time and effort away from employees' day-to-day tasks. When an organisation prioritises this investment in learning, but the employee does not, it is difficult to encourage engagement.

If your employee is focused on their individual achievements, then frame organisational learning as part of their employee development. Teaching skills beyond an employee's existing job description can be a catalyst for their own career growth.
Their individual success will ultimately lead to team success and managers should also emphasise team achievements through positive reinforcements.

No motivation for growth
The excuse "That's not in my job description" represents one of the most challenging barriers to organisational learning. Similar to the effects of resistance to change, employees who are not motivated for growth will not seek out opportunities provided by the organisations.

Not all organisational learning programs will be mandatory, even though they might still add value to an employee. This means the employee's personal motivation to learn and grow will determine whether or not they participate.

To overcome this barrier, try motivating your employees by explaining the future benefits of the learning initiative. You might also consider implementing a system for rewarding employees as they make progress.

Short-term focus
In business, it is often easy to focus on stop gaps to solve short-term problems without looking at the big picture. If an employee's job is not focused on the long-term vision of

Leading People

the company, it is easy to get caught up in short-term goals that do not include learning skills for the long-term benefit.
To solve this issue, encourage employees and managers to dedicate time for long-term goals and offer learning opportunities to fill this time.

Complexity

In the hyper-connected and always-busy world we live in today, complexity overwhelms the modern employee. In the digital workplace, we are often multi-tasking across multiple systems and platforms.

Picture the experience of learning a new software system. An employee may be taught in a webinar, given a link to a knowledge base online and the login for actually using the system. Even though all the information is there, when it comes time to implement their new skills, they may need to bounce between three or more tabs to successfully reach their objective. That is complex!

To overcome this barrier to organisational learning, training programs and materials need simplifying to deliver only the information they need in the simplest possible format. This will allow trainees to absorb the information and put it to use faster.

Leading People

Assessing Training and Development Needs

The following steps identify the stages needed to assess employees' training and development needs.

1. Understanding Employee Training and Development Needs
Firstly, any training you offer your employees will fall into one or more of these categories:

Organisational Analysis.
An analysis of the business needs or other reasons the training is desired. An analysis of the organisation's strategies, goals and objectives. What is the organisation overall trying to accomplish? The important questions being answered by this analysis are who decided that training should be conducted, why a training program is seen as the recommended solution to a business problem, what the history of the organisation has been with regard to employee training and other management interventions.

Person Analysis.
Analysis dealing with potential participants and instructors involved in the process. The important questions being answered by this analysis are who will receive the training and their level of existing knowledge on the subject, what is their learning style and who will conduct the training. Do the employees have required skills? Are there changes to policies, procedures, software, or equipment that require or necessitate training?

Work analysis / Task Analysis.
Analysis of the tasks being performed. This is an analysis of the job and the requirements for performing the work. Also known as a task analysis or job analysis, this analysis seeks to specify the main duties and skill level required. This helps ensure that the training which is developed will include relevant links to the content of the job.

Performance Analysis.
Are the employees performing up to the established standard? If performance is below expectations, can training help to improve this performance? Is there a Performance Gap?

Content Analysis.
Analysis of documents, laws, procedures used on the job. This analysis answers questions about what knowledge or information is used on this job. This information comes from manuals, documents, or regulations. It is important that the content of the training does not conflict or contradict job requirements. An experienced worker can assist (as a subject matter expert) in determining the appropriate content.

Training Suitability Analysis.
Analysis of whether training is the desired solution. Training is one of several solutions to employment problems. However, it may not always be the best solution. It is important to determine if training will be effective in its usage.

Leading People

Cost-Benefit Analysis.
Analysis of the return on investment (ROI) of training. Effective training results in a return of value to the organisation that is greater than the initial investment to produce or administer the training.

Not all employees will need all types of training. Sometimes the training needed may be even more fundamental. When staff have been "inherited" or recruited without using appropriate techniques and methodologies, they may have even more basic development needs. This could include competences which might normally be taken for granted.

Today's workplace often requires employees to be independent thinkers responsible for making good decisions based on limited information. This kind of work may require training if the employee does not have these skills. Below is a list of various knowledge, skills and abilities that employees may be required to possess in order to perform their jobs well.

Adaptability
Analytical Skills
Action Orientation
Business Knowledge/Acumen
Coaching/Employee Development
Communication
Customer Focus
Decision Making
Fiscal Management
Global Perspective
Innovation
Interpersonal Skills

Leadership
Establishing Objectives
Risk Management
Persuasion and Influence
Planning
Problem Solving
Project Management
Results Orientation
Self-Management
Teamwork
Technology

2. Conduct a Needs Assessment

Talking to your employees can help you optimise many aspects of your business from mental health issues to long-term sickness absence, to your employee rewards scheme.

Similarly, if you want to know what sort of training your employees need, all you have to do is ask. Schedule a friendly chat with every member of the team. Make it clear that it is not a performance review but ask them if there is any area of their role that they feel is lacking. Ask them if they have any comments about your current training programme and whether they feel that it supports their career goals.

At the same time, gather feedback from any managers and supervisors about the employees they oversee. Do they feel there are any skill gaps? You can also ask employees to rate their managers for performance. You will gather a lot of feedback and you will very likely spot patterns. The recurring themes in the feedback will effectively signpost the sort of training you need.

Other assessment techniques can include:

Leading People

direct observation
questionnaires
consultation with persons in key positions and/or with specific knowledge
review of relevant literature
interviews
focus groups
assessments/surveys
records & report studies
work samples

3. Set Clear Expectations and Goals

For every member of the team, you need to go beyond the job description. You need to set clear responsibilities, expectations and goals for everyone in your business. This will make it easier for you to measure everyone's performance.

When it comes to measuring performance, you may need an attitude shift. You are not measuring performance in order to catch out and reprimand employees. You are doing it as a means of supporting them.

- *Are they in a position to do their job to the best of their abilities?*
- *If performance is lacking, is there any training or development that might help improve performance?*

4. Create Personal Development Plans

This is an integral part of job satisfaction, staff retention and employee engagement. Developing a personal development plan for every member of the team will make them feel like you are actively investing in their success – which will, in turn, make them feel more invested in the business. Personal development plans can also help you to identify any training requirements. You need to routinely discuss personal development with your employees. You need to set goals and review them. Ask employees how they feel things are going. If they struggled to meet a goal, or if they did not quite hit their targets, perhaps some training will help?

5. Conduct Organisational, Task and Work Analysis

An analysis of the organisation should answer the question:

- *What are your business goals and what are your strategies for achieving them?*
- *What support will the senior management and managers give toward training?*
- *Is the organisation supportive and on-board with this process?*
- *Are there adequate resources (financial and personnel)?*

This should be followed by a task analysis.

- *Which tasks need to be completed in order to meet these business goals?*
- *How frequently are they performed?*

Leading People

- *How important is each task?*
- *What knowledge is needed to perform the task?*
- *How difficult is each task?*
- *What kinds of training are available?*

Observe the employee performing the job. Document the tasks being performed. When documenting the tasks, make sure each task starts with an action verb. Ask the following questions:

- *How does this task analysis compare to existing job descriptions?*
- *Did the task analysis miss any important parts of the job description?*
- *Were there tasks performed that were omitted from the job description?*

Organise the identified tasks. Develop a sequence of tasks. Or list the tasks by importance.

- *Are there differences between high and low performing employees on specific work tasks?*
- *Are there differences between Experts and Novices?*
- *Would providing training on those tasks improve employee job performance?*

Most employees are required to make decisions based on information.

- *How is information gathered by the employee?*
- *What does the employee do with the information?*
- *Can this process be trained?*
- *Or can training improve this process?*

Finally, there should be a work analysis.

- *What does everyone do all day?*
- *Is any time being spent on tasks that perhaps are not so pressing?*
- *Could you divert any resources to ensure that you are working towards achieving your organisational goals?*

A series of analyses will help to identify universal training needs. For example, some members of the team are spread too thin. Training an additional employee to take on some of their responsibilities will help relieve the pressure.

The CIPD calls this the RAM model – that means your focus is on Relevance, Alignment and Measurement. The idea is that training and development does not become a rigid box-ticking exercise. Rather, it is aligned with your business objectives and organisational requirements and all learning is linked to your desired business outcomes.

Leading People

Cognitive Task Analysis

Cognitive Task Analysis (CTA) is a psychological research method for uncovering what people know and how they think in order to study a task from a cognitive perspective.
CTA extends traditional task analysis to identify the cognitive skills and strategies needed to effectively tackle the task in question. The first step is to develop a model of the task which shows where the decision points are located and what information is needed to make decisions and the actions that might be taken based on that information. This model should be a schematic or graphic representation of the task. The model is developed by observing and interviewing the employees. The objective is to develop a model that can be used to guide the development of training programs and curriculum.

Job titles and descriptions should be reviewed to get an idea of the tasks performed. Observe the employee performing the job and review existing training related to the job. Both experts and novices should be observed to ensure an effective comparison.

Since training is often based on specific job tasks, employees may feel more comfortable taking the effort to participate in training when it is directed at what they really need to know.

Performance Analysis

This technique is used to identify which employees need the training. Review performance appraisals. Interview managers and supervisors. Look for performance measures such as benchmarks and goals.

Sources of performance data include:

Performance Appraisals	Accidents
Quotas met (un-met)	Safety Incidents
Performance Measures	Grievances
Turnover	Absenteeism
Shrinkage	Units per Day
Leakage	Units per Week
Spoilage	Returns
Losses	Customer Complaints

Are there differences between high and low performing employees on specific competencies? Would providing training on those competencies improve employee job performance?

Checklist for Training Needs Analysis

It is helpful to have an organised method for choosing the right assessment for your needs. A checklist can help you in this process. Your checklist should summarise the kinds of information discussed above. For example, is the assessment valid for your intended purpose? Is it reliable and fair? Is it cost-effective? Is the instrument likely to be viewed as fair and valid by the participants? Also consider the ease or difficulty of administration, scoring and

Leading People

interpretation given available resources. Click here for a sample checklist that you may find useful. Completing a checklist for each test you are considering will assist you in comparing them more easily.

Example training and development needs analysis checklist

Your training needs analysis should include the following:

- Know what the organisation is trying to accomplish.
- Know the history of training within the organisation.
- What "needs" will be addressed by the training?
- Any recent process or procedure changes?
- What resources are available for training?
- Who needs to be trained?
- Who can serve as subject matter experts?
- Are any staff going to do the training?
- Which companies provide training materials?
- What are the Knowledge, Skills and Abilities?
- Review Job Descriptions and Org Charts.

Leading People

Training and Development Methods

When selecting the appropriate training development methods, it is important to recognise an individual's preferred learning style should be taken into consideration where possible, should that be visual, auditory or kinaesthetic. It is important that you have an awareness of the various methods of learning available to support individuals to be high performing members of the team. The table below identifies a variety of methods and opportunities and the advantages and disadvantages of each. Selecting the appropriate method or a combination of the will motivate learners to achieve the desired outcome and contribute to the development of high-performance team

Activity	Advantages	Disadvantages
Coaching	can be arranged quickly does not always detract from the workload specific to the individual	personality clashes difference of opinions maybe time constraints due to logistics
Internal training course	usually low-cost can be arranged quickly	time away from workload familiarity
External training course	usually a formal qualification individual can take some time away from the office environment	cost time away from work
On the job shadowing	immediate sharing ideas and resources	personality clashes difference of opinions possible conflict
Secondment	retained within the business builds experience of the organisation	time away from main work role possible conflict-of-interest, dependent on work areas involved
Special assignment	provides ownership and accountability interesting and varied	Time required to monitor and review

With any development activity, it is important to monitor people's progress and provide clear guidance and feedback. Monitoring employees progress in giving appropriate and constructive feedback is vital every stage of their development. This will ensure staff members feel valued and that they are included within the whole work the whole process.

Learning and development should be a key factor in any set of objectives within any business arena. This may take any number of forms or guises, from ad hoc on-the-job training to attendance at more formal structured sessions with an accredited qualification as an end goal

There are numerous benefits to any business that adopts a structured formal approach to developing its staff, including harnessing a well-trained workforce, developing high levels of service delivery and reducing staff turnover and the costs associated with it. The business will also benefit from the increase motivation of staff who feel valued and will likely see improvements in job performance and the outputs associated with this and improvements in the brand's reputation in the businesses image.

Leading People

The employer is empowering a workforce that will be able to develop and amend their working practices and outlook as the needs of the business development change, therefore the employer is aligning personal development planning with the business's objectives. There are several benefits to the individuals also including:

- *an increase in job satisfaction as they will feel able to complete the role more effectively and efficiently*
- *an increase in their personal skills and competences*
- *an increase in the team's morale and improve attitudes that in turn could have a positive impact on their behaviour and improve their prospects for internal promotion*

Distance Learning

The world is rapidly changing since the onset of COVID-19. It will take some time before businesses resume operations as usual. Most likely, some employees will continue working remotely and offices will gradually begin housing workers again.

Organisational learning can still continue, even with a dispersed workforce. It requires technology to play a greater role to facilitate ongoing training, employee development and to support managers to ensure learning is effective.

Technology is the key to improve organisational learning

According to LinkedIn's 2019 Workplace Learning Report technology is cited as the tipping point to tackling day-to-day challenges and is strategic to proactively bridge skill gaps. More and more, companies are investing in online training versus instructor-led training.

Digital Adoption Platform (DAP) is a way to ensure that employees continue their organisational learning regardless of physical location. New software is easier to understand as DAP uses in-app guidance to lead users through business processes and workflows. Additionally, when DAP is enabled, tedious processes can be automated, thus reducing user-friction and giving employees more time to focus on immediate or urgent tasks.

More budget for online learning

	Online learning	Instructor-led training
spend less	9%	39%
spend more	59%	24%

Managers and DAP admins have visibility into how employees are using new or existing software which can pinpoint areas of confusion. Once identified, workflows can be adjusted, or helpful content can guide users through work processes.

A digital adoption platform is a tool that empowers organisational learning and can be used by employees and managers – anytime, anywhere.
Operational reasons for avoiding training and development

Leading People

- **Budgets.** When the first economic downturn hits, training and development budgets get chopped. Many companies fail to see training as an "investments."
- **The culture of senior management.** These leaders need to encourage, foster and believe in the training and development of their employees and influence the budget to align it with the strategy of the company.
- **Lack of vision.** Enhance the vision and have it be a key component before implementing the next "flavour of the month" best practice.
- **Time and staffing.** If these components are not valued, then there will always be a lack of time, funding and staffing assigned to training and development. There has to be sustainability, value and behavioural shifts which show tangible results.
- **Reactive vs. Proactive.** If we are always striving just to catch up, we will never make an impact on our businesses.
- **No perceived value.** If employees who attend do not see that they can use what is taught, then that is a much more critical loss of value than any financial issues will ever generate.
- **Attitude** – we have always done it that way.
- **Thinking it is an event, instead of a process.**
- **Cannot share information** – knowledge is power.
- **Work ethic.**
- **No link to the mission, vision and values.**
- **Risky because they are afraid to admit they do not know.**
- **Level of, or lack of, commitment.**
- **Job silos** – only know your job.
- **Reluctant to train others because you might lose your job.**
- **Got in trouble** – safety, harassment – no strategy.
- **No perceived value.**
- **Poorly qualified trainers** – they do everything.
- **Why train and invest in short-term employees.**
- **Why learn this week** – it will change next week.
- **Keep training and development separate rather than integrated.**

Delivering Training and Development

Training and development help improve how the employees perform within the company. It is also about how the company seeks to increase the self-fulfilment of its employees. This is done through a variety of education programs and methods.

Company Orientations
This is the most common kind of training method and helps ensure that new employees are successful in your company. Whether you carry out the training through some kind of handbook, a one-on-one meeting, or a lecture, the information you convey to the employees should contain the company's strategic and historic positions. The main people in authority in the company should also be mentioned, along with the structure of the company, as well as the specific departments. Employees should also be educated on

Leading People

exactly how their departments contribute to company objectives and help it accomplish its mission. The employee should also be educated about the rules and regulations of the company as well as its employment policies.

Training Lectures

Lectures are very useful when you need to get the same information to a large number of people at the same time. You do not have to carry out individual meetings with the employees, so that makes the lecture very cost effective. There are, however, some disadvantages to the lecture as a method of training employees. Since a lecture only works one way, with one person addressing the crowd, it may not be very interesting, making it less effective for training. It really depends on the oratory skills of the person delivering the lecture. If you are not good at grabbing and holding the attention of people for extended periods of time, then the attention of the crowd will soon shift. Another drawback is that the lecturer will not have an easy way of figuring out if the attendees have understood the message.

Case Studies

This method of training is nondirected. Basically, employees are given some practical reports of cases to analyse to learn the main points they need as part of their training. The case report will consist of an exhaustive description of some real-life situation employees may encounter. They should then analyse the problems presented as part of the case study and figure out possible solutions to them. They are typically encouraged to be independent in their thinking and even think outside of the box when possible. The employees should not rely on the direction of the instructor to perform their analysis of the case study. The main advantage that comes with the case study is that real-life stories are used. There is no better source of problems to analyse and come up with solutions. The employees gain practical experience in dealing with on-the-job problems. They do not have to deal with abstract theories that they might have a hard time practically applying to the job.

Role Playing

This training method asks people to take on various roles and play out those roles in a team. The facilitator of the training session will come up with a scenario that is to be acted out by the employees. The scenario is usually deeply rooted in practicality and the interpersonal relations that are simulated are quite genuine. The participants receive feedback immediately – from both the facilitator of the training session and the scenario they are carrying out itself. They will, therefore, have a much better understanding of their own behaviour as well as that of others. This method is quite cost effective and is often employed in management training and marketing training.

Simulations

The main difference between simulation training and role-playing is that role-playing is a subset of the simulation method. Basically, simulations are structured games and competitions that model the real world and seek to emulate scenarios that could plausibly occur in real life. The benefit of such methods is improvement of various employee skills, including problem-solving, understanding, decision making and the ability to perceive and respond to actual problems. They are also exciting enough to both capture and hold people's interest.

Computer-Based Training

Leading People

Computer-based training programs are focused on developing a structure for the learning process. Instructional materials are provided, via computer, to the new hires and they can complete it by themselves while bosses or trainers facilitate the process. The main benefit of this kind of program is that employees have the luxury to learn at their own pace and can learn at the times most convenient to them. The primary use of this method is in learning about operational equipment, computer hardware and computer software. Computer-based training is particularly important when it comes to learning about operational equipment, because the employee gets a simulated experience of operating the equipment without having to risk either damage to the equipment or injury. The operational equipment also does not have to face any downtime because it is simulated.

A particularly popular kind of computer-based training is web-based training, wherein people complete their training online, where there are additional resources; the company does not have to develop its own training materials but can use relevant materials that are already available online. Since more and more organisations have high-speed internet available, web-based training is becoming a lot more common.

Audio-visual Training Methods
These training methods include videotapes, film and television. They are similar to simulations and role-playing games in the sense that they also give employees access to real-world scenarios and are cost effective. The main disadvantage of this kind of training is that it is very hard to customise this kind of training for a given audience. Also, the audience does not get to participate in the training by asking questions during the presentation.

Team Building
This kind of training method involves the creation of effective teams with the same goals as the business or particular department within the company. It is not quite the same as the kind of ad hoc and informal use of teams in the workplace. Team building is a well-structured and formal process and is usually facilitated by some third party, typically a consultant. It is usually done to solve the issue of poor dynamics within groups and teams, manage relations between employees and management and also to improve productivity and quality of work.

The Effects of Culture

Collective behaviour and shared values
The tangible elements of a corporate culture can include a company's routines, stories and symbols; its outward facing Organisational structure and its hidden power structure. Culture can include what it says outwardly, but also what the company really means when it says it.

While it is common practice for companies to share their vision and mission with employees, this does not mean that all do an equal job of explaining what they mean. Some corporate cultures can be outward-looking and open, sharing much more about how they plan to reach their goals. Others are more secretive and operate on a need-to-know basis.

Formal or informal culture

Leading People

Corporate culture is unique to each company. Two companies in the same industry can have very different cultures.

Both IBM and Sun Microsystems manufacture computers and software. One is known as Big Blue, complete with a white-shirt-and-tie image. The other is California casual. One's historically regimented organisation and sheer scale gets the job done, while the other's entrepreneurial, innovative solutions regularly amaze its customers. Both have been highly successful because each company and its employees share an energy of related values and common business behaviours.

Corporate culture as an obstacle
A company that says it values its people, then lays them off and has them and their belongings escorted off the premises by guards, is not nearly as sensitive to the feelings of its staff as it would have people believe. Defining the culture of a new company and identifying how to fit into that culture is one of the most difficult things for an executive to do. Sometimes that is because the company states publicly that it is one kind of company but acts internally in a way that belies its words.

A new manager might be told that the company strongly endorses a team approach to process improvement. However, he quickly discovers that any suggestions are ignored or put down. Or the company might say that it promotes from within, but any time a senior position opens up, the job goes to an outside recruit.

Meshing leadership styles with corporate culture
Strong leadership is required to align a corporate culture with an organisation's strategy, especially if that strategy is a significant shift from the way things have been done. Risk-averse companies that set the goal to become innovative and nimble have to be taught an entrepreneurial culture.

Entrepreneurial in a command-and-control company
The primary leadership style in our society is what is called "command-and-control." It is accepted because it is efficient. Once workers learn skills, they generally repeat them and over time can come to resist change. This style is prevalent in large companies.
The opposite style, "leadership by worker responsibility," motivates people to thrive on challenge and change. This is precisely the environment cultivated in start-up and entrepreneurial environments.

While it is possible to be an entrepreneurial, mid-level leader within a regimented environment, it is not easy. To survive, the leader adopts a dual style: managing up as a line-skill manager and managing down as a motivational challenger, encouraging risk-taking and new skill acquisition.

Leading by motivation
A good leader uses more than one leadership style, depending on individual situations. Staff assessment is necessary to identify what style best motivates each worker. One employee might be completely self-motivated and independent and need minimal supervision. He is motivated by opportunities to be creative and can be highly productive. Another employee longs to find solutions and make decisions, is team-motivated and thrives on democratic discussion, change and responsibility.

Leading People

Still others might be motivated by goals and opportunity, by rewards and material prompts, or recognition and social status. Managing these employees requires skill in creating a work environment that provides enough motivational "honey"

Leading People

Equality and Diversity

Every employer has a responsibility to comply with the equality act which introduces a consistent basic framework of protection against direct and indirect discrimination, harassment and victimisation in work, education and public services. As an operations/departmental manager, usually by example when it comes to promoting equality and diversity in your own workplace. Your organisation will have its own equality and diversity standards and expectations and you will lead to understand these know how to adjust your working practices to include equality and diversity considerations. Workplaces are a cross-section of society and compromise people from many different backgrounds and cultures. It is important that you understand what promoting equality and diversity means

Promoting equality means

- *ensuring equal opportunities*
- *breaking down barriers*
- *eliminating discrimination*
- *ensuring access for all employment*
- *ensuring equal access to goods and services*

Promoting diversity means

- *celebrating people's differences*
- *valuing everyone*

Businesses that have effective equality and diversity policies that are embedded within their culture quite often attract a more diverse pool of applicants to any given post-there will be less conflict in the workplace and increase morale and productivity. The business and its brand reputation will be improved as it becomes common knowledge that the business values its employees.

The policy on equality of opportunity, diversity and inclusion to be effective, they should be written in clear, concise language and be available in a number of different languages required to ensure all employees of access to them. They should promote equality across the whole company, including to the directors and all staff members, who are full or part-time. They should include a commitment statement from an identified individual who will be responsible promoting the policies and ensuring there are adhered to.

Chapter 8: Managing People

Managing People

Managing People

People management is also referred to as human resources management and includes the recruitment, training and management of employees.

Good managers attract exceptional staff; they make the organisation a preferred employer; they help to increase market share and enhance profitability; they reduce costs. Their staff are engaged, committed and 'go the extra mile'. They are able to persuade the workforce to do things they might otherwise not do without causing a hint of unhappiness.

Criteria for successful management:

- *Promote a positive work culture.*
- *Promote commitment, trust and engagement between them and their workforce.*
- *Establish and maintain strong empathy with the workforce.*
- *Manage staff to achieve high level performance whilst ensuring their wellbeing.*
- *Ability to adapt behaviour to respond to crises without creating unhappiness in the workforce.*

Managing people is an essential skill of all managers

The key behaviours needed to inspire commitment, trust and engagement in others are:

- *Attentiveness*
- *Reliability*
- *Intellectual Flexibility*
- *Resolve Conflicts*
- *Encouragement*

These behaviours will:

- *Reduce costs due to unhappiness at work*
- *Reduce costs associated with presenteeism*
- *Improve innovation*
- *Improve staff engagement*
- *Increase productivity and performance*
- *Reduce staff turnover*
- *Achieve organisational targets and aims with minimum costs*
- *Improve team working*

Managing People

The role of a manager is not always smooth. At the beginning of your career, it is likely that you were responsible only for your own work, now it is your duty to inspire, lead and motivate your team to accomplish a set of goals for the organisation.

Not everyone is going to be easy to work with and ensuring everything is running without a hitch can often prove a challenge. So how can you go about being a great manager who displays authority and leadership, at the same time as maintaining respect from your peers?

1. **Improve your leadership skills**
   As a manager, employees look to you to lead them to meet the business objectives. Leadership involves making decisions about which employees are the most suited to different tasks. You will also need to provide clear and detailed direction for employees. Effective managers are able to mediate to resolve conflicts that arise within the team.

2. **Maintain good communication**
   Employees want to be kept in the loop about ongoing projects, goals and deadlines, so it is essential that you communicate well with them and inform them about goings-on within the organisation. It is also essential that you encourage feedback and that your staff feel that they can approach you with any questions or issues they want to address - making yourself accessible to your staff.

3. **Build positive working relationships**
   It is important to get to know members of your team individually, not only on a professional level but on a more personal level too. When you make the effort to get to know a bit more about how your colleagues are doing and what they are interested in, it will build a much better rapport among the team.

4. **Acknowledge good work**
   Do not be one of these managers who only gives feedback when you have got something to criticise! By providing your staff with positive feedback it will help to build their confidence and encourage them to get more involved in the future, so it is vital that you acknowledge their achievements and the effort that they are putting in. Encourage creativity and ensure that everyone is clear about what is expected of them.

5. **Be real**
   Your team does not expect you to be superhuman - if you are feeling the pressure and need a helping hand, do not be afraid to admit it and if you make a mistake, own up! By showing your human side and allowing your staff to get to know you a bit better, the team will feel more relaxed and comfortable approaching you.

6. **Be decisive**
   A good leader needs to be able to assert their authority and make important decisions for the team. There is no space for flakiness in a management role, so it is crucial that you stick to your guns and go with what you feel is best the business.

7. **Delegate jobs to the right people**
   Part of why it is vital that you establish a relationship with your team and get to know them individually is so you can assess what their strengths are. People perform better

Managing People

and are more engaged in roles where they feel they are employing their best skills - delegating proper functions that suit each individual will have a significant impact on the productivity of the team.

8. **Manage conflict**
   When there is conflict in the workplace, it must not be ignored. Turning a blind eye could lead to a negative atmosphere, which could have implications for staff productivity and communication among the team may suffer. When an issue arises, it is crucial that it is addressed straight away before it builds.

9. **Focus on training and development**
   In order to become a better manager, you must ensure that your employees are equipped to perform their tasks to a high standard. One of the ways to prepare the team is to give them access to suitable training and development opportunities.

   As an effective manager, you may also be responsible for hiring the right candidates to join your team. Individuals who want to become better managers view training and development as an ongoing process, which continues after a new hire has been through the onboarding procedure. Your job is to develop employees, so they are confident enough to take on new challenges to be promoted within your business

10. **Encourage team building**
    An effective manager is aware that they need the support of their team to be successful. To become a better manager, you should go beyond ensuring that your team is cohesive. You should seek to improve your team's reputation throughout the organisation. Team building efforts should include using objective methods to measure team members' performance and resolving any conflict that arises.

11. **Promote mentoring relationships**
    To become a better manager, you should seek to build a mentoring relationship with your employees. Being a successful mentor includes creating long-term developmental plans, giving professional advice and guidance and helping your employees to spot opportunities to advance their careers

12. **Set a good example**
    Staff will look to you for guidance and inspiration, so it is essential that you set a good example to gain their respect. If you expect them to behave professionally and commit to their work, it is vital that you do so yourself. Make sure that you are doing your job, continuing to develop your career and support your team in doing so too.

Managing People

Effective Team Management

Managing a team can be inspiring, rewarding and exhausting!

Busy working environments can leave little time for managers to check-in with team members and ensure they are feeling happy, creative and on track.

With good communication channels and plenty of opportunities to give feedback, you can provide your team with a strong support system. With this, managers can develop accountability, trust and a less hierarchical approach.

Core skills needed to manage a team

The first consideration as part of this process is to recall the difference between leading and managing

A good starting point is the quotation:

"Leaders are people who do the right things; managers are people who do things right."

Leadership involves creating a compelling vision of the future, communicating that vision and helping people understand and commit to it.

Managers, on the other hand, are responsible for ensuring that the vision is implemented efficiently and successfully.

The Importance of Delegation

The top priority for team managers is delegation. No matter how skilled you are, there is only so much that you can achieve working on your own. With a team behind you, you can achieve so much more: that is why it is so important that you delegate effectively!

Successful delegation starts with matching people and tasks, so you first need to explain what your team's role and goals are. A good way of doing this is to put together a team charter, which sets out the purpose of the team and how it will work. Not only does this help you get your team off to a great start, it can also be useful for bringing the team back on track if it is veering off course.

Only then will you be in a position to think about the skills, experience and competencies within your team and start matching people to tasks.

Managing People

Motivating a Team

Another key duty as a manager is to motivate team members.

People may have all the expertise in the world but, if they are not motivated, it is unlikely that they will achieve their true potential. On the other hand, work seems easy when people are motivated.

Motivated people have a positive outlook. They are excited about what they are doing and they know that they are investing their time in something that is truly worthwhile. In short, motivated people enjoy their jobs and perform well.

All effective leaders want their organisation to be filled with people in this state of mind. That is why it is vital that you keep your team feeling motivated and inspired. But this can be easier said than done!

McGregor's Theory X and Theory Y explains two very different approaches to motivation, which depend on the fundamental assumptions that you make about the people who work for you. If you believe that they are intrinsically lazy, you believe in Theory X, while if you believe that most are happy and willing to work, you will tend towards Theory Y.

McGregor's XY Theory of Management

Theory X and Theory Y were first explained by McGregor in his book, "The Human Side of Enterprise," and they refer to two styles of management – authoritarian (Theory X) and participative (Theory Y).

McGregor's XY Theory remains central to organisational development and to improving organisational culture.

If you believe that your team members dislike their work and have little motivation, then, according to McGregor, you will likely use an authoritarian style of management. This approach is very "hands-on" and usually involves micromanaging people's work to ensure that it gets done properly. McGregor called this Theory X. Many managers tend towards Theory X and generally get poor results.

On the other hand, if you believe that your people take pride in their work and see it as a challenge, then you will more likely adopt a participative management style. Managers who use this approach trust their people to take ownership of their work and do it effectively by themselves. McGregor called this Theory Y. Enlightened managers use Theory Y, which produces better performance and results and allows people to grow and develop.

Theory X
The assumption that employees dislike work, are lazy, dislike responsibility, and must be coerced to perform.

Theory Y
The assumption that employees like work, are creative, seek responsibility, and can exercise self-direction.

Managing People

The approach that you take will have a significant impact on your ability to motivate your team members. So, it is important to understand how your perceptions of what motivates them can shape your management style.

Theory X - 'Authoritarian Management' Style

Theory X managers tend to take a pessimistic view of their people and assume that they are naturally unmotivated and dislike work. As a result, they think that team members need to be prompted, rewarded or punished constantly to make sure that they complete their tasks.

Work in organisations that are managed like this can be repetitive and people are often motivated with a "carrot and stick" approach. Performance appraisals and remuneration are usually based on tangible results, such as sales figures or product output and are used to control staff and "keep tabs" on them.

This style of management assumes that workers:

- *Dislike their work.*
- *Avoid responsibility and need constant direction.*
- *Have to be controlled, forced and threatened to deliver work.*
- *Need to be supervised at every step.*
- *Have no incentive to work or ambition and therefore need to be enticed by rewards to achieve goals.*

According to McGregor, organisations with a Theory X approach tend to have several tiers of managers and supervisors to oversee and direct workers. Authority is rarely delegated and control remains firmly centralised. Managers are more authoritarian and actively intervene to get things done.

Characteristics of an X-theory manager

Perhaps the most noticeable aspects of McGregor's XY Theory - and the easiest to illustrate - are found in the behaviours of autocratic managers and organisations which use autocratic management styles.

The characteristics of a Theory X manager are some, most or all of these:

- *Results-driven and deadline-driven, to the exclusion of everything else*
- *Intolerant*
- *Issues deadlines and ultimatums*
- *Distant and detached*
- *Aloof and arrogant*
- *Elitist*
- *Short temper*
- *Shouts*
- *Vengeful and recriminatory*
- *Does not thank or praise*
- *Withholds rewards and suppresses pay and remunerations levels*
- *Scrutinises expenditure to the point of false economy*
- *Seeks culprits for failures or shortfalls*
- *Seeks to apportion blame instead of focusing on learning from the experience and preventing recurrence*

Managing People

- Issues instructions, directions, edicts
- Issues threats to make people follow instructions
- Demands, never asks
- Does not participate
- Does not team-build
- Unconcerned about staff welfare, or morale
  - Proud, sometimes to the point of self-destruction
  - One-way communicator
  - Poor listener
  - Fundamentally insecure and possibly neurotic
  - Anti-social

- Does not invite or welcome suggestions
- Takes criticism badly and likely to retaliate if from below or peer group
- Poor at proper delegating - but believes they delegate well
- Thinks giving orders is delegating
- Holds on to responsibility but shifts accountability to subordinates
- Relatively unconcerned with investing in anything to gain future improvements
- Unhappy

Managing an X-theory manager

Working for an X theory manager is not easy - some extreme X theory managers make extremely unpleasant managers, but there are ways of managing these people upwards. Avoiding confrontation (unless you are genuinely being bullied, which is a different matter) and delivering results are the key tactics.

- *Theory X managers (or indeed Theory Y managers displaying Theory X behaviour) are primarily results-oriented, so orientate your own discussions and dealings with them around results - i.e., what you can deliver and when.*
- *Theory X managers are facts and figures oriented - so cut out the incidentals, be able to measure and substantiate anything you say and do for them, especially reporting on results and activities.*
- *Theory X managers generally do not understand or have an interest in human issues, so do not try to appeal to their sense of humanity or morality. Set your own objectives to meet their organisational aims and agree these with the managers; be seen to be Theory manager sees you are managing yourself and producing results, the less they will feel the need to do it for you.*
- *Always deliver your commitments and promises. If you are given an unrealistic task and/or deadline state the reasons why it is not realistic, but be very sure of your ground, do not be negative; be constructive as to how the overall aim can be achieved in a way that you know you can deliver.*
- *Stand up for yourself, but constructively - avoid confrontation. Never threaten or go over their heads if you are dissatisfied or you will be in big trouble afterwards and life will be a lot more difficult.*
- *If an X Theory manager tells you how to do things in ways that are not comfortable or right for you, then don't question the process, simply confirm the end-result that is required and check that it's okay to 'streamline the process' or 'get things done more efficiently' if the chance arises - they'll normally agree to this, which effectively gives you control over the 'how', provided you deliver the 'what' and 'when'.*

Managing People

This is really the essence of managing upwards X Theory managers - focus and get agreement on the results and deadlines - if you consistently deliver, you will increasingly be given more leeway on how you go about the tasks, which amounts to more freedom. Be aware also that many X Theory managers are forced to be X Theory by the short-term demands of the organisation and their own superiors - an X Theory manager is usually someone with their own problems, so try not to give them anymore.

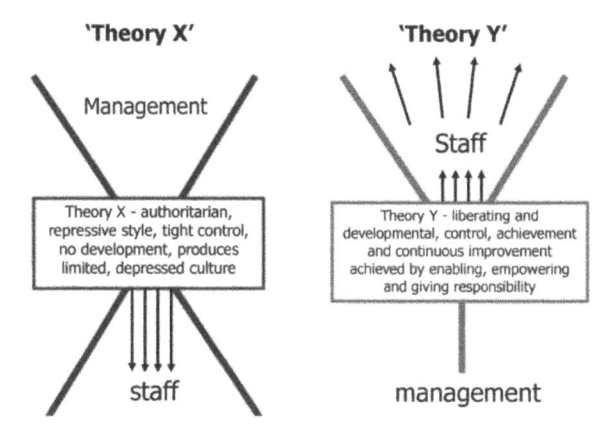

'Theory X'

Management

Theory X - authoritarian, repressive style, tight control, no development, produces limited, depressed culture

staff

'Theory Y'

Staff

Theory Y - liberating and developmental, control, achievement and continuous improvement achieved by enabling, empowering and giving responsibility

management

Theory Y - 'Participative Management' Style

Theory Y managers have an optimistic, positive opinion of their people and they use a decentralized, participative management style. This encourages a more collaborative, trust-based relationship between managers and their team members.

People have greater responsibility and managers encourage them to develop their skills and suggest improvements. Appraisals are regular but unlike in Theory X organisations, they are used to encourage open communication rather than control staff.

Theory Y organisations also give employees frequent opportunities for promotion.

This style of management assumes that workers are:

- *Happy to work on their own initiative.*
- *More involved in decision making.*
- *Self-motivated to complete their tasks.*
- *Enjoy taking ownership of their work.*
- *Seek and accept responsibility and need little direction.*
- *View work as fulfilling and challenging.*
- *Solve problems creatively and imaginatively.*

Theory Y has become more popular among organisations. This reflects workers' increasing desire for more meaningful careers that provide them with more than just money.

Managing People

It is also viewed by McGregor as superior to Theory X, which, he says, reduces workers to "cogs in a machine," and likely demotivates people in the long term.

> *Make sure that you fully understand these theories – they will fundamentally affect your success in motivating people.*

Whatever approach you prefer to adopt, you also need to bear in mind that different people have different needs when it comes to motivation. Some individuals are highly self-motivated, while others will under-perform without managerial input.

Theory Z - William Ouchi

First things first - Theory Z is not a McGregor idea and as such is not McGregor's extension of his XY theory.

Theory Z was developed by William Ouchi, in his book 1981 ' *Theory Z: How American Business can meet the Japanese Challenge* '. William Ouchi is a professor of management at UCLA, Los Angeles and a board member of several large US organisations.

Theory Z is often referred to as the 'Japanese' management style, which is essentially what it is. It is interesting that Ouchi chose to name his model 'Theory Z', which apart from anything else tends to give the impression that it is a McGregor idea. One wonders if the idea was not considered strong enough to stand alone with a completely new name... Nevertheless, Theory Z essentially advocates a combination of all that is best about Theory Y and modern Japanese management, which places a large amount of freedom and trust with workers and assumes that workers have a strong loyalty and interest in team-working and the organisation.

Theory Z also places more reliance on the attitude and responsibilities of the workers, whereas McGregor's XY Theory is mainly focused on management and motivation from the manager's and organisation's perspective.

Motivation Techniques

People are the main and the most important resource of each company. For achieving great results each leader needs to have a motivation strategy to create and maintain the spirit of enthusiasm among employees. Below are some effective ways for you to motivate your staff and ensure the continuous growth of your organisation.

1. **Share the organisational vision with each member**
   If everyone is aware of the collective vision, which will lead to prosperity and success of each team member, motivation and enthusiasm become the indivisible parts of all activities. Make sure that you continuously concentrate the attention of your staff on the glory of reaching that powerful vision.

2. **Communicate with your staff**

Managing People

You cannot learn about ideas, attitude or concerns of your team members without constant communication. Use each opportunity to interact with them and you will discover hundreds of new ways of organising your activities more successfully.

3. *Make people feel appreciated*
   One of the greatest needs of each person is the need of being appreciated. Very often appreciation is a greater reward than money. Show your sincere gratitude for the unique contribution everyone makes to the organisation.

4. *Support new ideas*
   Each team member will feel empowered by the opportunity to not only implement day to day tasks, but as well as suggest new ideas and make them a reality. Give people a chance to take initiative and you will be amazed by their ability to create brilliant ideas.

5. *Give challenging tasks*
   People cannot grow if they are constantly doing what they have always done. Let them develop new skills by giving challenging tasks. At the same time make sure the tasks are reachable and in the frames of the person's interests.

6. *Encourage Creativity*
   Supervising does not mean controlling each and every step. It means making sure that all the organisational activities are being implemented at the highest level. Give people the freedom to find their own unique ways of solving issues. Challenge them to think out of the box.

7. *Give each one opportunity to grow*
   If people know that everything is going to be the same way all the time, they will definitely lose the motivation to put their maximum efforts in work. They should be sure that the devotion and hard work will lead to new personal and professional achievements.

8. *Empower each individual*
   Very often people need just a little encouragement to believe in themselves and to realise that they have a greater potential within. Always show your confidence in the unique abilities and potential of your team members.

9. *Give as much support as you can*
   Even if people in your organisation are self-disciplined and creative enough for finding solutions to various problems, anyway they are always in need of your guidance. Support them as much as you can and they will be inspired to do the same for you and for the organisation.

10. *Manage each one individually*
    Every person has their strengths and weaknesses. Someone may be amazing at public speaking, while the other one has great writing skills. Give people a chance to operate in the frames of their strengths and they will be more confident and motivated in their activities.

11. *Do not let your people become bored*

Managing People

Do you want your team to be enthusiastic and productive? Then avoid routine. Routine is the enthusiasm killer. Let people explore and discover. Make the work as interesting and engaging as you can.

12. *Create healthy competition*
    For this purpose, you can effectively use the famous reward system. People contribute their efforts and ideas to the maximum when they know that outstanding excellence will lead to rewards. Just make sure that the reward system is absolutely transparent to everyone.

13. *Celebrate each success*
    Even the smallest achievements are worth being celebrated. The road to success consists of thousand small steps. Glorify each and every goal achieved. Show to your team that all of you made one more important step forward.

14. *Make sure there is a good working environment*
    Research showed that environment is more important to employees than money. This is a great chance for you to create extra motivation for your staff by making the work environment a beautiful place to work, rest and have fun at the same time.

15. *Create and maintain a team spirit*
    Team is like a family, where mutual support and trust are the most important values. Organise team activities both during working time and after. You will have the half of success by creating and maintaining a powerful team spirit at the workplace.

Managing a Large Team

How do you make the transition from managing a small team of specialists, to taking over the management and leadership of a larger team of multiple specialisms? This is a step that many managers will have to take at some point in their careers and it can prove challenging.

A small team can be relatively easy to manage as there are usually shared goals and objectives and a smaller demand on the manager to take the helm.

Where a whole department or large team needs management and leadership, there is a much bigger demand placed on the manager, the management style and priorities need to adapt. This increase in headcount, scope and responsibility can be daunting but providing you keep some key principles in mind, it is eminently achievable. Here are our key tips for managing a large team.

Build relationships across the team
Your most important professional relationships as leader of a large team are those you build with your direct reports or your management team. They are the ones who you will be in contact with most and the team that will be putting your strategy into action. They act as your conduit to the rest of the team, but it is important that you do not stop working on relationships there. All of you team down to the execs and assistants are valuable

Managing People

assets and should be treated as such. As the manager, you should show that you are invested in them and their work and endeavour to build some sort of working relationship. That is not to say that you have to befriend every single team member but try to build some rapport and show that you understand their role in the team. This will go a long way in ensuring that everyone is invested in what you are trying to do and pulling in the same direction.

Empower the management team
As mentioned above, the management team will be responsible for enacting the strategy and is your voice when projects are underway. It is crucially important that you build those strong relationships but also that you are empowering this team to excel and have confidence in themselves. You should be encouraging them to be decision-makers in their own right and to take ownership of projects. They are likely to be closer to the day-to-day operations of your set up and should be well placed to do so. However, this also helps them to boost their standing as managers in their own right. A motivated, respected and empowered management team can be your greatest asset as the leader of a large team.

Think about how you communicate
Communication is perhaps the most important thing to get right in any business. As a manager and in particular one in charge of a large team, it is absolutely vital that you establish clear communication channels within your teams. The key question to ask yourself is, how you can most effectively communicate with your team and how your team can most effectively communicate with each other? This will depend on the type of work you do and how the team is made up. It may be that a communication tool such as Yammer or Skype is the best approach. Alternatively, it may be that regular face-to-face meetings are the right way to go. You need to work out what works best and implement your solution.

Do not be afraid to delegate
Now that you are managing a larger team, your time and resources are likely to be stretched fairly thin. You are responsible for a large group of people and projects, each with their own set of priorities - it can be hard to juggle. Be willing to delegate tasks to members of your team that are capable and have the time and space, to absorb them. On the one hand, this will afford you more time to focus on other priorities, but it will also give those employees the opportunity to take on high-level tasks and to improve their skill sets. A vital part of management is empowering your direct reports and helping them to progress themselves. Delegating the right tasks to the right people can help with this.

Seek out and be accepting of feedback
Any manager should be open to feedback, both from those at the top and those who report in. It is a vital part of professional improvement and this does not stop when you reach these upper management positions. While you are unlikely to be offering an open forum for everyone under your remit to be putting forward their criticisms, it is important to be open to feedback. A good approach is to use your management team or team-leaders to act as information gatherers and also to encourage them to be honest with their opinions.

If you are seen to be open to feedback and willing to implement improvements, it can win you a lot of respect among your team.

Managing People

Managing Multiple Teams

When managing several teams to ensure high performance across each of them, it is recognised that collaboration and teamwork can make an important contribution to the success of the business.

For effective teamwork to be developed, departmental barriers need to be broken down both within and between teams to reduce the risk of misunderstandings and conflicts. Therefore, communication is the key to ensuring that all involved are fully aware of the importance of working in cooperation. Team member should be treated as individuals and time should be taken by managers to find out how they are motivated, how they prefer to be rewarded, what captivates them and what interests them. This will support them to consistently maintain high performing team members. It should be recognised that every employee contributes to the overall objectives of the organisation and this must be reflected when setting objectives for individuals and or teams by objective linking. This will ensure that everyone's objectives are aligned to the business as overall objectives, vision or mission statement.

Is important that all staff are aware of the organisations objectives which should be disseminated and communicated in a way that ensures an understanding at each level as to how individual objectives contribute to each teams and the managers objectives and to the organisations ultimate aim.

Managing multiple teams has its own challenges. You may be responsible for the management of teams and team leaders with different functions, for example, sales, accounts, Administration or production.

Often these teams will be interdependent and rely on each other to complete projects or activities, which need to be monitored and managed carefully to avoid conflict due to different rates of working.

As a manager, you will need to manage all teams to ensure a cohesive approach towards the achievement of goals. This entails managing consistency whilst remaining goal oriented. When managing multiple teams, the following points are important.

- *Support team leaders, delegate responsibility and give them all the autonomy to make decisions with clear guidelines-develop team leaders to be future managers.*
- *Give them the freedom to make mistakes, take ownership and responsibility and find their own solutions.*
- *Understand customers' needs and requirements and how they want to be involved and communicate this to the team effectively*
- *Time management is essentially managing multiple teams, build in contingency plans for emergencies, set aside time to deal with queries from teams. Prioritise and manage distractions and stay focus.*
- *Standardisation of processes and procedures*
- *Know your teams and their skills and utilise them effectively, supporting the acquisition of new skills and the improvement of existing practices*

Level 5: Operations / Departmental Manager

Managing People

- *Establish clear lines of communication and maintain contact*
- *Have consistent processes and procedures across teams*
- *Delegate responsibility and encourage decision-making and ownership*
- *Create opportunities for networking and information sharing*
- *Utilise an information management system*
- *Manager time and effectively between teams*
- *Make use of technology*

Remote or Multiple Teams

Dealing with multiple teams or people who may not be in close proximity creates a whole new challenge from managers, not only in the number of employees they may have responsibility for, but also ensuring that the locations culture and requirements are considered. It would suggest that this role would fall to a regional manager who will then have team leaders or managers to help carry out their managerial responsibilities.

Where this is the case, it would be logical to ensure that policies and practices remain consistent across locations as much as feasible. It should be recognised some occasions where the rancid requirements regarding working arrangements and purposes, however, having an employee handbook that is consistent across all locations will set the tone.

It is important as a manager of several locations to maintain a regular presence across all sites. This does not have to be physical visits, which might prove inefficient or costly, in some cases, but might consist of videoconferencing, telephone calls on a regular basis, especially with team departmental managers to ensure awareness of any progress and issues that may be arising. This will also demonstrate your team leaders and managers that your visible and available for support if required.

Managers with multiple teams and locations will need to be much more adept at delegating and ensure a level of trust is placed in those reporting to them. Defined lines of communication, which are open, must be implemented across all sites and all teams to ensure the information flows effective, even if and to simulate disseminated simultaneously

Qualities of an effective remote team manager paragraph the following qualities are essential for managers or managing remote teams and locations

> **Positivity**-*you need to be a brand ambassador across all teams and individuals, sharing and celebrating success. Having a positive and consistent approach will motivate team leaders and members to achieve and promote the brand.*

> **Encouragement**-*ensuring that each team or location has common procedures and guidelines clear lines of communication and team members are valued equally will promote a culture where there motivated and encouraged to succeed*

Managing People

Approachability-*an effective manager must be approachable and this is especially important when managing remote teams. You need to establish how you going to make yourself available and consider whether you can promote an open-door policy.*

Constructive and proactive-*an effective manager will think ahead and plan for foreseeable events having good contingency plans in place will support teams to deal with issues as they arise and it is important that they do so efficiently, especially when working in remote locations where your support may not be immediately available.*

Empathy-*you need to be aware of how remote team members may feel, especially those working in isolation from others. You will need to manage the psychological impact of remote working, involve all team members in discussions and maintain contact at least once a week, more often if necessary*

Understand team dynamics- *consideration needs to be made as to how different teams and team members interact with each other when remote working. Effective structures for communication between and within teams will need to be in place, this will help to prevent teams from becoming isolated and reducing consistency and conflicts from arising.*

Effective communicator-*as a remote team manager you will need to communicate effectively using active listening and respond appropriately and in a timely manner. Team leaders and supervisors should be trained to and empowered to use their own effective communication skills.*

In addition to these qualities there are some points that you will need to consider when managing remote teams and team leaders

- *establish a common vision and goals across and within teams*
- *use coaching and mentoring or implement body systems where practicable. This can be face-to-face periodically or by Webcam or social media in line with policies and procedures.*
- *establish clear expectations by setting monitoring and reviewing clear objectives*
- *arrange regular meetings it is good to bring everyone together once or twice during the year, this could be an annual conference or team building days.*
- *establish your availability, this could be set times during the day when you are available for team leaders and members to contact you. Inform teams of the times when you cannot be disturbed unless in an emergency.*
- *delegate responsibilities and empower team leaders*
- *maximise the use of technology using internal intranet, conference calling, email, e-learning and online training.*
- *remember to meet face-to-face, for example one-to-one meetings, supervisions are and annual appraisals or performance reviews.*
- *trusting your team and team members to get work task done and to meet deadlines. If you believe in the abilities of individuals and give autonomy to people rather micromanaging them, you will enjoy loyalty.*

Managing People

Virtual Teams

In the past, new managers often had the luxury of cutting their teeth on traditional teams located in the same building. Unfortunately, today's increasingly global work environment does not always afford that luxury. Many first-time managers find themselves assigned to a team of subordinates scattered far and wide.

You might assume that if you have managed teams before you will be able to manage a virtual team without any problem, but it takes a highly skilled manager to be able to build, manage and maintain a successful virtual team. You will need all those skills you developed when managing face-to-face teams – and a whole lot more.

A virtual team is a group of people that work together on common goals and projects but do not sit together and so communicate electronically rather than face-to-face – although they may occasionally meet in person. Virtual team members are sometimes homeworkers located in nearby towns but often they are based in offices across borders and continents. Virtual team working is notoriously challenging and it is often quoted that 50% of virtual teams fail to meet their objectives – and even when virtual teams do meet their objectives they very often do not want to work together again.

The absence of those informal opportunities to collaborate or those coffee machine moments where colleagues share a joke and build rapport means that it is much harder to build trust and create a sense of common purpose and engagement in virtual teams. The virtual manager needs to dedicate more time, energy and resources to establishing good relationships throughout the team, not only between themselves and the rest of the team but also between colleagues.

Specific skills needed when managing a virtual / distributed team

Managing a distributed team can feel overwhelming as it requires you to navigate many different types of distance related issues: geographic, temporal, cultural, linguistic and configurational (the relative number of members in each location).

Every one of these dimensions affects team dynamics and, therefore, has an impact on effectiveness and performance as well. Daunting as that may seem, there is good news in the form of a large and ever-increasing body of research and best practice on how to increase your odds of success. But first, it is important to understand which aspects of team dynamics are and are not, affected by distance.

The effects of distance

While all of the different types of distance listed above affect virtual / distributed teams, they do so primarily through two core mechanisms:

shared identity and shared context.

Managing People

Understanding these will help you develop a much more targeted plan of attack for managing from afar.

Firstly, distance affects how you feel about people. Dealing with the types of distance listed above (often grouped together and labelled "locational") triggers a sense of "social distance" – no sense of shared identity, or a feeling of "us vs. them." A lack of a shared identity has a far stronger impact on team dynamics than any of the types of distance individually.

It has been shown that unshared identity arising from social distance increases coordination problems and reduces group cognition in the form of transactive memory. When teams function with high levels of transactive memory, they know where different knowledge is held in the team and how to access it. For instance:

> *If everyone knows that Hector is a talented forecaster, the team will save time by assuming that Hector is responsible for any new information regarding forecasting.*

When transactive memory is impaired, however, the efficiency of the group suffers. Similarly, another study found that this sense of "us-vs. them" significantly increased levels of conflict within a major organisation.

Secondly, distance affects what you know about people. Catherine Cramton refers to this concept as "the mutual knowledge problem," put simply, it means that you do not know what they know – and vice versa.

Why does this matter? A shared sense of context, a shared understanding of not only what you do but how you do it and why, is a key driver of your ability to coordinate and collaborate. Teams with a shared understanding are more efficient. They do not waste time ensuring everyone is on the same page and they have fewer issues with miscommunication.

Taken together, this means that when assessing the effects of distance on your team, you need to keep in mind both how you feel and what you know, about your distant colleagues.

Though it may come as a bit of a surprise, distance does not change the fundamental rules of the game. A global virtual team is first and foremost a team — just because yours is distributed does not mean you should discard the prevailing wisdom about how the most effective teams operate. You need to arm yourself with a good model of team effectiveness and use it to assess and improve team dynamics and processes. A model provides structure and will help you organise your efforts as you tackle management for the first time. This is especially important for those who are dealing with the added complexities of distance.

Managing the effects of distance

Global, virtual, distributed teams are composed of people just like any other team. The more you and your team members can keep this in mind, the better your results will be. As the manager, encourage everyone to engage in some perspective taking: think about how you would behave if your roles were reversed. This is a small way of reminding your team that collaboration is not magic, but it does take some effort.

Managing People

Second, remember the basics. Arm yourself with a well-tested model of team effectiveness and use it to help structure your thinking.

Hackman's Team Effectiveness Model is an excellent starting point. It is based on a massive amount of rigorous research across a wide range of teams. This model stresses the importance of the team goal.

Building on Hackman's work, research shows that if you do only one thing, ensure that the team's goal is clear, challenging, consequential and commonly held as this yields the biggest benefit. This holds true whether your subordinates are down the hall or around the globe. In the end, being mindful about your team process is more important than which particular model you choose. Take that model and use it to assess how you have done, where you stand and where you are going.

Third, think (and talk) about how to overcome the negative effects that a lack of shared identity and shared context can have. To help your team combat "us-vs.-them" thinking, reinforce what is shared: the team's purpose. All teams are designed to achieve something and if the team is designed well, team members depend on one another to accomplish their goal. Remind your team that you are all working to the same end and that you need each other to get there. Doing so at the outset and intermittently throughout the project will help you build a strong sense of shared identity.

A shared understanding comes from sharing information. Team members working at a distance need to try to understand what is happening in each person's local context. Importantly, that includes information not only about the work being done but also about the environment in which people are working (e.g., structural changes, office politics, even personal life events). All of these affect the psychology of your dispersed colleagues and, therefore, how they react to you and the rest of the team.

One last note — it is easy to get fixated on either information or interpersonal dynamics to the exclusion of the other but that paints an incomplete picture. You need to consider the effects of both and how they reinforce one another. Always encourage team managers to have regularly scheduled check-ins not just to measure progress towards the team's goal but to discuss both its context (what it knows) and identity (who it is).

Transparent Communication

> *"The single biggest problem with communication is the illusion that it has taken place."* - George Bernard Shaw

Excellent communication skills are essential for virtual team managers who do not have the luxury of face-to-face communication but instead have to rely much more on text or voice only communication.

Without the benefits of non-verbal clues, it can be much harder to interpret the real intention of what is being said and know what the speaker is really thinking. As a virtual team manager, you must ensure that your communication is clear and unambiguous and that you make sure not only that you fully understand your team but that you are understood yourself.

Managing People

Ideas for virtual communication:

- *Communicate regularly and frequently but do not overload your team with information. Very long emails or online meetings should be avoided*
- *Make time for regular one-to-one communication with individual team members as well as group emails and meetings. Picking up the phone to see how someone is doing is usually appreciated and is certainly the best method if you have something sensitive to discuss*
- *Paraphrase and summarise when you are giving complicated instructions and check back that you have been understood*
- *Particularly with new team members be wary of using jargon or acronyms that they may not understand*
- *Listen attentively and be ready to read between the lines. Ask the right questions to check that you have understood*

Patience
Working virtually is challenging. Technology can let you down, response times may be longer if you are working across time zones and a lack of face-to-face communication can make it so much harder to interpret the real message.

You may also have language and cultural barriers to manage. Particularly in the early stages of your virtual team, you are going to have to flex your patience muscle: things will take longer, interpersonal irritations and upsets may well occur, people will not always say what they really think, meetings will not always go to plan and you will need to remain positive and focused on achieving your goals. You are likely to need a lot of patience!

Rapport-Building
Virtual teams risk losing the human element of the workplace and so their managers need to be highly skilled in building relationships and creating good rapport with their team members.

Make sure you allow time for the team to get to know a little more about each other's personal lives and factor in a few minutes small talk at the start of meetings – and do not be afraid to share a joke.

Remember that your team are human beings so from time to time check in on how they are feeling as well as what they are doing and engage sensitively when a team member is experiencing personal or professional challenges.

A regular quarterly or even annual face-to-face meeting will help enormously to build positive team relationships. Make sure you use any face-to-face time wisely and focus on team-building activities rather than on updates and reporting that can just as easily be done at a distance.

Results-Focus
All managers need to focus on results but one of the challenges of managing a virtual team is that you cannot see what people are doing or monitor their performance in the same way and

Managing People

so you can only really manage, measure and reward based on outcomes and results. When managing virtual teams, it is crucial to have clear individual accountabilities in place with agreed methods of monitoring and measuring performance.

Intercultural Skills

> *"Tolerance, intercultural dialogue and respect for diversity are more essential than ever in a world where people are becoming more and more closely interconnected."* - Kofi Annan

If you manage a virtual team the chances are that it is also an international team with members located across cultures and time zones. This means you will need to navigate values, communication styles and working preferences that may be at odds with your own or with other team members'.

Virtual team leaders need to manage multiple perspectives and decode different cross-cultural styles so that they can get the best from their individual team members and also maximise the diversity of the team as a whole. Be prepared to listen and learn about other cultural norms and move beyond nationality stereotypes. If colleagues in one location never seem to deliver on time, do not jump to conclusions but consider how milestones and deadlines are managed, how much support they are getting and if instructions are clear and accessible. If another colleague rarely contributes during online meetings, think about how the meeting is managed, if more materials could be circulated ahead of the meeting and whether they need additional language support – and make sure you make time to speak to them one-to-one.

Technology Skills

> *"The more elaborate our communication the less we collaborate."* - Joseph Priestly

Virtual teams rely on technology to interact with each other and share information and as the team manager you need to lead by example and demonstrate excellent technical skills. You must select the right tools and platforms for your team and match each task or interaction type to the most appropriate mode of communication. It goes without saying that you should be a competent user and be able to stay calm and trouble-shoot when technology lets you down.

Select a relatively small number of tools that can be used regularly and consistently but also be aware of how individual team members prefer to communicate. You might find you get a faster response from some colleagues by using an Instant Chat function while others prefer the human contact of a quick Skype call.

Managing People

Challenges for Virtual team members include:

- *Poor and infrequent communication*
  It can hinder innovation, effectiveness and decision making. Moreover, not being in regular contact can prevent team members from creating working friendships and can leave them feeling isolated. They may not see how their work and projects fit as a whole and become demotivated and despondent. Team leaders can create interdependent tasks and encourage partnerships within the team—but it is also every team member's responsibility to increase everyday interactions.

- *Lack of trust*
  Because virtual team members rarely work at the same time, they cannot see what others are doing and they do not get immediate responses. These problems can be averted by setting clear goals and expectations, as well as creating awareness of the contribution and achievements of every team member.

- *Diverse multicultural teams*
  They often comprise people with conflicting customs, work habits and values. Members prefer their own way of working and leaders must find common grounds to manage them. To minimise conflicts, all team members should agree on the fact that common, acceptable work ethics and team customs foster cultural understanding.

- *Loss of team spirit*
  Virtual teams can be more effective, cohesive and engaged through shared leadership. The team's leaders should create a clear direction for the other members, ensuring everyone accepts a common goal and vision.

- *Physical distance*
  It can foster cold, distant relationships among members—posing risks for the team's competence and cohesion. Members feel unable to ask questions and there are difficulties with the delegation. So, team leaders should pay individual attention to each member to create a sense of commitment and project ownership.

- *Time zone differences*
  Use collaboration tools in order to help you minimise the time overlap between members. This will also result in the reduction of virtual meetings.

- *An over-lengthy daily routine*
  It reduces worker concentration and motivation. Team members can feel exhausted if they are required to stay at their computers for many hours at a time to correspond with colleagues operating in different time zones. Encourage team members to work 'normal length' days, even if they are not 'nine-to-five'.

Managing People

- *Personal life and work-life imbalance*
  Virtual team members often work in the same physical space where they go about their personal lives. So, work can affect team members' personal life— and the other way around. Harmonising personal life and work life is crucial to the success of any virtual work.

- *Lack of clarity, direction and priorities*
  The hardest part of establishing a specific goal is maintaining it and keeping everyone focused. Overcoming this challenge for virtual teams requires planning, dedication, foresight, hard work—and getting all team members to engage with each other.

Virtual team working is becoming increasingly common, yet many teams struggle to perform effectively.

Virtual team managers need to consider how they adapt and expand their skills to adjust to the lack of human interaction – they need additional skills, but they also need to be aware of how and when they use the skills they have. Successful virtual and project managers are going to be in demand!

Managing People

Managing Managers

This is an issue for all of those managers who find themselves promoted or hired into a role where they are not just a manager — but a manager of managers. Is this brand of management any different? What should a new manager of managers consider in their role?

The Coach's Coach.
We all intuitively know that as a manager you are supposed to give people the freedom and room to do their best work. However, with managing managers, the need for autonomy becomes even more critical. Your success as a manager lies not in them delivering the work — but helping them to help their team deliver the work. The amount of space you give someone to do that as a manager, versus as an individual contributor, is much greater.

As a manager of managers, you play the role of "coach"- except this time, you are coaching a coach. You are in a manager's back pocket, ready to listen when they are stuck, frustrated, worried, or co. used about something. You are not helping them make progress on specific tasks but helping them think through sticky situations.

What is keeping them up at night? Who is the person on their team that is causing the problem? What they are trying to figure out how to perform better?

A sign of a great coach is one who asks a disproportionate number of questions to their team. As a coach's coach, consider:

> *Are you asking even more questions than you ever did before?*

Vision is undoubtedly important to share as a leader. After all, your team needs to understand where they are going and why it is important to get there. But when you are managing managers, this vision needs to be exceedingly clear. Why? Because the folks you are managing will need to answer the question, "Where are we going?" for their direct reports. Your managers will need to find ways to align the personal visions of their team members with the organisation's shared vision. So, if you have not made the answer to the question "Where are we going?" absurdly obvious, you can bet that the vision becomes watered-down or distorted in some way once your managers share it with their direct reports. As a manager of managers, you must clarify, repeat, reinforce, evaluate and again clarify and repeat the answer to "Where are we going?" over and over again.

Get comfortable criss-crossing.
When you are managing managers, your focus is much more cross-functional — you are working with business units across the entire organisation, instead of just one or two. There is a popular misconception that you get more freedom and control the "higher up" you go. But the reality is, when managing managers, your freedom and control is contingent on more moving pieces. You have more stakeholders to consider, more departments to coordinate with. Sure, you have the "final word" on more things and greater scope than when you were only managing individual contributors. But now, as a manager of managers, your view of the pie — and your responsibility of the pie — is bigger.

Managing People

You are not the domain expert anymore.
Domain expertise and domain leadership are not the same things. Knowledge, of course, is formative for decision-making and credibility, but it is not the driving force behind helping a group of people work together, get aligned around common objectives and make progress. The latter depends on your ability to build trust, to communicate honestly, to figure out what motivates each person and to lay out a clear path of where you are going and why it is important to get there. Remember this as you transition to managing managers.

You are likely further from being the domain expert you once were. It feels unnerving, to say the least — you are not up to date with the latest technologies or trends as you would like to be. But keep in mind that your priority is not in your fluency in the domain. Your priority is making sure the people on your team are the domain experts and that you are helping them do their best work to contribute to the organisation.

You are growing leaders, not just leading leaders.
Naturally, as a manager of managers, part of your role involves growing other leaders in the organisation. This does not necessarily mean putting formal training or mentorship programs in place (though, it can help). Growing other leaders can be as straightforward as carving out more dedicated time during your one-on-one meetings to ask questions like, "Is there anything outside your current role you'd like to be contributing toward?" or "What project have you been most proud to work on and why?" Essentially, you want to consider: Are you giving people a reason to want to continue to work in the organisation? Are you making it a place worthy for them to further their careers? Why would they want to stay?

This also means personally exemplifying the kind of leadership you would like to see across the organisation. Managers who are leading their teams are taking notes from you, watching you for cues on how to behave, make decisions and handle situations. Your actions are not just affecting your direct reports anymore — they are affecting their direct reports as well. Everyone is learning from your actions, implicitly. Keep this in mind.

You will notice that managing managers is not wholly different from managing individual contributors. The fundamentals are the same. Whether you are a manager of managers or of individual contributors, you are still helping a team achieve its desired outcomes. Rather, the points of emphasis differ: The amount of space you give your team, how exactly you spend your time and who you are interacting with on a day-to-day basis.

Managing a manager is both different — and not so different. Whichever way you choose to view it, in focusing on these elements, I hope your transition to becoming a manager of managers is smoother than you originally anticipated.

When you are managing managers, your responsibilities are two-fold: you need to make sure they are producing good work (as with any employee) and that they are effectively supporting their teams. You might know how to do the former, but how do you do the latter? Do you need to provide training? Coaching? And how do you serve as a good role model?

Managing People

Model the right behaviour
People learn how to lead from their managers, but your juniors do not just learn from you when you sit down for your one-on-one meetings. "It's not particularly authentic to say I'm going to be a role model on Thursday from 4 to p.m. People are watching all the time," Be sure that you are managing your people in the way that you expect them to manage their own teams. Always walk the talk. For example, if you want your direct reports to give their team members autonomy, be sure that you are doing the same for them.

Change the focus of your coaching
You spend time with your individual contributors talking about the specifics of their work but with managers, you will also need to explore their relationships with their direct reports. Instead of asking, "How's that project going?" you might ask "How are you working with Clara to get that project done?" or "How might you better support Clara on that project?" Talk directly about how they are coaching and giving feedback. "This sends a signal that these things are important,". Ask them how much time they are spending on coaching since they might be tempted, like many managers, to give this activity short shrift and you might regularly remind them:

> ## "We all have a responsibility to develop people."

Compliment them publicly
The people who report to you look to you for clues as to how they should feel about their managers. If you respect the person and the job they are doing, they will too. "Give people opportunities to demonstrate their credibility in front of others. Praise them publicly, ask for their advice in front of others, or assign them part of a presentation that lets them show off their expertise. Be careful: the same effect can work for negative comments. If you have criticism to offer, be sure to do it in privately.

Use an apprenticeship model
The best training for someone learning to become a manager is individualised attention from you, their manager. This should not just occur in meetings though. This will allow you to not only teach them but also to observe them in action. You are not going to sit in on all of their one-on-ones (hello, micromanaging!) but you should make time to do things like participate in their team meetings, watch them give feedback, or conduct job interviews. Whenever you are observing them, give immediate feedback as long as it is not in front of others in a way that undermines them.

Give them space
You do not want to dictate exactly how your employees do their job. You have to allow that individual to lead their own way. They need to figure out what is authentic to them. This is especially important when there are differences, such as gender, between you and your direct reports.

Go through the same training
Some organisations offer formal training for new managers or send up-and-coming leaders to executive education programs. If this is something you can do for your direct reports, select the same curriculum you went through. If you participated in a class that you found particularly helpful, suggest that your managers do the same.

Get to know their team

Managing People

It can be tricky to know how much you should interact with your direct reports' teams. On the one hand, you need to be familiar with the players so that you can give the manager relevant feedback and coaching. But, on the other hand, you do not want to undermine their authority. Any interactions should be above board with the explicit goal of trying to better understand the team and help the manager.

Find out how you are doing
You will be most supportive to your direct reports if you understand how you are performing as a coach and mentor. You can ask directly or use a 360 tool to assess how you are doing. Make sure that the questions get at indirectly and implicitly whether you are a good role model or not. Are you consistent in what you are asking for and what your expectations are? Also, do not wait for your annual performance review to ask for input. Feedback must be much more immediate and connected to the work you are doing.

Principles to Remember

Do:
*Treat your direct reports in the same way you want them to treat their team members.
Look for opportunities to observe them in action.
Spend time getting to know their team members.*

Do not:
*Dictate exactly how they should manage. Instead, give them advice and let them find their own authentic style.
Criticise them in front of their team. You should be looking for opportunities to bolster their credibility.
Wait until the annual review cycle to ask for input. Regularly seek feedback on how you are doing as their manager.*

Managing People

High Performing Teams

A high-performing team is a group of people who work together for a common goal and are able to achieve extraordinary results. High performance teams are created on a solid foundation of:

- *building productive communication,*
- *creating innovative solutions,*
- *delivering great performance.*

In other words, high performance teams are equipped with a high-performance team culture.

One of the areas a manager's main focus should be on, is developing teams that can work at the highest performance levels. You should help support individuals to develop by giving them the motivation they need to achieve the desired results. High performance teams have the necessary talents and skills to collaborate and high levels of innovation to produce excellent results.

There are several key features of high performing teams that need to be considered:

- *the businesses vision and values need to be communicated and understood*
- *team members roles must reflect individual skills and responsibilities must be clearly defined*
- *team members should be given autonomy, responsibility and accountability*
- *communication systems within and between teams should be effective and managed appropriately*
- *team members should support each other by communicating, giving feedback and making joint decisions*
- *team members should be encouraged to use their talents and strengths, which will increase motivation and therefore performance*
- *team members must be able to trust each other, with which develops team bonds and loyalty*
- *conflict should be handled effectively; this can create a positive culture where team members are able to discuss their differences of opinion and come to a consensus*
- *review of goal should be carried out regularly, outputs need to be evaluated and plans amended to ensure success*
- *achievements and successes should be shared and celebrated*
- *teams need to be adaptable and able to respond quickly to changes, adapting plans and working together to achieve outcomes*
- *teams need to have a strong sense of identity and belonging, this will ensure that a team is motivated and energetic and values and behaviours will be instilled in all team members*
- *individual team members will represent the same both internally and externally*

Managing People

Building a High-Performing Team

Teams do not simply happen. Indeed, teams are much more than groups of people. They occur when there are common goals, values and behaviours. And every leader has a part to play in building teams.

Model Excellence
You have probably heard the phrase: Behaviour breeds behaviour. This saying is illustrated by a simple model called the Attitude Behaviour cycle.

When stuck in a cycle of - mistrust, not taking responsibility, positive attitude and so on — it is up to the team leader to break the cycle and change attitudes.

Inevitably this has a positive impact on those around us. When we take charge and change our behaviour the team is more likely to follow our lead.

Open and Honest Communication
A hallmark of the high-performance team is a high level of open, honest, robust and transparent communication.

High performance teams increase trust by building a culture of partnership and shared values. This starts with open and honest communication.

When honesty and transparency are lacking there can be no trust.

Without trust, teams fail to solve problems or make decisions. Without trust teams are crippled by conflict.

A Supportive Environment
High Performance teams meet regularly and discuss progress, concerns and ideas for improvement.

Likewise, the team leader meets the individual to talk about their objectives, development and performance. The high-performance team supports its members by:

- *accepting difference and diversity,*
- *encouraging each other's strengths and*
- *supporting its members at times of personal or professional challenge.*

Understand the Expertise
Know your team's strengths and talents.

Motivation and positive attitude are more valuable to high performance teams than experience and negative character. The high-performance team motivates and coaches the individual. It helps and develops the less experience colleague. Moreover, the team listens to everyone and creates a sense of belonging. The team understands what each player has to offer and how they help achieve shared business objectives.

Managing People

Celebrate Success
Share good news. Make noise about successes.

Let everyone know when the team or a team member does something exceptional.

Finally, … encourage extracurricular activities for team members to forge close-knit relationships and build high levels of mutual trust and friendship

The following is a less detailed but fuller list of what managers should do to get people to work together to attain organisational goals.

1. **Define a very clear picture of the future—a vision for the team.** This is crucial because teams search desperately for specific targets. Consider the old expression: "If you don't know where you are going, any road will get you there." Journeys without a clear destination leave groups feeling flat and lost. Keeping teams informed on where they are headed and how best to get there means leaders must be prepared to acknowledge and adapt to changes in operational conditions and even objectives. Leaders cannot sit back and watch, but instead must create and recreate the vision and team spirit that stops people from losing heart and becoming lost.

2. **Be genuine, even if it means lowering your guard**. Leaders who create "click" have an uncanny sense about how and when to express their inner selves. They will even reveal their own vulnerabilities at the right time to gain the respect of those around them. They are not so concerned about projecting a perfect image: they know that high-impact leaders get results by laughing at their own flaws. They do not play make-believe, knowing it is more important "to be" than to "seem to be."

3. **Ask good questions**. They use inquiry and advocacy in such a way as to keep them abreast of what is really going on. They seem to use a simple formula of the 70-20-10 rule in conversations: 70 percent listening, 20 percent enquiring with just the right amount of advocacy and 10 percent tracking (i.e., summarising and synthesising information and providing possible courses of action).

4. **Talk about things—even the hard things**. A leader who gets their team to click is not afraid to talk about the tough stuff. They find ways to have the difficult conversations in the knowledge that burying problems does not make them go away. They also know that if they, as leader, do not talk about things, no-one will and, pretty soon, a culture will develop in which too many things are left unsaid. (I can always tell when teams are dysfunctional by measuring the amount of stuff not talked about, or what I call the "let's not go there" issues.)

5. **Follow through on commitments.** Leaders of high-performing teams find ways to build trust and maintain it, especially by making teams hold to their commitments and keeping the team's view of its goals clear. However, they also know how to distinguish professional trust from blind loyalty.

6. **Let others speak first.** In high-performing teams, members see themselves as equal in terms of communication. Leaders should therefore encourage this by putting the other person's need to express his or her agenda ahead of their own.

Managing People

7. **Listen.** High-performing teams are comprised of people who have mastered the art of listening without fear, of allowing others to speak without reacting strongly or negatively to what is being said, or what they anticipate will be said. The leader fosters and honours this attribute within the team by quickly putting a stop to bad conversational behaviour that cuts other people off and implies that their ideas are not valued. The leader knows that achieving higher levels of innovation requires team members to be unafraid to express unusual ideas and advocate experimental processes. They emphasise this by publicly thanking those who take risks–and by making sure that sharpshooters put their guns away.

8. **Face up to non-performing players.** This brings us to a very important characteristic of high performing teams, which is that their leaders do not tolerate players who pull the team apart. Interestingly, experienced leaders frequently maintain unity and discipline through third parties in the form of people we call "passionate champions." A leader may surround him- or herself with several passionate champions, who have established an understanding and close working relationship with one another and who are totally focused on and committed to, the team's objectives. They are capable of getting the job done–and not afraid to remove people who are failing to help them do so.

9. **Have fun, but never at others' expense.** High-impact leaders steer clear of sarcasm: they always take the high road. If they poke fun at someone, it is usually themselves. They have learned the lesson that reckless humour can be misinterpreted and backfire. They know that critics of the organisation can turn inappropriate remarks back on a leader who makes them.

10. **Be confident and dependable.** Somehow, over and above the daily struggle, managers who get teams to click, project confidence. They do this by preparing their conversations and not backing away from, or skimming over, real issues and problems, even difficult or confrontational ones.

    They always address "What's up?" and "What's so?" in the organisation. They do not try to be spin doctors because they know that, ultimately, this does not work. Rather, they are known as straight shooters–people who play hard, fight fair and never, never give up. At the end of the day, team members know that, whatever happens, their leader will be left standing. This gives them confidence that they will be standing, too. They also know that, should things get really bad, their leader will not desert them or try to shift the blame, but seek to protect them, even if it means standing in the line of fire.

Communicating and Working with a Team

Communication skills are essential for success in almost any role, but there are particular skills and techniques that you will use more as a manager than you did as a regular worker. These fall under two headings:

- *communicating with team members*
- *communicating with people outside your team.*

Managing People

Communicating with people in the team
As a team manager, you are likely to be chairing regular sessions as well as one-off meetings. Meetings of all kinds and regular ones in particular, are notorious for wasting people's time, so it is well worth mastering the skill of running effective meetings.

Many meetings include brainstorming sessions. As a team manager, you will often have to facilitate these, so you will need to be comfortable with doing this. There is more to this than simply coming up with creative ideas, as you do when you are just a regular participant in such a session: read our article to find out how to run brainstorming sessions. Make sure that you understand where they can go wrong and what you can do to avoid this.

Active listening is another important skill for managers – and others – to master. When you are in charge, it can be easy to think that you know what others are going to say, or that listening is less important, because you have thought of a solution anyway.

Do not fall into this trap. Most good managers are active listeners: it helps them detect problems early (while they are still easy to deal with), avoid costly misunderstandings and build trust within their teams.

Communicating with people outside the team
Your manager is probably the most important person you need to communicate with. Take time to understand fully what your manager wants from you and your team – if you know exactly what they like and how they prefer this to be delivered, you will be better able to meet with their approval.

Do not be afraid to ask your manager to coach or mentor you: you can usually learn a lot from him, but he may not be proactive about offering this. If you are approaching your manager for advice, make sure that you have thought things through as far as you can. Introduce the subject with a summary of your thinking and then say where you need help.

Also, as a manager, part of your job is to look after your team and protect it from unreasonable pressure. Learn skills like assertiveness and win-win negotiation, so that you can either turn work away, or negotiate additional resources.

Another part of your job is to manage the way that your team interacts with other groups. Use stakeholder analysis to identify the groups that you need to deal with. Then talk to these people to find out what they want from you and what they can do to help you.

Managing Team Discipline
However, much you hope that you will not have to do it, there comes a time in most managers' careers when they have to discipline an employee. Discipline may be subtly different from basic feedback because it does not always relate specifically to the employee's work. You can give feedback on their phone manner, for example, but handling problems with timekeeping or personal grooming can need a different approach.

Obvious breaches of the law or of company policy are easy to identify and deal with. But what of other situations? On one hand, you do not want to seem petty. On the other hand, you cannot let things go that should be dealt with.

Managing People

Use these rules-of-thumb to decide whether you need to act. If the answer to any is yes, then you need to arrange a time to speak to the employee in private.

Does the issue affect the quality of the employee's deliverable to the client (internal or external)?

A graphic designer regularly gets into work late, although he stays late to make up for this. Customers are sometimes frustrated by not being able to get through to him at the start of the day, particularly when he is working on rush jobs.

Does the issue adversely impact the cohesiveness of the team?
Individual designers tend to work on their own projects, with few meetings between design team members, so cohesiveness is not impacted. However, people are noticing his lack of punctuality and other people's timekeeping is beginning to slip.

Does the issue unnecessarily undermine the interests of other individuals in the team?
The designer sitting next to the latecomer is unhappy that she has to field calls from clients before he reaches the office and is unable to give a firm answer to the question "When will he be in?"

In this situation, the design team manager decides to speak to the latecomer because of the impact on the co-worker. They agree that coming in to work late is not a problem (they have a long commute, with heavy traffic en route) but that they will commit to being in by 9.30 a.m. every day to reduce the number of calls his co-worker has to field and also give them a fixed time to give clients. They will work late to make up time and will take on a task they do not like to make up for the extra phone handling.

When you are faced with a potential discipline issue, take time to gather information about the situation, decide what you are going to do and act. Discipline issues rarely go away of their own accord and they usually get worse, often causing considerable resentment amongst other team members.

Traps to Avoid
There are a number of common mistakes that inexperienced managers tend to make. Take care to avoid them! These are:

- *Thinking that you can rely on your existing job knowledge and technical skills to succeed as a manager. It is essential that you take the time to develop good management and people skills as well – these can be more important than your technical skills!*
- *Failing to consult regularly with your manager, in a misguided attempt to show that you can cope on your own.*
- *Approaching your manager without having thought a problem through and without having considered how the problem could be solved.*

Managing People

- *Embarrassing your manager or letting them get a nasty surprise. Follow the "no surprises" rule.*
- *Doing anything that requires your manager to defend you to others. This can cause your manager to "lose face" with their peers and superiors and it makes it look as if the team is out of control.*
- *Failing to talk to customers (whether internal or external) about what they want from yourself and your team.*
- *Using your authority inappropriately – make sure that everything you ask people to do is in the interests of the organisation.*
- *Many of these points sound obvious, however, it is incredibly easy to make these mistakes in the rush of everyday managerial life.*

Supporting the development of team members

Supporting individuals to develop will aid you as an operation/departmental manager to build high performing teams and include:

- *teaching them to follow best practices and procedures*
- *creating CPD plans for each employee*
- *giving them constructive feedback after they perform task*
- *setting an example by continually developing as an operation/departmental manager*
- *providing opportunities for them to expand their knowledge and learn new skills*
- *encourage them to challenge poor or risky practices*

You should always be on the lookout for new opportunities to motivate your team. Some individuals are self-motivated, but most team members require motivation from time to time.

As an operation/departmental manager, you need to ensure that your team stays motivated and you are on track to reach your organisational goals. You can do this in several ways, including:

- **Recognising the efforts of employees were job done well.** Simply say well done to a team member or thank you goes a long way to make them feel appreciated and give them a sense of achievement. Awarding an accolade such as an employee of the month is an effective way of recognising people's efforts and achievements publicly. Give praise wherever possible. As an operation/departmental manager, you should exude self-confidence and integrity and recognise the efforts of your team members. If a job is being well performed, do not hesitate to congratulate the team member-being appreciated boost morale considerably.
- **Offering rewards.** This can be financial rewards such as a pay rise, but it can also be time for prizes.
- **Offering a promotion or additional responsibilities.** Some people are motivated by the progress they are making are encouraged by the prospect of a promotion and additional, interesting challenges.

Managing People

- *Offering development opportunities, such as coaching or external training.* This adds to a person sense of achievement because they feel they are making progress in their careers.
- *Celebrating the team's efforts and achievements, for example, by organising a party after work.*

Motivating individuals involved:

- *letting them know that you can trust them by giving them more responsibility- this will also give them purpose*
- *being a role model and spreading positivity*
- *helping them to achieve a good work life balance*
- *setting them smaller, more achievable targets to achieve the desired results*

Development Plans

For any development plan to be effective, relevant and promote high-performance, the objectives should be set that arise from the organisations vision. Objectives should be set in the following order.

First for business directors, who will then identify objectives for their senior managers and then they will identify objectives for their middle managers and so on until all members of the team are aware of their own objectives. It should also be disseminated and communicated in a way that ensures an understanding at each level as to how individuals objectives contribute to managers objectives and to the businesses ultimate vision.

Professional development requirements should also be tied in with competences and role requirements, which can be found within either a job description and/or a job specification (ideally both). The information contained within these documents will not only reflect the specifics of the job role, but also the competences required of the individual to effectively perform the role.

A competency framework can be developed by collecting and combining competency information to determine standardised approach to performance across and within teams that is clear and accessible to everyone in the business. This can be utilised within the recruitment process to assist in the selection of candidates and to allow establish managers to compare current levels of competence with those desired, referring to the job description job specification and in line with the changing needs of the business.

Any form of personal development within the working environment should be agreed by the individual and their manager to ensure an increased likelihood of success.

There are several arguments that support the use of personal development plans, including that they:

- *enhance individuals existing skills*
- *help individuals acquire new skills*
- *provide opportunities for career development*

Managing People

During discussions with managers at one-to-one or appraisal meetings, individuals can contribute by identifying the career path that they would like to take and then decisions can be made as to the viability of the proposed development course.

Communication among team members is the key to ensuring that the business progression is in line with its objectives, vision and mission statement. Feedback from colleagues and managers will identify any developmental requirements. Completion of a skills, as in the example below can be utilised to also identified with the new skills are required to ensure objectives are met.

	Induction	Customer service	Commun-ication	Dealing with complaints	Operation of equipment
Team member 1	100%	75%	100%	50%	75%
Team member 2	75%	100%	50%	25%	100%
Team member 3	25%	75%	25%	25%	75%

The table can be adapted to display RAG ratings rather than percentages to indicate competency which will allow the manager to identify where learning and development is required at a glance.

The table can be as simple or as detailed as you need by adding elements such as a person's ability to train others or be a workplace champion certain areas of development

Managing People

Performance Management

Performance management, if conducted professionally, can motivate staff by functioning as a key component of the total organisational reward process.

The term total reward refers to all the benefits and investments that the business makes available to its employees. For example, pay, pension schemes, incentive payments and private health insurance and also includes things employees' value such as flexible working or career development.

Performance management can, of course, be associated with pay by generating data and information required to determine pay increases or bonuses that are related to a person's performance, competence or contribution, but it should be more about developing people and rewarding them in the broadest sense; therefore, approaches to using performance management to motivate people by non-financial means should be considered.

It is by using this approach that an environment will be created that more readily addresses the wider and higher-level needs of the individual rather than the base and always contentious financial level. It should also be noted that financial rewards may not always be available within the organisation and therefore more readily available non-financial reward may be all that the operations/departmental manager has at their disposal.

Generic Performance Management Cycle

To improve performance, a manager must know the current level of an individual's performance and this will be measured against the expected standards of performance previously agreed with the individual, shown in the following model

This model clearly focuses the process for addressing gaps in performance and not only reward. The example below includes this and the two models could be used in conjunction with each other to further motivate team members.

Performance may be measured in quantitative or qualitative terms.

Managing People

- *Quantitative relates to measuring or measured by the quantity of something rather than its quality.*
- *Qualitative relates to measuring or measured by the quality of something rather than its quantity.*

Quantitative measures are relatively straightforward to measure providing of course that there are output measures (what the individual has achieved) against input measures (what the individual has done). However, it becomes more difficult when qualitative measures must be used, as these may refer to behaviours or unquantifiable life outcomes rather than defined results.

Assessments can then become much more judgemental or subjective and therefore potentially biased, unfair or inconsistent, unless they are based on objective evidence of behaviour and the outcomes of behaviour. It is essential to ensure that factual evidence is therefore available on which to base these judgements.

Given that it has previously been identified that non-financial reward should be considered in addition to financial reward, it may be useful to suggest a wider range of performance measures or metrics. Five potential areas are offered for consideration as follows:

- **Finance**: *for example, income, shareholder value, added value, rates of return, costs*
- **Output:** *for example, units produced or process, throughput, sales, new accounts*
- **Impact**: *for example, attainment of a standard, quality, level of service, changes in behaviour, completion of work/project, level of take-up of a service, innovation*
- **Reaction:** *for example, judgement by others including colleagues and internal/external stakeholders or customers*
- **Time:** *for example, speed of response or turnaround, achievements compared with timetables, amount of backlog, time to customer market, delivery times*

It is further suggested the frequency of the performance management review should occur more often than the annual appraisal and should involve an informal element such as spontaneous discussion or informal supervision

Generic model of performance management frequency

Reviewing individual's performances
This can be done in several ways, including through appraisals, or more informal way such as brief discussions during the project. Whichever method is chosen, it is a valuable exercise to perform as it highlights the strengths and weaknesses of employees, giving them an insight into how they can improve. It also helps you as a manager to ensure that your team is working effectively as possible and any problems or issues of the person's performance are rectified as soon as possible. This feedback should always be constructive, which means it should

Managing People

concentrate not only on the negative aspects of a person's work, but also on the positive aspects to. This will motivate them, to learn, knowing their efforts are appreciated.

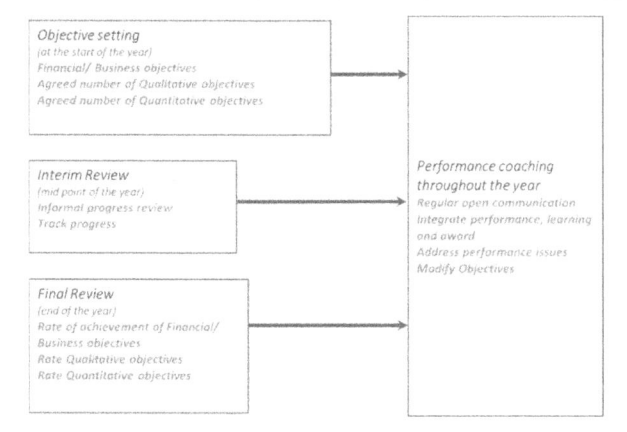

Objective setting
(at the start of the year)
Financial/ Business objectives
Agreed number of Qualitative objectives
Agreed number of Quantitative objectives

Interim Review
(mid point of the year)
Informal progress review
Track progress

Final Review
(end of the year)
Rate of achievement of Financial/ Business objectives
Rate Qualitative objectives
Rate Quantitative objectives

Performance coaching throughout the year
Regular open communication
Integrate performance, learning and award
Address performance issues
Modify Objectives

To review a managed performance or benchmark, the required standards need to be identified and communicated to individuals to ensure the expectations are understood. By having measures in place that can be monitored and reviewed, the management of an individual's performance can remain objective and following appropriate and effective progress process. These measurements should be set by utilising job descriptions and job specifications as well as any policies that are in place that provide specific information regarding lateness or dress code for example when following the information that has been provided and communicated effectively, the possibility of ambiguity and misunderstanding is reduced, subject to the information provided being explicit sufficient. Key performance indicators are also very good way of benchmarking performance and give the manager useful and unbiased tool to measure individuals against

Setting goals and objectives being able to set specific measurable achievable realistic and time bound (smart) objectives allows team members to work towards their goals and gives them the support they need to help the team succeed by spending time and effort to develop smart objectives for team members, you ensure that everybody has the knowledge and understanding needed to contribute effectively and comfortably to the team and business.

Conducting appraisals
Appraisal meetings are undertaken on a one-to-one basis in a structured and planned manner to allow employees to prepare their answers to questions and speak openly about their role and performance objectives should be set during an appraisal for the employee to complete during the year and a formal record of the meeting should be made. An appraisal is a two-way communication forum-it is not an opportunity for the manager to tour alone to talk

It suggested that individuals themselves are primarily responsible for progress in a performance plan and for ensuring that they play their part in its implementation. But it also recognises that, to different degrees, people will need encouragement, guidance and support. Managers are not expected to sit back and let their staff flounder; they have a role to play in helping is necessary in both the preparation and implementation of performance plan. The manager, therefore, has 5 key responsibilities as follows:

Managing People

- *Help produce action plans that are practical and achievable (SMART)*
- *support individuals in their efforts to learn and develop*
- *offer feedback at appropriate stages*
- *provide coaching when required*
- *encourage individuals to expand their risers and identify their opportunities.*

Fundamentally, it is the responsibility the manager to ensure that individuals are given the opportunity to implement performance plans which may require time away from the job and support, encourage and reward individual for their efforts.

Quality Management

Quality management techniques vary depending on the nature of the job the individuals are involved in. For example, the business is responsible for producing car tyres, the number of tyres produced may be the prime concern. This in turn may be the only measurement that is considered when making the decisions regarding someone suitability to work the business.

Other techniques and tools include checklist which can be performed hourly, daily, weekly, monthly or quarterly. A basic checklist can be used to identify the tasks that need to be undertaken with columns to be completed that identify when the task was completed and by whom. Training and development is another form of performance management, whether it is accredited training qualifications or on-the-job coaching, shadowing or secondment opportunities.

Absence Management

Having a contingency plan when people are absent from work is vital for the team and the business to run effectively. Understanding how absences can affect the team's performance and how best to prioritise resources and test when this happens, is the key to maintaining effective team during periods of absence.

Talent Management

Talent management should not be confused with succession planning. While succession planning should be included with it and within any talent management model, talent management is a far wider and more extensive picture of all the aspects of the management of personnel. Talent management is organisations attempt to recruit, keep and train the most gifted highest quality staff members they can find, afford and hire. Succession planning on the other hand is the identification and development of potential successors the key positions in an organisation, through a systematic evaluation process and training.

Talent management models include all aspects of sourcing and recruiting, performance management, succession planning and leadership development.

Approach to talent management

- **Definition** - *what does the business see talent management to be, what are the driving forces and why is it important?*

Managing People

- **Focus** - where is the talent needed, what are the roles to focus on and what issues or risks need to be addressed?
- **Process** - how will tele-management be achieved, was responsible and is the business prepared for the increment a should have clear structures and processes?
- **Action** - what are the desired outcomes and how will success be measured?

It is apparent that talent management is a key priority to many HR professionals and managers and seeks to attract, identify, develop, engage, retain and deploy individuals who are considered particularly valuable to an organisation or business this will result in positive outcomes:

- *early identification of the potential employees, their expectations and career aspirations*
- *filling vacancies and utilising knowledge and skills effectively*
- *staff retention*
- *opportunities for succession planning and promotion within the business*
- *valued and loyal employees*

Talent management can be achieved successfully by following the appropriate steps

- *identify the business's goals and priorities-job descriptions and specifications need to reflect the role*
- *search for and source the appropriate talent-access social networking websites as well as jobsite platforms and talent management/recruitment agencies*
- *recruit and select using appropriate and effective interview techniques*
- *retain employees by providing development opportunities, inviting ideas and innovations, promoting integrity, providing incentives and recognise and value and achievements*
- *provide opportunities for promotion and career growth*
- *planning conduct performance reviews/appraisals-identify potential for progression*
- *utilise succession planning-support the continual professional development of all employee employees to prepare them for future roles in the business*

To take the concept of talent management a step further, larger, global businesses are adopting the strategy and widening the search of potential employees to embrace diversity and recruit internationally. They will even go to the lengths of identifying potential future employees and grooming them for roles. Existing team members are also given the opportunity relocate, not only to fill roles but also to enable their own personal development.

Managing People

Recruitment and Selection

Every business will have its own unique process recruitment and selection; however, each will follow in general principles, the best practice and accepted for the recruitment and selection activity. The general principles will dictate that before a recruitment and selection activity takes place, a sound business case is constructed to establish the vacancy does exist; many organisations will use the potential vacancy is an opportunity to review the job role and see if it still necessary or perhaps could be incorporated into an existing job role. Thus, the person requesting a vacancy to be filled will be expected to offer a persuasive cost benefit analysis in the sport of the recruitment process.

When seeking to fill a vacancy, it is vital to remember that any candidate being recruited or selected for the vacancy should be judged on the appropriate mix of abilities, to not only be competent for the job role, but also to have the correct personal aptitude to operate efficiently and effectively in the environment where the job is to be performed. Too often, individuals selected for a job role merely based on possessing the right skills, only to discover later that their attitudes and behaviours render them inappropriate to perform the job in that particular work environment.

The link between attitude and behaviour is strong and the observational testing of behaviours will generally identify people's attitudes

Any recruitment and selection processes that is to have any degree of success will seek to identify the skills, attitudes and behaviours that are linked to the needs of the job role as identified in the job description.

The job description identifies a job and does not mention the type of person required to perform the role. To determine the type of person required, assistance will be sought from a person specification. This document will make explicit those attributes sort of a candidate for the job in question. There are two highly used plans in use today that will assist with developing a person specification.

Seven-point plan drawn up by Prof Alec Roger.

Area	Requirements
Physical make up	what is required in terms of health, strength, energy and personal appearance?
Attainments	what education, training and experience are required?
General intelligence	what is a job requiring terms of thinking and mental effort?
Special aptitudes	what kind of skills needed to perform the job?
Interests	what personal interest could be relevant to the performance of the job?

Managing People

Disposition	what kind of personalities required?
Circumstances	other any special circumstances that the job requires of the candidate?

This table can be further adapted to identify which of the seven points are essential for the job role or desirable. This is then used to grade a candidate accordingly.

The five-fold grading system as suggested by John Munro Fraser

The five aspects of this plan:

- ***impact on others***-embraces Rogers's physical make up on such aspects as dress, speech, manner and reactions
- ***acquired knowledge or qualifications***-general education, work experience and training and similar to Rogers's attainments category
- ***innate ability or brains***-ability to exercise intelligence and a range of situations, useful when few formal qualifications exist; it is about potential
- ***motivation***-how the individuals achieve their personal needs and ambitions rather than trying to identify those needs and ambitions
- ***adjustment***-emotional stability, maturity, ability to cope with stress, for example, basically the individual's reaction to presses pressures

Whichever method is chosen, this can only be done after the job description is been constructively formulated. The need for both the job description and person specification is essential as it allows for the job role to be formally analysed in some detail and then accurately mapped by means of the person specification to the correct person for the job. It provides a high degree of reassurance that the individual who has been chosen has great skills, attitude and behaviours for the job role and this is more likely to remain a competent and long-term employee.

All too often managers employ individuals on their skills alone and then wonder why, after short period of time, they find them unable to work within the team and able to interface with the customer and able to work with the conditions entailed by the job.

It is noted that some businesses combine job description and person specification into one document known as the job specification, however, if this is the case you should always ensure the key best practice principles about the job description and person specification are still included in the composite document.

Recruitment process

The organisation you work for will have its own procedures in place recruitment and selection and the following table shows only a generic process:

Managing People

- *established businesses need for the vacancy and secure approval*
- *analyse the job vacancy, review or construct job description and person specification*
- *determine essential and desirable characteristics to be used to selection criteria and whether they will be assessed at the application or interview stages*
- *advertise vacancy internal if required to determine the medium for advertising externally*
- *agree personnel to process and shortlist applications*
- *invite successful applicants for interview and inform those that were unsuccessful*
- *agree personnel to sit on the interview panel*
- *conduct first interviews against the essential and desirable criteria, repeat stages for 2nd interviews if required*
- *interview panel make the selection decision*
- *inform the successful applicant, request acceptance pending references and relevant security checks, agreed signing of the contract of employment and a great start date*
- *once the acceptance, references and security clearance been received and the contract signed, informed the unsuccessful applicants*
- *construct the induction programme taking account of any statutory and data requirements, agree objectives and probationary period, (the latter may be included in the contract)*
- *review the progress at the agreed frequency, make final decisions regarding employment before the probationary period expires*

Developing People

The development of your team members commences during the recruitment and selection process. The application interview records will start to identify gaps in knowledge and skills, enabling you to include these in an individual's organisational induction and continue this throughout the team members employment. Ongoing development will include the following elements

> **Induction**-*this should cover all but the new starter needs to know and understand about their job role, including any policies and procedures, reporting systems and important information, for example*
>
> **Initial and ongoing training**-*it is important that the new starters given the appropriate training, this will include mandated training such as health and safety, fire and customer service training and sector specific training for operating equipment, systems and processes and acquiring skills. It may also include coaching and mentoring.*
>
> **Probation period**-*the new starter will not only need to undertake the induction and training but will also require support and is in operation/departmental manager it is likely that you will delegate the responsibility to team leader. Often, a mentor or an experienced team member will be assigned to the new starter to shadow.*

Managing People

Personal development plan (PDP)*-PDP should be ongoing and used to support the team members development throughout their employment, from induction through to regular supervision is at and appraisals. It should include, as a minimum:*

- *development goals step*
- *steps to achieve the goals*
- *potential threats/Arista completing*
- *planned review/completion dates*
- *actual review completion dates*
- *review/completion comments*

Supervisions and reviews (3 months, 6 months)*-supervisions and review should be part of the PDP processor will provide the opportunity to review their progress toward goals, issues the team member encounters, work performance and give constructive feedback.*

Appraisal performance reviews (6 months, 12 months)*-appraisals and performance review should be planned so the team members prepared for the discussions. There should be no surprises as the points raised will have been discussed previously in supervision and reviews. The meeting is to review their progress throughout the previous year may also be pain related based on their performance.*

Continuous professional development (CPD)*-CPD plan is a record of a person's career development including their knowledge, skills and experiences, both formal and informal. It encourages team members to review and reflect on their own development. The CPD plan is usually collated in a foldable portfolio but could also record electronically.*

Conducting Appraisals

Appraisal meetings are undertaken on a one-to-one basis in a structured and planned manner to allow employees to prepare their answers to questions and speak openly about their role and performance objectives should be set during an appraisal for the employee to complete during the year and a formal record of the meeting should be made. An appraisal is a two-way communication forum-it is not an opportunity for the manager to tour alone to talk

It suggested that individuals themselves are primarily responsible for progress in a performance plan and for ensuring that they play their part in its implementation. But it also recognises that, to different degrees, people will need encouragement, guidance and support. Managers are not expected to sit back and let their staff flounder; they have a role to play in helping is necessary in both the preparation and implementation of performance plan. The manager, therefore, has 5 key responsibilities as follows:
- *Help produce action plans that are practical and achievable (SMART)*
- *support individuals in their efforts to learn and develop*
- *offer feedback at appropriate stages*
- *provide coaching when required*
- *encourage individuals to expand their risers and identify their opportunities.*

Managing People

Fundamentally, it is the responsibility the manager to ensure that individuals are given the opportunity to implement performance plans which may require time away from the job and support, encourage and reward individual for their efforts.

Employee Engagement

Employee engagement reflects the extent to which employees feel invested in and motivated by their work. The more engaged employees are, the more satisfied, productive and more likely they are to stay at your company.

The company as a whole has a greater impact on employee engagement than any other factor.

Organisational drivers
Organisational drivers can significantly improve employee engagement across the board, but given their bureaucratic nature, they can also be difficult to change. Pay close attention to these factors and make sure to challenge the status quo if necessary.

1. Direction & purpose
80% of employees are more engaged with work that aligns with the company's mission and core values. It is crucial for a company to have a clear direction with a well-defined mission statement, core values, culture code and employee value proposition. Setting organisational direction and purpose should be a collaborative effort that considers the future of the company while also considering its current state.

Establishing direction and purpose is also essential for recruiting great talent. It will help you find and hire people that will engage in their work beyond the bare minimum and help in developing a cohesive employer branding strategy.

2. Resources & tools
Resource limitations are an inevitability, but rather than concern yourself with limited resources, focus on how you can allocate what *is* available so it will have the greatest impact on your employees.
In order to know how to allocate resources, it is important to stay in close communication with teams to prioritise resources, whether they be financial, educational, experiential or sheer human power and consider their responses in relation to areas most in need of improvement in the company. While it may seem obvious to hire a new team member with more experience, it may be cheaper and more beneficial to provide more training to your current team to help them be more engaged and accomplish more collectively than a new hire.

3. Work-life balance
80% of people consider work-life balance a priority when considering potential employers and employees that identify as having good work-life balance work 21% harder than those who do not. Not only does providing work-life balance and flexibility attract more candidates, but they will work harder and be more engaged on a day-to-day basis.

Level 5: Operations / Departmental Manager

Managing People

4. Work environment
65% of employees report that environmental factors like lighting and temperature contribute to performance and productivity. Many companies are moving away from the dreaded cubicle-farm layouts and are incorporating various options for employees to tailor their work environment to their preferences.

While certain people work well in silence with bright lights, others prefer background noise and dim lights. Some companies even set up their office by work style rather than department. You may not be able to completely remodel your office in the near future, but you should regularly ask your employees what changes would improve their environment, because it could be as simple as dimming the lights or implementing quiet hours.

5. Transparency
70% of employees are most engaged when they are regularly updated by senior leadership about company strategy. In order for this to be successful, you need to make sure all of your board members, senior leadership and other stakeholders are on the same page with how to be effectively transparent with employees. The last thing you want is information leaked or rumours spread that will cause distrust and animosity among employees.

When you create a culture built around transparency, people will be more open to addressing conflict and concerns. Sometimes people do not know who to talk with or how to start a conversation and that can quickly escalate to decreased engagement, productivity and turnover.

6. Company culture
Unlike other drivers of employee engagement on this list, company culture starts at the inception of a company and evolves with each new employee. As a business grows, it becomes very difficult to alter culture, which is why it needs to be a priority for even the smallest start-ups.

Culture has a significant impact on the daily lives and engagement of employees. 77% of employees say that having strong relationships with colleagues is an important condition for engagement and 82% of employees have at least one friend at work.

HR Engagement Drivers
Human resources play a huge role in driving employee engagement. They are the primary resource during the hiring, onboarding and training of new employees as well as moderating conflict, fostering culture and ensuring transparency on a daily basis.
Due to the nature of their role in the company, they have a unique opportunity to gain insight into individual employee engagement and direct change. These are a few areas specific to HR.

1. Engagement surveys
Employee engagement surveys are the most popular way for companies to manage and drive engagement, which is great considering they are incredibly effective and simple to implement.

Managing People

Additionally, 89% of HR professionals find that regular feedback surveys positively impact their organisation. And just like that, the key to your engagement concerns can be solved, but where do you start? There is a plethora of related surveys available online and even platforms that send out automated questionnaires with metrics to determine key pain points to focus and suggest resource allocation.

2. Perks, benefits & compensation

While these factors may seem unrelated to an individual's daily work, they do affect engagement in a real way. The right blend of perks, benefits and compensation allow employees to design the ideal work environment, establish work-life balance, plan their financial future and much more, all of which have a direct impact on engagement.

36% of employees stay at their companies because of the benefits and perks they offer but designing the perfect package can be difficult. The best way to decide which benefits to prioritise, especially when you are on a tight budget, is to survey your employees to see what they want.

Depending on the various demographics of the employees, there will be different desired benefits that will change over time as your company and its people age. For example, there are significant generational differences when it comes to benefit preferences — 36% of Baby Boomers seek benefits like employee discount programs, 34% of Generation Xers want paid parental leave and 46% millennials value financial wellness programs.

3. Diversity & Inclusion

The impact of diversity and inclusion on corporate profitability have been proven time and again, but the benefits do not end at the ledger. Diversity and inclusion practices have also been shown to increase employee engagement and trust, as well. Creating a more engaging work environment goes beyond hiring diverse talent. Organisations need to ensure that all of their employees feel comfortable and welcome at work. Aside from hiring people who share those values, it is up to HR to implement diversity and inclusion programs that match their dialogue and vibe with employees.

4. Culture committees

Dedicated culture committees are the second most popular way to boost employee engagement behind engagement surveys (55% to 29%, respectively). Giving employees a seat at the table encourages them to take ownership and feel like their opinions are being heard. Depending on the organisation's culture, size and employee interests, there are a variety of culture sub committees for companies to consider, like party planning or events, diversity and inclusion and philanthropic committees.

Not only do committees contribute to creating a more inclusive work environment, but they will give you an insight into the interests of your current team. Smaller committees are unique in that they bring together people of similar interests — regardless of their role or seniority— to bond and implement change from the bottom up.

5. Hire, onboard & train

Here are a few facts to ruin your day: the national average time to hire sits at 44 days and of the employees that are hired, one third will quit within their first six months on the job. That is actually the good news, as the best thing a disengaged employee can do is leave.

Managing People

Here is the bad news: A staggering 85% of employees are either not engaged or actively disengaged with their work. The problem is these employees often remain in their current job as it is an easy pay cheque. They become a drain on the organisation.

These statistics are not used to give you heartburn, but to give you motivation to make engagement assessments part of your hiring and onboarding processes. Human capital is by far a company's most important asset and it is up to you to ensure that you are looking for more than the right skill set when hiring.

Senior Leadership Engagement drivers
As millennials rise into senior positions, they are pioneering new methods for leadership and mentorship. The generation known for its rebellious nature and refusal to adhere to standard workplace practices is changing the game to the benefit of both employers and employees.

But as traditional processes are ditched in favour of modern techniques, it is important to ensure that new leadership styles have a positive impact on employee engagement. Here are a few areas to keep an eye on.

1. Management/leadership style
42% of managers develop their leadership styles from recent managers and while this is not necessarily a bad thing, it does leave a lot to chance. It is important to respect your managers' individual leadership styles, but it is also crucial that employers provide adequate education and resources to train leaders on how to adjust their style to better communicate with and meet the needs of individual employees.

In particular, managers are becoming more empathetic and flexible with employees and their personal lives. Work-life balance has proven to significantly affect an employee's ability to engage with their work when they have time to relax and recharge.

2. Communication & feedback
It comes as no surprise that employees often find it easier to communicate with people close to their own age. 38% of employees find it difficult to communicate with colleagues of different ages and 77% of Gen Z prefer millennial managers. This is to be expected, but businesses must work to overcome communication gaps between younger (typically direct reports) and older (typically managers) employees.

To mitigate challenges among diverse teams, it is crucial for managers to initiate regular communication and feedback with employees. Not only does this help managers discover the learning style of individual reports, but it helps leaders adjust their own mentorship and communication style as well.

Unlike the one-sided performance reviews of the past, feedback needs to be a two-way conversation. Scheduling regular sessions and providing constructive feedback between managers and direct reports greatly helps both parties become more confident and engaged in their role.

While these conversations may feel intimidating, generational trends indicate that 97% of Gen Z are receptive to regular feedback from their superiors. Just like the company needs

Managing People

to provide guidance and direction for growth and development, leaders need to provide guidance and direction for their direct reports.

3. Recognition & appreciation
It does not take a rocket scientist to figure out that employees are more likely to be engaged in their work when they are recognised and appreciated for contributing to the success of the company at large. Not only that, but 22% of employees will look for a new job if they do not feel recognised for their work. It does not take much effort to create a program for employees to recognise each other's accomplishments and celebrate the wins and milestones, both big and small.

4. Growth & development
42% of employees indicate that learning and growth opportunities are a top priority when selecting an employer. This is to the benefit of both employees and employers and applies to all organisational levels.

Employees who are driven to learn and develop their skills are more engaged with their work because they are constantly being challenged with new material, thus improving their quality of work and elevating the success of the company. While these opportunities can be limited due to available resources and tools, leaders have experience and knowledge to provide in-house mentorship and training to employees at minimal cost to the employer.

5. Support & empowerment
Not to be confused with recognition and appreciation, support and empowerment pertains to providing co-workers (both managers and direct reports) with the tools and resources they need to excel in their role.

Whether that be providing training opportunities to improve a weakness, allowing employees to pursue passion projects or simply offering time off to improve work-life balance, it is up to leadership to figure out how they can better support employees to be successful and engage with their work.

Individual employee engagement drivers

Believe it or not, Generation Z is making its way into the workforce and with millennials rising into senior level roles, these youngsters have high expectations for their employers.

Employers are struggling more than ever to attract, retain and engage fresh talent who do not appeal to traditional employment opportunities. Here are a couple of drivers to home in on for rising generations.

1. Learning styles
Similar to leadership styles, every contributor has different learning styles that best resonate with them. While some people learn better through lectures and presentations, others may need to have hands-on experience before they fully grasp a new concept.

Managing People

Mixing individual learning styles with individual management styles can be quite challenging, so this is another area to focus on during the interview process to ensure your new employee has the resources they need to succeed.

2. Passion & commitment
76% of employees believe that having a meaningful job is a top condition for engagement, but meaningful work is a two-way street. Employers have to create roles that have meaning and employees have to find meaning in their work.

Identifying employees who are passionate and committed to their work starts with the hiring process. To find people who will be passionate and committed, it is important to be transparent about your company's goals, mission and values. Doing so can start as early as the job description and should continue in more depth during the interview process.
You should also continue to survey employees throughout their career to pinpoint areas for improvement. It is certainly not uncommon for employees to lose passion and commitment to their work and become burned out. Sometimes the solutions to employee engagement are much simpler than you expect.

3. Initiative & contribution
To be fully engaged at work, it takes a certain level of initiative from employees and from employers to help employees do work that contributes to the company in a way that is both meaningful to the employee and significantly impacts the company.

If you encourage employees to test experiments and pursue passion projects, they will become more comfortable and confident taking initiative with their own work and consequently become more engaged. Additionally, it is important for leaders to recognise and reward people who model this behaviour and build it into their culture.

4. Organisational culture
While we already touched on organisational culture under the HR section, it is important to note that culture is created by the collective differences and common interests of the individual employees. When organisations 'create culture,' they do so as a result of the people they hire and the opportunities they provide them to foster their own unique culture.

Making Training Effective

Training is an important part of preparing new employees for their roles and positions within the company and also helping existing employees stay current on the latest information about the company.

For a training program to be effective, it needs to have a purpose and then implement the right training methods. By understanding the factors affecting training and development effectiveness, you can either change your current training programs or develop them to meet the needs of your employees and your business. Here are some factors influencing the effectiveness of training programs:

Managing People

The purpose of the program
Of all the factors that affect work, the purpose is the greatest factor that will influence how the training program will be planned and executed. For you to be able to develop the right kind of training program, you will have to understand exactly what kind of knowledge and skills you want to impart to your employees. The training scope will also determine whether it will be possible to hold the training internally or you will have to contract a third-party consultant or institution to hold the training on your behalf.

The resources available to the company
The resources you have at your behest will determine the exact type and extent of your training program. Your budget, for example, will determine the type of training you will be able to afford. You might not be able to send all of your employees to a local college for training, but you might be able to call a few professors over for a series of training workshops. The space you have available in your workplace will also affect what is possible. You need a large enough space to train your employees. If you have limited space, you might have to do it in smaller groups. You will also need training materials to make your training program strong.

The audience of the training program
The kind of audience that attends your training sessions also affects how you develop the program. Some courses are made for all of your staff, while others are suitable only for a small section of it. You, therefore, need to understand the kind of background knowledge you need to develop a training session that is appropriate to the specific audience you are dealing with. You should know about any prior knowledge the participants of the training session have and build from there.

The training staff involved
The staff members in charge of the training program are also important to the effectiveness of the training program. Trainers who are educated and experienced in teaching professionals will conduct far better training sessions that those without that experience. You also want your trainers to understand the goals and values of the company and have enthusiasm for training your employees.

Quality training leads to job satisfaction
Employees who receive quality training will be better able to carry out their tasks on the job. They will also be able to constantly improve their skills and grow beyond their positions. The feeling of growth, as opposed to decline, is what leads to job satisfaction and lower employee turnover. You, therefore, cannot skimp on effective training for your employees.

Conflict can arise between HR/Training and other parts of the organisation, commonly due to differing priorities among performance management functions within a business and notably relating to training, development and welfare of staff. If so, you need to identify conflict and manage it.

Conflict is often caused by the different aims of the departments and you need to facilitate understanding and cooperation on both sides. This is especially important in order to achieve successful training needs assessment, training design, planning, delivery and optimal take-up

Managing People

and implementation. Aside from this there are very much deeper implications for organisations seeking to be truly cohesive, 'joined-up' and aligned towards common set of corporate aims and values. If you see any of the following symptoms of conflict, consider the root cause and facilitate strategic discussion and agreement, rather than limit your activity to simply resolving or responding only to the symptom.

- *management resisting release of staff for training due to day-to-day work demands*
- *short-term needs of performance management vs long-term outlook of HR*
- *HR have no line authority over trainees therefore cannot control training take-up*
- *Training is rarely well followed-through once delegates are back in jobs, despite HR efforts to achieve this via managers*
- *HR budgets are often cut if profits come under pressure*

Generally, conflict would stem from the values and priorities of directors, managers and staff involved and the aims and processes of the different HR functions. Here are some subject headings that serve as a checklist to see that the aims and priorities of HR/Training align optimally with those of other departments (the list is not exhaustive but should enable the main points of potential misalignment to be addressed):

profit, costs, budgets
well-being of staff
ethics and morality in treatment of staff
legal adherence
business strategy
training and development needs
succession planning
assessment and appraisals
promotion
recruitment
age, gender, disability
policies
harassment

counselling
workforce planning
management structure
decision-making and approval processes
outsourcing
contracts of employment
corporate mission and values
acquisitions and divestments
premises
pay and remuneration plans and market positioning
use of agencies
advertising and image

Managing People

Dealing with Conflict in Teams

Conflict abounds in the workplace. Research shows that each of us spends an average of 2 to 3 hours a week involved in some way in conflict. In the majority of cases, the outcomes are unsatisfactory and lead to fallouts, disharmony and distractions from the real purposes of work. The cost in lost productivity and human pain is considerable. That is why models of conflict resolution, such as the Thomas-Kilmann model, are vital to learning how to manage conflict more effectively.

Types of Team Conflict

Conflict is a common occurrence in teams. Conflict itself can be defined as antagonistic interactions in which one party tries to block the actions or decisions of another party. Bringing conflicts out into the open where they can be resolved is an important part of the team leader's or manager's job.

There are two basic types of team conflict: substantive (sometimes called task) and emotional (or relationship).

- **Substantive conflicts** *When deciding how to track a project, for example, a software engineer may want to use a certain software program for its user interface and customisation capabilities. The project manager may want to use a different program because it produces more detailed reports. Conflict will arise if neither party is willing to give way or compromise on his position.*

- **Emotional conflicts** *It is emotional conflict when two people always seem to find themselves holding opposing viewpoints and have a hard time hiding their personal animosity. Different working styles are also a common cause of emotional conflicts. Julia needs peace and quiet to concentrate, but her office mate swears that playing music stimulates his creativity. Both end up being frustrated if they cannot reach a workable resolution.*

Conflict can be beneficial

Not all conflict is negative. Just as some forms of stress can be beneficial, so can some types of conflict. Eustress (beneficial stress) is a positive reaction to stress that generates a desire to achieve and overcome challenges.

For instance, some people find that they produce their best work when a deadline is looming and the pressure to produce gets the adrenaline flowing. Team conflicts can also produce positive results when the conflict centres on substantive issues.

> *Conflict can spark new ideas and generate creativity.*

On the other hand, when people feel they cannot disagree or offer different opinions, new ideas cannot emerge.

Groupthink is the mindset that develops when people put too much value on team consensus and harmony. It is common when individuals are afraid to go against what most group

Managing People

members—especially dominant members—think. Some degree of conflict helps teams avoid groupthink and forces the group to make choices based on rational decision making.

If there is too much cooperation, the best ideas may never get shared and team effectiveness is sacrificed for the sake of efficiency. For the same reasons that diversity bestows benefits on a workforce, a mix of ideas and opinions improves team performance and decision making. If there is too much conflict, however, then nothing can get done. Employees on the team become less satisfied and motivated and may turn to social loafing or may even work against other members out of sheer frustration.

Resolving Team Conflict

Conflict is pretty much inevitable when you work with others. People have different viewpoints, and, under the right set of circumstances, those differences escalate to conflict. How you handle that conflict determines whether it works to the team's advantage or contributes to its demise.

You can choose to ignore it, complain about it, blame someone for it, or try to deal with it through hints and suggestions; or you can be direct, clarify what is going on and attempt to reach a resolution through common techniques like negotiation or compromise. It is clear that conflict has to be dealt with, but the question is how: it has to be dealt with constructively and with a plan, otherwise it is too easy to get pulled into the argument and create an even larger mess.

Conflict is not necessarily a bad thing, though. Healthy and constructive conflict is a component of high-functioning teams. Conflict arises from differences between people; the same differences that often make diverse teams more effective than those made up of people with similar experience. When people with varying viewpoints, experiences, skills and opinions are tasked with a project or challenge, the combined effort can far surpass what any group of similar individuals could achieve. Team members must be open to these differences and not let them rise into full-blown disputes.
Understanding and appreciating the various viewpoints involved in conflict are key factors in its resolution. These are key skills for all team members to develop. The important thing is to maintain a healthy balance of constructive difference of opinion and avoid negative conflict that is destructive and disruptive.

Getting to and maintaining, that balance requires well-developed team skills, particularly the ability to resolve conflict when it does happen and the ability to keep it healthy and avoid conflict in the day-to-day course of team working. Let us look at conflict resolution first, then at preventing it.

When a team oversteps the mark of healthy difference of opinion, resolving conflict requires respect and patience. The human experience of conflict involves our emotions, perceptions and actions; we experience it on all three levels and we need to address all three levels to resolve it. We must replace the negative experiences with positive ones.

The three-stage process below is a form of mediation process, which helps team members to do this:

Level 5: Operations / Departmental Manager

Managing People

Step 1: Prepare for Resolution

- **Acknowledge the conflict** – The conflict has to be acknowledged before it can be managed and resolved. The tendency is for people to ignore the first signs of conflict, perhaps as it seems trivial, or is difficult to differentiate from the normal, healthy debate that teams can thrive on. If you are concerned about the conflict in your team, discuss it with other members. Once the team recognises the issue, it can start the process of resolution.
- **Discuss the impact** – As a team, discuss the impact the conflict is having on team dynamics and performance.
- **Agree to a cooperative process** – Everyone involved must agree to cooperate in to resolve the conflict. This means putting the team first and may involve setting aside your opinion or ideas for the time being. If someone wants to win more than he or she wants to resolve the conflict, you may find yourself at a stalemate.
- **Agree to communicate** – The most important thing throughout the resolution process is for everyone to keep communications open. The people involved need to talk about the issue and discuss their strong feelings. Active listening is essential here, because to move on you need to really understand where the other person is coming from.

Step 2: Understand the Situation

Once the team is ready to resolve the conflict, the next stage is to understand the situation and each team member's point of view. Take time to make sure that each person's position is heard and understood. Remember that strong emotions are at work here, so you have to get through the emotion and reveal the true nature of the conflict. Do the following:

- **Clarify positions** – Whatever the conflict or disagreement, it is important to clarify people's positions. Whether there are obvious factions within the team who support a particular option, approach or idea, or each team member holds their own unique view, each position needs to be clearly identified and articulated by those involved. This step alone can go a long way to resolve the conflict, as it helps the team see the facts more objectively and with less emotion.

- **List facts,** assumptions and beliefs underlying each position – What does each group or person believe? What do they value? What information are they using as a basis for these beliefs? What decision-making criteria and processes have they employed?

- **Analyse in smaller groups** – Break the team into smaller groups, separating people who are in alliance. In these smaller groups, analyse and dissect each position and the associated facts, assumptions and beliefs.

    - Which facts and assumptions are true?
    - Which are the more important to the outcome?
    - Is there additional, objective information that needs to be brought into the discussion to clarify points of uncertainty or contention?
    - Is additional analysis or evaluation required?

    By considering the facts, assumptions, beliefs and decision making that lead to other people's positions, the group will gain a better understanding of those positions. Not only

Managing People

can this reveal new areas of agreement, it can also reveal new ideas and solutions that make the best of each position and perspective.

Take care to remain open, rather than criticise or judge the perceptions and assumptions of other people. Listen to all solutions and ideas presented by the various sides of the conflict. Everyone needs to feel heard and acknowledged if a workable solution is to be reached.

- **Convene back as a team** – *After the group dialogue, each side is likely to be much closer to reaching agreement. The process of uncovering facts and assumptions allows people to step away from their emotional attachments and see the issue more objectively. When you separate alliances, the fire of conflict can burn out quickly and it is much easier to see the issue and facts laid bare.*

Step 3: Reach Agreement

Now that all parties understand the others' positions, the team must decide what decision or course of action to take. With the facts and assumptions considered, it is easier to see the best of action and reach agreement.

If further analysis and evaluation is required, agree what needs to be done, by when and by whom and so plan to reach agreement within a particular timescale. If appropriate, define which decision making and evaluation tools are to be employed. If such additional work is required, the agreement at this stage is to the approach itself: Make sure the team is committed to work with the outcome of the proposed analysis and evaluation.

When conflict is resolved take time to celebrate and acknowledge the contributions everyone made toward reaching a solution. This can build team cohesion and confidence in their problem-solving skills and can help avert further conflict.

This three-step process can help solve team conflict efficiently and effectively. The basis of the approach is gaining understanding of the different perspectives and using that understanding to expand your own thoughts and beliefs about the issue.

Preventing Conflict

As well as being able to handle conflict when it arises, teams need to develop ways of preventing conflict from becoming damaging. Team members can learn skills and behaviour to help this. Here are some of the key ones to work on:

- **Dealing with conflict immediately** – *avoid the temptation to ignore it.*
- **Being open** – *if people have issues, they need to be expressed immediately and not allowed to fester.*
- **Practicing clear communication** – *articulate thoughts and ideas clearly.*
- **Practicing active listening** – *paraphrasing, clarifying, questioning.*
- **Practicing identifying assumptions** – *asking yourself "why" on a regular basis.*
- **Not letting conflict get personal** – *stick to facts and issues, not personalities.*
- **Focusing on actionable solutions** – *do not belabour what cannot be changed.*

Managing People

- **Encouraging different points of view** – insist on honest dialogue and expressing feelings.
- **Not looking for blame** – encourage ownership of the problem and solution.
- **Demonstrating respect** – if the situation escalates, take a break and wait for emotions to subside.
- **Keeping team issues within the team** – talking outside allows conflict to build and fester, without being dealt with directly.

Conflict Mode Instrument

The Thomas-Kilmann model was designed by two psychologists, Kenneth Thomas and Ralph Kilmann, to illustrate the options we have when handling conflict. There are two dimensions in the model. The first dimension, the vertical axis, is concerned with conflict responses based on our attempt to get what we want. Thomas and Kilmann call these the Assertiveness options. The other dimension, the horizontal axis, is concerned with responses based on helping others get what they want. Thomas and Kilmann call these the co-cooperativeness options.

These are the 5 options in conflict resolution in the Thomas-Kilmann model.

1. Competing. The Competing option is at the top left of the model which means you take a wholly assertive and un-co-operative approach to resolving the conflict. It means standing up for your rights, defending a position which you believe is correct, or simply trying to beat the other side.

2. Accommodating. The Accommodating option is at the bottom right of the model which means you take a wholly unassertive and co-operative approach. This might take the form of selfless generosity or charity, giving in to another person's orders when you would prefer not to, or yielding to another's point of view.

3. Avoiding. The Avoiding option is at the bottom left of the model which means you take an unassertive and un-co-operative approach to the conflict and do not deal with it. Avoiding might take the form of diplomatically sidestepping an issue, postponing an issue until a better time, or simply withdrawing from a threatening situation.

4. Compromising. The Compromising option is at the centre of the model because it is both assertive and co-operative but only to some extent. It is the approach of "half a sixpence is better than none". Both sides get something but not everything. It might mean splitting the difference between the two positions, some give and take, or seeking a quick solution in the middle ground.

5. Collaborating. The Collaborating option is at the top right of the model and is at the opposite extreme of avoiding. It means being willing to believe that when two parties are at loggerheads, it is possible for both sides to come out with what they want. Collaborating requires developed conflict resolution skills based on mutual respect, a willingness to listen to others and creativity in finding solutions.

Chapter 9: Managing Finance

Finance

Business

There are three principal sectors within business. These are:

- *Private Sector*
- *Public Sector*
- *Voluntary / Third Sector*

The private sector includes all the businesses which are in Private ownership and strive to make a profit. At its most simple, the self-employed which could be a one-man band or a partnership of two or more individuals who work together to make money. The people who operate it keep all the profits and divide it between themselves in a previously agreed manner.

The next type of organisation is a Private Company. A company is essentially a legal entity in its own right. It may or may not be limited. The term limited refers to whether or not the liability of the company is limited to the value of its shares and assets or whether the directors have absolute liability for all debts. There are tax benefits depending on the structure of the company.

The next type of company is a Public Limited Company. This indicates the company is owned by shareholders and those shares are available for purchase by anyone on the stock market. People will buy the shares in order to receive a dividend. The divided is paid once or twice a year and the amount paid will depend on the success or otherwise of the company.

Organisations are legally required to take care of their financial obligations. They need to keep records that can be used to show relevant stakeholders that operations are being run properly and in accordance with legislation, regulations and rules.

Depending on the type of organisation, the internal and external stakeholders that need to be satisfied about financial issues will vary.

Governance and Compliance

These are two key terms which are often juxtaposed or misunderstood. The term Compliance refers to compliance with legislation, whilst Governance refers to the way a business is governed to ensure the interests of those who have an interest in the organisation are met. The former is imposed by the Government and the latter, by the Senior Management of the organisation.

> **Compliance** - Organisations are required to comply with all legislation and regulations applicable to the conduct of the business. This can include the payment of taxes, alignment with financial regulations, provision of appropriate rights to employees and the return of details to Companies House annually.

Finance

Governance – is the system by which an organisation is directed and controlled. Depending on the type and size of organisation, governance will be implemented by the proprietors, business partners, a board of directors or trustees, etc.

Systems of Governance are put in place to ensure true and accurate records are collected to satisfy legislative requirements and protect the interests of those who have a stake in the organisation.

The organisation's internal processes, procedures and systems will focus on compliance with the various legislation and regulations that apply to its industry, environment, legal entity and circumstances.

In addition to compliance with external requirements, there will also be internal compliance created by the governance the management put in place.

Internal compliance requirements will arise from the conditions set out in the organisation's policies and procedures, for example:

- *how sales need to be recorded*
- *how often reports need to be generated*
- *how to use systems that track banking activities*
- *information needed for monthly reports sent to head office*
- *how to prepare quarterly reviews for shareholders*
- *systems to check and monitor compliance*

Purpose of Governance and Compliance

Broadly speaking, governance and compliance aim to avoid and mitigate issues such as:

- **fraud** – e.g., procedures to shred documents to prevent identity theft
- **theft** – e.g., using CCTV to monitor staff using a cash till
- **tax evasion** – e.g., procedures to make sure that cash payments are declared
- **criminal activity** – e.g., taking bribes or trafficking workers
- **misuse of funds and resources** – e.g., monitoring budgets closely to reduce waste and unnecessary spending
- **inefficiency** – e.g., from not monitoring waste or opportunities to steal cash or goods
- **money laundering** – e.g., Disposal of large sums of money which have been derived from illegal activity

Sometimes actions are deliberate and have a criminal intent – e.g., knowingly employing people who are illegal immigrants or those who have been trafficked, stealing products or cash. Some actions are due to negligence and ignorance – e.g., from someone not realising that they need to provide workplace pensions for their employees; under-declaring VAT due to lack of knowledge about the rules.

Finance

There are many more legal requirements imposed by external stakeholders. It is a requirement of all organisations to satisfy these legal requirements by, for example:

- *paying the right amounts of tax* – e.g., PAYE tax and national insurance, VAT or corporation tax
- *paying the correct level of minimum wage*
- *making contributions to workplace pensions* – e.g., to comply with the Pension Regulator's requirements
- *keeping adequate records* – e.g., audited accounts for large companies
- *using, storing and disposing of financial information correctly* – e.g., in accordance with the General Data Protection Regulations 2018 (GDPR)
- *submitting accurate returns on time* – e.g., to HMRC or Companies House
- *avoiding making bribes* – e.g., to conform with the Bribery Act 2010
- *satisfying industry-specific requirements* – e.g., FCA requirements for financial services organisations

Other Government departments and agencies are also external stakeholders and are responsible for applying finance-related legislation and regulations and the collection of duties and taxes. For example:

- **HMRC Annual return for PAYE and NI contributions**
- **Companies House** – where accounts and reports are held for limited companies as public records
- **the Financial Conduct Authority (FCA)** – for the financial services industry
- **the Prudential Regulation Authority (PRA)** – for banks and other financial institutions
- **the Pensions Regulator** – for workplace pensions

Costs associated with Governance and Compliance

There can also be costs associated with compliance – e.g., accountancy fees for preparing and submitting accounts; consultancy fees for compliance advice and strategy making and audit fees for verification. To achieve compliance, organisations need good governance – the system by which organisations are directed and controlled, such as a board of directors or trustees. Financial governance is necessary to enable organisations to:

- *keep up to date with new legislation and stakeholder expectations*
- *increase efficiency and revenue*
- *lower the costs of compliance*
- *avoid fines and penalties*
- *avoid damage to their reputation*

Value Added Tax

There is often confusion around VAT and its management as part of the financial process.

Finance

Her Majesty's Revenue and Customs (HMRC) are responsible for the collection of Value Added Tax and Income Tax / Corporation Tax

Income tax is paid by people who are self-employed whilst corporation tax is paid by businesses which operate as a limited company. Corporation Tax rate will be 25% of all profits from April 2023.

All business must be registered for the payment of VAT if their annual turnover exceeds £85,000 (in 2021) in a financial year (or part thereof). This is known as the VAT threshold.

VAT is currently set at 20% and is applied to many items we buy. (There may be temporary variations to the rate of VAT from time to time). VAT is added to the price the business wishes to charge for the item and is collected at the point of sale on behalf of HMRC. This money must then be paid to them, in full, at the end of each quarter.

In the event a business fails to pay the VAT, which is due, the management will be deemed to have committed a criminal offence which may lead to a prison sentence and very heavy fine. HMRC also have the authority to seize goods and chattels up to the value of the debt when an organisation is unable to pay.

Anyone who chooses to ignore any warnings from HMRC will not remain in business for very long.

VAT notes:

- *VAT replaced the former Luxury Tax which was applied to items deemed to be non-essential.*
- *VAT or Value Added Tax is charged on many goods and most services.*
- *VAT is added at the applicable rate to the price the organisation wishes to charge customers*
- *This money does NOT belong to the organisation - it is collected on behalf of HMRC*
- *This money must then be paid to H.M. Customs & Excise at the end of the VAT quarter*
- *This is paid after making a formal declaration on a VAT 100 form*
- *Some items purchased by the organisation will have VAT added to them - this can be reclaimed at the end of the VAT quarter.*
- *In order to manage VAT, there must be detailed and accurate financial records*

Finance

Financial Legislation

The legislation which defines how a business should conduct itself includes:

Companies Act	Defines the duties of the Directors of all companies registered in the UK
Financial Services and Markets Act	Regulates shares and securities
Financial Services Act	Applies criminal offences for making false claims or misrepresentation and creating false impressions
Insolvency Act	Governs the winding up of companies including liquidation and bankruptcy
Consumer Credit Act	Protects credit cards, loans and hire purchase agreements
Consumer Rights Act	Protects and assigns rights to the consumer including the right to compensation
Misrepresentation Act	Protects consumers from false or fraudulent claims
Payment Services Regulations	Protects consumers who are victims of fraud
Unfair Terms in Consumer Regulations	Defines the terms which are considered unfair in consumer agreements
Consumer contracts Regulations	Protects customers when buying items online

Accountability

A business is not just accountable to government, it is also accountable to its Stakeholders.

Internal stakeholders: need to be satisfied the organisation governs its financial procedures prudently and could include:

- **business owners** – e.g., sole proprietors or partners need knowledge of profit and cash flow
- **shareholders** – e.g., need assurance their investment is being properly managed
- **employees** – e.g., rely on the organisations success to maintain their standard of living

Finance

External stakeholders: could include:

- **banks and other lenders** – e.g., those who extend financial support to organisation
- **national and local government agencies** – e.g., those who collect taxes and provide grants
- **external customers** – e.g., those who buy and use the organisation's products and services
- **charity commission** – e.g., who examine accounts and are regulators of registered charities

> *Everyone involved with the business must have confidence in the way the business is operated and satisfied it is being managed equitably, legally and prudently.*

Financial management is required by law. Financial Reports must be submitted annually to Companies House. An Annual Financial Return must be submitted to HMRC for tax purposes and the quarterly VAT submission must be made along with payment by the last day of the month following the end of the VAT quarter.

Shareholders will need to examine the summary accounts before the annual general meeting so they can form a judgement on how to vote at the AGM or even whether to retain the shares they hold in the business

Lenders will expect to see evidence of positive business performance and evidence that the business is growing and viable.

Financial Reporting

Organisations must produce a range of financial reports, including:

- **income and expenditure statements** – to show income, expenses and profits over a period of time – enabling the organisation to see how well it is performing.
- **balance sheets** – giving a 'snapshot' of the assets and liabilities at any given time, usually at the end of the financial year.
- **cash flow statements** – to show what cash is available and moving through the organisation, so that managers can see what they can afford to do.
- **annual accounts and statutory returns** – to show a true picture of the organisation's income, expenditure, assets and liabilities at any given time, often after being audited by registered practitioners or chartered accountants.

Financial reports are used by managers when preparing business plans and to monitor progress. Investors and shareholders use the information to make decisions about funding

Finance

and investment choices. They are also used in the preparation of statutory returns and reports, including:

- **corporation or income tax returns sent to HM Revenue and Customs**
- **VAT returns**
- **PAYE returns** – *e.g., to declare tax and national insurance for the workforce*
- **audited accounts** – *e.g., to be submitted to the Charities Commission, shareholders or lenders*
- **annual returns to Companies House**

Reports may be provided in paper or computer derived formats, these will be identified in policies, procedures, training records and accounting manuals.

Audits

Audits are used to verify that the financial records which have been created are a true and accurate record of the business which has taken place.

Audits can take different forms, from simple stock takes to count how much stock is held on the premises including work in progress.

An example might be in a factory with a production line. It is all well and good counting all the items in the stock room and on the shelves, but stock is also tied in up work which is partly finished so these need to be included too.

Stock takes may take place as often as once a week in a pub or restaurant when staff will conduct an internal stock take or annually by an external organisation where a business produces just one product which is of low value.

An audit of an asset register may also be conducted from time to time. Many pieces of equipment to be found in the workplace will have a metal tag attached to it with a number. This item will be recorded on the asset register as an asset of the business and has a value. If the item cannot be identified in an asset audit, it will be deemed to have been broken or written off and its value will be removed from the list of assets owned by the organisation thereby reducing the value of the business.

A financial audit is used to provide stakeholders with assurances that financial statements are accurate.

A financial audit is a three-dimensional inspection and review of all aspects of an organisation to make sure that everything balances and complies with relevant regulatory requirements.

Finance

In a medium-sized company, for instance, a registered auditor from the firm's accountants will be tasked to check samples of records to make sure that reports are accurate and truly representative. They make look at, for example:

- **sales ledgers** – to check the level of income received
- **cash books** – to see that the income has been banked correctly
- **debtors** – to assess the amount of money owed to the company
- **stock** – to see that the stock records are accurate and to give the remaining stock a value as an asset
- **purchase ledgers** – to check that costs put through the business are correct, legal and compliant
- **bank reconciliations** – a process to check that payments in and out are all balanced and accounted for
- **creditors** – to see how much the company owes at the end of its financial year
- **payroll records** – to make sure that tax, national insurance and pension contributions have been dealt with and paid correctly
- **VAT returns** – to ensure that the correct amounts have been declared and paid

During the process, the auditor will check that other regulations are complied with – e.g., money laundering or data protection. Processes need to be robust and transparent to enable audits to be performed that can provide an accurate view of the organisation to internal and external stakeholders – e.g., shareholders, lenders and HMRC.

Implications of unresolved governance and compliance issues

There can be serious implications if governance and compliance issues are unresolved. Failure to address governance and compliance can cause internal issues that, for example:

- **result in theft and loss of income** – e.g., if sales and transactions are not monitored correctly
- **cause longer-term financial problems for the organisation** – e.g., from paying compensation and having to repay money that has been taken; from a drop in share value as investors lose confidence
- **lead to a breach of contract** – e.g., being sued for releasing information
- **cause a security problem** – e.g., a personal attack or terrorist threat if security arrangements are leaked; passwords and access codes being used by unauthorised people
- **cause embarrassment** – e.g., if personal details or financial records are made public
- **give competitors an advantage** – e.g., from gaining access to confidential operational data
- **increased compliance costs** – e.g., restructuring costs as a consequence of prosecution or loss of reputation
- **increased staff turnover and related costs** – e.g., from staff not wanting to work for an employer with a poor reputation

Finance

There can also be serious implications if an organisation's external stakeholders take action in response to governance and compliance failures – e.g., government agencies or customers who take enforcement or legal action. Actions could, for example:

- **result in fines and penalties** – *e.g., from paying insufficient tax*
- **result in compensation payments** – *e.g., to customers when financial data has been mishandled*
- **result in the organisation losing customers** – *e.g., from having a bad and unprofessional reputation*
- **cause financial problems for customers** – *e.g., if their bank accounts are hacked as a result*
- **lead to prosecution of the employer and/or employees** – *e.g., under the Data Protection Act, Bribery Act or Money Laundering regulations*

The consequences of failure can seriously affect an organisation's ability to survive and thrive due to additional costs and loss of reputation.

Management and Financial Accounting

Management accounting, and financial accounting are frequently used terms which are often used incorrectly. While both deal with numbers, that is where many of the similarities end.

Here are the differences between financial and Management accounting:

- *Management accounting is used strictly for internal purposes, while financial accounting provides financial information based on accounting standards.*
- *Management accounting frequently looks ahead, while financial accounting offers analysis of historical data.*
- *Management accounting typically runs a variety of operational reports throughout the month, while financial accounting runs financial statements at the end of the accounting period.*
- *Management accounting uses estimated amounts, while financial accounting only uses actual numbers.*

Management accounting

Management accounting centres around managing the ***internal*** needs of a business.

> *because management accounting centres around business potential and performance, it mainly deals with the future.*

Management accounting focuses on problem solving and devising strategies for making the company more profitable and efficient in the long term. Financial accounting does play a role in Management accounting. The financial statements are used as an information source when creating strategic plans, streamlining operations, solving log jams, and creating business budgets and forecasts.

Finance

Financial accounting
While the focus of Management accounting is internal the focus of financial accounting is **external**, with a focus on creating accurate financial statements that can be shared outside the company.

> For any public company, financial accounting processes must abide by the requirements of the Finance Act

Financial accounting uses a chart of accounts that has been created for the company, with set policies and procedures in place that govern how transactions are to be posted using these accounts, with the end goal to create factual financial statements for a very specific period of time.

However, it is important to remember that routine tasks such as creating an invoice or tracking accounts receivable balances, are also part of the financial accounting process.

Management vs Financial Accounting

Both management accounting and financial accounting are centred around numbers, but how those numbers are used varies greatly in these two types of accounting methods.

Management Accounting	Financial Accounting
Used internally	Used externally
Looks ahead	Looks at historical performance
Looks at operational and financial data	Only looks at financial data
Focuses on specific management needs	Reports on the entire company
Managers can choose the information they need	Information is provided based on outside regulators

> Management accounting looks at a way to solve specific management issues while financial accounting looks at the company as a whole.

Looking forward vs. looking back

- Management accounting is used to create strategic plans, tasking managers with creating budgets, and estimating upcoming income and expenses.

- Financial accounting analyses company results that have already been achieved, with those results contained in financial statements.

Finance

Reporting focus is different
Reporting is handled very differently in Management and financial accounting. In Management accounting, reports are run much more frequently and tend to focus on day-to-day operations.

Financial accounting focuses on performance for a very specific time frame. Another major difference is that Management reports are used internally, while financial reports are distributed to those outside the company, including regulators, investors, and financial institutions.

Management Reports	Financial Reports
Departmental reports	Balance sheet
Sales reports	Income statement
Inventory reports	Cash flow statement

Estimates vs. facts
While financial statements are frequently used as a starting point for creating a budget, budget estimates are usually created based on the needs and expectations of the manager(s) that are creating that budget. Financial statements are the results of events which have happened and cannot be reversed.

The information contained in financial statements must be accurate and is derived from the various financial transactions entered throughout the specified accounting period.

> *Remember, the facts contained in financial statements often play a role in Management accounting but estimates have no role in financial accounting.*

Legal requirements
There are no legal standards or requirements involved with Management accounting, which can be used by businesses as they wish. However, any business is required to prepare financial statements that follow set rules and regulations.

> *While many businesses use a combination of Management and financial accounting, only the financial statements produced using financial accounting processes are required to be audited.*

Finance

Similarities between Management and Financial accounting

Management accounting and financial accounting do have a few things in common.

Both need to have accurate numbers to work from: Management accounting to use as a basis for creating budgets and estimates, financial accounting to comply with standard accounting practice in order to be deemed accurate and in compliance with regulations.

While Management accounting works more as a problem solver, financial accounting shows you exactly what your business has accomplished to date.

> *In most companies, they are used simultaneously to create a more efficient, profitable business.*

Though some accounting software applications do offer budgeting capability, many businesses use a spreadsheet application such as Microsoft Excel to create budgets and estimates.

Management accounting and financial accounting are stronger together
While it is certainly possible for a business to use only financial accounting, putting management accounting into the mix will provide businesses with the best of both worlds: accurate financial statements and a way to plan for a brighter future.

Finance

Financial Management Process

The financial management process involves three stages. Planning, Trading and Year end. The year-end accounts are the result of a year's worth of trading and therefore a historic record of trading activity which cannot be changed.

The trading records are the tools used to produce the year end reports and are captured on a day by day, week by week basis throughout the trading period and therefore also record historical activity and likewise, cannot be changed.

> *It is the planning stage in Financial Management which is the key to business success.*

The planning stage records what is anticipated to happen during the forthcoming year and, because this is in the future, by carefully monitoring the progress during the trading period, changes can be made to any or all areas of the business, to ensure a successful outcome at the end of the financial year.

The planning stage uses data from the previous trading period as its basis and therefore it is easier to consider this process in reverse.

There are Standard Systems of Accounting Practice for different industries which set levels of budgetary control. A straightforward system requires seven levels of budgetary control. In other words, there are seven values which should be managed in a budget to ensure adequate control of the business, these are:

- *Sales*
- *Cost of Sales*
- *Gross Profit*
- *Variable Costs*
- *Operating Profit*
- *Fixed Costs*
- *Net Profit*

Financial Planning
Once detailed, accurate, trading figures are available, it allows the process of financial planning to take place for the next financial year. This will be much more difficult for a new start business without the benefit of prior trading figures. In this case, a conservative estimate is the best one can usually do.

The Trading, Profit and Loss Account

This is the basic financial calculation used in every business. When figures are added. this forms what is known as the Trading, Profit and Loss Account. It is created using the information used to set the seven levels of budgetary control.

Finance

```
Total Sales
            less Cost of sales  | Trading Account
Gross Profit                    |


            less Variable Costs |
Operating Profit                |
            less Fixed Costs    | Profit & Loss Account
Net Profit or Loss              |
```

When planning a budget for the forthcoming financial year the last two- or three-years TP&L accounts are a good place to start to get information to plan the budget.
This fairly short report provides the basis for almost all financial planning. In a small business the proprietor may compile the budgets, whilst in a larger organisation there may be specific teams assigned to deal with each level of budgetary control.

Example:

> A sales team will be responsible for calculating the anticipated sales for the forthcoming period whilst those responsible for buying the components or raw materials will be responsible for deciding what may happen to cost prices over the period and whether there will be the opportunity to obtain volume discounts based on the sales planned by the sales team.

These two teams will plan what they think will happen and this will allow the budgeted Gross Profit to be calculated. It will be for the head of finance to decide if this is acceptable or whether prices need to rise, sales need to increase, or costs need to be reduced. If that is the case, the two teams will go back to the drawing board and review the figures they have calculated.

Planning a Budget				
	y/e 2019	y/e 2020	y/e 2021	Budget
Total Net Sales	75,000	82,000	88,000	?
less Cost of sales	45,000	49,000	56,000	?
Gross profit	30,000	33,000	32,000	?
less Variable Costs	12,000	15,000	18,000	?
Operating profit	18,000	18,000	14,000	?
Less Fixed costs	16,000	15,000	15,000	?
Net Profit (or loss)	2,000	3,000	(1,000)	?

It would be foolhardy at best and downright incompetent otherwise, to try and manipulate the figures to achieve a desired outcome, without any plan or justification for how the proposed

Finance

figures might be achieved. It does not matter how grim the results are, that is the realistic situation and practical ways must be identified to work around the problem.

The next team to be set to work would be those responsible for the variable costs of the business.

Variable Costs

Variable costs are sometimes called controllable costs or controllable expenses. This is because they are directly controlled by the management of the organisation. They will also change or vary in direct proportion to the business as it increases and decreases.

As with everything, there is always an exception! There are also costs known as Semi Fixed / Semi Variable costs. These are costs which do not behave as we might expect. They are made up of both fixed and variable elements. These are dealt with in accounts by simply attributing them to whichever category represents the greater amount of money. An example of semi fixed, or semi variable costs is an energy expense. The total bill is usually made up of the standing charge – the fixed element and the energy used – the variable element. The costs for the energy would be allocated to whichever of the two elements is the greater.

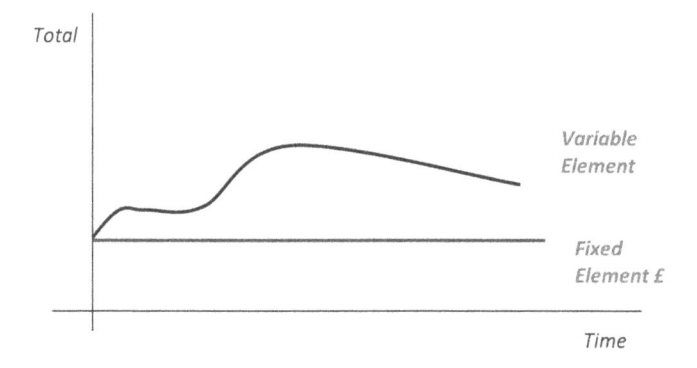

Another oddity is Stepped Costs. These costs behave as their name suggests. They will increase in a stepped manner. Unlike many costs which will increase gradually, stepped costs will increase in a significant jump when a certain level of business is reached, after which the remain constant until another level of business is reached when it will jump again.

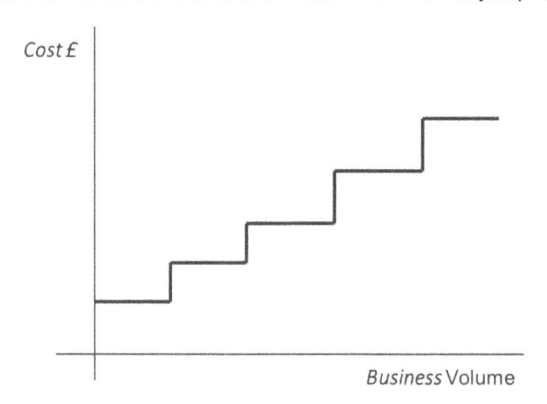

Finance

The classic example of stepped costs is wages. If we have one member of staff on duty, they will be able to handle a business volume of say up to £120 pounds an hour. After this point we will have to employ another member of staff which will cause the wage costs to increase significantly.

It is the duty of the team responsible for these costs to minimise them. In much the same way as we manage of own domestic costs by switching energy supplier, using different stores to buy certain items, economising, etc. so, it is the responsibility of this team to minimise the variable costs the business incurs.

> *By minimising variable costs the business can maximise the operating profit.*

The next level of control is the fixed costs. Unlike variable costs they do not vary with business volume. They remain constant for a reasonable period of time, typically a year, regardless of how much business is done. These include things like Rent, Rates, Loan Repayments, etc.

There is little one can do to reduce these costs apart from renegotiating rent, applying for a reduction on business rates and perhaps renegotiating insurance premiums. In larger organisations it may be possible to renegotiate car lease deals or take advantage of the relief of Duty for hybrid / electrical vehicles.

Finally, by subtracting the Fixed costs from the operating profit we arrive at the net profit or loss the business is likely to make at the end of the next financial year.

Interpreting Financial Figures

When analysing figures, it is almost impossible to compare numbers, one against the other, when they are expressed in monetary form.

To better understand the numbers, it is necessary to compare percentages one to another rather than numbers. Take a look at the numbers below - without percentages they mean very little

	2016		2017	
	£	%	£	%
Sales	362,000		427,000	
Cost of Sales	191,860		247,660	
Gross Profit	170,140		179,340	

However, when percentages are added the situation becomes clear.

Finance

	2016 £	%	2017 £	%
Sales	362,000		427,000	
Cost of Sales	191,860	53	247,660	58
Gross Profit	170,140	47	179,340	42

By adding the percentages, it is immediately clear that although sales rose in money terms, the cost of sales rose by more than 5% compared to the year before which, as a result, means that the Gross profit has dropped by 5%. This prompts the question, why this has happened and where has the money gone?

Once the percentages have been added, comparing year on year becomes far more straightforward and decisions as to the budget values become a little more straightforward to plan.

Planning a Budget								
	y/e 2019	%	y/e 2020	%	y/e 2021	%	Budget	%
Total Net Sales	75,000	100	82,000	100	88,000	100	?	100
less Cost of sales	45,000	60	49,000	60	56,000	64	?	
Gross profit	30,000	40	33,000	40	32,000	36	?	
less Variable Costs	12,000	16	15,000	18	18,000	20	?	
Operating profit	18,000	24	18,000	22	14,000	16	?	
Less Fixed costs	16,000	21	15,000	18	15,000	17	?	
Net Profit (loss)	2,000	3	3,000	4	(1,000)	-1	?	

Financial Forecasting

By now you will have deduced that there is little more than guessing involved in financial forecasting as there are so many influences which can both directly and indirectly affect the forecast made.

> *Who could have anticipated a global pandemic three months before it changed the World for ever?*

Finance

Some argue that a forecast could be referred to as a "Guesstimate" but, by following the guidelines listed below, it is possible to turn a "guesstimate" into a "Qualified Guesstimate" meaning its basis is founded in fact and there is tangible evidence of its derivation.

A financial forecast enables a business to:

- *Plan for the future.*
- *Create an action plan to achieve its financial objectives*
- *Measure performance against the planned objectives*
- *Plan contingencies for foreseeable financial risks*
- *Control how activities are achieved and moved forward*

There are a number of methods that can be used to develop a financial forecast. These methods fall into two general categories, which are quantitative and qualitative.

- *A quantitative approach relies upon quantifiable data, which can then be statistically manipulated.*
- *A qualitative approach relies upon information that cannot actually be measured.*

Examples of quantitative methods include:

Casual Methods
These methods assume that the item being forecasted has a cause-and-effect relationship with one or more other variables. For example, the existence of a cinema can affect sales at a nearby businesses, so the popularity of a blockbuster movie can be expected to increase sales in a nearby restaurant. The primary causal analysis method is regression analysis.

Time series methods
These methods derive forecasts based on historical patterns in the data that are observed over equally spaced time intervals. The assumption is that there is a recurring pattern in the data that will repeat in the future.

Three examples of time series methods are:

- **Rule of thumb.** *This is based on a simplified analysis rule, such as copying forward the historical data without alteration. For example, sales for the current month are expected to be the same as the sales generated in the immediately preceding month.*
- **Smoothing.** *This approach uses averages of past results, possibly including weightings for more recent data, thereby smoothing out irregularities in the historical data.*
- **Decomposition**. *This analysis breaks down the historical data into its trend, seasonal, and cyclical components, and forecasts each one.*

Examples of qualitative methods are:

Market research
This is based on discussions with current and potential customers regarding their need for goods and services. Information must be gathered and analysed in a systematic manner in

Finance

order to minimise biases caused by small data sets, inconsistent customer questioning, excessive summarisation of data, and so forth. This is an expensive and time-consuming research method. It can be useful for detecting changes in consumer sentiment, which will later be reflected in their buying habits.

Opinions of knowledgeable personnel

This is based on the opinions of those having the greatest and most in-depth knowledge of the information being forecast. For example, the senior management team may derive forecasts based on their knowledge of the industry. Or sales staff may prepare sales forecasts that are based on their knowledge of specific customers. An advantage of using the sales staff for forecasting is that they can provide detailed forecasts, possibly at the level of the individual customer. There is a tendency for the sales staff to create overly optimistic forecasts.

Delphi method.

This is a structured methodology for deriving a forecast from a group of experts, using a facilitator and multiple iterations of analysis to arrive at a consensus opinion. The results from each successive questionnaire are used as the basis for the next questionnaire in each iteration; doing so spreads information among the group if certain information was initially not available to everyone. Given the significant time and effort required, this method is best used for the derivation of longer-term forecasts

Finance

Budgeting and Financial forecasting

The key difference between a budget and a forecast is that a budget lays out the plan for what a business wants to achieve, while a forecast states its actual expectations for results, usually in a much more summarised format

Budgeting and financial forecasting are tools that companies use to establish a plan regarding where management ideally wants to take the company (budgeting) and whether it is heading in the right direction (financial forecasting).

Although budgeting and financial forecasting are often used together, distinct differences exist between the two concepts.

- *Budgeting quantifies the expectation of revenues that a business wants to achieve for a future period*
- *Financial forecasting estimates the number of revenues that will be achieved in a future period.*

In essence, a budget is a quantified expectation of what a business wants to achieve. Its characteristics are:

- *It contains estimates of revenues and expenses*
- *It predicts cash flows*
- *Illustrates expected debt reduction*
- *Compares the budgeted against actual values creating a financial model which allows remedial action to be taken when the actual values deviate from the budgeted values*
- *The budget is a detailed representation of the future results, financial position, and cash flows that management wants the business to achieve during a certain period of time.*
- *The budget may only be updated once a year, depending on how frequently senior management wants to revise information.*
- *The budget is compared to actual results to determine variances from expected performance.*
- *Management takes remedial steps to bring actual results back into line with the budget.*
- *The budget to actual comparison can trigger changes in performance-based compensation paid to employees.*

Conversely, a forecast is an estimate of what will actually be achieved. Its characteristics are:

- *Estimates a company's future financial outcomes by examining historical data.*
- *The forecast is typically limited to major revenue and expense line items.*
- *There is usually no forecast for financial position, though cash flows may be forecast.*

Finance

- *The forecast is updated at regular intervals, perhaps monthly or quarterly.*
- *The forecast may be used for short-term operational considerations, such as adjustments to staffing, inventory levels, and the production plan.*
- *There is no variance analysis that compares the forecast to actual results.*
- *Changes in the forecast do not impact performance-based compensation paid to employees.*
- *Management team can use financial forecasting to take immediate action based on the forecast data.*
- *Can help adjust production and stock levels.*
- *A long-term forecast might help develop a business plan.*

A budget is an outline of the direction management wants to take the company whilst a financial forecast is a report illustrating whether the company is reaching its budget goals and where the company is heading in the future.

the key difference between a budget and a forecast is that the budget is a plan for where a business wants to go, while a forecast is the indication of where it is actually going.

Budgeting can sometimes contain goals that may not be attainable due to changing market conditions. If a company uses budgeting to make decisions, the budget should be flexible and updated more frequently than a fiscal year so there is a relationship to the prevailing market.

Budgeting and financial forecasting should work in tandem with each other. For example, both short-term and long-term financial forecasts could be used to help create and update a company's budget.

A business always needs a forecast to reveal its current direction, while the use of a budget is not always necessary

Realistically, the more useful of these tools is the forecast, as it gives a short-term representation of the actual circumstances in which a business finds itself.

The information in a forecast can be used to take immediate action. A budget, on the other hand, may contain targets that are simply not achievable, or for which market circumstances have changed so much that it is not wise to attempt to achieve.

If a budget is to be used, it should be updated far more frequently than once a year, so that it has a direct relationship to current market realities. In a rapidly changing market, the assumptions used to create a budget may be rendered obsolete within a few months.

Finance

Planning a Budget

One can immediately see that budgetary planning for a small organisation would be a relatively straightforward process, but for a larger organisation, far more is at stake and the process is more complex.

The starting point would be the strategy of the business and the plans to which it has committed with shareholders and stakeholders. If growth is included in this plan, it must be reflected in budget. If there is a commitment to relocate to larger premises, the cost of this must also be reflected along with the impact it may have on Net Profit.

A good starting point when planning any budget would be to look back at past performance. Below we can see the sales over the last few years and for each year the percentage change that the sales have achieved. The percentage change is the increase or decrease in sales or costs when comparing one period to another.

Sales

The sales of the business are key to financial success – without sales – there is no business.

Sales are recorded for financial planning and management accounts, net of VAT. This is the actual revenue received by the organisation for the products and services it provides.

Historic Sales									
2016		2017		2018		2019		2020	
£	%	£	%	£	%	£	%	£	%
362,000		427,000	17.9	485,000	13.6	514,000	5.9	???	???

It is clear that sales have been slowly climbing over the last four years. The key question is why.

- Have prices risen each year to cause the increase in income?
- Has the business increased its customer base?
- Has the volume of sales increased due to the popularity of the product?
- Has the price reduced meaning more people can afford it?

It is important to answer these questions to underpin the budget value which is ultimately selected.

To answer these questions more information will be needed – production figures would show how many units were produced. Historic price data will indicate whether the price has changed. It should also be noted that the price will need to rise to keep in line with inflation, wage increases, economic changes, changes to the interest rate and other planned investments.

Consideration must also be given to advanced orders, planned sales campaigns, advertising campaigns, market location of the product, known plans of competitors, market saturation, new developments and products in the pipeline.

Finance

Cost of Sales

Planning cost of sales can be equally challenging and this is a task best assigned to the purchasing team along with the manufacturing team and maybe the research and development team who could be seeking ways to simplify the product or reduce the component the cost.

The task is to drive down the cost price per unit of production to the lowest point without compromising the quality of the finished item.

Again, historic figures can help with the development process by comparing them to sales.

	2016 £	2016 %	2017 £	2017 %	2018 £	2018 %	2019 £	2019 %	2020 £	2020 %
Sales	362,000	100	427,000	100	485,000	100	514,000	100	???	100
Cost of Sales	191,860	53	247,660	58	271,600	56	277,560	54		
Gross Profit	170,140	47	179,340	42	213,400	44	236,440	46		

Here we can see that the cost of sales has varied between 53 and 58 percent over the years. The why question needs to be asked once again.

- Has the product remained the same during this time?
- Is there more than one product being produced – if so, does this need to be broken down for each product first before being rolled up into a total for the whole organisation?
- Is one product less profitable than another?
- Have component prices risen, are they linked to market forces?
- Has wastage been an issue?
- Is theft an issue?
- Has a price increase for a component been overlooked?
- Are there any known plans in the pipeline to increase the cost of components?

These are all questions which need to be answered before a "qualified guesstimate" can be made as to what the cost of sales is likely to be next year.

Variable Costs

The next consideration is to look at the variable costs. These can be numerous in a large organisation and may be divided amongst the appropriate departments.

HR may be asked to look at staff costs, staff training, staff feeding, staff uniforms, etc. Consideration must be given to the changes to the National Minimum Wage and any planned wage increases which have been previously agreed.

Finance

Thought should also be given to significant changes which may be caused by the stepped effect of wage costs. It may be that at given volumes the staffing level is less efficient than if volumes were to increase. Energy on the other hand may be passed to the facilities manager to look for cheaper energy suppliers or more efficient ways of using energy, switching to low energy bulbs, changing the source of heating, etc.

As budgets are planned and calculated at departmental level. they will be returned for entry onto the master budget.

| | Historic Trading Profit and Loss Account ||||||||||
| | 2016 || 2017 || 2018 || 2019 || 2020 ||
	£	%	£	%	£	%	£	%	£	%
Sales	362,000	100	427,000	100	485,000	100	514,000	100	???	100
Cost of Sales	191,860	53	247,660	58	271,600	56	277,560	54		
Gross Profit	170,140	47	179,340	42	213,400	44	236,440	46		
less Variable costs										
Wages	65160	18	72590	17	82450	17	97660	19		
Energy	28960	8	38430	9	48500	10	41120	8		

Fixed Costs

Fixed costs include those which are unlikely to change in the short term, most will change annually, rent agreements, etc. are more likely to change over three or five years. Renegotiation of annual contracts can bring down fixed costs, but this tends to buck the trend of inflation. It should also be noted that salaries will be included in fixed costs and consideration should therefore be given to any salary increases or bonuses which have been promised or annual increments which may be due.

Finance

	Historic Trading Profit and Loss Account									
	2016		2017		2018		2019		2020	
	£	%	£	%	£	%	£	%	£	%
Sales	362,000	100	427,000	100	485,000	100	514,000	100	539,461	5.0
Cost of Sales	191,860	53	247,660	58	271,600	56	277,560	54	280,520	52
Gross Profit	170,140	47	179,340	42	213,400	44	236,440	46	258,941	48
Variable costs										
Wages	65,160	18	72,590	17	82,450	17	97,660	19	86,314	16
Energy	28,960	8	38,430	9	48,500	10	41,120	8	43,157	8
Total	94,120	26	111.020	26	130,950	27	138,780	27	129,471	24
Operating Profit	76,020	21	68,320	16	82,450	17	97,660	19	129,471	24
Fixed Costs										
Rent	18,100	5	18,100	4.2	18,100	3.7	22,014	4.3	22,014	4
Insurance	10,860	3	11,300	2.6	11,700	2.4	12,100	2.4	12,408	2.3
Total	28,960	8	29,400	6.9	29,800	6.1	34,114	6.6	34,422	6.4
Net Profit	47,060	13	38,920	9.1	52,650	10.9	63,546	12.4	95,049	17

Once the budget is completed, it is subject to scrutiny by all concerned. The difficulty, however, is that any changes to any element will affect every other element. This domino effect will mean many areas may need revisiting to review the impact each change has on the next value. A change to wages for example will directly affect the total variable costs which will affect the operating profit and ultimately the Net Profit.

Developing the Budget

Once the budget has been agreed, other reports can then be produced.

The first step is break down the planned budget into a monthly Trading forecast. Monthly sales volumes from previous years should be analysed and sales broken down proportionally, month by month.

Using the percentages from the budget the income and costs can be broken down to provide a monthly Trading Profit and Loss Budget.

From this a cashflow report can then be produced which anticipates when revenue will be received and when expenditure will happen.

The cashflow will record any cash sales – i.e., those which are paid for immediately and those which are payable by invoice in arrears. This will create an indication of any times during the year when cashflow may be limited due to the revenue stream being less than normal and may need intervention to arrange additional funding or an overdraft facility until the revenue stream reverts to normal.

Finance

In the example, this business might be involved in activities which warrant an increase in summer such as an ice cream manufacturer. As a consequence, business is quieter in the winter, but stocks are built up during this time in preparation for the busier summer period.

	Monthly Budget												
	2020		Jan		Feb		Mar		Apr		May		June	
	£	%	£	%	£	%	£	%	£	%	£	%	£	%
Sales	539,461	100	32,368	6	37,762	7	43,157	8	43,157	8	48,551	9	59,341	11
Cost of Sales	280,520	52	16,831	52	19,636	52	22,442	52	22,442	52	25,247	52	30,857	52
Gross Profit	258,941	48	15,536	48	18,126	48	20,715	48	20,715	48	23,305	48	28,484	48
Variable costs														
Wages	86,314	16	5,179	16	6,042	16	6,905	16	6,905	16	7,768	16	9,495	16
Energy	43,157	8	2,589	8	3,021	8	3,453	8	3,453	8	3,884	8	4,747	8
Total	129,471	24	7,768	24	9,063	24	10,358	24	10,358	24	11,652	24	14,242	24
Operating Profit	129,471	24	7,768	24	9,063	24	10,358	24	10,358	24	11,652	24	14,242	24
Fixed Costs														
Rent	22,014	4	1,835	6	1,835	5	1,835	4	1,835	4	1,835	4	1,835	3
Insurance	12,408	2	1,034	3	1,034	3	1,034	2	1,034	2	1,034	2	1,034	2
Total	34,422	6	2,869	9	2,869	8	2,869	7	2,869	7	2,869	6	2,869	5
Net Profit	95,049	18	4,899	15	6,194	16	7,489	17	7,489	17	8,783	18	11,373	19

Having produced an annual Budget for Trading, Profit and Loss, it can then be broken down into monthly budgets based on business volume across the year. In this case the business is busier in the summer months than in the winter months and this is reflected in the sales.

This monthly breakdown can be derived from historic data by comparing year on year sales volumes and establishing a monthly mean across the twelve-month period. Monthly sales can then be calculated and the cost of sales, and expenses are calculated by using the same percentage ratios they were in annual budget. This may not be wholly accurate but is more than sufficient for these purposes.

Finance

Projected Cashflow Forecast

Using the data from the projected budget, the data can be extrapolated into a Cashflow forecast for the next year which shows the flow of money in and out of the business.

	Jan	Feb	Mar	Apr	May	June	July	Aug	Sep	Oct	Nov	Dec
	£	£	£	£	£	£	£	£	£	£	£	£
Cash at bank b/f	11456	-10935	-18015	-17646	-18305	-12164	-12389	-16824	-433	26800	42757	5208
Cash sales	5503	6420	7337	7337	8253.8	10088	11005	9171	7337	6420	7337	5503
Credit Sales	3245	16234	26865	31343	35820	35820	40298	49253	53730	44775	35820	31343
Total Cash at bank	20204	11719	16187	21033	25769	33744	38914	41600	60634	77995	85914	88926
Cost of Sales	16831	19636	22442	22442	25247	30857	33662	28052	22442	19636	22442	16831
Gross Profit	3372	-7918	-6254	-1408	522	2887	5251	13548	38192	58359	63472	72095
less Variable costs												
Total	7768	9063	10358	10358	11652	14242	15536	12947	10358	9063	10358	7768
Operating Profit	-4396	-16981	-16612	-11766	-11130	-11355	-10285	601	27834	49296	53115	64326
less Fixed Costs												
Total	2869	2869	2869	2869	2869	2869	2869	2869	2869	2869	2869	2869
Cash at bank c/f	-10935	-18015	-17646	-18305	-12164	-12389	-16824	-433	26800	42757	52081	63292

When looking at this forecast one can immediately see that there is a problem at the end of January as it shows that the bank account will be overdrawn by £10,935 in January rising to a maximum of £18,305.

Whilst it would be normal practice to identify ways in which this could be minimised, it would also be prudent to set up an overdraft facility or arrange borrowing to cover the period. It is clear that from September the account returns to credit with over £63,000 pounds in December. Without having planned the budget and created a Cashflow forecast the business may have been unaware of the impending cash flow problems and struggled to survive

Set and Monitor Budgets

Even on a personal level, we need to draft a budget so that we can see:

- *how much money we have* – e.g., in cash or in bank accounts and savings
- *how much money we expect to bring in* – e.g., wages
- *how much money we need to spend* – e.g., for accommodation, food, transport and leisure

Finance

- ***how much we need to bring in or save to achieve our goals*** – *e.g., to buy a new car or go on holiday*
- ***how much we need to set aside for contingencies*** – *e.g., in case the boiler breaks down at home and needs replacing*

The challenges are exactly the same for organisations.

Financial resources need to be managed so that an organisation can meet its objectives and requirements.

Budgets show what money it has, what it expects to bring in, how much it expects to spend, and what it needs to keep to one side to achieve its future goals and cover potential problems.

"Play around with these figures, Harry. I've given you the total I want them to add up to."

Setting realistic budgets and planning for contingencies

When setting realistic budgets and planning for contingencies, managers need to consider a number of elements, including:

- *key components of a budget*
- *using information to set budgets*
- *the importance of accurate budgets and forecasting*
- *the purpose of contingency plans*

Key components of a budget
Budgets are estimates of income and expenditure for a set period of time. When setting realistic budgets, managers need to look at:

- *fixed costs* – **expenses that stay the same, regardless of sales rising or falling** – *e.g., rent and insurance*
- *variable costs* – **expenses that change according to sales volumes** – *e.g., raw materials used to make the products*
- *semi-variable costs* – **expenses that might be influenced by changes in sales** – *e.g., salaries and advertising*
- *income* – *known and likely income*

In addition, it is important to identify timescales, priorities and financial resources when preparing a budget to ensure that everything is accounted for:

- *timescales* – **to show when money is due to come in and out** – *e.g., when income is due; when sales invoices are issued; how quickly customers pay; how quickly purchase invoices need to be paid; deadlines for paying taxes*

Level 5: Operations / Departmental Manager   717

Finance

- *priorities – **to target resources correctly to support the efficiency and effectiveness of the organisation*** – *e.g., prioritising workforce costs, essential purchases and urgent capital investments*
- *financial resources – **to match funding with anticipated income and expenditure*** – *e.g., using an overdraft for short-term cash flow problems; financing long-term projects with business loans; anticipated increases in sales revenue*

There can be a main budget for the whole organisation, sometimes called the master budget, and there can be several budgets within that for different departments or activities. Each department will have their own budgets:

- *sales and marketing department*
- *manufacturing and production department*
- *transport and packing department*
- *a project to update IT throughout the whole business*

Each department or project may have a budget of what expenses it expects to have – e.g., stationery, transport, materials, payroll, building costs, or one-off expenses for a specific project.

Budgets can be done for any period of time that the organisation needs for its operations – e.g., daily, weekly, monthly, quarterly, annually, or for the period covered by particular projects or activities.

A budget for one item can appear in several places, and this can help provide a three-dimensional picture of the organisation. For example, staff costs can appear in:

- **each department's own budget** – *to show the wage costs for their part of the organisation*
- **the HR department's budget** – *to show the overall staff costs for the whole organisation, which include training, recruitment, pensions, employment benefits and expenses, management and HR costs as well as wage costs*
- **budgets for a project** – *to show the estimated staff costs for that project only*

Using information to set budgets

When developing a budget, it is necessary to use estimations. This is because a budget is a calculated guess or estimate and needs to have all of the expected figures in place. If something is missing, it can put the whole budget out of balance and make it unrealistic and unreliable.

Some of the estimated figures in a budget will be based on historical data – e.g., accounts from previous years; a previous, similar project; research of competitors' figures; projects run by a previous employer.

Finance

Some of the estimated figures will be based on current research and data – e.g., a range of prices found on the Internet; similar current projects; competitors' current charges; fixed costs that have already been calculated; current sales and expenses.
The remaining figures need to be based on educated and informed estimations, based on good knowledge of the industry and marketplace, current trends, likely inflation, worldwide and domestic political events, and any other relevant factors. Examples of influences could include:

- ***political and legal influences*** - *politics and legislation can affect every business. Changes to taxation are one of the most common factors which can have far reaching repercussions on many areas of the business.   is the creation and modification of taxes. Other political factors should also be taken into consideration, such as a change in government, war or terrorism. These can impact significantly on the stock market and the spending of both public and private money.*
- ***financial*** *– changes to interest rates can affect the cost of financial services and the cost of loan repayments as the cost of borrowing increases.*
- ***social influences*** - *social factors can have an influence on a business. A change in lifestyle patterns or behaviour can affect the way that people decide to spend money. A change in the population can also impact on the business. Other factors could include other issues such as the lowering or raising of the cost of living, etc*
- ***technology*** - *breakthroughs in new technology could put the organisation at a disadvantage. It may be necessary to make provision for the purchasing and implementation of new technology within the budget.*
- ***inflation*** *– the impact of inflation of cost and sales process*
- ***gross domestic product*** *– the government estimation of the overall growth of business over the forthcoming twelve months*
- ***natural disasters*** *– the arrival of COVID could not have been anticipated and the impact it has had across the World would have been inconceivable.*
- ***economic*** - *a growing economy is good for a business, because it gives businesses more opportunities to make profits however awareness of a downturn or stagnation of the market should always be considered.*
- ***anticipated revenue streams based on anticipated sales of a new product*** *– to help calculate a budget for new raw materials to make the next batch of the product*
- ***anticipated sales of existing products*** *– to help calculate possible sales revenue*
- ***estimated exchange rate between sterling and foreign currency over the next year*** *– to help calculate the value of future exports and the potential impact of increase cost prices*
- ***anticipated peaks and troughs in planned production*** *– to help calculate the cost of agency staff who might be needed to meet short-term demand*
- ***estimated birth rates in ten years' time*** *– to help to create a long-term budget for primary and secondary schools*
- ***estimate of the amount of consumables that may be used by a department*** *– to assist when preparing the departmental budget*
- ***climate change*** *– climate change has impacted on organisations and continues to do so. The impact has far reaching consequences across society from driving the development of new technologies, implementing environmental controls to the creation of new industries and new markets for the goods and services they produce.*

Finance

There are many different kinds of external influences on a business budget. Some of these changes are anticipated by looking at current trends, but some of them may hit as a complete surprise.

The Importance of Accurate Budgets and Forecasting

Budgets are needed to manage cash flow, control resources, plan for the future and secure financing. They are needed so that an organisation can estimate its income and expenditure in the days, months and years to come. This helps to make sure that there will be enough revenue to cover all expenditure and leave enough money to make a profit.
By making people accountable and responsible for a budget, an organisation can help to control its resources. Working to a budget helps staff to understand organisational objectives and motivate them to use resources efficiently and effectively.

Budgets can also show how a business plans to allocate its resources for the future. If a business wants to expand or make investments, it needs to know what its income and expenses are likely to be before it commits to plans.

For example, if a business wants to invest in new technology and buy a new, expensive, sophisticated machine, it needs to prepare budgets to estimate:

- *the capital cost of the new machine*
- *the running costs of the new machine*
- *the extra revenue that can be generated by using the new machine*
- *the potential savings in staff and maintenance costs from using a newer and more automated system*
- *how long it will take for the new machine to pay for itself*
- *the tax implications on investing in and operating the new machine*

Banks and other lenders will want to examine not only the financial accounts for the preceding years but also the budget before they agree to grant a loan or overdraft facility. Similarly, if an organisation applies for credit from its suppliers, it might be asked for a budget forecast so that they can negotiate discounts and payment terms based on the likely level of business.

Finance

The Purpose of Contingency Plans

It is normal to have contingency plans to deal with unforeseen circumstances. Sometimes it is impossible to budget exactly and managers can only estimate what may be needed to complete a particular project or objective. When renovating a building, for instance, it is not possible to get accurate costs for remedial work until some of the demolition has been done to reveal the inner fabric of the building.

Workplace and industry experience and risk assessments can help managers to estimate:

- **what may go wrong** – e.g., machinery breakdown or severe weather
- **unknown costs** – e.g., changes in world prices of raw materials
- **possible extra costs and other consequences** – e.g., increased costs of raw materials and delays in supplies and production
- **costs and delays when putting things right** – e.g., paying staff whilst waiting for supplies; employing extra staff to catch up and achieve targets
- **steps that can be taken to mitigate the risk** – e.g., having more than one supplier for key components
- **funds that need to be set aside** – e.g., a 20% contingency fund when building a new factory to cover unforeseeable and variable costs

By planning for contingencies, managers can:

- *incorporate the anticipated costs in their agreed budget*
- *reallocate funds if necessary*
- *have extra funds on standby in case they are needed*
- *avoid extra delays because the planning has already been done*
- *keep projects and progress of objectives on track*

Monitoring budgets
It is necessary to monitor budgets to ensure effectiveness and control costs. Managers need to be able to, for example:

- *assess whether targets are being met*
- *monitor variance of actual performance against the set budget*
- *monitor internal and external factors that affect budgets and cause variance*
- *revise a budget when required*

Assessing whether targets are being met
Organisations will have their own ways of assessing whether targets are being met, which could include, for example:

- **comparing results against SMART targets** – *measuring progress at key stages set out in SMART targets*
- **comparing actual costs with budgeted amounts** – *to evaluate the budget allocations and identify the causes of variance*

Finance

- ***analysing operational data*** – e.g., looking at productivity records to evaluate progress and output
- ***analysing sales patterns*** – e.g., to see if sales forecasts match actual sales
- ***progress reviews and team meetings***
- ***flow charts, graphs and Gantt charts*** – e.g., measuring progress against specific targets
- ***internal and external audits*** – e.g., completed by managers or registered auditors

Monitoring variance of actual performance against the set budget

As actual costs and income figures become available, managers can measure them against the estimated costs in their budgets. Fixed costs should be predictable and match forecasts and the amounts allocated in the budget. Variable and semi-variable costs need to be analysed more carefully to make sure that they are within the tolerances and amounts expected when the budgets and forecasts were prepared.

The frequency and formality of monitoring will depend on the project, objectives, activities and agreed working practices of the team, department and organisation. Variance in actual performance against the budget may take place:

- ***every day*** – e.g., when costs are entered into a company's accounts system that automatically compares performance against expectations
- ***monthly or quarterly*** – e.g., when departmental reports are prepared to show to the board of directors
- ***at agreed stages during a project*** – e.g., at critical review points during a building project

By having regular reviews, causes of variance can be identified as soon as possible and actions can be planned to address issues.

Internal and external factors that affect budgets and cause variance

Many internal and external factors can affect budgets and cause variance. Managers need to be able to identify and respond to them to make sure that budgets and plans stay on track. Some issues will come under the manager's area of authority. Others need to be escalated so that the issues can be addressed at an organisational level.

Finance

Reasons for change	Examples:	Suggestions about how to address issues. Managers may need to:
Objectives, aims and priorities change	A company decides to launch a new product A charity decides to abandon a project to run an open day for the public Business owners decide to move to larger premises An organisation decides to postpone buying new cars for staff and spend the money on a new IT system instead	Arrange discussions with decision-makers to establish revised objectives, aims and priorities Amend original budgets and plans, or prepare new ones to cover up-to-date plans once they have been agreed
Costs rise or fall	A rise in interest rates affects the plans to borrow money for expansion Weather problems and flooding damage crops and affect the cost of fruit and cereals	Make sure that there are several suppliers for key services, materials and components so that: • they work harder to be competitive • the risk of failure is spread • the manager can change suppliers Arrange to use the contingency budget to keep objectives on track
Demand for products and services rise or fall	A new tablet sells out after a successful marketing launch and the manufacturer needs to change its plans and budgets to increase production The demand for antiques and second-hand furniture drops and businesses cannot charge what they expected when selling items	Have contingency plans prepared for higher and lower volumes of output Have suppliers in the supply chain ready to cope with changes Address sales and marketing issues to boost awareness and trade Revise pricing strategies
Improvements in technology	New IT systems reduce the need for stationery and paper storage Videoconferencing technology improves and staff do not need to travel abroad for meetings so often A new website and online purchasing system increase sales dramatically	Revise operational procedures to: • incorporate relevant technology and processes • train staff in new methods • monitor their effectiveness • cope with changes in levels of production and sales
Plant and machinery need to be replaced sooner than expected	An expensive machine is expected to last 10 years and the budget is there to replace it then. However, it breaks down and is obsolete after 5 years, so it needs to be replaced early	Arrange discussions with decision-makers to gain agreement to: • gain agreement to replacing the machine • access the budget for replacing capital items • revise objectives to cope with the delay • revise the budget and forecasts for when the new machinery is in use

Finance

Reasons for change	Examples:	Suggestions about how to address issues. Managers may need to:
Unforeseen circumstances and unavoidable delays	Severe and exceptional weather affects production A cargo ship carrying supplies is lost at sea There is a fire at a factory	Inform relevant people Discuss contingency plans with other decisionmakers Implement contingency plans and access contingency budget if required
Estimations are found to be unrealistic	Estimations about sales turn out to be higher or lower than expected The actual running costs for new plant and machinery turn out to be much higher or lower than expected	Monitor data very carefully to check actual figures against estimates and look for errors Check the sources used when original estimates were made to test their validity Prepare revised plans, estimates and budgets Discuss contingency plans with other decisionmakers Implement contingency plans and access contingency budget if required
Changes in legislation and regulations	A change in the rate of VAT in the Budget New regulations about waste management have a financial impact on a company New regulations dictate that all staff must have or achieve recognised industry qualifications and organisations need to invest in training	Inform relevant people Discuss contingency plans with other decisionmakers Implement contingency plans and access contingency budget if required

Revise budgets when required

It is only through constant monitoring and control of budgets that problems come to light.

Managers are able to identify problems and issues when they study the budgeted and actual figures as they are updated and sometimes it may be necessary to revise budgets and plans.

The organisation's policies and procedures will show what needs to be done when budgets need to be revised. For example, they may have a tolerance that is agreed in advance that the manager can use at their own discretion – e.g., a 2% or £500 increase that can be implemented without seeking permission. Or managers may have several budgets under their control and be permitted to move funds from one budget to another – e.g., taking money from their stationery budget and putting it towards increased IT costs.

Finance

The main things that need to be established before revising a budget include, for example:

- *the manager's own limits of authority for making decisions and changes*
- *the decision-making process for when decisions need to be escalated*
- *the procedures for reporting variance and issues*
- *the procedures for making revisions and merging them with organisational budgets*

Finance

Delivering Value for Money

Responsible financial management includes delivering and receiving good value for money.

The concept of value for money

According to the Oxford dictionary, the phrase value for money is 'used in reference to something that is well worth the money spent on it'. The concept of value for money encourages organisations to make the best use of their resources to achieve objectives. Today, "value for money" has changed to become a term for something which is cheap. Value for Money supermarkets are considered to sell cheap lower grade products. A better term to bring this back into context is to think of the term "value for price"

Offering value for money/price helps an organisation to have a good reputation and stand out against competitors. In the workplace, when organisations concentrate on giving value for money, this can refer to:

- ***products and services that are provided for external customers*** – *e.g., supermarket goods, cars or legal services*
- ***services delivered to internal customers*** – *e.g., credit control staff who collect money owed to the organisation; maintenance teams who look after the buildings and other facilities*

Organisations also work to receive value for money when they manage, for example:

- ***operations*** – *e.g., refining policies and procedures to be as efficient as possible*
- ***suppliers*** – *e.g., services provided by specialist contractors and consultants, suppliers of raw materials and other goods*
- ***human resources*** – *e.g., employees, HR departments and management costs*
- ***physical resources*** – *e.g., equipment and machinery; factories, offices and retail outlets*
- ***finance*** – *e.g., finding the best business loans for a business venture*
- ***waste*** – *e.g., energy, time, human and physical resources*

Achieving value for money/price helps an organisation to operate efficiently and effectively, which is an important element when delivering profits to shareholders and securing jobs for employees.
Many organisations also have a statutory responsibility to achieve value for money – e.g., when using public funds.

Finance

Achieving value for money

There are many things that organisations can do to give and receive value for money when working with suppliers and customers.

Customers

Customers have expectations and they want:

- *an efficient and polite service before, during and after a transaction (buying or using products or services)*
- *good-quality and value-for-money products and services*
- *any complaints and problems to be dealt with properly*
- *their opinion to matter*

An organisation needs to offer good customer service and value for money at all times so that it can survive and thrive. If the customers are satisfied with the products or services, they return and they recommend the organisation to others. Quite simply, this keeps the organisation alive and means that their employees' jobs are safer.

Organisations offer value for money to customer through, for example:

- **the range of goods and services offered** – *e.g., offering budget and luxury ranges*
- **pricing** – *e.g., offering competitive prices; grouping complementary products together as a bundle*
- **discounts** – *e.g., buy one get one free*
- **Incentives** – *e.g., 10% off if customers buy today*
- **delivery options** – *e.g., free for standard delivery when customers spend above a minimum amount; charges for overnight or weekend delivery*
- **installation options** – *e.g., charges for installing household appliances like washing machines*
- **warranties** – *e.g., free or low-cost extended warranties on electrical goods that guarantee repairs or replacement if there are faults after the period covered by the manufacturer*
- **returns policies** – *e.g., rules about exchanges or refunds on returned items that are not faulty*
- **other value-added features** – *e.g., loyalty card points; membership and privilege cards*

Products and services need to be in line with the standards promised in catalogues, brochures, websites, customer charters, company policies, etc. They may also be covered in a Service Level Agreement (SLA) between two parties.

Suppliers

When working with suppliers, organisations can negotiate the same things because they are now the customers. In smaller organisations, managers and directors will make the decisions about how to obtain value for money when managing human and physical resources. Larger organisations can have procurement specialists and departments – e.g., in national supermarket chains or the Ministry of Defence.

Finance

Whatever the size of the organisation, the principles are the same. Physical resources need to be:

- **fit for purpose** – *of sufficient quality for the intended use*
- **sustainable** – *from sources that can maintain the supply chain for future purchases*
- **ethically and legally sourced** – *e.g., to comply with the organisation's own ethical policies*
- **able to be reused, recycled or reconditioned** – *where possible at the end of their useful working lives*

These factors are important when assessing value for money as money is not the only consideration. Even if something is incredibly cheap, if it is not fit for purpose, it will not provide value for money.

In parallel to these factors, organisations will also negotiate with suppliers to get deals – e.g., the best prices and discounts; favourable delivery and installation options; inexpensive and effective warranties and aftercare service; other added-value features that may be available.

Delivering value for money for the organisation

Teams and departments can also make the most of the organisation's resources and energy use to maximise value for money. There can be a mixture of obvious and hidden costs that need to be monitored as they all form part of the running costs that have to be met by the organisation.

Teams or departments can deliver value for money for the organisation by:

- *reviewing costs and operational activities regularly*
- *using resources efficiently*
- *using energy efficiently*

Reviewing costs and operational activities

Managers need to review how their team or department spends its budgets on a regular basis, to make sure that funds are being allocated in the most efficient way to achieve objectives and maintain quality. They need to look at all aspects to make sure that everything is fit for purpose and good value for money, for example:

- **fixed costs** – *e.g., machinery and equipment*
- **variable costs** – *e.g., raw materials or components*
- **human resources** – *e.g., to make sure that the right people are being employed at the right cost to achieve the team's objectives and quality standards*
- **working practices** – *e.g., to make sure that procedures are relevant and efficient*
- **outsourcing opportunities** – *e.g., analysing whether it is better to perform some activities in-house or to outsource them to specialist companies*

Organisations need a framework for discussing and reviewing all aspects so that managers and others can:

- *identify areas that need improvement*

Finance

- *address potential problems*
- *work collaboratively to make decisions about maximising value for money*

Using resources efficiently
When looking to improve the use of resources in the workplace that are related to external customers, managers need to consider, for example:

- **reducing packaging** – e.g., encouraging customers to buy loose vegetables and fruit; using smaller boxes, aerosol cans or plastic bags; cutting out unnecessary packaging; using refill packs of coffee rather than new jars every time
- **developing packaging that uses fewer resources** – e.g., boxes that stay together with folds rather than glue, reusable bags for customers
- **reducing consumables given out** – e.g., giving out one serviette per customer rather than letting them help themselves to a handful; smaller serviettes or tray liners; small hygienic packets of butter rather than a dish of butter that might be wasted

When keeping down operational costs of the team or department, managers may consider, for example:

- **reusing materials** – e.g., storage boxes and trays that can be used many times; using China mugs rather than disposable cups
- **avoiding scrap or waste** – e.g., managing portion control in a restaurant; training and monitoring production staff in a factory to help cut down on rejects and wasted materials; checking cutting patterns to make sure that they are as efficient as possible
- **reviewing, designing or adjusting procedures, products or services** – to maximise the use of resources
- **electronic communication** – rather than printed paper; emails or texts rather than paper memos
- **telephone and videoconferencing** – rather than travelling around the UK or abroad for meetings
- **using technology effectively** – e.g., using smart meters or sophisticated tills to measure consumption and target production efficiently; stock tracking systems to support Just-In-Time supply chain management; computer-based training for staff
- **working to improve staff retention** – e.g., managing the team well to avoid excessive recruitment and training costs that occur when there is a high turnover of staff
- **ensuring work practices support compliance** – e.g., to help avoid unnecessary investigations, legal proceedings, fines, penalties, compensation and loss of reputation

Managers need to be aware of changes to technology, products and processes to see if there are well-researched, better alternatives.

Using energy efficiently
When considering how to improve the use of energy and deliver value for money, managers will look at, for example:

Finance

- **more efficient buildings** – e.g., better insulation; improving weaker areas notes on the EPC (Energy Performance Certificate); good-quality glazing with thermal qualities; efficient heating and air conditioning systems; improving the layout within the building to maximise efficiency; solar panels
- **energy-efficient appliances and equipment** – e.g., heat pumps for heating and air conditioning; A-rated appliances, such as fridges; low-energy lighting where possible; reduced-energy standby modes on appliances
- **more efficient vehicles** – e.g., with low CO2 emissions; electric vehicles, especially for short trips; with more efficient engine technology; planning routes and times of journeys to reduce mileage and time spent in traffic jams
- **switching off unnecessary electrical items** – e.g., lights, office machines, air conditioning and heating when not in use
- **using more sympathetic packaging materials** – e.g., looking at packaging with a lower carbon footprint
- **consolidation of working hours** – so that the building only has to be fully operational for a shorter time
- **home working** – e.g., reducing an organisation's costs if they can use a smaller building; saves commuter time, expense and emissions, although there is an energy cost from using the employee's home
- **telephone and videoconferencing** – e.g., using technology to hold virtual meetings, especially when participants are many miles apart
- **longer but less frequent meetings** – e.g., making the most of people having travelled to meet up so that they do not have to meet so often
- **the carbon footprint of the different options** – e.g., having a small, low-energy photocopier might seem to be a good option, but if it cannot cope with the load and has to be replaced every six months, the overall costs will be higher over a year.

Finance

Financing Business

Raising funds to help support your business's growth is fundamental to financing a company, and in the unprecedented economic environment, this is an ever-increasing challenge for UK businesses.

Types of finance available

When looking to raise finance, whether it be to enable growth, to release value, to refinance or for any other reason, it is often advisable to explore alternative sources of funding beyond simply traditional bank debt.

With many finance options available, understanding which are right for your business can be difficult and assistance in identifying the most appropriate forms of finance can be helpful.

Bootstrapping
Often described as one of the most inexpensive ways for new businesses to gain financing, bootstrapping is likely to be your first port of call. Principally, it means using your own money as a method of raising finance for your business and getting it off the ground.

Bootstrap finance can result in one of the most important discoveries any business owner will make. If you keep on top of things and efficiently organise your finances, you will likely find capital with which you can invest and build the business. Here are some common bootstrapping methods:

- **Friends and family** – *If you can, ask those close to you. They know you; you know them, and you may find they would be delighted to help finance your new venture.*
- **Personal assets** – *Cash resources, credit cards – what have you got immediately to hand that would mean less reliance on outsiders?*
- **Co-founders** – *If you are going into business with someone, remember it is a joint venture. If you have exhausted your resources, have a frank and honest conversation with your partner. What can they bring to the table?*
- **Traditional bank loans**

Following the credit crunch of 2008, it would be easy to think bank managers will be less than generous with lending capital to new businesses. This really is not the case, but you need to prepare yourself before heading to your local branch.

That means writing a business plan. If the thought of it fills you with dread, it is worth employing an accountant who will help you and attend bank interviews if you ask.

Purpose of the loan – Be crystal clear on the use of the loan. Write a business plan which shows your experience, your target market, products/services and exactly where you will be spending every penny.

> **Your stake** – *Banks rarely lend 100%. They will feel uncomfortable if they (who have no day-to-day control of the business) are taking the lion's share of risk. Just in the way you*

Finance

need a deposit to buy a house, a bank will expect to see you have an investment in the business and may ask you to sign an undertaking not to withdraw it while they are still lending.

Repayment – *Demonstrate that you can repay the loan by detailing your projected revenue and cash flow in your business plan. The bank will want to ensure you have thought it through thoroughly and will have enough cash to survive. They will need you to demonstrate the business will be able to pay all its creditors, not just the bank.*

If it goes wrong – *Nobody goes into business expecting to fail but, up to 50% of new-starts do not last 5 years. To reduce risk for the bank it will usually demand some form of security for the loan (a property, for example).*

Asset finance
If you are familiar with hire purchase and leasing, you are on your way to understanding asset finance. Put simply, it is a way of financing your venture by obtaining the equipment you need to grow, usually by spreading the cost of the kit over an agreed period of time. Also, this type of finance can be used for a range of "capital items" or fixed assets including plant, equipment, vehicles, IT equipment and even far more specialist items like marine vessels and aircraft.

Invoice finance
This is suitable for B2B businesses where they can borrow against the value of work completed and invoiced. The two main products are factoring and invoice discounting although there are other hybrid services. It enables businesses to draw funds against sales invoices, before receiving of remittance from the customer. Done correctly, it will improve your cash flow and working capital. As a result, this type of finance is ideal for expanding businesses including new-starts.

Crowdfunding & Peer-to-Peer Lending
Perhaps one of the most exciting and modern forms of financing, crowdfunding and peer-to-peer lending are methods by which businesses can raise capital for new ventures by seeking investment from the general public. As a result, there are numerous specialists evolving all the time. Some offer to take a share of your business whilst others will lend to the business. In the same way that banks need to see an investment from you, investors and lenders will want to see that you have the confidence in your business and own ability to invest some of your own money.

Finance

Glossary of Financial Terminology

It is important to recognise and understand terms that are used when dealing with business finance. Here are some explanations of financial terminology:

Accounts – accurate records of the business income, expenditure, assets and liabilities – e.g., annual accounts that are prepared for companies and other organisations to use when making tax returns or applying for funding.
Assets – items owned by the business – e.g., vehicles, plant and machinery, equipment and buildings.
Balance sheet – this shows what the organisation is worth at any given time, showing its assets and liabilities.
Budgets – estimates and allocations of income and expenditure for a set period of time, used to measure and estimate financial aspects of all parts of a business.
Capital – money that is invested into a business – e.g., from owners, banks or shareholders.
Capital expenditure - money spent on long-term items such as cars, buildings and machinery with a long working life.
Cash flow – the amount of money coming into and out of the business in a given period.
Compliance – conforming to rules – e.g., standards, policies, regulations or laws.
Credit – there can be several meanings in business – e.g., a bookkeeping entry of money received; a credit note to give the customer an amount to take off their next purchase; a credit agreement for when a customer can have the goods now and pay later.
Creditors – people or businesses who are owed money – e.g., HM Revenue and Customs or suppliers who are waiting for payment.
Debt – money that is owed to someone else – e.g., if a company has a bank loan, it has a debt with the bank.
Debtors – people or businesses that owe money to the organisation – e.g., customers who have not paid their bills yet.
Expenditure – money paid out for materials – e.g., rent, payroll, marketing or travel.
Fixed costs – expenses that stay the same, regardless of sales rising or falling – e.g., rent and insurance.
Governance – the system by which organisations are directed and controlled – e.g., by a board of directors.
Gross profit - the difference between the revenue minus the cost of making the product – before deducting overheads, payroll, taxation and interest payments.
Income, turnover or revenue – money that comes in – e.g., from sales, planned sales, interest or investments.
Liabilities – the amount that a business owes to creditors – e.g., such as banks and suppliers.
Net profit - the actual profit after all working expenses have been paid.
Profit – the amount left over that can either be distributed, held or reinvested in the business.
Revenue – money received – e.g., from sales, grants, government funding, interest or investments.
Semi-variable costs – expenses that might be influenced by changes in sales – e.g., salaries and advertising.
Shares – units of ownership of a company that can be offered for sale – companies usually pay dividends to their shareholders, based on the level of their profits.

Finance

Staff costs *– all costs relating to human resources – e.g., wages, national insurance contributions, agency costs, welfare, uniforms and training.*

Turnover *– the amount of money taken by an organisation in a particular period – e.g., the annual turnover of a company.*

Variable costs *– expenses that change according to sales volumes – e.g., raw materials used to make the products.*

Working capital *– the amount of money left in a business once current assets and liabilities have been taken into account.*

Chapter 10: Project Management

Project Management

Projects

Projects have become an integral part of business management in the 21st century. Project management is rapidly becoming a standard way of implementing strategy in organisations. A typical organisation can accomplish a considerable part of its effort through projects.

Projects today are used for many purposes, not least:

- *deliver organisation's strategy*
- *achieve competitive advantage*
- *drive innovation,*
- *support decision making*
- *enable change.*

For many years, business leaders thought they only needed to design and communicate their strategy – and the rest of the organisation would take care of implementing it.

When the desired strategy was not realised, executives became frustrated, as they felt their strategic directives were being ignored. However, the reason strategy was not realised was more complicated.

Without determining a connection as to how it should be implemented, the strategy was merely loose words – pretty, perhaps, but without relevance to the worker's day-to-day jobs and the company's operations.

The realisation that the failure of the strategy was the result of a variety of causes, not least employees do not understand the strategy, managers do not have incentives tied to strategy, insufficient time is dedicated to revisiting, maturing and refining the strategy over time, and budgets are not linked to strategy has been key in the use of projects to drive organisational strategy.

At the simplest level, if projects are not directly linked to organisational strategy, there is a huge risk that one can push or pull the other in a direction which is disadvantageous to both, meaning there is no telling where the project or even the organisation may end up

Many factors limit an organisation from performing at its best. The limitations can be removed if employees better understand the strategy, understand the key initiatives and methodologies chosen to achieve it, and select the correct performance measures. This way they can more clearly view how what they do contributes to results. Projects can be the way to facilitate this.

As reliance on project management has increased, so too has the focus on achieving and measuring the consistency of project delivery and the organisational value projects provide. Essential to creating this performance orientation is a benefits management process and

Project Management

project delivery capability that aligns projects with corporate strategy development through an execution lifecycle.

Each day, whether at home or work we perform a wide range of routine tasks which we often regard as being chores. At work, in addition to the chores, some tasks will not be routine and are therefore called projects.

Definition:

A project is a unique, transient endeavour, undertaken to achieve planned objectives, which could be defined in terms of outputs, outcomes or benefits. APM

A project is usually deemed to be a success if it achieves the objectives defined in the initial charter, the acceptance criteria and is concluded within the agreed timescale and budget.

Time, cost and quality are the building blocks of every project.

- **Time:** scheduling is a collection of techniques used to develop and present schedules that show when work will be performed.
- **Cost:** how are necessary funds acquired and finances managed?
- **Quality:** how will fitness for purpose of the deliverables and management processes be assured?

Project management involves the concurrent management of a variety of tasks and the people responsible for those tasks. It includes planning and scheduling tasks and controlling the budget associated with delivering an end-product, in a finite time period. The final outcome will produce a significant change in an organisation or community and that change is what sets project management apart from business-as-usual management.

Project Management

Project Management

The core components of project management are:

- *defining the reason why a project is necessary*
- *capturing project requirements, specifying quality of the deliverables, estimating resources and timescales*
- *preparing a business case to justify the investment*
- *securing corporate agreement and funding*
- *developing and implementing a management plan for the project*
- *leading and motivating the project delivery team*
- *managing the risks, issues and changes on the project*
- *monitoring progress against plan*
- *managing the project budget*
- *maintaining communications with stakeholders and the project organisation*
- *provider management*
- *closing the project in a controlled fashion when appropriate*

Projects are separate from business-as-usual activities and occur when an organisation wants to deliver a solution to specific requirements within an agreed budget and timeframe.

Projects require a team of people to come together temporarily to focus on specific project objectives. As a result, effective teamwork is central to successful projects.

Project management is concerned with managing discrete packages of work to achieve specific objectives. The way the work is managed depends upon a wide variety of factors. The scale, significance and complexity of the work are obvious factors: relocating a small office and organising the Olympics share many basic principles but offer very different managerial challenges.

Project objectives may be expressed in terms of:

- **outputs** (such as a new HQ building)
- **outcomes** (such as staff being relocated from multiple locations to the new HQ)
- **benefits** (such as reduced travel and facilities management costs)
- **strategic objectives** (such as doubling the organisation's share price in three years)

Project Management

The Association for Project Management further defines Project Management as:

Project management is the application of processes, methods, skills, knowledge and experience to achieve specific project objectives according to the project acceptance criteria within agreed parameters. Project management has final deliverables that are constrained to a finite timescale and budget. - APM

Prince2 (Projects in Controlled Environments) defines it as:

A temporary organisation that is created for the purpose of delivering one or more business products according to an agreed business plan

For all but the simplest projects a formal approach to managing a project works best.

The control imposed by a formal approach is essential when there are complexities such as new technology, inter-dependent tasks, teams spread across several departments or companies, or where teams are located in different parts of the world: all common occurrences in many business projects.

Because every project will involve some type of change, change management should be an integral part of the project management process. Because projects almost always effect change, there are likely to be risks so risk management is also thrown into the project management mix.

Project Management

Change Management and Project Management

It is not enough to merely prescribe the change and expect it to happen; creating change within an organisation takes hard work and an understanding of what must actually take place to make the change happen.

Change Management

Change management is the process, tools and techniques used to manage the people side of change arising from projects, to achieve the required business outcome.

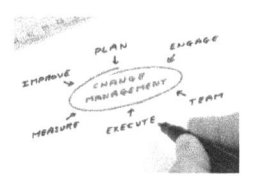

Change management supports moving an organisation from a current state (how things are done today), through a transition state to a desired future state (the new processes, systems, organisation structures or job roles defined by the project outcome).

Change management focuses on the people impacted by the change.

Any change to processes, systems, organisation structures and/or job roles will have a technical side and a people side.

The goal of change management is to help each individual impacted by the change to make a successful transition, given what is required by the solution.

Birth of the Project

A project usually begins when an idea is put forward and after discussion, is accepted as being a good idea and the decision to implement it is made.

This is the start of the project after which, plans and decisions will be made as to how the project should be implemented and planning process will begin.

The next step is the plan being implemented. The project does not end when the implementation finishes, this is only the end of the middle!

The project will end when the organisation has taken feedback and evaluated the whole of the project from start to finish.

A project therefore has a:

- *Beginning*
- *Middle*
- *End*

Project Management

Example

A company wishes to hold a charity dinner for its stakeholders to support a local charitable organisation. Tasks for the planning team might team could include:

- ***researching and planning the project*** – *finding a venue, booking caterers*
- ***working out timescales*** – *planning when things need to be delivered*
- ***finding and organising resources*** – *hiring service staff on the day; seating and tables; ordering portable toilets*
- ***sending out invitations the event*** – *publicity materials to news agencies and media; putting up posters; arranging TV, radio and press advertisements*
- ***contacting people coming to the event*** – *sending invitations and tickets; dealing with telephone and email queries*
- ***preparing the venue*** – *decorating the venue and dealing with queries from suppliers*
- ***host guests and performers*** – *arranging transport or giving directions*
- ***supporting staff after the concert*** – *taking care of lost property; taking unused programmes back to the office; dealing with queries*
- ***evaluating the success of the concert*** – *reviewing sales; responding to feedback, complaints and comments; helping to sort receipts and analyse the costs; assess monies generated*

In this simple example, the tasks to be undertaken are focused exclusively on the project and follow the defined plans and objectives. They are not part of the regular, routine, work of the organisation. Once the project is over, the tasks cease.

Working to strict timescales is critical. Things must be done on time as delays can have a knock-on effect on other people and tasks connected with the project. Projects crop up in almost all industries and businesses, for instance:

- Transport and infrastructure
- IT
- Product manufacture
- Building and construction
- Regulatory changes in finance and law

Project planning

There are standard project management processes used to plan and control tasks, budgets and schedules and to communicate between the different people involved and deal with risks. These processes are usually ongoing throughout the project.

There are also various phases of a project that will have a defined start and end within the overall project lifespan. The gathering of project requirements phase for instance, occurs in the early part of the project.

All of the necessary information and detail relating to the project is held in the Project Plan. The project plan is not just the schedule, although clearly this is an essential item, but it is a

Project Management

complete overarching plan for how the project will be managed from its outset to its conclusion, so it includes:

1. *A summary describing the aims of the project and the expected benefits, including any assumptions or constraints.*
2. *The processes that will be used to monitor and report on the status, and handle risks, change, quality etc.*
3. *Documentation of the scope, requirements and budget as well as a time and dependency-based schedule such as a Gantt Chart.*

In the simplest case a project management plan will include the following elements:

Project Management Plan	
Project aims	If the final deliverable of a project does not meet the requirements of the client, then it has not been successful. Therefore, you must establish what those requirements are (and prioritising them).
Project deliverables	These are the tangible items that will ensure the needs of the client are met and will include time estimates.
Project schedule	A list of individual tasks along with how long they are estimated to take, who will complete them, any inter-dependencies and any important milestones along the way. There are many software packages to help you do this efficiently.
Resource requirements	The project schedule will enable you to justify the project's resource requirements for time, equipment, budget and people. Identify individuals by name or skillset along with their responsibilities within the project.
Communications plan	Who needs to be kept informed about project progress and how will this be communicated? Typically, there will be various reports with differing levels of detail for different stakeholders that cover progress and planned work for the next period
Risk management	This involves the identification, monitoring and mitigating of risks.
Quality guidelines	You need to know what level of quality is expected and required so the definition needs to be detailed and measurable. It also needs to consider available budget and resources.

Putting together an effective project plan is essential but so too is sticking to it throughout the course of the project or adapting it as needs change, whichever is most appropriate for a particular project.

Project Management

Project Management Phases and Processes

Project Phases

Initiation
This first stage of a project defines the business case, the justification for the project, which will be used to ensure the project stays on track. It also states what the project is intended to achieve, how that will be achieved and the scope of the work; this is important for controlling subsequent change requests. In this phase, those involved in the project will be assigned their responsibilities.

Requirements
The requirements documentation describes the aims of the project in detail including timescales and constraints. It should also define the criteria that will constitute a successful project and will be used to manage the expectations of the stakeholders. Many projects use an iterative process to reach agreement on the requirements, although some projects take an 'agile' approach to project management.

Planning
The project plan includes details about how the project work will be carried out, how it will be monitored and controlled, how communication will be facilitated and information about costs and timescales. But once a project is underway it is typically the project schedule where most attention is focused.

All tasks need to be scheduled in the most efficient order to ensure tasks with inter-dependencies are completed when required and to enable several tasks to be performed in parallel. There are many project management tools available to assist with scheduling, one of the most common being the Gantt Chart.

Execution
The person or group assigned to carry out a task will need to know, in detail, what the task involves as well as any dependencies and timescales, and will also need to understand the criteria by which each task is deemed complete.

Closure
Once there is an approved end product the project can be formally closed and a final review held to learn from both the successes and the mistakes and take that experience forward to the next project

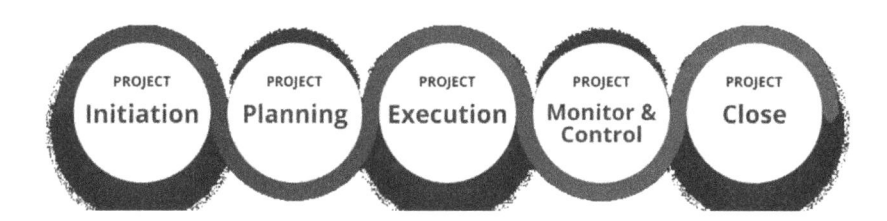

Project Management

Project Processes

Monitoring
Planning is carried out in the early stages of a project but there should be ongoing monitoring to ensure the project remains on budget and schedule; that resources are available and the expected benefits can be delivered. Estimates, deadlines and milestones may need to be altered as the project progresses.

Control
No project is without problems, but the project manager needs to control them, so they do not adversely affect the end result. The control phase also deals with risk management.

Communication
Good communication is one of the most important factors affecting project success. Many problems can be avoided if there is open, honest communication between everyone involved on a project; written and verbal, formal and informal.

People Management
A project manager is responsible for managing the individuals working on the project as well as the tasks and risks. In complex projects there may be segregated levels of people management, but every project manager will have some responsibility for individuals. That includes motivating people, delivering constructive feedback etc.

Project Management Methodologies

According to the Project Management Institute (PMI), a methodology is defined as 'a system of practices, techniques, procedures, and rules used by those who work in a discipline.'

> *Lean practices, Kanban, and Six Sigma are examples of project management methodologies*

Some are based on themes, some on principles, processes, standards, or a combination. They are essentially process' that aim to assist project managers with guidance throughout the project, and the steps take to complete the tasks.

Different methodologies have different strategies that aid in managing issues should they arise during the project's delivery.

There are many methodologies to choose from, each with their own set of rules, principles, processes, and practices. Which methodology is chosen depends entirely on the type of project to be undertaken.

> *the project management methodology is chosen to maximise the use of resources and time*

Project Management

While there are numerous methodologies to choose from, there is no such thing as the 'right' methodology. There will not be the one methodology that is perfect to use for every single project. Projects vary in scope and requirements, which means the right methodology to implement will also vary.

Agile

Agile is one of the more recognisable project management methodologies and is best suited for projects that are iterative and incremental. Originally created for software development, it was established as a response to the inadequacies of the Waterfall methodology, the processes of which did not meet the demands of the highly competitive and constant movement of the software industry. It is a type of process where demands and solutions evolve through the collaborative effort of self-organising and cross-functional teams and their customers.

Agile project management stems from the values and principles of the Agile Manifesto. A declaration cemented in 2001 by 13 industry leaders, its purpose being to uncover better ways of developing software by providing a clear and measurable structure that fosters iterative development, team collaboration, and change recognition.

It is made up of four fundamental values and 12 key principles:

Values

1. *Individuals and interactions over processes and tools*
2. *Working software over comprehensive documentation*
3. *Customer collaboration over contract negotiation*
4. *Responding to change over following a plan*

Principles

1. *Customer satisfaction through early and continuous software delivery*
2. *Accommodate changing requirements throughout the development process*
3. *Frequent delivery of working software*
4. *Collaboration between the business stakeholders and developers throughout the project*
5. *Support, trust, and motivate the people involved*
6. *Enable face-to-face interactions*
7. *Working software is the primary measure of progress*
8. *Agile processes to support a consistent development pace*
9. *Attention to technical detail and design enhances agility*
10. *Simplicity*
11. *Self-organising teams encourage great architectures, requirements, and designs*
12. *Regular reflections on how to become more effective*

Project Management

Because of its adaptivity, Agile methodology is commonly used to deliver more complex projects. It uses six main deliverables to track progress and create the product which are the product vision statement, product roadmap, product backlog, release plan, Sprint backlog, and increment. With these features, it establishes itself as a methodology that places an emphasis on collaboration, flexibility, continuous improvement, and high-quality results.

Best suited for: Projects that require flexibility and have a level of complexity or uncertainty. For instance, a product or service that has not been built by the team.

> *Agile is a methodology that has methodologies within itself, such as Scrum and Kanban*

It may be argued that Scrum and Kanban should be considered more as frameworks, they are used to develop and deliver a product or service and carry their own set of characteristics and terminology which, by default, makes them worthy enough to be included here.

Scrum

Scrum is comprised of five values: commitment, courage, focus, openness, and respect. Its goal is to develop, deliver, and sustain complex products through collaboration, accountability, and iterative progress. What distinguishes Scrum from the other Agile project management methodologies is how it operates by using certain roles, events, and artefacts.

Scrum team roles

- **Product owner:** Product expert who represents the stakeholders and is the voice of the customer.
- **Development team:** Group of professionals who deliver the product (developers, programmers, designers).
- **Scrum master:** Organised servant-leader who ensures the understanding and execution of Scrum is followed.

Scrum events

- **Sprint:** Iterative time boxes in which a goal is accomplished. Time frame does not exceed one calendar month and are consistent throughout the development process.
- **Sprint planning:** Where the entire Scrum team get together — at the beginning of every Sprint — to plan the upcoming sprint.
- **Daily Scrum:** 15-minute time boxed meeting held at the same time, every day of the Sprint, where the previous day's achievements are discussed, as well as the expectations for the following one.
- **Sprint review:** An informal meeting held at the end of every Sprint where the Scrum team present their Increment to the stakeholders and discuss feedback.
- **Sprint retrospective:** A meeting where the Scrum team reflect on the proceedings of the previous Sprint and establish improvements for the next Sprint.

Project Management

Scrum Artefacts

- **Product backlog:** Managed by the Product Owner, it is where all the requirements needed for a viable product are listed in order of priority. Includes features, functions, requirements, enhancements, and fixes that authorise any changes to be made to the product in future releases.
- **Sprint backlog:** A list of the tasks and requirements that need to be accomplished during the next Sprint. Sometimes accompanied by a Scrum task board, which is used to visualise the progress of the tasks in the current Sprint, and any changes that are made in a 'To Do, Doing, and Done' format.

Best suited for: Projects that consists of teams of less than seven people who need a flexible approach to delivering a product or service.

Kanban

Kanban is another popular Agile framework that, like Scrum, focuses on early releases with collaborative and self-managing teams.

The concept that was developed on the production line of Toyota factories in the 1940s. It is a very visual method that aims to deliver high quality results by painting a picture of the workflow process so that bottlenecks can be identified early on in the development process.

It operates on six general practices, which are:

1. Visualisation
2. Limiting work in progress
3. Flow management
4. Making policies explicit
5. Using feedback loops
6. Collaborative or experimental evolution

> *Kanban achieves efficiency by using visual cues that signal various stages of the development process.*

The cues involved in the process are a Kanban board, Kanban cards, and even Kanban swim lanes for those looking for that extra bit of organisation.

- **Kanban board:** What is used to visualise the development process, a Kanban board can be either physical (a whiteboard, sticky notes, and markers) or digital (like an online project management tool).

Project Management

- **Kanban cards:** Each Kanban card depicts a work item/task in the work process. Used to communicate progress with your team, it represents information such as status, cycle time, and impending deadlines.
- **Kanban swim lanes:** Flowing horizontally, Kanban swim lanes are a visual element on the board that allows you to further distinguish tasks/items by categorising them. Their purpose is to offer a better overview of the workflow.

While there are no set rules of Kanban per-se, it works by using a Kanban board to represent the stages of development from the beginning when ideas are produced, to the work in progress, to when the work has been completed.

The board's basic structure is three columns labelled as 'To-Do, Doing, and Done' — which is rather self-explanatory.

To-do	Doing	Done

Like most Agile frameworks, Kanban made its mark within the software development industry. However, due to its flexibility it has gained traction in other industries and is one of a few project management methodologies that can be applied to any project that requires continuous improvement within the development process.

Best suited for: Like Scrum, Kanban is appropriate for projects with smaller teams, who need a flexible approach to delivering a product or service. Kanban is also great for personal productivity purposes.

Lean

The Lean methodology promotes maximising customer value, while minimising waste. It aims to create more value for the customer by using fewer resources. With its roots in the Japanese manufacturing industry, its values suppose that:

> *'as waste is eliminated, quality improves while the production time and cost are reduced.'*

It identifies three types of waste: Muda, Mura, and Muri, also known as the 3Ms.

Muda
Muda is about getting rid of waste and refers to an activity or process that does not add value. It can either be something that is a physical waste of your time or something that is a waste of your resources. Characterised as seven original wastes, they are:

1. **'Transport:** The movement of product between operations and locations.
2. **Inventory:** The work in progress (WIP) and stocks of finished goods and raw materials that a company holds.

Project Management

3. **Motion:** The physical movement of a person or machine whilst conducting an operation.
4. **Waiting:** The act of waiting for a machine to finish, for a product to arrive, or any other cause.
5. **Overproduction:** Over producing product beyond what the customer has ordered.
6. **Over-processing:** Conducting operations beyond those that customer requires.
7. **Defects:** Product rejects and reworks within your processes.'

Mura

Mura is about eliminating variances in the workflow process at a scheduling and operation level so that everything flows evenly. For example, when publishing a magazine, if an editor spends too much time editing an article, it means that the design team will have less time to create the spread before the publishing deadline comes. Therefore, you would reduce the editing time and ensure every department's timeframe spent on the article is the same.

Muri

Muri is about removing overload so that the nothing slows down. It refers to managers and business owners imposing unnecessary stress on their employees and processes due to things such as poor organisation, unclear ways of working, and using incorrect tools.

Instead of implementing certain processes, Lean is more about adhering to a set of principles. The five main principles are:

> *specify value by the customer*
> *identify steps in the value stream*
> *make product flow continuously*
> *allow customers pull value from the next upstream activity*
> *manage towards removing unnecessary steps.*

Best suited for: Often mistaken for specialising in manufacturing industries, Lean methodology is ideal for any business or organisation that is not looking for a process as such but is interested in transforming how they conduct doing business.

Project Management

Waterfall

One of the more traditional project management methodologies, Waterfall is a linear, sequential design approach where progress flows downwards in one direction — like a waterfall.

It originated in the manufacturing and construction industries, but its lack of flexibility in design changes in the earlier stages of the development process is due to it becoming exorbitantly expensive because of its structured physical environments.

The methodology was first introduced in an article written in 1970 by Winston W. Royce (although the term 'Waterfall' was not used) and emphasises that you are only able to move onto the next phase of development once the current phase has been completed. The phases are followed in the following order:

System and software requirements
Analysis
Design
Coding
Testing
Operations

Waterfall is a project management methodology that stresses the importance of documentation. The idea is that if a worker were to leave during the development process, their replacement can start where they left off by familiarising themselves with the information provided on the documents.

Pre-Agile saw the Waterfall methodology being used for software development, but there were many issues due to its non-adaptive design constraints, the lack of customer feedback available during the development process, and a delayed testing period.

Best suited for: Larger projects that require maintaining stringent stages and deadlines, or projects that have been done various times over where chances of surprises during the development process are relatively low.

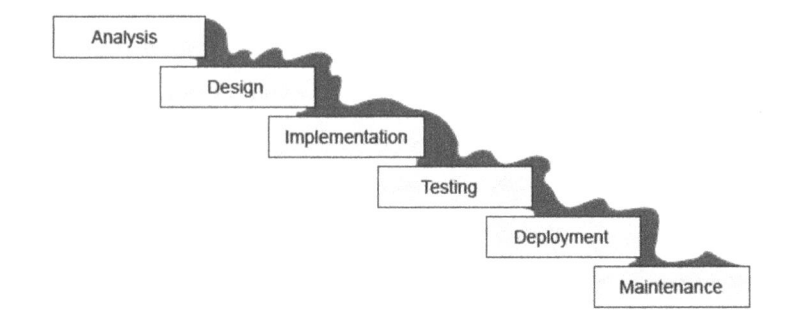

Project Management

Six Sigma

Six Sigma is project management methodology first introduced by engineers at Motorola in 1986. It aims to improve quality by reducing the number of errors in a process by identifying what is not working and then removing it from the process. It uses quality management methods, which are mostly empirical and statistical, as well as the expertise of people who are specialists in these methods.

There are two major methodologies of Six Sigma carried out by Six Sigma Green Belts and Six Sigma Black Belts and are supervised by Six Sigma Master Black Belts. They are DMAIC which is used for improving business processes, and DMADV which is more for creating new processes, products or services. The letters stand for:

Define the problem and the project goals
Measure in detail the various aspects of the current process
Analyse data to, among other things, find the root defects in a process
Improve the process
Control how the process is done in the future

Define the project goals
Measure critical components of the process and the product capabilities
Analyse the data and develop various designs for the process, eventually picking the best one
Design and test details of the process
Verify the design by running simulations and a pilot program, and then handing over the process to the client

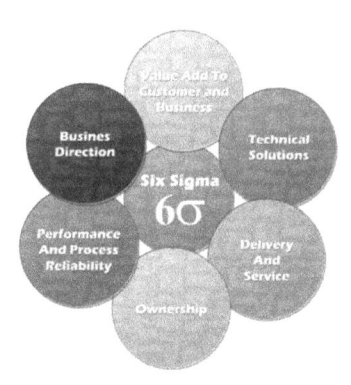

There is also a Lean Six Sigma methodology which is committed to improving team performance by systematically eliminating waste and reducing variation.

Best suited for: Larger companies and organisations that want to improve quality and efficiency through a data-driven methodology.

Project Management

PMBOK

PMBOK stands for the Project Management Body of Knowledge and is a set of standard terminology and guidelines for project management. It states that there are five process groups that are prevalent in almost every project. They are:

1. **Initiating:** *Defining the start of a new project or new phase of an existing project.*
2. **Planning:** *Where the scope of the project, objectives, and how the objectives will be achieved.*
3. **Executing:** *Actually, doing the work defined in the project management plan.*
4. **Monitoring and Controlling:** *When you need to track, review, and regulate the progress and performance.*
5. **Closing:** *Concluding all activities across all Process Groups to formally close the project or phrase.*

Along with this, it includes best practices, conventions, and techniques that are considered the industry standard. Regularly updating their guide to ensure that they echo the most up-to-date project management practices, the PMBOK is currently up to its sixth edition which was published in print and online in 2017.

Best suited for: Because it is more of a reference guide than an actual project management methodology, you cannot implement PMBOK to a project. However, it can be used for when you want to assess the best practices for your project.

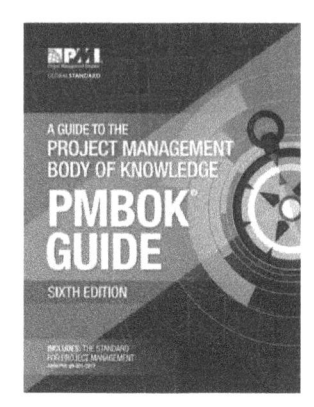

P3 Management

Project, programme and portfolio (P3) management is concerned with managing discrete packages of work to achieve objectives. The way the work is managed depends upon a wide variety of factors.

The scale, significance and complexity of the work are obvious factors: relocating a small office and organising the Olympics share many basic principles but offer very different managerial challenges.

Scale and complexity are not the only factors. Managing a major infrastructure development for delivery to a client will need a different approach to internally managing the merger of two banking organisations.

A good distinguishing factor is often to look at the nature of the objectives.

Objectives may be expressed in terms of:

- *outputs* (such as a new HQ building)

Project Management

- **outcomes** *(such as staff being relocated from multiple locations to the new HQ)*
- **benefits** *(such as reduced travel and facilities management costs)*
- **strategic objectives** *(such as doubling the organisation's share price in three years).*

*A **Project** is deemed to be work of a lesser scale and complexity, leading to an output*

*A **Programme** is work that combines projects with change management to deliver*

*A **Portfolio** is a collection of projects and programmes designed to achieve strategic objectives.*

However, some undertakings that only deliver outputs may be very large and complex, while some work that delivers benefits and encompasses the management of change may be relatively small and straightforward. Small organisations will have strategic portfolios that are nowhere near as complex and expensive as, say, a large government IT project.

Although projects, programmes and portfolios are often spoken of as being mutually exclusive approaches, they are actually just convenient combinations of managerial tools and techniques used to describe typical sets of circumstances.

The concept of projects, programmes and portfolios should be thought of as just points on a gradual scale of managing effort to deliver objectives.

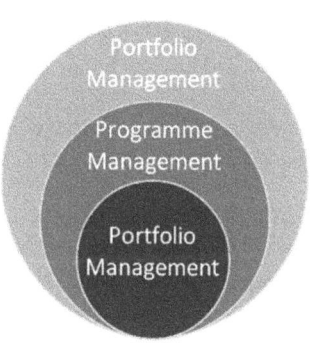

Manages

Portfolio Management — Strategic objectives, economic cost and corporate risk

Programme Management — Benefit realisation, project interdependencies and structured change

Portfolio Management — Time, cost and resources

Project Management

P3 Project Life Cycle

Definition

A life cycle defines the inter-related phases of a project, programme or portfolio and provides a structure for governing the progression of the work.

All projects, programmes and portfolios are designed to deliver objectives. These objectives may be expressed as outputs, outcomes or benefits. A P3 life cycle illustrates the distinct phases that take an initial idea, develop it into detailed objectives and then deliver those objectives.

All life cycles follow a similar high-level generic sequence, but this can be expressed in quite different ways. Life cycles will differ across industries and business sectors.

The most common type is the linear life cycle, sometimes known as the linear sequential model or waterfall method. In addition to the linear model, other life cycle formats include:

- ***parallel*** – this is similar to the linear, but phases are carried out in parallel to increase the pace of delivery.
- ***spiral*** – this is often employed where many options, requirements and constraints are unknown at the start (e.g., in prototyping or research projects).
- ***'v'*** – this is applied in software development where requirements are defined and the development tools are well known.

The phased structure facilitates the creation of governance and feedback mechanisms:

- ***stages*** – development work can be further subdivided into a series of management stages (usually referred to as 'tranches' in programmes) with work being authorised one stage at a time.
- ***gate reviews*** – these are conducted at the end of a phase, stage or tranche. Senior management will consider performance to date and plans for the next phase, stage or tranche before deciding whether it is viable.
- ***post-reviews*** – learning from experience is a key factor in maturity. Post-project and programme reviews document lessons learned for use in the future.
- ***benefit reviews*** – these measure the achievement of benefits against the business case.

All phases of the life cycle are important. No phase should be omitted but they may be adjusted to accommodate the development methodology and context of the work.

Project Management

Delivering the Project

It is true to say that no two projects are the same and everyone will have different objectives, parameters, budgets, constraints, outcomes, etc.

As a consequence, every project will need to be managed differently with different emphasis on different elements. There cannot therefore be a definitive guide as to how a project should be delivered and everyone should be assessed and planned on its own merits before a delivery plan is drawn up.

Key project documentation

Given that no two projects are the same and therefore a standard set of documentation cannot be prescribed to a project. The documentation will be unique to each project. Key pieces that may be used to deliver a project can include:

- *a brief and terms of reference*
- *project plans*
- *definitions of project roles*
- *a risk log (RAID) or register*
- *project monitoring records* – *e.g., Gantt charts or progress reports*

A brief and terms of reference
During the initiation stage, a brief and terms of reference to provide a framework for the project must be produced. By agreeing these early in the process, everyone can agree their role and commitment to it, and the project managers can check whether or not the project is viable. This needs to be agreed before the organisation commits to planning and using its resources, finances and stakeholders' time.

It is important to show what is not covered by the project too. This is key in large organisations in particular, where people may look at a project and assume that it covers their area when it does not.

Project plans
The project plans will include all aspects of the project, including:

- *timescales, deadlines and critical review points*
- *human and physical resources*
- *the budgets that relate to the project*
- *contingency plans*

The plan needs to go into detail about how the different timescales and tasks will overlap and affect each other.

Definitions of project roles

Project Management

The various people involved with the project need to have their job descriptions in definitions of project roles. Having these together helps the project manager to have an overall view of who is tasked to do what, so that they can make sure that all aspects and tasks have been covered.

A Risk Log or Register

An important element of the planning stage is to prepare a risk log or register and put in measures to minimise risk. A risk assessment needs to be performed for each aspect of the project, and these are kept together in a risk log.

For example, organisations can use a RAID log for their projects:

- **Risks** – *events that will have an adverse effect on the project*
- **Assumptions** – *factors that are assumed to be in place*
- **Issues** – *something that is going wrong on the project and needs managing*
- **Dependencies** – *events or work that are dependent on the result of the project, or things on which the project will be dependent*

Risks can be defined in many ways – e.g., financial risk when investing or borrowing money; reputation when making decisions that affect the organisation's image and good name; weather or other external influences; health and safety.

According to the Health and Safety Executive, there are five main steps to risk assessment. Many organisations use these as guidelines when designing and implementing their own risk assessments:

1. *Identify the hazards*
2. *Decide who might be harmed, and how*
3. *Evaluate the risks and decide on precautions*
4. *Record findings and implement them*
5. *Review the assessment and update as necessary*

These risk assessment guidelines can be modified to apply to any type of risk as they help everyone to see and understand the potential hazards, and to take steps to reduce the chance of harm by having control measures in place.

A risk management log could include columns such as:

- **risk impact** – *high, medium or low*
- **probability of occurrence** – *high, medium or low*
- **risk descriptions**
- **project impact** – *timescales or resources that may be affected*
- **risk area** – *budget, resources or schedule*
- **symptoms** – *human resources are not fully decided when a project is about to start*
- **triggers** – *24 hours before bad weather is inevitable, contingency plans to cancel will come into effect*
- **risk response** – *mitigation*

Project Management

- **response strategy** – *allocate extra resources, reschedule or cancel*
- **contingency plan** – *bring in qualified agency staff to cover short term*

Project Monitoring Records
Once the project is underway, documents are needed for monitoring the project's progress against plans and objectives. These could include, for example, Gantt charts or progress reports.

Project Management Tools
A variety of project management tools can be used at appropriate phases of the project. They may be used:

- **during the planning phase** – *to provide a clear structure for the project*
- **when monitoring progress** – *using plans, progress charts, actions plans and risk logs when communicating with stakeholders*
- **when reviewing a project** – *to illustrate and explain progress and plans during review meetings*

Tools can include, for example:

- SWOT analyses
- Work Breakdown Structures (WBS)
- PERT Diagrams
- SMART objectives
- Gantt charts
- Plan on a Page
- RACI matrix
- Time management techniques
- Kotter's 8-stage change model

SWOT analyses
In the workplace, a SWOT analysis can be used in many different situations to identify and measure:

- **Strengths of a project** – *e.g., well supported; well financed*
- **Weaknesses of a project** – *e.g., very short on time; not enough trained staff to do all the tasks effectively*
- **Opportunities to improve** – *e.g., recruitment drive to bring in the staff needed*
- **Threats to progress** – *e.g., competition from other employers who need to recruit staff with the same skills*

The SWOT analysis can be applied at any scale and can be simple or more detailed. It acts as a snapshot and does not track progress or interdependency of tasks, goals or resources. It can be used in any part of the project that needs a simple, focused analysis on where we are now, where we need to be and how we are going to get there.

Work Breakdown Structures (WBS)

Project Management

A WBS is a useful project management tool that breaks down a project into smaller components. The tasks and responsibilities are broken down into manageable sections that align to ensure that overall objectives can be met.

A WBS is useful in the earlier stages of planning so that:

- *tasks can be broken down into small pieces*
- *an overall picture of how elements will work together can be seen at a glance*
- *different people can see how the tasks may overlap and work together*

Below is a small sample of a simple WBS planner for the Charity Dinner example. It could be developed to go into more detail about the actual days of the month, and names and contact details for all of the internal and external team members.

	February	*March*	*April*	*May*	*June*	*July*	*August*
Tickets	Print tickets by 1st April				Launch sales 5th June	Last boost for tickets	
Caterers	Identify potential candidates	Meet shortlisted companies	Appoint caterers			Finalise menu	
Volunteers			Publicise and start recruitment	Recruit & do phone interviews	Recruit & do interviews Provisional order of uniforms by 16 Jun	In-house training Final order for uniforms by 22 Jul	Training at venue Give out uniforms
Performers	Confirm bookings and contracts		Make contact to stay in touch		Check rehearsal dates are OK	Contact about special requests – food, drink etc. Book transport	Venue rehearsals 20, 21, 22 Aug Event 23rd Aug
Transport		Research taxi & limo companies	Reserve transport for performers, guest speakers			Confirm transport bookings OK	3 limos, 6 taxis, 1 minibus needed 22, 23 Aug

Programme Evaluation Review Technique (PERT) diagram

Another project management tool is a PERT diagram, which stands for Programme Evaluation Review Technique.

This chart is a graphic representation of the project's schedule and it is used to schedule, organise and coordinate tasks within the project. It was developed in the 1950s by the US Navy to manage the Polaris submarine, an extremely complex project.

A PERT diagram usually shows:

Project Management

- the sequence of tasks and milestones
- how these are prioritised
- a three-point estimation technique that shows the duration of each task as being 'optimistic', 'pessimistic' or 'most likely'

The main feature of a PERT diagram that is made using software is the instant calculation of timelines with every change in the workflow. The project manager can instantly see how one changed timescale affects other parts of the project. Its main benefit is to have an overall view of the whole project, rather than individual details, showing how parts of the project can move and impact each other.

Below is a simple PERT diagram about making and packing a teddy bear that has a customised T-shirt:

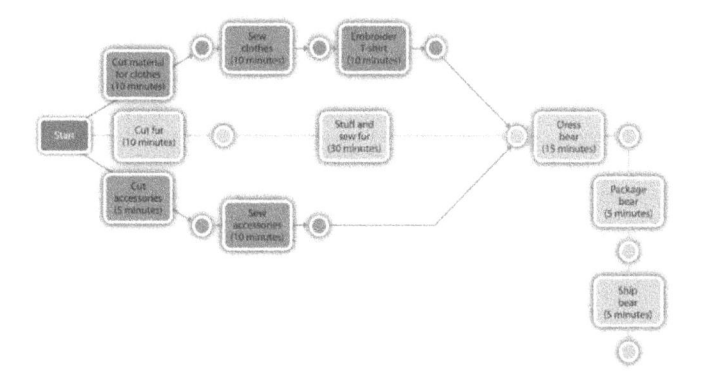

SMART targets or objectives
Another tool to use is the familiar SMART targets or objectives. As we see in many aspects of management, SMART targets are:

Specific
Measurable
Achievable
Realistic
Time-bound

As with SWOT analyses, they can be used for the project as a whole or for small tasks within the project.

Gantt Chart
The underlying concept of a Gantt chart is to map out which tasks can be done in parallel and which need to be done sequentially. If we combine this with the project resources, we can explore the trade-off between the scope (doing more or less work), cost (using more or less resources) and the time scales for the project. By adding more resources or reducing the scope the project manager can see the effect on the end date.

Project Management

A Gantt chart displays information visually as a type of bar chart in a clear and easy-to-understand way and is used for the following activities:

- *Establish the initial project schedule*
- *Allocate resources*
- *Monitor and report progress*
- *Control and communicate the schedule*
- *Display milestones*
- *Identify and report problems*

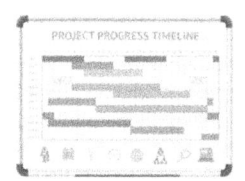

To create a chart, you need to know all of the individual tasks required to complete the project, an estimate of how long each task will take and which tasks are dependent on others. The very process of pulling this information together helps a project manager focus on the essential parts of the project and begin to establish a realistic timeframe for completion.

Project management solutions that integrate Gantt charts give managers visibility into team workloads, as well as current and future availability, which allows for more accurate scheduling. Gantt charts have been around for nearly a century, having been invented by Henry Gantt, an American mechanical engineer, around 1910. Below is a simple example of a Gantt chart which reflects the data in the Pert chart above:

Activity/Day	1	2	3	4	5	6	7	8	9	10	11	12	13
Cut fur	■	■											
Stuff and sew fur			■	■	■	■	■						
Cut material	■	■											
Sew clothes			■	■	■								
Embroider T-shirt					■	■							
Cut accessories	■												
Sew accessories		■	■										
Dress bears									■	■			
Package bears											■		
Ship bears													■

Lot size: 100 bears

All activities are scheduled to begin at their earliest start time.

■ Completed work
▨ Work to be completed

Project Management

Disadvantages of a Gantt Chart

Gantt charts are not perfect and all too often they become overly complex with too many dependencies and activities. This is a trap many new project managers fall into when they start using planning tools.

It is much better to produce a clear and simple plan that shows the main work packages in summary, than a plan with so much detail the overall impression of project progress is lost. Let the work package manager put together the day-to-day detail of the activities within a work package, while the project schedule concentrates on the interfaces between project teams.

Neither are they good at showing the relative priorities of individual tasks and the resources expended on a task. Tasks are prioritised on the amount of float not their importance to the project. For example, they can clearly show the elapsed time of a task but cannot so easily communicate how many people may be needed to complete that task. So, if not backed up by other data they can give a misleading impression to stakeholders. This is where using additional techniques such as a precedence diagram (sometimes called a PERT chart), for instance, becomes useful

A precedence diagram is another powerful project management technique which is particularly useful for identifying complex inter-dependencies and showing relative priorities of activities and, hence, highlighting the tasks most critical to project success.

Setting up a Gantt Chart

- *When you set up a Gantt chart, you need to think through all of the tasks involved in your project and divide them into manageable components.*
- *Then decide who will be responsible for each task and delegate to the team.*
- *Identify task relationships and decide on the completion date sequence for each task, showing the expected time duration of the whole project and the sub tasks. A Gantt chart will show the tasks in a sequential order and display task dependencies (i.e., how one task relates to another).*
- *Determine and allocate your resources.*
- *Anticipate the risks and problems you may encounter and create a contingency plan for potential problems.*

Project Management

Plan on a Page

This is a simple tool that condenses the whole project down to one page of information. It is particularly useful to, for example:

- **help the project manager focus on the main points of a project** – when making presentations to people outside the project
- **show stakeholders a very quick overview of the entire project** – when applying for extra funding or resources from new sources
- **show the media the main points of the project** – when launching a new product
- **use as a leaflet** – when distributing information to the local community about a project that will affect or involve them

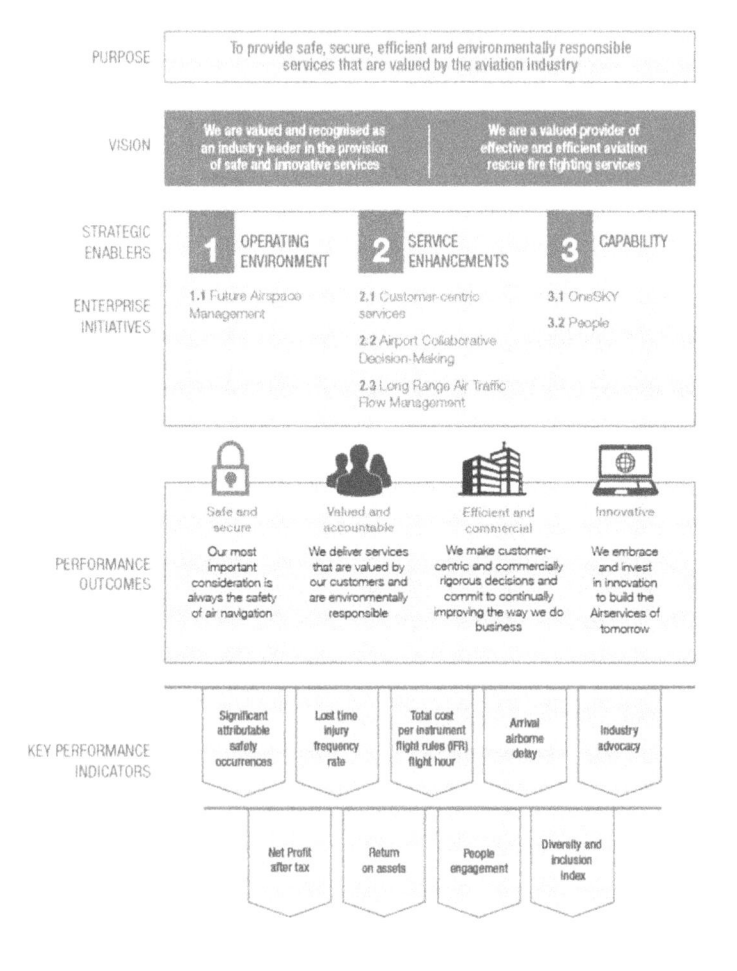

RACI Matrix

Project Management

The RACI model is a straightforward tool that is used in project management to identify roles and responsibilities. It stands for:

Responsible – *the person who does the work to achieve the task*
Accountable – *the person who is accountable for the correct completion of the task – e.g., the project manager who approves the Responsible person's work*
Consulted – *the people who provide information for the project in two-way communication – e.g., subject specialists*
Informed – *the people who are affected by the outcomes of tasks and need to be kept informed about progress in one-way communication – shareholders, directors or senior managers who are not involved with the day-to-day running of the project*

This helps to avoid confusion about the decision-making process by providing a clear illustration for all relevant stakeholders to see who is responsible for tasks, and who needs to be informed along the way. A RACI model can help the project manager to manage expectations and identify roles and responsibilities early in the project.

Time Management Techniques

The tools used for project management help managers to:

- *plan ahead for each element and stage*
- *keep elements of the project on time*
- *predict busy and quiet times*
- *prioritise human and physical resources to meet deadlines*

Time management techniques can be extremely valuable for the project manager and their team members. For example:

- *allow time each day to plan activities*
- ***prioritise communications*** – *e.g., deal with urgent messages and accept that some emails and telephone calls do not have to be answered immediately*
- *factor in some time for interruptions and unplanned activities*
- *plan meetings and be firm about time spent*
- *remove distractions when focus is needed*

An Eisenhower grid or matrix can be designed to give an overview for personal time management, for example:

Project Management

	URGENT	NOT URGENT
IMPORTANT	**1) DO NOW** • emergencies • complaints • planned tasks and projects due now • staff needs • problem-solving	**2) PLAN TO DO** • planning • preparation • research • networking • system development • strategy planning
NOT IMPORTANT	**3) REJECT AND EXPLAIN** • trivial requests from others • ad hoc interruptions • distractions • pointless routines or activities	**4) RESIST AND CEASE** • 'comfort' activities – computer games, excessive breaks • chat, gossip • daydreaming and doodling • reading irrelevant material • unnecessary travel

Kotter's 8-stage Change Model

Developed in 1996, the stages of Kotter's change model can be used as a tool and an overall change management framework when managing a project. The eight stages are:

1. **Establish a sense of urgency** – *when initiating the project and presenting the project plans.*
2. **Create a guiding coalition** – *convince people that the project has value and benefits; bring together a strong coalition or team of people from different departments to guide the team.*
3. **Develop a shared vision** – *create a strategy to deliver the objectives of the project.*
4. **Communicate the vision** – *communicate the purpose, aims and objectives of the project efficiently; address concerns openly.*
5. **Empower people to act on the vision** – *remove obstacles that may stop progress.*
6. **Create short-term wins to motivate with success** – *set smaller objectives that can be achieved, praised and rewarded.*
7. **Consolidate and build on the changes made by the project** – *analyse each 'win' for success and areas for improvement; set goals to continue the momentum.*
8. **Institutionalise the change** – *talk about progress; include relevant lessons learned during the project within the organisation's training and recruitment practices.*

Project Management

Managing Resources

When managing the project's resources, a range of the tools above can be used. They can help to provide an up-to-date, three-dimensional view of the project at all stages, which helps the project manager to, for example:

- *make sure that resources are available on time for each stage of the project*
- *identify problems and potential risks as soon as possible*
- *find solutions to address problems, issues and risks*
- *make decisions about how to reallocate resources*
- *provide evidence to support requests for increased resources and timescales*
- *show more senior decision-makers how they are managing the project*

When managing resources, the purpose, scope, aims and objectives for the whole project need to be very clear. This gives a focus so that time, human and physical resources can be geared up to achieve goals without unnecessary waste.

Human Resources

When managing human resources for a project, managers perform the usual functions associated with people management, for example:

- *planning and allocating work to match the skills, experience and knowledge of team members*
- *developing and maintaining a common sense of purpose and a positive working environment*
- *working to retain team members*
- *recruiting and training team members*
- *making sure everyone understands aims and objectives*
- *supporting team members in career and skills development*
- **ensuring compliance with legislation** – *e.g., health and safety, data protection and equality and diversity*
- *monitoring work and taking action to improve performance*

In addition to these management tasks, the project manager's main focus is to make sure that people with the right skills are available when required for each stage of the project. During the planning stage, they can:

- *identify exactly which human resources are going to be needed for specific parts of the project*
- *work out the lead times for preparing and recruiting staff*
- *ensure that existing team members have the right skills*
- *recruit new team members, from inside or outside the organisation*
- *train and brief all team members in time*
- **emphasise the importance of timescales and quality** – *and how these can affect other areas of the project*

Project Management

- ***ensure that team members have the equipment they need to perform their duties*** – *e.g., Hi-Viz jackets, stationery, laptops, tablets, travel tickets, radios or mobile phones*

During the delivery and control stage, these points need to be monitored, supported and reinforced, as necessary.

Physical Resources

Projects are very focused and visible, which often means that the resources are under more scrutiny than in other business activities. As projects are usually stand-alone activities, every physical resource needs to be planned and allocated to them – e.g., venues, desks and stationery.

The project team is accountable and responsible for managing resources effectively and may have to answer to, for example:

- ***senior managers and directors*** – *who need the project to make a profit for the organisation*
- ***clients*** – *customers who have commissioned and paid for the project*
- ***sponsors*** – *companies who have associated their brand with the project*
- ***government agencies*** – *enforcing regulations on the environment or health and safety*

Due to the temporary nature of a project, with its beginning, middle and end, resources need to be flexible. This means that everything needs to be planned in great detail, which requires a considerable amount of management to keep things on track. For example, the project manager for our charity dinner example will have to manage:

- ***the venue for the dinner*** – *checking its capacity and suitability; booking it; setting up kitchens for the dinner; dismantling everything afterwards*
- ***resources needed at the venue*** – *sound and lighting systems; hiring toilets and changing rooms for the artists; parking facilities for staff and artists; rest areas, training rooms and catering facilities for volunteers*
- ***office space for staff*** – *at the venue and within the organisation's premises*
- ***office equipment*** – *integrated IT and telephone equipment at the venue and head office*
- ***vehicles*** – *hiring cars and vans for volunteers, artists and full-time staff to use*
- *catering and other resources for the artists– extra portable toilets; catering outlets; smoking areas*
- ***sales, marketing and ticketing*** – *printing and distributing tickets, leaflets and posters*
- ***insurance and inspections of resources*** – *insurance for the venue, public liability, vehicles and rented equipment; dealing with the health and safety representatives from the local council who inspect the venue*

Every item has a cost and a lead time, so careful management is required to make sure that:

Project Management

- *each item is fit for purpose and satisfies regulatory requirements*
- *it is available on time*
- *the quality is as agreed and expected* – as set out in a service level agreement
- *waste is kept to a minimum*
- *there is a plan for all resources at the end of the project* – handing rented venues, equipment and machinery back in good condition; selling purchased items that are no longer required; returning equipment and supplies to head office

Financial Resources

Budgets are usually strictly controlled for projects and the project manager is accountable and responsible for agreeing, controlling and managing budgets. They need to consider, for example:

- **timescales** – to show when money is due to come in and out – when money from ticket sales and sponsors is likely to be available
- **priorities** – to target resources correctly to support the efficiency and effectiveness of the organisation – prioritising workforce costs; assessing and arranging payments for urgent, planned and essential purchases
- **financial resources** – to match funding with anticipated income and expenditure – helping to arrange business loans to finance long-term projects; dealing with increases and decreases in revenue and expenses
- **contingencies** – negotiating and setting aside budgets and resources for unpredictable and unforeseen circumstances

Project Management

Management Tools for Monitoring Progress

By using management tools, the project manager can monitor progress and see when it is time to implement the next stage of delivery of the project. The example of the volunteers working at the charity dinner, the sequence might include:

- *establishing the uniform sizes needed for the new recruits*
- *giving a provisional order to the supplier* – so that they can start to prepare
- *finishing recruitment of volunteers*
- *confirming the uniform sizes that are needed and making the final order a month before the dinner* – the company needs two weeks to print and deliver the uniforms

Until the volunteer recruitment has been finalised, it is not possible to make the final uniform order. As a contingency, a few extras of the standard sizes will be ordered. By tracking all of this information using, for example, a PERT diagram or a Gantt chart, the project manager can identify critical points and make sure that everything is on track.

Examples of how management tools might be used to monitor progress in the recruitment and training of team members in the charity dinner are as follows:

Tool / Method	How this could be applied to monitoring progress
SWOT analysis	To track the strengths and weaknesses of recruitment policies compared to expected targets; to review the opportunities for finding the right people if there are issues; to review the threats to progress to make sure that they are still relevant
Work Breakdown Structures (WBS)	To monitor the job descriptions set out in the initial WBS to make sure that the right people are being selected; to monitor training programmes set out in the WBS to make sure that they are relevant and suitable
PERT diagrams	To have a visual record about how a delay in advertising vacancies has a knock-on effect on applications, interviews and training
SMART objectives	To review levels of recruitment and training against the SMART targets on a regular basis
Gantt charts	To see how the recruitment and training elements of the project are progressing in relation to all other aspects of the project, such as physical resources and finance
Plan on a Page	To prepare a quick overview for progress meetings and interim management reports
RACI matrix	To use as a guide to make sure that communication is as expected and agreed between different stakeholders – to ensure that the relevant directors and external stakeholders are being informed of progress

Project Management

Another useful tool to use when monitoring a project's progress is to show the RAG status – red, amber, green. During the planning stage, the planning team can set parameters about what the colours mean, for example:

> **Red** – *major problems that will affect the viability of the whole project and cannot be resolved by the project manager – the matter should be escalated to the project board member*
>
> **Amber** – *problems that have a negative effect on one or more aspects of the project's viability and performance – problems can be dealt with by the project manager and their team, who then notify the board about progress*
>
> **Green** – *the project is performing to plan – all problems are within tolerances and expectations and can be dealt with within normal limits of authority*

RAG can really help to keep everyone involved and motivated by letting them know how things are going. If the news is not very good, it can help to reassure everyone, so that they work harder to get back on track and understand the problems behind the problems and potential issues. If things are going well, the team and other stakeholders benefit from knowing and getting some positive praise and feedback. This lifts morale and helps to keep people motivated and focused.

There can be drawbacks to the traffic-light system; it can oversimplify a project's progress and it is very dependent on the integrity of the information that can turn an element from red to amber or green. As a visual aid, it is effective as it draws attention to the problem areas and shows when everything is on track.

Project Management

Managing Project Risks and Issues

Difference between project risks and issues

A **risk** is the probability of harm happening. It is only a 'what if' and the harm may not happen at all, especially if measures are put in place to minimise the risk of harm to the project. For example, there can be a physical risk of harm from:

- **slips, trips and falls** – due to unsafe flooring, obstructions, wires, badly-positioned equipment or other trip hazards
- **working at height** – up ladders or on scaffolds
- **cross-contamination when handling food and drink** – when staff do not wash their hands and pass on germs to customers
- **illness and injury** – from poor crowd control, excessive alcohol or excessive noise; if loose wires on machinery are not dealt with correctly

Projects are also at risk due to, for example:

- **failure of an event or task** – from insufficient planning
- **financial failure** – if revenue is too low or costs are too high
- **equipment failure** – due to inadequate maintenance
- **changes in external factors** – planning rules or employment laws; world prices; national or international political influence; weather; local community action
- **changes in internal factors** – reorganisation of premises, workforce or management structures; organisational culture

An issue that affects a project, has actually happened. It is something that is real and actually has an impact on the project. Despite every effort to minimise risk, there are some things that cannot be mitigated and they do cause issues for the project team. If any one of the identified potential risks becomes a reality, it becomes an issue that the project management team needs to address. Examples of issues that affect projects include, for example:

- **weather** – leading to cancellation or reorganisation of an event; leading to increased costs from having to use extra resources to deal with the consequences
- **inability to recruit sufficient, good-quality team members** – due to insufficient local supply or competition from other organisations
- **illness or injury to team members or others** – following an accident in the workplace
- **increased prices of supplies** – due to a change in world prices of raw materials
- **decreased revenue** – as a result of bad weather
- **political change** – changes in tax legislation

As risks and issues can both affect how a project is run, they need to be managed and tracked. The project team need to do all that they can to minimise the risks of harm to the project, and to make plans and forecasts about how they will deal with issues that do arise.
The implications of failing to mitigate risks and plan how to deal with issues can be extremely serious – from physical harm to people to the failure of the whole project or the organisation.

Project Management

Identifying and mitigating Risks
When identifying and mitigating risks, the project manager needs to:

- *identify potential hazards and risks during the planning stage*
- *create a risk log or register – and use it to mitigate risk*
- *maintain awareness of potential risks*
- *consult stakeholders to agree approaches to risk management*
- *use leadership skills to manage risks that materialise*
- *amend plans when risks have an impact on the critical path or other timelines*

Managing Project Risks
One of the most important elements of risk management is complete honesty. Without an honest approach to the risks involved there will always be unvoiced issues and these can be the biggest risks of all.

So how can you be sure that, once you have (honestly) identified your risks, that your risk management procedures are effective and add value to the project?

1. Document the risks
Create a risk log listing each risk with a description, stating who is responsible, the likely impact and the mitigating actions that could be taken. It needs enough information to be useful in monitoring and reporting on risks but not so much that it cannot be easily updated. A straightforward, up-to-date risk log will be useful during the whole life of the project.

2. Prioritise the risks
In order to prioritise effectively you need to understand what factors could make the risk more likely to occur and what impact that would have on cost, timescale and scope/quality of the final deliverable. So, prioritise the risks using a combination of a probability rating and an impact rating. Some risks may be very likely to occur but have low impact; others may be less likely to occur but have a major impact, so the overall priority needs to take this into account.

3. Plan the response
For each identified risk decide, firstly, what could be done to minimise the chance of it occurring and, secondly, what action could be taken if the risk does occur. You will then be better prepared to deal with it if you have to (any risks that could not be anticipated are, of course, another matter).

The usual options to mitigate risks that are threats (rather than opportunities) are:

- *Accept*
- *Avoid*
- *Transfer*
- *Reduce*

Project Management

Risk management can and does help ensure more successful projects and it should be an integral part of the project management process, but it should not be so large a task that the effort expended is out of all proportion to the size of the project or the potential impact of the risks. Finally, make sure the responses are implemented. Without following through on the risk reduction measures then the risk management process will add little value overall.

Managing Issues

There are a huge number of unknown variables with any project, no matter how well you plan. It would be naïve to think that a few conversations regarding potential risks at the beginning of your project will be enough to ensure that you do not encounter any hurdles or stumbling blocks along the way.

All managers from experienced leaders to project manager apprentices should expect problems to arise and should develop issues management skills which will help to deal with these issues timely and effectively in order for the project to continue.

Issues that arise during a project may be unforeseen, but they also may be from risks which had been identified during the planning phase of the project. In order to get closure on the issue and to minimise the effect the issues have on the project; you need to have your action plan kick in quickly and get the issue resolved before it grows into a serious problem.

When managing issues, the project manager needs to:

- **understand the nature of the issue** – *the reasons why recruitment of new team members is so difficult, maybe using a PESTLE analysis (to look at political, economic, social, technological, legal and environmental impacts)*
- **evaluate the scope of the issue** – *how big a problem this could be and how the recruitment problem could either ease or get worse*
- **evaluate the impact on the project** – *how the recruitment problems could cause extra work for current team members or complete failure of the whole project*

Doing a SWOT analysis as soon as an issue has been identified could be an effective activity to focus attention and aid the decision-making process. By looking at the strengths, weaknesses, opportunities and threats to progress of each possible solution, the project manager can evaluate the issue and work out how to limit or eliminate the impact of the issue. For example, a project manager still needs another 50 stewards to run an event. They normally have trained volunteer stewards. However, with only one month to go, they do not have enough people to steward the event, and there is a legal requirement to have sufficient stewards on duty whenever the public are in the venue.

All stewards need to have a full day's training if they do not hold a current Spectator Security qualification. The project manager does a SWOT analysis to help them identify the pros and cons of each option:

Project Management

	Option A – increase publicity to attract new applications from new volunteers – e.g., advertise, make public appeals, approach organisations that place volunteers	Option B – approach another organisation that has large numbers of trained volunteers who might help for this one event	Option C – employ an event company who use qualified, paid staff
Strengths	New team members add to the pool of talent for future events and projects Control over type of person selected Control over training and monitoring Low cost	Volunteers already used to work at large events Good to have relationship between organisations that can help each other out from time to time	Staff can be provided in time Identifiable costs The company's service history should indicate reliability Staff will be qualified and will know how to operate without further training Less input required from the project team as the event company will manage the 50 staff and associated resources
Weaknesses	Time taken to deal with advertising, applications, interviews and recruitment of new volunteers No guarantee that enough people can be found, recruited and trained in time Unknown numbers for uniforms and other resources until the last-minute Cost of advertising	Volunteers might not be available or willing to work with a new project team The other organisation might not want to lose its volunteers Restricted choice in the actual individuals who join the team Staff training time required	Need to rely on the event company to choose suitable individuals High costs Volunteers might resent paid staff doing the same job as them
Opportunities	Local radio is running a volunteer campaign next week One week to advertise, then two weeks to interview and recruit Training sessions for all volunteers booked in 4 weeks' time	Three or four well-known groups in the local area that could be approached Three weeks to sort out before training is due	Plenty of event companies and staff available if researched online and using trade networks Could be arranged quickly
Threats to success	Lack of time – leading to a high chance of failure, which would put the whole event at risk Other events might be competing to recruit volunteers	Lack of cooperation from others Other events might be competing to recruit volunteers	High costs might not be covered by contingency budget Other events might be competing to recruit staff for the same day

Once you have managed the issue and your plan has been actioned, you cannot simply just forget about it and move on. It is very important that you go back to the person, team or process which had been impacted to see whether your plan of action has been successful in resolving the issue. If it has been resolved, it is also important to understand the ensuing effects in case they pose a further risk to the project. Circling back and re-examining the issue

Project Management

and how you resolved it also gives you information for future risk management strategies to avoid similar events in future projects.

Following the PDCA cycle devised by J Edwards Deming can also help the project manager to focus on how to manage issues:

- **Plan** – identify the problem and root causes; collect data; set objectives; allocate resources and training
- **Do** – implement the plan and take action
- **Check** – review and measure progress against objectives; analyse strengths and weaknesses of the plan
- **Act/Adjust** – praise success; identify further improvements; communicate any changes to the people involved

The most important thing to do, though, is to act promptly when a potential or actual hazard, risk or issue is identified, and to take steps to minimise or eliminate the causes before the effects become even more serious. A combination of actions may be required that might include, for example:

- **reallocating human resources** – e.g., to cover emergencies or sickness
- **reallocating physical resources** – e.g., moving equipment to where it will be used more efficiently
- **negotiating extra funds or time** – e.g., a contingency budget or an extension on a deadline
- **asking people for help and advice** – e.g., team members, colleagues or industry contacts due to an emergency
- **escalating issues** – e.g., when decisions are outside the limits of authority, or the project is in danger of failing

Effective management of risks and issues can be a large part of your role as a project manager so your specific project management skills in this area are crucial to your career development. You will need to be able to provide customers, stakeholders and senior executives with explanations of why your project stalled, was delayed or exceeded the budget, and this will happen at some point in your career. Showing you have the right attitude to work efficiently and effectively to identify and mitigate the impact of issues and risks will demonstrate your competence as a project manager even if your project has not been entirely successful.

Reviewing Project Performance

The project manager needs to evaluate a project and look at all of the data that has been collected, so that the team can, for example:

- **compare the outcomes with the original objectives** – to see if the project has achieved its intended aims and the correct quality standards
- **understand how the project has achieved its purpose** – or why it has failed

Project Management

- *identify how the project used human resources* – to analyse the skills used and identify career development opportunities
- *identify how efficiently the project used physical resources* – comparing budget forecasts with actual costs; reviewing the levels of waste
- *identify problems and potential improvements*
- *advise stakeholders and decision-makers* – about how to repeat, develop or improve actions and plans for future projects
- *identify needs for further project work* – to set up a new project to solve major issues that were discovered when working on the first project

When evaluating a project, the data needs to be reliable and relevant to be of use. We need to consider what we want to know, and what we want to measure, to be able to identify what data we need and how we will collect it.

Organisations will have their own ways of evaluating a project, which could include, for example:

- *comparing estimated costs with actual costs* – to evaluate the budget allocations and identify the causes of variance
- *collecting and reviewing feedback from customers and other users of the services and products covered in the project* – e.g., independent surveys, feedback forms, forum comments, focus groups or satisfaction surveys
- *analysing operational data* – e.g., looking at patient records in a hospital to evaluate changes in services
- *reviewing progress reports* – e.g., final 'wash-up' reports from staff and other stakeholders about their experiences and recommendations
- *analysing sales patterns* – e.g., to see when tickets were purchased and by whom; to see if business changes have affected sales as expected
- *analysing changes in activity and comments on websites and social media* – e.g., to illustrate a change towards Internet shopping following a project on online sales

The methods selected will depend upon who needs and wants to see the evaluation of project performance. The media, for example, might only be interested in the initial financial impact of changes made by the project, whereas the organisation's HR department will be more interested in evaluating the impact on staff skills, experience, training and career development. Reviews of project performance need to be presented in ways that satisfy the needs of stakeholders.

In general, the project team's review needs to:

- *show the successes of the project*
- *praise everyone who contributed to the success*
- *identify areas of weakness and lessons that can be learned for future projects*
- *illustrate the project team's value to support bids for future projects*

Chapter 11: Delivering a Project

Project Delivery

Project Planning Process

The success of a project depends on the effort and endeavour which goes into its planning. The starting point for any project is at the point where the need for a project is first identified. This could involve a relatively minor change to the organisation of an office, to the complete upgrade of an organisations IT systems and platforms.

At some point, the need for such a project has been identified and the preliminary planning will begin. This is where the idea will be assessed and justified for implementation. This can be a chicken and egg situation as finance and practicality send to always be in conflict. Is it worth funding a second rate upgrade to keep costs low when a premium upgrade is really needed, but would cost significantly more?

As a result, a business case would need to be produced which consider the cost of the project and the practicalities of it. Once this has been produced a feasibility study can be conducted which identifies all the possible options and variations which are open to selection.

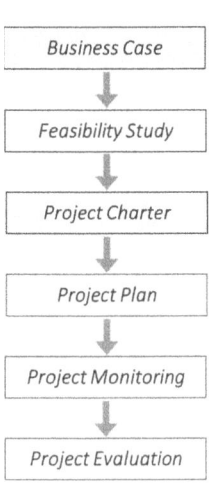

```
Business Case
      ↓
Feasibility Study
      ↓
Project Charter
      ↓
Project Plan
      ↓
Project Monitoring
      ↓
Project Evaluation
```

The Business Case

A business case is used to explain the reason for starting a project. The business case shows how the use of financial and other resources are in support of a business need.

A business case will be adaptable, fitting the size and risk of the proposal, but it will structurally be the same from project to project. It deals not in technical issues, but the business concerns of the project, and it needs to be comprehensive.

Ideally, the business case should be easy to understand, clear, logical and relevant. The key aspects need to be tracked and measured and justified. There also must be accountability and commitment for the delivery and costs involved.

The business case should include a detailed description of the problem or opportunity set out with headings such as:

- *Introduction*
- *Business Objectives*
- **Executive briefing,** which includes what the project is, what the results of that project will be and why it should be undertaken
- *Assumptions and Constraints*
- *A list of the alternative solutions available*
- *An analysis of the business benefits, costs, risks, and issues*
- *A description of the preferred solution*
- *Main project requirements*
- *A summarised plan for implementation including a schedule and financial analysis*

Project Delivery

Feasibility Study

Once the business case has been approved, the next step is taking a feasibility study, which documents potential solutions to the opportunity or business problem that the project is proposed to address. It directs you to the right way to approach the project.

A feasibility study researches the opportunity and documents what is required to complete a successful project. It will also identify any other solutions, if available. Risks and issues are outlined at this time, as well as what the proposed solution to each will be if they occur.

The Project Charter

A project will start when the sponsor (the person who has asked for the research to be done) first identifies the need for change. If the project aligns with their business objectives, they will pursue it. The next step would be to produce a cost benefit analysis to see if it is actually profitable.

A project charter outlines the purpose for the project and how it will be structured and executed. In it, the vision, objectives, scope and deliverables for the project are all detailed. Responsibilities for the project team and stakeholders are also described.

A project charter helps to identify the project vision and objectives clearly. It defines the scope of the project and lists all the deliverables.

The project charter will also list the roles and responsibilities of the project team and identify the project's customers and stakeholders. It is at this point that the project is organised structurally, documenting the project plan and listing all risks, issues and assumptions.

This is sometimes called the "Project Definition Document." It gives the project manager the authority to direct and complete the project.

A concise project charter will include the following details:

- *The appointed project manager*
- *A definition of the project scope*
- *The budget*
- *The defined milestones*
- *A list of the important / key stakeholders*
- *The technical characteristics of the project deliverable*

Project Delivery

Project Plan

A project plan is used to plan a project from its initial stages through to its planned conclusion. It is produced by the project manager who will have spent a great deal of time ensuring every detail and element of it is correct and they will use their expertise and judgement to do this.

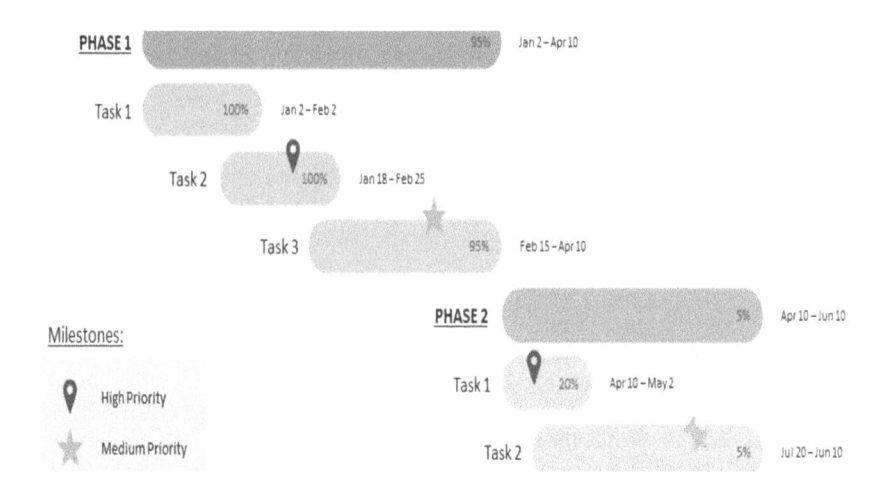

PHASE 1 — 95% — Jan 2 – Apr 10
- Task 1 — 100% — Jan 2 – Feb 2
- Task 2 — 100% — Jan 18 – Feb 25
- Task 3 — 95% — Feb 15 – Apr 10

Milestones:
- High Priority
- Medium Priority

PHASE 2 — 5% — Apr 10 – Jun 10
- Task 1 — 20% — Apr 10 – May 2
- Task 2 — 5% — Jul 20 – Jun 10

The project plan is not one single document but rather a compound document made up of a number of other documents each of which have a specific role and purpose.

Every project is unique in what it addresses, the scope, scale, value, etc. which means there cannot be a single, standard, document which can be created and tailored to suit each project, however, there are some specific elements which should be included in every project plan. This will help to avoid confusion and forced changes during the project execution phase.

Project Plan
The Project Charter
Project Goals
Project Scope
Milestones and Major Deliverables
Work Breakdown Structure
Budget
Human Resources Plan
Risk Register
Communications Plan
Stakeholder Management Plan
Change Management Plan
Timeline

Project Delivery

Project Goals

Project goals are defined in the project charter, but they should be included in the project plan as well to explain the goals of the project or be included the charter as an appendix to the plan.

No matter how a project manager chooses to incorporate the goals into the project plan, the important thing is to maintain a clear link between the project charter—a project is first key document—and the project's second key document, its project plan.

> *A project goal is a tangible statement of what a project should achieve.*

The project goal defines the questions that will be asked at the end of the project. What has the project accomplished? That is the project goal.

Examples:

- Improve employee satisfaction by introducing flexible working hours.
- Introduce mobile devices for sales staff to reduce average order time and increase customer satisfaction.
- Upgrade network infrastructure to increase bandwidth and eliminate network outages.

A project goal should be tied to a higher purpose.

Example:

- increase sales
- cut cost
- increase profitability
- increase safety
- protect the health of people

This is where the goal can be linked to the Mission, Value and Goals of the organisation. If the goal is not tied to these, it may just end up as another wreck at the bottom of the sea. Simply because it did not bring the results it was supposed to deliver.

Project Goals		
Importance:	Goal	Ownership
1.	Build a new warehouse in the Northern region to better serve our customers in the Borders and Scotland.	Project Team

Project Delivery

Project Scope

Like the project goals, the scope of the project is defined in the charter and should be further developed and refined in the project plan. By defining the scope, the project manager can begin to show what the project's goal or finished product will look like at the end. If the scope is not defined, it can get expanded throughout the project and lead to cost overruns and missed deadlines.

Example:

> *if you are leading a marketing team to create a brochure for a company's product line, you should define how many pages it will be and provide examples of how the finished product might look.*

For some team members, a corporate brochure might mean two pages, while others might consider ten pages to be more appropriate. Defining the scope can get the entire team on the same page at the outset.

This should be written as a definitive of statement of what the project will achieve and what it will not achieve. It should be written in a style which can be understood by all – it should not assume and prior technical knowledge.

Project Scope
What is included:
What is Not included:

Project Delivery

Milestones and Major Deliverables

The key stages in a project are called milestones and the work which is achieved at these key stages is called a major deliverable. They both represent the big components of work on a project. A project plan should identify these items, define them, and set deadlines for their completion.

If you were building a house, a key stage is when the roof is completed. So, the completed roof would be a major deliverable. This would be identified in the project plan, stating when it must be delivered (completed) by.

Following those, the project could have milestones for internal completion, electrical testing, client acceptance testing, and the date for the handover of the keys. These milestones have work products associated with them, but they are more about the processes than the products themselves.

Milestone and major deliverable deadlines do not have to be exact dates, but the more precise, the better. Precise dates help project managers break down work structures more accurately.

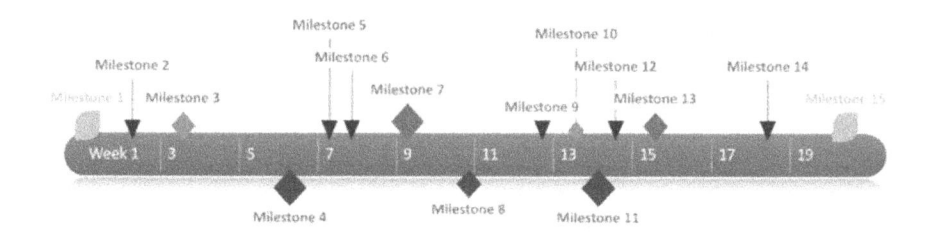

Milestones and Major Deliverables		
Week	Milestone	Description
1	1	Formation Meeting
1	2	Planning application submission

Typical Milestones in a Project

Project Approval

While not as commonly noted as other project milestone examples, the first milestone in the course of any project is the initial approval that allows the project to move forward.

For internal projects, this milestone often comes in the form of an approval from a department director or other high-level stakeholder. For other projects, this milestone is usually marked by the completion of a sales contract and scope of work. Once the project

Project Delivery

is approved, project managers begin inputting elements of the project into their chosen project management tool.

Requirements Review *(Major projects)*
Most enterprise projects involve a lengthy process in which the project requirements are defined and gathered through a series of meetings, review sessions, and document exchanges. The project team then typically interprets and consolidates their notes and presents the client with a detailed description of the requirements as they understand them.

When the client or customer agrees that the requirements are accurately documented, another major project milestone has been reached.

Design Approval *(Major projects)*
After gathering the customer's requirements, a project team needs to design a solution that will meet the requirements and fulfil the terms of the scope of work. When the initial design is complete (which often takes months or even years for large projects), the customer needs to review the proposed solution and confirm that it will satisfy the project objectives.

This design approval is a significant milestone for projects in fields as diverse as software, construction and marketing, just to name a few.

Project Phase Milestones
Once the project team begins to actually build or implement the proposed solution, the project manager will typically define project-specific milestones related to the components of the work being done.

In a construction project, for example, the project manager might need to mark milestones (and arrange milestone payments) for the completion of phases such as framing, concrete pouring, plumbing installation and interior finishing.

Final Approval
The most significant of all project management milestones, of course, is the one that marks the completion of a project. This milestone typically comes at the end of an extensive testing and inspection process, and a final review session in which all stakeholders agree that the work is complete and meets the project requirements.

Upon reaching this milestone, successful project managers typically hold a follow-up meeting with the team to discuss what worked, what could have been better and how to work even more efficiently and effectively on the next project.

Project Delivery

Work Breakdown Structure

A work breakdown structure (WBS) breaks down the milestones and major deliverables in a project into smaller chunks so one person can be assigned responsibility for each chunk or element. In developing the work breakdown structure, the project manager will consider many factors such as the strengths and weaknesses of project team members, the interdependencies among tasks, available resources, and the overall project deadline.

Work Breakdown Structure is defined as a:

> *"Deliverable oriented hierarchical decomposition of the work to be executed by the project team."*

Project managers are ultimately responsible for the success of the project, but they cannot do the work alone. The WBS is a tool the project manager uses to ensure accountability on the project because it tells the project sponsor, project team members, and stakeholders who are responsible for what. If the project manager is concerned about a task, they know exactly who to meet with regarding that concern.

The WBS is a hierarchical reflection of all the work in the project in terms of deliverables. In order to produce these deliverables, work must be performed.

A typical approach in developing a WBS is to start at the highest level, with the product of the project. For example, you are assigned as the project manager of a New Product Development project. The new product you are developing is a new toy for children. The objective of this product development project is to increase the revenue of the organisation by ten percent.

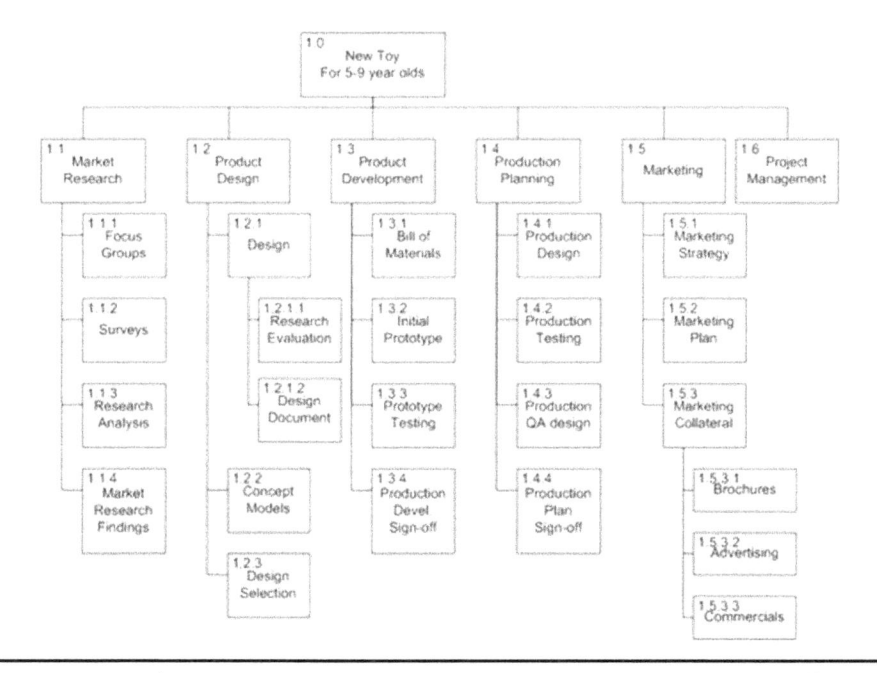

```
                              1.0
                           New Toy
                        For 5-9 year olds
   ┌──────┬──────────┬──────────┬──────────┬──────────┬──────────┐
  1.1     1.2        1.3        1.4        1.5        1.6
 Market  Product    Product   Production Marketing  Project
Research Design   Development  Planning            Management

 1.1.1   1.2.1      1.3.1      1.4.1      1.5.1
 Focus   Design    Bill of   Production Marketing
 Groups           Materials    Design    Strategy

 1.1.2   1.2.1.1    1.3.2      1.4.2      1.5.2
Surveys Research   Initial   Production Marketing
        Evaluation Prototype   Testing     Plan

 1.1.3   1.2.1.2    1.3.3      1.4.3      1.5.3
Research  Design  Prototype  Production Marketing
Analysis Document  Testing   QA design  Collateral

 1.1.4   1.2.2      1.3.4      1.4.4      1.5.3.1
 Market  Concept  Production Production  Brochures
Research Models    Devel       Plan
Findings          Sign-off    Sign-off    1.5.3.2
                                         Advertising
         1.2.3
         Design                           1.5.3.3
        Selection                        Commercials
```

Project Delivery

Above is an example of a WBS for this new toy. Each level of the WBS is a level of detail created by decomposition. Decomposition is the process of breaking down the work into smaller, more manageable components. The elements at the lowest level of the WBS are called tasks. In the example above, brochures, advertising and commercials are all work packages or tasks.

The decomposition of a schedule will continue at varying rates. 'Brochures' is a task identified at the fourth level of decomposition, while the 'marketing plan' is also a task but defined at the third level of decomposition.

As a project manager, the level of decomposition will be dependent on the extent to which you will need to manage. The expectation is that each task will have a single owner and the owner is expected to manage and report on the work necessary to deliver the task. This person is called the 'task owner.' If you cannot assign a single owner, or you need to have additional visibility into the progress of that task, additional decomposition is recommended.

Work Package	WBSID	Activity	Predecessor	Duration in Weeks	Resource Type
Focus Group	1.1.1.1	Identify Focus Group Targets			
Focus Group	1.1.1.2	Prepare Focus Group Objectives			
Focus Group	1.1.1.3	Perform Focus Group			
Surveys	1.1.2	Perform Survey			
Research Analysis	1.1.3	Perform Analysis			
Market Research Findings	1.1.4	Create Market Research Findings			
Research Evaluation	1.2.1.1.1	Review Market Research Findings			
Research Evaluation	1.2.1.1.2	Develop Design Options			
Research Evaluation	1.2.1.1.3	Present Design Options			
Design Document	1.2.1.2.1	Draft Design Document			
Design Document	1.2.1.2.2	Design Document Review			
Design Document	1.2.1.2.3	Final Design Document			
Concept Models	1.2.2	Develop Concept Model			
Design Selection	1.2.3	Review Concepts			
Bill of Materials	1.3.1	Create Initial Bill of Materials			
Initial Prototype	1.3.2.1	Develop Initial Prototype			
Initial Prototype	1.3.2.2	Revise Initial Prototype			
Prototype Testing	1.3.3	Test Prototype			
Production Design	1.4.1	Design Production Process			
Production Testing	1.4.2	Design Production Testing Process			
Production QA design	1.4.3	Design Quality Assurance Tests			
Marketing Strategy	1.5.1	Develop Marketing Strategy			
Marketing Plan	1.5.2.1	Develop Initial Marketing Plan			
Marketing Plan	1.5.2.2	Final Marketing Plan			
Brochures	1.5.3.1	Create Brochures			
Advertising	1.5.3.2	Create Ads			
Commercials	1.5.3.3	Create Commercials			
Production Plan Sign-off	1.4.4	Production Plan Sign-off			
Production Devel. Sign-off	1.3.4	Production Devel. Sign-off			
Project Management	1.6	Project Management Activities		LOE	

Once all the deliverables of the project have been identified, tasks will be performed in order to create the deliverables. In some cases, these activities are the physical deliverables, but in other cases they are the actions that need to be performed. A physical deliverable, for example, might be an image (an actual file) that is needed for the brochure. Listing out each of the tasks to be performed will result in an activity list as demonstrated below.

Budget

Project Delivery

Project budget management is a process of formally identifying, approving and paying the costs or expenses incurred on the project. Project budget management involves using purchase order forms to state each set of project expenses, such as training, consulting services, equipment and material cost, etc. Usually in the process, the project manager plays the role of "Approver" (a person who approves a budget for a project) and the finance unit (e.g., Finance Department) acts as a "Recorder" (an organisational unit that tracks and audits budgeting activities and reports to the project manager).

		Project Budget					
		Salaries and Wages		Cost		Materials and Equipment	
WBS ID.	Work Element	Rate - £/hr	Hours	Budget	Actual	Amount	Cost
1.1.1.1	Identify focus group targets	£25.75	6	£154.50			

Budgeting Process

The process of determining budget for a project is an activity of combining the cost estimates of individual activities, or a work package, to develop the total cost estimate that allows setting a formal minimum cost for that work package.

This minimum cost figure may differ from the figure which is finally recorded as the Project Manager may decide to add money into the minimum cost in case there are changes to the planned prices or the project hits a problem and is delayed. These are known as contingencies. This will be repeated for each work package until all the planned activities have been identified and funded. These values will then be used as a way to control the budget and provide valuable data to the project resource management process.

The project budgeting process is conducted at the initial steps of project planning, and typically it is performed in parallel with the project scheduling process. The steps of the process are highly dependent upon the cost estimations, task durations and allocated resources. The process is also known as "the project budgeting process". The budgeting serves as a cost control mechanism that allows comparing actual project costs to the items of the authorised project budget. The process allows developing a budget considering key cost factors associated with time durations of project tasks.

When working on the project budgeting activities, the project manager should collaborate with people responsible for managing the work efforts as well as for estimating project costs (the cost estimating team). They will develop and give the cost estimates of individual activities, or work packages, so that the project manager can actually start performing budgeting activities.

Project Delivery

The project manager should use the Work Break Down Structure (WBS) of the project, the cost estimates, historical data and records, resource information, and policies in order to identify the monetary resources required for the project.

Budgeting and Risk Management

The budgeting process will not be complete and effective if no risk assessment and assignment have been applied. Without assessing risks surrounding the project, uncertainties and threats that happen regularly during the project implementation will affect the project's bottom line. Cost estimates should be developed with reference to conducted risk assessing activities but identified risks should not be considered a factor influencing the increase in the overall price of the budget. Risk assessing activities allow representing risks as actual costs incurred over the course of project development. Usually, risk assessments cover such areas as development team experience, reliability of the technology used, time shortages, availability of project resources, etc.

Once analysed, a scope and percentage can be assigned to each identified risk.

Human Resources Plan

The human resources plan shows how the project will be staffed. Sometimes known as the staffing plan, the HR plan defines who will be on the project team and how much of a time commitment each person is expected to make. In developing this plan, the project manager negotiates with team members and their supervisors on how much time each team member can devote to the project. If additional staff are needed to consult on the project, but are part of the project team, that is also documented in the HR plan. Appropriate supervisors are consulted, as necessary.

	Project Manager	Design Engineers	Implementation Manager	Training Leads	Functional Managers	Department Managers
Requirements Gathering	A	R	R	C	C	I
Coding Design	A	R	C		C	I
Coding Input	A	R				
Software Testing	A	R	C		I	I
Network Preparation	A	C	R		I	I
Implementation	A	C	R	C	C	C
Conduct Training	A			R	C	C

Key:
R – Responsible for completing the work
A – Accountable for ensuring task completion/sign off
C – Consulted before any decisions are made
I – Informed of when an action/decision has

Project Delivery

Risk Register

Many things can go wrong on a project. While anticipating every possible disaster or minor hiccup is challenging, many pitfalls can be predicted. In the risk management plan, the project manager identifies risks to the project, the likelihood those scenarios will happen, and strategies to mitigate them. To formulate this plan, the project manager seeks input from the project sponsor, project team, stakeholders, and internal experts.

Mitigation strategies are put into place for risks that are likely to occur or have high costs associated with them. Risks that are unlikely to occur and ones that have low costs are noted in the plan, even though they do not have mitigation strategies.

A risk register is used to identify potential risks in a project or an organisation, sometimes to fulfil regulatory compliance but mostly to stay on top of potential issues that can derail intended outcomes. The risk register includes all information about each identified risk, such as the nature of that risk, level of risk, who owns it and what are the mitigation measures in place to respond to it.

A risk assessment needs to be performed for each aspect of the project, and these are kept together in a risk log.

Organisations can use a RAID log for their projects:

- **Risks** – *events that will have an adverse effect on the project*
- **Assumptions** – *factors that are assumed to be in place*
- **Issues** – *something that is going wrong on the project and needs managing*
- **Dependencies** – *events or work that are dependent on the result of the project, or things on which the project will be dependent*

Risks can be defined in many ways – e.g., financial risk when investing or borrowing money; reputation when making decisions that affect the organisation's image and good name; weather or other external influences; health and safety.

According to the Health and Safety Executive, there are five main steps to risk assessment. Many organisations use these as guidelines when designing and implementing their own risk assessments:

- *Identify the hazards*
- *Decide who might be harmed, and how*
- *Evaluate the risks and decide on precautions*
- *Record findings and implement them*
- *Review the assessment and update as necessary*

These risk assessment guidelines can be modified to apply to any type of risk as they help everyone to see and understand the potential hazards, and to take steps to reduce the chance of harm by having control measures in place.

A risk management log could include columns such as:

Project Delivery

- **risk impact** – high, medium or low
- **probability of occurrence** – high, medium or low
- **risk descriptions**
- **project impact** – timescales or resources that may be affected
- **risk area** – budget, resources or schedule
- **symptoms** – human resources are not fully decided when a project is about to start
- **triggers** – 24 hours before bad weather is inevitable, contingency plans to cancel will come into effect
- **risk response** – mitigation
- **response strategy** – allocate extra resources, reschedule or cancel
- **contingency plan** – bring in qualified agency staff to cover short term

			Risk Register						
Index	WBS	Category	Description	Effects	Probability	Impact	Risk Rank	Owner	Response Plan
001	3.2.4	Scope	Implementation depends on completion of 2.4.3	Delay	7	10	70	D Smith	Monitor closely
002									

Communications Plan

A communications plan outlines how a project will be communicated to various audiences. Much like the work breakdown structure, a communications plan assigns responsibility for completing each component to a project team member.

In this step, it is important to outline how issues will be communicated and resolved within the team and how often communication will be opened to the team and the stakeholders or the boss. Each message has an intended audience. A communications plan helps project managers ensure the right information gets to the right people at the right time.

Communications Plan	
Project:	Project Renew
Summary:	Redesign Website to support new brand image
Communication Goals:	
Keep Stakeholders informed of project timeline, budget and project needs	
Provide a clear insight into any decision's needed or roadblocks	
Provide structured opportunities for feedback from stakeholders	
Give to stakeholders as needed to gain acceptance of the project	

Project Delivery

Stakeholder Information					
Person	Role Title	Frequency	Format / Channel	Notes
Dave Smith	Assistant CEO	Major Milestones	High Level budget by email	Prefers audited and approved files
Joan Greaves	HR Lead	Weekly	Weekly F2F meeting & emails	Must authorise additional labour

Stakeholder Management Plan

A stakeholder management plan identifies how stakeholders will be used in the project. Sometimes stakeholders only need to receive information. That can be taken care of in the communications plan. If more is needed from stakeholders, a stakeholder management plan outlines how it will be obtained.

Because of how much power Stakeholders wield, the project manager needs to balance the requirements from key stakeholders with finesse.

What are their primary goals with this project? What are they hoping to invest? The more you can tease out what each of their goals and requirements are from the outset, the better.

Because there are many different types of stakeholders, you will want a well-rounded stakeholder management plan.

Stakeholder Register						
Name	Title	Role	Power	Interest	Requirement	Concern
R Jones	Accountant	Sponsor	H	H	Maintain strict budget controls	Expenses only received monthly
M. Shah	Programmer	Team	L	H	Complete stage 14 by planned date	Network Issues

List the Stakeholders
Internal stakeholders are easy to identify. They are typically those within the organisation that have a key interest in the completion of a project. They are usually department heads, such as heads of Marketing, IT, Development, Operations and more. These stakeholders can affect the project either directly or indirectly by influencing the direction of their department on the given project.

Project Delivery

External stakeholders are not typically part of the organisation itself but are made up of investors, users/customers, the media, neighbouring businesses or governmental oversight authorities.

Prioritise the Stakeholders
Prioritise which stakeholders are going to have a bigger influence over the project and note at which stage their influence becomes lesser or greater.

Start by considering how to manage the stakeholders on your project, and then start prioritising their demands and goals. Understand that those priorities can flex at different project points. For example, at certain points, say, during a website design project, the stakeholder with a special interest in the design will have their goals prioritised. Then, as you move into the development phase, the stakeholders with a special interest in development will have their goals elevated over design.

Interview the Stakeholders
Working with new stakeholders can be tricky at the start—some are easier to manage than others. Depending on the type of project, there will either be many voices from outside the company with different personalities and demands, or many voices inside the company with competing goals.

Try to get a solid understanding of whether or not the stakeholders feel positively or negatively about the project, and at what stages their perspectives might shift. Also, identify which ones have a stronger set of views and which ones are more flexible and open to compromise. This will help to mitigate any possible stop gaps down the road.

Develop a Matrix
A quick mock-up of a quadrant to sort the findings will help easily distinguish those with high interest, high priority versus low interest, low priority. It will also help to sort all those in between.

For example, those with a high interest but a low priority are typically the best confidants. They are ready to get work done and will cheerlead the project on. Those with low interest and high priority might be the squeakiest wheels—keep the lines of communication open with them but keep a firm boundary so as to not spend all the time focusing on them.

They say the squeaky wheel gets the grease, so remember that even those in the low priority, low interest or high priority, low interest still need to be continually communicated with to ensure that their voices are heard throughout the project.

Set & Manage Expectations
Once the matrix is outlined and priorities and interests have been identified, create the project plan. Clearly identify which stages each key stakeholder will be involved in, and timelines by which their feedback is needed.

Include a schedule of office hours for them to easily make contact so that they can have time to provide feedback either in a private setting or in a group. As always, be realistic, transparent and honest at every project phase—the stakeholders can tell and will be thankful for it.

Project Delivery

Risks of not having a Stakeholder Management Plan
Since stakeholders usually involve multiple key contacts across many different avenues, it is important to communicate with them effectively and efficiently. Not having interviewed them ahead of time or gauging their priority or interest, could mean spending a great deal of time trying to validate the requirements of a stakeholder with low priority and low interest, leaving those with a high priority feeling frustrated at the process.

Project Delivery

Project Change Management Plan

A change management plan lays out a framework for making changes to the project. (This should not be confused with the Change management in a Human Resources context which may run in parallel to the project itself) . Although project managers tend to want to avoid changes to the project, they are sometimes unavoidable. The change management plan provides protocols and processes for making changes. It is critical for accountability and transparency that project sponsors, project managers, and project team members follow the change management plan.

There are several steps involved in writing a change management plan.

Demonstrate the reasons for the change.
Make sure that the reasons for the change effort are clearly defined. When stakeholders have a clear understanding of why the change is needed and how it will improve business or the way they work, they are more likely to support rather than resist the change.

Determine the scope
The next step in writing the change management plan is determining who the change will affect. Also determine what the change will impact, including policies, processes, job roles, and organisational structure.

Identify stakeholders
In large projects a change management team may be created to deal with changes to the project in smaller projects it will be the role of the Project Manager. The composition of this team is extremely important and it must be led by a credible leader. The change management team interacts with stakeholders, addresses concerns, and oversees a smooth change transition. Roles within the team require clear definition, including outlining each member's responsibilities.

Clarify the expected benefits
These benefits should be clearly delineated so that everyone involved understands the advantages of proceeding with the change.

Establishing well-communicated and achievable milestones are vital to the success of any change plan. These milestones become symbols to employees that the plan is working, progress is happening, the direction is still right, and the effort is worth it."

Create a change management communication plan.
There are three basic elements to communications in the context of change management.

- *Identify the stakeholders and those impacted by the change.*
- *Schedule regular face to face interactions and email communications to keep stakeholders updated on progress.*
- *Communications should be consistent, thorough, and regular. Communications should also clearly explain the change, define the reasons for change, present the benefits of the change, and always include change owner's contact information*

Project Delivery

Project Monitoring

Project monitoring is a crucial element of all project management plans.

It refers to the process of keeping track of all project-related metrics including team performance and task duration, identifying potential problems and taking corrective actions necessary to ensure that the project is within scope, on budget and meets the specified deadlines. Without it, you cannot see where or why projects fail. It essentially comes down to keeping tabs on all project-related measurements, proactively recognising possible problems and taking the necessary steps to guarantee the project is completed on budget, on time and in scope.

The process of project monitoring begins during the planning phase of the project. During this phase, it is important to define how the project success will look like and how the goals can be measured using KPIs (Key performance indicators).

Project monitoring exists to make sure you are implementing a project as competently as possible. It should always be a cohesive and constant part of project management, and vital decisions should never be made without it. The project management lifecycle has five phases: initiating, planning, executing, monitoring, and closing.

During the initiating & planning phase, the project receives the necessary approvals, a plan has been created, and the work actually begins on the tasks. The executing phase and the monitoring phase happen concurrently. This means that you are monitoring your progress while you are completing tasks.

Executing and monitoring of projects happen concurrently.

Once the project plan is finalised and approved, the project manager monitors the progress making sure that the tasks are completed accordingly.
It is vital to monitor projects diligently and use the data you gathered both before and during the project to come up with intelligent decisions. Here are some questions answered through project monitoring:

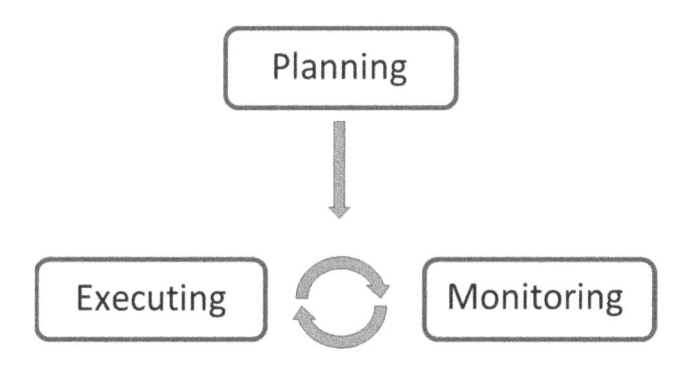

```
            ┌──────────┐
            │ Planning │
            └──────────┘
                 │
                 ▼
┌──────────┐   ↻    ┌────────────┐
│ Executing│        │ Monitoring │
└──────────┘        └────────────┘
```

Project Delivery

- *Are tasks being carried out as planned?*
- *Are there any unforeseen consequences that arise as a result of these tasks?*
- *How is your team performing at a given period of time?*
- *What are the elements of the project that needs changing?*
- *What is the impact of these changes?*
- *Will these actions lead you to your expected results?*

Project Monitoring can be attained via:

- *Staff Meetings, which can be conducted on a Weekly, Monthly or an Annual basis.*
- *Partner's meeting, Learning forums (FGD, Surveys) or Retreats.*
- *Participatory reviews by the stakeholders*
- *Monitoring and Supervision Missions that can be Self, Donor or Joint.*
- *Statistics or Progress reports*

Project monitoring aids various purposes. It brings out the problems which occur, or which might occur during the implementation of the project and which demands solutions for smoother progress in the project. Effective monitoring helps in knowing if the intended results are being achieved as planned, what actions are needed to achieve the intended results during the project execution, and whether these initiatives are creating a positive impact towards the project execution.

- **To assess the project results:** *To know how the objectives are being met and the desired changes are being met.*
- **To improve process planning:** *It helps in adapting to better contextual and risk factors which affect the research process, like social and power dynamics.*
- **To promote learning:** *It will help you learn how various approaches to participation influences the outcomes.*
- **To understand stakeholder's perspectives:** *Through direct participation in the process of monitoring and evaluation, learn about the people who are involved in the research project. Understand their values and views, as well as design methods to resolve conflicting views and interests.*
- **To ensure accountability:** *To assess if the project has been effectively, appropriately and efficiently executed, so that they can be held accountable.*

Project Delivery

Project Control

Project control is a "project management function that involves comparing actual performance with planned performance and taking appropriate corrective action (or directing others to take this action) that will yield the desired outcome in the project when significant differences exist."

Essentially, project controls are a series of tools that help keep a project on schedule. Combined with people skills and project experience, they deliver information that enables accurate decision making.

The project control process mainly focuses on:

- *Measuring planned performance vs actual performance.*
- *Ongoing assessment of the project's performance to identify any preventive or corrective actions needed.*
- *Keeping accurate, timely information based on the project's output and associated documentation.*
- *Providing information that supports status updates, forecasting and measuring progress.*
- *Delivering forecasts that update current costs and project schedule.*
- *Monitoring the implementation of any approved changes or schedule amendments.*

Monitoring and control keep projects on track. The right controls can play a major part in completing projects on time. The data gathered also lets project managers make informed decisions. They can take advantage of opportunities, make changes and avoid crisis management issues.

Put simply, monitoring and control ensures the seamless execution of tasks. This improves productivity and efficiency.

Implementing Project Monitoring and Control

Monitoring and control processes continually track, review, adjust and report on the project's performance. It is important to find out how a project's performing and whether it is on time, as well as implement approved changes. This ensures the project remains on track, on budget and on time.

On the surface this sounds simple enough, until one stops to think about the depth and breadth of the monitoring and controlling activities described throughout the PMBOK® Guide, which include:

- *Comparing planned results with actual results*
- *Reporting performance*
- *Determining if action is needed, and what the right action is*

Project Delivery

- *Ensuring deliverables are correct based on the previously approved definitions and/or requirements*
- *Acquiring sign-off on deliverables by authorised stakeholders*
- *Assessing the overall project performance*
- *Managing risks*
- *Managing contracts and vendors*

In other words, project managers use the monitoring and controlling processes to translate project execution data from information into knowledge. This knowledge is then used to make the right management decisions and to take the right actions at the right time. Generally speaking, project managers face two choices in most situations:

- *Recommend the implementation of appropriate changes, which are planned and approved by the change management process*
    or
- *Allow the project to function "as is"*

Project Delivery

Evaluating a Project

Evaluating a project means performing a rigorous analysis of completed goals, objectives and activities to determine whether the project has produced the planned results, delivered the expected benefits, and made the desired change.

Evaluation can be a simple, do-it-yourself process, or a full-scale, professional study. The choice of how to evaluate a project or program is usually determined by:

- **The scope of the project:** *A tiny one-day event does not warrant big-time evaluation.*
- **The funding source:** *Some sources, particularly large organisations, will tell you what kind of evaluation they want to see.*
- **Your needs:** *Do you need to prove a concept? Show outcomes to raise money? Or just satisfy your curiosity?*
- **Your resources:** *Do you employ someone who could evaluate the project, or the money to hire someone out of house?*

Most project evaluations, however, are do it yourself exercises that require some careful planning and thinking.

Evaluation can help you to:

- *learn from the experience*
- *record what has been learnt, and share it with other stakeholders*
- *check progress*
- *check whether what is happening is still what the organisation wants or needs*
- *identify strengths and weaknesses in the project*
- *create a basis for future planning*
- *demonstrate whether you have used the resources – time and money – effectively*
- *explain to funders, and others involved in the project, what you have achieved and how successful it is*

Measuring the success of projects and learning from failed projects can make a big impact on small businesses. Companies that employ successful project management create confidence in their staff and their customers.

As a process, project evaluation takes a series of steps to identify and measure the outcomes and impacts resulted from project completion When evaluating a project, it is important to make the evaluation complete and honest. Ask multiple stakeholders -- employees, management and customers -- to evaluate each project, and review the results with the project manager.

When starting, monitoring and evaluating a project, there are three over-arching questions at the start, middle and end of the project:

Project Delivery

1. What happened?
2. Why? (the story behind what happened)
3. Why do these results matter and what is next?

As a process, project evaluation takes a series of steps to identify and measure the outcomes and impacts resulted from project completion.

Project Management Success Criteria

These are only three criteria that pertain to the project itself and its accomplishment. They help measure the internal efficiency of the organisation to deliver projects. These are:

- *Project is completed on time*
- *Project is completed within budget*
- *Project meets quality targets*

More criteria can be added such as:

- *Project includes all items within scope*
- *Project satisfies commercial objectives in terms of revenue and profit*

Or criteria about different stakeholders:

- *Project team satisfaction*
- *End-user satisfaction*
- *Supplier satisfaction*

Success Indicators

The project evaluation process involves an analysis of different components or indicators that characterise se the project's progress towards the achievement of its goals and objectives. These components/indicators are Outcomes and Impacts.

Outcomes
These are any measurable and auditable changes that can be obtained as a result of the project's successful accomplishment. They determine the extent to which the identified problems have been mitigated, resolved, or eliminated.

In terms of project evaluation and management, outcomes define the measurable results and benefits that are observable within the targeted environment once the project is done. They serve as the general indicator of project progress towards successful implementation of project goals and objectives.

Project Delivery

Outcomes describe short-term and medium-term effects generated by the project. Several examples of project outcomes are:

- *New skills and competencies obtained by personnel*
- *Improved knowledge*
- *Increased understanding of business environment*
- *Proactive participation in decision making*

Impacts

These are the indicator of changes that can be specifically linked to the project's implementation activity. Impacts determine and measure the extent to which goals and objectives of the project are achieved.

In terms of project evaluation and management, impacts define the tangible and intangible effects (consequences) of the project upon the environment in which this project is implemented. They measure the change made by the project and show how close the goals and objectives are achieved.

Some examples of project impacts are as follows:

- *Increased quality of a product/service*
- *Decreased incidence of diseases in the targeted region*
- *Higher number of students wishing to obtain master's degree*
- *Enhanced productivity of personnel*

The key difference between impacts and outcomes is that impacts produce a long-term, lasting effect that is observable for months and years after project completion.

Evaluation Criteria

The criteria to be evaluated are exactly the same as those monitored during the project. The reason for this is anything being evaluated at the end of the project should also be assessed during the project's life cycle, or the targets set may not be achieved.

1. Schedule

Project management success is often determined by whether or not it kept to the original timeline. Experienced project managers know how hard that is, but it is a little bit easier if you continually monitor the progress as you go. Measure the success of the schedule against the initial Gantt chart in the project plan. Look at the major milestones and check if they fell on the same dates. Work out the slippage, if any, and assess the impact of this on the project as a whole

2. Quality

At the end of a project phase is a good time for a quality review. You can check both the quality of your project management practices – has the change management process been followed every time and have the deliverables been achieved

Project Delivery

3. Cost
Many executives would rate cost management as one of their highest priorities on a project, so evaluating how you the project has performed financially is crucial. Compare actual spend to the budgeted. If there are variances, look to explain them.

4. Stakeholder Satisfaction
The wider team – the stakeholders – are essential in getting much of the work done, so it is worth finding out how they feel about the project.

This is difficult measure to document statistically, although there is nothing to prevent them from giving a rating out of 10. Even if the evaluation of satisfaction is subjective, it is still a useful exercise.

5. Performance to Business Case
Finally, evaluate what you have achieved with what was originally agreed. Check that the planned benefits have been delivered. Sometimes project teams work on initiatives that sound great but by the time they are finished the business environment has moved on and the project is redundant. If no one bothered to check the business case during the project's life cycle - no one would have realised that the work was no longer needed.

Evaluation Tools

Tools come in two groups; the best known are quantitative tools, which measure how many, how much, how big, and so forth. Qualitative tools allow evaluators to measure intangible things like awareness, attitude, and appreciation.

In some cases, quantitative tools are all you need, because your project has simple, measurable goals. Typically, these are the straightforward projects that aim to lower or increase something easily measured. For example: increase grades; decrease addiction; increase employment; decrease homelessness. Did it work? To find out, just measure rates within your target audience before and after your program was implemented. Quantitative tools include basic, well known methods such as:

- **Head count:** How many people attended?
- **Testing:** Pre and post tests to see how many more correct answers attendees could get after participating in your program.
- **Data analysis:** What percent of people who attended your program graduated, increased grades, became employed, etc.
- **Comparison:** How many came to the events before your outreach project; how many came after your outreach project.

More interesting and complex are qualitative evaluations which look at intangible outcomes such as attitude, awareness, and so forth. These measures are used to evaluate projects with goals like "participants will appreciate the importance of textiles as a tool for exploring culture and history" or "participants will become more fully aware of the importance of diet and exercise in maintaining good health."

Project Delivery

While it may seem impossible to actually measure such intangible outcomes, there are tools for doing just that kind of evaluation. You have probably used or at least heard of all of them. They include:

Surveys
Typically, surveys are carefully crafted tools that allow you to take the pulse of a group of people before the start of a project, and then again after the project is completed. Surveys can measure almost anything, from prior and post knowledge of content you are teaching to attitudes, preferences, achievements, self-esteem... you name it. When you survey your intended audience, you are setting the bar for success. If your post-program survey shows improvement, you have done what you set out to do. Surveys can be conducted in one of several ways: electronically (using online systems like SurveyMonkey), with paper and pencil, or through a person-to-person interview. Electronic surveys offer the great benefit of being easy to distribute and easy to tabulate, but users may share limited information. Paper and pencil surveys are a good way to start a program that requires participants to show up, sit down, and engage in a classroom like situation. Interviews are versatile and flexible and may gather a good deal of information – but they are time consuming and expensive.

Observation
How do you know that youngsters are more interested in fine art after a workshop than they were before the workshop? One way to find out is to observe the group prior to and after the workshop. Using a stopwatch, you can compare the amount of time they spend in front of individual works. Listening to conversation, you can hear which words they use to discuss and describe the art. You can also note body language: are they zipping past the works? Stopping to look? Pointing and discussing? All of these observations are data points to help you assess outcomes.

Case Studies
Your non-profit is running a program that prepares unemployed individuals for job placement by crafting resumes, building interview skills, honing business skills, and providing career-appropriate clothing. Each week, dozens of people go through the program. You know that X number are getting jobs – but you do not really know which part of your program is most useful, or how clients feel about their experience.

One way to find out is to conduct a series of case studies, in which you choose representative individuals and study them in depth. In the end, you will come out with transcripts of interviews, pre- and post-test results, and other data to help you tell the story of how several unique individuals arrived at your door, experienced your program, and either succeeded or failed in reaching their goals.

Focus Groups
Your youth development program helps teens improve grades, build self-esteem, get involved with community service projects, and learn study and workplace skills. You have lots of participants, but you really do not know how those participants' attitudes and abilities changed as a result of their experience. To find out, you might run a focus group. A focus group usually consists of 3-5 individuals who, together, represent a cross section of your target audience. Through directed, open-ended questions, you can learn a great deal about how they perceive and are impacted by your program before it begins, as it runs,

Project Delivery

and after it ends. Focus groups are typically "facilitated" by someone with specific experience, recorded, and transcribed.

Interviews

Have you ever walked into a museum or zoo and been accosted by a person carrying a clipboard who asks whether you will answer a few questions? If so, you have seen the interview process in action. Typically, interviews are used to gather marketing information (who is coming, why are they coming, what are they coming for, are they satisfied, etc.) – but interviews can also be used to assess knowledge, interest, and so forth. For example, a museum might interview visitors to find out what they already know about the Impressionists, what they might like to know, which Impressionists they prefer, and so forth. That sort of information can provide a baseline for later comparison.

Whatever your project or your budget, there are tools available to evaluate your level of success. When you use those tools, you improve your ability to make your case for support, you gain critical information for refining your program, and you build a database of knowledge for developing new programs and projects for the future.

Evaluation Plan

Exploration and analysing of the relationships between project outcomes, impacts, goals, objectives, and activities can be managed under a project evaluation plan.

Such a plan provides a set of tools to measure progress in implementing the project and its key components, such as goals, objectives, and activities. A project evaluation plan also focuses on assessing project effectiveness and efficiency through exploring and analysing the outcomes and impacts.

A Project Evaluation Plan is a detailed document that defines and sets forth practices and sequence of activities for analysing and examining the project by certain evaluation criteria. This document aims to determine project effectiveness and efficiency through tracking progress on each objective, completion of activities, and dates of completion.

There is no exact number of indicators or evaluation criteria that must be used in evaluating projects.

There is also no predefined set of activities for running the evaluation, because every project is unique and has certain goals and objectives.

In designing a project evaluation plan, the following general guidelines are suitable for project evaluation:

Identify outcome and impact

You can use status of the goals and objectives of your project as the framework for project evaluation. Achievement of a goal or objective is achieved creates certain short- or middle-term results and benefits, which are outcomes. Through measuring outcomes, you can understand the extent of goal achievement.

Project Delivery

Outcomes generate certain long-term effects which are impacts. Through evaluating project impacts you can identify the project overall effect on the environment it is targeted to.

Choose evaluation method

What project evaluation method will be used to measure outcomes and impacts? In your evaluation plan you need to include a method that helps determine whether the goals and objectives are completed and whether the project generates desired change. Your evaluation method will focus on results and benefits (outcomes) as well as effects (impacts).

Report on the evaluation

The final item in is reviewing the work done and creating a project evaluation report. Such a report includes the conclusions about the project's ability to produce desired change and accomplishing pre-set goals and objectives.

The evaluation criteria will establish whether the project was undertaken in a manner consistent with the original plan and whether project activities contributed to project success. In other words, it confirms whether goals and objectives are fully achieved during the course of the project and whether desired outcomes and impacts have been reached.

Once developed, the evaluation report should be submitted to the management team for review and further decision making.